Managing Operational risk

20 Firmwide Best Practice Strategies

Founded in 1807, John Wiley & Sons is the oldest independent publishing company in the United States. With offices in North America, Europe, Australia, and Asia, Wiley is globally committed to developing and marketing print and electronic products and services for our customers' professional and personal knowledge and understanding.

The Wiley Finance series contains books written specifically for finance and investment professionals as well as sophisticated individual investors and their financial advisors. Book topics range from portfolio management to e-commerce, risk management, financial engineering, valuation, and financial instrument analysis, as well as much more.

For a list of available titles, please visit our website at *www.WileyFinance.com*.

Managing Operational risk

20 Firmwide Best Practice Strategies

DOUGLAS G. HOFFMAN

John Wiley & Sons, Inc.

Published by John Wiley & Sons, Inc., New York
Published simultaneously in Canada.

This publication is designed to provide accurate and authoritative information in regard to the subject matter covered. It is sold with the understanding that the publisher is not engaged in rendering professional services. If professional advice or other expert assistance is required, the services of a competent professional person should be sought.

Library of Congress Cataloging-in-Publication Data:

Hoffman, Douglas, 1955–
    Managing operational risk: 20 firmwide best practice strategies/Douglas Hoffman.
        p. cm.
    Includes bibliographical references and index.
    ISBN 0-471-41268-6 (cloth: alk. paper)
        1. Finance. 2. Risk management. 3. Capital market. 4. Banks and banking. 5. Financial institutions. 6. Corporations—Finance. I. Title.

HG173 H585 2002
    658.15'5—dc21   2001026853

Printed in the United States of America.

10 9 8 7 6 5 4 3 2 1

For Claudia, Whitney, Chelsea,
and my Mother and Father
for their love and support

acknowledgments and credits

I would like to take this opportunity to acknowledge all of the organizations and individuals who have contributed to the advancement of operational risk management in recent years, and directly or indirectly to the development of this book.

I have had the privilege to work with many talented, creative, and intelligent people in numerous aspects of operational risk management and related areas of the risk management field. Some have been my mentors. Others have been team members, students, or interns who have gone on to forge their own programs and advancements in risk management. The list also includes current and former clients and colleagues in the industry. Space limitations do not allow me to recognize each and every one of them, but I would like to thank them generally for their contributions. Wherever possible I have sought to showcase or reference their work through this book. We will all benefit from their contributions.

One additional thought, recognizing the work of my colleagues and others, is in the area of sharing our experiences. The Lessons Learned section that appears in most of the chapters is intended to share with the reader my own varied experiences and that of my teams in operational risk management. Equally important, this book reports on lessons learned by people I have had the privilege of working with throughout the years who have been kind enough to share their experiences with us on these pages.

Individually, I would like to acknowledge a number of people who contributed directly and indirectly to the development of this book. Most books, and this one in particular, are truly the result of a concerted effort.

I would like to recognize and thank Mark Balfan, George Vojta, and Simon Wills for reviewing my manuscript. In particular, I would like to thank Barbara Matthews for her extra effort in poring over my early drafts despite all of their jumbled paragraphs and sentences and providing helpful suggestions for improvement.

There are a number of other people I would like to recognize and thank for their contributions to individual chapters. I'll do so in the order that their contributions appear.

The Executive Summary, Operational Risk 101, in Chapter 1 is partly an update and revised version of a chapter entitled "New Trends in Operational

Risk Measurement and Management" that I wrote in 1998 for *Operational Risk in Financial Institutions,* published by Risk Books (now Risk-Waters) and sponsored by Arthur Andersen. I would like to acknowledge and thank Risk-Waters and Financial Engineering, Ltd. for their agreement to allow the reproduction of parts of it here and in several other chapters.

The Best Practice Strategies, first presented in Chapter 2, and then interwoven throughout the book, are the result of catalyst conversations with colleagues, clients, regulators, and consultants. They are intended to distill as much of the current consensus on Best Practices as possible from both financial services and non-financial corporations. I have found it particularly satisfying to undertake this process as an independent consultant without any specific bias toward one or more methods or products. Although many contributed to this effort, specifically, I would like to recognize Felix Kloman, a long-time mentor and partner, for his critique and editorial contributions to my early draft.

Definitions have been at issue since people began talking about operational risk. What better way is there to help define the issues than to showcase some loss events? The Introduction, Chapter 3 on Definitions, and several other sections are far better for these cases. I would like to recognize and thank Penny Cagan and Zurich IC Squared for their numerous contributions of loss case descriptions from their IC Squared First Database, providing the loss cases used in Chapter 3 and elsewhere in the book as illustrations of various operational risk class definitions. In addition, I would like to recognize and thank Penny for the bibliography of operational risk sources that appears in the Appendix. She developed and contributed the entire document. Prior to working at Zurich IC Squared and on their First Database, Penny headed our information center at ORI and OperationalRisk.com, and before that, she headed the Information Center at Deutsche Bank in New York.

I would like to take this opportunity to thank Mike Levin of KPMG for his insightful piece in Chapter 4 on Corporate Culture and Risk Taking, and Chris Rachlin of Royal Bank of Scotland for his contribution on creating Risk Aware Cultures. The latter is reprinted here with permission of Risk-Waters and Financial Engineering, Ltd.

Relative to Chapter 5, I would like to recognize and thank Marta Johnson and Pat Medapa for our early work together on the unpublished study on share price relative strength and methods to quantity reputation risk that form the basis of part of this chapter. Marta was an integral member of my management team from 1992 to 1998 and managed the day-to-day workings of our Operational RAROC team and models during much of that period. Pat was also a member of our team during much of that period. I would also like to acknowledge and thank *Institutional Investor* for its agreement to reprint my article entitled "Operational Risk Management: A Board Level Issue," published in their *Bank Accounting and Finance* journal in Winter

2000, and I would also like to recognize Kate McBride for her assistance on the article.

Relative to Chapter 6, I would like to extend my appreciation to Denis Taylor and Commonwealth Bank Group (CBG) of Australia for his work in drafting and coordinating the case entitled Building Effective Roles and Working Relationships. Denis was a member of my operational risk management team in Sydney, Australia at Bankers Trust and later a member of our staff at ORI and OperationalRisk.com.

My appreciation goes out to Matt Kimber for his contributions to Chapter 7 on the operational risk management unit. Matt was formerly a member of my operational risk management team at Bankers Trust and a founding member and regional director at ORI and OperationalRisk.com. He now heads operational risk management at Halifax Group in London. My thanks also go to Robert Huebner of Deutsche Bank in Frankfurt for contribution of his exhibit on role and responsibilities.

Chapter 8 on Risk Response Framework features several key strategies. I would like to recognize the work of my former business continuity planning team managers and members, Walter DeCanio, Peter Giacone, Andrea Schaja, and Lori Stern. Our work together over the years gave rise to the substance of the section of Chapter 8 on business continuity and in Chapter 9 entitled The Business Continuity Risk Assessment Analogue.

The book features four firms and case illustrations in Chapter 9 on Risk Assessment. In order of appearance, I would like to thank Mark Balfan of the Bank of Tokyo Mitsubishi for his case illustration on Control Self-Assessment, Marie Gaudioso of the Bank of New York for her work on their case on Collaborative Risk Assessment, and Hansruedi Schuetter of Credit Suisse Group for his contribution entitled Leveraging Internal Audit Reviews. Last, I would like to recognize Dan Borge and David Fite, my co-pioneers on Long-Tail Event Risk analysis, on which I based the section of the same name.

In 2000, Margaret Levine and I wrote a piece titled "Enriching the Operational Risk Data Universe" for Informa's book entitled *Operational Risk,* published in March 2000. That piece has been reproduced in part at the end of Chapter 9 on Risk Assessment, and partially in Chapter 10 on Databases and Consortia. I would also like to thank Catherine Kwong for her contributions. Both were formerly of Operational Risk, Inc. and OperationalRisk.com. I would also like to thank and acknowledge Informa, the publisher of my article on operational loss data consortia entitled "Into the Valley," which first appeared in *Risk Professional* in December 2000/January 2001, which is also partially reproduced here.

Chapter 11 features a partial reprint and updates to an article that Denis Taylor and I wrote for Risk-Waters' *Operational Risk* Supplement in October 1999. I would like to recognize and thank Denis for his work and contribution to the chapter and Risk-Waters Group for their permission to reprint. In addition, I would like to recognize and thank Joe Swipes and Dresdner Bank for their case illustration. Joe was a member of operational risk teams at Bankers Trust and Deutsche Bank, then our team at ORI and Operational-Risk.com. He is now an operational risk manager at Dresdner Bank in New York.

I would like to recognize and thank Dave Sommer, FCAS, and vice president of Am-Re Consultants, Inc. for his contributions to Chapter 12, especially for his work on the loss distribution part and for his editorial assistance on this chapter overall. Dave played a key role in support of our developments of the loss distribution and actuarial analyses portions of our models for operational risk at Bankers Trust from 1995 to 1999. I would also like to recognize and thank Karolina Kalkantra and Riaz Karim of West LB and David Syer of Algorithmics for their work and contribution on the Bayesian Belief Network/OpVar case. I also extend thanks to Jerry Miccolis and Samir Shah of Tillinghast-Towers Perrin for their contribution on System Dynamics models, and to Jeevan Perera of NASA for his contribution on Neural Networks.

Chapter 13 on Dynamic Risk Profiling and Monitoring contains several additional informative cases. Three are continuations of the early cases or contributions from Deutsche Bank, Dresdner Bank, and the Bank of Tokyo Mitsubishi. I add my thanks for the case from Ammy Seth and his staff at Halifax Bank for their work on their Dynamic Enterprise-wide Risk Profiling, and to Corinna Mertens of Commerzbank, Irina Schaf of Accenture, and Dr. Hans-Peter Guellich of RCS Risk Management Concepts Systems for their contributions to the Commerzbank case. Last, I would like to thank Tony Blvnden, Matt Kimber, and Leanne Long for their work on profiling examples that gave rise to examples shown on pages 309, 310, and 316.

I would like to acknowledge the good work of Russ Opferkuch and Antonina Basile on risk finance and insurance over the years, and their indirect contributions to Chapters 14 and 15. Russ headed my risk finance and insurance management team at Bankers Trust from 1989-99 and Antonina was a key member for several years. I would also like to recognize Tim Boyle for his part in our work together on the insurability of operational risks.

The last segment of Chapter 16 is a detailed discussion of Bankers Trust's Operational RAROC approach, including its evolution, details of implementation, and lessons learned. Because of the ongoing interest in our groundbreaking work and methodology, and its continued relevance to recent industry developments, I have dusted off and am featuring this case overview of our early work on Operational RAROC. This section of Chapter 16 is an update largely based on an overview of the models that was developed by Marta Johnson and myself for *Treasury and Risk Management Magazine* in 1997. The overview is also provided courtesy of Deutsche

Bank, which acquired Bankers Trust in 1999. I would also like to take this opportunity to recognize and thank Marta for her indirect contribution to Chapter 9 in the form of the early work we did together on Business Vulnerability Analysis.

Early in 2000 Matt Kimber and I wrote a chapter for Informa's *Operational Risk* book entitled "Operational Risk Management and Capital Adequacy." Many of the issues raised in that chapter remain relevant in the regulatory discussion today, so parts have been reprinted here in Chapter 17, Regulatory Capital and Supervision, for your consideration. I would like to take this opportunity to recognize and thank Matt Kimber not only for his work on the original, but for his contributions to the update of Chapter 17. Parts of the update are reproduced here courtesy of Informa Business Publishing.

Special thanks and recognition are due to David LaBouchardiere of IBM in London for his extensive work in authoring Chapter 18, An Operational Risk Management Case Study: Managing Internet Banking Risk.

I also owe special thanks to Anand Sahasram for his contributions, overall review, and suggestions for Chapter 19 on Operational Risk Technology and Systems. Anand was a founding member of our team at ORI and OperationalRisk.com, and served as our Chief Information Officer there. He is now IT Director at McKinsey and Company in New York. I would also like to recognize and thank Debbie Williams of Meridien for her exhibit on operational risk systems architecture and Craig Spielmann of J.P. Morgan Chase and Carmine DiSibio of Ernst and Young for the case study they contributed on automating self-assessment programs at J.P. Morgan and an overview of the Horizon Tool. This chapter also includes continuations of the Halifax, Commonwealth Bank Group, and Commerzbank.

I would like to acknowledge others who have had the greatest impact on the evolution of my own views about risk management. Among them are E. J. Leverett, Jr., who recruited me into the field back at the University of Georgia, and Felix Kloman, who was my mentor for many years in the early part of my career. Others include Mitch Cole, Hugh Rosenbaum, Jim Trieschmann, Bob Almeida, Dan Borge, David Fite, Randy Cooper, Dan Mudge, Ken Abbott, and Clinton Lively. I would also like to recognize their many contributions and challenges over the years.

Last, but certainly not least, as I finished proofing this manuscript, the United States has suffered brutal terrorist attacks on New York and Washington, D.C. My prayers join those of millions for the victims and their families. It is only fitting that I use some of this space to give thanks for being here today to write about it. I was due to be at the World Trade Center on the afternoon of September 11, 2001.

Although we will never be the same in the wake of the tragedy, we will move on and be even stronger for it. We cannot help but grieve for all those lost. As risk practitioners, we can take some comfort in knowing that in some small ways, operational risk management contributed to the safety of so many thousands more and the survival of many businesses through evacuation plans, safety measures, engineering advancement, diversification strategies, backup sites, redundant systems, and crisis management.

contents

introduction

Operational risk is everywhere. Its presence is felt in every facet of our personal and business lives today.

The connected world in which we live has rung in a new era of prosperity, productivity, and opportunity. And yet along with those rewards, we are periodically reminded of the risks that accompany them, lurking just below the surface of such a promising exterior.

Operational risks are those of our interconnected world becoming disrupted on a large scale, or locally in our workplaces or neighborhoods through acts of man, or of nature. They involve our global systems becoming disrupted through malicious or careless omission. They are the risks that unbridled acts of co-workers cause massive losses or embarrassment to our companies. We might see competitive forces run amok resulting in disputes between company and customer, employees or regulators, or in misdeeds by management or staff alike. Or, we may find our companies become embroiled in landmark legal judgments and settlements, accounting improprieties, fraud, improper sales practices, terrorist acts, corporate sabotage, attacks on systems, regulatory violations, or damages resulting from earthquake or windstorm.

These are risks that lie in wait, quietly hidden for the most part. But they are especially dangerous because the errors, omissions, and control failures that underpin them are most often viewed and experienced as routine nuisances— the larger versions of these losses occur far less frequently. This infrequency is a good thing, of course. But it is also the very feature that makes them all the more dangerous because they are too often ignored as being insignificant, improbable, or uninteresting. And therein lies the challenge to managing them. The challenge becomes one of balance: maintaining just enough focus to control them, without becoming so obsessed and overbearing that the operational risk management effort becomes an unreasonable drag on productivity.

FAMILIAR RISKS, TRANSFORMED BY THE TIMES

There's still no complete consensus on a definition of operational risk. With the ongoing discussions in the financial services industry and series of releases from the Basel Committee on Banking Supervision, and its Risk Management Group [1] in Basel, Switzerland, however, one is emerging. With the exception of some fringe areas of debate, operational risk has generally become understood to mean the risk of loss from inadequate or failed internal processes, people, and systems, or from external events. The basic descriptions of those risks are anything but new. But watershed changes in society, technology, science, and the interconnected nature of global society and business today make them more relevant than ever before. Whether a consensus definition emerges from this version, or some variation of it, the discipline is probably very close to reaching common ground on a definition. The final version, however, must reach beyond that overview description to clarify the details of risk classes and subclasses.

It is no exaggeration to say that people have felt the effects of operational risk since the beginning of time. Maslow's hierarchy of needs provides an interesting backdrop for the history of operational risk priorities. For instance, he placed food and shelter and, essentially, survival at the first rung of the ladder. Basic physical risks of loss were among the first to be felt as man struggled for survival in the more rugged past, and occasionally on the frontiers of exploration, even today. In his best selling book, *Against the Gods,* Peter Bernstein makes another connection as he tours the history of risk. It is no surprise that some of the earliest risks to commerce that he cites are operational risks—losses caused by the risks of early trading and shipping, and by the ravages of early wars.[2] During more recent centuries, operational risks have continued to dominate the risk spectrum, but priorities have transitioned to reflect further changes in society. Thus, more recently, operational risks are found to be equally embedded in human nature and our reliance on technology as they are in physical risks.

For banks, the management of operational risks also reach back to the origins of banking itself, when early bankers took great pains to protect the currency and precious metals in their care from robberies and burglaries. In the more recent past, the face of operational risk has changed a bit, but the human behavioral aspect is still very much a part of it all. For financial services firms on a global basis, operational risks have spanned numerous headline losses in recent years, from old standby categories like loan and accounting fraud, to newer ones like rogue trading, legal liabilities, and networked computer system vulnerabilities. Whether it is a function of human error, or the darker function of greed and fear, the spectrum of investment emotions, many of the most significant operational loss events through time can be traced directly to human behavior.

The urgency for operational risk management has been underscored numerous times, as headlines in the 1990s and early 2000s alone have been filled with loss events. They ranged from rogue trading to system failures, accounting improprieties, fraud, improper sales practices, landmark legal judgments and settlements, terrorist acts, systems attacks, sabotage, product recalls, environmental disasters, and regulatory violations, to name only a few. The first shock of the decade was the landmark 1991 case involving the Bank of Credit and Commerce International (BCCI) and its $15 billion loss, described in Exhibit I.1. Although other losses have since taken dubious credit for the operational risk management movement, the BCCI case was most noteworthy because of its magnitude and international complexity, both of which began to underscore the challenges to come in operational risk management. The case involved a complex web of international operatives, but it boiled down to a massive case of old fashioned loan fraud. Nevertheless, the sheer magnitude of the case and its reach throughout the international regulatory community served as the first of a series of high-profile losses throughout the remainder of the decade.

Along with the shocking size of the loss itself was the reminder that losses of this magnitude all too often involve not just a handful of employees but entire management teams as well. It underscored the potential impact of management collusion and fraud, both within a firm and to its counterparties. In addition, it served as a wake-up call for the regulatory community. Although the case heralded in the 1990s, the BCCI loss was not the first, nor will it be the last major debacle of its kind. It was just one of the many landmark cases throughout the 1990s and into the new century, however, that have kept attention focused on the subject of operational risk.

THE MAGNITUDE OF THE PROBLEM

It is painfully apparent that operational risk and associated losses can drag down or sink an organization completely. We have seen it happen time and time again. Business libraries and case histories are littered with the names of companies that have been torpedoed by these silent killers.

But these cases are not news so that begs the question: If everyone is already well aware of these risks—they have been around for some time, and are everywhere—why has the discussion of operational risk become such a hot topic in *recent* years, and even been gaining momentum?

In order to answer that question, we must look at the risks again. Clearly the risks *have* been felt more intently by all organizations in recent years. Whether an organization spent millions preparing its computers for 2000 (Y2K), has been plagued by litigation over product or service liabilities (derivatives, tobacco, silicon litigation), has faced employment practices liabilities, or rogue trading losses, it has come head to head with operational risk. In short, there has been a recent recognition that the major headline losses are not isolated events. They can, and have, hit some of the most established and admired firms. The accumulation of both large and smaller losses and the underlying risk trends are difficult to ignore.

On July 5, 1991, an operational loss event that has been described as the biggest bank fraud in history came to a head when regulators in seven countries raided and took control of branch offices of the Bank of Credit and Commerce International (BCCI). Monetary losses from the scandal were huge, totaling $17 billion. This case developed over nearly two decades, and encompassed an intricate international web of financial institutions and shell companies, which escaped full regulation, and were reportedly involved in a number of suspect transactions, in addition to legitimate banking activities. BCCI's scheme was so complex that, even a decade after the institution closed, its activities are not completely known.

The Bank of Credit and Commerce['s] . . . multinational platform supported a conglomeration that became increasingly complex over time. BCCI's international nature helped the company avoid a large number of regulations because no one country had full jurisdiction over the firm.

Although institutions such as the CIA and the Bank of England reportedly had some knowledge of BCCI's activities before the scandal broke, regulators worldwide were unable to take action against the bank because inadequate communication among agencies prevented the spread of vital information on its activities. [For example] . . . One such signal was the bank's involvement in money laundering and finance of arms trafficking. The U.S. Custom's Service completed an undercover operation that led to the arrest of several BCCI figures, who were convicted of money laundering on July 29, 1990. The bank itself pled guilty to the laundering charge and was fined $14 million.

BCCI's use by cartels was just one facet of a much larger event. . . . The regulatory probe that exposed the bank's losses was brought about by its illegal control of several American banks. The largest, First American Bankshares, was based in Washington, D.C. . . . The bank's international web began to unravel in 1990 when *Regardies,* a Washington-based magazine, published a story that questioned the true ownership of First American. After the article was published, the Fed began an official probe into the alleged connection between the banks. In March 1991, BCCI admitted that it had acquired a 25% stake in First American, without the approval of regulators. The Fed then ordered the bank to sell the shares in question. The investigation continued, and in June, Price Waterhouse informed the Bank of England that it had found evidence of widespread fraud in BCCI's operations.

The fraudulent activities primarily involved loan practices and record-keeping. Throughout its history, BCCI made large loans and did not properly secure them. These included funds received by individuals as well as companies. When these loans went bad, the bank had no legal recourse, and was forced to absorb the losses. This "strategy," which ran counter to common sense and all principles of good lending, racked up huge losses for BCCI. The firm covered this problem by creating a matrix of false accounts that hid the

EXHIBIT I.1   Bank of Credit and Commerce International
Reprinted with permission from Zurich IC Squared First Database

losses for years. When BCCI's problems were uncovered in the 1991 probe, regulators in seven countries moved quickly to take over the bank's branches. On July 5, offices in the U.K., U.S., France, Spain, Switzerland, Luxembourg, and the Cayman Islands were seized, and the bank's business activities were frozen. BCCI's assets were ultimately liquidated, and a pool was established to reimburse depositors who had lost their funds when the bank shut down.

The BCCI case may never be fully understood. For the purpose of this analysis, general fraud, a subset of the People Risk category, is considered the primary trigger of the incident: The bank's untenable loan strategy and practice of hiding the massive losses that resulted were the problems that ultimately led to its downfall. These were compounded, though, by many other elements, including a bad trading strategy that created further losses. The case also involved several types of Relationship Risk, including BCCI's numerous regulatory violations and legal liabilities. Other contributory factors included omissions on the part of regulators, who should have taken action against BCCI long before 1991, and organizational gaps, which confounded outsiders who tried to sort out the tangle of the bank's subsidiaries.

[There have been numerous] . . . settlements and fines: . . . [associated with the loss. For instance] . . . in December 1991, BCCI made the first of many contributions to the depositors' restitution pool, when it pled guilty to criminal charges and agreed to forfeit $550 million. . . . [Then in 1996] . . . BCCI . . . made a payment of $2 billion to the depositors' pool. The company made its second such payment in 1998, again for $2 billion. Several other agreements were reached that year, one of which involved Price Waterhouse, the firm that had served as BCCI's auditor.

EXHIBIT I.1   Bank of Credit and Commerce International

Nothing—not even BCCI—really seemed to spark a management reaction, however, until the Barings rogue trading debacle that broke in February 1995. The storied loss of $1.2 billion by Nick Leeson proved itself to be the defining event for operational risk management. Others had come before even BCCI, but in the wake of the landmark Barings case and a string of other operational risk cases since and capped by the September 2001 terrorist attacks on the World Trade Center in New York and Washington, D.C., financial service firms and regulators alike have become highly focused on the problem. They have begun to consider operational risk with renewed interest and a new set of glasses—with a view towards assessment, measurement, and mitigation.

The magnitude of loss and impact of operational risk and losses to date is also difficult to ignore. Based on our years of industry loss record-keeping from public sources, large operational risk-related financial services losses have averaged well in excess of $15 billion annually for the past 20 years, but this only reflects the large public and visible losses.[3]

Many see this as merely the tip of the iceberg. They believe that the actual loss costs are easily a multiple of this figure, some believing the multiple is as high as 10 times that amount when one includes all the losses that you never hear about because organizations don't want them out in the public eye.

On an individual loss basis, the numbers are nothing short of staggering. Our research has yielded nearly 100 individual relevant losses greater than $500 million each, and over 300 individual losses greater than $100 million each. Exhibit I.2 is a listing of major operational losses.[4] Interestingly enough, in both cases the majority of these losses have occurred in the 1990s alone. It is also interesting to note that the majority of these losses have occurred in financial services, which explains the industry's leading focus on operational risk management (ORM).

Operational losses are measured by the direct economic loss and indirect expense associated with business interruptions and legal risk. Some also include "immeasurable" exposures such as reputation risk. With no concrete statistics attached to it, operational risk can be seen as a looming danger, which has the potential to trigger us into panic, following an apparently unassailable company's high-profile disaster. So, it is no wonder that global business and risk managers are waking up to the importance of this subject.[5]

In addition to the losses, the challenges presented by operational risk have been accentuated by the speed of change in technological and sociological developments toward globalization. The business environment has changed dramatically in recent years. Technological advances, the information revolution, open global markets, financial product advancements, and most recently the advent of electronic commerce have all driven this change.

Related trends have included but not been limited to increased transaction values and volumes, increased costs of regulation and litigation, and high-profile losses. These have all contributed to bringing the collective universe of operational risks into a high state of visibility. So, coupled with the headline losses, it is no wonder that within a very short time, the subject of operational risk has assumed a prominent position on the agenda of senior management at major financial institutions and corporations alike. But this is also a function of the realization that more creative actions must be taken to deal with the increasing complexities and risk involved with the management, people, and systems underpinning organizations. In addition, organizations have come to realize that operational risk and losses are having a substantial impact on their bottom lines, not to mention their reputations and franchise values.

The year 2000 (Y2K) computer scare put operational risk on the radar screen for many senior executives. This was a major issue that caused firms worldwide to invest in both vulnerability analysis and system remediation in order to avoid large scale business disruption and losses.

Company	Loss Amount	Date	Description
Numerous Financial Institutions and Others	$20,000,000*	2001	Terrorists hijacked four commercial airliners and crashed them into the World Trade Center. Over 6,000 lives lost. Countless businesses impacted.
Bank of Credit and Commerce International	$ 17,000,000,000	1991	Regulators seized about 75 percent of The Bank of Credit and Commerce International's (BCCI) $17 billion in assets in a major fraud.
Long Term Capital Management	$ 4,000,000,000	1998	Huge market losses due to model risk and inadequate controls. The breakdowns at LTCM include an overexposure to leverage, sovereign, model, liquidity, and volatility risk. In addition, the firm lacked the diverse revenue streams of the Wall Street investment banks of which it liked to compare itself. Overall, the fiasco portrays a failure of LTCM to implement a balanced risk management strategy.
Texaco, Inc.	$ 3,000,000,000	1984	Pennzoil sued Texaco alleging that Texaco "wrongfully interfered" in its merger deal with Getty. In 1987, Texaco appealed the judgment, and the Texas Court of Appeals upheld the $7.53 billion award in actual damages but reduced punitive damages to $1 billion. In 1988, Texaco settled the dispute alleging that it improperly lured Getty Oil away from a merger with Pennzoil in January 1984 by paying $3 billion to the Pennzoil Company. This settlement ended Pennzoil's litigation over Texaco's "tortious interference" in Pennzoil's 1984 agreement to acquire Getty stock.
Sumitomo Corporation	$ 2,857,000,000	1996	Sumitomo Corporation incurred huge losses through excessive trading of copper. The scheme that produced this loss had continued for more than a decade, and provides a classic example of rogue trading.

Continued

EXHIBIT I.2 Top Operational Risk Losses

*Initial Estimates

Company	Loss Amount	Date	Description
Cendant Corporation	$ 2,850,000,000	1985–1998	The largest and longest-running accounting fraud case in history. Former executives conspired to inflate earnings in order to meet earnings expectations, and inflate the company's stock price.
Tokyo Shinkin Bank	$ 2,300,000,000	1990–1991	From July of 1990 through August of 1991, the manager of the Imasato branch of Asaka-based Tokyo Shinkin Bank forged 19 deposit certificates with a face value of 416 billion yen. The deposit slips were used to raise money for stock deals worth 172.5 billion yen in stocks and debentures. The value of forged certificates almost equaled the institutions's total deposits. Tokyo Shinkin was broken up in 1992.
Dow Corning	$ 2,000,000,000	1994	The company agreed to pay millions in settlements to 18 women who reported that silicon-gel breast implants made by the company made them ill.
Saint Francis of Assisi Foundation	$ 1,980,000,000	1999	Insurance fraud case in which Martin Frankel allegedly stole as much as $1.98 billion from the St. Francis of Assisi Foundation, a bogus charity he established the year before in the British Virgin Islands. Charges included securities fraud, racketeering, wire fraud, money laundering, and conspiracy.
Banca Nazionale del Lavoro	$ 1,800,000,000	1992	Former employees pleaded guilty to conspiring to arrange from $5 billion in unauthorized loans to Iraq.
Metallgesellschaft	$1,800,000,000	1991–1993	Loss due to liquidation of oil supply contracts. This oil futures scheme brought down the company in just two years. The lessons learned from this case include the necessity for firms to employ classic risk management strategies such as stress testing, multiple scenario analysis, and independent risk oversight.

EXHIBIT I.2 Top Operational Risk Losses

Company	Loss Amount	Date	Description
Owens Corning Fiber Glass	$ 1,680,000,000	1980s–1990s	Settlement of asbestos-related claims, many of which stemmed from the now defunct Owens-Corning factory that produced insulation materials containing asbestos.
Orange County	$ 1,600,000,000	1994	One of the largest people risk class cases in financial history. It involved the use of leveraged derivatives, and resulted in the largest investment loss ever registered by a municipality, which led to bankruptcy, and the mass layoff of municipal employees.
Atlantic Richfield Company	$ 1,500,000,000	1986–1990	Settlement of North Slope oil royalties dispute with Alaska. ARCO was one of several oil companies charged with undervaluing the crude oil they pumped and tax avoidance.
Kashima Oil	$ 1,500,000,000	1994	Firm accumulated a vast number of FX forward contracts to buy dollars and then, when the currency market moved against it, used lax accounting rules to disguise the losses by rolling the contracts over at the end of each month instead of charging them off.
Showa Shell Sekiyu	$ 1,500,000,000	1989–1993	In a people risk situation, this major oil refiner in Japan faced losses from forward currency transactions.
Prudential Securities Inc., Prudential Insurance Company, Prudential-Bache	$ 1,400,000,000	1994	Prudential found itself burdened with a serious relationship and reputational risk situation when it settled charges of securities fraud with state and federal regulators. The incident stemmed from charges of improper management practices, sales misrepresentation, and an executive management structure that promoted profits above all else.

Continued

EXHIBIT I.2 Top Operational Risk Losses

Company	Loss Amount	Date	Description
Drexel Burnham Lambert	$ 1,300,000,000	1998–1993	Former employees filed a class action suit charging the company with fraud, breach of duty, and negligence in connection with employee purchases of the firm's common stock. In 1989 three employees charged Drexel's top managers with breach of contract and violation of their fiduciary duties. In 1991, Michael R. Milken of Drexel and Kohlberg Kravis Roberts & Co. were sued for $1 billion for misappropriating state employee's pension funds. Investors' money had been put into junk bonds that Milken sold at Drexel.
General Motors	$ 1,200,000,000	1996	Heavy losses suffered due to three strikes.
Diawa Bank	$ 1,100,000,000	1983–1995	Loss due to unauthorized trading by an employee who was in charge of both securities trading and the custody department, and used these positions to carry out and cover up his scheme.
Phar Mor	$ 1,100,000,000	1992	A former president of the firm defrauded it of $1.1 billion in an embezzlement scheme. In what has been called the "biggest corporate fraud," the former executive overstated the firm's profits and diverted $11 million.
Barings	$ 1,000,000,000	1995	This catastrophic loss has become a benchmark for operational risk. The loss was larger than the bank's entire capital base and reserves, and created an extreme liquidity crisis. An employee, Nick Leeson, was able to hide the losses in a special account that he controlled. He was violating a central tenant of good operational risk practices: lack of dual controls and checks and balances. He was the acting settlement manager for both the back and front office, and was able to hide his accumulating losses for more than two years.

EXHIBIT I.2 Top Operational Risk Losses
Source: Excerpts from IC Squared First Database.

Last, but certainly not least, has been the move toward enterprise-wide risk management. With its advent has come the realization that operational risks, unlike credit and market risks, touch or are touched by everyone in the organization. That realization presents an enormous challenge, but also a golden opportunity. It is the recognition that if we can harness that opportunity for risk management involvement, not only will we be able to lever risk management to become a more effective discipline, but we can also catapult the effort squarely in the camp of value creation for all stakeholders.

Why has operational risk *management* remained such a nebulous area? One reason, as we well know, is that much of operational risk is embedded in human behavior. It represents a very different set of risk classes than those most people are used to. Operational risk has a unique set of data availability and characteristics, complex causation considerations, subjective control variables, and a different notion of portfolio and transactions views. Until recently, most banks, brokerages, and financial institutions did not track operational risk and losses very closely. It is difficult to quantify, more elusive, and much less defined. So clearly, risk practitioners and management teams alike must put in their time to get their hands around the problem.

WHY LOOK AT OPERATIONAL RISK IN ISOLATION?

Some who have moved onto enterprise-wide risk management (covering market, credit, operational, liquidity, and other risks) more broadly have asked, 'Why not simply cover this topic as part of the larger whole?' After all, many of the basic principles and even some of the strategies we will be discussing here can and should be applied to all risks, not just operational risks.

For some, the point is well taken. For others, however, the answer is simple. Unfortunately, some firms have moved on to that bigger picture, but are ill prepared to do so. That is, they don't have a full understanding of the nature of the risk classes themselves, some of the techniques for measuring and managing them, the nature of regulation, and aspects of hedging them, all of which are unique in many ways. Once we have mastered these peculiar aspects, by all means, let's move on to the bigger picture of enterprise-wide risk management.

There is also a disturbing level of confusion out in the industry about operational risk management. At one extreme it is interesting to see how many firms become one dimensional in their program design, framework, and implementation. Probably the best example of this in recent years in the financial services industry has been the focus on impending regulatory developments for operational risk management. As the pall of potential regulatory capital hangs over the industry, many firms have found themselves caught up in debate over definitions, measurement, modeling, and the impact of those charges, rather than on development of sound education, assessment, and mitigation processes. There seems to be an assumption that because operational risk has been around for some time, there's nothing new in risk management processes other than risk measurement.

At another extreme, there are so many tools, techniques, and developments (e.g., loss databases, loss consortia, self-assessment, measurement models, regulatory capital charges) emerging that confusion among practitioners and regulators alike is clear. In addition, there are even camps forming that have begun to suggest that one group is going about this far more intelligently than the other (i.e., some who use quantitative models have scorned "self-assessment," and vice versa). Debate is healthy, but at a point it becomes entirely unproductive. In the wake of it all, many executives and line managers are simply looking for direction. In my own experience, many of the techniques in the market have their value and their place, but where and how one should apply them is not at all clear to many.

Operational risk practitioners, and business managers alike, have been groping for some perspective on Best Practices. In approaching me to write this book, Wiley targeted the work of my colleagues and I in developing operational risk assessment programs, models, and integrated risk finance dating back to 1990, and related programs for much longer, and suggested that our experience and perspective would be particularly beneficial at this point in time. Admittedly, it is very satisfying to see that many of the techniques we were developing and implementing back then are now being adopted broadly in the marketplace today. But it seems that while some firms are finding solutions, others are just now beginning to encounter, or are on the verge of encountering, some of the same problems and challenges that we encountered a few years into our implementations.

So this book is intended as a road map in sharing our experiences and that of others who have found success to identify Best Practices and the dead ends, and to steer around the obstacles that we encountered along the way. It is intended for management and operational risk management practitioners grappling with the problem of designing or fine-tuning operational risk management programs on a firmwide and enterprise-wide basis. There is no such source as yet that covers the entire spectrum of management issues, ranging from broad perspective on the operational risk management opportunity and considerations in the investment community, to some of the practical aspects of risk assessment, measurement, mitigation, finance, economic and regulatory capital, and technology and system development. With all of these issues in mind, we will attempt to simplify the subject a bit and begin to drive a stake in the ground on what should be considered the current range of Best Practices for operational risk management. This book is not intended as the last word, but instead it may be considered one of the first in a developing discussion about operational risk *management*.

OPERATIONAL RISK MANAGEMENT BEST PRACTICES

The nexus of lessons and proven strategies borrowed from respected business leaders, together with the birth of operational risk management, has yielded an initial set of Best Practice strategies for enterprise-wide operational risk management programs. Some are rooted in customer-focused Six Sigma, quality, and strategic value-based management, some in traditional risk and insurance management, Internal Audit, operations management, and others, more recently, from newer leading edge risk management practitioners.

Operational risk management is still at an early stage as corporate functions go. With the help of best of breed practices from other functions, however, a number of strategies have begun to emerge that pave the way for enhanced shareholder value. Together they are already beginning to bear fruit in the form of enhanced performance at a handful of firms. The evidence suggests that operational risk management is not just another management fad.

So, this book presents a variety of alternative tools and techniques that fall under a proven set of risk management principles and Best Practice strategy headings. Extensive discussions, debate, and pioneering work by individual firms has already yielded a variety of emerging best practices. The development and evolution of these processes and practices are the foundation of the book.

A QUICK TOUR

Before we begin, it might help put things into context if we take a brief tour of the contents of the book overall. First of all, it is positioned and organized to be the first definitive work on framing the broad topic of operational risk management, written in a style intended to be attractive to business leaders at multiple levels, not simply for risk management practitioners. It is intended to give the reader a complete tour of the subject of operational risk and operational risk management. More importantly, it will provide a roadmap to those proven strategies and essential best practices.

Line managers, business executives, and risk practitioners alike will find Chapter 1, Operational Risk Management 101: An Executive Summary, to be a useful primer and starting point for effective management. The book contains many practical business tools, including but not limited to those that have often been solely the purview of risk management practitioners. It also advances the notion that sound operational risk management, once implemented, embedded, and practiced continually firmwide makes for a far more effective organization in facing this increasingly competitive global marketplace. Thus, this book is based firmly on the premise that a company can and should position itself to reap far greater benefits than simply protecting itself in the face of downside.

Following the executive overview in Chapter 1, we unveil the Best Practice strategies in Chapter 2, then explore them more fully throughout the book. In fact, they will serve as much of the framework for the text. Going beyond the strategies, we will present the various approaches that some firms are taking toward each strategy and share alternative tools and tactics for program development. Where available, we include case studies written by industry practitioners themselves. For ease of reference, the practices have been organized as 20 firmwide strategies for effective operational risk management, and within the framework of six basic principles or building blocks.

With this as a background, we continue to explore the complete evolution from the definition of operational risk, its causation, and underlying trends, as well as the complete spectrum of organizational response. This will include setting objectives, motivating management and staff to deal with the risks firmwide, organizing and staffing, coordinating operational risk management functions, a tour of various approaches to risk assessment and measurement, as well as case examples on techniques for mitigating operational risk. Then, we will move on to a variety of financial considerations, including economic capital and regulatory models for operational risk, and also risk finance treatment.

Last, but certainly not least, a key part of the mission here is to simplify what has become an unnecessarily arcane world of risk management. I'll mention three other features before we begin. They are the Myths, Lessons Learned, and operational losses sprinkled throughout the book.

Myths, and Debunking Them   There has been a great deal of head-scratching in the industry today about operational risk. For instance, the conversation overheard in the hallway at a recent conference provided as much insight into operational risk management's state of evolution as the sessions inside. One attendee was overheard saying, "Well, it's clear to me that operational risk management has matured—the 'quants' have taken over; I'd better brush up on my statistics." Another replied: "I disagree, operational risk management will not have matured until someone figures out a way to simplify all the complexity, and manage risk more effectively, not make it all even more complicated."[6]

And so the head scratching continues. These comments are noted in stark contrast to the frenetic search for singular "truths" and methods underway in anticipation of various Basel Committee deadlines. In their pursuit of *the ultimate answer,* some risk managers seem to have rushed off tangentially, pursuing one-dimensional positions, without defining many of the risk management questions, objectives, and implementation challenges.[7]

I chose to emphasize some of these concerns as Myths and sprinkle them throughout the text.

Lessons Learned   As Indiana Jones put it in the famed film *Raiders of the Lost Ark,* "It's not the years, it's the mileage." It is with some reluctance that I admit having logged 25 years to date in risk management. Although many important lessons have come from those years, like Jones' brand of archeology, it is the mileage that counts more than the years in risk management. The mileage—in our case the experiences, victories, failures, and yes, especially managing through the operational losses and crises—have been invaluable. So one of my objectives has been to write a book that shares a number of "Lessons Learned" in operational risk management, some of which come from the experience of my teams and I, but many others courtesy of numerous other contributors as well.

So, in addition to the case illustrations, I will end most chapters with Lessons Learned both as a recap and an easy reference tool. I know how difficult it can be for a busy executive or risk manager to find the time to read a thick book like this from cover to cover. The conclusions and Lessons Learned at the end of each chapter are included for easy skimming. Then, when a topic is timely and relevant, you can refer back to the detail in the chapter text.

Operational Losses   I find loss case studies to be invaluable sources of ideas for risk management. So, I have sprinkled as many anecdotes and loss descriptions as possible throughout the book. Where it was not possible to identify them, individual and company names have been omitted for reasons of privacy protection.

LEARNING FROM A VARIETY OF INDUSTRIES

One final introductory thought is in order. Although operational risk management is a hot topic in the banking and financial institutions circles, and there is much to cover in banking and finance alone, this book will draw from and feature Best Practice strategies already being applied in many different industries, and those that have evolved from predecessor fields. Much can be learned from the trends and events that have occurred, regardless of the industry. If one is willing to take a broad perspective on risk and keep an open mind, it is easy to imagine how circumstances from another industry and its losses might be applied to one's own firm and industry.

While overseeing insurance and risk finance management at Bankers Trust (Bankers Trust was acquired by Deutsche Bank in 1998) in the late 1980s, I was particularly struck by litigation trends a few years earlier both within and external to our own industry. In the mid-1980s, many banks were suffering from legal action levied against them in what was being referred to as "lender liability suits." Elsewhere, public accounting firms were suffering from litigation at the hands of depositors, shareholders, and regulators alike, who were leveling legal action against them for their alleged errors or omissions relative to auditing savings and loans during the crisis of 1981, which cost United States taxpayers billions of dollars. Couple that with active litigation and litigation threats in the United States involving asbestos, silicone breast implants, and impending concerns at the time about tobacco litigation, and it wasn't much of a stretch to think that financial services might see yet another wave of lawsuits.

So, my team and I concentrated on what financial structure might best protect the corporation in the event of another class of lawsuits in the 1990s, regardless of their origin in financial services. We did well to pay attention to what was going on in other industries, and other sectors of our own, because it was not long before Bankers Trust and other firms found themselves embroiled in litigation in the mid-1990s over complex derivative financial structures. Had we kept blinders on, and focused on financing only the risks obvious in financial services at the time, we may have missed this loss potential and the opportunity to tailor a risk financing program accordingly. By looking at other industries, we realized that another wave of litigation might be brewing on the horizon for financial services, just as it had already impacted accounting, tobacco, chemical, and asbestos manufacturers, not to mention savings and loans and their accountants in the 1980s. So, with this lesson in mind, this text will include illustrations from other industries, where relevant.

CHAPTER 1

Operational Risk Management 101

An Executive Summary

THE ACCELERATED DEVELOPMENT OF OPERATIONAL RISK MANAGEMENT

Operational risk has been a challenge for financial service firms for years, but because of the infrequency of losses, it has not been recognized for its full potential until recently. Large loss events had occurred before. One-off events had caused both mass embarrassment and/or collapse, but they were widely considered to be extremely remote and perhaps even aberrations. Thus, operational risk didn't attract such significant attention until the 1990s, when a series of life threatening or fatal operational loss events at a number of different financial firms caused reorganization, management shakeup or a refocus on control environments, and a new focus on operational risk. Even more noteworthy was that operational losses were occurring at high profile and respected firms in the United States and Europe (i.e., Barings, Prudential, Kidder Peabody), thus further underscoring the danger of ignoring this area.

This series of loss events, coupled with a changing risk landscape, has perhaps forever changed management's perceptions and priorities. At one time, operational risk could be defined as an area characterized by frequent small and predictable events such as processing errors, reconciliation breaks, or system glitches, accompanied by the one-in-five-or-ten-year large system failure and loss, defalcation, or customer dispute. More recently, however, these larger loss events have become far too commonplace and visible in the industry news for management's comfort. Couple this with the advent of increased management and directorship accountability forced by legal actions against officers and directors and a chain reaction has been set in motion.

Recent trends in business complexity, highly visible operational losses, and the need to manage risks associated with them have given rise to a new field called operational risk management (ORM). Many of its underlying component parts, like the existence of various control functions, have been in place for years. There is a new recognition, however, of the importance of identifying, understanding, and measuring operational risks more intelligently, as well as weaving an effective web of approaches to managing them given their complexity and potentially devastating impact on firms today.

Management, bank boards, and regulators have been forced to ask questions like, "What else besides credit and market losses can put our firm at substantial risk? What is operational risk? How do we define, measure, and best manage it? Can we hedge it? Perhaps we should be thinking more holistically about risk on a truly enterprise-wide basis so we are not blindsided in the future."

This chapter is an overview—an executive summary, focused on key trends in operational risk management, as well as on the changes in the underlying risk factors that could well serve to increase the focus even further.[1] It covers executive management needs and perspectives, ORM trends to date, the ORM upside opportunity, risk assessment, performance measures and risk finance. Last, it includes a brief overview of Bankers Trust's early work on operational risk measurement, including our advancements on operational risk-based capital, and in the general implementation of operational risk management. As a credited pioneer in operational risk management, the work of Bankers Trust (BT) on risk measurement and risk financing still remains a beacon of insight and innovation even today.

EXECUTIVE MANAGEMENT NEEDS AND PERSPECTIVES

In the wake of headline losses and business and technology changes, chief executives and senior managers at the best firms have concluded that they must:

- Understand more fully the extent of the impact of operational risk (i.e., risk identification and risk capital measurement).
- Obtain management information about operational risk: its sources and causative factors.
- Determine capital adequacy for operational risk just as they have done for market, credit, and liquidity risks.
- Effect risk response through clearly assigned ownership and responsibility for risk management.
- Provide incentives for risk management through performance measures such as risk capital attribution and links to incentive compensation.
- Make better-informed decisions about hedging or risk financing (e.g., risk reserves, insurance, and other financing techniques).

- Combine the net impact of operational risk with credit and market risk potential for a firmwide view of risk and aggregated risk capital adequacy.
- Balance risk management investment against upside from operational risk management efforts.

Before we begin to discuss the practical details of operational risk management, it is important that we dispel a common myth. (ORM Myth: "Risk Measurement = Risk Management."). No one actually makes this statement, of course, but it is often implied. Many risk practitioners and consultants say risk *management,* when they are actually practicing risk *measurement.* Risk measurement is a subset, of course, of risk management (i.e., once you identify risk, you should evaluate, analyze, and *measure* it, before mitigating it through risk controls, and financing or hedging it). Although measuring risk adds much value in drawing attention for mitigation and management purposes, in isolation the measurement process does not have much *value until the numbers are integrated back into management, for instance, and used in a performance management or behavior modification sense.* Without a doubt, the most effective methods are those that have a direct impact on incentive compensation. For instance, quantifying the possible loss costs of weak controls in sales or trading systems is all well and good, but you haven't achieved much unless you reduce or withhold a manager's bonus until such time as the controls are strengthened.[2]

What are we actually going to do about the risk once we have identified it, understand it, and have dimensioned it? Here we want to look into the various types of control measures, behavioral modifications, and other means of mitigating risks that we are looking to minimize—or shed altogether—from the organization.[3] The primary objective of risk mitigation is simple enough: to reduce the risk of operational losses. It's the strategies, methods, tools, and style of implementation that make up the complex part.

It is also important to clarify a few key points about operational risk mitigation. Few, if any, have suggested that operational risk management subsume existing control infrastructures. So, a key part of the risk mitigation challenge will be to provide support and enhance the existing risk-control environment. To do this we need to do two things: First, create incentives for the business manager to improve upon control and behavioral risk-indicator results, thus improving the overall state of operational risk management in the firm; second, provide incentives to support existing functions, such as policy and procedures and internal audit, and link those to the numbers in operational risk management.[4]

However, we want to go even one better than that. The logical objective argument from a business manager's perspective will be even more progressive, and perhaps seem a bit radical relative to the traditional risk management perspective. Thus, armed with information, incentives, and leverage, we will support strategic decision making and strategic advantage. As such, we will be seeking to "turn" the firm's risk profile into a competitive advantage.

THE REAL OPPORTUNITY: BUILDING MORE EFFECTIVE ORGANIZATIONS

Many people believe that operational risk only consists of a downside. That is unfortunate. The position goes something like, "If we can simply limit the losses caused by operational risk, then we will have fulfilled our mission and will be in a much better position overall." Or, another perspective limits its sights on finding the most technically correct calculation of risk in order to minimize the impact of prospective regulatory capital charges by the financial service regulatory community. Although both are noble goals in and of themselves, and will contribute, there *is* a far greater cause here.

The opportunity is to propel the new strategies, tools and techniques forward to transform not just a part of risk management, but to fill an important gap in the management of business strategy and day-to-day business operations for an upside: enhanced shareholder value. We have arrived at a point in time that corporate strategy and shareholder value initiatives are in need of the very tools that are emerging in the operational risk management discipline. This direction is far more than just some grand scheme to elevate the stature and importance of operational risk professionals. In order to be successful, operational risk management needs to hold the attention of senior executives, managers, and staff alike if it is to achieve its own goals of risk mitigation. One might do so by focusing on critically important targets like shareholder value.

Throughout this book we will be seeking to take all of this operational risk management effort to yet another level, to lobby for the real endgame: to link with broader enterprise-wide strategies that are seeking to build shareholder value through more effective organizations. Few would argue against the notion that General Electric has created real shareholder value with its management and control initiatives grounded in its Six Sigma quality approach. Similarly, few would argue with the statement that J.P. Morgan enjoyed a stellar reputation for quality and integrity during the course of most of its storied history in financial services, or that firms like HSBC (Hong Kong Shanghai Banking Corporation) and The Bank of New York have created value for their shareholders through their own unique control-oriented styles. In the broadest sense, these cases are all examples of the *optimizing benefits* of operational risk management.

RISK-ADJUSTED PERFORMANCE MEASURES (RAPM)

Peter Drucker introduced the world to results-oriented business and performance measures as early as the 1960s.[5] Over time the best firms have continued
to excel using performance measures. As risk management has matured, firms
have begun to harness the power of risk-adjusted performance measures. And
now, the challenge has become finding ways to leverage the risk–reward possibilities from more effective management of operational risks.

Some firms, particularly corporate entities, are already using Economic
Value-Added (EVA) measures to determine true economic benefits. These can
provide a foundation. For financial firms, Daily Price Volatility (DPV) or Value
at Risk (VAR) have become common measures of risk and might seem like an
obvious place to start. But when it comes to operational risk, daily or short-
term variations would be extremely difficult to measure because many types of
operational losses occur so infrequently. The basic idea of calculating exposure
to operational risk makes good sense. Thus, the underlying concept of VAR
over a longer term, of say one year, is much more relevant and compelling.

These measures become most useful for managing risk and influencing
behavior, however, when linked to performance measures and incentives. It
is only at this point in which we move from measuring risk to begin the
process of managing risk.

At Bankers Trust, Risk-Adjusted Return on Capital (RAROC) was our
primary risk-adjusted performance measure for many years. We completely
overhauled our approach to Operational RAROC during 1991 through
1995 and reintroduced these models into production during and following
the banks leveraged derivative transaction troubles during the first quarter
of 1996. The models were based on long-term Value-at-Risk calculations in
our risk measurement model (one-year time horizon, 99% confidence level).

The decision to develop measurement tools was an easy one. RAROC
had been an applied concept at BT since the 1970s. And since its time horizon and confidence level characteristics are far more relevant to operational
risk's more gradual evolutionary tendencies, it served as an appropriate basis for our new operational risk models.

Our next challenge was to find an analogue for market price volatility.
After some deliberation, we concluded that actual operational loss experience, and the variance of loss experience from expected ranges, would fit the
bill. Observing actual losses at all firms in the global marketplace at large
painted a valuable picture. The variance of losses from small routine errors,
reworks, and claims, to larger scale failures, redesigns, and legal costs provided operational risk's own unique picture of volatility.

One of our previously noted objectives was to confirm capital adequacy.
Thus, we reintroduced our risk measurement model in a significantly

upgraded analytical format. Another objective was to support our risk-control environment. To meet this second objective we needed an incentive-based system. The concept of Operational RAROC seemed perfectly aligned with this objective. Under our system, operational risk capital was attributed to business units based on model measures of their operational risk profiles, thereby raising the performance hurdle for the business, and engineering operational risk management into the business managers' agendas. A third objective was to support strategic decision making.

EMERGING OPERATIONAL RISK MANAGEMENT FUNCTIONS

There are at least five perspectives on operational risk management organizational structures emerging in the financial services community today. They include focus from that of risk management analytics and risk measurement, the control group focus, business line management teams, insurance risk management, and enterprise-wide multidisciplined operational risk management functions.

In this latter and broadest enterprise-wide risk management group, practitioners believe that the most effective operational risk management programs will select the most effective tools of all four of the analytics, control group, insurance risk management, and business risk measurement groups. They intend to apply those tools to dimensioning the size of the operational risk challenge, applying the most effective risk management and risk control tools, and also monitoring risk drivers and indicators. They will use these tools—key risk indicators, scores, event data, analytics, and management information systems (MIS)—like warning lights for the business manager pilot in the cockpit, with an objective of creating a comprehensive operational risk management program. Taken together, information from all of these efforts contributes to what we have begun to refer to as a firm's *operational risk profile.*

This optimal blend of objectives, strategies, methods, and tools is poised to emerge as accepted industry practice, and thus is important background. Exhibit 1.1 outlines some of the progress and emerging trends in operational risk management.

ORGANIZATIONAL FRAMEWORK FOR OPERATIONAL RISK MANAGEMENT

Most risk practitioners live by the principle that responsibility for risk management should reside with those in the best position to manage it. This generally dictates that line management own the risk and is held accountable for its management. In practice, however, risk management is addressed by a part-

The best firms are making heroic strides toward risk definition, data collection, aggregation, and first-level analysis.

Some of the key trends include:

1. Enterprise-wide risk management and operational risk recognition are on the rise.
2. Early consensus is beginning to emerge on the definition of operational risk.
3. Companies and risk managers have recognized the value of operational risk data and creating internal risk loss event database systems.
4. External commercially available databases have become available.
5. Corporations have begun to set up internal accounting codes to trace losses resulting from operational risk.
6. Firms have begun to track risk issues on both corporate and business line levels.
7. Organizations use external risk data (commercial vendors) to supplement their internal risk loss data for statistical analysis in support of experimental risk capital calculations.
8. Regulators are beginning to impose industry standards and guidelines for handling operational risk, data, and capital.
9. Risk mitigation is being enhanced through the interpretation of operational risk data.
10. Incentives are being developed for operational risk management through performance measures such as risk capital attribution and links to incentive compensation.
11. Insurance risk managers recognize that they too will need operational risk data for effective evaluation of insurance and risk finance hedge structures.
12. New risk information measures and technology applications have begun to emerge for improved operational risk management decision making.
13. Firms are recognizing that there is an upside value to managing operational risk!

EXHIBIT 1.1 Operational Risk Management Trends to Date

nership between line and corporate management. Line management should have the responsibility for strategy and day-to-day management of operational risk, both expected and unexpected. In contrast, corporate management is usually in the best position to capture an enterprise-wide perspective of the firm's risk profile, including the larger scale impact of operational interdependency and concentration risks, and capitalize on economies of scale in hedging the risk. Thus, a corporate (or group) risk management function should add significant value by sharing perspective (and analytics) on the bigger picture with line management who must manage it on a daily basis.

From both a corporate and business line management perspective, generally speaking, the contribution to risk management can be categorized in two ways. One is in providing a businesswide or firmwide *process and framework* that is needed to assure consistency in approach. At both line management and corporate levels, this role generally involves policy setting, developing risk management standards, monitoring, and portfolio management (of data or of hedges, etc.) of measuring firmwide operational risk capital. The second is a *transactional role,* such as active involvement and consultation in deal review because of specialized knowledge (e.g., of risk management techniques such as contract engineering, or of insurance and risk finance, for instance, at the corporate level). In short, the two dimensions—process and transactional—lessen the danger that a centralized operational risk management function might either find itself too detached from the firm's business flow or miss the big picture (e.g., tail risk).

OPERATIONAL RISK ASSESSMENT AND MEASUREMENT

Risk assessment and risk measurement are fundamental in the initial steps of the process. Understanding and measuring the risks are key. Because of the difficulty in measuring operational risk, however, a balanced qualitative and quantitative approach is necessary in order to achieve a complete picture of the risk.

Scenario analysis is an important *qualitative* strategy. The objective is to come up with forward-looking scenarios and then do the scenario analysis itself. One way to do this is to use the Delphi technique. This consists of pulling a number of people that represent the area, along with experts from the field, into a room together to get their opinions on what may go wrong.[6]

An effective *quantitative* technique that can be valuable is using statistical and actuarial projections to come up with a number, or series of numbers, that represent the loss potential. Risk capital calculations would then use those numbers as a means of representing the risk to the firm's capital structure, should they occur in either the "normal" expected loss sense or the extreme or catastrophic loss scenario.[7]

A third component is the use of an operational risk management information system (ORMIS) that draws useful qualitative and quantitative information about all the different types of variables and risk indicators, whether they are people-related, technology-related, tracking issues, loss incidents, or actual losses themselves.[8]

OPERATIONAL RISK DATA AND INFORMATION

Information is the key to business operational risk management. Operational risk information is becoming critically important for both business line management and at corporate levels at many financial firms. In fact, it is becoming clear that in looking ahead some of the most successful risk managers will be adept at collection, analysis, and presentation of relevant risk information, balanced with effective hands-on risk mitigation measures.

At the outset, one must recognize that he or she is confronted with unique challenges in managing operational risk. The first, and most significant, problem is the availability of data, not to mention information, in usable formats. With the exception of relatively small loss events, most of which represent processing risk (e.g., errors, outages, system glitches), data on larger and "unexpected" losses is not readily available. This is either because they have not occurred, have only occurred very infrequently, or that have not been documented and collected. Second, most organizations that *have* attempted to measure their own operational risk have done so in a vacuum and thus are only working with their own firm's (hopefully) limited experiences with operational losses. This yields an incomplete picture at best (i.e., an insufficient statistical sample). Third, although loss events can be dissected, post mortems conducted, and lessons identified, at best the exercise results in observations of circumstances that were in place prior to, and at the time of, the loss. The relationship between cause and effect has all too often not been proven statistically. Neither have control variables been proven statistically. Thus, in both areas there is room for data collection and correlation analysis.

The data challenge caused us to create some of the first operational loss databases to support our early modeling efforts (see Chapter 10, "Databases and Consortia," and Chapter 16, "Economic Risk Capital Modeling").

RISK MEASUREMENT: TYPES AND CONCEPTUAL FOUNDATIONS OF MODELS

From a modeling standpoint, an obvious difference between operational risk and credit or market risk is the availability of data. For the more liquid financial markets, price data for market risk measurement are plentiful. For credit risk, although default and other data may not be nearly as plentiful, they have been more so in recent years. In contrast, operational data, predictors, and models are still in their relative infancy. Another challenge in operational risk modeling is the need to represent tail risk in such a way that makes a convincing case with a business manager for its importance.

In response to managers' desire for a full and complete view of firmwide risk at their firms, operational risk must be represented on terms comparable to market and credit risk. Thus, before beginning any modeling exercise, a key consideration will be to achieve a result that can be aligned with other risk disciplines. The last thing you want to do is find yourself in a modeling vacuum. Thus, successful risk practitioners have worked to align with credit and market risk measurement to find a common language.

There are a number of possible conceptual foundations for operational risk modeling, of course. As examples, one could make a case for one or more of the following:

- **Economic Pricing Models:** These base forecasts on economic models. One such operational risk model uses the Capital Asset Pricing Model (CAPM) to suggest a relative distribution of pricing of operational risk among the other price determinants for capital.
- **Scenario Analysis/Subjective Loss Estimate Models:** Used to capture diverse opinions, concerns, and experience/expertise of key managers and represent them in matrix and graphic form.
- **Expected Loss Models:** Simplistic models based on expectations of loss and derived by a multiple of expected frequency and expected severity.
- **Statistical/Actuarial/Loss Distribution Loss Models:** Actual loss data are used to construct representations of loss frequencies and severities in the form of statistical probability distributions. Simulation techniques are then used to combine the distributions in modeling expected losses for the future.
- **Factor-derived Models:** Apply loss and/or causal factors to build a bottom-up prediction of loss expectancies. For instance, these models are being applied in operations and processing units in conjunction with Baysean Belief Networks and Value at Risk.

In most cases the best firms will conclude that a combination of model types will yield the best results. This was our conclusion at Bankers Trust after having experimented with several of the model types above in the 1980s and early 1990s.

PUTTING INSURANCE AND RISK FINANCE TO THE TEST

When structured properly, insurance and risk finance programs will serve as an economic hedge for operational risks. As a first step in applying them, however, we must break out of insurance conventions and insurance-like risk classes that drive many risk finance and insurance programs, with all of their *Definitions and Constraints.* Operational risk-based capital provides some with a conceptual escape. That is, it forces the practitioner to work with a broad definition of operational risk (e.g., loss from people, process, systems and external events), not more narrowly-defined insurance risk, classes. Insurance convention forces a risk practitioner to think in classes like Blanket Bonds with their very specific definitions of crime risk, for instance, rather than starting more broadly with all the possible sources of crime or fraud losses. The same is true with technology and processing risk, and so on.

Risk Finance Objectives

In order to keep the value of risk finance and insurance in perspective, we cannot lose sight of two key objectives. Most financial firms arrange for risk finance and insurance programs for two key reasons, even though they might not identify them explicitly. These are either (1) to protect their earnings, or (2) to protect their balance sheet, or perhaps (3) both. Nonfinancial corporate firms might also arrange for risk finance and insurance to protect cash flow or liquidity, but that is often not necessary as a prime objective for financial entities.

Ironically, these key objectives also find themselves at the nexus of contention between insurers and insureds when one relies on insurance alone to hedge risk. That is, there are timing problems with regard to traditional insurance claim settlements and loss accounting periods. In addition, traditional insurance limits have not provided true catastrophe protection.

Risk Finance and Insurance Performance

Based on several different surveys of our database of industry losses, we found that aggregate insurers' coverages respond to only about 20 to 30% of OR losses. (Because of the complexity of insurance terms and conditions, it is difficult to settle on a precise rate of performance.)[9] To achieve the higher end of that range you must assume that payments would be made in cases where the claim situations contained one or more parts that might be problematic from a claim perspective (i.e., might run afoul of policy terms, conditions, or exclusions). This is probably an unlikely assumption, indeed.

The winds of change are beginning to blow, however. Already some insurance underwriters (e.g., at Lloyds of London, in continental Europe and the United States) are beginning to entertain more holistic and coordinated insurance approaches for operational risk classes, rather than just for insurance classes. In addition, capital market solutions have been explored to bring increased limit capacity to the traditional insurance markets.

Thus, a more comprehensive result for risk finance strategy at a financial firm might involve "earnings protection" or loss accounting smoothing at relatively low levels of risk; attempts at improving the timed alignment of accounting treatment for losses and recoveries; and targeted large loss structures as a start toward "balance sheet protection."

ACHIEVING A FULLY INTEGRATED FUNCTION

An organization derives several key benefits from using a fully integrated approach to Operational Risk Management (ORM). The organization is able to:

- Create forums for collaboration by getting different groups to work together
- Measure exposures more completely
- Develop incentives for productive behavior
- Clarify transaction and deal flow
- Streamline internal risk controls, eliminating redundancy
- Derive value from management information systems (MIS) by using them to support operational risk management

By definition, these activities are collaborative between corporate, or group level, and business line level. Internal Audit, in contrast, differs by its necessary independence and arms length. Key sources of enterprise-wide operational risk data are varied: loss data and analysis, qualitative self-assessment or risk assessment, and process risk assessment—from throughout the firm. Many are paper-based today but will be automated with loss and data capture. For process-risk analysis of key performance and risk indicators, at both a business level and firmwide, the key is integrating that data and making it available to corporate and business managers.[10]

DYNAMIC AND INTERACTIVE RISK MANAGEMENT

Some aspects of operational risk management have already become abundantly clear. For instance, one-dimensional and territorial operational risk management thinking and tactics are destined to fail. The complex operational risks of today demand a flexible series of multidimensioned solutions working in tandem. We will be far more effective as risk managers if we recognize this and blend a number of the tools and initiatives—from risk indicators to qualitative risk assessment, from issues tracking to quantitative analysis, and from risk systems to risk finance—into a mosaic, not exclusively as individual tiles of limited individual interest and value.[11]

OPERATIONAL RISK MIS AND TECHNOLOGY

In addition to modeling operational risk, there is much to be said for simply improving on the availability of information about operational risk information for management decision making. For instance, much value can be gained by simply reporting on some or all of the following:

- Losses and loss cause analyses
- Linking analyses to outstanding control issues
- Specific risk variables/indicators (e.g., compilation of extensive technology or other risk class data)
- Risk class/concentration-of-risk representations
- Identification of candidates for incentives and accountability
- Risk factor comparative and trend analyses
- Risk finance coverage alignments
- Impact on the balance sheet and the P&L (profit and loss)

Technology will be the essential mortar needed to aggregate, cement, and simplify all the pieces in place, thereby linking all of the functional areas, initiatives, and data sets, both hard and soft, firmwide. Aggregated operational risk reporting will become commonplace, much as portfolio market and credit risk reports have. Because of the softer issues involved, like the vagaries of human behavior (i.e., people risk), however, a mix of tools will be needed to represent operational risk fully. The risk complexities will also require more effective risk management programs to link initiatives and variables together not just periodically, but continuously, and with the speed of "Internet time."

REGULATORY DEVELOPMENTS

One noteworthy development is the relatively rapid series of releases on Operational Risk Management by the Basel Committee's Risk Management Group (RMG) from September 1998 to the present. To quote the first such document, "managing operational risk is becoming an important feature of sound risk management practice in modern financial markets," and the BIS "encourages banks to share with their supervisors the development of new techniques to identify, measure, manage and control operational risk." Certainly, the Basel Committee was not finished. At the time of this writing, there are several proposals on the table to levy a regulatory risk capital charge for operational risk, as outlined in the committee's January 2001 release.

CONCLUSION: WHERE ARE WE NOW?

We are at the precipice of a new risk management frontier with operational risks and clearly there is still much farther to go. Perhaps the situation can be summed up as follows. Recently, when asked if he had come up with a way to allocate economic capital for operational risk, the vice-chairman of one major U.S. bank responded, "We're trying."

Leading up to and in the wake of the January 2001 release from the Basel Committee, risk managers have clearly been trying, and in the process groping for definitions, data, and tools. In its broadest definition, operational risk represents the danger posed by potential disruptions in service or resulting damage to an institution's reputation, revenues, or productivity. Whether the operational risk event is a failure in internal controls, information processing, or is a result of malicious or fraudulent actions by individuals, or any other unpredictable events, risk managers already know that measuring and managing it will take a dedicated effort to persevere. To have any real power in this area, risk pioneers will have to develop a framework to explicitly identify, measure, and monitor operational risks. In most cases this implies updating existing data resources, risk structures, and risk-tracking procedures.

Operational losses have become more visible and painful, operational performance demands are greater than ever, the Basel Committee will require an explicit capital charge for operational risk, and management and shareholders are demanding answers.

It seems clear that understanding the history, the issues, the emerging analytics, and the relevant management structures and styles will all be key to progressing the topic. Thoughtful objectives and firmwide program implementation are all too often omitted, however, from the debate that has gone on in the last several years about the definition and measurement of operational risk. There has been far too little discussion about setting objectives, understanding the risks, and understanding how broad or narrow the scope of mitigation efforts and the program is overall. It is critically important to turn these conflicting objectives into opportunities: opportunities to reduce risk at both a business/product/profit center and at a corporate or firmwide level, while at the same time understanding risk and control and behavioral issues throughout the firm.[12]

Clearly the direction that an individual firm will take on the management of operational risk will depend on the style of its management and the firm's overall culture. Whether it places all of its emphasis on more granular audit-based control systems, blends them with risk measurement and incentive systems at a higher firmwide level, or introduces softer, perhaps less measurable risk factors, all depends on their expected impact in influencing human behavior in a positive risk management way.

Dynamic and integrated risk mitigation will be key; measurement and modeling should be only one piece of the overall operational risk management puzzle. But now, more than ever, in the midst of regulatory capital-at-risk discussions, if we are not careful, their relative value can be blown out of proportion in operational risk programs. We want to strive for fully integrated operational risk management systems and programs firmwide and at all levels, and along with them, more effective and competitive organizations for our stakeholders.[13]

We can certainly expect a greater emphasis and investment on data collection and analytics, with a view toward more heroic attempts at building operational risk models for measurement, analysis, and management of these risks. Senior managers are seeking better definition and better MIS. Thus, risk information will also be key and performance measurement tools will be essential in creating incentives/disincentives for effective risk management behavior.

On the regulatory front, because of the stakes involved, it is simply a matter of time before operational risk measurement and management is much more closely scrutinized on a regular basis, and discrete regulatory capital will become a requirement.

Organizationally, firms will have to invest in operational risk management groups and analytics. The challenge will be in coalescing teams of people schooled in the broad range of disciplines represented by the underlying operational risks.

Last, there are encouraging signs that the financial and insurance markets will continue to evolve toward providing more effective "hedges" for broader areas of operational risk than has been addressed by the insurance markets alone in the past.

The precise direction that risk practitioners responsible for operational risk modeling, measurement, management, and risk finance will take in future months and years is unclear. What is clear, however, is that operational risk itself can be expected to grow in size and complexity given the anticipated evolution of systems and the increased interdependency of organizations. And if recent industry losses are any indication, the need for risk management will continue to evolve along with it.

All of these trends make for interesting times ahead. In the following chapters we will explore all of these concepts more fully.

CHAPTER 2

The Best Practice Strategies

O perational risk management is a new management discipline with the goal of enhancing management performance through the early identification and avoidance of business disruption. Its specific focus is on the failings of people, process, systems, or external events. The discipline introduces a new corporate mandate, strategies, framework, function, business practice, tools, techniques, analytics, metrics, processes, and technology, plus a coordinating unit, all rolled into one. The operational risk management movement is certainly not simply about a new *department, position* or *even about new capital models* alone.

The operational risks themselves, however, are not all that new. Most of them have simply morphed, albeit substantially, from more familiar risks given the watershed changes in the business environment. Those changes have made once familiar risks more dangerous than ever before. The good news is that the discipline and tools used to manage them have been changing to keep up. This evolution of management practices has been dramatic. During the course of a relatively short period of time, a variety of practices have evolved to combat these newly evolved risks.

So, perhaps rather than asking about the risks at this point, the more interesting question may be, "What are the characteristics that define enterprise-wide operational risk management?" Today, an operational risk management program and process will consist of many or all of the following components and concepts:[1]

- An enterprise-wide recognition that there is an urgent need, opportunity, and upside in managing operational risk.
- A dedicated and independent risk assessment function by business, and for operational risks at the corporate level, not solely an audit function.
- Use of quantitative analysis for risk assessment at all levels of the organization, applying sophistication appropriate for the organization and its culture.
- Specific firmwide risk assessment and control projects (e.g., e-business, systems integration, merger, and acquisition due diligence).

- Development of operational risk mitigation programs and incentive systems.
- Development of operational risk capital attribution and/or allocation methods for operational risks.
- Focus on strategic reputation management in alliance with public relations (PR) and senior management.
- Linkage with risk and insurance management functions for the mutual benefits of enhanced risk assessment and broader risk financing.
- Enhanced development and dissemination of management information about operational risks (e.g., risk indicators, incident, issue, and loss data), performance measures (e.g., business-risk goals and industry benchmarks) at all levels in the organization.
- Assimilation of all of the above risk functions into a firmwide ideological vision (e.g., quality management efforts like Six Sigma or other programs).
- Recognition that operational risk management is a key component of enterprise-wide risk management, including credit, market, operational, and strategy risks.

Admittedly, some of these features bear striking similarity to those of enterprise-wide risk management. The reality is that operational risks are pervasive. As such, they have more enterprise-wide implications in many firms than credit or market risks alone, which may not be present in some business units. As a result, operational risk management, when implemented within the broad context of the best practice strategies we will be discussing, will serve as an important launching pad for an enterprise-wide risk management function.

This chapter will be the linchpin for the remainder of the book. It will continue to elaborate on this answer and lay the groundwork for the remainder of the book in the context of key principles, strategies, tools, and tactics for program development, and explore ideas, illustrations, and cases along the way.

SOME BORROWED, SOME NEW STRATEGIES

Early work on operational risk management began as an evolution from other risk management-related disciplines in the early 1990s. As one example, our formation of a team to address the interrelated management needs of risk assessment, operational risk capital, and risk finance/insurance management at Bankers Trust in 1991 has been credited by many as a groundbreaking effort in the field. Numerous other firms began pioneering their own versions of operational risk management at about the same time. Despite one-off programs, however, it wasn't until 1996 that the subject began receiving widespread attention by firms, industry associations, and conference promoters.

So, in a relatively short period, the subject and industry progress has evolved dramatically. But credit for a great deal of this push must be attributed to the large losses that have gripped our attention in the headlines, and certainly as a result, regulators as well, who have pressed the issue. Their push has culminated most recently in a series of releases from the Basel Committee on Banking Supervision, which proposes regulatory capital for operational risks.

In some respects, operational risk management is beginning to define the next phase of evolution of corporate risk management. In financial institutions, sophisticated market and credit risk management have been most visible in stature and in the commitment of resources over the past two decades. Until the last 5 to 10 years, however, these techniques have been used only by a relatively small number of sophisticated risk managers, traders, and sophisticated lenders (to the extent credit risk modeling has become more widely accepted in the latter case), and by specialized risk functions within larger firms.

Because of its pervasiveness, on the other hand, operational risk touches every individual in an organization. A number of different and disjointed strategies and techniques—from internal audit control assessments to insurance risk management risk class assessments and actuarial quantification techniques—have existed for years in managing operational and event risks. The recent convergence and combination of these strategies and tools now have the potential of creating a risk management discipline that will affect and influence more organizations and people than ever before. In addition, just as market risk practitioners have come to realize in the wake of Long-Term Capital Management (LTCM), there is recognition that a balance of qualitative and quantitative operational risk assessment techniques is an improvement over one or the other alone.

In developing a fully integrated operational risk management program, companies will take full advantage of the better risk management practices that may already be in place throughout a firm. This may seem like a simple first step, but it is an important push in the right direction.

Operational risk management itself has roots in many management and control functions that already exist throughout an organization. But that might beg the question, Why is a *new* operational risk management function necessary? Well, first and foremost, the function is generally designed to focus on the facilitation of operational risk response *by linking with and leveraging* existing corporate risk and control-related programs and units.

It would help to describe it in the context of the functions that contributed to its birth and development. For instance, as will be apparent from the following chapters, some of our own breakthroughs on operational risk model development had their roots in insurance-related actuarial modeling, coupled with market and credit risk capital modeling. Elsewhere, some of the performance metrics used now in tracking operational risk indicators were borrowed from business management, operations, and processing groups. Qualitative risk assessment scenario analysis and control self-assessment work have blended risk assessment techniques borrowed from both internal audit functions and risk and insurance management practitioners.

Advancing the best practices from these functions can go a long way toward an integrated, holistic approach to operational risk management. The next step in building an advanced operational risk management platform is to outline an operational risk framework definition and vocabulary, so that everyone is on the same page across the entire organization.

KEY BUILDING BLOCKS AND 20 BEST PRACTICE STRATEGIES

Even in the short time that it has been a recognized function to date, operational risk management has begun to sprout some best practices. But the term *best practices* implies a function that has matured. It begs the questions, Best practices in whose opinion? Where's the proof? Some might argue that the discipline is too new to sprout best practices.

The best practices showcased here emerged from numerous discussions and debates with senior management teams, practicing risk managers, and members of the regulatory community, each of whom exhibited nearly a passion for one or more of these methods and approaches. In addition, as already discussed, operational risk management has the advantage of having evolved from years of work in several other well-established business and corporate functions.

This section introduces the key building blocks (or component principles) and strategies that are setting the stage for best practice in operational risk management. I will introduce each one briefly for now, then explore them much more fully in the ensuing chapters. *Note:* the 20 Best Practice Strategies that follow are outlined in the order that they appear in the text. They provide a logical flow for thinking through and understanding the issues of operational risk and the arguments for an integrated program of operational risk management. This is not necessarily the order in which they would be applied, however, in developing an operational risk management program.

In discussing these 20 strategies with clients and colleagues, some have suggested that 20 is too many—it is too hard to remember all of them. That may be a fair observation, so for ease of reference and memory, I offer six key principles—building blocks that serve as our foundation for the strategies. They are:

I. Enterprise-wide Vision, Culture, and Commitment
II. Organizational Framework and Responsibilities

III. Framing Strategies for Operational Risk Response
IV. Dynamic Risk Monitoring and Management
 V. Financial and Regulatory Management Positioning
VI. Operational Risk Management Technology

The best firms and most successful operational risk management programs will address all six of them. Each one serves as the foundation for one or more strategies. The six building blocks and 20 strategies are outlined below.

I. Enterprise-wide Vision, Culture, and Commitment

Any enterprise-wide program must be evident to stakeholders both internally and externally. The commitment must be as clear to the investment community as it is to the employee and client base. Thus, it is essential to begin with top-level issues of vision, reputation, culture, and definition.

1. Define Operational Risk for the Organization   Operational risk must be defined and that definition communicated throughout an organization before it can be measured or managed effectively. It is nearly impossible for a staff at large to be focused on and committed to a topic if the topic is not well defined or understood.

2. Demonstrate a Vision, Mandate, and Objectives   The firmwide vision, values, and mandate will be formulated at the highest levels of the organization and communicated outward. It will be communicated at three levels. The first is the company's own ideological vision statement. That sets the stage. The second is a statement on enterprise-wide risk management, of which operational risk will be a recognized part. The third is a specific statement on operational risk management, which will be much more specific as to the key objectives, roles, responsibility, and functional scope. Taken together, the statements will serve as clear evidence of buy-in at both the board and most senior management levels of the organization. They demonstrate not only internally, but also externally, the firm's commitment and also serve as an enhancement to shareholder value.

3. Foster a Culture of Integrity and Risk Management Awareness   More often than not corporate culture and ethos are the least recognized components of an operational risk management program but, at the same time, can have the greatest positive or negative impact on an organization's risk profile. A senior level commitment and a risk-aware culture are both essential.

4. Manage the Risk to the Firm's Franchise, Reputation, and Brand   The best firms will have a clear understanding of the potential effect of operational risk on their franchise and franchise value. A vision and mandate are not enough. In addition to continued positive reinforcement of the company's franchise and brand, reputation management requires ongoing discipline, a tested strategy, and a plan for managing crises that might impact their reputation and franchise.

II. Organizational Framework and Responsibilities

Without a clear vision, mandate, framework, and responsibilities, operational risk management will fail.[2] Day-to-day management of operational risk is the responsibility of the business units. Corporate management is charged with enterprise-wide policy and standards, supporting and holding the business units accountable.

5. Empower Business Units with Responsibility for Risk Management   The framework will delineate risk management roles and responsibilities of the business units. Business units on a local level manage operational risk most effectively. The best firms will support and empower business units and profit centers with responsibility, accountability and authority for management of their own operational risks.

6. Support and Leverage Corporate Units' Capabilities and Contributions   Define roles and responsibilities of corporate units firmwide. Structure operational risk management programs such that they reinforce key aspects of existing control and risk management programs, including but not limited to those of Control Self-Assessment, Internal Audit, Compliance, Legal, Security, and other risk management functions. Support and leverage their contribution. Avoid redundancy of effort. A mission statement and objectives will be set for those units contributing to the firmwide function, not limited to the group operational risk management unit.

7. Designate an Operational Risk Management Unit to Serve as a Facilitator   Form a coordinating unit for operational risk management headed by a senior manager and staffed with top talent to coordinate operational risk management efforts firmwide. In some firms the manager will head operational risk exclusively. In others, the individual may also serve as Chief Risk Officer. In any event, business units will direct their own operational risk efforts, but a separate corporate operational risk function will support and monitor their activities. In some industries (e.g., financial services), the function will be separate from Internal Audit.

III. Operational Risk Response Framework

Although arguably all of our efforts are or will be geared toward mitigating or optimizing risk, there are several strategies that will be identified as providing an overall framework for risk mitigation efforts firmwide. We refer to these as the risk mitigation framing strategies. They consist of strategies that must emanate from the corporate organization in support, reinforcement, and scrutiny of the business unit efforts.

8. Disseminate Useful Management Information and Reports   Provide clear, useful, and actionable information about operational risks, losses, and the status of risk response and control efforts such that business unit managers and staff firmwide are in a position to manage them on a day-to-day basis.

9. Use Incentives and Disincentives in Managing Operational Risk   Use incentives *and* disincentive systems as a means to balance strategic risk and reward. For instance, use risk-adjusted performance measures (RAPM), such as risk-based economic capital allocation or attribution processes, to highlight operational risk intensive businesses. Provide both incentives and disincentives for management of risk. Use capital as a means to optimize risk and reward.

Far too often, risk management only focuses on negatives, and thus risk managers fall in the trap of penalizing staff and units for risks identified, poor performance, and loss results. The most effective programs balance this with a system of rewards for productive risk management behavior and investment by both business and corporate units and staff alike. Some examples might include reduction of risk through upgrades in systems or manual processes, enhanced issue tracking systems, and timely clearance of self-identified risk issues or issues identified by Internal Audit.

Focus attention beyond organizational units to individual behavior. Build operational risk considerations into incentive-based compensation plans (e.g., bonuses, stock options, deferred compensation) in order to assure that staff members are focused on mitigating and optimizing operational risk on a day-to-day basis.

Develop a program of benchmarking and goal setting to track progress on a consistent basis over time and relative to peers on a unit-by-unit basis and firmwide (e.g., peer comparisons, incident and loss results over time, cost-of-operational risk analyses and reporting).

10. Employ Segregation and Diversification Strategies   Pursue high-level diversification techniques to combat the potentially catastrophic effects of process. Reinforce diversification and segregation of duties in critical processes. Balance risk and reward in diversification of physical asset concentrations.

11. Leverage Firmwide Defenses for Business Continuity   A key aspect of operational risk management will be to assure the smooth continuity of business operations. Enhance and leverage strategic business continuity efforts beyond traditional areas of focus, such as physical hazard risk. Address the vulnerabilities such as risk to key revenue streams, reputation, stakeholder and regulatory standing, and one-time risk of loss. Include strategic investments in systems and processes. Seek opportunities to showcase business continuity as a competitive advantage.

IV. Dynamic Risk Monitoring and Management

Understanding the risk profile of the organization is an essential first step in managing it. Use of data and metrics is essential for making the subject more tangible and retaining management and staff attention to the issues at large.

Traditionally, risk management had been viewed as consisting of separate and distinct elements. They have been recognized to include risk identification, assessment and/or measurement, and mitigation or control. Although the process has always been continuous, it was often viewed to require formal and orderly risk identification reviews, followed by analysis, then a focus on controls. Today, rates of change in technology and business processes have accelerated to such a point that separate analyses are too often out of date before they are even completed. Thus, the need for continuous and dynamic reviews is more evident today than ever before. Fortunately, advancements in technology, frequent reporting, and interactive systems will support a more timely response.

This principal entails the building block strategies for moving toward dynamic risk profiling and management.

12. Implement Bottom-Up Processes to Identify, Evaluate, and Manage Operational Risks
Effective operational risk management begins with each employee having an understanding of the potential benefits and harm in each risk faced. This requires a process at a sufficiently detailed and specific level for identifying and evaluating new risks on a continuous basis (e.g., independent risk assessment, control self-assessment, process analysis).

13. Use a Portfolio-based Approach to Evaluate Firmwide Loss Potential   Although bottom-up process reviews are helpful for individual business unit and line managers, they sometimes miss the big picture. In addition, senior management at a firmwide level must have an aggregate view of operational risk. This is where the portfolio level analysis comes in (e.g., firmwide, risk mapping, portfolio-level actuarial analysis).

14. Coordinate Event and Risk Indicator Data Firmwide   Track operational risk issues, incidents, and losses by developing a process to capture and track them, including their cost and causative factors, at both business and corporate levels firmwide. Identify and track predictive indicators and drivers of operational risks. Capture both quantitative *and* qualitative driver data and

descriptive information. Provide indicator reports and scores to management levels appropriate for action.

15. Apply Analytics to Improve ORM Decision Making   One of the most significant advancements in modern operational risk management is the introduction of quantitative techniques for risk assessment and modeling of future loss scenarios. Apply analytics to support operational risk management decision making on a day-to-day business level, as well as in strategic risk–reward decision making on a portfolio level. Apply levels of analytic sophistication appropriate for your individual firm's size, culture, and business mix.

16. Implement Dynamic Risk Profiling and Monitoring   The most successful programs have been built around a continuum of risk tools for effective identification, assessment, mitigation, and finance. Advancements in risk monitoring include risk profiling and dynamic risk profiling. Risk profiling recognizes the need for combining different types of assessment and measurement and control tools for a complete picture of an organization's risk. Dynamic risk profiling requires a continuous and timely process, enabled by interactive technology. Work to apply them for more effective and timely day-to-day risk management.

V. Financial and Regulatory Management Positioning

This set of strategies is focused on the firm's financial and capital structure, from both management and regulatory perspectives.

17. Enhance Risk Finance Hedging of Operational Risks   Align insurance and risk finance programs to operational risks. Measure program performance over time. Re-engineer programs to attain an optimal coverage and cost trade-off. But conventional insurance provides only a partial solution. Enhance risk financing through the use of effective alternative risk financing structures. Use self-insurance, captive, excess-of-loss reinsurance, credit, and capital markets to construct effective protection for expected, unexpected, and catastrophe operational risks.

18. Apply Operational Risk-Adjusted Performance Measures and Economic Risk Capital Models   Use risk-adjusted performance measures (RAPM) and economic risk capital models to calculate and monitor the effect of operational losses on firmwide and business unit levels. Monitor capital structures on top-down and bottom-up bases. Embed the models and processes to drive strategic and tactical risk-based decisions firmwide. Work toward application of the models in product pricing.

19. Monitor the Emerging Regulatory Capital and Supervisory Environment and Position Accordingly   Participate in regulatory discussions and monitor the evolution of requirements. Financial service firms should monitor developments from the Basel Committee on Banking Supervision, as well as regulatory interpretations and actions on a local level. Monitor the emerging operational risk regulatory capital guidelines and options. Ensure that economic risk capital models are in sync with regulatory model developments and then position accordingly to optimize risk capital models and the balance sheet.

VI. Operational Risk Management Technology

Technology is an essential part of our everyday lives today. It is just beginning to become appreciated as an essential part of enterprise-wide operational risk management programs, however. Because of its importance, we dedicate a separate section and strategy to its development.

20. Leverage Risk Management Efforts through State-of-the-Art Technology Assure program efficiency by leveraging technology in enterprise-wide data gathering, analysis, and information delivery. Web-enabled systems will support the flow of data and information both internally and externally. Use powerful database and data warehouse technology to prepare for the flood of data that will be required to manage operational risk effectively in the future.

A WEB OF BEST PRACTICES

These best practice strategies have been drawn from numerous projects, and years of collective experience of business managers and risk practitioners alike. The list is not intended to represent industry consensus by any means, but rather establish some early lines in the sand for those who must begin managing operational risks now. They are intended, however, to prompt the industry toward a broader discussion over regulatory capital than currently exists.

Major high-profile operational losses and incidents have a pronounced effect on individual firms. They tend to spark action and creativity and, incidentally, serve as a more powerful motivator than regulation. It may be more than just an interesting coincidence that several of the firms selected as case studies in the following chapters for their advances in operational risk management or pioneering efforts have also attracted publicity for some high-profile operational events. Examples include General Electric, Bankers Trust, The Bank of New York, and Halifax Bank Plc. These firms were selected for the development and use of best practices, not because they had suffered losses. The reality, however, is that virtually all large firms have suffered at least one high profile event. Another reality is that of the firms featured here, in almost every case their best practice operational risk management strategy was in development or in early stages of implementation when the event occurred. Perhaps the more interesting point is that in virtually all cases the events had one beneficial effect: they prompted additional aware-ness and investment in risk management enterprise-wide.

Few would argue that General Electric is one of the most respected com-panies in North America, if not the world. They are featured in Chapter 4 for their use of Six Sigma, quality, and excellence programs. These programs have really come into prominence after the high-profile trading scandal at Kidder Peabody (summarized in Chapter 6), one of the firm's business units.

Second, as an independent firm, Bankers Trust was known and revered for its risk management pioneering systems, including portfolio-level RAROC and Operational RAROC. There too, the latter RAROC development was still in its design phase when the firm's troubles with customer disputes involving leveraged derivatives first began to surface in 1994. Not surprisingly, additional investment in funding and resources came after those cases emerged.

Third, The Bank of New York is featured in Chapter 9 for its respected work involving independent risk assessment and controls. There too, it was be-ing implemented when the bank's incident of alleged Russian illegal wire trans-fers took place in 1999. Although highly visible, the incident ultimately caused no direct monetary loss, but had the positive effect of confirming the bank's commitment to its risk management framework.

Fourth, Halifax Group is included in Chapters 13 and 19 for its work in moving toward technology-based dynamic risk profiling. Again, it is a coinci-dence that one of its systems problem was selected for use in Chapter 3 because it serves as a useful illustration in the definitions chapter. Here too, however, these technology glitches helped to spark management to work even harder on its more recent developments in its operational risk management program.

Operational risk management is still in its infancy and will continue to evolve and build upon current best practices. I am not aware of any indi-vidual firm that has yet adopted *all* of the listed strategies framed here in their program. Chalk this up to management style or corporate culture, or the relative embryonic stage of the discipline. Elsewhere, the reality is that some firms and/or managers have embraced certain strategies fully, while re-jecting others. This is most clearly evident when it comes to risk assessment and modeling methods and styles. Some are adamant about certain strate-gies, and even seem passionate about them over others.

Balance is key. The best firms have come to realize that there is much to be said for implementing one quantitative risk assessment and modeling strategy and balancing it with one qualitative or subjective strategy. Just as there are few, if any, firms that practice all of the risk assessment and modeling strategies, there are probably few or any that practice each of their selected strategies to perfection. Having said that, there certainly seems to be a relationship between the performance of firms in the marketplace and their use of these strategies.

When the practices are implemented as a comprehensive framework, however, they will provide the greatest potential for mitigation of operational risk, reduction of loss frequencies, and along with some luck, reduction in aggregate losses over time, and will increase effectiveness of the firm's business overall.

Last, by definition best practices are elusive. It is presumptuous and discouraging to think that we have already found the ultimate best practices and that there will be no further progress on the subject of operational risk management. The list will be a moving target. It is my expectation, however, that evolution will come in the form of refinement of the strategies outlined herein, around the fringes as it were, rather than as wholesale changes to the list.

PHASES OF IMPLEMENTATION

The majority of firms are in one of three phases of operational risk management: realization, basic implementation, and advanced integration.[3]

- **Realization:** As with any major issue, the first step is to accept a problem. Most firms have passed through the first phase. They realize that operational risk is a major issue, understand the framework of operational risk, and have embarked on operational risk programs.
- **Basic implementation:** Firms in the second phase are implementing one-off initiatives, experimenting with self-assessment, employing risk indicators on an isolated level, using various management tools, using management information systems (MIS) for individual business lines, and perhaps doing some high-level modeling of certain areas of risk.
- **Advanced integration:** What firms are really striving for is phase three, integrated or holistic operational risk programs, including multiuser web-based platforms and systems. They are seeking to support input and access of data and information throughout the firm, conduct various types of analyses to support the efficiency of the business overall, and reduce the cost of operational risk and loss.

At this level, programs and systems are fully integrated and distributed. There is risk assessment and mitigation throughout the firm. Risk capital is being used to understand the impact on the capital structure of the firm, and blended risk finance—insurance, reinsurance, self-insurance, capital markets, finite risk, or financial insurance coverages—is a reality. The management framework is in place, or at least being created, for dealing with the risk of complexity: integration risk, merger and acquisition risk, dealing with cultural changes, and things of that nature.

The last part of this phase is to weave operational risk management into an enterprise-wide risk management program that serves to address financial, operational, and strategic risks.

A FINAL THOUGHT: PROGRAMS MUST
BE TRANSPARENT AND UNDERSTANDABLE

Modern day advancements in both financial (market and credit) and operational risk management add enormous value. For instance, the move toward sophisticated quantification techniques takes some of the guesswork out of risk–reward business decision making. Before these advances, managers had little basis on which to make decisions about risk reductions, risk finance, and the efficient use of risk capital. Now operational risks will be included in these risk–reward calculations.

The flip side of this advancement, however, is that as the topic has become more sophisticated for some, it has become more arcane and less comprehensible for many. Arcane classifications, analyses, capital calculations, and financing structures serve to make the entire subject more confusing for many, at a time when simplicity and involvement by the masses on an enterprise-wide and industrywide basis is most critical.

You can hear the complaints throughout many organizations, at conferences, and even in the boardroom. "Give me something I can grasp. Give me something I can use. Give me something I can apply in the real world. Give me something I can communicate to line managers and staff so they can get involved in risk optimization on a day-to-day basis." Risk professionals should not lose sight of transparency and simplicity.

CONCLUSION

Enterprise-wide operational risk management addresses an incredibly wide range and diverse set of issues. To be effective, this management discipline must cover much ground in a short period of time, and yet many firms have just begun their development. Once they do, they recognize the enormity of the task.

On closer examination, it is clear that in some cases it is simply a matter of realigning existing functions and resources for more effective results. Take the case of a control self-assessment, a legal, and an internal audit department all operating independently. Each uncovers risk issues, but they are tracked and handled independently and inefficiently. With a coordinated issue and action tracking system, combined with an operational risk capital allocation system, the groups will work more effectively and efficiently.

A roadmap of Best Practice Strategies will simplify what can otherwise become an insurmountable task. The 20 strategies outlined in this chapter and throughout this book are being applied successfully in varying degrees at numerous firms. Individually, however, their benefit is limited. Firms are now discovering the benefits of weaving them together into a comprehensive risk management program.

CHAPTER 3

What Is Operational Risk?

Operational risk is "the risk of loss resulting from inadequate or failed internal processes, people and systems or from external events" *

Basel Committee on Banking Supervision 2001[1]

O ne can scarcely pick up a newspaper without reading a story about an accounting embarrassment, fraud, legal action, or some other operational disaster. Operational risk seems so prevalent that one might wonder if it is too broadly defined to be useful to those in the field. How should we narrow our definition? Where should we set boundaries on operational risk? It is with these questions in mind that we begin our search for a proper and useful definition.

No discussion of operational risk would be complete without some commentary on definitions. So many have approached the subject from different perspectives that finding common ground at the outset is not just important, it is essential. For instance, the subject has been approached from operations and processing managers, corporate risk managers, insurance risk managers, market and credit risk managers, auditors, regulators, and consultants. Each has brought a different but important perspective.[2]

Despite the definition of operational risk in the opening quote, complete consensus has not been reached, for reasons that we will explore more fully in this chapter. For one, although the Basel Committee notes in its January, 2001 release that the definition includes legal risk, it excludes reputation risk. Presumably the reason is that reputation risk is too difficult to measure, and

---

*We might like to imply by this quote from an influential and standard-setting global regulatory body that there is full consensus on the definition of operational risk. But in reality, there is not, at least not *full* consensus just yet as evident by the references to definitions and risk classes throughout this book.

BP STRATEGY #1—DEFINE OPERATIONAL RISK FOR YOUR OWN ORGANIZATION

Operational risk must be defined and that definition communicated in any given organization before it can be measured or managed. It is nearly impossible for a staff at large to be focused on, and committed to, a topic if the topic is not well understood.

measurement is a key part of the Basel Committee's focus. But the danger in excluding reputation risk is that this might cause some to take their eye off the ball relative to the importance of reputation risk. It, therefore, remains critical that firms work to refine their own definitions and understanding of operational risk both individually and as an industry. Organizing a firmwide effort to manage operational risk before defining it is like going to war against an unknown adversary. The battle would be futile.

Even though there is still no "generally accepted" definition, some basic components have begun to emerge, as the Basel Committee's definition implies. This chapter will explore various considerations relative to operational risk definitions. It will address the what and why in the evolution of early definitions used by practitioners, produced by industry surveys, and adopted by regulators. It will draw a distinction between *operational* risk and the more narrow areas of *operations* risk. We will draw from research and case examples in Zurich IC Squared's First Database[3] to illustrate the significant impact of operational risk events.

BACKGROUND: OPERATIONAL RISK TRENDS AND DRIVING FORCES

We all know that operational risk itself is not a new subject. In some sense, neither is operational risk management. Various functional groups within organizations have been managing these risks for years.

Recent developments and trends, however, have brought new attention to the discipline. In describing the growth of operational risk, the word *geometric* may not be too strong. What is it about operational risk that has altered the risk landscape in recent years?

There are a number of key factors that warrant study before we analyze definitions. For one thing, financial products and transactions are all more complex than ever before. Second, technological advances in the 1980s and early 1990s have given rise to financial engineering, affording firms the ability to dissect and analyze multiple dimensions of financial risks, applying hedges where advantageous. This evolution has been key in transforming corporate risk profiles and enabling reduction of the financial (i.e., market and credit) risk profiles for corporations and financial service firms alike. At the same time, however, this evolution has given rise to an entirely new phenomenon: greater complexity.[4] Many of these financial structures cross many markets and product types.

The underlying technology has also facilitated greater transaction velocity. In turn, however, the management of the complexity of those structures themselves has caused an even greater reliance on key systems—both central and distributed on desktops—along with key people who understand them. Thus, there are greater challenges in controlling and monitoring them, and less ability to operate manually should the technology itself fail. And so the cycle continues. The advances themselves have contributed to the expansion of operational risk. Today the advent of electronic commerce has ushered in yet another phase of change in the business and risk landscape, along with risk issues of confidentiality, identity, compromise, and repudiation.[5]

Several other factors are contributing to the growth of areas of operational risk. They include the continued global societal trend toward litigation as the method of choice for settling disputes, an increased frequency of large-scale natural disasters in recent years, constant change and evolution in the regulatory landscape, and problematical issues in operational risk transfer. The latter being the ability of insurance and other risk transfer products to align effectively to operational risk classes.[6]

More specifically, following are the factors that have prompted the acceleration of change underlying operational risks and industry emphasis on an operational risk management.

1. Headline Financial Services Losses/Recognition of Risk Costs: We have already discussed the loss figures in the introduction. Whether one focuses solely on the public figures of $15 billion annually over the past 20 years, or chooses a multiple of that amount industry-wide, the numbers cannot be ignored. As noted, some believe that the figure may be ten times the public figures. At that aggressive multiple, the figure may be closer to $150 billion. Even at a conservative multiple, however, we may be looking at $45 to $60 billion annually.

2. Other Life Threatening Corporate Events: In addition to the losses, numerous firms have been brought to their knees over operational risks and losses. The demise of Barings and Kidder Peabody are commonly given as examples. On a smaller scale, operational risk and loss have factored in firms' decisions to exit certain businesses, or be forced into mergers because of mounting operational risk losses.[7] In addition, there are scores of instances in which firms' reputations have been damaged severely, and which now face a long slow recovery.

3. Advances in Technology: The advances in technology, processing speed, and increases in capacity have been evident throughout organizations.

Whether we are looking at trading operations in a financial institution front office, or origination and execution of transactions, more generally, in any organization the impact has been clear. The ability to conduct business, including necessary recordkeeping, at a far more rapid rate than ever before has been enabled by technology. Nothing underscored the pervasiveness of technological advances in the 1990s better than Moore's Law, which states that, every 18 months, processing power doubles while cost holds constant. In other words, every 18 months you are able to buy twice the processing power at a constant price. Stated another way, every 18 months, the cost of your processing power is cut in half![8]

Obviously, these technological advances have enhanced competitiveness, but they bring with them some cost, if only in terms of a variety of operational risk challenges such as the ability to process, structure, and execute increasingly complex transactions at greater than ever speeds!

In the 1970s and 1980s, the greatest operational risk challenge, or one of them, was to protect an organization's centralized data processing facilities. As time went on, technological advances gave rise to desktop computing, client-server and networked computing, and then with the advent of the Internet, open environments. Thus, whereas once the greatest challenge was in protecting the centralized data processing facility, along with software and data storage, today that challenge has been compounded many times over. Applications and data reside both in central data facilities and can reside in "miniature data centers" on virtually every desktop throughout the organization. In the perfect world, the loss of individual desktops would not present a threat to the organization. But as we all know, all employees maintain some degree of critical data on their desktop computer hard drives despite their employers' efforts to stop them from doing so.

4. Societal Shifts/Complexity of Business: Global competition is probably the single most dominant factor driving the complexity of business today. But there are a variety of other factors as well, including changes in society, the workforce, and the needs of people. Increases in the number of two-income families, single-parent families, the dispersion of the workforce, including the advent of telecommuting, and the need to support remote workers—again supported by advances in technology, including the advent and dominance of the Internet—all contribute to additional business complexities and operational risks.

5. Societal Shifts/Global Litigiousness: Several current trends have also contributed to the rise of operational risk. One of these is the global propensity toward litigation. Not so long ago litigation was largely a phenomenon of the United States and, to a lesser extent, European and Australian society. Today we are seeing much more pervasive litigation trends around the world. Litigation has become more common in recent years even in global regions such as Asia, where it previously had been shunned. The apparent notion that there must always be a guilty party and that someone else must pay when there is a loss raises the standard of care, or at least the level of caution, and certainly reduces the margin for error in all business dealings today.

Another phenomenon, particularly in financial service dealings, is the spectrum of fear and greed. Although discussions of the spectrum of fear and greed have always been present in psychological discussions among and about traders, they have only recently become part of the discussion about operational risk.

6. Increased Competition/Squeezed Margins: Increased competitiveness has also driven increased attention to operational risk and operational risk management. Simply stated, there is far less profit margin and thus far less room for error in business dealings today. In banking, for instance, whereas institutions once enjoyed generous margins on virtually all their products and services, today margins have been squeezed on all product lines to the point that some commodity-type products and services are barely profitable even before considering the cost that risk is applied to in those products and services. A risk-adjusted return might yield little or no profitability for those same businesses. Thus, operational losses, whether a function of customer dissatisfaction, booking error, or any other type—even the smallest—will be noticed. And given the increased volumes and velocities enabled by technology as discussed previously, the operational losses may be larger than what was once the case.

7. Regulatory Developments: In response to the speed of change in business, including new products, services, and processes, the global regulatory community has been scrambling to keep pace. Thus, regulations have emerged as a subsidiary factor to some of the societal and business changes. In turn, organizations must work to navigate product and service regulatory requirements and changes enacted. The patchwork of these regulations in individual countries, as a function of product and service changes, such as the proliferation of derivative markets and/or the need to navigate changes across borders, all present additional operational compliance and risk challenges.

More recently, the Basel Committee's Risk Management Group has issued a series of releases that have jolted the banking industry into action on operational risk management.

8. Problematical Insurance Environment: The presence or absence of viable insurance and risk financing solutions for operational risk has little relationship to the underlying risk trends themselves. Without a doubt, however, when left uninsured, operational losses are all the more evident. Studies have shown that the typical financial institution insurance program covers only 20–30% of the broadly defined universe of operational risks.[9] Recognition of this statistic in recent years has underscored the importance of exploring areas of mismatch between operational risks and areas of insurability.

9. E-Commerce Activity: For the most part, Internet commerce has brought little in the way of new risks to the operational risk discussion. It has, however, accentuated some existing ones. Internet commerce has shed additional light on a variety of operational risk issues, such as security of the transaction for both buyers and sellers, legal risks relative to representation on the Internet, and vulnerability to acts of sabotage and website vandalism. All of these risks are already present in the marketplace. They are just now accentuated with a different emphasis. It is precisely this heightened emphasis, coupled with the proliferation of the Internet in society today, that has presented greater focus on operational risk and operational risk management. In fact, it can be argued that operational risk management will become an enormous part of e-commerce and e-business strategies as the Internet and use of the Internet mature.

As the e-business marketplace matures in the very near future, there will be far less forgiveness for interruptions of service, less than optimal performance or service, and anything less than continuous and high-speed processing. Whereas once chief executives were primarily facing a strategic risk of not being represented on the Internet, by 2000 the issue became one of optimal performance and operational risk management of online services. Incidentally, the only new risk presented by e-commerce is probably repudiation risk, which is the risk that a party denies that they were present and a party to a transaction at all. (Chapter 18 provides a case study on risk management involving the implementation of an e-commerce business strategy.)

10. Frequency of Natural Disasters: Physical losses in the form of fire, windstorm, flood, and earthquake are the oldest form of operational risk. Many firms have been reminded of this since the 1990s as sizable windstorms have threatened the East Coast of the United States, the United Kingdom, and Europe, and earthquakes were felt in Japan, Latin America, and on the West Coast of the United States.

11. Interest in Enterprise-wide Risk Management: Last, but certainly not least, more holistic perspectives on risk in recent years, and the advent of enterprise-wide risk management programs, have placed a significantly new focus on operational risks. These developments have uncovered risks that have, heretofore, not been addressed in most financial service firms' risk capital recognition systems.

AN EVOLUTION OF DEFINITIONS

Definitions of operational risk have progressed through several iterations since widespread discussion began on the topic in the mid-to-late-1990s. In this section we will explore the thought process.

As part of our operational risk management strategy at Bankers Trust, we began in about 1990 with a serious study of operational risk by asking a very simple question: What risks were our market and credit risk management models and functions *not* addressing? Answering this question led us to identify the risks associated with key resources of the firm, such as its relationships, people, technology/processing, physical assets, and other external sources.[10]

The journey was instructive. Because having a full understanding of the thought process is important for any organization developing its own definition and risk classes, we will take a quick tour of our own thinking and experience before moving into the details of definitions.

A PLACE TO START

Anything That Is Not Credit- or Market-Related

Despite the fact that consensus on definitions of operational risk is just beginning to emerge, agreement has come a long way in a very short period time. When we began our initial study of operational risks in 1990, it was not at all clear what the area should and should not cover. By now, there has been much said about our initial parameter: ". . . anything that does not fall in the market risk or credit risk categories." This description has been soundly criticized industry-wide, as is appropriate. For our purposes, at the time, it served as a very practical beginning point. That is, since we did not know what we were dealing with, we decided to begin looking at actual cases to help us formulate a definition. This was the origin of our initial construction of an operational loss database. The process was quite simple. We began gathering information on any loss that was not market-related (i.e., caused by asset price movements) or credit-related (i.e., caused by an inability to meet payment obligations).

As such, we captured a variety of both industry and proprietary losses and began to categorize them. Once we had several hundred of them in an Excel™ spreadsheet, we began to draw some conclusions about categories, causation, and the like. This then took us in the direction of an *inclusive* definition. And, after awhile, we noticed some patterns beginning to form in our collection of losses.

SAMPLE DEFINITIONS AND RISK CLASSES

Following some trial and error we arrived at a definition that spanned several risk classes. We liked this approach in particular because it served as a means to categorize the various loss scenarios that we were observing in the marketplace and at our own firm. The risk classes were helpful for risk modeling purposes as well. That is, we were in a position to capture losses by risk class and began to analyze them accordingly. These ranged from simple mathematical totals and averages to actuarial simulations of expected and possible loss outcomes by risk class.

Following is the definition we developed. It established a framework for us that was key for risk identification, measurement, management, and mitigation.

> *The risk of loss from business disruption, control failures, errors, misdeeds, or external events*

We then specified that operational risk will manifest itself in five key risk classes. We settled on five because they represent responsibility and accountability, either on a firmwide basis or within individual business lines or profit centers.[11] We also found it essential to apply the MECE Principle. That is, we wanted to be certain that our categories were Mutually Exclusive and Collectively Exhaustive.

The five primary operational risk/exposure classes were people/human capital, relationships, systems and technology, physical assets, and other external sources.[12] Brief definitions follow:

1. **People Risks:** The risk of loss caused intentionally or unintentionally by an employee (e.g., employee error, employee misdeed) or involving employees, such as in the area of employment disputes.
2. **Relationship Risks:** Non-proprietary losses to a firm and generated through the relationship or contact that a firm has with its clients, shareholders, third parties, or regulators (e.g., reimbursements to clients, penalties paid).
3. **Technology and Processing Risks:** The risk of loss by failure, breakdown, or other disruption in technology and/or processing. It also includes loss from the piracy or theft of data or information, and loss from technology that fails to meet its intended business needs.
4. **Physical Risks:** The risk of loss through damage to the firm's properties or loss to physical property or assets for which the firm is responsible.
5. **Other External Risks:** The risk of loss caused by the actions of external parties, such as in the perpetration of fraud on the firm or, in the case of regulators, the promulgation of change that would alter the firm's ability to continue operating in certain markets.

All five exposure classes included several dimensions of risk, including direct economic loss, the economic impact of indirect loss or business disruption, and/or legal liability.[13]

The first four risk classes were logical and convenient given our objective—proactive risk management—because they relate back to functions and managerial responsibility, such as sales and marketing relationship managers, senior business management, human resource management, operations management, and senior technologists. Others, such as the compliance, legal, and security functions, can also take on matrixed responsibilities for managing risk.[14] The fifth category captured certain external areas such as regulatory risk and fraud risk.

Note that recent regulatory discussions have combined the scope of these risk classes. I have chosen not to do so here partially because at the time of this writing, the regulatory developments are still fluid, and they are not universally accepted yet, as shown by some of the case studies included herein. In addition, rather than re-write history, I prefer to share the evolution of our thought process here and in other parts of the Bankers Trust case throughout the book.

KEY OBSERVATIONS

Along the way, we came to several observations and conclusions:

- **Recognize the Dimensions of Loss:** As noted, we looked at multiple dimension loss scenarios involving each of the five risk classes, including their direct impact and cost, their indirect business disruption and interruption, and legal considerations.[15]
- **Broaden Perspective to Operational Not Just Operations Risk:** For the most part, there is consensus today that the universe of operational risk includes, but is broader than, operations or processing risk alone. It transcends all business lines, not just information and transaction processing businesses (i.e., *operations* risk). Operational risk spans front, middle, and back office business operations. It is broader than just conventionally insured risk. And it is broader than studies of control failures alone.[16]
- **Represent the Business Process:** Operational risks relate to all phases of the business process, from origination to execution and delivery. Exhibit 3.1 illustrates this intersection. Can these risks and their associated loss costs be sorted so that each risk and loss fits neatly into one category without overlapping one another? Is it possible to identify categories that would both be logical to senior managers and imply risk management responsibility? It was critical to the development of Operational RAROC that the answer to these questions be a resounding *"yes."*[17]
- **Focus on Cause, Not Just Effect:** First and foremost, being that our ultimate objective was to manage risk, we recognized early on that we were most interested in loss causes. Where were the losses coming from? For example, we were more interested in knowing that *people's errors* or *lack of training of people* were causing losses than in knowing that we had an operational trading loss on our hands. We would be interested in where the loss had manifested itself too, of course, but that was not our first classification concern.[18] In doing so, we found that we could get closer to the

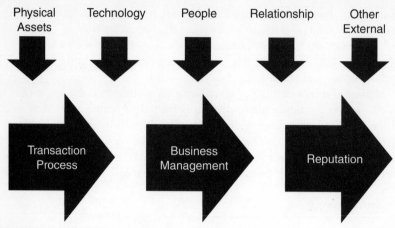

EXHIBIT 3.1 Risk Class vs. Business Process Intersect

underlying source, circumstances, and causative factors for each loss event. For instance, by focusing on people risk one may be more inclined to analyze the human behavior that might cause negative outcomes, whether they are simple carelessness, inadequate control, cultural, peer pressure, or dishonest tendencies. In contrast, conventional approaches to risk definition, whether borrowed from auditing, regulatory, or insurance communities, for instance, often tend to focus on the outcome or symptom (e.g., "it was a compliance, reporting, or legal risk"), rather than the underlying behavior. Although the latter terms might be useful for classification purposes and in reengineering control functions, they have limited value in analyzing causation. After all, the objective should be to facilitate and promote effective risk managed behavior, not to only measure compliance with controls alone. So whatever categories one chooses for analyzing operational risk, they should have a solid foundation for practical risk management and behavioral modification.[19]

- **Target Functional Responsibility for Risk Management:** In addition, and perhaps more importantly, these five risk classes served a useful purpose for risk response. As of this writing, we have used them for many years now in risk systems because they focus on responsibility and accountability; they are not simply a convenient way to measure operational risk. Each class is multidimensional. In each class, where a loss occurs, there is direct economic impact, but there is also indirect impact. Operational loss is measured by *direct economic loss, indirect expenses* associated with business interruption and legal risk, and sometimes can include *immeasurables,* such as the negative impact operational loss has on a company's reputation or brand.

Risk Categories	Examples	Functional Responsibilities
People	Human error; internal dishonesty; staff unavailability (i.e., physical injury or competitive loss)	Business line human resources; Security
Relationship	Legal and/or contractual disputes	Sales and marketing; Business management; Legal; Compliance
Technology and Processing	Failure of technology; damage caused by virus/cost of eradication; loss costs due to antiquated system.	Business line technologists; Central infrastructure; Data center; Operations
Physical Assets	Loss of physical environment/business interruption; loss of negotiable assets	Operations Management
Other External	Changes in regulations; external fraud	Business line compliance; Regulatory; Security Services

EXHIBIT 3.2 Mapping Operational Risk Categories to Functional Responsibilities[20]

Exhibit 3.2 is a matrix that we developed to begin aligning the risk classes with various functional areas of primary responsibility. That is, we envisioned that both on a firmwide basis and a business unit basis that people risks will be presented to business managers and human resource managers for their attention. Similarly, relationship risks will be aligned to business management and sales and marketing managers for attention. Line managers, chief information officers, and operations managers will address technology and processing risks, and chief administrative officers and corporate real estate managers will manage physical risks.

Last, we wanted to quantify operational risks so that severity and frequency distributions could be developed and analyzed. We were interested in events that had been experienced by our own firm, of course, but our risk exposure is broader than just our experience. We wanted a database of events that reflected relevant parts of the financial service sector's direct and indirect exposure. An example of indirect exposure was first witnessed during the 1980s litigation over lender liability, when lenders were sometimes held liable for the operational risk exposure involving tort litigation over tobacco, silicon, and asbestos. The legal theories, outcomes, and size of exposures in these cases can be analyzed and used in the development of risk management tools and predictors.[21]

And if all this didn't present enough challenge, although they have backed away from the notion more recently, when we began, regulators had been anxious to see *reputation risk* considered alongside of operational risks. In any case, it is a key consideration and factor in many operational events, particularly for banks and where human behavior is concerned. Admittedly, however, it is probably the most difficult area to quantify.[22]

DISSECTING RISK CLASSES AND SUBCLASSES

Regardless of the high-level definition and whether there are four classes (i.e., people, process, systems, and external), five classes (i.e., people, relationship, technology, physical assets, and external), or just one aggregate risk class, a firm must have a series of meaningful subclasses. They play an important role and basis for analysis.

This is also the place and point at which the definition begins to hold meaning for day-to-day business managers. It is a bit difficult for a manager to manage against a forecast number for "people risks," for instance. On the other hand, if an analyst can provide greater detail, for instance, with numbers for people risk or losses due to employee turnover, or due to employee errors, or because of employment disputes, then the numbers have more relevance and can be addressed by management and staff alike.

Regardless of your choice (or the industry's choice) of overall definitions, therefore, it is key that the operational risk practitioner be clear about the contents of that definition.

The development of the risk categories was the turning point in our early work on operational risk. We found that the operational risks had been defined so broadly that any one risk might fit into a number of classifications. In order to develop a rigorous model, we needed to be able to place each risk in one, and only one, class. We have had to continue to evolve the definitions and risk categories, but the changes have been relatively minor.[23]

The following examples are *illustrative only* for our original five risk classes. They are not meant to represent industry consensus on definitions or examples. In fact, as noted, that consensus has not yet been finalized. Thus, I present our original definitions for purposes of discussion here. In any event, it is also quite possible to combine these five classes in different ways. For example, although we always found it useful to keep them separate, some might choose to combine the People Risk class below with the Relationship class. Such combinations at a risk class level would serve to produce the evolving industry consensus classes, if desired.

People Risk

The risks associated with the employment of people (e.g., that an employee intentionally or unintentionally causes loss to the firm; losses involving employment liabilities) is the first risk category. Exhibit 3.3 is an illustration. Some examples of specific loss scenarios are employee errors, employee misdeeds, employee unavailability, and employment practices.

Employee errors cause a disruption in the business processes due to an employee's mistakes:

- Documentation and keying-in errors
- Programming errors
- Modeling or pricing errors

Employee misdeeds cause a disruption in the business processes resulting from an employee's dishonest, fraudulent, or malicious activities against a firm. It does not include employee theft of a physical asset, which is included under the main risk category of *physical asset risks*.

- Insider trading/rogue trading
- Theft from a client's money into employee's own account

Employee unavailability results in a disruption in the business processes due to personnel not being available at vital times or the risk of key people leaving the firm.

- Loss of intellectual capital when key employees leave the firm
- Loss of key employees due to death, illness, or injury
- A strike by employees

Employment practices cause losses to a firm due to discrimination within the firm, harassment of employees or other civil rights abuses, wrongful termination of employees, and employee health and safety issues. It includes former employees, current employees, and job applicants but does not include discrimination of clients/customers. Examples include allegations of:

- Improper terminations
- Sex, race, age discrimination toward employees with regard to promotions
- Discrimination with regard to hiring

Typically, the head of human resources or personnel is responsible for hiring "the best and brightest." Good operational risk practices here can enable a firm to control the flip side of the human equation: human error, employment-related liability, fraud, or misdeeds.

The Orange County case is one of the largest *people risk class* cases in financial history. In December 1994, Orange County in Southern California publicly announced that its investment pool had suffered a $1.6 billion loss. This was the largest investment loss ever registered by a municipality and led to bankruptcy, and a mass layoff of municipal employees.

The loss has been blamed on the unsupervised investment activity of Robert Citron, the county treasurer. In 1998, the Los Angeles District court upheld Citron's authority to invest in derivative securities, despite the fact that he made "grave errors" and "imprudent decisions." It was difficult for Citron to represent himself as an "inexperienced investor" and "lay person" after he testified that he had more than 20 years experience in the investment industry . . . . Citron had delivered returns that were 2% higher than other municipal pools in the state of California, and was viewed as a "wizard" who obtained better than average returns in difficult market conditions.

Citron placed a bet through the purchase of reverse repurchase agreements (reverse repos) that interest rates would fall or stay low, and reinvested his earnings in new securities, mostly 5-year notes issued by government agencies. The strategy worked until February 1994 when the Federal Reserve undertook a series of six interest-rate hikes that generated huge losses for the fund. The county was forced to liquidate Citron's managed investment fund in December 1994, and realized a loss of $1.6 billion. It is worth noting that, according to Philippe Jorion in his case study on Orange County, a huge opportunity was lost when interest rates started falling shortly after the liquidation of the fund, and a potential gain of $1.4 billion based on Citron's interest-rate strategy was never realized. He found the county most guilty of "bad timing." The lessons learned from this debacle include the lack of employment of classic risk management techniques by Citron, and his investors, including the use of Value-at-Risk (VAR), and the lack of intelligent analysis of how the county was managing to realize above-market returns.

EXHIBIT 3.3 Illustrative People Risk Case: Orange County, California
Reprinted with permission from Zurich IC Squared First Database.

Here, too, human resources and business management can monitor risk and even encourage positive behavior by looking at the correlation between turnover rates, training levels, and customer complaints, and the overall quality of the people a firm is hiring: their education, experience, and the number of years of relevant expertise they bring to a company (see Exhibit 3.3).

Relationship Risks

Nonproprietary losses caused to a firm and generated through the relationship or contact that a firm has with its clients, shareholders, third parties, or regulators is the second risk category. Exhibit 3.4 is an illustration.

In February 2000, Bear Stearns & Company agreed to pay $39 million to settle a *relationship risk* suit brought by Granite Partners L.P., Granite Corp., and the Quartz Hedge Fund. These three hedge funds were driven into bankruptcy when the value of their collateralized mortgage obligations (CMOs) sharply fell. The hedge funds charged the New York brokerage firm with misconduct in its sales of risky CMOs.

The suit alleged that Bear Stearns and two other brokerages committed fraud by selling the hedge funds' manager, David J. Askin, esoteric mortgage-backed securities with derivative factors such as floaters and inverse floaters that peg the security's coupon and value to an independent financial benchmark. In addition, it alleged that Askin, Bear Stearns, and two other brokerages colluded on the sales of these instruments for the fees and commission they generated. It also claimed that the brokerages loaned the hedge funds money through repurchase agreements (REPOS) in order to allow Askin to leverage the funds' holdings. In a REPO transaction, the borrower gives securities to the lender in exchange for cash. The REPO is similar to a forward contract in that the borrower is obligated to repurchase the same securities at a specified price and date in the future. When the Federal Reserve Board unexpectedly raised interest rates several times in 1994, the value of the collateralized mortgage obligations decreased by $225 million, leaving the funds unable to meet their repurchase commitments. The brokerages then liquidated the funds' REPO collateral, forcing Askin into bankruptcy.

EXHIBIT 3.4 Illustrative Relationship Risk Case: Bear Stearns
Reprinted with permission from Zurich IC Squared First Database.

The *submodule* is determined by the parties affected or by the source of dispute or complaint.

Some examples of specific loss scenarios are client-originated, shareholder-originated, third-party-originated, and regulator-originated.

Client-originated are losses to a firm resulting from negligence or professional errors or during the business process. Examples include:

- Faulty or inappropriate products/services causing a suit by a customer
- Tort or professional negligence causing a suit by a client

Shareholder-originated are losses to a firm resulting from shareholder lawsuits. Examples include:

- Unrealistic profit projections, misleading financial statements
- Improper business ventures or investments

Third-party-originated are losses to a firm stemming from interactions with third parties or suits taken by regulatory bodies. Examples include:

- The holder of a patent sues over infringement
- Contractual disputes with third parties

Regulator-originated are losses to a firm stemming from fines and charges extracted by regulatory bodies. Examples include:

- Enforcement of securities laws and issuing fines for breach of same
- Enforcement of environmental regulations and charging cleanup costs

Well-managed relationships are key to a company's success and encompass everything from relationships with customers, regulators, and other companies to relationships with stakeholders, colleagues, media, and the public. For example, an individual or group is charged with maintaining those relationships. If any of those relationships is handled poorly or neglected, the direct operational loss includes lost sales, customers, revenue, and opportunity and higher expenses; the indirect operational loss may result in additional legal expenses, impact on reputation, and—potentially—a lower stock price.

Systems, Technology, and Processing Risks

The risk that a firm's business is interrupted by technology-related problems is the third risk category. Exhibit 3.5 is an illustration. Some examples of specific loss scenarios are external disruption and systems maintenance.

External disruption is a disruption in the business processes due to systems failures outside of the firm. Examples include:

- Failure of exchanges (equities, futures, commodities, etc.)
- Third-party systems failure

Systems maintenance is a disruption of the business processes due to the firm's technological (hardware and software) failures. Examples include:

- Software problems
- Systems outdated and unable to handle firm's needs
- Computer viruses
- Systems integration risks
- Systems developments being delayed and over budget

Most firms today have a chief information officer or chief technologist who is accountable for the firm's technology and processing resources.

On November 26, 1999, a technology problem caused reputational losses, as well as unreported monetary losses, for Halifax Bank. Sharexpress, its online share trading system, experienced a security breach, which Halifax attributed to a technology glitch during a software upgrade. In analyzing this situation, Simon Goodley and Steve Ranger wrote that "Inadequate software testing seemed to be at fault for . . . (the) . . . security breach at Halifax's online share dealing service." The computer glitch occurred after system modifications and testing by Halifax's software supplier TCA Synergo. Trading began at 8 AM but was suspended at 10:30 AM on Friday morning. . . . The security breach allowed Sharexpress customers to access other customers' personal details online. Even worse, customers were able to buy and sell shares through other Halifax customers' accounts.

In dealing with this security issue, Halifax contacted its customers to verify that accounts were in order before restoring the service. Halifax said customers' accounts were not affected by the breach. A statement issued by the firm said that after conducting a comprehensive audit, it was found that "all trades carried out on Friday were legitimate and that customers accounts are in order." According to a statement by Halifax, "The fault, which was identified on Friday [the day of the security breach] has now been eliminated." Sue Concannon, Halifax's share dealing managing director, said "the error was due to a combination of factors that the system hadn't seen before." Ms. Concannon agreed that similar situations could be avoided as companies gain more experience in e-commerce.

A spokesman for TCA said Halifax had implemented additional controls following this problem. Halifax said that the incident affected 10 customers, but that no erroneous trades were carried out. After a weekend shutdown, Halifax's Sharexpress resumed trading at 8 AM on Monday, November 29, 1999. This problem was a severe embarrassment to Halifax because the firm was working to turn itself into a leading e-commerce player by spending GBP 100 million to set up its Internet bank. Other e-businesses were annoyed because security breaches like Halifax's tend to erode consumer confidence in e-commerce security across the board. As a result of this technology issue, one customer was quoted in the press as stating that he planned to change his account, move his portfolio, and cancel all standing orders and direct debits. Reportedly, Sharexpress customers had complained of technical difficulties from the time of its launch in September until this event in November 1999.

EXHIBIT 3.5 Illustrative Systems and Technology Risk Case: Halifax Bank
Reprinted with permission from Zurich IC Squared First Database.

A fire ravaged the Paris headquarters of Credit Lyonnais in May 1996 in an incident that initially appeared to fit squarely in the area of physical asset risk. . . .

There were, however, press murmurs from the beginning that the fire might have been an act of sabotage. A government report was released in 1998, two years after the fire, stating that it was started in two separate places before spreading rapidly through the bank's trading floor and eventually destroying a large portion of the historic headquarters building (and a highly prized art collection). The report strongly suggested that the fire had been set deliberately and was linked to an incident that broke out in August 1997 in a bank warehouse just a few days after records were requested by the government. The earlier fire also destroyed substantial documents and files that are alleged to have shed light on the fraud case. (As of the time of this writing) an ongoing investigation into allegations of gross mismanagement of the French bank continues (as of 2001) five years after the 1996 fire and touches the bank's operations in several European countries and the United States.

In spite of the separate investigation, the case underscored the significance of concentration-of-risk concerns relative to trading floor operations from the standpoint of key people (top traders) and concentration of systems, and the need for reliable business continuity plans.

EXHIBIT 3.6 Illustrative Physical Asset Risk Case: Credit Lyonnais
Reprinted with permission from Zurich IC Squared First Database.

Physical Asset Risks

The risk to a firm's business processes and key facilities due to the unavailability or improper maintenance of physical assets is the fourth risk category. Losses also include the cost of replacing items. Exhibit 3.6 is an illustration. Some examples of specific loss scenarios are crime, disasters, and product/facility damage.

Disasters:

- Natural disasters include earthquakes, tornadoes, and hurricanes
- Unnatural disasters are bombs, fires, and explosions

Product/facility damage is damage to physical plant, facility, or product leading to losses. Examples include contamination (i.e., air, water, raw materials) and product recalls.

Usually, the chief administrative officer, chief of staff, or the chief operating officer has responsibility on a corporate or business line/profit-center level for a firm's physical assets.

This 1999 case involves a number of insurance companies, Liberty National Securities and Martin Frankel, a money manager who is being investigated in connection with the disappearance of funds entrusted to him by the insurers. Frankel used his home as an office for his investment firm, Liberty National Securities. He was not a registered broker as his license to trade securities had reportedly been revoked by the Securities and Exchange Commission in 1992 due to investor complaints.

According to the FBI (U.S. Federal Bureau of Investigation), Frankel had been defrauding insurance companies since at least 1991. Reports indicated that a dozen Southern U.S. insurance companies were missing at least $218 million that they entrusted to Frankel. Several of the companies have filed a joint lawsuit in which they represented they were missing $915 million. Frankel is alleged to have set up several corporate entities under different aliases in order to gain control of insurers' assets. He allegedly defrauded investors by falsely promising to invest their cash and profits in his brokerage firm. In reality, Frankel "systematically drained" the insurers' assets by laundering their funds through bank accounts he controlled in the United States and abroad and by purchasing untraceable assets. The insurance companies were headed by John Hackney and were related to a holding company, Franklin American Corp. They are reportedly controlled by Thurnor Trust, which is headed by Mr. Hackney. Hackney alleged that Thurnor Trust was owned by Frankel's charity, the St. Francis of Assisi Foundation. Frankel was charged with wire fraud and money laundering, but the insurance companies suffered huge losses in this case of alleged external fraud.

EXHIBIT 3.7   External Loss—Liberty National Securities and Various Insurers
Case excerpted from IC Squared First Database.

Note that some risk class categorizations have included physical asset risk in the external category.

External Fraud/Regulatory Change Risks

Risk to business processes stemming from people or entities outside of the firm is the fifth risk category. Exhibit 3.7 is an illustration. Some examples of specific loss scenarios are external fraud and regulatory changes.

External fraud are losses to a firm due to the fraudulent activities of nonemployee third parties (including clients).

Regulatory changes are losses to a firm due to changes in regulations, such as the cost of implementing new procedures to comply with the regulatory change (e.g., SEC reporting modifications). They do not include fines for noncompliance of regulations.

Chief legal counsel and/or the compliance officer and head of security would be responsible for this category of operational risk, which includes regulatory change from a business and strategic-planning standpoint, external fraud, or other environmental change.

BUSINESS PROCESS RISK

In addition to classing risks by the five "asset- or resource-related dimensions" previously outlined, we believed that there is a business process dimension of each. In other words, each of these risks classes impacts business processes throughout a firm, and vice versa. The business process is divided into four categories: (1) origination, (2) execution, (3) business line management, and (4) corporate.

Origination

This includes all aspects of structuring a customer deal involving high-level customer contact. Examples of activities include, among others:

- Advising/educating the customer about a product/service
- Consulting with customers about their needs
- Defining product and service procedures
- Defrauding customers/clients
- Designing contracts
- Front office activity
- Full and timely disclosure of information to stakeholders
- Insider trading
- Market manipulations
- Misleading shareholders/clients
- Misrepresentations in an IPO prospectus
- Negotiations
- Nondisclosure of company relationships (e.g., conflicts of interest)
- Overbilling
- Price fixing/antitrust/monopolies
- Pricing risk
- Bribes to obtain sales contracts
- Selling and marketing
- Stock price inflation due to release of misleading information by the company
- Structuring and customizing a contract

Execution

This includes all aspects of implementing the deal and associated maintenance. Examples of activities include, among others:

- Breach of contract not related to a product
- Development of systems to complete contract
- Breach of fiduciary duties
- Environmental damage
- Execution and processing trades or transactions
- Health and safety of customers/nonemployees
- Customer service and relationship management errors or omissions
- Documentation issues
- Product liability
- Professional malpractice
- Securities violations/industry regulatory violations

Business Line Management

This category includes aspects of running a business not directly linked with the creation and sale of a particular product or service, but related to the management oversight. This will include the following examples of activities, among others:

- Business and technology strategy
- Fraudulently obtaining loans to support one's business
- Health and safety of employees
- Employment practices (e.g., discrimination with regard to employees)
- Labor dispute/strike
- Excessive management control (e.g., liabilities)
- Money laundering
- Obstructions of justice
- Patent infringement
- Product strategy
- Tax fraud

Corporate

This fourth category includes events over which an individual business line has little or no control. Corporate management, on the other hand, may have control. This will include events such as:

- Physical damage due to natural disasters (i.e., earthquakes, storms, floods, etc.)
- Physical damage due to a major incident or nonnatural disaster (i.e., fire, terrorism, explosion)
- Segregation of businesses (to avoid conflicts of interest)

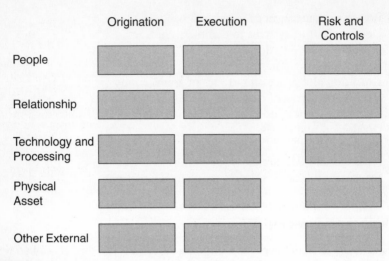

EXHIBIT 3.8   Operational Risk Class Worksheet

Once combined with the risk classes, the introduction of business process provides a much more complete understanding of the risks. Exhibit 3.8 is an example of an operational risk class worksheet.

AN INDUSTRY DEFINITION EMERGES

In 1998 and 1999 the British Bankers' Association (BBA), International Securities Dealers Association (ISDA), and the Risk Management Associates (RMA), and their members, sponsored a study on operational risk management. The associations retained the services of Pricewaterhouse Coopers (PWC) to conduct the project. That effort consisted of yet another, far more detailed survey of operational risk management at banking firms than those of the past.

The sponsors and consultants (PWC) coordinating the BBA, ISDA, and RMA survey attempted to conclude consensus on a definition of operational risk in its 1999 final report. They noted that "while the definitions in each specific firm are different, the underlying message is the same: Operational risk is the risk of direct or indirect losses resulting from inadequate or failed processes, people, and systems or from external events." Several key factors went into their decision to conclude this definition. They noted that it is a positive statement, rather than a negative definition, such as "everything other than credit and market risk"; they agreed that individual firms should elaborate on the stated definition with some classes of risk; and they recommended a firm's chosen definition be included in operational risk policies in order to support and promote a common language for operational risk management.[24]

Loss Databases and Consortia

In Chapter 10 we will discuss loss databases and consortia in detail. Clear definitions are essential for maintaining consistency in the construction and maintenance of a loss database. In another attempt at achieving an industry standard on definitions, and consistency in the databases, each of the loss consortia initiated their efforts with a definition of operational risk. In another attempt at reaching consensus on an industry definition, while promoting its consortium effort, during February 2000, NetRisk, the promoter of the MORE Exchange loss consortium, released its proprietary methodology for classification of operational losses and risks available to the public.[25]

The Institute for International Finance (IIF) and The Industry Technical Working Group on Operational Risk (TWGOR) Definition

The Institute of International Finance (IIF) is a private research and advocacy group that serves large international banks. In 1999–2000 its Working Group on Operational Risk (WGOR) and a subset of it, the Industry Technical Working Group on Operational Risk (ITWGOR) were formed consisting of representatives from a number of large international banks. A key objective was to respond to the Basel Committee's June 1999 consultative paper on the revision to the 1988 Basel Accord. The ITWGOR is an independent body, but sometimes serves as a subcommittee of the WGOR and the IIF.

The WGOR/IIF and ITWGOR have each released the papers on operational risk. In an October 2000 document,[26] among its discussion of measurement approaches (specifically the Internal Measurement Approach), they advanced the following commentary on definitions:

Definition of Operational Risk   The ITWGOR adopted and advanced the following definition of operational risk used by the Institute of International Finance:

> The risk of loss resulting from inadequate or failed internal processes, people, and systems or from external events that are not already covered by other regulatory capital charges (i.e., credit, market, and interest rate risks). Business, strategic, liquidity, and reputation risks are expressly excluded.

Definition of Operational Risk Losses   The WGOR continues by noting that, "In any attempt to quantify operational risk, it is necessary to define what types of losses or costs are to be included in the measurement. We are using the following definition:

> The direct loss, including external direct cost or write-down involved in the resolution of the operational loss event, net of recoveries.

The definition of operational risk losses specifically excludes timing mismatches, opportunity costs, indirect losses, and near misses."[27,28]

Last, the ITWGOR proposed the following list of the loss types with definitions, as part of its discussion of measurement approaches:

- **Legal Liability:** Consists of judgments, settlements, and other legal costs
- **Regulatory, Compliance, and Taxation Penalties:** Consists of fines, or the direct cost of any other penalties, such as license revocations
- **Loss of or Damage to Assets:** Consists of the direct reduction in value of physical assets, including certificates, due to some kind of accident (e.g., neglect, accident, fire, earthquake)
- **Restitution:** Consists of payments to clients of principal and/or interest by way of restitution, or the cost of any other form of compensation paid to clients.
- **Loss of Recourse:** Consists of payments or disbursements made to incorrect parties and not recovered
- **Write-downs:** Consists of the direct reduction in value of assets due to theft, fraud, unauthorized activity, or market and credit losses arising as a result of operational events[29,30]

THE BASEL COMMITTEE DEFINITION

The most important developments toward consensus, however, involved in the actions of the Basel Committee's Risk Management Group.

The Basel Committee issued its first paper in September 1998. That document was the result of a survey of 30 major banks. It was the first of several regulatory working papers intended to define the state of operational risk management at major institutions, and advance the discipline. As a subsidiary objective, the Committee has been seeking to finalize a definition of operational risk.

The most recent release from the risk management committee as of the time of this writing was the Consultative Document dated January 2001. This paper proposed the definition that appears at the opening of this chapter. Clearly, in writing this document, the Committee picked up on the definitions from the IIF, the ITWGOR, and the RMA/BBA/ISDA/PWC study as a reference to the definition it would be using. The paper states that, "In framing the current proposals, the committee has adopted a common industry definition of operational risk, namely: 'the risk of direct or indirect loss resulting from inadequate or failed internal processes, people and systems or from external events.' " They continue, in a footnote, to clarify that the definition includes legal risk.[31]

SOME OTHER PERSPECTIVES

The industry seemed to breathe a collective sigh of relief when consensus began to emerge on an overall definition. After all, definitions had been debated at industry conferences and industry association meetings for several years. To many, the debate has seemed endless.

Individual firms would do well, however, to continue working on their own definitions. Most recognize that even this most recent development from Basel requires far more refinement in the development of risk classes and subclasses, and further work on the definition itself. In addition, most firms recognize that although some consistency will be required relative to regulation and data sharing, it is most important to maintain a definition that is meaningful, generally understood, and effective within one's own organization.

In addition, some make the distinction that in the toil to arrive at a positive or inclusive definition certain risks have been left on the table. The simple phrase "people, process, systems, and external events" is not all-inclusive. Although it is convenient and provides some clarity for risk measurement purposes, it is lacking for risk management purposes. As a result, some suggest that in managing risk, firms should continue to focus on the more inclusive negative definition ("everything other than credit and market risk"). As one example, the Committee has been clear to omit reputation risk from their definition because it is so difficult to measure (understandably so). In doing so, however, they have omitted a major dimension of operational risk concern. The best firms will not lower their standards in managing risk simply because it cannot be measured conveniently.

CONCLUSION

Numerous business, societal, and technological changes have sparked a dramatic growth in operational risks on a global scale. Perhaps because of its far-reaching nature and many dimensions, the debate over a definition of operational risk has been one of the most painstaking aspects of the disciplines evolution, with the single possible exception of more recent discussions about measurement and modeling.

In hindsight, however, the discussion and debate have been appropriate, because it is critically important to have a definition in place before beginning the process of managing risk. The evolution began with a simple catchall phrase: "anything that is not market- or credit-related." It has evolved through several studies sponsored by the British Bankers Association, and more recently together with RMA and ISDA, with the help of Pricewaterhouse Coopers.

Most recently, the Basel Committee has picked up on the discussion and based its recent releases on the generalized definition that operational risk is

" the risk of direct or indirect loss resulting from inadequate or failed internal processes, people and systems or for external events." As this book goes to print, additional thoughtful treatment of definitions was released by the Institute of International Finance.[32] There was not time to include commentary on it here.

Clearly the discussion will continue for some time yet. From an individual firm's perspective, however, it is most important to adopt and communicate a consistent definition internally, such that there is a basis for discussions about the topic of operational risk management. At the same time, there should be flexibility to allow for some consistency with the ultimate regulatory definition.

LESSONS LEARNED AND KEY RECOMMENDATIONS

- Define operational risk for *your* organization. Operational risk must be defined and that definition communicated before it can be measured or managed. It is nearly impossible for any staff at large to be focused on, or committed to, a topic if the topic is not well understood (BP Strategy #1).
- Operational risk has come to be defined by some in the industry and by regulators as "the risk of direct or indirect loss resulting from inadequate or failed internal processes, people, and systems or for external events." Although this development represents progress, and is helpful in risk measurement, it does not include strategic or reputation risk. Beware of the "out of sight, out of mind" syndrome.
- Definitions should include subclasses for greater specificity and focus on causative factors, as opposed to those that focus only on the effect or symptoms of operational risk and losses.
- The underlying risk trends and factors shed light on the real drivers of operational risk and the need for operational risk management. Studying and understanding these trends sheds additional light on where resources should be committed for mitigating causative factors.
- Although it is important to remain in sync with regulatory developments, it is more important to use a definition that works for your organization rather than one that conforms precisely to an industry definition. That is, you can align to regulatory definitions as a subset of your internal definition. You should also consider whether you intend to make extensive use of industry benchmark data by risk class or intend to participate in an operational loss consortium. In managing their own risks, the best individual firms will be mindful of, but not limited to, regulatory definitions.
- Keep the definition simple and comprehensible. It is more important to communicate the scope of your operational risk program to staff at large simply and concisely rather than to communicate a definition that is completely comprehensive and all-encompassing. Save your all-encompassing

definitions for your data standards and for those who will be most involved in the data gathering process.

- Operations or processing risk is a key component of operational risk but should be recognized as a subset. The risk characteristics of operations risk generally fall in the high-frequency low-severity category, whereas other risks in the universe represent more catastrophe loss potential (i.e., low-frequency/high-potential severity).
- Although the earlier "exception" definition of, "anything that is not market- or credit-related" is not specific enough for risk measurement purposes, it remains an all-inclusive definition and is useful for maintaining a broad management perspective.

CHAPTER 4

The Real Opportunity

Creating More Effective Companies

THE IRONY OF UPSIDE

It is certainly no revelation that operational risks and the large losses associated with them have caught the attention of regulators in financial services and other industries. They have focused on risk both at individual firms and in the industry at large. As I write this in mid-2001, most recently they have directed that focus toward applying pressure on organizations to bring more discipline to the analysis, measurement, and management of it. Financial service regulators have made their long anticipated announcement of their intention to levy a regulatory capital charge for operational risks. Discussion, analysis, and debate over regulatory capital and supervision are at an all time high.

It is a bit troubling, but not entirely surprising, that many in banking and financial services today have allowed much of the initial focus on operational risk to be driven by regulatory pressures. This suggests that banks have not yet recognized the larger potential and upside opportunity from a more effective management of these risks and use of new tools and techniques being pioneered today. It's not simply about regulation or even about surviving these risks and losses; there's a far more exciting opportunity before us today. And to add further insult to this missed opportunity, first irony of upside is that line and corporate risk management functions alike often become frustrated with traditional approaches to corporate risk management and control effort because neither focuses on this *real* upside (Hint: not just eliminating losses).

In its broadest sense, operational risk permeates the fabric of the organization, from its culture to its strategy; its business plan to its day-to-day execution; its chief executive to its mail clerk; and its overall franchise, brand, and image to its individual product and service transactions. In the same way, both the vaccination and the antidote must flow throughout the organization's veins.

Interestingly, the terms *operational risk* and *operational risk management* are hardly noticed by many in organizations that "get it" on an enterprise-wide basis. They already understand the benefits and upside of effective operational risk management—quality and excellence—and they ironically "get" the execution of operational risk management right as a side benefit.

In contrast, those who do *not* "get it" and ignore its importance often pay the price in the form of diminished competitiveness, frequent embarrassments or highly visible losses. Unfortunately, some firms may not even survive long enough to regret having missed the point. Operational risk is viewed by many who do not understand it as a routine and unexciting subject. That observation generally comes from an assumption that we are talking about relatively routine or expected loss scenarios.

There should be no confusion about the objectives for operational risk management, and thus the scope of this book. Although regulatory considerations are important, operational risk management is a far broader topic than regulators' interest in proper measurement or adequate risk capital.

THE OPPORTUNITY PROGRESSION

Risk management is perhaps an unfortunate title. In reality risk management often ends up being discussed only in negative terms. Many believe that operational risk and loss only represents the downside. The argument goes something like, "If we can simply limit the losses caused by operational risk, then we will save money for the firm overall." Or, another perspective focuses on finding the most technically correct calculation of risk in order to minimize the impact of impending regulatory capital charges by the financial service regulatory community. Unfortunately, although correct, both views are rather shortsighted.

Intuitively, most people understand that risk management is intended to minimize losses and/or loss potential, thereby *enhancing the performance of a business* overall. Unfortunately, this primary objective sometimes gets lost in the day-to-day strategies and tactics applied by some risk managers.

The larger opportunity is often lost in a series of tasks such as data collection, loss analysis, modeling, contract negotiations, and rule and guideline development. Unfortunately, because all of the activities appear to lack a vision, the end result is all too often that risk management feels like a burden on the business, rather than an enhancement to its performance.

Felix Kloman, editor and publisher of *Risk Management Reports,* recently observed that most attempts at defining operational risk ". . . overlook the positive or beneficial aspect of risk. They overcater to the insurance thinking that all risks are negative."[1] In order to see the greater opportunity, however, one must widen his or her perspective.

The Next Generation of Effective Organizations

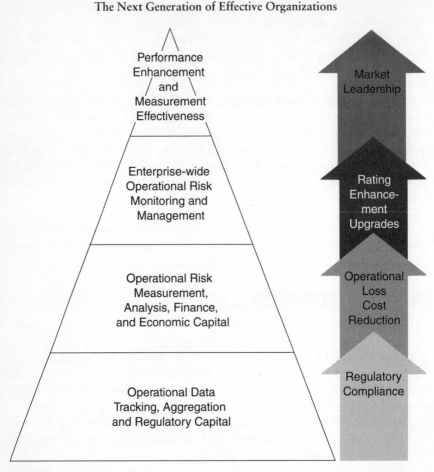

EXHIBIT 4.1   Value Pyramid

Leaders often point to goal setting and performance measures as keys for success. And history has shown that there is a relationship between the companies that are performing the best in the marketplace and those that use many of the same performance metrics and best practices that are developing in operational risk management. In short, they manage operational risk well. A logical extension of this thinking is that effective operational risk management will lead to building the next generation of effective organizations.

Exhibit 4.1 portrays the progression from baseline regulatory compliance through to operational loss cost reduction, rating enhancement upgrades, and ultimately achievement of market leadership. As an organization continues to invest intelligently in risk measurement, analysis, finance, and operational risk monitoring, it positions itself well to reap increasing benefits from these programs. As it progresses through the sophistication of these programs, implementing a coordinated enterprise-wide program, linking risk and performance measurement and enhancement metrics, it is ultimately in the position to enhance its position as a market leader.

Perhaps better terms for framing all risk management are *risk optimization* or risk response. The concept is easily understood in areas like credit and market risks, but less so in operational risk management. In financial risk management this term is used to mean that the risk manager and business manager alike are continually confronted with the choice of "shedding" or hedging unwanted risks, while retaining those that can best be managed, all with a view toward enhancing and optimizing the business' desired performance.

There is a broader silver lining in operational risk management, and in all forms of risk management, for that matter, that is far too often overlooked. The upside potential of risk reduction is not limited to the absence of losses, it is the creation of value and quality. Thus at the other end of the loss spectrum is the creation of more effective companies. Here it speaks to the balance of applying effort to manage the risks commensurate with their relative loss potential and their upside opportunity as well. For instance, rather than the risk practitioner and business manager focusing their full attention solely on the downside—on customer legal actions, or even customer complaints that might be an earlier indicator of legal actions—their risk management efforts should balance that focus with emphasis on quality and customer satisfaction initiatives. Thus they would enhance the firm's position in the market and balance effort on both downside and upside risk.

As operational risk practitioners begin to broaden their perspective and look beyond the downside, they may find that senior managers have warmed to the idea. In *The ValueReporting Revolution,* the authors encourage companies to move forward in risk reporting by answering three questions:

1. What do you do to create value?
2. What can happen to destroy value?
3. What degree of confidence do you have in the estimated distribution of outcomes?[2]

It is interesting to find that in discussing these questions, the authors go on to describe how companies respond to each presently. In the first instance, they note that in discussing the *opportunity dimension of risk,* most companies describe the upside almost exclusively—the good things that might happen when they take risks. Here they argue for expansion to report on the corresponding downside. In illustrating current communication in the second area, they note that companies sometimes go to great lengths to report on the hazard dimensions of risk, as in the disclosures that took place on Y2K exposures. For the third, they mention banks' advancements in value-at-risk reporting.[3]

They came so close, but they themselves missed an opportunity to go one step further in highlighting a practical solution for closing the upside–downside disconnect, and move toward further improvement of risk reporting. That is, the key is to bring the advocates of each position together for a coordinated result. On the one hand you have legal counsel and risk practitioners often pressing for reporting on the second and third areas—hazard and value-at-risk dimensions—but perhaps missing their own opportunity to connect with senior management on the first area—the upside–downside trade-off, or *opportunity dimension of risk*. On the other hand, the authors are arguing for companies to do a better job of reporting on the *risk dimension of opportunity*. If the authors are right, that senior managers are listening, and we are in fact on the verge of a reporting revolution, a window of opportunity may have just opened for risk practitioners to climb through. In the process they find their companies already looking in from the outside.

Why is it important to make this connection? Well, as anyone who has toiled with internal lobbying for risk management will attest, it is very difficult to keep a business manager's attention focused on the importance of managing risk when the best you can do is have no losses. On the other hand, when the best outcome will be business improvement—as evidenced by enhanced corporate image, more satisfied customers, increased retention of customers, increased sales, market share and profitability, you will get much further. This implies a change in thinking from pure downside to a risk–reward mentality. In essence, then, this is a second irony of upside: for years practitioners have argued that there is only a downside to operational and event risks. Many have resisted the upside argument, until they find themselves struggling to sell the concepts to management. Then they wonder why no one will listen!

At the top level, the new operational risk management will support strategic decision making. Risk professionals in the credit and market risk environment already have a handle on strategic decision making, using a risk–reward scenario. Here is a classic market risk risk-adjusted return on capital (RAROC) example: When buying a U.S. Treasury, the relative risk is so low that the yield itself can be relatively low; if one were to buy a high-yield, or junk, bond instead, one would need a much higher yield to justify the much higher risk.[4]

Now look at the relative risk–reward of stable, well-managed, well-controlled businesses versus those unstable, poorly managed businesses facing the relative unknown of a new business line, product area, geographic area, or new markets—where the control infrastructure is much less predictable. The former is in a far better position to handle the uncertainties of today's Internet-paced business environment. In addition, when you lay market, credit, and operational risk side by side, the overall risk–reward picture for a firm becomes much clearer.[5]

"JUST GOOD MANAGEMENT?"

So, the upside opportunity is far bigger than a discipline of simply assessing risks and measuring losses. To borrow but slightly modify a phase from the U.S. presidential election in 1992, "It's the strategic opportunity for market leadership, stupid!" There is a huge opportunity here; it's not just about losses and risk trends, or even regulation. However, the third irony of upside is that banking and financial institutions only seem to have picked up on operational risk management as a discipline because of regulatory pressures. And if the recent developments are any indication, there is the risk that a disproportionate part of the effort could go the road of an obligatory capital management function, with far too little emphasis on management of the risk or the opportunities.

> *Myth: We don't have to worry about an operational risk management program, isn't it "just good management?"*

Some have suggested that any discussions beyond risk assessment tools, losses, risk measurement, and regulatory capital are simply about "*good management.*" That may be so, but if it is all that simple, why aren't more companies overflowing with "good managers and good management?"

Effective operational risk management *is* good management. Generally speaking, I have no issue with this statement, but it is disappointing that some leave the discussion there. It is too vague and intangible, and it adds no value toward improving the situation. More focus is needed.

This position also trivializes the subject of operational risk management. Although there is certainly a direct relationship between good management and good operational risk management, the relationship begs the question: How do we achieve good operational risk management, good and effective management, and thus more effective organizations?

Some of the best management teams have developed means of tracking and mitigating risks within their business lines or profit centers. But until recently, this has been mostly an ad hoc, manual exercise. Now, however, there are techniques, backed up by technology, that give managers operational risk management and control tools to enable them not only to automate and build best practices on their own but also to track and optimize their business by tracking control variables in real time. Further, they can implement these practices across an entire firm. But perhaps more to the point; these tools were not available until recently.

Meanwhile, firms in some industries have applied the concepts in a larger sense and for greater reward. The first step toward seizing this opportunity is to bring the two developments—a larger strategic application and day-to-day tactical tools and techniques—together for better management firmwide. In essence, along with all of the tactical developments, such as quantitative modeling, performance metrics, benchmarking, goal setting, and greater accountability in operational risk management, has come a strategic recognition that by focusing attention on operational risk management and improving a firm's risk profile it stands to enhance stakeholder value.

In fact, when the loss magnitude is coupled with the macro technological, societal, and business trends, along with recognition of the *operational risk management opportunity* in front of us today, interest in the topic of operational risk will grow at a breakneck pace. In short, you ain't seen nothing yet from this new discipline.

ENTERPRISE-WIDE STRATEGIC VISION AND CORE IDEALS

Now for a fourth irony of upside: one of the most important parts of a solid operational risk management foundation does not actually come in the form of a risk management policy statement. It is not even discussed in most risk management texts. The first-level strategic and firmwide mandate is actually outlined by management in the firm's strategic vision. It speaks to the broad issues of corporate quality, vision, and "being" in laying the foundation for a strategic corporate mandate on risk management.

Statements on corporate vision and quality management have particular relevance to operational risk management programs. If effective risk management is an extension of quality products, service, and a conscientious management team, then the most effective mandates are founded on firmwide values, and embedded into the organization's culture. All the risk management in the world cannot compensate for a flawed corporate vision and culture. In point of fact, a risk management group will beat its collective head against the wall if the organization at large is not focused on the prime directive of creating a culture of teamwork, excellence, and risk awareness and managing risk along the way. We have seen this happen time and time again in the financial community.

In research for their important book, *Built to Last,* James Collins and Jerry Porras examine numerous company statements on vision and values. They note that most of the statements can and should be boiled down to three to five themes overall. An interesting observation is that often embedded in them are one or more themes that can provide an important basis for enterprise-wide risk management. Consider these examples of core ideology themes from their work:[6]

- Honesty and integrity (3M, Ford, GE, Merck)
- Tolerance for honest mistakes (3M)
- Worldwide reliability of services (American Express)
- Tackling huge challenges and risks (Boeing)
- Product safety and quality (Boeing)
- Interdependent balance between responsibility to customers, employees, society, and shareholders (GE)
- Individual responsibility and opportunity (GE)
- Contribution and responsibility to the communities in which we operate (Hewlett-Packard)
- Go the last mile to do things right (IBM)
- Continual self-improvement (Merck)
- Unequivocal excellence in all aspects of the company (Merck)
- Continual improvement in all that the company does—in ideas, in quality, in customer satisfaction (Motorola)
- Honesty, integrity, and ethics in all aspects of business (Motorola)
- Continuous improvement, never being satisfied (Nordstrom)
- Product excellence (Procter & Gamble)

Collins and Porras note one of their findings is that many companies do not articulate their core values and purpose in their core ideology.

Clearly one key focus of their work and book was to advise corporations to develop core ideologies and statements on vision, thereby taking an initial step toward becoming "visionary companies." This should serve as both a challenge and a golden opportunity for risk practitioners—to encourage management toward the development and promulgation of such statements, and in the process to weave in one or more themes that would support the risk management effort enterprise-wide.

A word of caution: Some management teams go to great lengths to develop and publish far-reaching mission statements for the corporation overall. These can be useful in laying the groundwork for many aspects of the company, including its personnel both internally and externally, and thus have relevance for risk management as well.

The statements can either be a raging success or fall flat on their faces, taking the brunt of scoffs internally and externally. Much of the relative success depends on management's own actions. If members of management ignore the statement and behave in a way that is contrary to the mission without repercussions, then the statement will most certainly fail. It all comes down to the role model set by management itself.

Many readers will relate to a parenting analogy. An example is the case in which the parents lecture their children sternly to behave with the finest social graces, attend religious services faithfully, but do not show

BP STRATEGY #2—DEMONSTRATE A VISION, MANDATE, AND OBJECTIVES

The firmwide vision, values, and mandate will be formulated at the highest levels of the organization and communicated outward. It will be communicated at three levels. The first is the company's own ideological vision statement. That sets the stage. The second is a statement on enterprise-wide risk management, of which operational risk will be a recognized part. The third is a specific statement on operational risk management, which will be much more specific as to the key objectives, roles, responsibility, and functional scope. Taken together the statements will serve as clear evidence of buy-in at the board and most senior management levels of the organization. They demonstrate not only internally, but also externally, the firm's commitment and also serve as an enhancement to shareholder value.

consideration or compassion themselves. When the next lecture comes around they recognize that their own failings may have been noticed by their children and offer the counsel, "Do as I say, not as I do." But who's kidding whom? How often does that one really work? The lectures to the kids ring a bit hollow after that.

It's no different with management and employees, or the market at large, for that matter. Take the situation of a company that communicates to the world through its mission that it cares about customers, service, and its own people, but then ignores customer concerns and its own people's needs. If management takes pains to write a flowery customer care statement but does not take even the first measure to respond to customer complaints, and favors revenue at all costs over quality products and service, the statement tends to become a bit of a joke.

For the best firms that are intent on making the statement work—and live it on a day-to-day basis—it can be a very powerful tool indeed. The statement is reinforced through actions of management with rewards to business units and staff that have epitomized the mission statement through their own actions; then the strategy stands an excellent chance of succeeding.

SIX SIGMA AND QUALITY PROGRAMS

One has only to look at some of the most successful corporations to get an appreciation for firmwide values and mandates. Take General Electric, for instance. It is a huge conglomerate, with significant financial service operations, and has achieved the top position on Fortune magazine's list of America's Most Admired Companies™ for several years in a row. The company has ranked among the top three for quality of management and use of corporate assets and produced a total annualized return for shareholders of 46% during 1994-99.[7] GE and other highly regarded corporations have adopted Six Sigma programs for performance enhancement. A logical side benefit of these programs is an enhancement to the focus and a refinement of the organizational culture, which yield a more risk conscious employee base.

The parallels between Six Sigma programs and the upside opportunity in risk management are striking. It may not be an overstatement, in fact, to suggest that Six Sigma programs and their associated advantages are the other side of the operational risk management coin.

What is Six Sigma? Technically, the term *Six Sigma* refers to its primary objective: striving for virtual perfection in meeting customer requirements.[8] The authors of *The Six Sigma Way*, however, define it as "a comprehensive and flexible system for achieving, sustaining and maximizing business success. Six Sigma is uniquely driven by close understanding of customer needs, disciplined use of facts, data, and statistical analysis, and diligent attention to managing, improving, and reinventing business processes."[9] All of that sounds familiar.

First of all, like operational risk management, Six Sigma is not new. The discipline is an outgrowth of quality management programs that have gone before it. A key difference is that Six Sigma was developed with customers in mind. That is, the first objective was to refocus and reorganize a corporation to align genuinely with its customers.[10] The concept and its implementation extend well beyond the customer, however.

In fine-tuning a firm's focus, much of an operational risk management effort is intended to enhance business performance by involving the entire organization. It entails improvements to management processes, performance standards, metrics, and financial and regulatory management. With similar goals, Six Sigma refocuses the entire organization on the upside opportunities that flow from its customers, its most valued asset. Interestingly, the authors of *The Six Sigma Way* highlight a number of methods and tools that complement its strategy. Among them are continuous process improvement, statistical analysis and analysis of variance, balanced score cards, process management, and the metrics behind statistical process controls.[11] See Exhibit 4.2. Coincidentally many of these are also driving the development of operational risk management.

As operational risk management practitioners toil over their own data, analyses, and measurement advancements, all with a view toward creating effective performance measures, there is one last observation on Six Sigma worthy of note. As this book goes to print, insiders at General Electric, one of the most visible corporate advocates of Six Sigma, report that there too management's focus has most recently been on enhancing the company's Six Sigma program to include better metrics for performance measurement. It seems clear that enterprise-wide operational risk management has met its soul mate.

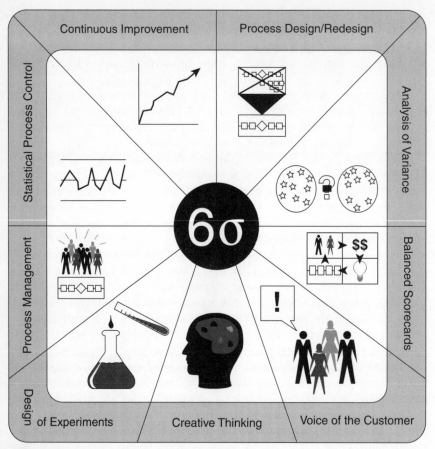

EXHIBIT 4.2 Essential Six Sigma Methods and Tools.

The Six Sigma Way Peter S. Pande, Robert P. Neuman, and Roland R. Cavanagh, McGraw-Hill, p. 422 5/00.

CORPORATE INTEGRITY AND CULTURE: MANAGING DOWNSIDE RISK AND UPSIDE OPPORTUNITY

Clearly only the more progressive companies will seize operational risk management in its broadest sense as one of their levers toward market leadership. This is purely a matter of opportunity and choice. Regardless of the degree to which a firm presses the operational risk management opportunity, however, there is a piece of the market leadership puzzle that cannot be ignored—corporate culture.

Corporate culture can be an incredibly powerful motivating force. It should not be underestimated as an ally or obstacle to a successful operational risk management effort. With a supportive culture on your side, op-

BP STRATEGY #3—FOSTER A CULTURE OF INTEGRITY AND RISK MANAGEMENT AWARENESS

More often than not corporate culture and ethos are the least recognized components of an operational risk management program but at the same time can have the greatest positive or negative impact on an organization's risk profile. A senior level commitment and a risk aware culture are both essential.

erational risk management efforts can flow almost effortlessly. On the other hand, a corporate culture that seems to run counter to creating risk awareness in the organization can put the risk practitioner in the role of the proverbial salmon swimming upstream.

Referring again to *Built to Last,* Collins and Porras also examined a number of companies and industries over the long term (throughout their life spans) and in direct comparison to others. Their research was focused on boiling their key findings down into a framework of underlying ideas, with the end goal of identifying some of the key characteristics of visionary companies. In their chapter entitled "Cult-Like Cultures," they highlight anecdotal evidence about companies like Johnson and Johnson, Merck, Hewlett-Packard, and Wal-Mart. They note that visionary companies work toward creating an "empowered" or decentralized work environment. First and foremost, they impose a "tight ideology, screen and indoctrinate people into that ideology, eject the viruses, and give those who remain the tremendous sense of responsibility that comes with membership in an elite organization."[12] Wow! That's powerful stuff. It would be tough to swim in any direction other than with that flow. So, why bother? Harness that potential to maximize the value of culture in driving your operational risk management program.

Certainly, Collins and Porras were highlighting these strong cultural visionary company characteristics to make their point. Not every company has a culture that strong, but every company has a *unique* culture, and it is critically important to be mindful of that when attempting to fulfill one's own mission. Whether a company has a culture that is entrepreneurial risk-taking, quality-oriented, an EVA (Economic Value Added), a VAR- (Value at Risk) based, control oriented, or with no particular distinction at all, its culture will contribute to setting the stage for the success or failure of an operational risk management program.

A firm's corporate culture will make or break a risk assessment program. It must be factored in whether a program is positioned for loss reduction at one extreme or market leadership at the other. A firm should leverage its cultural attributes, if predisposed toward quality and risk control, into successful operational risk management. If not, it should leverage operational risk management in such a way as to enhance risk awareness attributes of its culture and its employee population.

There is much discussion about creating "risk aware cultures" in firms. Some is in order here. Most of the ideological vision statements referenced in the prior section give some reference to risk management. Some are specific, but most are vague, at best. With or without a vision statement, it is important to take some specific steps toward creating the desired environment.

Following is a case illustration of values that the Royal Bank of Scotland (RBS) has worked to instill in its culture. Their emphasis on personal responsibility combined with attempts at removing the tendency to blame others for problems are important characteristics. Most employees tend to be comfortable with reasonable levels of responsibility, but as Chris Rachlin, Group Operational Risk Manager at RBS explains in the case, the combination of responsibility and a "blame culture" creates a tendency to hide problems until they can be hidden no longer. The end result often becomes the discovery of a major loss with potentially catastrophic impact that might have been avoided or at least been much less severe if discovered sooner.

CASE ILLUSTRATION

Promoting "Risk Aware" Cultures

The Royal Bank of Scotland

The culture of an organization is very difficult to express tangibly. There has been much talk in recent years about instilling a "risk control culture" in banks, but it is difficult to define exactly what is meant by this.[13]

If defining organizational culture is difficult, changing it is even more challenging. While we cannot cover in detail the rich topic of change management here, the following are some starting points:

■ **Remove the "Blame Culture":** Most organizations find it easy to criticize and difficult to praise. If it appears to the employees that the bank's only communication about operational risk is to sack or severely reprimand poor-performing personnel after a major operational risk incident, the example set is that it is acceptable to do things badly providing you do not get caught. This will lead to staff trying to cover up what they are doing wrong. Problems will tend to be discovered only once they have grown to be very sizable.

To avoid this, the performance appraisal process must be designed to pick up poor management and staff at an early stage so that, when appropriate, employees can be counseled well before an incident happens. When an incident does occur, the staff involved should be helped to improve and made to feel less concerned about admitting their mistake. In this way, small incidents can be stopped from turning into major ones.

■ **Promote Personal Responsibility:** Many banks suffer, to an extent, from what might be termed *silo thinking*. This means that staff only focus on the narrow range of tasks they are asked to do without thinking about the impact of what they do on others in the bank.

This can result in departments "throwing rubbish over the fence into the next-door yard." For example, to meet a schedule, a department may complete their processing to a substandard level and pass it to the next department who are left to "clean up" the transactions—or pass the problem on to the next department in the chain. Yet a small error in a transaction in one part of the bank can end up being a major operational risk issue in another.

Two ways to engender a culture of personal responsibility are:

1. Ensure that all parts of the organization have full knowledge of the business and the business processes from end to end, not just their part of the process, so they understand the significance of what they are doing.
2. Develop department performance targets that explicitly consider the quality of the output and information that flow to other areas.

    At the Royal Bank of Scotland, the introduction and eventual certification of processes under ISO 9000 has helped a number of departments improve the quality of work and reduce errors.

■ **Raise the Status of Operations-related Functions:** Historically, banks have focused their brightest and best staff on developing new business and looking at credit-related issues. In some cases, operations-related functions have had to make do with the staff that other areas did not want. An effective bank operations area needs good managers who have the resources to hire and motivate bright staff.

■ ■ ■

CASE ILLUSTRATION

Corporate Culture and Risk Taking

There is another important dimension of corporate culture. This one involves relative risk taking. The following section was developed and contributed by Mike Levin of KPMG Consulting on the importance of understanding and leveraging corporate culture in risk taking.

A complete response to the problem of operational risk demands that a firm seek to understand exactly why its executives and employees respond to risks in the ways that they do. Why does a managing director seem to ignore obvious signs of trouble in a trading desk? Or, why does a middle manager reject a needed investment in a new database technology that, if successful, would save the firm millions of dollars, but, if failed, would cost the firm relatively little?

Understanding why these individuals make these decisions shows the way to improving the processes underneath the decisions. The managing director or middle manager might explain their decision with an appeal to the firm's "corporate culture," yet little is really known about what makes up a firm's culture, and even more, how that culture influences how executives and employees take on and manage risk in a firm.

A professional society recently grappled with this very problem. Its CEO sought to improve risk management in its operations and sensed that its particular "culture" influenced its risk taking and management. In particular, the CEO wondered why the institution was not taking even slight risks and how cultural factors might make all employees harmfully and wastefully risk averse.

A framework for understanding the cultural factors underlying risk averse and risk-seeking behavior was needed. The Risk Culture Model in Exhibit 4.3 divides risk-taking behavior into two areas: risk perception and risk propensity. Risk perception prescribes how an individual "frames" or views individual risk opportunities, including how it analyzes and interprets analyses of uncertainty or risk arising from an opportunity. For the professional association, risk perception involves how individual managers describe a given risk opportunity, including how much emphasis the analysis places on the relative advantages and disadvantages of that opportunity. Thus, before anyone makes a decision, how an individual describes the situation and the available alternatives can influence that decision, as any savvy manager well knows.

Risk propensity is divided into three areas: definition of risk, attitude toward risk, and response to risk. Individuals define risk in different ways, as "hazard," "opportunity," or "variability," and the mere definition suggests whether an individual is risk averse or risk seeking. The definition in turn influences the attitude toward risk, including thoughts and feelings about risk, and whether an individual seeks more or less of it in his or her decisions. These attitudes provide further evidence about risk-averse and risk-seeking behavior. Finally, risk attitude will, in part, drive the actual response to risk: eliminate it completely, reduce it, or take more of it. In all three areas, the professional association was able to classify specific behaviors that they had observed with respect to whether they were risk averse or risk seeking.

The Risk Culture Model provides a way to understand how specific examples of behavior and decision making are risk averse or risk seeking. The professional association used data and observations from formal interviews, reviews of internal documents, informal participation in meetings, and other

EXHIBIT 4.3 Risk Culture Model—Part 1

Observed Activities and Behaviors	Risk Averse (low variability, low return situations)	⟷ (high variability, low return situations)	Risk Seeking (high variability, high return situations)
Risk Propensity			
Definition of Risk How the firm views or conceives of risk in its business, operations, or activities	• downside only • hazards, threats to operations "cost," "expense" "uncertainty," with largely unknown outcomes and likelihoods	• variability in results • material deviation from expected outcome "risk," with knowledge of possible outcomes and likelihoods	• upside only • opportunities, growth businesses "revenue," "income"
Attitude toward Risk How the person or firm feels or thinks about the presence of risk in its business, operations, or activities	• avoid/eliminate hazards and threats from operations • view in isolation, with no pooling of impact on firm	• accept and manage risk as natural component of opportunities • view risks as portfolio with net positive impact on firm	• seek/exploit opportunity from operations • view in isolation, with no pooling of impact on firm
Response to Risk How the firm makes decisions and deploys resources to make choices about risks; how the firm selects, controls, and transfers specific risks	• absolute control over processes • hedge, insure, and transfer completely	• balance control with respect to capital or investment • cost/benefit analysis of hedging, insurance, and transfer	• minimal control over processes • little or no hedging, insurance, or transfer
Risk Perception How the firm "frames" or views individual opportunities, including how it analyzes and interprets analyses of uncertainty or risk arising from an opportunity	• bias toward downside impact of risk on firm • analyze hazards and threats arising from opportunity	• consider both upside and downside impact of opportunity • analyze net impact of risks on firm • analyze impact of hazards and income with respect to investment, capital	• bias toward upside impact of risk on firm • analyze revenues and income arising from opportunity

Source: March, James G., and Zur Shapira, 1987. Managerial Perspectives on Risk and Risk Taking. *Management Science*, Vol. 33, No. 11 (November), pp. 1404–1418. Sitkin, Sim B., 1992. Reconceptualizing the Determinants of Risk Behavior, *Academy of Management Review*, Vol. 17, No. 1 (January) pp. 9–38.

Observed Activities and Behaviors		Risk Averse ⟷ Risk Seeking	
Risk Perception		• current fiscal situation limits risk capacity and magnifies perceived riskiness of opportunities • analysis focuses on severity of adverse events and "worst-case" scenarios	• Internal analysis reviewed range of possible outcomes
Risk Propensity	Definition of Risk	• focus on significance (not likelihood) of hazards or adverse events • zero-defect approach to decisions • no common risk language	
	Attitude toward Risk	• no shared view of risk, as individuals bear entire risk on own and seek cover in processes, committee deliberations • no shared spirit of success arising from good decisions • little connection between attitude and rewards, except for extreme adverse outcomes, with absolute punishment • avoid conflict, constructive debate on issues and decisions due to fear of criticism and blame	• Internal decision embraced constructive conflict • Certain subsidiaries include elements of risk-taking and risk management in compensation
	Response to Risk	• control individual areas tightly and intrusively, and respond to issues and problems with process, not solutions • slow decision process	
Possible Drivers	executives (BoD, senior staff)	• low trust, high-control environment • significant conflict avoidance	
	vision, mission, strategy	• clearly expressed • inconsistent understanding among staff	
	structure	• isolated executives and functions • policy and business activities	
	metrics	• currently, budget and anecdotal rewards and punishment	

EXHIBIT 4.4 Risk Culture Model—Part 2

sources to complete the model in Exhibit 4.4 for themselves. Not surprisingly, most of the observed behavior falls under the risk averse heading:

- Internal analyses tend to emphasize downside events only.
- Risk is defined as the severity of a potential hazard.
- Employees are typically fearful of risk and see risk as leading only to damage or harmful personal consequences.
- Consequently, the organization seeks to control risk tightly and eliminate it completely.

Interestingly, in some decisions the organization did exhibit more risk-seeking behavior. One division incorporated variable components into compensation, with salespeople putting their bonuses "at risk." In another, a critical decision to enter into a new venture featured a complete analysis of both advantages and disadvantages of the venture, thus "framing" the decision in a risk-neutral manner, and limiting the influence that the format of the description and analysis (as opposed to the substance) might have on the decision. But, for an extremely risk-averse organization, these examples were rare.

A critical extension of the analysis involved trying to identify the drivers of these various observed behaviors. The association could then respond to these drivers with specific initiatives. Drivers of these behaviors include some critical components of the current corporate culture:

- Isolation of business and functional units from one another
- Lack of trust within levels (executive, managerial, staff) of the organizational hierarchy, and among different levels of the hierarchy
- Atmosphere of conflict avoidance at all costs

These drivers explain many of the behaviors that were observed, and the organization has since designed and implemented initiatives to respond to these problems, including reorganization that limits isolation of units, executive leadership to surface and respond to conflicts, and education and training in trust-building in the organization.

In this way, this organization developed a deep understanding of how its corporate culture influences the level of risk taking, and how to change that culture in order to make the organization more of a risk taker.

■ ■ ■

OPPORTUNITY COST EQUALS OPPORTUNITY LOST

There is a great deal of attention being paid to operational risk management today, especially in banking and finance in response to recent regulatory activity, but is it lasting? Consider all the time, effort and resources, and commitment made to prepare all organizations worldwide in 1998 and 1999 for the much anticipated, much touted Y2K meltdown. As we now know, it never happened, and many of those efforts were quickly forgotten and lost in the blur of the New Year in 2000, particularly when it all turned out to be a nonevent.

Operational risk practitioners would do well to take necessary measures to fight off a similar fate. That is, when the buzz over new regulatory capital charges recedes, these programs are at risk of fading into the woodwork, with minimal real business improvement impact on organizations going forward. At that point, the real risk would be that organizations evolve in another direction, and operational risk management simply becomes another necessary regulatory compliance appendage, with little added value to show for itself. If this were to occur, we will look back on this period as a missed opportunity.

But relevance must be earned. If operational risk management is seen simply as a necessary evil, then it may be lasting but only in a minimal way: to address capital and supervisory requirements. Firms would do well to position these programs such as to achieve relevance and add real value for their shareholders.

CONCLUSION

As we progress throughout all the various aspects of operational risk management in this book we should keep the upside potential firmly in the forefront.

The real opportunity here is that operational risk management not only serves as a key part of the real "blocking and tackling" for firmwide risk management effort, but also an enterprise-wide strategy for enhancement of the business. The new tools and techniques being explored (e.g., first-time linkage to a firmwide strategy, new quantitative tools, new senior management committees, new risk finance programs) all speak to new horsepower that the forerunners of operational risk (traditional risk and insurance, traditional internal audit, isolated risk assessment programs, and even quantitative-only analysis) have not enjoyed up to this point.

Even short of setting grand ideals for a risk management function, too few risk programs have focused on leveraging the unique aspects of their own corporate ideals and values in developing their risk management statements. The risk practitioners would do well to harness the power of the corporate ideals in propelling their own efforts forward. With corporate ideals as a key foundation, the development statements on enterprise-wide operational risk management, more specifically, begin to fall into place.

There is little question that when properly positioned, framed, focused, and resourced an operational risk management will serve to enhance our firms' shareholder values, efficiency, and competitiveness. But even on a smaller scale day-to-day it will serve to add additional validity to the struggles of operational risk practitioners as they fight for investment, resources, attention for the subject, and cooperation from senior management and line managers alike.

Integral to this focus is the importance of understanding corporate culture, molding that culture to focus on quality, appropriate risk taking, and management. Corporate culture will make or break any risk management program.

LESSONS LEARNED AND KEY RECOMMENDATIONS

- Demonstrate a vision, mandate, and several objectives. The firmwide vision, values, and mandate will be formulated at the highest levels of the organization and communicated outward. It will be communicated at three levels. The first is the company's own ideological vision statement. That sets the stage. The second is a statement on enterprise-wide risk management, of which operational risk will be a recognized part. The third is a specific statement on operational risk management, which will be much more specific as to the key objectives, roles, responsibility, and functional scope. Taken together, the statements will serve as clear evidence of buy-in at both the board and most senior management levels of the organization. They demonstrate not only internally, but also externally, the firm's commitment, and also serve as an enhancement to shareholder value (BP Strategy #2).
- Operational risk management *is good management.* There is no argument there, but there is much more to it than that. Operational risk management has introduced best practices from a variety of other disciplines, including the use of performance measures, analytics, and improved capital and financial management, to name just a few.
- The most effective mandates are evidenced in the form of firmwide values. They cannot be viewed as window dressing; however, they must be embedded into the organization's culture. We can find numerous examples of expertly constructed risk management programs that have been thwarted by faulty corporate cultures.
- Foster a *culture of integrity* and risk management awareness. More often than not corporate culture and ethos are the least recognized components of an operational risk management program, but at the same time can have the greatest positive or negative impact on an organization's risk profile. A senior level commitment and a risk aware culture are both essential (BP Strategy #3).
- One should think about risk management in terms of risk balance and optimization. That concept is easily understood in areas like credit and market risks, but less so in operational risk management. Here it speaks to the balance of applying effort to manage the risks commensurate with their combined relative severity and likelihood of occurrence. The

reward either takes the form of a better managed business, fewer losses, or better focused control expenditures, or all three.

- A risk culture model may be helpful for understanding the cultural factors underlying risk-averse and risk-seeking behavior. It provides a way to understand how specific examples of behavior and decision making can be harnessed for greater results.

- An operational risk management program will leverage the organization's culture. That is, if it is analytic and metric-driven, metrics will be a key lever for your operational risk program. If there is a VAR or RAROC culture, capital allocation methods may well become the foundation for operational risk management. If it is audit and control driven, then independent assessment or control self-assessment will probably be key. If quality programs have been permeated in the firm's culture, then they will provide a springboard for numerous relevant tools and strategies.

CHAPTER 5

Operational Risk and Market Perception

Franchise, Reputation, and Brand Risk

It takes a lifetime to build a reputation,
and a heartbeat to lose it.

There is a natural tendency when reviewing operational losses to concentrate on the aspect of operational risk that is most tangible and measurable—the direct economic loss costs themselves. Operational losses can have a huge impact on a company in the marketplace and with the investment community at large, however, in the form of damage to reputation and brand.

This chapter will address the impact of operational risk on loss of market share and shareholder value. At the outset, we explore the importance of a good reputation and the value of brand, one of a firm's most valued assets. Next, we look at the characteristics of reputation risk, from pre-loss considerations to loss cost components, and examine a few case studies that represent attempts to quantify the impact of operational loss on share price. Then we look at a few reputation metrics. Last, we go to the heart of the matter: Management's need to take proactive steps to protect their firm's reputation, both on a pre- and post-loss basis.

FRANCHISE AND REPUTATION RISK MANAGEMENT

A Senior Management Priority

Protection of the firm's reputation and brand is certainly an area that is near and dear to the hearts of the board, senior management, and the employee population at large. Enhancing and protecting a firm's shareholder value has a direct relationship to its financial performance, its reputation in the market, and with the investor community.

Building and protecting a solid reputation benefits the firm in many ways. From the perspective of the financial community, it can mean creating and enhancing a high market valuation, better standing with the investment community, and generally improved access to capital markets. In the customer arena, it often equates to greater market share and enables premium pricing for product and services. From the perspective of its cost structure, it can mean greater negotiating leverage with vendors. For the employment experience, it translates into attracting and retaining top talent, and high employee morale and productivity. And with the general public it can often mean preferential treatment by special interest organizations and better standing with the media.[1]

There is no question that senior management is focused on these advantages. A recent survey of CEOs reported that more often than ever today they are looking for external endorsements for their companies as a means to enhance their corporate image. The survey went on to report that many CEOs consider external image-making to be absolutely crucial for attracting and recruiting key people—that being the name of the game in today's highly competitive business environment.[2]

From an operational risk and loss standpoint, it is more likely that a major hit to a firm's reputation will sink a once-viable entity than the economic components of most losses, with the possible exception of the largest financial losses conceivable. And studies show a direct relationship between a high company valuation and how well it handles itself in the market, particularly in times of crises, when the firm is most vulnerable to losing the market's confidence.[3]

Despite all of these factors and the importance of reputation and brand generally, far more time and attention in operational risk circles is spent on the direct economic impact of operational losses. Some practitioners ignore events that have no measurable economic loss component but entail reputational consequences. From a regulatory standpoint, the Basel Committee has excluded reputation risk from its first round of regulatory proposals. The likely reason, of course, is that the economic dimensions of loss are more measurable than the reputation dimensions.

Although arguably reputation risk does not belong in a regulatory capital change, it is unfortunate that "degree-of-difficulty" may have become the deciding factor in prioritizing which dimensions of operational risk will be addressed first. Although this is understandable from a measurement perspective, of course, a concern remains that the banking industry will devote precious little management attention to reputation risk as a result.

Market Share and Customer Service

Customer and market perception can make or break a company. Positive perception can spread like adrenaline to energize every corner of the firm.

> ## BP STRATEGY #4—MANAGE THE IMPACT OF OPERATIONAL RISK ON THE FRANCHISE, REPUTATION, AND BRAND
>
> The best firms will have a clear understanding of the potential impact of operational risk on their franchise and franchise value. A vision and mandate are not enough. Reputation management requires a tested strategy, plan, and ongoing discipline for protecting corporate integrity and managing crises that might impact their reputation, brand, and franchise.

Negative perception can spread like a cancer, destroying everything in its path that hundreds or thousands of dedicated employees have labored to create. Consider the following illustrations from General Electric, Delta Airlines, American Airlines, Bankers Trust, Ford and Firestone.

CASE ILLUSTRATION

From the Outside-In: The Customer as First Priority

General Electric

General Electric is held in high esteem as one of the most admired companies in America, if not the world. Much of the credit for that achievement has been attributed to its chief executive, Jack Welch, and management's focus on quality, excellence, and the customer (a visible part of its Six Sigma strategy). The following quote from Welch in January 1999 speaks well to the company's customer focus:

> The focus on the customer . . . will change General Electric forever. It will absolutely make this company totally different. 'Outside in' is an enormous thought. 'Outside in' is a big, big idea. We've been 'inside out' for over 100 years. Forcing everything around the 'outside in' view will change the game. . . . With the company focused on the customer, no one in this company can ever again at the end of a month, at the end of the quarter, at the end of a year do anything . . . to make a financial number at the expense of customer satisfaction. . . . You talk about sins—that's the ultimate sin. . . ." [4]

■ ■ ■

CASE ILLUSTRATION

Operational Risk and Care for the Customer

Delta Airlines and American Airlines

It's the little things that matter for customers and the public . . . little things like customer service, especially in times of unsettling, or worse, life-threatening operational events. Chris Duncan, Director, Risk Management at Delta Airlines recently described the airline's shift in policy toward caring for passengers who were engaged in an "incident." As the airline expression goes, Delta had recently "bellyflopped" an airplane on the runway in San Francisco following a major landing gear malfunction. Having been recruited into the senior risk management role at Delta, he was new to the company and unclear about their policy toward customer care. His inclination was to contact the passengers individually. After all, from an insurance risk management perspective, it has been a long-held claims management rule of thumb for any risk manager to arrange for contact to injured customers following an accident involving injuries. The move sends a message of caring to the public. As a side benefit, it serves as both a useful information-gathering move, and a litigation deterrent strategy.

Duncan and Delta took the idea further, however, and decided to contact everyone on the aircraft they could find within 24 hours of the incident, regardless of injury. Their plan was to extend the message of caring even further by providing, with no (legal) strings attached, an apology letter telling each passenger what had transpired in this incident, and accompanying travel vouchers for a free first class round trip ticket. Delta also placed additional phone calls (with passengers' permission) in the following weeks to check on each person individually. Based on the conversations that he and his staff had with passengers and their surprise at receiving a phone call—even those who had not been injured—the strategy was a raging success. Few, if any, passengers even considered the idea of pursuing a claim against the airline, and many were left with a good feeling about the company.

Contrast this to my own personal experience on an American Airlines flight in the 1980s that was forced into an emergency landing in Milwaukee, Wisconsin, in early February. Despite what would have been the normal weather conditions there, it was not snowing at the time. Instead, we had encountered a freak thunderstorm at a very high altitude and, we surmised later, our plane had been struck by lightning. As we later overheard, the pilot had observed a fire detection alarm for one of the engines, which caused him to undertake an emergency landing. This had been an overnight "red eye" flight returning from Los Angeles to New York. The emergency landing procedure required us to exit the aircraft via the emergency slides. Half asleep (it was still the middle of the night), we complied with the hurried instructions—removing our shoes, leaving our personal belongings behind, which, I should add, included suit jackets, sweaters, and overcoats—and found ourselves gliding down the inflatable slides into a cold Wisconsin mid-February rainstorm. We landed feet first in icy puddles in our stocking feet.

Of course, none of us would have minded in the slightest if there had been an actual emergency and I, for one, appreciate the captain's cautionary moves. We were all relieved to learn that the fire detection had indicated a false alarm. Apparently there was little danger after all, other than a bit of strain on our nerves, having dropped from nearly 30,000 feet to a landing in less than five minutes and sliding into icy puddles on the tarmac. After a bit of a delay while standing in the rain, we collected our nerves, our luggage, boarded some local school buses, and were shuttled to the terminal from our remote location on the runway. Eventually by mid-morning we were directed onto other flights.

The point of all this is not to simply recount a harrowing tale, but instead to highlight the end result. You see, many of us tried to make light of the situation, joking about the extra frequent flyer miles that surely we came to be entitled to for our troubles. In reality, however, as a passenger, I never heard another word from American Airlines about the incident. There was no explanation that morning nor was there a follow-up contact. This left more than just a bad taste in our mouths for the airline. Couple that to the recollection of the harrowing tale itself and many customers are left with plenty of opportunities to tarnish the airline's reputation over dinner conversations about how *not* to manage a corporate brand and reputation event.

Without question, *good operational risk management has an upside.* How many companies let opportunities to not only maintain, but enhance, their reputations slip through their fingers? Contrast that to the new Delta Airlines policy, the goodwill and reputation management that a few simple phone calls have engendered.[5]

■ ■ ■

CASE ILLUSTRATION

Operational Risk—When Customer Perception Goes Bad

Bankers Trust

Exhibit 5.1 is a brief summary of the case involving Bankers Trust and Proctor and Gamble, which was one of the high-profile leveraged derivative transaction cases that tarnished the bank's reputation. From a risk monitoring standpoint, Bankers Trust thought it was doing many of the right things, not the least of which included following standard industry practices with regard to documentation of trades and taping conversations on the trading desk to confirm the accuracy of customer conversations. But when some high-profile customers suffered extreme losses on leveraged derivatives following an interest rate spike in 1994, the behavior of sales and marketing staff were put under a microscope. What resulted

In 1996 in a major reputational, and relationship risk case, Bankers Trust (BT) and Proctor & Gamble (P&G) settled a highly publicized dispute over the sale of leveraged derivative transactions. The case involved two swaps contracts that eventually led to huge losses in 1994 when interest rates spiked upward as the Federal Reserve raised interest rates numerous times and in rapid succession.

Under terms of the settlement, P&G agreed to pay $35 million of the $195 million it owed BT on the swaps contracts, leaving BT with an approximate $160 million loss. If the trial had gone forward, it is conjectured that a series of audio tapes would have been presented that allegedly would have left the appearance that BT sales people and relationship managers misled their client about the risk of the derivatives contracts. Other allegations included accusations of racketeering, mis-selling, and fraud. P&G's defense would have involved a contention that they were not "sophisticated investors" and did not understand the terms of the derivatives agreement that they had entered into.

EXHIBIT 5.1   Bankers Trust—Procter & Gamble Case

Source for the above: Zurich IC Squared First Database. Key lessons here: (1) Reputational— The behavior of certain Bankers Trust sales and relationship managers and traders did the company no favors when brought to light in its fight for its corporate reputation and corporate life in the wake of these allegations of misconduct. Get the entire employee base involved in reputation management on a day-to-day basis. (2) Know Your Customer always applies in complex transactions. Get acknowledgment of sophistication in writing.

was the release of numerous tapes of "locker room talk" involving sales, marketing, and trading staff. The conversations of certain individuals reflected poorly on the bank overall, and would have played very badly in front of a jury. The result was an out-of-court settlement and a multiyear process of recovering the entire firm's reputation, including changes involving senior management members at the top.

■ ■ ■

CASE ILLUSTRATION

Operational Risk—When the Company's Position toward the Customer Is Questioned

Firestone–Ford

The Firestone–Ford case has become another classic case of reputation damage involving operational risk and loss. Here, as outlined in Exhibit 5.2, both companies' reputations have suffered in the wake of their failure to heed early warnings about recalling problematic tires. To many, the fin-

In an example of what can go wrong when firms pay insufficient attention to quality warnings, Firestone, its parent, Bridgestone, and the Ford Motor Company in a reputational risk case, announced in August 2000 the recall of 6.5 million tires after reports linked them to a series of tragic automotive accidents. The estimated number of fatalities linked to the faulty tires was 174 at the time of this writing [January, 2001]. There were 280 personal injury lawsuits outstanding in the courts, with one high-profile case settled for an undisclosed amount estimated to be in the range of $30 million, and involving a public apology on the part of Ford lawyers at the hospital bed of a paralyzed victim.

The scale of the tire recall is reportedly the second largest in history; the largest being a 1978 recall action by Firestone. Ford Motor's best-selling sports utility, the Explorer, was the primary end-user of the recalled tires, and the difference in how the two companies reacted to a crisis that is predicted to cost Firestone $350 million and Ford $500 million and to perhaps ultimately top $2 billion is noteworthy. Both companies might have avoided costly mistakes (both in terms of reputation and actual dollars) if they had heeded early warnings and taken appropriate action. But once the story hit the press in August, 2000 alleging that there were an unusual amount of accidents involving the Explorer and attributed to tread separation on the automobile's tires, the two firms responded very differently. Firestone's initial response was considered appalling by the public, with the then CEO of the Japanese parent firm blaming the problems on improper consumer maintenance of the tires. These initial statements are rumored to have cost Firestone far greater in terms of its reputational capital than was necessary. Ford, on the other hand, took immediate action toward rescuing its reputation and sprinted into a crisis management mode. The company's executives offered sympathy and concern for the victims of this tragic story, and assured the public that it would take steps to make sure such problems never resurfaced again. It is difficult to draw conclusions from such a complex case. But Ford has managed to retain market-share of its popular Explorer brand, and its share price weathered the storm relatively well, while Firestone experienced considered pain and found itself at odds with a major end-user of its product after blaming the problems partially on the design of the Explorer.

The incident has also created reputational problems for other manufacturers of automobiles, and automobile parts, with the consumer public worldwide now more suspicious of all such products and unsettled by finger-pointing. The U.S. courts have also become willing to be increasingly aggressive with their demands for product recalls. Firestone is deemed to have made serious public relations blunders and dragged down its brand by failing to

Continued

EXHIBIT 5.2   Firestone/Ford Motor Case

accept responsibility for the fatalities. It may have been motivated solely by its legal defense strategy. Reports released on the causative factors of the tire problems were inconclusive, with most experts agreeing that it is not possible to isolate a single factor. At the time of this writing [January, 2001], the problems appear to have been caused by a number of factors, including underinflated tires, poor manufacturing, temperature conditions, and automobile weight. (In an interesting aside, Bridgestone Corporation announced the recall of 98,000 tires, mostly used on the Nissan Altima SE brand on February 20, 2001. This recall is not related to the earlier one, but the company attributed it to an early-warning system that it has put in place that identifies issues before they become problems.)

EXHIBIT 5.2   Firestone/Ford Motor Case
Reprinted with permission from Zurich IC Squared First Database.

ger pointing between the two companies seemed unprecedented. As of the time of this writing, the two companies had just broken off a 100-year-old relationship over the dispute. Initially it appeared that Ford had survived the ordeal with only marginal reputational and market capitalization damage, but that is no longer clear. As this book goes to print, *Business Week* has just featured a cover story entitled, "Ford: It's Worse than you Think." [6] In spite of all this, its share price has been volatile, but held up reasonably well. Meanwhile, Firestone's parent, Bridgestone, has lost an estimated $8 billion in market capitalization during the depth of the crisis.

These reputation lessons are easily transferable between industries. Consider the bank that contacts customers following a web site denial-of-service attack, or a trading scandal that would inform customers about its investigation of the situation and what action it is taking to avoid a reoccurrence. Or how about the case that is held out as the model of how to best manage corporate reputation in the face of crisis—the handling of customers by Johnson & Johnson in the 1980s following the Tylenol poisonings.

How does a company engender this type of customer service in its employee base? It all goes back to management's moves toward creating a culture of teamwork and caring about the organization and its customers.

■ ■ ■

SHAREHOLDER VALUATION THEMES

Let's return to the message from the quote about reputation risk that opened this chapter—a good reputation takes years, perhaps decades to build, but only moments to destroy. Can we quantify the impact?

Shareholders are generally focused on several primary issues when making investment decisions. Return on their investment, of course, is obvious. But what are the other characteristics of a good equity investment? Rather than look at investment and valuation theory, let's consider the views of some that are among the most influential on shareholder and investor decision making: investment advisors and fund managers.

Investment advisors keep the drivers to a short list. For instance, Peter Lynch, the highly respected former manager of Fidelity's Magellan Fund, has written several books on equity investing. In them he gives much good advice about selecting solid companies as investments for the long term. He provides a number of perspectives on special investment situations and opportunities to watch for, but one of the themes he keeps coming back to is earnings. His advice: "What you are asking here is what makes a company valuable, and why it will be more valuable tomorrow than it is today. There are many theories, but to me, it always comes down to earnings and assets. Especially earnings."[7]

William O'Neill, editor and publisher of the business newspaper *Investors Business Daily*, has also had a good deal of influence on the investment community. He balances earnings growth and stock price momentum in his seven-point stock selection system. Specifically, among the seven points he includes issues like quarterly and annual earnings growth, new products, new management, company and/or product leadership, and institutional sponsorship.[8]

These factors have interesting implications for operational risk and operational risk management. But what undercurrents lie below the surface? One can conclude that shareholders and prospective investors alike expect that there will be:

1. **Enhancement to market value** of the company, and thus its share value, preferably without significant volatility, caused by attitude swings toward the company
2. **Consistency of earnings growth,** and thus, almost by definition, elimination of negative surprises, generally resulting in a negative variance in earnings
3. **Stability or upgrades to management** and management quality
4. **A quality corporate image** based on performance, and perhaps social responsibility, both of which serve as a further enhancement to market value

These observations fall into two simple categories: expectation that downside risk will be minimized, and expectation that there will be an upside on their investment. When reality falls short of any of these expectations, prospective investors look elsewhere, and existing shareholders become discontent, or worse, when reality falls significantly short, they may become litigious.

In their insightful work, *Street Smarts,* and cleverly titled chapter on "Zookeeping," Smith and Walter have yet another view. Their study of securities firms has even more direct relevance for operational risk practitioners. They observe two perspectives or sets of values of these firms—market values and professional values—and go on to point out the frequent conflict between the two. Market values "reflect economic results, and professional values that reflect the positive (or negative) intangibles associated with each firm's business franchise." The market often struggles with the conflict between these values, however, which shows up in its difficulty in valuing or certainly in placing a premium on these firms. They note that "so much of the wealth created by the firms' efforts can easily be destroyed by fines, penalties, adverse judgments in litigation, and reputation losses."[9] Sound familiar?

REPUTATION AND BRAND RISK: CHARACTERISTICS OF EVENTS

First, we should recognize that negative surprises do not impact all companies the same way. Some companies weather storms better than others do. For instance, Johnson & Johnson is often cited as the company that "did it right" in its quick recall and public relations response to the product tampering involving its Tylenol product in the 1980s that caused a number of deaths. It recovered quickly. In contrast, it took Bankers Trust several years to recover from its leverage derivatives cases. It also took Lloyds of London years to recover from their scandals involving the mistreatment of names (investors) in the late 1980s and early 1990s. Firms like Kidder Peabody never recovered from theirs.

What makes some companies and their reputations and images more vulnerable to negative surprises than others? Well, it is a bit difficult to generalize, but there are some patterns that have emerged.

For one, the ability of a company to weather storms in the eyes of *all* stakeholders—clients, shareholders, bondholders, regulators—lies in the form of an established track record. The characteristics of that track record include some or all of the following:

- **Credibility of management (pre-event):** Is management a known quantity?
- **An established and highly respected position in the marketplace:** Is your firm a bastion of conservatism, with a 100-year-old reputation?
- **Earnings track record:** Has it been stable, predictable?
- **Quality of products and services:** Are they highly regarded, or unproven in the market?
- **Behavior of the company and its representatives, including sales and service to customers:** Is the firm a cocky start-up full of "cowboys" with a non-descript identity?
- **Market share:** How large is it? Do you dominate the market?

- **A long-standing image enhancing the advertising program:** Is it credible?
- **Social responsibility and standing in its marketplace:** Is the company seen to make a contribution to society at large?
- **Quality of the employment experience:** Does management have a reputation for caring?

When confronted with negative surprises, however, having scored well on this list increases a company's chances of faring well during a reputation crisis, but alone does not guarantee that a company will weather the storm. It only buys management a bit of breathing room. It gives a company a leg up when confronting the event. And when confronting today's impatient investment community, it might allow the best and most established of companies an extra day or two to respond. For those with less of a record, it might buy an extra few hours. In short, it only delays the inevitable, because once an event occurs, all bets are off.

EXPLORING RELEVANT OPERATIONAL RISK MEASUREMENT: REVISITING THE LOSS COMPONENTS

Returning to our opening premise, for all the discussions about operational risk to date, ironically enough, there has been relatively little discussion about just how much these events cost companies on the reputation side of the equation.

Where does the cost of reputational damage fit into the overall cost scheme? A dissection and review of loss costs is in order. One way to think about the cost breakdown is that any event consists of the *direct loss costs,* the monetary cost incurred when controls failed and employees went astray, the fraud that was perpetrated, or the fire or flood that occurred and damaged property and records; then there are the *indirect financial costs,* the out-of-pocket costs associated with an event, such as costs of investigation, legal liability, if any; and third, the less tangible *reputation costs.* Exhibit 5.3 is an outline showing the three categories—direct loss costs, indirect financial losses, and risk to reputation—and their component parts.

The reputation risk costs are inherently the most difficult to quantify, and have recently been explicitly omitted from regulatory capital discussions, as is logical. Neither of these realities make protection of a firm's reputation any less important, of course.

Even though it is difficult to quantify, reputational damage can be very costly indeed. A little digging around in loss databases can show just how costly. One gauge of reputational damage has been the action of a firm's share price. Take the case of the acquisition of Republic New York Corporation by HSBC Holdings in 1999. The cost in terms of a decline in share price in that case was pegged at $450 million. Exhibit 5.4 is a synopsis of the

Following is a breakdown of operational event loss costs, with emphasis on the impact of reputational risk costs.*

- **Direct Loss Costs:** Most discussions of operational risk are limited to hard economic losses themselves, for instance, whether that consists of a monetary transaction and related loss; or loss of financial or physical assets.
- **Indirect Financial Losses:** Consist of the hard loss costs associated with an event. These are sometimes difficult to capture and track, but it can be done. They include:
  - Costs of investigation (consultants, accountants)
  - Costs of "repair" (improved processes, standards)
  - Fines, penalties
  - Legal liability, if any
  - Medical costs, if injuries involved
  - Extra expense to continue operations (alternative sites)
- **Risk to Reputation:** Associated soft costs. Usually less tangible and sometime immeasurable loss costs in a direct economic sense. Examples:
  - Management and staff downtime
  - Lost customers/reduction of continuing revenue
  - Decline in share price
  - Other people costs: defection of employees/increased costs of hiring
  - Decline in market share
  - Increase in funding costs
  - Additional advertising costs

EXHIBIT 5.3 Loss Cost Breakdown
*N.B. This is a management view of costs, not a regulatory one.

case. It can get worse from there, of course. We have already discussed the extreme cases—those in which the company does not survive. Their shareholders have paid the ultimate price—in corporate terms, of course.

Another challenging aspect of operational risk is that it is embedded in a business and cannot be stripped out easily. That is to say that its reputational consequences cannot be escaped simply because of the existence of a hedge. In the case of technology systems or processing risk, either the firm suffered an outage or it didn't. It doesn't much matter if the processing operations had been outsourced or whether the event had been insured. Either the firm's own trading or settlement operations were disrupted or they weren't. So we can make the distinction that perhaps the economic impact can be hedged away in either the insurance or outsourced instance, but the firm still lives with the disruption and any reputational impact that might come with it.[10]

In May 1999, HSBC Holdings PLC made an offer to acquire Republic New York Corporation (Republic) for $10.3 billion. While the offer was still being finalized, the Princeton Notes Scandal broke. Republic was the custodian of funds from the sale of Princeton notes. The proceeds from this sale were transferred into the chairman of Princeton Economics International Inc.'s accounts and used to pay personal debts. Republic New York Corporate faced huge lawsuits related to its custodial role.

The merger was put on hold while the two parties discussed the ramifications of the scandal. When the scandal first became public, Republic's shares fell to $57, while the original HSBC offer price was $72.00 per share. In the end, the principal shareholder of Republic, Edmond Safra, agreed that HSBC could pay him $450 million less than the May agreement stipulated for his shares, which left the other shareholders' stock price undiluted. He also offered personal guarantees that provided that he would meet 60% of any liabilities between $700 million and $1 billion. The agreement remained in force through his estate, as Mr. Safra passed away before the deal was consummated.

The net result was that Republic, and specifically Mr. Safra as its major shareholder, took a huge financial loss on the deal because of operational risk and its reputational impact.

EXHIBIT 5.4   Republic New York Corporation Case
Reprinted with permission from Zurich IC Squared First Database.

CASE STUDIES: AN EMPIRICAL LOOK AT SHARE PRICE IMPACT

There have only been a few known studies that have looked at the cost of reputational damage.

Early Analytic Work at Bankers Trust

During 1996–1997, following the rollout of production models for Operational RAROC at Bankers Trust, and in the wake of our reputation problems following our leveraged derivative transaction scandals, we were encouraged by regulators to push forward with our work on measuring the impact of operational risk on reputation. As such, we experimented with a variety of methods of quantification, and implemented a reputation risk component to our economic capital models in late 1997.[11]

As a foundation for that work we turned to our proprietary industry database of operational loss events once again. We also looked to some additional highly publicized credit and market loss events for comparison. In all, we selected 68 loss cases from 1988 to 1997 to analyze. Of the total,

75% of these cases were financial service firms of one type or another. Our intention was to review and understand fully the relative and absolute impact of different types of events, which is why we did not limit our review to operational loss events, selecting instead a variety: 12 were credit-related, 11 were market-related, and the remaining 45 were operational losses. For the purposes of our study, our primary focus was on the amount of decline in share price during the first 30 days after a company's event had been made public. Last, we netted the declines against an appropriate equity index in an attempt to remove other market "noise" from the case in question.

From the sample and the analysis we observed the following:

- **Magnitude of Declines:** There was a 6.2% absolute decline (net of index) in share price on average during the first 30 days after the event for all cases, and 6.9% decline for cases involving operational risk.
- **People or Relationship Risk:** 60% of the operational risk events were either people or relationship-related.
- **Notable Loss Scenarios:** The cases involving the largest declines and longest periods of decline involved accounting irregularities, scandal (e.g., Salomon Treasury Auction Scandal), unauthorized trading, or fires that affected key operations (e.g., Credit Lyonnaise trading floor fire and fire at a steel plant that impacted 33% of the firm's production).

The Templeton Study

The Templeton College at Oxford University published an interesting study entitled *The Impact of Catastrophes on Shareholder Value* (Knight and Pretty).[12] (The insurance broker, Sedgwick Group, sponsored the study.)

In the course of their research, Knight and Pretty sought to identify the impact of catastrophes by tracing changes in share price following major catastrophes at fifteen major corporations. Based on their relatively small sample, their analysis revealed that "[i]n all cases the catastrophe had a significant negative initial impact on shareholder value." Following the initial negative impact, which averaged a loss of 8%, the study noted that on average there was a full recovery in just over 50 trading days."[13]

The more interesting finding, however, involved the variance of recovery between the different corporations and loss situations analyzed. The study categorized individual corporations as "recovers" and "nonrecovers." In essence, it appeared that investors used the opportunity to vote with their capital against the management teams who appeared least able to handle their individual crisis, and who may have contributed to the catastrophe by not implementing safety procedures, internal controls, or other risk control measures. Conversely, those management teams who appeared relatively blameless, and handled the catastrophe's aftermath respectably, received votes of confidence in the form of additional investment and a recovered share price. The authors noted that "paradoxically, [the catastrophes] offer an opportunity for management to demonstrate their talent in dealing with difficult circumstances."[14]

More specifically, Knight and Pretty also noted the essential distinctions between recovers and non-recovers to be:

- "There is among non-recovers an initial negative response of over 10% of market capitalization.
- "In the first two or three months the magnitude of the estimated financial losses [were] significant among non-recovers.
- "There [were] a large number of fatalities. This seems to govern recovery in the first two or three months; and thereafter, the issue of management's responsibility for accident or safety lapses appears to explain the shareholder value response."[15]

INFLUENCING FACTORS DURING AND IMMEDIATELY AFTER THE EVENT

Generally speaking, in our own study of reputation damage cases we have observed for individual case studies and one-off observations in the marketplace that the size and duration of reputation damage is influenced by a variety of factors characteristic of the event or events themselves. Thus, we add to our previous list of pre-loss reputation risk factors the following post-loss factors:

- **The duration of the event itself:** Was the loss a point-in-time event, such as a fire in which the outcome is known within a day or two, or does it involve uncertainty of duration—a factor most abhorred by the financial markets—such as in the case of an ongoing investigation by the company itself, its auditors, or regulators?
- **Isolated event:** Was the event isolated to the firm in question, or did it involve the entire industry, or sector?
- **Market expectations:** Whether the market has high earnings or market share expectations for the company.

These factors are not solely a function of operational risk and loss, but often are observed in the equity markets generally, such as during times that companies miss analysts' earnings estimates when announcing their actual results.

CASE ILLUSTRATION

Troubles in the Investment Community

Lucent Technologies

Lucent Technologies' share price and market value troubles of 2000 and 2001 are a good illustration of the combination of these factors and reputation risk phenomenon. In the years after its spinoff from AT&T in 1996, the company could do no wrong. It was truly a "Wall Street darling." Beginning in early 2000, however, after disappointing Wall Street analysts and the investor community several times—with missed earnings, warnings about the probability of missed earnings, the need for restructurings, and finally a report of accounting irregularities, its operational risk icing on the cake—the investor community lost all confidence in virtually anything that Lucent's management had to say. Clearly management's credibility had been ruined. Share price recovery from an operational loss event, such as its accounting problems and Securities and Exchange Commission investigation toward the end of this period of eroding confidence would be met very differently from another company that was held in high esteem by Wall Street just before the operational risk event was announced. For Lucent, its share price recovery will likely be a slow painful process. In contrast, the company guilty of only a "first offense" disappointment or operational loss would more than likely see a quick "V-shaped" pummeling and then recovery in its share price, all else being equal.

■ ■ ■

MANAGING RISK TO THE FRANCHISE

What is the implication for operational risk management? The role of operational risk management practitioners in the protection of a firm's reputation is twofold. On the one hand, there is some interest today in attempting to measure the impact of operational losses and associated crises in confidence on a firm's franchise value. As such, risk analysts will explore possible quantification techniques applied to the ripple effect of operational risk and loss on reputation. Some have been charged with making sense of it all.

In a second, and perhaps more tangible, sense, when armed with this information on the impact of a crisis in confidence, the operational risk management process can bring tremendous value to an organization by contributing to executive management and public relations in enhancing the coordination of crisis management planning and execution.

Certainly management of the firm's external relations is the responsibility of executive management and public relations groups. Operational risk management will often bring value, however, as a facilitator. Risk practitioners can play a key role in assuring that a crisis plan has been worked out, and that executive management is on board with it.

So in the next section we explore some findings to date with respect to these two roles—the measurement of reputation risk, and well as some insights on reputation crisis management.

A UNIQUE MODELING CHALLENGE: REPUTATION RISK— DEFINING THE METRICS

How do we quantify the costs of reputational damage? At the time of this writing in early 2001, there have been very few metrics developed. In our early research we looked at a variety of measures of the impact of an operational loss on reputation and brand. The objective was to determine a reasonable measure to include in our operational risk economic capital models. The methods fall into at least four general categories as follows.[16]

Option 1: Post-Loss Share Price Relative Strength

The idea here was to use post-loss share price moves as a basis for reputation risk valuation. This method involved using the data set created during the course of our early analysis of operational loss on share price referenced earlier in this chapter.

In summary, a dataset was created that captured the absolute difference between stock price movement and an appropriate market index (i.e., the S&P index for large banks). The dataset consisted of 68 datapoints. Each individual datapoint was assigned to its relevant risk category (i.e., Credit (12), Market (11), or Operational (45)).

The analysis matched the movement in share price to the relevant initial period of publicity generated by the event. The timeframe of measurement was set to less than or equal to one month (30 days), and only instances that satisfied (exhibited movement in beta) the above criteria were considered. Further, care was also taken in the selection and measurement of an appropriate index (stock price movements measured against S&P index of money center banks over the same timeframe) that served as a benchmark with which to relate the individual stock price movement.

In arguing for this approach, stock price represents the market value of the firm at any given time. Under the semistrong form of the Efficient Markets Hypothesis, stock price reflects all publicly available information. Analyzing stock price movement relative to an appropriate index at the time of public disclosure of a significant failure of controls that could not be reasonably anticipated should reasonably allow for capture of the public's "perception" of a firm and allow for a defensible base for quantifying reputation.

On the other hand, one can argue that stock price movement and weakness in relative share price strength are too sensitive a variable to allow for isolating the impact of any single event. As such, the extraneous noise created by all other contributing variables to a firm's value—economic conditions, marketshare, type of product, etc.—would rule out attributing variance in relative price strength solely to reputation. In addition, one must identify a means of segregating the impact to individual business lines/profit centers in the organization.

Option 2: Deviation from Historic or Expected Results

This approach uses historical growth rate(s) as a benchmark against actual performance in the relevant period, and identifies any abnormal variance. Alternatively, it uses plan versus actual figures to identify abnormal variances that correlate to the periods of failure of controls.

The first instance, the historical method, can be applied if the forecasted data are unavailable. One would plot the historic performance of the line of business prior to the year under study (between five and ten years experience is sufficient) and establish a pattern of behavior. Based on that historical experience, the analysis forecasts the performance for the year under study. Then it will compare the forecast calculation to the actual performance. If the variance is larger than historical experience, the balance can be attributed to the damage to reputation.

A second approach, the expected method, will compare the actual performance of a line of business with the forecasted performance over a period of five years preceding the year under study. Then one will determine the absolute value of the difference between the two for all given years. Use the average of these figures as the figure within which performance in the year under study can differ from the actual. Expand upon that average to create a range using factors to account for peripheral influences affecting the outcome. If the actual performance falls below the negative end of the range set above, then the balance will be attributed to the damage to reputation.

The advantages of this option are that the data consistency and availability firmwide allows for the drilldown of any aggregate estimation of reputation. The disadvantage, however, of the historic approach is that it assumes a static world—the past reflects the present. For the expected approach, a disadvantage is that limited resources, over/underestimation of performance, and other factors besides failures of control or other operational losses could affect the outcome.

Option 3: Estimate of Reputation Costs

At the outset of this chapter, we explored the dimensions of operational loss, including indirect costs and estimates of reputation risk and loss. Thus, our third quantification option involves using estimates for each of those categories as an overall representation of reputation risk.

To recap, among others, these costs include cost of management/staff downtime, the cost of lost customers and potential reduction of income, and other people costs, such as wholesale staff departures and difficulties in recruiting.

Other issues include the impact of analysts' ratings, frequency of press meetings and level of management involved, and advertising costs to identify the impact that negative publicity has on the firm's image. Here we also look to assess the impact of various factors such as the importance of specific publications based on circulation and frequency of readings, and the extent to which analysts incorporate the firm's image into a rating.

One benefit of this approach is that it forces management to think through the risk of loss and associated costs of reputational damage. Once the exercise is completed, it is more defensible than the use of any quantitative data to assign a value to as fuzzy a variable as reputation. It can be refined, as well (i.e., the number of variables expanded).

As noted, of course, the disadvantage is that these costs can be extremely difficult to estimate. Being that they are qualitative in nature increases the scope of assumptions. In addition, driving the aggregate estimate to specific business units could be an issue.

Option 4: Peer Group Comparisons

Fourth, we can look at peer group composite characteristics, such as relative share price performance, relative P/E ratio performance and price-to-book ratios, and benchmark them against appropriate members of a peer group.

This method seeks to benchmark the factors that represent those firms with top reputations in the group against an individual member, then focus on the differential. More work is needed in this area, but it is particularly interesting because it represents the upside of operational risk management. That is, the theory is that the top companies will already be perceived as managing themselves well and will exhibit performance measures accordingly, and will serve as a goal for others.

THE REPUTATION RISK MULTIPLIER

Exhibit 5.5 presents a reputation risk multiplier worksheet. This tool is intended to showcase yet another dimension of reputation risk impact. That is, different types of operational loss will carry varying levels of reputation risk. For instance, as we have seen in individual cases, the market will often forgive a company for a physical disaster much more readily than a case of fraud, or mismanagement. This generally occurs assuming, of course, that in

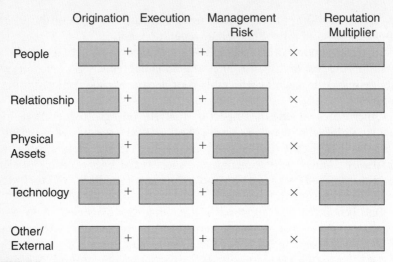

EXHIBIT 5.5   Operational Risk Worksheet: The Reputation Multiplier

the former instance management had taken reasonable precautions toward business continuity planning. As such, the worksheet can be used to illustrate the multiplier effect of a direct loss when combined with its reputational damage counterpart, assigning a higher weighting to people and relationship risk cases, and a lower weight to physical damage cases, for instance.

MANAGING CRISES INVOLVING REPUTATION AND BRAND

In today's 24/7 society, not only will a firm be continuously "online," but it must be continuously vigilant for possible harm to its reputation, or to "crises in confidence" as it is sometimes termed, whether that threat is real or contrived. According to public relations experts, in many cases management may have as little as 15 to 20 minutes to respond to a breaking story on the news wire or Internet before damage is done. Risk to reputation has become real time. In the "old days," firms had a bit more time—perhaps a leisurely hour or so—to respond to more established media, such as radio or television, before the damage set in. Even then, there was no assurance that the firm could manage its way out. Few would suggest that the uncertainty for success is any reason not to be prepared.

A study of a number of high-profile operational events in numerous industries, from Salomon's bond scandal in 1991 to the Exxon Valdez oil spill in Puget Sound, have yielded some instructive points about preparing for and dealing with crises in confidence. These include: (1) development of a statement on reputation management, (2) formation of a reputation crisis team, (3) dissemination of guiding principles for reputation crisis management, and (4) creation and maintenance of a briefing repository. As with all business continuity planning exercises, it is also true here that the *process* of planning, testing and the lessons and experience gained by those who ultimately must manage the crisis can be more valuable than the plan itself.

1. **Development of a Statement on Reputation Management:** Some firms have gone to great lengths to protect their image and reputation. A framework step will be to communicate the seriousness of reputation management to all staff in a statement. Exhibit 5.6 is a sample for a fictitious firm, the Integrity Company.

2. **Guiding Principles for Reputation Crisis Management:** A second step in effective reputation crisis management will entail the development and dissemination of guiding principles for crisis communication. The reality is that few people have a depth of experience in managing crises in confidence. Even though they may be reluctant to admit it, even CEOs often appreciate some guidance in this area.

   Exhibit 5.7 is a set of guidelines and lessons learned from reputation management sucesses and disasters. It is offered as a handy reference tool for action during and after an event.

3. **The Briefing Repository:** One of the most critically important resources is an up-to-the-minute repository of news items and issues that is accessible by all employees. The information must be available to all employees, because if anyone is denied access, they will see it as an attempt to stonewall the issue and hide the truth. This can be very dangerous because due to the widespread access, there will be natural concerns about litigation risks and the need to protect legal defense positions should litigation arise at a later date. Thus, the statements available on this database will naturally be very limited in nature but should be updated periodically with more fulsome descriptions as information becomes available and can be released. Typically, firms are best served in being forthcoming with the truthful description of the scenario early on in the crisis rather than later on. Time is your enemy in a reputation crisis.

4. **The Reputation Crisis Team:** When the crisis actually comes, the firm should be prepared with its precrisis tools and measures, and a predesignated reputation crisis team.

We all know that in our "connected" world, the media has no patience for responses like "no comment," or "I'll get back to you." We also know that when a crisis breaks, the media will file its report and it will be written with or without the company's help. We also know that the company fully understands the need to respond quickly. The dilemma internally, of course, then becomes one of determining what and how much to release and how to balance the need for open and honest disclosure again with the need to protect legal defenses should allegations of wrongdoing emerge either immediately or at a later date.

The Integrity Company values its reputation for unquestioned integrity, excellence, and a strong financial position. The firm will take every appropriate action to protect its reputation in the face of any circumstance that poses a threat. Toward that end, every employee of the firm has a responsibility to guard the firm's integrity and reputation and use his or her best judgment in the marketplace at all times.

Proactive communication is key. Although situations vary, experience of other companies that have encountered reputational and integrity crises is instructive. They illustrate the importance of a realistic, tough-minded (rather than hopeful) forecast of how an episode is likely to be treated in the public arena. The key lesson from crises in confidence and reputation is that we must operate within a framework proactive communication internally and externally.

The Communication Team at the Integrity Company is charged with the responsibility for media relations. It is most important that the firm's communications managers be promptly advised of any episode of a significant potential that may be seen as a breach of the firm's integrity, competence, or financial strength. Early notice will allow time for the gathering of facts and for an assessment of the potential damage to our reputation among the firm's principal constituents: employees and potential employees, clients and prospects, stockholders and the investment community, regulators, and legislators. Concurrently, a judgment will be made on the likelihood that the matter will become public (if it is not already) and a forecast will be offered on how the episode is likely to play out in the public arena, using the absence of communications management as the starting point.

Based on this forecast, the communications managers can determine and implement the actions that are best suited to safeguard the firm's reputation, including early public involvement of executive management. Actions will range from proactive statements to be used in response to standard inquiries, to proactive communication for specific situations and each constituent group. Communications will be direct and through the media, telling them what happened, what we are doing about it, and what we will do to make it less likely that it will happen again. Communications managers for each constituent group will be appointed in coordination with senior officers worldwide.

All employees of the firm have the responsibility for referring episodes that have the potential for harming the firm's reputation to the communications team. Employees should not take it upon themselves to manage a media situation. Always use best judgment in assessing individual situations. When in doubt, the communications team should be contacted.

Every reasonable attempt will be made to keep employees advised of an emerging situation, including use of the integrity company broadcast messaging system, via voicemail, e-mail, and videoconferencing facilities.

EXHIBIT 5.6   The Integrity Company Statement on Reputation Management

A *timely and effective communications strategy* is key to managing crises in confidence and reputation under stress, but which specific actions have worked and which have hurt companies? The following guidelines have been developed based on a review of numerous cases of operational loss, and associated reputation damage and/or recovery in a variety of industries worldwide.

1. **Integrity and Honesty**
   - Put customers and the public before profits during the crisis. Behave before, during, and after the crisis as any company would that values its reputation for ethics, honesty, and credibility (e.g., Johnson & Johnson 1982).
   - Procrastinating product risks is a dangerous practice (Dow Corning 1991; Bridgestone/Firestone 2000).
   - Scapegoats—blaming an entire event on others and/or suggesting that policies and procedures are flawless can be disastrous to a firm's reputation (e.g., Bhopal–Union Carbide 1983; Salomon Treasury Auction scandal 1991).
   - Accountable senior officer—the visible presence of a senior official (on site, where applicable) would have helped some firms during their time of crisis (e.g., Exxon 1989).

2. **Proactive Communications during the Crisis**
   - Develop an instinct to tell it first, fully, and accurately. The firm should back away from these guidelines only after the most careful consideration of all implications (i.e., reputation versus legal).
   - Active communications—take control of communications rather than relinquish them to others through inaction. As long as a firm keeps up a steady information flow of information, chances are good that the media will be *less* likely to dig for dirt (e.g., Exxon 1989).
   - Internal communication will be a top priority.

3. **Tangible and Credible Actions**
   - Be responsive to those most affected by the crisis.
   - Independence—consider using a credible and visible independent in a key role during the crisis such as an analyst or auditor, if possible (e.g., Salomon 1991).
   - Actions speak louder than words—visible cleanup actions are an essential first step to reputation damage control, not to mention averting fines and penalties (e.g., Salomon 1991).

4. **Manage for the Worst Case**
   - Prepare and manage for the worst case scenario; apply Murphy's Law and assume that the event will deteriorate into the worst possible collection of circumstances and prepare to manage accordingly (P&G–Bankers Trust Case 1994–1996).
   - Opt for more disclosure rather than less (e.g., Salomon 1991).

EXHIBIT 5.7 Effective Communications Strategy: Guidelines for Reputation Crisis Management

A proactive public relations crisis manager or operational risk practitioner will act swiftly to get all parties in a room and get the ear of the CEO. Certainly, the more risk-attuned CEO will call the meeting himself or herself.

In his book, *Crisis Response*, Jack Gottschalk makes an excellent argument for the need for a levelheaded operational risk management perspective when managing crises. For instance, a critical decision will be to balance legal concerns, which although important, may be short-term, against potentially fatal damage to the firm's reputation.[17] Deciding this balance is where risk officers' and CEO's careers are made or broken.

Recent discussions of reputation risk management have shifted, appropriately enough, to the risk of damage to a company's brand involving online abuse. This new dimension of reputation risk management was addressed in a recent issue of *Business 2.0*.[18] In the spirit of learning from the operational events and misfortune of others, the article outlined six cases in which companies' brands were targeted and attacked both in and out of cyberspace. One of the most notable cases of online fraud involved an 23-year-old Camino Community College student who attempted to manipulate the stock of Emulex, a fast growing network computer company, for personal gain. The individual posted an Internet wire release falsely reporting that the company's CEO had abruptly resigned and that the company's earnings had been misstated. Its stock price dropped almost immediately from $115 to $45 and in the wake of this activity, lawsuits were filed against Bloomberg and the Internet wire, which had both picked up the fictitious story.[19] This case provides ample evidence of the need to manage reputation risk cases in real time and shows why it is essential to prepare tools and teams in advance of events.

CONCLUSION

We have already discussed the importance of an ideological vision and of nurturing integrity and a risk aware corporate culture in our discussion about the opportunity or upside of managing risk in Chapter 4.

An interrelated topic is that of managing the intangibles of risk to reputation and brand. In this section we discuss risk management measures that should be taken to protect the firm's franchise, reputation, and brand not only with the investment community, but with clients, regulators, and the public marketplace at large.

LESSONS LEARNED AND KEY RECOMMENDATIONS

- Manage the risk to the firm's franchise, reputation, and brand. The best firms will have a clear understanding of the potential impact of operational risk on their franchise and franchise value. A tested strategy and plan is key for managing crises that might impact their reputation and franchise (BP Strategy #4).

- Research shows that operational and credit loss events appear to have impacted reputation and share prices more often and extensively than market losses.
- Although the risk is difficult to measure, reputation is one of a firm's most important corporate assets. Protection of the organization's reputation will be a key component of an operational risk management program, but because it is not easily measured the discussion of reputation risk management is often left out of operational risk management discussions. Ironically, damage to the firm's reputation is usually far more devastating than the direct loss costs.
- Firms have several options for *measuring* reputation risk. Among them are calculations based on stock price movements, deviations of plan versus actual results following operational losses, loss and expense cost tracking associated with operational loss events, and peer group comparisons. Generally, however, the results are soft, at best, and although useful for developing a sense for the cost of a reputation crisis, they have not been particularly useful in economic capital modeling to date.
- Senior management and directors will be held responsible for pre- and post-loss actions. Management preparation and response during an event are key in protecting or enhancing the firm's reputation.
- Operational risk management programs must address risk to reputation—prepare management and remain vigilant for threats. Four simple components for managing reputation risk include the use of:
  1. A statement on reputation management
  2. Reputation management guiding principles
  3. A briefing repository
  4. A reputation crisis team

CHAPTER 6

The Enterprise-wide Framework

Corporate Governance, Mandate, and Roles

INTRODUCTION

The risks involving people, processes, and systems touch everyone and every part of an organization. Because operational risk is so pervasive, one essential factor for success in managing risks is to involve the entire organization in the process. Operational risk management cannot be practiced in a vacuum. Sometimes discussions about the topic place so much emphasis on the risk managers' roles that they almost suggest that the function is discreet and entails only a handful of individuals dedicated to assessing and managing operational risks. Clearly an isolationist view would be misplaced. But what should architecture of an effective enterprise-wide operational risk management effort look like?

Chapter 2 introduced the 20 Firmwide Best Practice Strategies. In many respects it is the interwoven fabric of these strategies that comprises the component parts of an ORM framework, ranging from ideology to risk management technology. We have already discussed the importance of a firmwide ideology, vision, and mandate, but those only represent the first step. The framework we discuss in this chapter also involves the entire enterprise, not just a single risk management department. It picks up where we left off on corporate vision and covers (1) corporate governance, beginning at the Board level; (2) a specific mandate for risk management generally, and operational risk, more specifically; and (3) roles and responsibilities of business and corporate groups in operational risk management. Last, but certainly not least, we explore the implications of operational loss and reputation damage for senior management and the Board of Directors. Given that reputation and brand are among a firm's most important assets, damage to them may well have directors' and officers' liability repercussions.

FRAMEWORK ENVIRONMENT AND COMPONENT PARTS

There are numerous moving parts to an enterprise-wide framework for operational risk management, and for all risk management for that matter. They range from the mandate and the board of directors outward to senior management teams, corporate culture, policies and procedures, management committees, business line management team roles and responsibilities, corporate risk management and control functions, and personal responsibilities of individuals firmwide. Without clarity on these components and, in particular, senior management and board commitment, operational risk management will fail.

Following is a brief description of each component area and its role.

- **Board of Directors:** The board of directors is responsible to the firm's shareholders. Just as they have the responsibility to ensure that the firm has a reasonable strategy and business plan, and the means to execute it, they have the ultimate responsibility, on the shareholders' behalf, to ensure that a process exists for the day-to-day management of downside risk.
- **Vision and Values:** We cannot overemphasize the importance of a vision, and leveraging the corporate ideology at the corporate level. Risk management may be referenced, albeit as part of a very broad vision, in a statement such as "the firm is committed to excellence and quality in the delivery of products and services. . . as such, management will make every effort to make certain that it conducts its affair with the highest standards of integrity."
- **Firmwide Risk Management Mandates:** Beyond the firmwide ideology, there are two additional levels of mandate. In this chapter we cover the second and third levels: the enterprise-wide risk management level and, then more specifically, both corporate and business line operational risk management units. All of these integrated statements form a critical basis for the entire program framework and the single overriding goal or objective of the program.
- **Senior and Executive Management Teams:** A commitment is essential at the firmwide and business line management levels to create and ensure momentum in individual business and corporate units.
- **Corporate Culture:** As already discussed, corporate culture will make or break a risk management program. If quality and risk management is stressed at senior levels and driven throughout the organization, the operational risk management program will be more likely to succeed. In contrast, if control is simply viewed by management or conveyed in the culture as an obligatory task, but not nearly as important as developing new business, serving clients, and producing revenue, then the operational risk management effort will fail.
- **Operational Risk Management Committee:** A management committee will be comprised of senior business line representatives and senior

corporate risk and control representatives and will serve as one of the focal points for monitoring operational risk management efforts. The committee will serve as the glue that holds the parts of the program together firmwide.

- **Policies and Procedures:** Specific directives on operational risk, quality, and control policies, along with specific procedures, become integral parts of the program.
- **Business Line Risk Managers and Teams:** The existence of a dedicated risk manager, and perhaps a risk management and/or control committee within the business line, are key parts of the framework. Each should have clear roles and direct responsibilities for the management of risk and loss by the business.
- **Corporate Risk Management and Control Functions:** There are a variety of corporate functions that contribute to an overall operational risk management framework. These range from other risk management functions, such as credit and market, to internal audit, legal, compliance, security, technology, operations, and insurance risk management.
- **Risk Juries:** As an optional part of the Operational Risk Management Committee, or a related function, the organization might have one or more risk juries that evaluate risk findings and judge progress toward risk mitigation. Some firms have found the collaborative approach of a risk jury to be effective in drawing in more of the organization to the risk management effort.[1]
- **Individual Roles:** The role and responsibility of every individual in the firm should be defined in firmwide communications and statements, whether they are employed within the business line itself, or within corporate functions.

Every organization will apply its own unique personality and culture to conveying the right recipe for combining each of these ingredients of a program framework. Exhibit 6.1 is a composite of the parts.

FOCUS ON THE BOARD OF DIRECTORS

Defense against operational risk and losses flows from the highest level of the organization—the board of directors and executive management. The board, the management team that they hire, and the policies that they develop, all set the tone for a corporation, its external face and image, and its internal culture. At the end of the day, they will have a huge impact on the chances for success of most initiatives, including an operational risk management program.

As guardians of shareholder interests and shareholder value, boards of directors must be acutely attuned to market reaction about negative news.

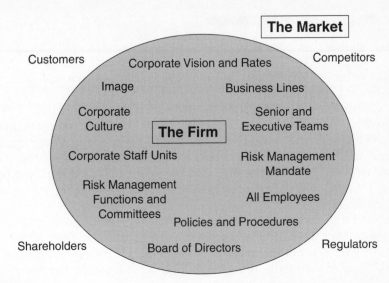

EXHIBIT 6.1 Operational Risk Management: The Environment and Component Parts

In fact, they can find themselves on the firing line if the reaction is severe enough. As representatives of the shareholders, Boards of Directors are responsible for policy matters relative to corporate governance, including but not limited to setting the stage for the framework and foundation for enterprise-wide risk management.

Not long ago, when risk management was thought of, in financial firms, primarily in terms of managing credit risk or market risk, many board members were comfortable with risk oversight at the credit committee or treasury level. The past decade delivered the recognition that firmwide risk could not be represented by market and credit functions alone.[2]

Now, operational risk management is a topic of discussion for regulators and in boardrooms across the United States and, as I write this, even more visible in Europe. In the wake of the 2001 releases from the Basel Risk Management Committee, banks now have further insight as to regulators' position on the need for regulatory capital for operational risk. Meanwhile, shareholders are aware that there are means to identify, measure, manage, and mitigate operational losses that add up to billions of dollars every year and include frequent, low-level losses and also infrequent but catastrophic losses that have actually wiped out firms, such as Barings, Kidder Peabody, and others. Regulators and shareholders have already signaled that they will hold directors and executives accountable for managing operational risk.[3]

Corporate Governance Considerations

Senior management, and certainly the board of directors, have the key responsibility for shareholder value. Inherent in this charge is recognition that enhancement to shareholder value is inextricably intertwined with the risk–reward equation.

Clearly these individuals are focused on upside opportunities for their firms. Their focus is evidenced by key questions like: What is the state of the macroeconomic environment? Do we have the right product mix? Have we allocated reasonable resources to research and development? Is our business positioned well to take advantage of market conditions and opportunities? Have we developed the right business plan? Have we hired the right people to execute it?

From a risk standpoint, there is a companion list of issues that entail questions like: What are the competitive threats that we might be facing? What are the risks in the financial environment? What errors or mistakes could cause damage to the firm or franchise? What is the legal environment? Have we addressed regulatory and compliance issues sufficiently?

What becomes clear immediately is that senior managers and the board already share many of the same risk sensitivities as operational risk managers. The fact is that senior managers and the board have always focused on these issues. Some have simply done a better job of it than others.

Although the recognition of these risks has always been present—for reasons discussed in terms of societal, technological, legal, and regulatory trends—the environment has been changing. Another change is that today there is a recognition that tools and techniques have been developing. Couple the changes in the environment with the fact that there is greater recognition of these risks, and that measurement techniques have been improving, and the result is that the bar has been raised relative to the professional standards expected of both organizations and their corporate governance.

This combination provides some interesting foreshadowing for the future. Certainly there is an expectation from industry financial services and other regulators that operational risk and operational risk management processes will be addressed. As such, if processes are lacking, one would expect that regulators will have a greater tendency to hold management and the organization accountable. Similarly, one can expect that shareholders will have their own expectations about the development and rigor of risk management programs. For their part, shareholders will remain silent on the issue for as long as the firm sails on an even keel. But if unexpected losses, and certainly if catastrophic, losses rock the boat, then shareholder legal action will not be far behind. Take the case of Kidder Peabody & Company and its infamous trading profits case involving Joseph Jett in 1993 and 1994. As described in Exhibit 6.2, in the

Directors' and Officers' Liability Implications

In March 2000 the General Electric Company agreed to pay its shareholders $19 million in a long awaited settlement of a class action lawsuit. This suit related to the Joseph Jett bond trading scandal, a case that government regulators called one of the largest in the history of the securities industry. It was a classic example of a loss involving allegations of inadequate supervision and people risk. The legal case contended that actions by Joseph Jett, a former bond trader for the now defunct Kidder Peabody and Company, a former G.E. subsidiary, inflated Kidder's net worth and deceived shareholders about the value of G.E. stock. In the suit, investors claimed that they overpaid for G.E. stock in 1993 and 1994 because Jett created phony profits that overstated Kidder's financial performance by $350 million. Jett later asserted that he was following standard Kidder procedures, and used trading models that the firm had put in place. G.E. executives denied any knowledge of wrongdoing and ended the case "for the purpose of avoiding continuing additional expense, inconvenience, distraction, and risk of this litigation."

The Joseph Jett bond trading scandal was one of a series of problems that plagued Kidder Peabody and eventually prompted the sale of the once highly profitable firm by the parent entity, General Electric, to PaineWebber. The scandal was a classic example of improper employee supervision. The SEC accused Kidder of lax supervision, poor management judgment, and for creating an environment where "employees were unwilling to ask tough questions when money was being made." Joseph Jett was the head of Kidder's government bond trading desk, and was billed as a rising star who quickly rose to stardom while at Kidder. It was eventually discovered that Jett had faked $350 million in profits, and hid $85 million of real losses. He was dismissed after his superiors became convinced that he had generated false profits and caused the firm to report hugely inflated earnings to its parent, General Electric. In a very short time Jett went from being Kidder's "Man of the Year" (in 1994) to the catalyst of its failure. He was later partially exonerated by a 1996 arbitration panel that determined he was under the impression, no matter how mistaken, that his trades were making money. He claimed that his trading practices involved the legitimate use of computer-model bond-trading strategies, while Kidder labeled these strategies the equivalent of a "ponzi scheme." Jett's formula was a simple one: "if the strips were underpriced in relation to bonds, buy them, reconstitute them into a bond, then sell the bond. If the strips were overpriced, sell them, then buy and strip the bond." In short, Jett would finance various bond instruments for less interest than they would later yield.

Postscript: Kidder currently exists on paper with no current operations. G.E. sold Kidder's main operation in 1994 to PaineWebber Group Inc. under the stipulation that G.E. assume all future liabilities in connection with the scandal. Jett was fired from Kidder shortly before the change of control.

EXHIBIT 6.2   Kidder Peabody Bond Trading Scandal
Reprinted with permission from Zurich IC Squared First Database.

aftermath General Electric's directors and officers have found themselves dealing with a lawsuit involving disgruntled shareholders, who alleged that the Directors should be held responsible for overpaying for Kidder Peabody. Their situation is not all that unique, however, when shareholders are confronted with
high-profile operational loss events.

The point here is not to suggest that senior management and corporate boards have had a deaf ear to operational risk issues as much as it is
one of recognizing the changing backdrop: a changing environment and
changing expectations of regulators, investors, and clients alike. Suffice it
to say that directors' and officers' liability risks add further confirmation
that a program for the management of operational risks will become
a high priority at organizations, coupled with other quality and control-
oriented programs.

Sending a Wake Up Call to the Board

On the international scene it was the BCCI and Barings debacles that created a stir for risk controls and operational risk management. Controls for
fraudulent financial reporting and the responsibility at the Board level were
already on management's radar screen, however. Felix Kloman, editor and
publisher of *Risk Management Reports,* recently noted that "Treadway [and
other] Committees raise risk issues to the Board level. Major financial
catastrophes force an enterprise view of risk. . . . Like it or not, the risk management discipline is becoming more integrated, as new governance mandates and practical considerations demand a fresh look at formerly fragmented
efforts inside organizations."[4] In the United States, the numerous failures of
savings and loans and other financial institutions gave way to the enactment
of national legislation, entitled the Federal Deposit Insurance Corporation
Improvement Act (FDICIA), in 1991.

Following is a sampling of key developments and reports:

1. The Treadway Report and COSO: In 1987 the Committee of Spon-
soring Organizations (COSO) issued *The Report of the National Commis-
sion on Fraudulent Financial Reporting,* more commonly known as the
Treadway Report. The common name referenced the committee's chairman,
James C. Treadway. The sponsoring organizations included the American
Institute of Certified Public Accountants (AICPA), the American Accounting
Association, the Financial Executives Institute, the Institute of Internal Au-
ditors, and the Institute of Management Accountants.

The report contained 50 recommendations that address the mitigation
of financial reporting fraud. The findings represent the external audit per-

spective, of course, of the COSO's sponsoring groups. In addition, as one would expect, this private sector initiative provides a general perspective and some latitude in interpretation and implementation.

From the perspective of corporate governance and a Board of Directors, however, the report conveyed several key themes including compliance with applicable laws and regulations and the reliability of financial reporting. Even more relevant for operational risk management are the five components that COSO saw as key for effective internal controls. These include the control environment, risk assessment, control activities, information, and communication and monitoring.[5]

2. The Federal Deposit Insurance Corporation Improvement Act (FDI-CIA): The rules of U.S. banking changed in 1991 with the enactment of the FDICIA. The Act introduced sweeping changes that impacted both corporate governance and internal controls. It drew from the private sector work introduced in both the Treadway from the United States and the MacDonald Report in Canada.[6]

From an operational risk management standpoint, some of the key developments introduced by FDICIA included the requirement that the CEO and Chief Accounting or Financial Officer of a financial institution insured by the FDIC attest to the firm's internal control systems. Specifically, they must provide a statement of management responsibility for the establishment and maintenance of an adequate internal control structure and a fiscal year end assessment of the effectiveness of that structure. Both the statement and assessment must also attest to compliance with safety and soundness laws and FDIC regulations.[7]

3. The Turnbull Report: The Turnbull report was released by a working party at the Institute of Chartered Accountants in England and Wales in 1999. It has been credited with having a dramatic impact on the responsibility of boards of directors, particularly as regards internal controls and risk management programs. Anthony Carey, project director, and Nigel Turnbull, chairman, of the Internal Control Working Party recently summarized what they believe to be the key points in the Report. Their points, which follow, evidence an even stronger link to corporate governance and operational risk management strategies:

- A key responsibility of the board is to review the effectiveness of the group's internal control system.
- The report seeks to promote best practices by "adopting a risk-based approach to designing, operating, and maintaining a sound system of internal control."
- It encourages the board to disclose whether there is an ongoing process for identifying, evaluating, and managing significant corporate risks,

and to confirm that the process is regularly reviewed by the board, and to the extent that it is in compliance with the board's expectations.

■ "In determining the company's risk profile, the board should review information from senior managers on the significant risks it faces at a group level."

■ The report "stresses that control be embedded in the culture and processes of the business. It is better therefore to build appropriate mechanisms into existing management information systems than to develop entirely separate risk reporting models."

■ "Key risk indicators and the results of embedded monitoring should be regularly supplied to the board or designated committees."[8]

Other reports have added to the advancement of controls and risk management on various fronts. For instance, the MacDonald Report, issued in Canada in 1988, contains many similar findings and recommendations as the Treadway Report. It was followed by the release of *Guidance on Control* by the Canadian Institute of Chartered Accountants in 1995, commonly referred to as COCO. In the United States, additional COSO recommendations were released in 1992 under the report title, *Internal Control—Integrated Framework*. In 1995 Australia and New Zealand published its joint standards on risk management (AS / NZS 4360). These were later revised and re-released in 1999. It is perhaps the only instance of national standards in existance, and promotes the risk management process, ranging from the headings of Context, to Risk Identification, Risk Analysis, Risk Evaluation, and Risk Mitigation. In 1998 Germany passed its *KonTraG* (Gesetz sur Kontrolle und Transparenz im Unternehmensbereich) law, which requires German companies to implement risk management in the form of risk identification, assessment, and communication.[9]

Given that the board already has this oversight responsibility, operational risk management practitioners should not miss the opportunity to lever its power firmwide. This can and should take the shape of everything from negotiating a firmwide mandate, policy statement, and gaining support for framework, reporting, and systems.

In the spirit of learning from our own mistakes and those of others, there is a wealth of knowledge that has been collected in post mortem reports, and other corporate governance reports and best practice reports. For our purposes here, we will outline only the sections of the key reports that appear to have the greatest direct bearing on corporate governance responsibilities.

The G-30 Report

The Group of 30 (G-30) is a private nonprofit organization that consists of and represents both private and public sector firms, as well as academia. In

1993 they issued a report intended to be a self-governing document for financial institutions and corporate entities in the use of derivatives. The report has since been seen in a larger context as serving to define a number of best practices for risk management generally. Relevant to our discussion here is one of the 18 key findings entitled "role of senior management." It advises that "dealers and end-users should use derivatives in a manner consistent with the overall risk management and capital policies approved by their boards of directors. . . . Policies governing derivatives use should be clearly defined, including the purposes for which these transactions are to be undertaken. Senior management should approve procedures and controls to implement these policies, and management at all levels should enforce them."[10]

The G-30 Report is particularly instructive because it outlines standard of care practice for both senior management and the board of directors. The report also addresses various best practice recommendations on valuation, risk measurement and management, documentation, systems, professional expertise, and authority. We will not explore each of these points in detail here, however it is worth noting that senior management and the board may well find themselves held to these standards if and when questions about reasonable corporate governance were to arise.

Report on the Collapse of Barings

In 1995 the Bank of England released its *Report of the Board of Banking Supervision Inquiry into the Circumstances of the Collapse of Barings.* The disaster and ultimate demise of Barings is often cited as a landmark case for operational risk management instruction. Not only is it a useful illustration of the failure of controls, including lack of segregation of duties, insufficient oversight and supervision, but the Barings case is also cited as a prime case of unauthorized and rogue trading. Upon further investigation, however, it was found that senior management and the board of directors had knowledge of the activities in question and so the case is used to underscore the failings of management and board supervision, as well as corporate governance as a whole. Following are several key findings that should serve as important markers for boards of directors:[11]

- **Management Understanding and Involvement:** Management teams have a responsibility to understand fully the businesses they manage. Senior Barings management later claimed they did not fully understand the nature of their business, which is clearly an untenable and unacceptable position from the standpoint of shareholders.

- **Relevant controls:** Internal controls, including clear segregation of duties, are fundamental to any effective risk control system.
- **Resolution of control weakness:** Any weakness identified by an internal or external audit must be addressed quickly. An internal audit report in the summer of 1994 had identified the lack of segregation of duties as a significant weakness. Yet this was not addressed by Barings' top management.

Report on Long Term Capital Management (LTCM)

More recently, the case of LTCM, its near collapse, and the shock waves that this event sent through the financial system in 1998 gave rise to formation of the Counterparty Risk Management Policy Group (CRMPG), an organization formed from a collection of representatives of the LTCM investors. Although not directly an operational risk event, it had many relevant implications. Of the 12 key findings of the group and its report, 3 stand out as having relevance for senior management and the board in the context of corporate governance:[12]

- **Management Role:** Senior management should communicate its tolerance for risk, expressed in terms of potential loss. This implies the need for reporting processes that enable management to monitor the firm's risk profile.
- **Risk reporting:** Senior management should receive regular reports on large risks and exposures to loss.
- **Concentration analysis:** Senior management should be informed about concentrations of market and credit risk due to positive correlations between the firm's own principal positions and camera party's positions.

Each one of these findings mentions senior management, however, given the magnitude of the LTCM disaster, one might naturally conclude that these responsibilities would be extended to the board if such a disaster was to reoccur.

THE RISK MANAGEMENT MANDATE

Certainly operational risk has already caught the attention of most boards and senior officers, so it should not be a stretch to parlay that interest and concern into the design and communication of an appropriate enterprise-wide mandate. If protecting the firm's reputation and shareholder value is, in fact, the end game, then the best firms will memorialize that position in a public statement on quality management and prudent risk management at all levels.

There are at least two and perhaps three levels of the operational risk management mandate. The first is strategic and serves as an umbrella for a

> ## BP STRATEGY #2, REDUX—DEMONSTRATE A FIRMWIDE VISION, VALUES, AND OBJECTIVES
>
> The firmwide vision will be formulated at the highest levels of the organization and communicated outward. The company vision will be used to leverage risk management efforts firmwide and serve as clear evidence of buy-in at both the board and most senior management levels of the organization. Additional statements on risk management and a mission for operational risk management will be linked.

firm's visions overall, which we covered in Chapter 4. To recap, statements on corporate vision and quality management can have particular relevance and serve as an important foundation for risk management programs in general, and operational risk management programs, in particular. Effective operational risk management is an extension of quality products, service, and a conscientious management team.

The next levels of statements are more specific and tactical in nature. They will cover enterprise risk management at the second level. Then, more specifically, a mandate and mission for the unit or units coordinating operational risk management will be the third level and statement.

Before we move on to the specific risk management objectives, we must reconcile the organizational placement of operational risk management relative to the movement toward enterprise-wide risk management. How do the two disciplines align? Are they one in the same thing? How does an operational risk management function align to financial (market and credit) risk functions, or treasury-based risk-based functions? All of these questions must be addressed in the tactical mandate as well.

OPERATIONAL AND ENTERPRISE-WIDE RISK MANAGEMENT

No discussion of the operational risk management framework could be complete today without addressing the question of the interrelationship between operational risk management and financial risk management functions, at one level, and in the context of enterprise-wide risk management programs, more generally.

At first glance, there is much similarity between operational risk management and other areas of risk (e.g., market and credit) and the management techniques applied by them. At a strategic and conceptual level the principles that must be applied are nearly identical. Both areas must assess and measure their respective risks. Principles of concentration of value and segmentation of risk apply to both. In fact, many of the broader risk mitigation strategies that we will be discussing in later chapters bear striking similarities. In addition, there is interest in hedging both areas of risk to the extent it is economical to do so, albeit in different markets and with different tools. Thus, when communicating a risk management vision, the two areas should certainly be integrated under coordinated enterprise-wide communications. At a more detailed level, however, there are numerous differences, ranging not only from the risk classes at the heart of the discipline to the types of skills needed for risk treatment (perhaps with the possible exception of analytics).

A key question, however, is whether the operational risk management function should be integrated fully into an existing financial function. In banks that might entail the question of merging operational risk management into a portfolio risk management (market and credit) function. In some banks and other types of corporations, the question might be whether to merge the two within a Treasury function. In the intermediate-to-longer term, the answer is most assuredly "yes." An enterprise-wide function should be formed with a broad scope and mission.

On a short-term basis, however, the answer will largely depend on an individual firm's defined scope of all three areas. If it has adopted an enterprise-wide risk management approach, then how has it been defined? Does enterprise-wide mean enterprise-wide from the perspective of managing economic capital only, or does the function play a broader role? Do operational and financial risk management programs have the same basis? That is, if the financial function is highly quantitative in nature, but the operational risk function primarily uses qualitative risk assessment, alignment may prove to be difficult.

Over time, however, the alignment should be progressed in any event. There are many aspects that must be orchestrated between them (risk capital, risk financing, risk reporting), but management must recognize that the risk classes and approaches, the internal alliances, and to a degree even the audiences may be different from one business unit to the next.

Where present, a Chief Risk Officer (CRO) will have the responsibility to recognize the nuance of different risk functions, their unique risk characteristics, different analytics, often different audiences (beyond the senior most management levels, that is), and manage the functions accordingly. It is not a simple task to recognize the nuances that must be applied to them, even for those who specialize in one or the other area. For a highly quantitative CRO, there can be a tremendous temptation for him or her to take the attitude that because operational risk management models are still being developed and are not well defined, there isn't an appropriate role for the risk management group to play. Some have fallen into the trap of assuming that a qualitatively-based operational risk management function should be entirely the domain of internal audit.

Generally speaking, operational risk management programs represent significant unique complexities of their own. For some organizations one reasonable approach may be to allow an operational risk management function to develop initially as a separate, but aligned entity, then fuse it organically together with financial risk functions as it begins to mature.

The point here is that management should not simply assume that in every case the seeds of an operational risk management function can be planted within a financial risk function and expected to grow naturally. These functions will require special attention in the near term. In addition, CROs are still a rare commodity as it is. It is even more unique to find one who can relate to, represent, and serve as a balanced advocate for the management of all three major classes of risk—market, credit, *and operational risk.*

ENTERPRISE-WIDE STATEMENTS ON RISK AND RISK MANAGEMENT

Every company should develop and promote an overall statement on risk management including its objectives enterprise-wide. There should be no confusion: Operational risk management is a component part of the firmwide risk management effort. It should be addressed as a component part of a much larger whole.

An effective statement on risk and risk management will include the following component parts:

- **Objectives:** Describe the key objectives for managing risk. Relate them to the corporate vision and objectives. This presents an opportunity to set the stage for themes of risk response and mitigation on an enterprise-wide basis.
- **Impact of Risk:** As an attention grabber, describe both the upside of risk management and the impact of loss on the firm.
- **Description of Risk Classes:** Given the transformation to enterprise-wide risk management in recent years, it is advisable to describe the spectrum of financial and operational risk classes that form the subject matter of the statement.
- **Framework and Responsibility:** The statement should be clear that risk management is the responsibility of all employees firmwide and not solely that of the risk management department.
- **Process:** Describe the process of risk management including identification, assessment, response, mitigation, and financial management.
- **Reporting Relationship:** Describe the reporting relationship and accountability of the risk function(s).

Exhibit 6.3 is a sample statement for a fictitious firm that we will call Global Financial Services (GFS). It outlines typical enterprise-wide risk

Statement of Mission and Objectives

Global Financial Services (GFS), its subsidiaries and affiliates shall manage the balance of risk and reward on a continuous basis in all business operations worldwide. The ability of the corporation to manage risk effectively is essential relative to our vision and objectives for integrity and continuous self-improvement. Effective risk management is also central to the need for safe and sound operations, consistent with our responsibility to shareholders and clients alike. Protection of the firm's integrity, reputation, and continuous operations are of utmost importance.

To the risks of loss, GFS will apply the risk management process. Key steps are a systematic and continuous identification of loss exposures, the analysis of these exposures in terms of frequency and severity probabilities and risk–reward opportunities, the application of sound risk response procedures, and of the financing of risk consistent with the corporation's financial resources.

Risk Management Focus: On an ongoing basis, the corporation will identify, analyze, monitor, and control all major risk classes. These include credit risk, the potential loss of asset values due to a change in the ability of an obligor to perform as agreed on a payment obligation. A second is market risk, or the potential loss in value due to unfavorable changes in market prices and value of financial contracts. A third is liquidity or funding risk, which is the risk of the firm's inability to meet its own obligations through funding sources or liquidation of assets in a timely manner. A fourth is operational risk, which includes the risk of business process disruption caused by failure or losses involving the performance of people, relationships, systems, physical assets, or losses from external sources.

Management Framework: GFS will apply several key principles in the ongoing management of risk and reward. These principles include continuous investments in corporate integrity, management information and tools, incentives and capabilities, diversification and segregation of processes and assets, controls, diligence and legal risk management, and business continuity defenses. The firm will apply the Risk Adjusted Performance Measures (RAPM) framework and tools to qualify and measure its risks, attribute capital, measure risk adjusted returns, and create incentives for all business units and staff worldwide for the ongoing management of risk.

Responsibility: Business line management has primary responsibility for continuous identification, assessment, and response to the risks of their own business operations. Enterprise Risk Management, working in conjunction with line risk management officers, Corporate Treasury, and Legal, has primary responsibility to support the business units with tools, analysis, and management information for a coordinated risk management process firmwide.

EXHIBIT 6.3   Enterprise-wide Risk Management

The Board of Directors has the final responsibility of assuring that any prudent risk management program is in effect at all times.

Reporting: Enterprise Risk Management and line management will work in concert to ensure that the firm's enterprise risk management system contains current and accurate reporting of relevant risk information at all times. Enterprise Risk Management shall report to the Board of Directors on the state of risk management at least quarterly; business line management will report as needed.

EXHIBIT 6.3   Enterprise-wide Risk Management

management objectives, description of risk classes, risk management framework, responsibility, and reporting.

BUSINESS LINE RISK MANAGEMENT

Risk is best addressed by those best positioned to manage it. That usually equates to business management and process controls being owned and managed at desk and unit levels.

For instance, on a regular basis, major exposures to loss must be identified, assessed, and controlled by business lines themselves in the context of firmwide standards for risk management and/or internal control. These standards are often embedded in a control self-assessment program, or in business line risk assessment programs, more generally.

In essence, the business line will have its own operational risk management team or unit. Depending on the size of the firm, of course, that unit may consist of as many as two to three people, or be the full or part-time role of one individual. The most effective operational risk unit in a business line will be headed by a senior manager, such as the business line head's chief of staff or business manager, who serves as liaison to corporate and/or operational risk management

BP STRATEGY #5—EMPOWER BUSINESS UNITS WITH RESPONSIBILITY FOR THE MANAGEMENT OF OPERATIONAL RISKS

The framework will delineate roles and responsibilities between various corporate areas and business units. Business units on a local level manage operational risk most effectively. The best firms will support and empower business units and profit centers to manage their own operational risks. This means giving them the responsibility, accountability, and authority to do so.

and other corporate functions. In some respects, the individual or unit will be a microcosm of the corporate operational risk management group. See Chapter 7, "The Operational Risk Management Group," for further insights.

INTERRELATED BUSINESS AND CORPORATE ROLES

Firms will be creative in developing their operational risk management functions. There should be no need to create an entirely new infrastructure to support the program. Rather, once again, it should leverage existing resources in as many ways as possible.

For instance, integrated strategic business continuity planning (BCP) framework structures can provide a useful analogy and, in some cases, a launch pad for a *business line* operational risk management function. For that matter, if the right talent is present, it may provide a reasonable home at the *corporate* level as well. This assumes, however, that the firm has taken its BCP function seriously and elevated it to an appropriate senior and strategic level in business line and the corporate center.

Many firms' enterprise-wide strategies for BCP already consist of a coordinated business line and corporate effort. Individual business lines have primary responsibility for mitigating the risk of business interruption in their operations. Corporate groups, such as the BCP group, operational risk management, if different, Human Resources, the Information Risk Management unit of Computer Systems Processing, Real Estate, Security, and other corporate units are charged with supporting business line risk management efforts.

In this scenario a partnership between operational risk management and other corporate units will be formed to develop and implement firmwide standards and policy on operational risk management. The operational risk management group becomes the logical coordinator, of course, but cannot operate in a vacuum. The group must work on an interrelated front with other corporate units that have quality management and risk control responsibility.

Many of the aspects of the framework for enterprise-wide BCP apply to operational risk management more broadly:

- **Planning Responsibility:** Every business line, corporate staff unit, and location firmwide is expected to develop, maintain, and test a business continuity plan. Planning standards are generally developed and promulgated for each of these groups such that the process is facilitated by a simple and common methodology. The model implies that this will be the case for assessing and managing operational risks as well.
- **Coordination Role:** Each firm location worldwide will designate a "home" for the business company planning function (except in large firms this equates to a part-time coordination role by one person), which

will be responsible for location plans and be available to assist resident business lines and staff units as they develop their specific risk assessment efforts, plans, and management initiatives.

- **Guaging Event Severity:** In BCP, the planning process is designed to respond to two types of events: (1) those in which the business interruption potential is localized to a department or division, and (2) those in which an entire office location or several locations would be affected. The latter necessitates that all affected business line and corporate units would activate their plans on a decentralized basis and the corporate infrastructure would activate its plan to set up an emergency communications/command center. The same risk response and crisis management concept can be leveraged to a broader mission in operational risk management, as well.

- **Tracking System:** BCP and operational risk management will both maintain a tracking system relative to the status of each business line, corporate units, and location on planning, testing, and risk management, more broadly. Technology groups are already focused on BCP and obviously have a major role to play in the management of operational risks as well. For instance, a technology group will keep an inventory of application systems especially in the wake of Y2K. Internal audit will review plans and testing against established standards. Business line units deemed critical and urgent from the standpoint of business continuity standards and operational risks will be held to a higher planning standard or management requirement than those whose disruption will have less immediate impact.

Exhibit 6.4 is a more detailed outline of the typical BCP framework considerations.

With emphasis on the corporate level first and foremost, it is key to recognize that many corporate functions will be included in the operational risk management program. One of the first simple steps that an organization can take toward structuring a firmwide operational risk management effort is to bring these groups together, enlist their talent and resources, and gain contributions from each. In doing so the program will extract the best practices from them, all with a common objective of managing people, processes, and systems risks.

In developing operational risk management best practices it is also key to understand that operational risk itself has roots in many management and staff functions that already exist throughout an organization. Traditionally, however, many of these functions have operated independently and without coordination on some of the same risk issues. As a result, there is often an opportunity lost. Instead, corporate risk management should be aligned

Summary

Each division and profit center is responsible for the successful recovery of its business within the downtime tolerance that they set. They know their business better than any corporate group and it is their bottom line that will be affected by any interruption. Corporate entities will provide assistance and support in assuring that the integrated business continuity planning process is workable during an actual recovery.

Interdependencies

There are many tools available to assist in the BCP process:

- Firmwide standards have been developed and define what should be included in a business line plan (e.g., technology requirements and interdependent groups) and how it should be tested.
- Business line risk assessment, combined with firmwide risk assessments conducted by corporate operational risk management teams highlight the key risks (in terms of revenue, reputation, risk of loss, and regulatory risk) that the business division or profit center faces. These work products also serve to identify the interdependence that the businesses have and provide the business line with a high-level view of its recovery as well as giving the bridge vital information for managing the crisis.
- Central crisis management teams provide additional assurance that there is an effective strategy to fight the disaster and that appropriate corporate resources are deployed efficiently. Support from the central crisis team allows the business units freedom to concentrate on their own recoveries.

Responsibility

The business lines have the ultimate responsibility for risk assessment, planning and testing. It is their responsibility to ensure that they can recover their business operations to a reasonable degree because:

- They know their business better than any corporate group
- It is their bottom line that will be affected by any interruption

The corporate business continuity risk management team (or operational risk management), including corporate technology and telecommunications groups will:

- Develop the firmwide standards
- Monitor compliance with the standards
- Develop and update a crisis management reference guide to ensure that the crisis team is reasonably equipped to handle an event
- Organize centralized testing

EXHIBIT 6.4 Business Continuity Planning Framework

> ■ Provide technical support for the business units and ensure that their plans contain relevant technology needs and provisions.
> ■ Advise business units in all aspects of the planning/testing process.
>
> Other corporate units (real estate management, security, etc.) will provide assistance to all business units. This response will be coordinated by the emergency communications center. Internal audit groups will provide independent review and confirm compliance of the business plans and tests against firmwide standards.

EXHIBIT 6.4   Business Continuity Planning Framework

BP STRATEGY #6—SUPPORT AND LEVERAGE CORPORATE UNITS' CAPABILITIES AND CONTRIBUTIONS

Define roles and responsibilities of corporate units firmwide. Structure operational risk management programs such that they reinforce key aspects of existing control and risk management programs, including but not limited to those of control self-assessment, internal audit, compliance, legal, security, and other risk management functions. Support and leverage their contributions. Avoid redundancy of effort. Corporate risk management and risk control-oriented units should be aligned and coordinated in such a way as to maximize their contribution.

with other staff functions in the most creative way such as to maximize their contribution.

CONTRIBUTIONS FROM CORPORATE RISK CONTROL FUNCTIONS

There are a variety of corporate units that already contribute to firmwide operational risk management, although perhaps they have not been recognized as such. In fact, a number of these functions contributed in one way or another to the development of operational risk management.

Here are some of the places where the best firms find practices that are worth leveraging and/or adopting as part of their firmwide operational risk management effort:[13]

■ **Quantification and Risk Capital:** Many people who focus on quantification and risk capital come from the market-risk or credit-risk analytics areas. As such, they are schooled in statistical and actuarial sciences and are looking for a mathematical representation of risk.

- **Operations Management:** In operations risk management, people focus on operations and processing—the back office or middle office of business management—thinking about process flow and key risk indicators (KRIs). They have developed many good practices using process and indicator tools within these functions. Many people in operations have been heard to say, "I've been involved in many of these disciplines in the past, so the broader operational risk field is a natural extension for me."

- **Line Management:** A business line manager, similarly, often looks at key performance indicators (KPIs) or key risk indicators (KRIs) as a way of managing the business. Many proactive managers have pioneered excellent work in using these indicators. We can borrow some of their proven tools and methods and apply them to broader, firmwide applications. These tools track all kinds of things, from inherent risk variables (such as the fixed number of computers and applications necessary to run the business) to control-oriented risk indicators (those things that management can tweak, such as the ratio of dollars spent on training to the number of customer complaints).

  Business managers, understandably, zero in on customer relationships: customer satisfaction, quality assurance levels, customer complaint rates, and customer retention rates. Also, many business managers concentrate on problems on the processing side—and this can overlap with operations managers—such as reconciliation rates, trade fail rates, and a variety of other variables, such as system downtime or system failures versus maintenance investments.

- **Internal Controls / Internal Audit:** Internal controls and internal audit groups have been concentrating on risk-ranked audits, businesswide risk assessment, and more granular self-assessment processes in recent years. All three areas of risk assessment are helpful in building a fully integrated operational risk management function.

- **Insurance Risk Management:** Insurance risk managers bring more of a firmwide look at risk assessment and management, not so much at the product or process level but at the level of the firm's entire portfolio. They ask, "What are the catastrophic or large-loss exposures that can impact the firm?" Here, too, some of the more progressive insurance risk management practitioners have brought actuarial quantification techniques to the table. Some of the best ones have also taken on leadership roles in their organizations in assessing risk on both insurable and uninsurable loss exposures; interacted proactively with security, audit, and legal functions on risk control activities; and been active on contingency/disaster planning and crisis management. More recently they have also been proactive in coordinating their activities in a consistent way with financial risk managers within their organizations.[14] Unfortunately, far too many others have not. In too many cases the risk and insurance function has been so closely associated with the administration of insurance programs alone for so long that senior managers often do not even consider them when contemplating the impact on uninsurable risks or, for that matter, the control of risks, whether insurable or uninsurable. The irony here is that in order to develop and maintain an effective program that focuses primarily on risk financing and insurance, a manager must have a thorough understanding of the risks of loss and have controls in place to manage those risks.[15] As such, too many risk and insurance management units admittedly have not played a key role in the management and control of operational risk.

■ **Corporate Risk Management Functions:**[16] Financial service firms certainly don't have a monopoly on the development of risk management techniques. Some of the more progressive risk assessment, mitigation, and finance techniques have been pioneered by major multinationals in other industries. Operational risk practitioners at financial firms would also do well to monitor those developments.

The best firms derive the best of breed and teamwide from these corporate staff units. Including as many of the best practices as possible from each of these functions can go a long way toward an integrated, holistic approach to operational risk management. Key first steps in building a coordinated operational risk management platform are to outline an operational risk framework definition, vocabulary, and vision, then to form a senior risk management committee, working group and/or risk jury system so that everyone is on the same page across the entire organization.

Data availability will drive how many of these tools, techniques, and measurements can be coordinated. Newly created forums and the formation of a senior management control committee for operational risk should be supplemented by using MIS to integrate the data flow and availability.[17] We will discuss data flows and risk information at length in Chapters 10, 11, and 13.

A word of caution: Some of the things we have to keep in mind—and deal with—in coordinating these disparate views involve human nature and turf issues. Many of the functions we have discussed had been distributed throughout the firm and are part of the turf of different control groups. Now we are talking about aligning them in different ways, even if only informally, and issues may arise.

The following case on creating effective roles and working relationships was contributed by Denis Taylor of Commonwealth Bank Group.

CASE ILLUSTRATION
Building Effective Roles and Working Relationships

Commonwealth Bank Group (Australia)

The Commonwealth Bank Group (CBG) was a relatively early adopter of operational risk quantification and modeling, with a central function (Operational Risk Management) charged with the responsibility for the development and consistent implementation of our methodology in the mid-1990s. The subsequent years have yielded a wealth of experience in better understanding the operational and strategic risk profile of the organization, while operational risk remains an integral component in our integrated risk management framework for the group.

Divisional Roles: CBG's Bottom-up Approach   Initial objectives for operational risk management not only focused on the immediate needs for accurately allocating capital, but also in establishing and maintaining risk ownership, accountability, understanding, and the facilitation of change.

With these objectives in mind, top-down macro measures for operational risk were evaluated and subsequently discounted, and from the outset the CBG concentrated its efforts into partnering the business to develop direct estimations of individual risks at a divisional and business unit level. The group has completed a number of annual assessments using this approach.

Workshops or smaller working meetings are the primary mechanisms used to engage the business in the identification and assessment of risks, controls, insurance benefits, and correlations between risks.

Each division has identified its most significant risks having due regard for key strategies, critical business processes, and occasionally by analyzing scenarios gleaned from publicly reported external events. The assessment for each risk is based on the articulation of a scenario equation for a given likelihood of occurrence. An appropriate risk distribution (from the seven standard distributions we have used for modeling) is then applied to this point estimation and results in a single measure of the profit and loss impact of a risk.

A risk aggregation process that accounts for correlations through a Monte Carlo simulation results in an Economic Equity calculation for operational risk.

CBG attributes its relatively early success in implementing such an approach largely to the following:

- Continuing the involvement of the group's senior management throughout the project
- Ensuring that all center initiatives serve both group-wide and divisional business needs, accentuating and maintaining the high visibility of value created
- Forging cooperative working relationships with divisional personnel
- Designing and implementing an enduring process for direct assessment, including the development of software to facilitate the process.

Senior Management: The Critical Ingredient   A select group of senior and executive management personnel is instrumental in the establishment of a central operational risk function and methodology, and in communicating objectives.

The broadening of involvement across executive and senior management teams of all divisions was given impetus by an active interest undertaken by the Managing Director and the group's Audit Committee.

The risk management team at CBG believes that its risk ownership, accountability, and capital allocation objectives were instrumental in capitalizing on senior and executive managements involvement and maintaining their participation. The allocation of capital, and the resulting impact on a division's Return on Target Equity (ROTE), naturally yields significant management attention.

It is, of course, a significant challenge to maintain the importance and relevance of Operational Risk Management within a dynamic organization and rapidly changing industry. In recognition of this, CBG's operational risk scope also expressly includes the potential variations in the value of the group's businesses due to *strategic and business decisions*. By attuning its framework to incorporate the subject matter nearest to the heart of senior management, a greater buy-in appears to have been afforded.

For instance, regular reporting on large exposures by each of the group's divisions to the Managing Director and the Audit Committee contributes to maintaining the visibility of operational risk. This reporting accentuates significant changes in the risk profile of a division, while Risk Indicators and Triggers alert these stakeholders to material concerns.

Some lessons learned are:

- It's a tired old adage but it still rings true: The active support and conceptual understanding by executive management is the key to gaining quick wins.

- Dynamic organizations require flexible and dynamic methodologies for operational risk.

Design to Focus and Deliver on Business Needs   Alignment of all new operational risk initiatives to both group-wide and divisional needs is essential in articulating the value proposition for each phase of development of our operational risk framework. The resulting shared vision of the value created, and the demonstrated benefits of better understanding and more effective, consistent, and transparent operational-risk management, significantly increases CBG's chances of a successful implementation.

   Some lessons learned are:

- Understanding and delivering on stakeholder needs is an elementary consideration in developing new initiatives or enhancing methodologies.
- A business case approach to new operational risk initiatives can be instrumental in sharing a vision and leveraging other divisional activities.

Divisional Role and Cooperative Working Relationships   Sharing a vision is important; however, maintaining a cooperative working relationship with all divisions is CBG's modus operandi. To ensure a consistent and intrinsic adoption of its group-wide methodology, a position was formalized within each division with responsibility for coordinating, educating, and driving operational risk within the division. These senior Divisional Risk Managers (DRMs) invariably have a detailed understanding and interest in the business operations, and have been trained in the detailed mechanics of the methodology, including the rationale behind CBG's seven standard representative risk distributions. This working relationship provides an ideal basis for soliciting a divisional perspective prior to, and subsequent to, new assessments or initiatives.

   Some lessons learned are:

- Appropriate empowerment of divisional representatives has enabled a cascading effect firmwide in relation to operational risk methodologies and practices.
- Delivering an education on the methodology is targeted to each audience (not everyone is interested in the math!).
- Leveraging demonstrated wins from Business Continuity Management (BCM) for operational risk initiatives is worthwhile.

   Note: This case is continued in Chapter 19, Operational Risk Technology and Systems, with additional insight on the development of in-house technology and systems support.

■ ■ ■

CASE ILLUSTRATION
Teamwork Alliances

Bankers Trust

Another illustration of corporate and business line interaction is the development of our own risk-based capital and performance measurement program (Operational RAROC) at Bankers Trust.[18] The project was initiated jointly by the General Auditor, the Chief Corporate Strategist, and this author, when I was head of Operational Risk and Insurance Management (ORIM), and at various times during our evolution, the CEO, CFO, Chief Corporate Strategist, General Counsel, General Auditor, Global Risk Manager, Chief Credit Officer, Management Control Committee, Asset/Liability Committee, Operating Committee, and Board of Directors all endorsed and participated actively in the effort.

The project evolved from risk management work at Bankers Trust. During most of its development and implementation, the effort was managed by our unit although the effort has been collaborative with many internal departments.

Following the project's initiation, ORIM maintained day-to-day responsibility for the project, with periodic meetings with the firm's General Auditor, Chief Corporate Strategist, and Market Risk Manager. ORIM was later moved into the Corporate Risk Management Department, which evolved into an enterprise risk management function overall. The operational risk effort interfaced with all business lines and departments in refining the project's strategy, defining goals, presenting information to senior management (including the Board of Directors), and developing risk management tools for use by the business line.

■ ■ ■

THE OPERATIONAL RISK WORKING GROUP OR COMMITTEE

The most common strategy for deriving best practices from other corporate staff functions is to form a committee, or better still, an active working group, that seeks synergies between various businesses, departments, and teams through a common purpose.

In many firms there is already a senior risk working group or committee in place. Admittedly, such groups are generally formed under the heading of Control Committee or Operational Risk Committee, but a "working group" would have the connotation of being much more involved and hands-on. Regardless of the format, the bottom line is that these groups and their methods work far better in concert than individually.

Having such a group in place is certainly a positive step and a necessary one to effect real change. A unified senior level voice will go a long way towards promoting and encouraging the implementation and change necessary.

Beyond the title, the form that the group should take will be a matter of organizational style and preference. An excess of committees or even working groups can dilute the decision-making process and confuse the messages coming from senior management. So, for some firms one approach will be to leverage the agenda of existing committees' scope, as long as the operational risk management agenda is not lost in the larger picture. There is always a risk of this happening when a market- or credit-risk committee or an asset-liability committee is expanded to address operational risk issues.

The agenda for the committee might address some or all of the following:

- Results of risk assessment efforts
- Progress reviews on risk management investment efforts (systems upgrades, control upgrades, new MIS)
- Summary MIS on risk indicators, incidents, losses, and forecasts calculations
- Review of outstanding control issues
- Review recent operational losses and post mortem studies
- Periodic economic capital calculations and trends
- Quality, control, and compliance issues and initiatives
- New product and business lines
- High-level disaster recovery planning

Once formed, the group will be in a unique position inasmuch as it will have a view of the entire organization and its risk profile. The more effective committees will actually have an array of useful metrics at their disposal, with emphasis on the word *useful*. Committees and their individual members will have little patience for being inundated with raw data. Thus, there must be a filtering or distillation process applied. This will require robust technology to be able to provide the data and information feeds necessary to track multiple facets of the organization firmwide and globally.

CORPORATE CULTURE, AGAIN: SQUARE PEGS AND ROUND HOLES

It is critically important to achieve balance between the operational risk management framework and the organization's corporate culture. All too often there is the assumption that a framework can be transferred from one organization to another. The fact is organizations are a lot like the people that comprise them—each one is different and unique. A framework and strategy that works well for one organization simply may not be transferable to another. For instance, some firms are highly control-oriented, while others establish broad guidelines for operating units within an overall corporate hierarchy and allow them to operate independently. In fact, one division may even have an entirely different culture from another.

A good illustration of an organization with a unique control orientation is HSBC (Hong Kong Shanghai Banking Corporation). The company operates its control structure by the book, literally. It has developed a "bible" that contains the policy and procedures that must be followed by each division. When a new entity has been acquired, the book is distributed and that organization is expected to comply fully. This approach seems to work quite well for them, mainly because it has been operated under the clear mandate and direction of senior management and ingrained in the firm's corporate culture.[19] Clearly, however, it is unique to HSBC. It would simply not fit with many other corporate cultures that operate with greater freedom and flexibility line-by-line. Although seemingly very effective for them, the HSBC approach may not be readily transferable to other firms, and vice versa.

DIRECTORS' AND OFFICERS' (D&O) LIABILITY CONSIDERATIONS

In some respects, D&O liability is the operational risk of not managing operational risk. Management teams and boards of directors that do not heed the warnings from industry losses and advice in resultant post mortem reports will find themselves in the position of having to defend their actions or inactions. Consider the following:

- **Business Judgment Rule:** The business judgment rule is generally seen to be the most important defense for a board of directors. It is based on the premise that provided the directors act in a "reasonable" manner and in the interest of shareholders, they will enjoy legal protection.
- **Professional Standard of Care:** The extent to which an individual or organization met or exceeded an existing professional standard of care is generally seen to be the basis of professional liability legal actions and defense strategies. Given the magnitude of financial industry disasters in recent years, however, and the number of resultant corporate goverance reports, it is not at all unreasonable to expect that the professional standards outlined in these reports may be applied to managers and boards in a corporate governance context.
- **Directors' and Officers' Liability Experience:** Tillinghast-Towers Perrin publishes an annual survey of D&O liability. There is no specific evidence of claims against directors and officers for the specific failure to

set appropriate risk management policy or establish reasonable risk management programs as yet, but one has to wonder whether these cases are simply buried in the numbers. Their 1999 survey reports that 33% of D&O cases relate to breach of general duties, and 15% for all other shareholder issues, for a total of 48% of cases. Given the attention on large-scale disasters in recent years, and the culpability of management and boards relative to errors or omissions in corporate governance, it may simply be a matter of time before we see more specific suits for wrongful acts relative to the governance of risk management specifically.[20]

People who believe that the risk begins and ends with the board of directors would be kidding themselves, of course. In addition to doing a diligent job of risk management, risk practitioners would do well to take the extra step to familiarize themselves with Exhibit 6.5 and its D&O liability indemnification and insurance protection issues. A little career risk management never hurt anyone.

Another Operational Risk Management Myth

One trap that some boards of directors, and many of the rest of us, often fall into is in relying too heavily on models, numbers, and reports without questioning their assumption and methods. The area of corporate governance brings at least one of our ORM myths back to mind.[21]

> **ORM Myth:** *We have little to worry about: our risk measurement models are second to none.*

Risk management is not the same as risk measurement. In short, risk measurement is a subset of risk management, and the sooner that balance between the two moves onto the broader board and senior management-level agenda, the better off the industry will be.

Business case studies are now rich with the names of financial firms that were recognized as having had some of the best analytics but still suffered life-threatening or even fatal operational losses, among them Long Term Capital Management, Drexel Burnham Lambert, and Kidder Peabody.

Risk measurement models have been proven to be extremely helpful in dimensioning risk, but they can be dangerous to a firm's survival. They often create a false sense of security, particularly at the board and senior management levels. There becomes a misconception that the risks have been measured and thus bounded; that management understands the issues and has dealt with them; and, therefore, that the board can move on to other priorities.

Indemnification and Insurance

A discussion of boards of directors and operational risk would not be complete without some treatment of the potential for liability, as well as methods for addressing it.

Firms must be prepared for the possiblility of a shareholder action being leveled against the board of directors and/or senior management following a catastrophe operational loss event. This will likely be the case if there is a suspicion that proper precautions had not been taken by the corporation or its board to manage the risks involved. Anyone studying or having responsibility for operational risk management should understand the liability ramifications for boards of directors and senior managers who might find allegations of insufficient attention to the matter protecting shareholder value.

The typical corporation provides financial protection for directors and officers against third-party allegations of "wrongful acts" through its corporate bylaws, and secondarily by its directors' and officers' (D&O) liability insurance. The situation can be summed up as follows:

- **By-law Indemnification:** The first line of defense is the legal indemnification provided under the corporation's bylaws. A corporation's bylaws typically outline the specific circumstances under which the corporation will protect and defend the director or officer against allegations of wrongdoing, typically with the exception that it will not protect those individuals for allegations of illegal or fraudulent activity.
- **Company Reimbursement Insurance:** The second consideration is the company reimbursement portion of a D&O liability insurance program. It is designed to reimburse the company for any amounts paid as indemnification for the directors or officers as dictated by the bylaws or statutory provisions. The protection typically extends to legal liability judgments, settlements, legal fees, and other defense costs. Note: these insurance programs do not provide any financial protection to the corporation for its portion of any liability if it, too, is named in a lawsuit.
- **Directors' and Officers' Liability Insurance:** There is typically an individual coverage part of the D&O policy that provides coverage directly to the individual board members or officers in the event that protection or indemnification is not permitted by law or statute. The insurance protection is subject to specific terms and conditions of the policy, of course.

Thus, it is the combination of corporate bylaws and D&O liability insurance that would respond to allegations that the board of directors or senior managers have not done enough to govern the development of a risk management program. D&O insurance protects individual directors and officers for personal loss arising out of suits against them in a director and officer capacity. The definition of "wrongful acts" will vary from policy to policy, but may include coverage for charges of "errors, misstatements, misleading statements, acts, or omissions, neglect, or breach of duty."

EXHIBIT 6.5 Directors and Officers Liability

CONCLUSION

There are few aspects more important than setting an overall firmwide mandate and defining and setting program objectives for the risk management program. The mandate will drive all other considerations, from framework to data collection, system implementation, and financial management. In essence, it is the first step in establishing a firmwide framework.

In addition, the overall mandate and statement will help to form an important basis for the corporate framework and participation of business units and numerous corporate groups in the overall process. The second step, then, is to delineate roles and responsibilities for both business units and corporate groups. In Chapter 7, we will explore the role and responsibilities of a designated operational risk management unit in specific detail.

LESSONS LEARNED AND KEY RECOMMENDATIONS

- Communicate firmwide vision, values, and objectives for operational risk management. The firmwide vision will be formulated at the highest levels of the organization and communicated outward. It should serve as clear evidence of buy-in at both the board and most senior management levels of the organization (BP Strategy #2, Redux).
- Prioritization of objectives and methods will be a key part of the firmwide mandate. *Recognizing* that risk management is a continuous or circular process is one thing, identifying the priority and emphasis on each element—identification, assessment, risk capital, risk finance—is another thing entirely. Priorities, roles, responsibilities, and flow of information between the participant groups are all key for a successful effort.
- Recent landmark cases, events, and ensuing reports have provided an important framework and guidance for the corporate governance responsibilities of the board and senior management. Many of the findings of these reports, including the G-30 Report, the Report on the Collapse of Barings, and the Report on Long Term Capital Management, and others, set standards for responsibility in setting policy and process for internal controls and risk management. Many of these reports and findings are directly relevant for setting a framework for operational risk management programs.
- A key milestone in operational risk management will be the development of a fully integrated function. An operational risk management group office or department can be a logical coordination point but must have continual interface with business line and other corporate groups.
- Empower business units with responsibility for the management of operational risks. The framework will delineate roles and responsibilities

between various corporate areas and business units. Business units on a local level manage operational risk most effectively. The organization will support and empower business units and profit centers to manage their own operational risks. This means giving them the responsibility, accountability, and authority to do so (BP Strategy #5).

■ Support and leverage corporate units' capabilities and contributions. Define roles and responsibilities of corporate units firmwide. Structure operational risk management programs such that they reinforce key aspects of existing control and risk management programs. Support and leverage their contributions. Avoid redundancy of effort (BP Strategy #6).

■ An operational risk management committee, chaired by a member of the executive committee, can be very effective as the focal point for operational risk management issues, action tracking, and initiatives.

■ Internal audit, in particular, plays a key role in the operational risk management program, including but not limited to extensive risk assessment both pre-audit and during audits. Both internal audit and operational risk management should link to the issue or action tracking system that captures all major operational issues firmwide. In addition, it is only logical that internal audit provide independent reviews of the operational risk measurement and capital allocation system.

CHAPTER 7

The Operational Risk Management Group

INTRODUCTION

In view of recent regulatory developments in financial services, many firms have just recently begun to confront the prospect of forming an independent operational risk management unit. In Chapter 6, we introduced the key premise that business line is responsible for managing their own day-to-day operational risks. We also discussed the roles and responsibilities of other corporate units. That might leave some wondering about the nature of a central operational risk management group (sometimes called a Group Operational Risk Management function). Where do its role and responsibilities begin and end?

Certainly a central risk function must avoid redundancy with either the business lines' individual efforts or those of other corporate units, such as internal audit. Simply suggesting that the central function is required because of the regulatory developments, or because the topic is now in vogue, will not survive in today's lean and highly competitive business environment.

Like any other function, a central operational risk group must add value in its own right. The unit must be proactive and effective, plain and simple. In most cases its contribution should take the form of helping to facilitate the active management of operational risks, including continual interaction with business lines, executive management, and corporate functions such as audit, legal, controllers, operations, compliance, security, and other corporate staff functions that support the business lines.

Before we delve too deeply into the operational risk management group's role, one key clarification is in order. One should not confuse the operational risk group and operational risk practitioners with the much larger concept of an enterprise-wide operational risk management program. The former is a facilitator; the latter is the sum of the many component parts.

BP STRATEGY #7—DESIGNATE AN OPERATIONAL RISK MANAGEMENT UNIT TO FACILITATE FIRMWIDE

The best firms will form a coordinating unit for operational risk management headed by a senior manager and staffed with top talent to coordinate operational risk management efforts firmwide. In some firms the manager will head operational risk exclusively. In others, the individual may also serve as Chief Risk Officer. In any event, business units will direct their own operational risk efforts, but a separate corporate operational risk function will support and monitor their activities. In some industries (e.g., financial services), the function will be separate from internal audit.

This chapter will address the design and structure of a value-added firmwide group, along with a discussion of implications for design of its component parts.

STRATEGIC POSITIONING

Let's return to one of our opening questions. What is it that the individual firm is seeking to accomplish in operational risk management, and how does its objective help to formulate a mandate and mission for the in-house operational risk management unit? In fact, the answers will probably align with the organization's perspectives more broadly on enterprise-wide risk management, views on economic capital and performance measures, the role of Internal Audit, and its views on organizational structure (e.g., corporate roles versus decentralized business line roles).

There are at least five different perspectives emerging in the financial services community today on the structure and positioning of an operational risk management unit. They range in focus from risk management analytics and risk measurement, to the control group focus, to business line management teams, to enterprise-wide multidisciplined operational risk management functions. It is only natural that if the operational risk management group is headed by a senior manager from one of these areas, the ultimate program and function may have some bias toward his or her roots. Each is described as follows:

1. Risk Measurement: Advancements in analytics for operational risk have become one of the hallmarks of the new operational risk management function. In some cases a unit's formation may have been driven by recent bank regulatory urgings; in others, by relentless pursuit of analytical precision. This perspective has focused entirely on risk measurement—finding a number or a series of numbers to represent the range of possible outcomes. The analytic focus is often first on modeling in the belief that a number is critical for emphasis, for attention, and for focus of purpose. The greatest challenge for these analysts will be in proving not only that they have achieved analytic precision, but also that such measures may be used to improve behavior.

2. Internal Controls: The second perspective represents the opposite end of the spectrum: those who have practiced operational risk management in the form of one or more control disciplines (e.g., Internal Audit, Compliance, Self-assessment groups, etc.), whose focus has been on maintaining tight controls and risk management structures. It is tempting, and in some cases conceivable that a move to the emerging discipline of operational risk management is only a minimal step from their current role(s).

3. Business Management: The third view often emerges from the ranks of hands-on business management. Managers in this group may have operated their businesses armed with key performance indicators, balanced scorecards, or other performance measures. For this group, the move to track and analyze risk indicators is certainly not foreign and may only require a slight refocusing with additional enterprise-wide information being available to them.

4. Insurance Risk Management: A fourth group consists of a perspective from insurance risk management practitioners. This group is becoming more visible in the operational risk management discussion, as evidence of the firms' desire for more effective operational risk hedges versus less effective traditional insurance coverages.

5. Multidisciplined Operational Risk Management: There is a fifth group now emerging at some of the best managed firms. Practitioners in this group believe that the most effective operational risk management programs will select from features of all four of these prior schools of thought. First, they use risk measurement tools for dimensioning the size of the operational risk challenge. Second, they apply the most effective risk management and risk control tools. Third, they monitor risk drivers and indicators, like warning lights for the business manager pilot in the cockpit, through the use of risk indicators and management information systems (MIS) tools—all with an objective of creating a comprehensive operational risk management program. Fourth, they will apply risk finance and insurance tools as "operational risk hedges."[1]

SETTING PRIORITIES: DEPARTMENTAL MISSION, GOALS, AND OBJECTIVES

The subject of operational risk management is so far-reaching in an organization that it is easy to lose one's focus and clarity on the issues and priorities. Assuming that we have established the upside strategic opportunity in the collective corporate mind, or even a tactical risk mitigation focus, the questions become, "Where do I begin, and what are the most important steps to take?"

Should you begin with self-assessment, with the areas that caused the largest losses last year, with an economic or regulatory risk capital scheme, or perhaps with enhanced training of employees? It should come as no surprise that once again the answer is embedded in the formulation of a clear vision, strategies, tools, and tactics, along with expert execution of the plan overall. Because it is so easy to lose one's focus in the broad scope of ORM, both day-to-day and even year-by-year, it is critically important to carefully consider, and define objectives before establishing a program and hiring staff.

The process of defining operational risk objectives and priorities is not nearly as obvious as one might think. Even for established functions, risk issues, loss events, and specific risk response projects will arise on a regular basis, distract a team for weeks or months at a time, and hinder progress in the bigger picture. That is true whether we are talking about the focus of an ORM *unit,* the firm's entire risk management or just its ORM *strategy.* Consider the impact of Y2K preparations. One-off events and projects certainly can be important, but an organization must work to determine and revisit its priorities for its risk management resources continually. It is not only conceivable but also entirely likely that without a clear set of objectives and priorities, the entire function and organization might find itself lost on a tangent or in the details of a specific project, thus taking its collective eye off the ball of the impact it might have had with enterprise-wide programs.

It is both difficult and presumptuous to give generalized recommendations about the appropriate content of a mission statement, along with specific objectives and goals for all ORM functions, without having an intimate knowledge of the organization, its priorities, and culture. There are some generalizations that can be applied, however, as one goes about considering the construction of an appropriate statement and the specific design of a department or function. Similar to the statement on risk management that we discussed in Chapter 6, here too we will want to cover areas like objectives, strategy, roles and responsibility, and the component parts of the risk management process-risk identification, assessment, communications strategies, mitigation, and risk finance, as appropriate.

A logical place to start this discussion is in revisiting "Operational Risk Management 101." Any risk management program should support a continuous flow of risk identification, risk analysis and assessment and/or measurement, risk mitigation, and risk finance. Exhibit 7.1 presents a sample

Objectives and Strategy

The Operational Risk Management unit's mission is to facilitate operational risk management firmwide. A key focus should be the anticipation and mitigation of risk of operational disruption at all levels of the organization. Operational disruptions are broadly defined as internal control failures or external events that give rise to loss events in the areas of people, process, systems, and external events.

Roles and Responsibility

Scope of responsibility includes facilitation of risk identification, assessment, mitigation, and financing strategies.

- **Risk Identification, Assessment, and Communication Strategies:** These include ongoing risk assessment reviews with the firm's business lines and drawing from risk information available from other control groups. The unit facilitates operational risk assessment by the firm's business lines and operational vulnerability analysis at a firmwide level. It communicates information about operational risk, risk indicators, and event trends through risk and performance measurement tools including the firmwide Operational RAPM program.
- **Risk Response:** Facilitation of risk reduction efforts of the firm's business lines by providing tools for effective risk management, such as standards and tracking systems (e.g., business continuity planning, vendor standards). The group provides consultations about the practical and efficient mitigation of one-off operational and event risk issues. Crisis management, business line deal review, operational risk factor reporting, claims management, and other targeted efforts also contribute to risk mitigation.
- **Risk Finance Strategies:** A proactive effort should balance self-insurance, insurance, reinsurance, and (noninsurance) business contract engineering, where efficient and economic, in order to smooth Cost-of-Operational Risk. Cost-of-Operational Risk, in its broadest sense, is defined as the sum of loss costs, insurance, reinsurance premiums, self-insurance reserves, and administrative costs, less recoveries. All major insurance, reinsurance, and self-insurance decisions on behalf of the firm worldwide are coordinated through the Operational Risk Management unit.

Reporting

The Operational Risk Management unit is part of the Enterprise Risk Management group and reports to the Chief Risk Officer, who in turn reports to the CEO.

EXHIBIT 7.1   Sample Mission Statement for Operational Risk Management

Role	Business Lines	ORM Group Office
Risk Assessment / Risk Measurement	Direct	Direct
Risk Response / Risk Mitigation	Direct	Consultative
Risk Finance and Insurance Management	Consultative	Direct*

EXHIBIT 7.2 Corporate Operational Risk Group: Direct and Indirect Roles and Responsibilities
* If included in the ORM function, of course.

broad-based operational risk management mission statement that serves as a starting point and can be adapted to fit any organization.

Exhibit 7.2 illustrates the broad direct and indirect responsibilities of an operational risk management function. It is interesting to note the similarities between the direct responsibility of the operational risk management function and how it relates to those direct responsibilities of the financial risk management function.

These are useful guidelines for openers, but the new operational risk management practitioner will be faced with some important decisions relative to setting an agenda for his or her part of the enterprise-wide mandate. Even the seasoned risk management strategist should revisit goals and objectives periodically as a reality check on priorities. Like virtually every other corporate function, one key consideration will be decisions about the allocation of the manager's scarce resources, whether it is the time and energies of the manager or his or her team.

When our group began its initial work on operational risk management at Bankers Trust, our primary directive was to devise an economic capital model for operational risk. Anyone now engaged in this exercise may relate to our initial experiences. Our team first set out to study individual business lines with a view toward determining how to classify and analyze risks that were both inherent in the business, or otherwise controllable. As one might imagine, this exercise took us through numerous interviews, reviews of documents, loss experience, and the like. We superimposed our own risk management experiences and filters on these business operations.

For us, a corporate unit, the process took us deeper and deeper into the business units, and all the while we invested numerous person-days in devising risk assessment questionnaires. We found ourselves developing a risk assessment process, not unlike the control self-assessment programs in use at many firms today. As time dragged on, however, we realized that at the rate of speed we were running, our small team would take months, if not years, to complete the exercise. At the same time, however, we realized that we were evolving a risk assessment program and had strayed from our risk capital mission. In retrospect, the digression was helpful for us to confirm our capital perspective. We had strayed, however, in that our mandate did not yet take into account the full spectrum of enterprise-wide operational risk management as described here.

One of the most challenging aspects of operational risk management is that the risks are so pervasive. Because they are embedded in human behavior, in systems, in processes at all levels, and in all corners of an organization, there are numerous possibilities and opportunities for managing them. A key to success, then, is to apply the best techniques from many functions and disciplines in different settings and at different levels throughout the organization. Remember that we are seeking to *support and leverage* the best practices of each in building comprehensive risk management firmwide. But, where does this leave a firm and operational risk management group in positioning its overall operational risk management mission, objectives, and strategies?

Some guiding issues and questions might be helpful in determining where the unit might have the greatest impact for enhancing line efforts toward mitigating risk firmwide. As a starting point, consider some of the following:

- Is there a quality management program already in place enterprise-wide?
- Is ORM already embedded in the firm and its culture?
- Is there an enterprise-wide risk management function in place or in development?
- Is there a risk-adjusted performance management (RAPM) culture in place?
- Where have operational losses occurred in the firm *and* in its market sectors?
- Where do specific control problems lie?
- Is there an opportunity to align with a strategically focused enterprise-wide business continuity planning function?
- How do regulatory risk capital developments apply to the firm?
- Have there been any recent regulatory issues of concern at the firm or in the industry?
- What is the status of the firm's risk finance and insurance programs? Is there further alignment possible?

Armed with the answers, or at least some guidance on the issues, the best firms will begin to determine some priorities for positioning the central operational risk function.

ROLE IN RISK ASSESSMENT

It is clear that in order to fully assess new exposures before they become losses, one must have a complete knowledge of the firm's operations and loss exposures.[2] This is an area that has received some discussion over the years at various risk management forums, but practically speaking, some of that discussion can be characterized as lip service. Generally speaking, a key role of the central operational risk function is in adding value to business lines' own risk assessment processes in two ways:

1. **As a facilitator and a consultant** to provide an independent view and a second opinion on local risk assessment activities in order to achieve the most thorough and complete results. As such, an ORM function should strive to maintain ongoing risk assessment discussions with all key business lines and functional areas and may have responsibility for coordinating economic and/or regulatory risk capital calculations, and attributions or allocations.
2. **As a conduit** to obtaining specialty risk assessment and control resources and services either from within or outside the firm. For instance, these resources might provide technology, systems, operations or environmental risk assessment, specialty engineering risk mitigation for physical or natural disaster risks, health, safety, ergonomic consultants, business continuity planning and recovery, and other risk-related services. In contrast, business lines themselves would probably have the best access to specialists in their own areas, such as trading operations, securities processing, and the like.

Exhibit 7.3 is an outline that delineates the split of roles and responsibilities between the business division level and the corporate level at Deutsche Bank. Note the clear responsibility of business lines for risk identification, management, and reporting on operational risk at the division level. Those concerned with managing risk must exhibit very proactive involvement. ORM practitioners must reach out to the business lines and become involved. They cannot wait for their phones to ring.

The area of risk assessment and measurement may well be one of the most significant areas of change and involvement by operational risk practitioners in the future. The new breed will have to have a full working knowledge of the business of their institutions, become much more proactive and much more worldly and aware.

At the very least, individuals responsible for operational risk management will have to understand the results of other risk assessment processes already in place. And to truly add value to risk assessment and control efforts,

Business Division versus Corporate Operational Risk Responsibility

Business Divisions

- Identify, manage, and report on operational risks
- Define risk appetite for operational risk in their activities

Divisional Operational Risk Officer

- Implement operational risk management framework in the division
- Roll out operational risk management tools in the division
- Establish regular divisional operational risk report
- Set divisional operational risk standards
- Ensure divisional crisis management

Chief Operational Risk Officer*

- Chair the operational risk committee
- Owner of the group guidelines
- Establish the operational risk framework
- Set firm- and group-wide reporting standards
- Establish regular firm- and group-wide operational risk management report
- Develop firm- and group-wide reporting and management tools
- Develop firm- and group-wide calculation methodology
- Develop knowledge pool to support divisional operational risk officers
- Ensure cooperation between specialist functions and divisions

EXHIBIT 7.3 Deutsche Bank
* Firmwide role at corporate office.

those individuals will have to have a complete understanding of the specific business lines and be in a position to develop and disseminate information on losses elsewhere in the industry that will be useful to the business managers and staff.

One important risk assessment objective for an ORM function in a large, decentralized financial institution, then, can be to develop and disseminate guidelines or standards for risk assessment and control. This may take the form of managing a Control Self Assessment or independent risk assessment program. Another objective may consist of educating the units on the need for operational risk management in the first place. A third may include a response to the need for a "big picture" assessment of corporate issues like business disruption, executive protection, management succession, business risk concentrations, and geographic market risk exposures. But all this implies the need for the ORM function and the individuals associated with it to attain a great deal of respect enterprise-wide. For most, that means that in order to have an impact they had best earn respect by exhibiting an understanding of the business that they are in, and by focusing on risks and loss exposures that rank among the highest corporate priorities.

Clearly, the first capital adequacy requirements evolved because credit and market risks were at the top of that list. Aside from operational losses, another area that is just as critical as an opener for risk assessment discussions is the potential for loss of public confidence and reputation. Such "losses" can result from *any unmanaged* catastrophic loss, ranging from a computer disaster to a huge adverse liability judgment.

Initially, market- and credit-risk managers may have an inherent advantage in understanding the business—they are often firmly entrenched in it. The point here is that the most successful operational risk practitioners will have a working knowledge of all of the key risks (operational and financial) facing the organization in order to apply consistency in managing and financing risk. In the past, all too often a great deal of time and effort has been expended by predecessor risk functions in focusing on the relatively mundane and "inexpensive" expected-level operational risks, while the unexpected and more complex and potentially disastrous ones may have been overlooked.

Consistent with their increased involvement, the best operational risk practitioners of the future will become increasingly sophisticated in techniques of risk assessment and loss forecasting.

RISK RESPONSE

The more successful operational risk management groups will also look for opportunities to become involved in many facets of risk response, mitigation, and control. Some primary roles will include:

- Responsibility for the operational risk management committee
- Communications and risk reporting
- Design and management of an enterprise-wide operational risk management information system
- Risk capital analysis and allocations for performance measurement
- Strategic business continuity planning, especially as it relates to operational risk management

The evolution of operational risk management will demand more networked systems and more and better data on exposures and industry losses. The ORM group function will play a key role here. The objective will be better forecasts of expected, unexpected and catastrophe losses in support of more professional and credible risk management decision making. Operational risk systems will have to be designed to provide early warnings and anticipate and respond quickly to questions from senior management.

A strategic role in business continuity planning can also be very advantageous, assuming that the stature of the function is not relegated to the most junior staff in the firm. Inherent in the involvement in BCP is a need to continually reassess major exposures to loss and risk response measures. Operational risk management may have the responsibility for setting standards relative to the decentralized development of business continuity plans. In addition, the unit might serve as a facilitator and consultant in the development of these plans, as needed.

Other day-to-day roles might include:

- **New business and new venture reviews:** Assistance to the business lines in evaluating client and new business ventures from an ORM perspective to determine the firm's direct and indirect exposures.
- **Property protection and safety:** In combination with in-house resources, operational risk management will have access to manage relationships for specialty services.
- **Contract review:** Working in conjunction with business lines, legal, and other corporate staff units, as appropriate, operational risk management might play a key role in structuring major vendor lease and client agreements and contracts. The focus is on equitable risk transfer through indemnification, risk of loss, insurance, and other contract provisions.

RISK FINANCE AND INSURANCE MANAGEMENT

An important development in operational risk management at the more progressive firms is the alignment with risk finance and insurance programs. This will be a healthy evolution of the function in order to confirm the relevance of coverage. The implication is that operational risk practitioners will also need to have a broad working knowledge and understanding of risk finance and insurance programs.

COMMUNICATIONS

The inability to communicate clearly and concisely both laterally and with senior management is probably cited as the single greatest shortcoming of predecessor attempts to evolve operational risk management. Operational risk practitioners will position themselves appropriately in order to provide relevant communications at the most senior levels.

Brief but practical one-to-three year plans for ORM will be key. These plans should be shared and submitted to senior management for acceptance of their conceptual approach.

The following is intended as a sampling of options in structuring roles and responsibilities for a new or existing operational risk management group, all of which can add significant value, and may not currently be addressed by any other group in the firm.

Leadership and Facilitation Roles

- Design and implement a firmwide Quality and Excellence program (e.g., Six Sigma, ISO 9000).
- Develop firmwide policy statements on operational risk management.
- Chair an operational risk management committee or working group.
- Chair a firmwide business continuity network.
- Develop a reputation risk response program.
- Design, enhance, or support a firmwide control self-assessment program.
- Develop strategic firmwide operational risk capital attribution or allocation models.
- Design a firmwide operational risk information system, and develop specifications for technology that will be used to collect data, manage reporting, and compare and contrast business line operational risk management performance.
- Leverage the *strategic* business continuity planning portfolio efforts to support a broader mandate to include broad-based people, processes, systems, and external and reputational operational risks.

Direct Management Roles

- Develop portfolio-level quantitative risk measurement for economic risk capital and RAPM, or to determine appropriate levels of risk finance protection.
- Conduct firmwide qualitative vulnerability analysis studies.
- Manage a system of capital allocation.
- Manage a firmwide operational risk information system.
- Manage firmwide risk finance and insurance programs, including insurance, reinsurance, self-insurance, captive insurance, and capital markets programs, as well as claims.
- Allocate operational risk costs (e.g., risk finance and/or insurance, risk mitigation investments such as redundant facilities for disaster recovery)
- Coordinate the necessary data and respond to operational risk regulatory capital guidelines.

Continued

EXHIBIT 7.4 Operational Risk Management: Functional Roles and Responsibilities

Exhibit 7.4 summaries a range of functional responsibility options for the corporate role. As outlined, implications for positioning the unit can be characterized into the areas of risk assessment, risk capital calculations

■ Manage a firmwide business continuity planning program.
■ Provide senior management and board level reporting on firmwide operational risk management progress.

Consultation and Participatory Roles

■ Consult on the development and maintenance of operational risk-related firmwide policies on specific issues (e.g., intellectual capital, information security, professional standards, vendor standards, travel), linking with human resource, legal, security, and other areas.
■ Due diligence risk consulting on new business (e.g., mergers and acquisitions, new business formations).
■ Offer specialist operational risk consultation on transactions (e.g., investment banking or lending deal reviews).
■ Contract analysis on operational risk issues (e.g., development of contract standards for risk of loss, indemnity, insurance requirement), in conjunction with legal department and others.
■ Participate in firmwide risk assessment efforts as part of a formal program, or on an ad hoc basis.
■ Review individual audit reports to identify a control weakness and consult with business units on action plans.
■ Participate in various corporate committees on new business, new technologies, and special risk concerns.
■ Participate in crisis management teams.

Notes: (1) Firms will design their own operational risk management programs to include some or all of these roles and responsibilities. Similarly, firms will differ on the assignment of certain roles in the previous categories (e.g., whether a role falls in the Facilitation category, Direct Management category, or is structured as a Consultation Role). This explains why some roles are listed more than once here, in different contexts. (2) The mission of a group operational risk management unit will be reviewed at least annually to confirm that it is still appropriate and relevant for changes in the organization. In reality, the result of those reviews may not result in any sweeping changes to the mission but may cause management to reconsider the scope of individual functional responsibilities. In contrasting corporate and business unit roles, the Deutsche Bank illustration (Exhibit 7.3) also provided some insight on that firm's actual assignment of responsibilities.

EXHIBIT 7.4 Operational Risk Management: Functional Roles and Responsibilities

and allocations, development and administration of operational risk management information systems (ORMIS), communications, reporting, decentralized structures, divisional alliances, risk mitigation, and risk finance.

LEADERSHIP, ORGANIZATIONAL POSITIONING, AND REPORTING STRUCTURE

First and foremost, in view of the broad scope of the subject matter and the mission outlined here, there should be a senior and very visible manager for the group. The position must be senior enough to gain respect, with a support base provided to address firmwide priorities.

In some firms the senior officer might be the Chief Risk Officer as long as that individual has the time and perspective to devote to the function. In any event, the ultimate choice will depend on the specific mission of a given firm and the capabilities of those persons available. Organizational factors will determine the exact positioning of the function.

Locating the Operational Risk Function

The location of the operational risk function will undoubtedly influence the perception of it throughout the organization. That is, there have been cases where the function has been created with reporting responsibility to the internal auditor, as an ancillary function of Internal Audit, and as such has been viewed as just another audit activity. This can limit its scope. In other cases, where it has been aligned to a market-risk analytics function, it has been viewed solely as a risk capital analysis function. In short, the best firms will position the function where it will have the maximum scope and reach for influencing behavior and risk response decisions.

Independent Unit

The operational risk function should be established as a separate and independent discipline and unit for a number of reasons:

- Operational risk departments must promote themselves as a facilitator function. This can be accomplished easier without direct reporting or affiliation to another department with different control missions (e.g., the evaluative or supervisory role of internal audit or compliance).
- It becomes established as a separate center for resource planning, which will become more important as the group becomes more sophisticated.
- It will promote the group internally as having more significance from the perspective of senior management and will enhance buy-in for its programs and initiatives elsewhere in the firm.
- Independence can be seen as positive by external auditors and regulators (enables objective opinions, less reliant on the politics of a particular area).

- It will aid in promoting operational risk as an equally important risk category in the minds of others; this is also important as the capital allocation methodology evolves.
- The group must be objective and have a "birds eye" view of the business as a whole.

Relationship to the Financial Risk Management Function, Revisited

A key part of the challenge for an emerging ORM department remains building a companion and highly respected sibling function or global portfolio to develop financial risk management functions.

As discussed in Chapter 6, there are many good reasons to tie market-, credit-, and operational-risk groups together under a heading of group risk. For one, a consolidated function can help in the coordinated analysis of risk issues. In addition, it can promote a unified voice on risk for the firm overall.

If No Group Risk Function Exists, Then What?

The first question should probably be: Why not? In any event, if a consolidated risk function is simply not in the cards, then certainly there are many other options for positioning an operational risk management function. Reporting structures vary greatly from one firm to another around the world. A firm will have to determine its own "best fit." The factors to consider are:

- Where is the operational risk initiative being driven from (Audit, Risk, Operations, Compliance, etc.)?
- What is the political climate? Where does the support lie?
- What is the strategic growth of the department? For example, if capital attribution and allocation are the ultimate goal, would it not make sense to leverage off the modeling techniques and expertise of credit and market groups?
- Is there a risk–reward orientation for the function from the perspective of quality and Six Sigma-type programs? If so, the group could be situated almost anywhere among the executive management ranks.
- What are the objectives of the operational risk department? Some institutions merely want the operational risk function to "police" areas such as Internal Audit issue clearance. In this particular instance it may make sense for the function to report to Internal Audit. Part of the problem here is that it may be seen as an enforcer, not a facilitator.
- Where is the information flow that the operational risk group wants to tap into and exploit (e.g., loss reporting)?
- What is the risk culture at the firm? Do businesses actively consider their risk profile when approving new products and businesses?

STAFFING CONSIDERATIONS

In most firms the operational risk department will consist of more staff than the senior officer alone. The subsequent members of the team will be chosen with a view toward their fields of expertise (e.g., varied business line experiences and functional experience, such as audit, technology, legal, insurance, security). Operational risk is a very broad discipline with a huge diversity. Thus an operational risk department can benefit a great deal from different specialists on staff. Key advantages are as follows:

- It adds credibility when interfacing with and seeking buy-in from a business line if the operational risk person is fluent in the terminology and issues of the business.
- When discussing business risk drivers, risk, and loss scenarios, it is much more effective if the operational risk representative can prompt the conversation with relevant business or technical examples.
- Senior management will come to view the area as a real asset in that very few areas of a bank ever really have a holistic view with specific expertise in a number of different businesses and functions. This is key when assisting on specific projects such as merger and acquisition or new product due diligence.

CREATING VALUE WITH SCARCE RESOURCES— ADMINISTRATIVE EFFICIENCY

Last, but certainly not least, as a new function, operational risk management and operational risk professionals will have to prove their salt.[3] That is to say, there will be no fiat or assumption at the onset that a grand operational risk management function is needed beyond some base level risk assessment and regulatory risk capital compliance resources. One could certainly attempt to argue that given the risk trends and magnitude of losses at stake, any function contributing to the management of these risks should be one of the last to sacrifice resources, but there are no guarantees.

Operational risk management is critically important now more than ever, given that most firms can scarcely afford to bear unexpected losses. But in all probability, as in every other corporate function, senior management will still want to see proof of the group's worth, preferring instead to challenge operational risk professionals to "do more with less."

To the extent that there is any discrepancy between views here, it is probably one of focus, not substance. The objective should be to make routine (that is, some administrative) functions more efficient, while emphasizing the highest priorities: risk assessment and response. With that in mind, here are a few suggestions to get you started:

- Prioritize, prioritize, prioritize. . .
- Hire and retain the best, brightest, most enthusiastic, and efficient staff (albeit fewer of them)—you can't afford anything less.
- Automate more. Get started with technology as soon as possible. If time and resources are limited or nonexistent, begin with one piece at a time. Start with basics like database management. As your universe of operational risk data becomes more complex, the problems will multiply quickly.
- Don't waste time building your own external databases. At one time this might have made sense, but several are now available in the marketplace.
- Apply time management techniques that work (e.g., avoid unnecessary meetings that waste valuable time).

Above all, don't lose sight of the fact that you are working to preserve time for risk response and risk assessment activities. Be careful; the minute you or your group sacrifices this in order to have enough time to rework data collections, models, etc., you may find yourself regressing. The net stereotypical characterization could become one of suggesting that ORM is a function that is "just one more necessary corporate evil, but really out of touch with the business lines and the issues and risks of the firm." It will be critically important to maintain the proper balance such that ORM is providing maximum impact and visible added value to the business lines and firm overall.

Last, in most sectors decentralization is here to stay, along with head count pressures on corporate staff. Operational risk management functions will have to germinate and flourish in this difficult climate without the luxury of large departments. Given lean corporate staffs, there will be a need for more effective and focused use of outsiders—vended contractors and consultants—with clear direction from the clients operational risk function.

CONCLUSION

The more successful operational risk professionals today are expanding their horizons and taking on a more holistic view of the issues and their organizations. Practitioners in this group have come from a variety of disciplines, including the business units themselves. They generally believe that the most effective programs will select the best features and practices from all related disciplines. As such, they are applying performance measures and risk indicators from progressive business managers, process analysis tools from operations managers, quantitative analysis from market risk managers and risk finance/insurance risk managers, and risk assessment tools from Internal Auditors, to name just a few.[4]

Clearly an operational risk management group's own mission will be driven by the firm's vision first and foremost, then its risk management philosophy, and to a more specific extent, the ORM unit's own mission statement. There will be both a clear strategic positioning and a more tactical day-to-day role.

The unit will have at least one core role and mission. That might be the creation of a Six Sigma program, creation and/or administration of an operational risk capital system, an ORM information system, administration of a risk assessment program (control self-assessment or independent risk assessment), or some combination of these functions and others. In any event, without a core role, the unit's value will soon be questioned, and it could well become an example of corporate dead weight.

The day-to-day management of operational risks will be left to various line management teams. Thus, in forming a central operational risk management function, the natural question becomes one of delineating areas of responsibility between the central operational risk unit and line management teams.

If properly focused, staffed, resourced, and managed, the central operational risk management unit can serve not only to facilitate the operational risk response with line managers, but it can help to transform the firm into a more competitive force overall.

This new breed of operational risk management practitioner will apply the most effective tools and technology available to monitor and communicate about risk indicators, risk assessment issues, initiatives, incidents, loss events, and quantitative analysis. They are using the combination of them, like warning lights in the cockpit for the business manager/pilot, to create a more effective holistic operational risk management program. But they are not stopping with their own use. These risk practitioners have come to recognize the value of forums and technology platforms that empower risk management throughout their firm, by placing the tools and technology in the hands of scores of people firmwide, not just in the risk management department itself.[5]

LESSONS LEARNED AND KEY RECOMMENDATIONS

- Designate an Operational Risk Management Unit to Serve as a Facilitator. The best firms will form a coordinating unit for operational risk management headed by a senior manager and staffed with top talent to coordinate operational risk management efforts firmwide. In some firms the manager will head operational risk exclusively. In others, the individual may also serve as Chief Risk Officer. In any event, business units will direct their own operational risk efforts, but a separate corporate operational risk function will support and monitor their activities. In some industries (e.g., financial services), the function will be separate from Internal Audit (BP Strategy #7).

- Responsibility for operational risk management and the essential strategies will be distributed throughout the firm. Although the operational risk management department should be charged with implementing a number of the strategies, it has direct responsibility for only some of them, and indirect responsibility for many.

- The operational risk management officer position should be senior enough to be able to accomplish his or her mission, have a seat on senior risk and control committees, and the like. That would probably imply a Managing Director or Senior Vice President level in most large firms, or a minimum Vice President position in smaller ones.

- An operational risk team is best staffed by individuals with a diverse set of backgrounds. Representation of business units and backgrounds in risk analysis, financial control, legal, and Internal Audit are all important additions to the team. The goal should be to combine a variety of perspectives.

- The location of the operational risk function will undoubtedly influence the perception of it throughout the organization. Position the function where it will have the maximum scope and reach for influencing operational risk management behavior in a productive way.

CHAPTER 8

Risk Response Framework and Strategies

OUT OF PLACE?

"Isn't this chapter in the wrong place?" you ask. Every other risk management book or article text you and I have ever read has placed the subject of risk control and risk mitigation (titled Risk Response here to represent both upside and downside potential) after those of risk identification and risk assessment. So why, you might ask, are we exploring this topic before them in this book?

Well, granted, it is out of place relative to the conventional steps in the risk management process, but it is here to make an important point. Too often we delve into tools, data and analytics without establishing a proper framework. If we remind ourselves that focusing on the customer and enhancing shareholder value are our ultimate objectives, then it is only natural that our initial and primary risk management focus should be on risk mitigation and risk optimization. In essence, all of our other risk management activities should be prioritized and work to support the risk response framework. Logistically, placing risk response after all those activities in the traditional way would result in risk response being Chapter 17 of 20. That just seems like the wrong message.

Let's face it. Corporate resources will always be scarce. So in maintaining a lean and focused stance, everything else that competes for scarce resources in the risk management program should be driven off of the risk response framework. Why do risk practitioners work to identify and assess risk at all? For the simple reason that we suspect that we will find risks that are unacceptable to the organization, of course. Those risks must be targeted, addressed separately, and balanced for maximum shareholder value.

But the next question becomes, What is the most efficient and effective way to assess those risks? Why do we track losses, build databases, benchmark our performance, and model loss potential? All for the very same reason: We are seeking to assess and then balance the firm's risk profile. Stated another way, if all of those activities are not targeted toward risk response strategies, then, we should question why we are pursuing them in the first place.

Before we launch into labor-intensive and granular control self-assessment programs, extensive database construction projects, and model development, we will be clear about our framework for risk response and mitigation, our framework for the program overall, and a reasonable level of resources. This is not to play to a self-fulfilling prophecy—that is, just because we have or don't have the resources, we should or should not do all those things. Instead, it is intended to suggest that we be sure to define our risk response goals and objectives, and to frame our risk identification, assessment, and financing programs accordingly.

Most of the 20 best practice strategies are ultimately positioned to assist an organization in balancing its risk profile and enhancing shareholder value. Response to risk will flow from that process. Although this chapter will begin to provide a framework for some of the explicit risk response strategies, one should keep in mind that risk response and risk mitigation are *implied and embedded* in virtually all of the strategies that remain, even though they may not fall under a risk response heading expressly.

One last perspective on beginning with risk mitigation is this: Because the process is circular, we can actually begin at any point in the cycle. So, why not start with the most important element. We'll use this chapter as a framework for risk response to set the stage at the outset, then reevaluate it after risk assessment and risk finance.

RISK RESPONSE: WHERE THE RUBBER MEETS THE ROAD

Within the complete cycle of risk assessment, risk response and risk finance, a business management team will have at its disposal a seemingly endless list of strategies, tactics, tools, and techniques that a firm can employ in managing operational risk. Once again, they are confronted with a balancing act. Finding the right recipe for optimizing the operational risk profile of an organization requires a combination of skill and experience in dealing with people, both individually and in organizational structures.

There are a number of pieces in the risk response/mitigation puzzle that fit well together. In reality, one such piece picks up where risk assessment leaves off: self-assessment/risk assessment linked to decentralized controls, which is a very granular, low-level, individual task-level orientation. On another plane, capital attribution or allocation is a high-level look at a firm's entire risk portfolio and can be very effective when linked to incentives.[1]

Performance management with goal setting, results tracking, and risk-based incentive compensation makes it possible to attack risk at a human level. Operational-based strategic decision making, with links to the risk-control environment, is really about incentive and control on a staff level but supports a more senior level. Each one of these should be linked into an enterprise-wide operational risk effort; none of these should be considered to operate independently of the others.[2]

In the end, the most important factor in designing an effective risk mitigation framework is setting an overall coordinated strategy. Then, it involves knowing what might work and what probably will not, given your firm's management style and culture, and knowing when to apply each of them. Generally, risk management success is often a function of the Latin phrase — *carpe diem* (seize the day). Seizing opportunities to promote a risk aware culture, to install features of risk management programs, to improve the organization during and as a result of managing crises, all serve to achieve risk management success.

MANAGEMENT TECHNIQUES: HARD AND SOFT RISK RESPONSE STRATEGIES

The challenge here is that successful risk response, mitigation and/or optimization are much more art than science. One reason is that we are dealing with people and human behavior, of course. So before we get too deeply into the details of risk response, it is worth taking another moment to step back to look at the bigger picture. We have already discussed the importance of an accommodating corporate ideology, a quality-driven and customer-focused culture, and leveraging or creating risk awareness in the culture. Admittedly, all of these strategies speak to a softer side of risk management that is difficult to pin down. They also serve as recognition that the process of response is another one of the balancing acts that we face in risk management.

By now, management theorists and practicing managers alike have had considerable time to cogitate on and experiment with Douglas McGregor's work and theories on management and employee behavior—titled Theory X and Theory Y. Generally speaking, Theory X suggested that most people are inherently lazy, do not want to work, and prefer direction to self-direction. In contrast, Theory Y suggested that given the right opportunity and conditions, most people want to work, want to take pride in their jobs, prefer to participate in the decision-making process, and can help to find creative solutions to problems in the workplace if given the opportunity.[3] As it turns out, these theories have some interesting application in risk management as well.

Theory X has always been evident in operational risk management discussions, and for that matter risk management discussions generally. The very reference to risk mitigation under the heading *risk control* implies more structure in the "Command and Control" sense, and less of a trusting environment. Perhaps this phenomenon is embedded in the part of operational risk management that has evolved from auditing functions. But in any event the title implies that the best way to control risk is to control the people who create it—whether those people are traders, lenders, clerks, or other managers.

In contrast, Theory Y, and the more recent introduction of Theory Z, might imply that the rigid command and control tactics of risk management should be balanced with the softer side of management, as well. Theory Z was introduced by William Ouchi in the 1980s and argues for a more democratic empowerment in management circles in the 1980s and 1990s. This alternative perspective is characteristic of both Theories Y and Z.[4] Exhibit 8.1 is an interpretation of the risk response in the context of all three of these key management theories.

Since the time that McGregor introduced his theories in the 1960s, there has been a belief that between Theory X and Theory Y the latter was certainly the preferred approach. No manager wanted to be perceived as all controlling and nontrusting of his or her employees. And as the 1960s gave way to the 1970s, 1980s, 1990s, and a new century, theories of empowerment were truly taking hold. When the New Economy dawned in the later half of the 1990s, *The Wall Street Journal,* in one of its workplace columns in June 2000, actually declared that the military style of Command and Control management is dead in business today. They implied that managers had better get with it because the new workforce is virtually (no pun intended) in the driver's seat now.[5] Interestingly enough, a mere six months later a January 30, 2001 *Wall Street Journal* article, "Managers Are Starting to Gain More Clout Over Their Employees," opened with the statement "Suddenly bosses have the upper hand again."[6] The point here is not to suggest that one article is right and the other wrong, but simply to point out the rate of change in thinking, and that balance and flexibility are certainly important. Whichever style is in vogue, a blend of management (in this case, risk management) styles is key.

Recent history certainly has proven the value of empowerment and responsibility at some of the most successful firms. These softer management methods should flow through to driving responsibility and empowerment for risk management as well. But there is also still an important place for Theory X risk control. Since its introduction, application of this theory had always been thought to make sense in many routine functions, such as back office processing and money transfer, but there is a larger consideration in which it remains very relevant in banking and finance as well. In short, as we have seen time and time again, greed is a very powerful motivating force that must be kept in check.

Unfortunately the "less trusting" controls of Theory X are necessary in banking and finance to serve as a counterbalance at all levels in the organization. For instance, when the infamous Barings demise is discussed, the name Nick Leeson first comes to mind. But the loss investigation actually showed that senior management and the board of directors back in London

Theory	Description	Risk Response Implication
McGregor's Theory X	• Hard management style • People do not like to work • People require a rigid management structure to be effective • Managers must motivate and energize staff • People do not want responsibility	• People find risk management boring, they do not like to think about it, and must be pressured into thinking about control gaps and ways to strengthen risk management and controls • Often evidenced in routine functions (e.g., wire transfer key entry), but has real implications for trading environments as well
McGregor's Theory Y	• Soft management style • More participative in nature; managers share decision making with staff members • Work is like play; people are creative and eager to work • People respond to responsibility	• Implies that when presented with the risk management opportunity (risk/reward), they will participate and get involved in finding creative solutions to risk problems/opportunities
Ouchi's Theory Z	• A blend of strict American management style (Theory A) and Japanese style (Theory J) • Company will value family, cultures, and traditions • Workers can be trusted to perform to their ability, have discipline and a moral obligation to work hard • Features job rotation, broadening of skills, generalization over specialization, continuous training of workers	• Employees and business lines can be trusted to manage their own risks as a natural part of their roles and responsibilities • Employees and business units can be trusted to control risks on their own (e.g., control self-assessment (CSA) programs)
Peters' & Blanchard on Empowerment	• Redesign roles and job descriptions to allow for more decision making by individuals	• Business lines will identify and manage their own risks • Support for employees' recognition of risk and CSA, again

EXHIBIT 8.1 Management Theories and Risk Management Implications

were well aware that something out of the ordinary was going on, and in all probability that the risks being taken were at least commensurate with, if not well in excess of, market gains. Yet rather than stop the process, they rolled the dice, and out of greed "bet the House" on the trades that Leeson was making. It is for actions such as these that Theory X remains relevant at *all* levels in firms. Thus, when the powerful human emotions of fear and greed are involved, harder controls are key.

THE RISK RESPONSE BEST PRACTICE STRATEGIES

In studying some of the most successful companies, and combining the results with original work in risk management, we have observed that there is an interesting blend of hard and soft principles that will be applied. The hard side gets a lot of airtime, as it should. Greed is a powerful force. Whether an individual is being motivated directly into unauthorized activities or dishonesty for direct personal gain or indirectly to cut corners in striving for incentive compensation, hard controls are often necessary.

"I think risk professionals often put too much emphasis on the 'hard side' of risk management, such as risk policies, systems and reports. We need to place more emphasis on the 'softer side' of risk management, such as people, culture, values, accountability and incentives." Such was a quote from James Lam in October 1987, then chief risk officer for Fidelity investments, now CEO of eRisks, the on-line risk management portal.[7] While I agree with his premise that this statement is appropriate in risk management generally, I think it has particular relevance to operational risk management because the element of human behavior is so dominant here.

There are other factors to consider, as well. Let's revisit our discussion of trends and changes in the marketplace that drive operational risks from Chapter 3. One must also consider the opposing forces of the excitement and pressures of today's high stakes market environment and the personal career risk and uncertainty, which drive the need to attract, retain, and motivate the people best suited to cope. Balance this, however, with the counterbalancing need to maintain a culture of high professional standards. It is a difficult combination, at best, and one that requires balanced risk management leadership from the top down and throughout the organization.[8]

True to our premise about creating an equilibrium, risk response strategies will range from those that represent the softer side of risk management, or those that fit Theory Y and Z strategies such as corporate integrity, incentives, and capabilities, to those that are much "harder" and tangible in nature (Theory X), such as process controls, diligence, and legal risk management. If one were to categorize risk response strategies, several groups emerge. Following is the range of important management principles that serve as our foundation for risk response strategies:

1. Enhanced corporate integrity franchise and reputation risk management
2. Enhanced management reporting information and tools
3. Incentives and disincentives
4. Diversification and segregation of processes and assets
5. Controls, diligence, and legal risk management
6. Business continuity defenses

These principles have already proven their worth in numerous successful companies. However, it is encouraging to note that they already exist to one degree or another in most firms, so risk practitioners should look for opportunities to target and leverage them further. For our purposes here, we will use them as an important backdrop and integral addition to our list of operational risk management Best Practice Strategies. We explore them individually and more fully as follows.

CORPORATE INTEGRITY, FRANCHISE, AND REPUTATION RISK MANAGEMENT

These principles were significant enough to merit strategies of their own. See Chapter 4 for a full discussion of corporate ideology, vision, integrity, franchise, and reputation risk.

MANAGEMENT REPORTING: INFORMATION AND TOOLS

Management cannot focus in the absence of useful information. When well-conceived and positioned, risk information can be a powerful motivating force. Thus, BP Strategy #8 involves the development and distribution of useful information about risks and risk mitigation opportunities at numerous levels throughout the organization.

Operational risk practitioners should seize the opportunity presented by the need for periodic management reporting. Whether performance-based systems are in place or not, the best firms will develop and provide senior management and line management information on the state of operational risks and operational risk management firmwide.

Management information can range from simple data displays to more complex reports:

■ **Simple Operational Risk and Loss Data Displays as Mitigation Tools:** Simply aggregating operational risk management information system (MIS) data, drawn from numerous sources throughout an organization, aggregated and/or reformatted in useful ways, can provide valuable aids to senior management. For day-to-day management at a business line level, business managers can use MIS to get to more efficient targeting

BP STRATEGY #8 — DISSEMINATE USEFUL OPERATIONAL RISK MANAGEMENT INFORMATION AND REPORTS

Provide clear, useful, and actionable information about operational risks, losses, and the status of risk response and control efforts such that managers and staff firmwide are in a position to manage them on a day-to-day basis.

of risk assessment risk-indicator tracking, risk-class concentration, and support risk analysis. Armed with these data, managers can monitor their business better, reduce losses, and reward the staff accordingly.[9]

- **Sophisticated Risk Reporting as a Mitigation Tool:** One simple and clear way to see a firm's risk profile is to apply risk-index techniques by business line and across the entire firm. More complex reporting applications will include calculating an overall risk profile and capital adequacy.[10]

Responsibility and Accountability

In either case, the data and reports should be aligned with business units consistent with ownership and responsibility for operational risk management throughout the firm.

The best firms already maintain performance summary reports by business unit. These summary reports are developed and distributed on a regular basis, then discussed in logical forums, such as at senior and executive management meetings. With performance reports as a background, some chief executives seek to create a sense of competition between their business unit managers. The better ones do not limit this competition to bottom line results alone. They find it particularly effective to create a competitive spirit around other factors, such as the results of risk management and control efforts, internal audit findings, incident and loss reporting, due diligence relative to meeting firmwide standards for internal control, business continuity planning, and the like.

The dissemination of information about operational risk and operational risk management should not end with reports to senior and line managers, however. The firm should get its employee population-at-large involved and focused on key risks. The range of audiences should include:

- Board level
- Executive management
- Business line managers
- Profit center unit managers
- Select committees
- Newsletters to the employee population-at-large (e.g., orientation training, articles in employee communications, and electronic newsletters)

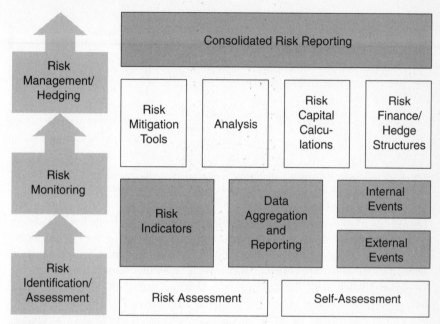

EXHIBIT 8.2 Building Blocks for Integrated Operational Risk Management

In essence, management reporting needs set the stage for much of the work undertaken by risk practitioners and the design of integrated ORM programs. Exhibit 8.2 illustrates this concept. At the top of the figure we show management reporting. Below it are some of the tools and analyses needed to drive the reporting.

For now, we will focus our attention on the management information *needs and priorities* in this regard. Later in Chapter 12 and beyond we elaborate on the implications of those information needs for reporting, data interpretation, and risk measurement. In Chapter 13 we will explore some samples of the individual report types. In other words, some of the reports described here will make much more sense as we move on to consider the data flows, analytics required, and provide samples.

Following is a sampling of categories of useful reports and management information:

- Consolidated dashboard or heat map risk profile
- Individual risk indicator reporting
- Risk indicator composite views
- Customized risk index
- Key risk driver analysis

- Issue tracking system and management reports
- Risk management initiative and/or project tracking
- Causal analysis predictor report
- Incident and loss displays
- Incident trends and forecasts
- Loss forecasts
- Risk monitoring during threshold events
- Economic risk capital analysis and reports
- Regulatory risk capital analysis and reports
- Cost of operational risk (COOR) reports
- Risk finance/insurance decision reports
- Risk mitigation reports

This series of management reports will serve as a useful basis for discussion and action. Exhibit 8.3 is a description of each in terms of the key information needed or questions that might likely have prompted it, which are then aligned to the most appropriate audience. The exhibit shows that much can be accomplished with the basic data and some simple mathematics alone. Many of the individual reports, data needs, and implied analytics shown are self-explanatory from the exhibit. Later, a logical place to begin our discussion of risk measurement and risk profiling will be this Management Reporting and Decision Tools Matrix.

Feeling overwhelmed yet? The next natural question in a world of information overload becomes, which are the highest priority issues and areas for risk reporting, especially given that both line and senior managers are already overburdened with information flow? Couple this with the practical reality that the operational risk management team may have just recently been formed. Alternatively, it may have been formed, but it is more than likely already overwhelmed, understaffed, and under-resourced. In short, focus and efficiency are key.

With all of this in mind, in the short term the operational risk team can be more targeted perhaps on risk assessment summaries, incident and loss reporting, and on some basic forward-looking indicators. In the intermediate term the team will focus on evolving toward providing as close to the full list of reports as soon as reasonably possible.

It is important, however, to provide a broad perspective on operational risk management to the audience (i.e., as many of these reports as possible), even if they are not yet backed by highly sophisticated analysis. For example, it would be more important to present some rudimentary loss presentations and simplified projections, along with presentations of outstanding risk issues, risk assessment findings, and compilations of incidents, than to focus solely on a highly sophisticated and detailed loss analysis (i.e., retro-

Classification of Management Report and Tools:
- Business Line Tools (B), Risk Measurement Tools (RMT), Capital Attribution/Allocation Report (C)
- Dynamic Monitoring and Management Tool (MM) or One-time Decision Tool (D)

Management Need and Implied Reporting	Key Audience, Question, and Further Description
1. **Consolidated Risk Profile Dashboard,** including Indexes for Indicators, Issues, Incidents, and Losses (B,MM)	BL (Business Line) Manager, BL risk manager, Operational Risk Management Officer, CRO, CFO.
Ongoing monitoring need, with view toward identifying operational risk "hot spots" in the organization. Use a "heat map" construct. Monitoring might take the form of monitoring staff or system adequacy, efficiency, etc. Decisions might involve the reallocation of resources, the need for new technology investments, the need to investigate errors, or the need to apply additional control processes.	Different levels/different views. Wants to monitor "near real time" individual indexes for indicator, issues, incidents, and losses by profit center, by business, enterprise-wide, by risk class, or by his or her own risk categories to be defined by user. Wants to drill down on component parts.
2. **Risk Assessment Tracking (B,MM)** To monitor the status of business line risk identification and assessment, control self-assessment and other similar efforts.	Senior business line and corporate managers, risk management staff, and others.
3. **Individual Risk Indicator Report and Monitoring (B,MM)** To track one or a handful of key risk and/or performance indicators to maximize the business' efficiency and minimize loss costs. Implies: Ongoing monitoring of one individual indicator by a unit manager (e.g., error rates, turnover rates, or customer complaints against certain tolerance levels). Probably rare that a single indicator graph would be used, except against a goal. Chances are better that a table might be used.	Manager at any level in the organization might want this feature. Useful for business managers, risk managers, corporate area managers (HR, audit, risk), or operational risk committees.

Continued

EXHIBIT 8.3 Sample Management Reporting Needs: Description and Audience

4. Risk Indicator Composite Reviews (B,MM) To pinpoint risk predictors for improved management performance.	Key Question: Is there a combination of risk indicators that might serve as a predictor of certain risks or losses?
5. Customized Risk Index (indicator index) creation (B,MM) To monitor special indexes meaningful to certain business lines or sectors, or of use in firm's peer group for benchmarking purposes.	Key Questions: What are the telltale signs of **operational stress**? What risk indicators should be included in an operational stress index? A standard risk index dashboard will produce indexes business by business and by risk class (people, relationship, technology, assets, and external), however. . . Many more areas are to be addressed here.
6. Key Risk Indicator (Driver) Analysis (B,D) Individual client managers would prefer to track and manage only a handful of indicators, not hundreds, for his or her business.	Key Question: What are the most important operational risk indicators or drivers? Managers will want to determine which risk indicators are most important predictors of operational risk and will want to apply 80/20 rule to risk indicator data capture and monitoring.
7. "Issue Display" and Management Report (B,MM) Managers must minimize the number of outstanding risk issues (e.g., self-assessment, audit, regulatory, and other known risk issues and circumstances for their areas).	Business manager or risk manager wants to track outstanding audit, technology, compliance, or other risk issues for his or her business line, profit center, etc. Who is responsible? What is the deadline? The status?
8. Risk Management Initiative (Project) Tracking (B,MM) Need to track the status of certain new risk management investments (e.g., a newly automated process, such as straight through processing [STP], or a new control process).	Manager wants to use an event-oriented application to track the status of investment in risk reduction initiatives (e.g., STP system).

EXHIBIT 8.3   Sample Management Reporting Needs: Description and Audience

9. Causal Analysis Predictor Report (B,D) Desire to monitor combinations (series) of circumstances that can give rise to losses. Probably most useful in operations or processing environments.	Key Question: Can a firm determine the probable outcome of a series of business decisions (e.g., reduction in staff, training expenditures, increase in transaction volume, etc.)?
10. Incident Displays (B,MM) Management is concerned about any concentrations of incident frequencies that might be developing in a certain product area, process or operations processing unit (e.g., FX).	Key Questions: Is there a certain type of incident that is occurring in the business more frequently than others? What are the top five most frequent incident types?
11. Incident Trends and Forecast Needs (D, RMT) See item 10. Management is concerned about the trends of incident frequencies that might be developing in a certain product area, process, or operations processing unit (e.g., FX).	Key Question 1: Where is incident trend headed, by incident type? Key Question 2: Can we identify any specific risk indicators that might cause an acceleration of that trend?
12. Loss Forecasting (D, RMT) Management wants a forecast of losses by type and/or in the aggregate (1) by business unit, (2) by product line, or (3) firmwide. Information might be used in product pricing decisions at the product or business level, for reserve decision making, or for risk finance/insurance decision making.	Operational Risk Officers (corporate and business level); Operational Risk Committee; CRO Key Question: What is the loss potential firmwide or by area?
13. Monitoring Risk During Threshold Events (B,MM) Need to monitor the potentially heightened state of operational risk during mergers, acquisitions, management changes, restructurings, and the like.	Key Question: What information will be available to support management during change (merger, aquisiton, integration, reorganization), or a crisis?

Continued

EXHIBIT 8.3 Sample Management Reporting Needs: Description and Audience

14. Economic Risk Capital Analyses and Reports (RMT,C,D) Need to determine the possible impact of operational losses on the firm's capital base.	Senior management and the corporate risk management function is the probable user/audiences. In the short term, however, there is minimal consensus on approach.
15. Regulatory Risk Capital Analysis and Reports (RMT,C,D) Need to produce a periodic report on risk capital required by regulatory supervisors. Many firms will want to pilot some analyses in anticipation of new regulatory requirements.	Numerous possibilities exist here too, although for many firms probable short-term result will be a simple calculation using some revenue, expense, headcount, transaction, and/or other high-level data.
16. Cost of Operational Risk Reports (MM,RMT) Corporate management will need to understand the overall cost of operational risk to the organization. This will be a key program metric.	Analysis implies the capture of (1) firm's total of operational losses by accounting period, (2) expenditures on insurance, reinsurance, other risk finance (RF), (3) control investments, and (4) insurance/RF recoveries.
17. Risk Finance/Insurance Decision Reports (D) Need to determine whether the client organization is purchasing the right combination of insurance/risk financing.	Key Question: What percentage of industry losses would be covered by the firm's own risk finance/insurance program?
18. Risk Response Reports (B,MM) Need to monitor the status of certain risk mitigation efforts — various types. Example: Business Continuity Planning Status Report.	Key aspects would involve descriptions of the effort, cost/benefit summary, business unit, and persons responsible and dates.

EXHIBIT 8.3   Sample Management Reporting Needs: Description and Audience

spective view) in isolation. In other words, it is more important to present a multidimensional view of operational risk, even if the analytics and reports are somewhat rudimentary but reasonably accurate, in their initial stages, than it is to provide a detailed view of only one dimension of operational risk.

CASE ILLUSTRATION

Operational RAROC Communications-Forum and Media

Bankers Trust

The global diversity of Bankers Trust required us to use a wide forum and various media to communicate the objectives and progress on Operational RAROC to business managers and to other interested parties, such as our Management Committees and the Board of Directors.[11]

A communication strategy was developed that outlined the objectives for each phase and subphase of our risk capital effort, the primary and secondary method of communication, the target audience, and the time frame in which to accomplish each objective. The strategy was based on the firm's culture of senior managers' desire to participate in the development of firmwide risk management initiatives.

The media used to implement the communication strategy included:

- One-on-one meetings with multiple levels of business line management at all major firm locations
- Presentations to major business line committees
- Monthly memos highlighting each business line's amount of attributed risk capital and financial performance sent via e-mail
- Hard copy and e-mail copied reports distributed to the firm's senior business line management, risk management, and controller contacts
- Audio or video conferencing with staff located outside New York (home office location)
- Hard copy reporting and presentations to various management committees, and aggregated into Corporate Risk Management reports to the board (including market, credit, and operational risk information)
- Integration with risk finance and insurance reports to senior management and the board (e.g., operational risk data included in Cost-of-Operational Risk calculations)

■ ■ ■

INCENTIVES AND DISINCENTIVES FOR RISK MANAGEMENT

BP Strategy #9 is one of the most important. It strives to create and promote incentives for risk management throughout the firm. There are a variety of tools, techniques, and activities that can be taken to provide this support and leverage existing processes and function on both a business unit and an individual basis.

BP STRATEGY #9—USE INCENTIVES AND DISINCENTIVES IN MANAGING OPERATIONAL RISK

Use incentives *and* disincentive systems as a means to balance strategic risk and reward. For instance, use risk-adjusted performance measures (RAPM), such as economic capital allocation or attribution processes to highlight operational risk intensive businesses. Provide both incentives and disincentives for management of risk. Use capital as a means to optimize risk and reward.

Far too often risk management only focuses on negatives, and thus risk managers fall in the trap of penalizing staff and units for risks identified, poor performance, and loss results. The most effective programs balance this with a system of rewards for productive risk management behavior and investment by both business and corporate units and staff alike. Some examples might include reduction of risk through upgrades in systems or manual processes, enhanced issue tracking systems, and timely clearance of self-identified risk issues or issues identified by internal audit.

- **Reward Business Units for Effective Risk Management Investment and Progress:** There are several tactics here that work. They include risk capital systems, action tracking systems, and best practices tracking. Again, we want to provide real incentives, not just disincentives.
- **Capital Attribution or Allocation:** The advent of risk-based capital systems can be a key focal point in creating incentives for productive operational risk management behavior. Unfortunately, most first phase attempts at creating such systems primarily result in creating system disincentives. That is, the programs serve primarily to penalize business units by assigning incremental capital amounts for risks that are identified and measured.
- **Incentives for Risk Issues Outstanding:** Develop an incentive system for clearing outstanding risk issues. It is common to maintain tracking systems in internal audit departments for control issues that have been identified through internal audits. These systems may be expanded to provide economic capital relief for clearing operational risk issues more broadly, including but not limited to control self-assessment issues and risk assessment issues.
- **Risk Mitigation Investment Tracking:** Monitoring management investments toward risk mitigation (e.g., technology, processes) can provide additional information about a firm's risk profile, especially when distilled into data displays. This is beneficial for:
  - Highlighting the upside of operational risk management
  - Highlighting best practices

- Assigning credits to risk aware or proactive units
- Creating links to incentive compensation systems
- Example: implementation of a proactive risk management action tracking system

■ **Provide Appropriate Individual Incentives:** Beyond focusing on business units as consolidated entities, the effective incentive-based risk management strategy will include features that influence individual behavior. For instance, it is generally insufficient to attribute or allocate capital to a business unit alone, particularly if there is no trickle down effect from the unit to the individual. On the other hand, if incentive compensation (e.g., bonus distributions) is made or at least influenced by returns on risk capital, an individual will feel its effect, and chances are good that the system will get his or her attention.

Specific individual incentives will be addressed in staff training, goal setting, incentive compensation, and in aligning interests with shareholders, as follows:

- **Staff Training:** Organizations would do well to reassess the adequacy of product and service training on a periodic and continual basis. This training should include, but not be limited to, an understanding of risk and reward. Employees that are ill prepared for their roles and responsibilities can hardly be expected to manage the risk of their day-to-day operations effectively.
- **Goal Setting as a Mitigation Tool:** The best firms use performance measures to modify behavior. By setting goals and benchmarks to help manage risk-indicator trends, organizations can mitigate risk. For example, this will involve setting goals for risk issue clearance. Audit, technology, compliance, and regulatory issues may have been identified and need to be addressed and cleared. To the extent that they are known but have not been cleared, they are an inherent risk to the firm.[12]
- **Use Incentive Compensation as a Motivator:** Build operational risk considerations into incentive-based compensation plans in order to assure that staff members are focused on optimizing operational risk on a day-to-day basis.

Referring back to our primary objective of creating value, a key principle of value creation in a firm is to create or modify the compensation system such that people at all levels of the firm are motivated to contribute.[13] That should include risk reduction and optimization. From an incentive standpoint, some techniques can include polling corporate control and risk management functions on outstanding operational risk management achievements prior to annual bonus reviews and awards. These could include the development of a new issue tracking process or improvement of a procedure that has caused problems in the past involving either customers or transaction processing. The individuals involved can be recognized and rewarded publicly. Conversely, the firm might punish individuals responsible for deleterious actions concerning operational risk and loss.

■ **Align Employee and Shareholder Interests:** The firm should be seeking an alignment between employees and shareholders as a means to promote a risk awareness and productive risk management behavior. The alignment between employee and shareholder is particularly evident when employees are awarded shares or stock options. Then they are more likely to discuss openly their views on various decisions that might impact shareholders. For instance, some of the better managers are prone to say in meetings, "You are all shareholders, what do you think?" or by saying, "Answer the question as though you are spending your own money."

Few would argue with the power of carefully crafted incentives that gain attention and commitment to a cause. Unfortunately, all too often once a system is in place human nature causes people to assess an incentive system and focus more time and energy on figuring out ways to play the game. The incentives often drive people to play for maximum result rather than focus on the objective at hand. Clearly a system has limited value, or perhaps no value whatsoever, and may even work to its detriment when the entire employee population is focused on playing the game. The trick here, of course, is in achieving genuine commitment, as opposed to the creation of an incentive gaming system.

DIVERSIFICATION AND SEGREGATION OF PROCESSES AND ASSETS

BP Strategy #10 involves the simple principles of diversification and segmentation. Concentration of risk and concentration of power too often set the stage for large-scale operational losses. We have seen this time and time again, from the Barings debacle in the context concentration of process and the lack of segregation of duties, to large-scale physical asset disasters where a firm has concentrated its data processing, trading, or back office processes at a single location. On the face of it such concentrations appear to have been a wise move from the standpoint of efficiency; however, these firms are running a significant operational risk in the event of misdeeds by those with concentrations of control, authority, or power. Similarly, relative to physical asset and physical locations, firms concentrating their operations into a single process or at a single location run the risk that an event might disrupt their entire business. In essence, firms must work to create diversification by location, business, and product and implement reasonable backup facilities.

BP STRATEGY #10—EMPLOY SEGREGATION AND DIVERSIFICATION STRATEGIES

Pursue high-level diversification techniques to combat the potentially catastrophic effects of process. Reinforce diversification and segregation of duties in critical processes. Balance risk and reward in diversification of physical asset concentrations.

CASE ILLUSTRATION

Physical Concentrations—Trading, IT, and Processing Operations

There are often compelling synergistic business reasons to locate all traders, information technology (centralized data processing), settlement operations, or key data processing operations at a single location. Events during the 1990s to date, however, have elevated concerns over the long-tail (i.e., highly improbable, but potential devastating) risk of concentration of property, technology, people, and key business drivers all in one building. Events in major cities like London and New York introduced several risks that have elevated concern over the concentration of property, technology, and people—a financial firm's most important asset.

One reality risk is terrorism. Although terrorism has been a sad reality in London, Europe, and elsewhere for some time, it is a newer phenomenon on U.S. soil. Analysis of the major bombings that have taken place in London, most notably the Bishopsgate bombing in 1992, showed the devastation that a bomb can cause to surrounding buildings (i.e., building contents were literally blown out of the opposite side of buildings nearby). In that case, Londoners were fortunate that the bomb had been detonated after business hours.

New York and Washington, D.C. were not nearly as fortunate during the terrorist attacks of September, 2001. In addition to the horrendous loss of life and destruction of the World Trade Center (WTC) itself in New York, surrounding buildings were severely impacted as well (the attacks took place between 8:45 and 9:15 AM on a business day). Whether impacted directly or indirectly by a large-scale disaster, should a firm concentrate its key operations, it faces the reality of a long-tail event of this nature during business hours and stands to risk its entire operation, and possibly some key staff (e.g., key traders, relationship managers, corporate executives). Since the Bishopsgate bombing and the original 1993 WTC bombing, a typical operational risk management move has included the decision to outfit a second facility (e.g., trading floor) in a separate location and configure the two such that they could serve as partial backup locations to one another. Another option is to configure a second location with prewired and partially equipped expansion space to serve as a backup. In short, segregation and diversification are just as important in operational risk as they are in any other area of risk management.

■ ■ ■

CASE ILLUSTRATION

The Segregation of Duties Rule

Exhibit 8.4 describes the Barings case in which rogue trading activities were free to occur because of a lack of segregation of duties. One key lesson here, of course, is to enforce segregation of duties control standards, especially where large values are concerned.

Barings PLC

Barings PLC, a venerable institution with roots going back 233 years, suffered a catastrophic loss of $1.3 billion in February, 1995 that has become a benchmark for operational risk.

The loss was larger than the bank's entire capital base and reserves, and created an extreme liquidity crisis. Barings was forced to declare bankruptcy and was later purchased by the Dutch bank ING for the token amount of one pound sterling, and an agreement to assume the fallen bank's substantial debts. The event shook the world's financial markets, and ultimately led to an increased awareness on the part of banks, trading houses, and regulatory agencies of inherent operational risks. Nick Leeson, a 28-year-old trader with Baring Futures Singapore . . . a trader from a humble background who had emerged as a star in the rough and tumble derivatives world, was given a great deal of latitude by Barings' management. He had worked in Singapore since 1992 and had registered significant profits on Barings' books by betting on the future direction of the Nikkei index.

No one looked very closely at the nature of Leeson's profits either because derivative trades appeared too exotic to be understood in the early 1990s, or because management was thrilled to register Leeson's gains and did not care to investigate further. Instead of generating substantial profits, . . . (Leeson) was [in fact] losing money. (He) . . . was able to hide these losses in a special account that he controlled. He was violating a central tenant of good operational risk practices: lack of dual controls and checks and balances. He was the acting settlement manager for both the back and front office, and was able to hide his accumulating losses for more than two years. It is speculated that Leeson was given these dual duties by Barings as a "cost cutting measure." And while Leeson continued with his "charade" he was pulling in over a million dollars in salary and bonus payments annually. By

Continued

EXHIBIT 8.4 Lack of Segregation of Duties and Dual Controls

December 1994, with $512 million in losses already under his belt, he bet heavily on Tokyo's stock index. When it did not rise as expected, and Japan's post-bubble economy continued on its downward path, Leeson continued to buy Japanese futures contracts. The country was recovering from the devastating Kobe earthquake, and he had bet that the rebuilding effort would help boost its economy. Instead, Japan's economy continued to head downwards. Over a period of three months Leeson had bought more than 20,000 futures contracts in hopes he would recoup his accumulating losses. Three-quarters of the $1.3 billion that Barings eventually lost can be traced to these trades.

While Leeson is the obvious culprit in this fiasco, Barings' management [was] also responsible. An internal memo circulated two years before its collapse warned of the dangers involved with having Leeson manage both the front and back office settlement process. The Monetary Authority of Singapore (MAS) also cautioned Barings about the inherent dangers of this arrangement. There is no record of the bank having acted on this information. In fact, it continued to finance Leeson's trades. Barings' losses have left the world a noteworthy legacy in the form of "lessons learned" and the emerging attentiveness to operational risk issues. The general sentiment in the banking community is that a Barings type event will happen "never again."

EXHIBIT 8.4 Lack of Segregation of Duties and Dual Controls
Reprinted with permission from Zurich IC Squared First Database

■ ■ ■

More generally, there are some ongoing methods that can be taken to provide support for the diversification and segregation of processes and assets:

■ **Limit Relative Size of Any Single Exposure:** An important example of this type of analysis is to gain an understanding of the exposure a firm has to physical/environmental disaster at any single location. The classic concentration of exposure illustrations in the 1970s and 1980s involved centralized data processing facilities. Today, similar risks exist in concentrated trading floor and processing facilities.
■ **Develop Portfolio of Exposures:** Monitor/map revenue and income streams against different types of operational risks to make certain that no undesirable concentrations of risk develop. Specifically, a firm may seek to map net income streams by type of operational risk, or by geographical or locational exposure.

CONTROLS, DILIGENCE, AND LEGAL RISK MANAGEMENT

We already introduced the BP Strategy of reinforcing existing risk control programs and resources. The heading of controls, diligence, and legal risk

BP STRATEGY #6, REDUX — SUPPORT AND LEVERAGE CORPORATE UNITS' CAPABILITIES AND CONTRIBUTIONS

Define roles and responsibilities of corporate units firmwide. Structure operational risk-management programs such that they reinforce key aspects of existing control and risk management programs, including but not limited to those of Control, Self-assessment, Internal Audit, Compliance, Legal, Security, and other risk management functions. Support and leverage their contributions. Avoid redundancy of effort. Corporate risk management and risk control-oriented units should be aligned and coordinated in such a way as to maximize their contribution.

management refers to the risk control infrastructure already in place to review, assess, and enhance control processes on a day-to-day basis. As introduced in Chapter 6, the ORM program should be designed to support and leverage these processes and functions. This section offers some specific tactics to that end.

There are a variety of specific activities that can be taken. Some examples follow:

- **Control Self-Assessment or Independent Risk Assessment:** A program of self-assessments by individual business units will be developed, with standards, from a corporate team whether it be from group operational risk or internal audit. Alternatively, the firm may choose ongoing risk assessments by an independent group, in conjunction with business units.
- **Due Diligence and Assessment of New or Existing Risks:** An effective process for review of new business proposals by various control groups should be in place and monitored on an ongoing basis. For each review, generally a representative from the control groups will be designated as responsible for coordinating the operational risk analysis (i.e., collecting the comments and findings of all groups). The process will be reviewed in a senior management forum.
- **Leverage Internal Audit:** The firm's operational risk effort will maximize the impact of the internal audit department, and its reviews, at a minimum. This can be achieved by a variety of means, including the use of scorecards and/or allocation of operational risk capital based on the relative ranking of the units on a risk-adjusted basis.
- **Action Tracking and Scoring System:** As referenced in the incentives section, develop and use a system to monitor outstanding risk issues (e.g., internal audit, regulatory) actively, communicating their status and length of time outstanding to senior management teams on a regular basis. Some

firms have found it effective to use such a system as a basis to include outstanding, and especially delinquent items, within any special area of operational risk economic capital charges.

■ **Use Legal Structures to Control Liability:** The best firms are proactive in the use of corporate structure (e.g., separate subsidiaries) and other forms of limited liability to provide flexibility and protection in the event of operational legal liability. An ongoing review of such structures will include an evaluation of guarantees and obligations within the firmwide system.

BUSINESS CONTINUITY DEFENSES

BP Strategy #11 recognizes the singular relevance of business continuity management. In Chapter 6 we explored the relevance of aligning the business continuity framework, function and roles, here we expand upon relevance and explore key steps in the process.

As a practical matter, business disruption should be one of the key concepts embedded in any definition of operational risk. It is interesting that the Basel Risk Management Committee did not pick up on this nuance in its adopted definition. In practice, the distinction between simply a "risk of loss" and a "risk of business disruption and loss" is an important one. The former implies no solution. The latter implies that we can leverage a business process already in place to manage some of these risks: strategic business continuity planning (BCP) programs.

There are a number of interesting parallels between the task of building a business continuity planning function and rolling out an enterprise-wide operational risk management program. For one, the two are focused on many of the same risks. What is more, for the sake of cost efficiency business continuity management programs already exist in most firms and will be leveraged by the best ones for operational risk management on a larger scale. For this reason, in this section we will explore the component parts of effective business continuity programs.

We must make an important distinction here, however, between a business continuity or contingency planning effort that is focused primarily on physical events and loss (fire, flood, earthquake) and one that is focused on those, plus strategic business issues. The latter would include the risk of loss involving disruption of systems, unauthorized activities, risk of loss to reputation, and the like. From an operating standpoint, it is critical to remain vigilant for disruptive factors and have in place a structure to respond effectively to the events at hand.

In a strategic business continuity management scenario, a firm's senior management will emphasize that business interruption risk must be mitigated at all levels firmwide. In order to do this in most firms, all business lines and corporate staff units (as well as joint ventures and other associated

---

BP STRATEGY #11—LEVERAGE FIRMWIDE DEFENSES FOR BUSINESS CONTINUITY

A key aspect of operational risk management is to assure the smooth continuity of business operations. Enhance and leverage strategic business continuity efforts beyond traditional areas of focus, such as physical hazard risk. Address the vulnerabilities such as risk to key revenue streams, reputation, stakeholder and regulatory standing, and one-time risk of loss. Include strategic investments in systems and processes. Seek opportunities to showcase business continuity as a competitive advantage.

---

entities) must ascertain all vulnerabilities to business interruption through an assessment or evaluation of their core business functions. This evaluation can be used as a road map in developing, testing, and maintaining an effective business continuity plan (BCP) for the business.

Whether managed by a separate corporate business continuity management team, or an operational risk team, the effort often involves two key initiatives: a business continuity risk management process and a crisis management process.

Development of Enterprise-wide Planning Standards

One key component of the program is the development of enterprise-wide standards for business continuity risk management. The standards are used by the business line to perform a risk assessment, and develop and test business continuity plans. Business continuity planning is a key part of an enterprise-wide effort to ensure that it remains in business following any business interruption event. A separate technology group often develops specific standards for technology infrastructure, systems, and applications.

Business Line Planning and Testing Process

Each business line will undertake its own business continuity risk management process consistent with the enterprise-wide standards. Generally the process contains four key steps, as outlined in Exhibit 8.5. The objective of the process is to focus line management on those aspects of the business which are most vulnerable to business disruption, prioritize them, and develop and test plans to mitigate the risks.

1. **Business continuity risk assessment** is the most critical step. It requires an evaluation of the business line's inherent risk relative to revenue, rep-

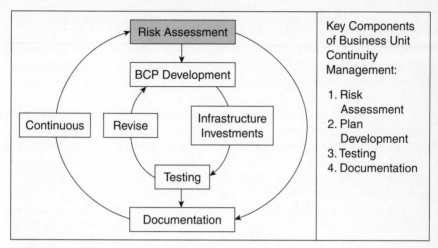

EXHIBIT 8.5   Business Continuity Management Cycle

utation, risk of one-time loss, and regulatory requirements. The identification and prioritization of key resources required to resume business
will be decided upon during the risk assessment phase. When the risk assessment is completed in a thorough manner, it will serve as a road map
for the development of a business' plan as it will focus attention on those
aspects that hold the greatest risks. The critical resources required to enable the business to recover and its downtime tolerance are determined
as part of the risk assessment.

2. **Development of a business continuity plan** involves using the information gathered in the risk assessment process as the foundation for planning. This stage will capture specific information about the resources required to perform priority functions (e.g., applications, communication
equipment, and workspace requirements) and guide infrastructure investments in alternate or backup sites. Responsibility for and expenses
associated with business continuity arrangements will be the responsibility of the affected business.

3. **Testing is key** and involves a combination of physical exercises, periodic
scenario analyses, and walk-through exercise discussions involving sufficient participation from business line staff. The process will ensure that
the unit has an adequate level of awareness to recover the business successfully. A physical exercise will ascertain the viability of an alternate
site by highlighting any shortcomings (e.g., availability of critical information, technology connectivity, suitability of environment). A
scenario-based exercise brings together a wider range of staff and interdependencies to stress test the plan's content and accuracy.

4. **Documentation** of the risk assessment, the plan, external agreements, and tests is important, particularly given the rate of change and reorganization within business lines (e.g., staff, technology, products). The risk assessment and plan will be reviewed and updated as appropriate, but at least every 12 months.

Crisis management procedures will also be developed at each firm location. They cover corporate infrastructure issues not addressed at the business line level. They also serve together all business unit plans and their technology. Issues include safety and emergency evacuation, designation of an emergency communications center, property protection, interaction with the public/media, and the like. For a firm's larger locations, the crisis management team will consist of members of areas ranging from the business units themselves, to business continuity or operational risk management, technology, security, legal, public relations, human resources, insurance risk management, property management, and information security.

A crisis center will play a pivotal role in enabling business line senior management and corporate support groups to convene and manage the crisis. Therefore, it is key that business lines designate a representative to liaise with the crisis team and establish a central point of contact at the business' alternate site to facilitate communication during an interruption. In smaller locations, the primary business line resident will handle these crisis management responsibilities.

Scoring and Risk Ranking Implications

In another instance of leveraging business continuity planning programs, like audit risk assessments, business continuity planning self-assessments by business units are tracked by the better firms for operational risk-scoring purposes. The scores are included in operational risk information systems, economic capital models, and/or overall operational risk reporting. In any event, senior business managers should be provided updates on business continuity planning and technology disaster recovery planning status for risk monitoring and comparison. And there is an insightful reading on the interrelationship between inherent risk versus control risk here — the business units that classify themselves as "critical" or "urgent" must have taken the proper measures to plan or test their ability to respond and recover in the event of disaster!

CONCLUSION

Risk response, the balancing of risk and reward, including the reduction or elimination of risk and loss, is the first line of defense and ultimately the most important element in any risk management effort. Traditionally, it is considered to be the end game. At the end of the day, many would argue that we are looking to mitigate, neutralize, or eliminate the negative aspects of a firm's operational risk profile and leverage rewards where possible along the way, such as the increased quality of products and services that will result. The systematic application of new tools, software, and incentives has recently made mitigation of operational risk and its attendant losses a more attainable goal.

LESSONS LEARNED AND KEY RECOMMENDATIONS

Too often we delve into tools, data, and analytics without establishing a proper framework. If we remind ourselves that focusing on the customer and enhancing shareholder value are our ultimate objectives, then it is only natural that our initial and primary risk management focus should be on risk response — risk mitigation and risk optimization. In essence, all of our other risk management activities should be prioritized and work to support the risk response framework.

The effective risk response framework will be a balance of "soft" and "hard" strategies. They will range from those that fit Theory Y and Z management theories, such as enhancing corporate integrity, incentives, and capabilities, to those that are much harder and tangible in nature (Theory X) such as process controls, diligence, and legal risk management.

- Disseminate useful management information and reports. Provide clear, useful, and actionable information about operational risks, losses, and the status of control efforts such that managers and staff firmwide are in a position to manage them on a day-to-day basis (BP Strategy #8).
- Use *incentives and disincentives* in managing operational risk. Use incentives *and* disincentive systems as a means to balance strategic risk and reward. For example, use risk-adjusted performance measures (RAPM), such as economic capital allocation or attribution processes to highlight operational risk intensive businesses. Provide both incentives and disincentives to both units and individuals for management of risk. Use capital as a means to optimize risk and reward.

  Far too often risk management only focuses on negatives, and thus risk managers fall in the trap of penalizing staff and units for risks identified, poor performance, and loss results. The most effective programs balance this with a system of rewards for productive risk management behavior and investment by both business and corporate units and staff alike. Some examples might include reduction of risk through upgrades in systems or manual processes, enhanced issue tracking systems, and timely clearance of self-identified risk issues or issues identified by internal audit (BP Strategy #9).

- In developing an economic risk capital allocation system, consider development of a system of capital credits under which business units might qualify for reductions in capital. Candidates for credit might include evidence of bona fide advancements in control and risk management, data collection, action tracking and clearance and metrics, all with a view toward improving the business unit's risk profile.
- Employ segregation and diversification strategies. Pursue high-level diversification techniques to combat the potentially catastrophic effects of process. Reinforce diversification and segregation of duties in critical processes. Balance risk and reward in diversification of physical asset concentrations (BP Strategy #10).
- Leverage firmwide defenses for *business continuity*. A key aspect of operational risk management is to assure the smooth continuity of business operations. Enhance and leverage strategic business continuity efforts beyond traditional areas of focus, such as physical hazard risk. Address the vulnerabilities such as risk to key revenue streams, reputation, stakeholder and regulatory standing, and one-time risk of loss. Include strategic investments in systems and processes. Seek opportunities to showcase business continuity as a competitive advantage (BP Strategy #11).

CHAPTER 9

Risk Assessment Strategies

risk 1: *possibility of loss or injury: PERIL 2; a dangerous
element or factor; 3 a : the chance or loss of the perils to the
subject matter of an insurance contract; also, the degree of
probability of such loss* . . .

Webster's Ninth New Collegiate Dictionary

INTRODUCTION

Isn't it interesting that Webster's still has no reference to an upside in its definition of risk? Our endgame is balancing risk and rewards. Risk response and risk mitigation are the top priorities in risk management. We covered those strategies before risk assessment and measurement to underscore that very point and to set the stage for activities required to achieve them.

Practically speaking, before we can deal with risk we need to identify the sources and types of it, define them, and understand the underlying characteristics and behavioral issues as well as the external forces involved. Then, we must quantify the risk: What are the probabilities of a low-level loss versus a catastrophic loss, and how severe is it likely to be?

We will include in our broad category of risk assessment the component processes of risk identification, analysis and evaluation. Risk assessment is another critical step in the risk management process. Suggesting that one should assess risk before deciding on the appropriate risk treatment measure is like saying that it would be wise to learn how to fly before getting in the cockpit. The tricky part comes in when we begin to discuss what risk assessment method is most appropriate for your organization.

In this chapter we will explore the two key dimension of risk assessment: bottom up versus top down and qualitative versus quantitative. Then we will explore various qualitative approaches here. We limit our exploration of quantitative approaches for now to the last section of this chapter, "Introduction to the Data Universe." It serves as a preface to the next several chapters on loss databases and consortia, risk indicators, risk measurement and analytics, and risk capital modeling.

OBJECTIVES AND GOALS FOR RISK ASSESSMENT

There are at least three key objectives here. First, determine the types of loss scenarios that we face. What risks do existing business activities, or new ones, such as e-commerce or e-business, bring in terms of operational risk? One way to do that is to determine what characteristics new businesses and older established businesses have in common and to use those as a starting point.

Second, recognize the causes and how large the potential losses are. Identify the relative probabilities and loss potential. We want to fully understand what is causing the losses: Is it a quality-of-people issue, a know-your-customer issue, or a quality-of-systems issue? What are the common threads? Is it a lack of adequate supervision? Are the potential losses frequent and modest or uncommon and potentially catastrophic? How can we measure the possibilities?

Third, complete the cycle by applying the results to risk mitigation. Determining capital at risk is important, but alone it is insufficient. People or organizations that are concentrating solely on capital adequacy are targeting only one of the objectives and may be missing other potential weapons in the operational risk arsenal.[1]

DIMENSIONS OF RISK ASSESSMENT

There are two key dimensions of risk assessment. The first is the continuum from top down, high level portfolio-based views to specific bottom up processes. The second is the continuum from subjective to quantitative assessments.

The First Dimension: Top Down versus Bottom Up

In the process of risk assessment, the focus should be on those exposures that can significantly impact the ability of the firm to continue operations. This is relevant at all levels in the organization, although the specificity will differ depending upon the objective of the risk assessment being undertaken. For instance, a business manager will need specific insight on individual exposures in risks in order to make prudent decisions about running the business.

In contrast, operational risk practitioners who are charged with developing operational risk capital models may only need portfolio views of individual profit centers and business line operations. Similarly, insurance risk managers may only need exposure information by risk class in order to make decisions about constructing and fine tuning risk finance and insurance programs to hedge the risks in question.

The best firmwide risk assessment programs, however, will be designed to meet these information needs at multiple levels. Hence, there is a need for both specific or granular level risk assessment processes on one hand, and more generalized, higher or aggregated portfolio-level risk assessments on the other. These have come to be known as *bottom up* and *top down* risk assessment strategies, respectively.

Bottom-Up Strategies   Three types of bottom up strategies all involve business level scenario analysis, often in the form of control self-assessment, independent audit reviews, and collaborative risk assessments.

In concept, bottom up self-assessment processes represent an excellent way for business management to get a handle on control process gaps. If well structured, they can identify key risks in both origination and execution of transactions. But by definition, many of these analyses become extremely detailed in nature. The fact is that most bottom up self-assessment processes become so granular and time-consuming that some lose sight of the bigger picture. What is worse, they are often delegated away from busy line managers for completion—often to consultants, interns, or new junior hires—because line management simply does not have the time required to conduct the analyses. Thus, in the process, the exercise oftentimes becomes divorced from business managers themselves, thereby defeating the entire purpose! Another drawback is that too few self-assessments are conducted continuously and in "real time." The trick is to strike a careful balance between detail, relevance, and priorities.[2]

Top-Down or Portfolio-Level Strategies   Top down risk assessment is defined as a determination of risk potential for the entire firm—the entire business, organization, or portfolio of business. By its very nature, it is a high-level representation. It cannot get involved in a transaction-by-transaction risk analysis.

A criticism often leveled against top down methods, however, is the direct opposite of its cited benefits. That is, although useful for a manager at the corporate center, it is relatively useless for managers (or risk managers) in line positions.

These portfolio-level strategies seek to arrive at an aggregate representation of the risk in a business unit, an overall business line, or for the firm as a whole. Alternatively, they might seek to take a firmwide representation of risk-by-risk class (e.g., by the broad classes of people, processes, and systems across the entire firm on a global basis). Portfolio-level strategies range from various types of scenario analysis to risk mapping strategies, or actuarial analysis.

The reality is that once one considers a full spectrum of enterprise-wide ORM objectives, a debate over top down versus bottom up is pointless. The two analyses have different uses. It all comes down to the objectives of the specific audience. The important first step is to determine one's objectives in both risk measurement and in risk management. How broad or granular is your focus? Are we only attempting to determine the firm's total exposure to operational risk, or are we attempting to go deeper? Do we want to understand loss potential and risk control quality by risk class (e.g., subrisk class), by business, by profit center, or even by product? From an economic capital objective, it is probably more a question of measuring the former aggregate perspectives, but from a business management view it is clearly much closer to the latter detailed views. To a line manager it is far more important to understand the loss potential in his or her processing system, or in e-commerce, than to a broader risk class like technology generally.[3]

Both top down and bottom up views add value in risk measurement and management, but here again neither should be used in isolation. Top down analyses are often useful for senior management (i.e., across business lines) in identifying large-scale risk management priorities (i.e., need for enterprise-wide technology initiatives, talent upgrades, etc.), or for firmwide capital-at-risk analyses. At the same time the top down analyses will have relatively less value to line managers, confronting day-to-day risks embedded in business transactions and processes. A carefully designed bottom up (i.e., self-assessment or risk assessment) approach, on the other hand, can be useful for line management in identifying control gaps, flaws in front-to-back trade processing, or staff management issues, for instance. Exhibit 9.1 is an overview of the scope of bottom up versus top down techniques.

Let's begin with bottom up best practices. When pressed, many admit that they are striving for a bottom up approach in the end because it is seen as bringing immediate tactical value to the business. By definition it is more specific as to individual business processes and yields a more detailed and complete picture of the risks embedded there.

BP STRATEGY #12—IMPLEMENT A BOTTOM-UP PROCESS TO IDENTIFY, EVALUATE, AND MANAGE OPERATIONAL RISKS

Effective operational risk management implies having a clear understanding of the risks that can cause serious harm to the organization. This requires a process for identifying and evaluating new risks on a continuous basis (e.g., independent risk assessment, control self-assessment, process analysis).

	Bottom Up Strategy	Top Down Strategy
Objectives	To identify, evaluate, and quantify the risk potential at a transaction or business unit level.	To identify, evaluate, and quantify the risk potential at an enterprise-wide and/or top line business level.
Uses	• To assist in day-to-day risk–reward business decision making. • For the allocation of risk control resources, control technology expenditures.	• To support firmwide risk quantification and/or risk capital calculations. • For the allocation of enterprise-wide Internal Audit resources. • To assist in making risk finance and insurance decisions.
Tactics and Techniques	• Control self-assessment • New product reviews • Business unit level scenario analysis • Process analysis VAR calculations. • Unit level interviews.	• Risk inventories. • Risk maps. • Businesswide or enterprise-wide scenario analysis. • Risk class or enterprise-wide level VAR analysis. • Mid-to-top level interviews.

EXHIBIT 9.1   Risk Assessment Strategies: Bottom Up versus Top Down

The Second Dimension: Qualitative versus Quantitative Risk Assessment

In another dimension, there are the extremes of qualitative or subjective risk assessments on one hand versus numeric or quantitative analyses on the other. Both extremes bring value to the process. For their part subjective risk analysis accommodates for the complexities of operational risk. In contrast, there's enormous value in getting to a number. Most of us are now familiar with the adage "You can't manage what has not been measured." This is probably a bit extreme, but it certainly drives home the idea that having numeric points of reference is extremely valuable when attempting to convince a reluctant manager that he or she must invest scarce resources to address a risk. How many times have you attempted to convince a reluctant audience that they must do something and your only ammunition is a statement like "because it is important, critical, or we could have a loss if we don't do this?"

	Bottom Up	Top Down
Qualitative	Business Unit Level: • Control Self- Assessment (CSA) • Risk Assessment Interviews	Firmwide Level: • Interviews • Delphi Scenarios
Quantitative	Business Unit Level: • Unit level trends, regressions • Loss Distribution Analysis • Causal/Baysean Belief Network Analysis • System Dynamics Approach	Firmwide Level: • Trends/Regressions • Loss Distribution/ Actuarial Analysis • Score cards

EXHIBIT 9.2   The Quadrants and Tools of Risk Assessment

It is far more convincing to say, "We measured the loss potential to a 95% confidence level. In other words, it is highly probable that we could face a loss upwards of $100 million if we don't address this risk."

Of the two dimensions (or four quadrants) of risk assessment illustrated in Exhibit 9.2, there is no single correct approach for all organizations. One can make a strong argument for saying that an organization should use a blend of these methodologies to reach a reasonable representation of their loss and risk profile. Finding the right "blend" all depends on your own firm's organization, culture, risk management experience, and related objectives.

THE QUANTITATIVE VERSUS QUALITATIVE TUG-OF-WAR

One danger created by the evolution of operational risk management from existing disciplines is that some practitioners will have difficulty letting go of their prior perspectives in isolation. For instance, some will continue to argue that modeling is the extent of operational risk management. Others might argue that control self-assessment defines it. Others still may argue that their business line risk control work is operational risk management. In fact they are all parts of a larger whole. One perspective and practice is simply not complete without the others.

In the short time since the discipline has been developing, it has already become apparent that there are two very distinct camps forming on how best to manage these risks. On one side is a group that formed quickly and rallied around the belief that quantification is by far the most important activity for advancement.

Elsewhere, there are risk practitioners that are convinced that softer qualitative risk management methods, such as self-assessment, risk mapping, and scenario analysis, are the superior techniques. Some members of this group believe that quantification of operational risk is a waste of time and far better results would be obtained in focusing on these softer techniques together with behavior modification.

My own experiences suggest that the best results have been obtained in applying a balance of both qualitative and quantitative techniques. It is simple enough to find illustrations of the fallacy of embracing one technique exclusively over the other.

IN RISK MANAGEMENT, BALANCE HAS BECOME EVERYTHING

Long live qualitative reviews and stress testing! In case there was any doubt about the future of qualitative reviews, the Long Term Capital Management (LTCM) debacle in 1998 settled the debate. The case serves as a great illustration of embracing quantitative techniques while completely ignoring the softer qualitative approaches, including scenario analysis. LTCM may cast a long shadow on the sophisticated quantification techniques practiced by financial risk managers. Regardless of whether the case is classified as market or operational risk, the principles and the fallout are the same. After all, the management team at LTCM included some of the most sophisticated financial engineers in the industry. Their highly sophisticated models failed them in considering extreme loss scenarios, which may have also left the population-at-large questioning the wisdom and value of quantitative modeling, but certainly questioning the wisdom of quantitative modeling in isolation.

Conversely, organizations such as Barings occurred while qualitative techniques such as internal auditing were already in place. In short, employing both approaches can tighten the weave in the net to catch weaknesses in the firm's risk profile and risk management defenses.

Last, because operational risk management has evolved from both qualitative and quantitative disciplines, it has the potential of making a far greater impact on the evolution and transformation of enterprise-wide risk management through balance and the inclusion of an organization's mainstream population in the discipline.

BOTTOM-UP RISK ASSESSMENT METHODS — SCENARIO ANALYSIS

There are a variety of qualitative methods in use. The remainder of this chapter will be devoted primarily to qualitative assessment techniques. They include interviews, Delphi-type scenario analysis, such as using the business vulnerability analysis part of business continuity planning as control self-assessment, collaborative risk assessments, internal audit reviews, and new product reviews. Chapters 10–12 will examine a variety of aspects of quantitative techniques — that is, risk *measurement*.

The Risk Assessment Interview

Risk assessment scenario analysis strategies can range from simply asking a few easy questions to get people thinking about the risks, the business, the processes, and the vulnerabilities, to the completion of a few grids, to very detailed process reviews. Everyone should be involved in risk assessment at one level or another. Senior managers generally think of risk intuitively. But it doesn't hurt to ask a few high-level risk questions to get a manager's creative juices flowing. For instance, ask key questions like: What keeps you awake at night? What is the worst thing that can happen in your business? When is the worst time it can happen? Questions such as these can bring to mind the following nightmare loss scenarios:

- Loss of market share, major customer or market segment
- Market crash or rate spike, extreme volatility, or significant losses to market positions
- Technology failure, large-scale systems fault, or business interruption
- Control failures, errors, or unauthorized activities
- Large credit loss
- Class action legal risk
- Combination of events

Operational risks make the list in several places.

Delphi-type Scenario Analysis

Delphi-type scenario analysis involves a number of people in the process of devising loss scenarios through collective judgment. A good example of the exercise is the typical business continuity planning risk assessment exercise.

The Business Continuity Risk Assessment Analogue

Once again, there is a useful analogy to business interruption risk assessment processes that should already exist in most firms (See Exhibit 9.3). There is much to be said for leveraging these existing processes.

Businesses that focus their business interruption risk management efforts toward determining where they are most vulnerable or most at risk will be better able to recover. Plan development should prioritize the urgency

A Strategic Perspective — Four Risk Dimensions		
Risk Dimensions	**Definitions**	**Examples**
Revenue and Expenses	The impact on both short term and longer term *revenue streams* if the business is not able to resume normal operations in a timely manner. This might include an expense associated with being unable to perform a business function.	Destruction of dealing room(s) means that traders cannot generate income and that expenses are incurred in business recovery.
Reputation and Franchise Value	The impact on current and long-term ability to attract and maintain customers. Consider the firm's *position in the market* where it is a significant player and/or where its absence might have a significant impact on the market. Also consider the impact on customers/counterparties.	If the outage lasts more than a day then the firm may struggle to regain its former position or maintain its client base. For some business lines, appearing "open for business" is critical in order to retain customers/ counterparties.
Risk of Loss	The cost of significant *one-time losses* due to an inability to operate. Crisis management expenses, commitments made in contracts (both to customers and internal units), and guarantees should be considered.	Because a trade could not be confirmed, a payment was sent to a counterparty in error who is reluctant to return the funds.
Regulatory and Legal	Central *compliance/ regulatory requirements* and the cost of noncompliance.	Failure to comply with regulations could lead to fines or more serious regulatory interruptions of business

EXHIBIT 9.3   Business Disruption Risk

of each business function. Businesses will identify their interdependencies, both internal and external, and have an understanding of how a group providing a key service would manage its own interruption.

The business continuity risk assessment process is meant to help each business line evaluate their vulnerability to business interruption risk. A risk assessment enables the business to prioritize its functions and highlight creative alternatives if a major supplier of information or service (either another internal unit or an outside vendor) is not available. By measuring and assessing the risks over time the business can determine its need for an alternate site and outline required alternate operating procedures. Business lines that must resume key functions within hours will require a site that is fully wired and can be operational quickly. Those whose operations are not as time sensitive will not require the same level of readiness. Identification of critical resources is a natural outcome of the prioritization process.

All business units will review and update their risk assessment as appropriate, but at least every 12 months.

Business continuity risk assessment can be organized into a three-part process. The phases include analysis of the impact of individual loss scenarios on the business unit's functions over time, identification of critical resources, and assignment of a downtime tolerance threshold to use for classifying the criticality of the business. The outcome of each plays a key part in the development of a business continuity plan.

1. **Analysis of Interruption Scenarios' Impact on Business Functions.** The objective here is to identify and analyze various interruption scenarios against four risk dimensions: revenue, reputation, risk of loss, and regulatory/legal requirements from the time of an event onward, as outlined in Exhibit 9.3. The result is a prioritization of business functions for the various interruption scenarios against the four dimensions over time.

Here the goal is to define the critical objectives of the business. We prioritize key business processes and identify the dimensions of interruption risks given a range of scenarios. The business continuity risk assessment process begins with an analysis of the ways in which the scenarios impact a business unit's product and service offerings. The nature of the business, including the complexity of transactions, will be taken into consideration, of course, when determining the scope of the risk assessment.

The following steps assist in the analysis and prioritization of business functions.

(a) **Exposure Identification:** Identify key exposures, or the business processes that may be vulnerable to interruption. This can consist of a brief description or flow chart of the operating/business environment.

(b) **Scenario Identification:** Identify the possible scenarios that could interrupt the business. These will cover situations involving building access and application availability. A thorough risk assessment will cover the complete range of possible scenarios from short-term outages to more severe longer-term interruptions.

(c) **Loss Potential:** Evaluate the potential severity of an event on each dimension of business interruption risk (revenue, reputation, risk of loss, and regulatory. Based on a full range of interruption scenarios, business lines will study their priorities and the degree of risk attached to each.

The decentralized functions in a business line and their rate of change require a periodic and continual review of priorities by all functional groups to ensure all critical functions are represented. This review will include the recovery procedures of interdependencies and key resources, as these may impact the level at which the business can develop an effective plan and recover following a disruption.

The risk dimensions are designed to prioritize those business functions that need to be completed in order to protect the business. It is important to remember that while all business functions have a purpose, they do not all have the same priority, nor do they require the same level of resources.

For some of the risk dimensions (especially reputation) it may be difficult to apportion an accurate dollar impact. The aim is not to have an exceptionally detailed analysis of the dollar impact of a business interruption but rather to identify the speed and severity with which the business line will be affected and necessary time frames for recovery.

To develop the analysis it may be useful to plot a rough graph of dollar impact versus time. For example, a business that processes a heavy volume of high-value transactions may be vulnerable very quickly; such a business should consider having a dedicated "hot site," with data being replicated on a real-time basis, etc. On the other hand, a relatively new or developing business may not have the same degree of vulnerability and might not require such extensive recovery capabilities.

Risk assessment will be performed at all levels of the organization. For instance, exercises at the individual profit center level will complement and be consistent with more comprehensive analyses performed at the business division level.

2. **Identification of Critical Resources and Interdependencies:** Once a business' priority functions have been established, the critical internal and external resources required for recovery will be identified. The objective here is to identify the key staff, equipment, and connectivity to applications.

The result should be a list of resources needed to recover high-priority business functions. For instance:

- **Key Staff:** Identification of staff to perform key functions. This includes identifying where there are only one or two people who can fulfill a function.
- **Applications:** Both proprietary and nonproprietary applications that operate on internal equipment or at a third-party site.
- **Types of Equipment:** Personal computers, market data services, palmtops, printers, phones, faxes, photo copy machines.
- **Types of Connectivity:** Internal and external voice and data connections.

3. **Downtime Tolerance:** The objective here is to determine a business' overall downtime tolerance to an interruption of operations. The resultant downtime tolerance threshold is a criticality rating that equates to the speed of recovery needed by each core business.

In this phase, the planning team determines the threshold for the unit's core business activities. This rating identifies a time frame in which its core business functions must recover. If the time frame varies based on the time of the day, week, month, or year, then businesses will err on the side of greater urgency (i.e., base the business' risk classification rating on the most vulnerable time a business interruption event may occur).

Downtime tolerance thresholds are self-assigned because the business itself is the most qualified to ascertain the margin of time between an interruption and when significant losses or exposures are incurred. A business unit's self-assigned downtime tolerance threshold (i.e., for its core functions) will drive many other business continuity risk management considerations. Examples of these are the need for a fully readied alternate site, the frequency and thoroughness of testing requirements, and crisis management resource allocation. The classifications, might range from as little as 1 or 2 hours, to a maximum of 3 to 5 days.

Management Considerations   A business' downtime tolerance assessment might be linked to its key technology applications' downtime tolerance, but the two are not necessarily the same. In some cases, alternate-operating procedures may enable the business to manage its risk sufficiently until the applications are available. Conversely, applications can have downtime tolerances less than the business if transactions can be processed without the business being fully operational. Depending on when applications can be recovered (i.e. "start of day" versus "point of failure"), plans will have operating procedures that adequately mitigate the interruption exposure.

In summary, it is clear from this overview that the business continuity risk assessment process has numerous parallels to a separate operational risk assessment exercise. The better firms will coordinate business continuity risk assessment and operational risk assessment efforts for greater efficiency overall.

Control Self-Assessment

Control self-assessment (CSA) is the process by which individual business units analyze their own business processes step by step to identify the strength and weaknesses of their risk control programs. In so doing, they identify control gaps and risks. In certain respects, CSA applies scenario analysis. That is, the development of a sequence of events, when projected into a variety of outcomes, will employ various counterbalancing risk mitigation measures.

CSA programs have come into vogue in recent years with the recognition that business units can be empowered to control their own business architectures on a local level, including but not limited to management of local control infrastructures. CSA programs have been developed and installed to supplement internal audit reviews, not replace them. When designed properly, a portion of the control infrastructure can be moved from internal audit to the local business line in keeping with the notion of local empowerment. This alignment does not relieve internal audit of its role for conducting independent reviews.

Many risk practitioners see CSA as the cornerstone of an operational risk management program. In many respects, use of control self-assessment also fits very neatly with our BP Strategy #5 — Empower Business units with responsibility for risk management.

CASE ILLUSTRATION
Control Self-Assessment
The Bank of Tokyo Mitsubishi

The Bank of Tokyo Mitsubishi (BTM) has used control self-assessment as an important foundation for its operational risk management program in New York. Mark Balfan, SVP, who heads market risk and operational risk management there, outlines their approach in this section.

Background　The concept of self-assessment has been around for many years, as has operational risk. How we manage and think about operational risk has undergone, and will continue to undergo, major changes. However, self-assessment continues to be performed in much

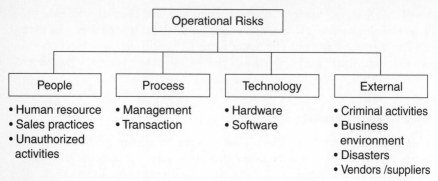

EXHIBIT 9.4   The Bank of Tokyo Mitsubishi Risk Class Hierarchy

the same manner as it always has. Either through flowcharting or process analysis, someone determines a set of controls that should exist or do exist and assembles a set of questionnaires for each business based on those controls. The questionnaires are usually yes/no-based and tend to get stale as processes and technology change. Further, since every business is different, the set of questions in each questionnaire is different, which makes aggregation and analysis at a higher level almost impossible.

Goals and Objectives   The primary goal for self-assessment at BTM was to use it as a tool in identifying and measuring operational risk. In order to achieve that goal, it was essential that self-assessment be integrated with every other aspect of operational risk assessment. In order to achieve that integration, a common hierarchy of risks was established across all tools. Exhibit 9.4 is the risk class hierarchy for BTM.

The hierarchy was divided into 103 subrisks. These risks formed the basis of the self-assessment. Every business was asked by operational risk management to evaluate their risks and controls for the same exact set of 103 risks. This allowed for easy aggregation and analysis.

A second goal for self-assessment was that it should be risk-focused. By risk-focused we mean that rather than evaluating a long list of controls, the focus was on evaluating the risks. We continued to evaluate the controls separately as a means to manage the risks, but risk was paramount. While this distinction may sound academic, we believe it is an important one. Our experience shows that most businesses would prefer not to sound any alarm bells. As a result they tend to understate the net risk in the business. However, by focusing on risk separately from controls, we have been able to achieve more honesty and consistency in the responses received from the departments. For example, most managers are quite willing to acknowledge the existence of a major risk but will most likely say that that risk is well managed. By focusing on risks separately from controls we can at least identify the high-risk areas.

While these were our two main objectives, others include quantification of risk and satisfaction of regulatory purposes such as compliance with FDICIA. To achieve these additional objectives one must design the self-assessment differently to elicit the necessary information from the businesses.

Design Exhibit 9.5 is a sample screen from our self-assessment program. Notice several items. (1) The business is initially prompted with a definition of the risk to be evaluated. These are from the 103 risks that we discussed before. Exhibit 9.5 is an example of question 61 which deals with data entry. (2) The business is then asked to evaluate the amount of the inherent risk to their business for that question. Inherent risk is divided into the maximum potential loss (i.e., severity) and the potential frequency. Severity and frequency combine to arrive at total inherent risk. We deliberately separated the inherent risk assessment into severity and frequency to allow for better management and control of the risk. For example, higher frequency/lower severity risks may be managed through increased controls whereas higher severity/lower frequency risks may be better managed through insurance or simple assumed by the business. (3) The controls are assessed through a very simple control effectiveness percentage (between 0 and 100%). Percentages were preferred over the standard high, medium, and low to allow for more consistent responses across businesses and to allow for easier aggregation and analysis later on. (4) We then asked business units to provide us with a list of risk indicators they use to manage that risk themselves. It's easy for a business to say they have an effective control, but to monitor the effectiveness through indicators confirms that effectiveness. Further, providing us with indicators facilitates one of our group's missions, which is to collect and analyze risk indicators. (5) Finally, we asked if the business has ever sustained a loss from that risk. A yes response to that question is followed up with a phone call to understand the nature of the loss and where in the organization that loss was recorded. This facilitates our loss collection efforts.

Thus, it is critical to design the self-assessment in such a way so as to ensure consistent responses and to allow you to leverage off the responses for some of your other risk management initiatives such as collection of risk indicators or losses.

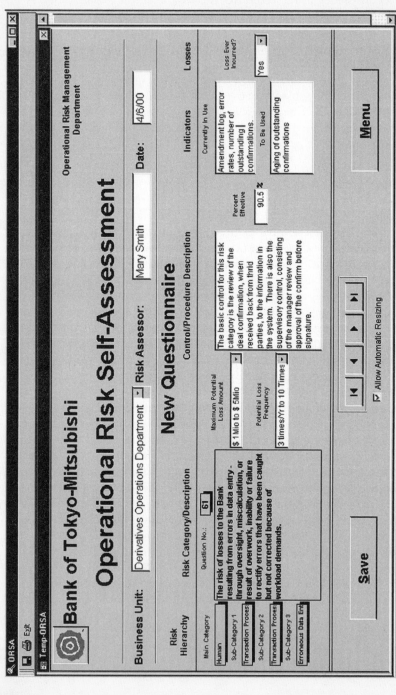

EXHIBIT 9.5 The Bank of Tokyo Mitsubishi Self-Assessment Data Entry Screen

Implementation Once you have designed the self-assessment, getting the forms out to the businesses and back from them can be a monumental task. Technology has certainly assisted us in that effort. A bank's intranet can be perfect for such a task. We distributed the forms to businesses and collected them back on the net. Receiving information electronically also allows for easier aggregation at the end.

There are also various software packages out there to accomplish the tasks. However, it is impossible to judge them against each other especially if you are not very familiar with self-assessment. They all have unique strengths and weaknesses. We initially looked at them and decided to go it alone. Now that we've been through the process once, we are in a much better position to judge each of them.

Validation Self-assessments cannot be used unless there is an in-depth validation process in place. We have three levels of validation. The first and most detailed is done by internal auditors during their annual audit cycle for each business. Each response is assessed and the control effectiveness verified. Other institutions may find it easier to conduct a special audit during the self-assessment to ensure that the responses don't become stale by the time the audit is conducted.

Our risk specialists do the second validation. Each specialist receives the results for the risks assigned to them. We ask the specialists to opine on the risk in total and not on each department's assessment. Thus they look at the severity and frequency distribution along with the economic risk calculations and determine their appropriateness in total. Finally, our Operational Risk Management Committee reviews all of the summary analyses and raises any issues that need to be investigated further.

Follow-up The whole point of self-assessment is to improve the control environment. Without a formal issue tracking process, the self-assessment just winds up as some pretty graphs. Any issues that arise from this process should be tracked and followed up on just like all other institutional issues.

The Bank of Tokyo Mitsubishi case is continued in Chapter 13 Risk Profiling and Monitoring.

■ ■ ■

Collaborative Risk Assessment Approach

Some firms prefer to take a different approach. Rather than leave the assessments *completely* in the hands of the business units, or leave them entirely in the hands of Internal Audit as an independent group, they take a collaborative approach. The assessments in the following Case Illustration below are conducted by the independent operational risk management team in combination with the business units themselves. This approach can benefit from greater consistency in the results, along with the added advantage of an independent review, but requires adequate resources to get the job done. Marie Gaudioso, Vice President of The Bank of New York describes their program below.

CASE ILLUSTRATION

The Bank of New York Case

Organization Structure The Operational Risk Management division of the Bank of New York was established by senior management in 1999, as an independent function, to develop a framework for assessing, monitoring, measuring, and reporting on *operational risk* throughout the organization. Operational Risk Management, while independent, works with the business units to define the key risks in each business and assess those risks in terms of severity and probability or likelihood of occurrence. The bank's definition of operational risk is:

> *Operational risk is the potential for unexpected financial losses, damage to reputation, and/or loss in shareholder value due to a breakdown in internal controls, information system failures, human error, or vulnerability to external events.*

The Operational Risk Management unit is an independent function reporting to the Chief Risk Officer of the bank, who reports to the Chairman. The department consists of the Department Head and staff, called Business Risk Monitors, who physically reside in and are responsible for assessing the risks in specified business units.

The Business Risk Monitors are responsible for identifying, assessing, monitoring, and reporting on the operational risks in those businesses. The initial stage of their job responsibilities includes mapping business processes and conducting risk assessments. Exhibit 9.6 is a sample **risk assessment profile,** which is created for each business and identifies risks and contains recommendations to mitigate those risks. In addition, the Business Risk Monitor is the coordinator of the Business Infrastructure Group, a multidisciplined group that meets regularly to review all current and outstanding risk issues and initiatives within each business unit and reports on the status of all risk management efforts.

The second stage builds upon the risk assessments and establishes a risk monitoring process. Operational Risk Management has developed a methodology for the identification and tracking of key risk indicators

(KRIs). The process identifies both the drivers of risk and related metrics to enable the organization to highlight potential high risks and monitor, track, and report on the level of risk in each business unit.

The third stage involves measuring losses arising from operational risk events to determine the level of regulatory capital needed to support each business and to further refine our capital allocation methodology.

Operational Risk Management Objectives The Bank of New York's Operational Risk Management unit has several objectives, namely to:

- Develop a uniform and comprehensive operational risk management framework and risk assessment methodology for the organization.
- Develop risk profiles and monitor the status of risk mitigating action plans and other risk management initiatives in the business units.
- Align controls with the business objectives.
- Ensure that all material risks are identified and managed in accordance with management's expectations.
- Provide senior management with risk-related information and the status of implementation plans.
- Develop and track key risk indicators.
- Promote control awareness among staff and throughout the business lines by sharing best practices and recommendations for improvement.

Strategy and Approach This initial stage involves the use of a qualitative risk assessment model that determines an Operational Risk Score, which incorporates an *inherent risk score* and a *business risk assessment score*. The central objectives of the evaluation process are (1) a meaningful assessment of operational risk, and (2) a balance between risks and controls that best suit the organization, provides appropriate incentives, and results in continuous improvement and resolution of operational problems. The Business Risk Monitor facilitates the risk assessment with the business unit managers and provides a level of independence.

- **Inherent Risk Score:** The inherent risk score measures the degree to which the business unit being assessed is exposed to a set of inherent risk criteria, such as average transaction values (e.g., transaction volumes, settlement risk, transaction complexity, regulatory complexity, technology fail exposure, etc.), adjusted by a scaling factor.
- **Business Risk Score:** The business risk score is derived from a binomial model in which the risk impact of an event and its probability are rated. The risk impact denotes the degree of severity should the event occur (using a scale of 1 to 5), in terms of economic loss, damage to reputation, or loss in shareholder value. The probability is rated on a similar scale based upon the quality and effectiveness of the control environment, processes, people,

Dept	Objective	Significant Risks	Impact on Objective	RI	Key Controls
	Objective 1: Sufficient counterparty margin/ collateral or underlying collateral that is properly controlled or valued. The corporation's interest in underlying collateral is perfected on a timely basis.	1. Margin/collateral that is due is not tracked for timely receipt.	Bank could be exposed if customer defaults with insufficient margin.	3	1) System calculations to measure exposure periodically. 2) Notification of limit excesses.
		2. Margin/collateral is not periodically marked to market.	Bank could be exposed if customer defaults with insufficient collateral value.	4	1) Vendor feeds of asset pricing. 2) Multiple feeds daily. 3) Multiple vendors. 4) Conservative valuation techniques.
		3. Margin/collateral is not adequately safeguarded against inappropriate access.	Bank could suffer financial loss, reputation risk, or fraud if a customer defaults with insufficient margin.	4	1) Dual system controls. 2) System password/security methods. 3) Strong procedures and collateral confirmation methods.
		4. Records of margin/collateral are not adequate.	Bank suffer financial losses if customer defaults with insufficient margin.	3	1) System specifications ensure proper records exist for audit trail. 2) System overrides are subject to dual controls and senior approval.
		5. BNY's interest in the underlying collateral is not perfected.	Bank suffer financial losses if the lien is not perfected.	4	1) Periodic review of appropriate law with Legal Department and external counsel conducted. 2) Client agreements in place to document contract. 3) Legal Department and External counsel are engaged for client contract.

EXHIBIT 9.6 Bank of New York Operational Risk Management Risk Assessment of Division ABC

Risk Drivers/ Issues	Prob	Risk Score	TRS	Action Plan	P/I	RC	Priority H/M/L	Due Date/ Responsibility
1) Technology-Batch processing creates timely delays. 2) External-Prices are often not updated, so stale prices are used. 3) People. Insufficient number of staff to process and monitor this function.	3	9	3	1) Develop real time processing. 2) Review staffing levels. 3) Institute review of stale prices.	−6	O	M	1) Thomas 2Q2001. 2) Thomas/ Smith 3Q2001. 3) Smith 4Q2001.
1) External-Prices are often not current so prices may be stale for certain assets. 2) Diverse collateral types complicate the valuation process. 3) Asset price volatility. 4) Hard to price assets.	3	12	8	1) Create reports that age the length of stale pricing. 2) Analyze stale pricing to determine trends/categories. 3) Develop a strategy to decrease stale pricing from 2 above.	−4	O,M,C	M	1) Thomas 2Q2001. 2) Thomas/ Smith 3Q2001. 3) Smith 4Q2001.
Lack of supervision for segregation.	1	4	4	Current environment requires no action plan.	O	O	Not Applicable	Not Applicable.
1) External-Potential litigation and disputes from clients and counterparties. 2) External-Complexity of client requirements. 3) Process-Manual error.	2	6	6	Current environment requires no action plan.	O	O	Not Applicable	Not Applicable.
1) People-Lack of knowledge by staff of current law. 2) External-Changes of existing law. 3) Process-Lack of execution of periodic filings.	2	8	4	Expand Tickler system functionality to periodically review security instrument filings with appropriate jurisdictions.	−4	O,L	M	Jones 3Q2001.

Potential financial impact or reputational damage would be described as follows for the various operations risks:

Risk Impact Rating (RI)

1. Minor expense, industry acceptable risks type; no damage to reputation — **1**

2. Moderate expense and/or damage to reputation; acceptable industry risk type — **2**

3. Significant expense and/or damage to reputation; unusual financial risk type — **3**

4. Substantial economic loss including loss of shareholder value and damage to reputation; unacceptable or unusual nature or extent of risk — **4**

5. Major economic loss including loss of shareholder value and damage to reputation — **5**

Risk Probability (Prob)	Probability Weight
Very High	5
High	4
Mod High	3
Medium	2
Low	1

Definitions:

Risk Score: The Risk Score represents a numeric factor based on potential risk impact and the probability based upon the existing key controls of the Impact occurring for each risk. The Risk Score is computed by multiplying the Risk Impact $\times$ Probability Weight.

Target Risk Score (TRS): This is the adjusted Risk Score assigned to the particular risk should the action plan be fully implemented. It is computed by taking the Risk Impact Rating (RI) and multiplying by the new Probability Weight resulting from the Risk Mitigation Plan.

Potential Improvement (PI): This is the potential gain to be derived from the full implementation of the Action Plan. It is the difference between the Risk Score and the Target Score.

Risk Category (RC): Operations (O), Credit (C), Legal (L), Market (M), Liquidity (Q).

Overall Risk Score: It is computed by taking the total aggregate Risk Scores and divided by the aggregate number of risks.

EXHIBIT 9.6 The Bank of New York Operational Risk Assessment Legend

adequacy of systems, and management oversight. The product of the risk impact rating times the probability rating is the overall business risk score (the higher the score the higher the overall perceived operational risk).

■ **Operational Risk Score:** The overall Operational Risk Score is calculated by multiplying the Inherent Risk Score by the Business Risk Score. This score can be improved once the business unit implements the recommended action plans and controls.

This model provides a "risk assessment profile" of the business overall and creates a platform to develop action plans for risk mitigation, which is monitored and updated periodically as action plans are implemented.

Link to Economic Capital Allocation   The risk assessment methodology is also used in the allocation of economic capital to the business lines. The allocation of economic capital is based upon a composite rating derived from the ratings from the operational risk assessments and other related factors. The Benefits for the Bank of New York are that the process:

■ Assigns accountability at the business line level
■ Provides incentives and motivates behavior to drive continuous improvement of internal processes
■ Allocates capital based upon the risk profile and quality of the risk management and control processes in the business line
■ Allows for proactive monitoring of risks over time and alerts management to rising levels of risk
■ Provides flexibility in determining internal measures appropriate to the organization
■ Provides a platform for decision making and risk mitigation strategies

■ ■ ■

Leveraging Internal Audit Reviews

The assessment of operational risk has always been included in internal audit departments' charters, whether expressly or implied. The role and reporting relationship of auditors is such that their focus is a bit different, by definition, however, than that of operational risk management. Internal auditors have responsibility and reporting relationships to the board of directors, thereby underscoring their independence from the business operation itself. An operational risk management function has a bit more flexibility in this regard.

For the purposes of operational risk management, however, the work of internal auditors is entirely relevant and integral to firmwide operational risk assessment. As evidence of this, at Bankers Trust, for instance, our operational risk management department was born out of collaboration from Internal Audit, Corporate Risk and Insurance Management and Strategic planning. The firm's General Auditor played a key role in driving the development forward. Over time, however, as a bank it became advisable to separate internal audit from operational risk management. A productive working relationship remained, however.

At Bankers Trust, we used internal audit reports as part of the qualitative side of our risk-based capital models. A review of the audit reports, their ratings, and the status of business management's response formed the basis for additional risk-based modification to our statistically derived risk capital.

Other firms have also used audit reports as part of their operational risk management programs. Along with their many other tools and techniques, Hansruedi Schuetter, Group Operational Risk Manager for Credit Suisse Group, has found these reports to be extremely helpful as an independent source of documented risk information. He offers his advice on the use of them in the following section, which he authored.

CASE ILLUSTRATION

Leveraging Internal Audit Reviews

Credit Suisse Group

Internal Audit is the Chairman's personal team of experts who perform regular independent health checks on the business. It may be safe to assume that internal auditors generally satisfy the highest integrity standards and are not driven by any profit and loss or bonus considerations in their assessments.

Given the pole position that Audit enjoys, management must strive to use Audit as a powerful ally and rich source of insight and information that may otherwise be hard to obtain. This must appear as a trivial statement, however, the reality is that in many institutions, Internal Audit's existence is considered as some sort of a necessary evil. There is probably nothing more frustrating for an auditor than knowing that nobody really cares about most of his output. Barings' auditors pointing to Nick Leeson's concentration of power in Singapore bears grim witness of this.

At Credit Suisse Group, we pay great attention to every single audit report. Due to its early establishment and top down implementation, Internal Audit applies consistent methodologies and uniform standards. For the Operational Risk Manager, a detailed analysis of audit reports is of particular value because it provides:

- Firmwide coverage at all areas, all departments, all levels
- Examiner commands broad company knowledge and overview
- Uncompromising, but fair, scrutiny
- Findings based on documented facts

- Tailor-made recommendations
- Business response to findings
- Commitment of deadlines for remediation
- Early warning signals of potential danger

Shortcomings consist of:

- Freeze frame type inspection
- Irregular inspection intervals
- Valuable, but potentially time-consuming, routine checks

The first two shortcomings are probably in the nature of Audit's mandate and resources, whereas the last one is different from firm to firm. Auditors at Credit Suisse Group endeavor to dig deeper into nonroutine aspects, without neglecting to produce the necessary statistical findings. This not only enriches the auditor's job, but also requires a much more detailed knowledge of the nature of the business inspected.

How does Operational Risk Management use Audit Reports? At the Corporate level, we track audit points routinely across all business units as well as per individual unit. These high-level statistics are presented quarterly to the Executive Board and the Group Risk Coordination Committee as indicators of where management attention should be directed.

As Operational Risk Manager, I sometimes have my own opinion of what is a good or a bad report. Mostly, my opinion will coincide with Audit, but often I tend to be more demanding and critical. Completely opposing overall judgments are seldom, but it has happened, mostly due to differing judgment criteria. A report calling for a few dozen labor-intensive improvements is undoubtedly one that would carry a "major action required" tag, however they may represent a limited indicator only of the overall risk posed. Things I would personally consider in my own judgment would include:

- Management attitude to the audit points
- Deadlines proposed
- Number of issues resolved by the time the report is delivered to senior management

Occasionally, cultural differences in the business environment may be applied when deciding on a subjective management rating. The CRO, the CFO, or the Chairman will follow up on unsatisfactory audit reports if they contain points that have not been resolved since the previous inspection or point to a substantial risk of any sort for the bank. These follow-ups are intended as a clear message to the business lines that senior management all the way at the top cares. As a consequence, it is encouraging to observe the percentage of bad reports decreasing steadily, whereas the very good reports remain at a stable 20% across the group.

In summary, the use of internal audit reports as a prime management tool results in:

- Greater recognition, importance, and impact of Internal Audit
- Closer integration of Audit with the business
- Comprehensive management overview
- Judgmental health certificate (versus, e.g., VAR or similar numbers)
- Early warning signals of potential danger
- Senior management follow-up as clear message
- Additional bonus relevant factor

Audit reports are a powerful, value-adding tool only if senior management is prepared to fully support Internal Audit and insist on remediation of all audit points raised, something that Credit Suisse Group's top management has committed to.

■ ■ ■

New Product Review Processes

Corporations have struggled with new product and new process review processes for many years. The concept is simple: Put in place a system of review such that new products and/or processes are evaluated by risk management and control groups prior to roll-out. New product and process reviews usually involve a team of diverse corporate staff functions such as operational risk management, market and credit risk, legal, compliance, audit, technology, insurance risk management, and others, as appropriate.

The challenges are also easy to understand: Business units are anxious to roll out their new products and processes. Speed to market is key and any roadblock that appears to slow things down unnecessarily is resented and often skirted, if at all possible.

TOP-DOWN (PORTFOLIO-LEVEL) RISK ASSESSMENT STRATEGIES

In this section we will examine a qualitative portfolio-level method— namely, the process of building risk inventories.

CASE ILLUSTRATION

Early Operational Risk Management Work

Bankers Trust

At Bankers Trust,[4] we began looking strategically at operational risk management as a part of an early attempt at strategic firmwide risk

> ### BP STRATEGY #13—USE A PORTFOLIO-BASED ANALYSIS TO EVALUATE AND MANAGE FIRMWIDE LOSS POTENTIAL
>
> Bottom up process reviews are important for individual business unit and line managers. At a firmwide level, however, senior management must have an aggregate view of operational risk for strategic planning and decision-making. This is where the portfolio-level analysis comes in.

management. We had already developed models for market and credit risk, and now the question was: What's missing? Thus, in 1990 we began capturing risks outside of our market and credit risk measurement criteria (i.e., beyond 99% confidence level) and calling them long-tail event risks. We also began capturing risks of a nonmarket and credit variety. The trick was not only identification of them, but at a later stage, measurement of them.

Our first pass involved simple scenario analysis from the corporate level; asking questions of key managers about the loss scenarios most likely to "keep them awake at night." Admittedly many involved credit and market risks, but oftentimes there was also an operational risk dimension (e.g., large-scale failure of key systems, overarching regulatory change, class action legal concerns, loss of key people). The exercise involved a systematic pass through risk identification, identification of past losses, assessment of projected probabilities, frequencies and severities, risk finance and/or insurance in place, and most important of all, effective risk response measures.

At the time, the cornerstone of Bankers Trust's work on operational risk was a long-tail event risk assessment project initiated in 1990 by our team, Operational Risk and Insurance Management, together with the strategic planning group. The study was intended to identify and assess all major "long-tail" event (LTE) risk classifications (i.e., event risks under the tail of the firm's RAROC probability distribution curve, but not captured by those models at the time). This assessment led to a continuous process of work with others enterprise-wide toward enhanced management controls for each risk.

Risk identification and assessment efforts in this area resulted in an extensive inventory of risk classes. Early on in the process we began to differentiate between two general areas of event risks. They were business-specific risks and universal-corporate risks. One of the first efforts that developed from this study was work based on the need to integrate defensive actions into the fabric of the firm and its day-to-day operations. Specific results of this effort were (1) the

Hypothetical Entry for Professional Liability Risks

Risk Description	Risk Assessment	Risk Response Activities
Professional Liability Risks Legal liabilities for errors, omissions, or "wrongful acts" with respect to fee-based financial services or other activities of the firm. There is no limitation to the reach of this risk; it is present in virtually every business unit of the firm.	Financial services' professional liability is becoming a major problem for financial service firms worldwide, as have liabilities for other professional disciplines, such as medical, accounting, legal, engineering, and architectural firms. The expected annual loss exposure to this risk on a firmwide basis is estimated at less than $5 million. This estimate is comprised primarily of legal defense costs. Firmwide interviews, scenario analysis discussions, and a review of external industry loss data have implied that the firm's exposure to this risk can range, however, from $5 to $500 million! Specific areas of concern firmwide include: • Conflicts of interest allegations involving client relationships with two or more business lines, where there is the potential for inappropriate sharing of confidential information. • Improper management of credits, particularly where the firm has responsibility as adviser or agent for a loan facility or participation. • Breach of fiduciary duties, where errors may be alleged in the handling of customer assets. • Failure to perform or execute trading commitments that result in a client's or counterparty's inability to meet obligations. • Investment performance involving real or perceived guarantees of investment returns. • Special loans/workouts situations in which it is alleged that the firm has become involved in the wrongful management of the customer's business. • Improper or inadequate advice in structuring complex financial transactions. • Fraudulent misrepresentation in allegations of breached transaction warranties. • Valuation errors or omissions in investment banking transactions.	The business divisions have the responsibility to manage the individual risks represented by these scenarios. Some of the measures being taken to respond include: • Special sales and marketing product and compliance training • Product disclosures • Indemnification agreements • CSA reviews to identify and address specific vulnerabilities • Active review of customer satisfaction and/or complaints It was identified that the firm's Structured Products Group has a very effective risk response program in place, which should be promoted as a best practice for improving other divisional programs firmwide.

EXHIBIT 9.7 Portfolio-Level Risk Inventory

firmwide standards for long-tail event risk and business continuity risk, (2) introduction of broader-based operational risk management research and development, and (3) the operational risk group's coordination of round table discussions with business lines where risks were identified and management controls discussed. Exhibit 9.7 presents a fictitious illustrative risk inventory entry from this type of scenario analysis exercise.

We continued this approach over several years as our early attempt at tracing large-scale firmwide long-tail event risks, as we were calling them. A key benefit of the process was the identification of low frequency/high severity risks that had not previously been in focus. In 1992 and 1993, we set out to identify a methodology that might actually align to our market and credit risk functions. Our objectives were simple enough. They spanned (1) risk measurement, in supporting capital adequacy and attribution; (2) risk management, in support of strategic decision making (i.e., invest, disinvest, or divest), and to provide support of the risk control environment; and (3) risk finance, in providing tools to support decision making relative to risk finance designs and insurance/reinsurance purchases.

This time we initiated our scenario analysis approach by business. After several detailed reviews, however, we realized that while the analysis served as an informative exercise, from a loss potential perspective its results were too subjective to be completely convincing and comparative in the absence of other approaches. This observation caused us to work toward supplementing these analyses with quantitative analysis for more consistent risk-based capital measurement and allocation purposes, particularly for uses that might involve strategy decisions. Thus we move on to the universe of operational risk data.

■ ■ ■

INTRODUCTION TO THE DATA UNIVERSE

Risk practitioners are thirsting for operational risk data, whether it is for modeling or simply for benchmarking purposes.[5] The need for operational risk management data sets is fundamental to understanding the potential for operational risk. By way of historical perspective, operational risk and losses have always existed in financial services firms. Operational risk management has come alive in recent years because of a string of large-scale and colorful losses. So when it comes to arguing the importance of loss data, you don't have to take anyone's word for it. The losses speak for themselves.

BP STRATEGY #14 — COORDINATE EVENT AND RISK INDICATOR INFORMATION FIRMWIDE

Coordinate data and information about operational risk issues, incidents, and losses by developing a process to capture and track them, including their cost and causative factors, at both business and corporate levels firmwide. Identify and track predictive indicators and drivers of operational risks. Capture both quantitative and qualitative driver data. Provide indicator reports and scores to management levels appropriate for action.

A first critical step is to begin to quantify risk and losses so that we can get our arms around the depth and breadth of the problem. Once we quantify risk, it becomes both a cost and an opportunity. Operational risk data are key to understanding, measuring, and evaluating the myriad mounting risk losses cutting into the bottom line. In operational risk management, regardless of data type, the most valuable data for risk profiling will be your firm's own. It would be ideal if operational risk data were as available as other sets such as market and economic indicator data. Unfortunately, it is not. There are several constraints that make it difficult to gather historical loss information. As a partial solution, risk management practitioners have come to realize the value of using historical industry data to supplement their own firms' loss histories and distributions for analysis and corporate learning.

What will this universe of internal and external consist of? How do we go about tracking, gathering, and organizing our data universe? Where will the information come from? Developing an operational risk data framework is the first step.

When we begin to construct a framework and risk profile, we do so with the universe of information known about the organization's *experience*. Then we move on to look at predictors of risk. These include broad categories of *risk indicators:* inherent risk variables, management controllable risk indicators, composite indicators, and model factors. Thus, the two major categories are:

1. **Experience/Event Data:** The capture of operational loss data has for quite some time now been a fundamental feature in support of risk management processes, in particular insurance risk management. Along with issues and incidents it represents a whole dimension of operational profiling.
2. **Risk Indicators/Predictors of Risk:** These enable risk managers to monitor and track several different types of data sets. Broadly defined, they include inherent risk variables or exposure bases, management control risk indicators, composite indicators, and model risk factors.

The use of risk indicators and analysis is still relatively new. Before we begin, it is important to understand the subtle difference between inherent risk variables and control-oriented risk indicators. Inherent risk variables are those exposure bases or factors that describe characteristics of a business: numbers or values of transactions, assets, and fixed costs. Control-oriented risk indicators are things a manager can control, such as investments in training or systems maintenance.[6] Most important of all, each variable or risk indicator must be evaluated on the basis of its significance, or predictive capabilities, to ensure accuracy and relevance throughout the various levels of the organization.

The next two chapters expand the discussion of event data and risk indicators, respectively, in detail, both in preparation for the subsequent chapters on risk measurement and modeling, capital models, and risk profiling and monitoring.

CONCLUSION

One of the most important steps in the risk management process is risk assessment analysis of the uncertainty of all outcomes. Understanding not only the range of possible economic impacts, but understanding the circumstances that might contribute to a loss, the scenarios that have occurred at your own firm or at other firms before, contributing factors, and the likelihood of the event are all important to analyze and understand.

Every competitive organization must have a perspective on threats to its forward progress, its strategies, and certainly its survival. This is what risk assessment is all about. Viewed in this way, operational risk assessment becomes a critical part of the business, its strategy, evolution, and execution of key business plans, certainly not just a necessary evil mandated by the corporate center and industry regulators. So, regardless of the simplicity or complexity of risk assessment, the process itself is an essential part of business success.

LESSONS LEARNED AND KEY RECOMMENDATIONS

- There are two key dimensions of risk assessment. The first is the continuum from top down portfolio-based views to specific bottom up processes. The second is the continuum from subjective to quantitative assessments and risk measurement. Each of the four quadrants of risk assessment adds value to the firm. Once again, balance is key.
- Bottom up analyses (i.e., process-level scenario analyses, such as control self-assessment) are very useful for (1) identifying specific control weaknesses in discrete processes, and (2) providing the basis for the most tangible remedial or mitigation action steps.

- Implement a bottom up process to identify, evaluate, and manage operational risks. Effective operational risk management implies having a clear understanding of embedded risks that can cause serious harm to the organization. This requires a process for identifying and evaluating new or existing risks on a continuous basis (e.g., independent risk assessment, control self-assessment, process analysis) (BP Strategy #12).
- Bottom up risk assessment can be very effective for analyzing specific business processes. One should be careful, however, since one size does not fit all. That is, the strategy will have to be tailored for different types of businesses. For instance, some CSA programs often result in resistance if an organization attempts to apply without modification across the entire firm. For instance, the detailed nature of these programs often work best in analyzing certain routine processes, such as money transfer or settlement businesses. Without modification, they may be rejected by non-routine functions, such as investment banking and capital markets businesses.
- Use a firmwide portfolio-based approach to monitor operational risks. Although bottom up process reviews are helpful for individual business unit and line managers, senior management at a firmwide level must have an aggregate view of operational risk. This is where the portfolio level analysis comes in (BP Strategy #13).
- Firmwide or top down analyses (i.e., class loss analyses, actuarial analyses, risk inventories, risk maps) are most useful for (1) Strategic planning and portfolio-level decisions about allocations of capital and (2) risk class-based decisions about enterprise-wide risk financing and insurance programs.
- Use of internal audit reports *by operational risk management* can leverage the audit function for even greater impact and, on occasion, provide a second opinion on audit findings (useful to avoid the Barings' syndrome).
- One key feature that differentiates modern-day operational risk management programs from its predecessor programs of the past is the concept of identifying risk classes, gathering data, and beginning to prove causation. All of this plays to a need for a universe of data to profile, understand, and track various characteristics of the risks.
- Coordinate *event and risk indicator data* firmwide. Track operational risk issues, incidents, and losses by developing a system to capture and track them, including their cost and causative factors, at both business and corporate levels firmwide. Identify and track predictive indicators and drivers of operational risks. Capture both quantitative and qualitative driver data. Provide indicator reports and scores to management levels appropriate for action (BP Strategy #14).

CHAPTER 10

Databases and Consortia
Working Through the Details

THE PAST IS PROLOGUE

The past is a useful predictor of future risk. As one key starting point in profiling a firm's operational risk, there is no doubt about the value of creating an inventory of past experience.

Astonishingly, however, few firms had even attempted this until recently. They have no idea what operational risk losses cost them on a firmwide basis each year. Many firms have yet to track them; others are still not even clear where to begin or how to dimension or measure the underlying risk. In contrast, firms that have begun to track their operational losses have determined that the cost is very significant, indeed. For instance, one firm recently completed a five-year analysis of its operational losses and discovered that in the aggregate those losses had cost it over $1 billion from its bottom line. A second global bank did a multiyear analysis and found that the number was well over $5 billion![1]

Beyond simply collecting past loss data to benchmark their own business lines or organizations against others, many risk management practitioners have concluded that data-based calculations are an effective foundation for modeling operational risk. Unfortunately, however, because so few have collected the data, many do not yet have access to enough of it to even begin an analysis, or to prove or disprove their program or model's value.

In this chapter we explore more fully the event side of the data universe. That is, we look at the conceptual progression of operational risk issues, incidents, and losses. First we will define the terms, then we will look at the benefits of the various data categories, and last we will take a detailed look into loss databases and data consortia.

BP STRATEGY #14, REDUX—COORDINATE EVENT AND RISK INDICATOR INFORMATION FIRMWIDE

Coordinate data and information about operational risk issues, incidents, and losses by developing a process to capture and track them, including their cost and causative factors, at both business and corporate levels firmwide. Identify and track predictive indicators and drivers of operational risks. Capture both quantitative and qualitative driver data. Provide indicator reports and scores to management levels appropriate for action.

GETTING AHEAD OF THE LOSSES

One of the most logical places to begin is to create an inventory of past experience (e.g., incidents and losses). Couple these with risk circumstances, or "issues" that are known, and an interesting progression of risk emerges. These data classes are defined as follows:

- **Issues:** Circumstances that have been identified and may lead to a loss in the future (e.g., outstanding internal audit, compliance, and technology issues).
- **Incidents:** Occurrences that might well have resulted in monetary loss, or a reputation loss, but due to the credit of either loss control measures or just plain good fortune did not.
- **Losses:** Incidents that resulted in direct or indirect economic or monetary loss (e.g., business disruption or legal liability). Losses can also include reputation, brand, franchise, and other difficult-to-value losses.

Embedded in risk control strategies since "the beginning of time," the idea here is that a firm wants to catch events early enough in the progression to keep them from becoming losses. Exhibit 10.1 introduces the conceptual progression of events from issues to incidents and losses.

Issue Tracking

As an example, once a weakness in controls in a trading or settlement system is identified (an issue), it should be addressed as soon as reasonably possible. Conceptually, if it is not, then the risk may begin to manifest itself in the form of limit breaches, settlement breaks, or fails (incidents) that have not yet resulted in monetary loss. If the incidents are not addressed, they may grow in number and the chance of them costing the firm increases (i.e., they result in actual losses).

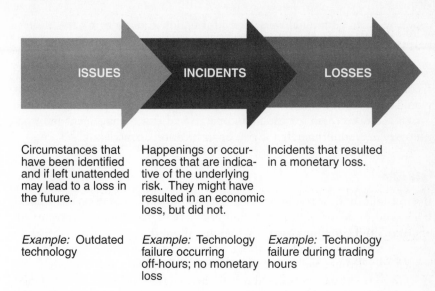

ISSUES	INCIDENTS	LOSSES
Circumstances that have been identified and if left unattended may lead to a loss in the future.	Happenings or occurrences that are indicative of the underlying risk. They might have resulted in an economic loss, but did not.	Incidents that resulted in a monetary loss.
Example: Outdated technology	*Example:* Technology failure occurring off-hours; no monetary loss	*Example:* Technology failure during trading hours

EXHIBIT 10.1 Leveraging the Event Progression: Issues, Incidents, and Losses

Interestingly enough, if this progression is not recognized or addressed the loss developments may result in even greater risk costs and the introduction of indirect risk. For as long as the incident or weakness is left unchecked, it exposes the organization to even greater risk. Although, it may have initially resulted in loss, now because management is aware and has not acted, the potential for regulatory, customer, and/or shareholder liability risk may enter the picture.

In the spirit of upside when tracking risk issue data one should not ignore the benefit of tracking the inverse of risk issues—productive operational risk mitigation investments, particularly from the perspective of internal best practice efforts. In an economic capital sense, such tracking might even result in assigning credits to the business or unit, and reflecting those results in incentive compensation rewards. However used, this issue, as well as the risk mitigation investment tracking exercise, can add much to the emerging universe of operational risk data.

Incident Data

The key to effective risk assessment is to examine risks before losses occur, or at the very least before a series of incidents becomes a large-scale operational risk and loss. Much has been written about self-assessment, process engineering or re-engineering analysis, and, for that matter, internal controls and audit standards. For our purposes here, it is useful to note that these areas can provide an additional wealth of information about a firm's risk profile, particularly if distilled into useful data displays.

One approach is to attempt to assign a downside loss value to the risk issues and incidents identified and work those values into a scenario analysis or risk mapping exercise for management information displays. Another would be to risk-rank issues and incidents identified by those processes and assign values to them for use in an operational risk management information system, and ultimately for risk quantification or modeling.

Loss Data

If a tree falls in the forest and no one is there to hear it, did it make a sound? If a loss occurred in your business four or five years ago, and no one recorded, analyzed, and communicated any findings about it, would anyone benefit a year or two from now? How about in the scenario in which the staff have turned over? Might the new team wind up making the same mistakes?

Given the choice between internal and external loss data, internal data are the most useful. They are the best representation a firm can use in profiling its own risk. They are the closest representation of the firm's own business mix, its control infrastructure, and culture. There are a few hitches, however. First, with the exception of the most recent losses, each of those variables will change over time. Thus, the older losses are not as accurate a representation of the risk profile as the most recent ones. Second, the good and bad news is that most firms don't have enough large losses to give a reasonable representation of large loss potential by using internal data alone. These concerns aside, internal loss data are the most valuable source of data for analysis of a given firm's risk.

The trouble is that all too often corporations give the appearance of being in denial about losses. It is unfortunate that far too few have collected their past losses, no less studied them in the form of post mortems or database construction. It is only natural to attempt to keep financial statements in a positive light, of course, seeking logical offsets and recoveries to net against losses when they occur. The fact is, however, that when it comes to operational risk losses, most companies spend more time burying and hiding them than they do analyzing them.

The problem is tough enough at the business unit level, but at a corporate level, the challenge is even greater. So it is even more important to begin the process of getting managers on board and aligned to firmwide operational risk management and data collection goals. Some of the most fertile areas of a firm for sourcing incident and loss data are: Accounting/Controllers (Errors and Claims accounts), Audit, Technology, trading, sales, back office (fails/breaks), front office (clearing, cash management, custody), security, Human Resources, and the Legal Department.

CASE ILLUSTRATION
Early Database Investments

Bankers Trust

In the early 1990s, we began construction of one of the industry's first operational loss databases at Bankers Trust.[2] We had already been maintaining an internal database of insurable losses in our insurance and risk finance unit. With the introduction of our new operational risk management initiative, we expanded upon that insurance-related project to cast our net wider in seeking to understand the universe of operational risk. At the same time we began a second project, and the creation of a second database, which involved the collection of industry (external) losses. All told, when the time was tallied, it took us something in the order of two person-years before we were to the point in 1995 that we felt comfortable enough with the data to begin modeling on a firmwide basis across all business lines. Was the time and effort worth it? Most definitely yes.

The exercise helped us to develop our own definition of operational risk and to learn much about loss causes and actual loss costs in the interim. Initially we began by capturing and studying the characteristics of any loss event that did not have its basis in a market or credit loss (i.e., was not caused by a market move or the inability of a party to meet its obligations). Our early analysis resulted in observations that: (1) because of sparse data at Bankers Trust alone (thankfully), we would use industry data to supplement our own; (2) we should hold our numbers of risk classes to a minimum; and (3) we could class the losses by a type distinction that will be meaningful for future analysis (i.e., by resource/asset or causation).

With these considerations in mind, one result of the effort was that operational risk classes developed an identity of their own. After that, we began focusing our attention on a definition of operational risk that centered on business disruptions related to:

- **People/human capital** (e.g., employee errors; injury to, or loss of, key people, intellectual property; employment-related liability)
- **Relationships** (e.g., customer-, regulatory-, shareholder-related matters)
- **Physical assets** (e.g., loss of physical business location or property, loss of customer assets)
- **Technology resources** (e.g., systems failure, programming errors, hacking; loss of hardware, applications)
- **Other external/regulatory** (e.g., external fraud risk or regulatory change risk)

We concluded that classifications of loss to, or involving, the firm's key resources and related functional responsibilities, as outlined above, was most relevant from a risk management standpoint. These risk classes also allowed us to focus on the direct loss exposures (i.e., risk of loss of key technology, for instance) and indirect consequences (e.g., legal liability or business disruption involving technology). They also served as important classes and bases for our operational risk models.

Another benefit of our databases included analyzing past mistakes and/or causes of loss for future risk control procedural changes and investments. In addition, by reviewing causes and outcomes we were in a better position to make appropriate refinements to our insurance and risk finance programs and enhance coverage for the future.

■ ■ ■

BUILDING A LOSS DATABASE

As a result of regulatory pressure, many other firms have now set themselves to the task of collecting data from throughout their organizations on everything from errors and claims to trade fails, shortages, property losses, external frauds, and legal actions. Some specific categories being discussed in a regulatory context include write-downs, loss of recourse, restitution, legal liability, and loss of or damage to assets. The task can be daunting and take years, but is well worth it.[3]

The creation of a loss database, whether an internal or external one, has become recognized as being of utmost importance in any operational risk effort. A well-designed and thorough database will enable the user to delve into key facts and trends, which can be used to perform rigorous analysis. To underscore their value in shedding light on the causes and nature of risk and loss, risk practitioners might go as far as to refer to these tools as knowledge bases internally because of their value.

Factual information is key. Examples are:

■ The identification of the institution or department that incurred losses
■ The amount of loss suffered as a result of the loss incident
■ The date the loss was realized
■ The occurrence period, or the time interval for the reported loss
■ The insurance recovery, if any, of all or a portion of the loss
■ The location of the reported loss

Descriptive and Interpretive Information

The catalogue and easy availability of the information allows a risk manager to address and answer relevant questions to help mitigate risk. Following are some of the pertinent questions that relate to direct observations:

■ Can we draw any conclusions about significant event periods (e.g., are there specific trends where operational stress is most rampant)? For instance, the 2000 Technology bubble, the 1987 Stock Market crash, or the Asian crisis in 1997.

- Are there any obvious trends in large legal settlements and how have companies been affected?
- Are there any possible generalizations relative to the loss events at specific firms? This implies the idea of "learning from the past mistakes from others." But instead of learning on a case by case basis, loss events of a particular competitor, business sector, or product line could be compiled and examined, and some instructive conclusions made about their weaknesses.
- What have been the effects on individual firms (earnings, share price, market perception)? Do highly publicized loss events lead to a significantly larger impact to share price?

Interpretive risk management information is a more advanced feature, and much harder to come by. It is entirely dependant on the detail and quality of data capture. Interpretive information will help answer questions like:

- How was the loss detected?
- What are the most effective checks and controls?
- What are the underlying factors that led to the loss?
- Was the loss a result of control failures or firm wide corporate culture?
- Which business functions in the company have the highest inherent risks?
- Are there products and services, or features of them, that are more risk prone than others?
- What are other possible loss outcomes if the courts ruled and granted claimants their initial demands?
- Is there a correlation between occurrence period and the amount of loss? Is it possible that the longer the risk went undetected the higher the loss amount? How about between causative or contributory factors and size?
- Were risk finance and insurance strategies effective?
- Were international cultural differences a factor? For example, did companies suffer losses because they failed to localize their operations (e.g. securities scandals in various countries)?

Distilling Causes and Effects

Ask yourself the question at the outset: Am I capturing symptoms of the operational risk problem, or am I getting to the underlying causes? This is a trap one can fall into with the use of historical loss data and databases. That is, if we only look at the outcome of the losses, and draw inferences from them, are we considering the appropriate issues? Or does it make more sense to dig into losses more deeply and look at the causative factors? I would certainly argue that the latter is more appropriate. For instance, have we achieved anything if we capture, aggregate, and project all trading losses that were not caused by market conditions? Or is it more appropriate to separate the losses that were caused by trades outside of authorized limits versus operational losses caused by traders with different levels of training, supervision, and experience? These are the types of classification issues that must be considered early on.

THE NEED FOR DATA STANDARDS

When it comes to the universe of data, certainly the adage of "garbage in, garbage out" suggests that, as far as data are concerned, much planning and standardization must be applied in any viable data model. This is even more important for consistency of analysis.

The need for data standards is an important aspect of the internal and external database picture. Starting out with an agreed upon definition of operational risk can help to insure that everyone is on the same page. The definition would then determine which types of events would be appropriate for your database. You can limit the database to only risk cases that fall into predefined risk categories. In short, you will need to incorporate data standards in every field in your database. Some of the questions you will come up against include:

- What losses will you include (again)? Have a complete data dictionary of what an "operational loss" consists of and define each class and subclass explicitly.
- Decide on a standard for entering data in each of the fields; for instance, date fields, currency fields, geographic location fields, and text fields. Build these standards into your database model to create uniformity and make it easy to do analysis on the data.
- Define and assign a standard risk class to each item. Have clear definitions of each risk class so that the codes are accurate.
- Understand and define the width and breadth of the data you are collecting such that they are uniform across all entries.
- Use uniform names for all departments, businesses, and products so that you can aggregate them under one larger heading. Alternatively, create an authority file for each department so that whichever way the name is input, it will always aggregate the same way, under one business, such as money transfer, for example.
- Have a field for the source of information (person, manager, periodic report, etc.) for tracking purposes.
- Document all dates including the date the record was entered, who entered it, and a comment field for future observations.

There is little one can do to sidestep the commitment of time and effort required to build an internal incident and loss database. Initially, much of the effort will be manual as analysts are required to sift through disparate records of errors and claims in one place, customer issues in another, systems outages in a separate location, and so on. Unfortunately, the enormity of the task of collecting proprietary data might stand in the way of gathering a sufficient amount of it. The best firms will develop data sourcing and capture formats and harness technology and internal accounting systems to achieve a more automated data capture process. This will cut the time and cost somewhat initially, and more dramatically as time goes on. Even with an automated data capture process, you will find yourself wanting for staff resources to enter and scrub all the data. Without one, however, your own team's resource needs will be far greater due to manual sorting, counting, aggregating, data access, and analysis.

At this point, you may be sold on the idea of collecting event data, and you have developed your data standards and collection process for your own firm. Both fortunately and unfortunately, you may encounter another problem on a business-by-business basis.[4]

". . . BUT WE HAVEN'T HAD ANY LOSSES"

The senior manager at a large multinational bank sat reviewing the capital allocation for his unit and blurted out, "We haven't had any operational losses here. We are far less risky than this report would suggest. I simply don't accept these findings or allocations." In this case, the resourceful risk manager had maintained a database of operational losses, however, and nimbly slipped out of the room during the course of other conversations just long enough to retrieve loss data relevant to the industry sector in question. You see, the business manager had in fact suffered two losses over the past two years, which he had conveniently forgotten. In addition, although the business manager and his team had not suffered many losses themselves, their industry sector had, and in a very big way. One look at the list of both internal and external losses was met with comments like "Oh, yeah, I was aware of this one, everyone is, but what is this? . . . And this? . . . And this one?" Each loss was a bit more significant than the last, in terms of size, scope, and circumstances. Could it happen to him? It was easy enough to deny one, two, three, even a half dozen cases, but certainly not all of them. Ten major loss cases later, the conversation moved on to the allocation methodology.

As you can see from this illustration, some have the enviable problem of not having had many losses, and therefore do not have sufficient data to populate a benchmarking scorecard, or the body or tail of a loss distribution, or whatever tools you are looking to populate. They may have either managed their business well or have been just plain fortunate. Either way, from the

There are three types of databases in use today: (1) a firm's own ("internal") losses, (2) losses of other firms ("external" losses), and (3) consortium loss databases. Each has its own advantages and disadvantages, but when taken together, they are complementary and can be very effective

Database Type	Advantages	Disadvantages
Internal Losses	(1) Serves as the best direct reflection of a firm's own loss experience and potential. (2) Taken in isolation, internal losses are too inward-focused.	(1) A firm's own experience would normally be light on "tail risk" losses, thus making it difficult to use alone in forecasting future events.
External Losses	(1) Natural bias of loss information in the public domain is toward large, newsworthy events generally underrepresented in internal databases (i.e., "tail losses") (2) A firm can learn much by studying and avoiding the mistakes of others, not to mention dodging the monetary loss.	(1) Losses may not be directly relevant to any one firm; user must select relevant losses from the overall population. (2) Few databases have sufficient detail about circumstances, control environments, etc. involved in the losses for adequate benchmarking.
Consortium Losses	(1) Can be used to fill in necessary data for either the body or tail of the distribution.	(1) In sanitizing losses, they may not provide sufficient detail about circumstances, control environments, etc.

Databases are important weapons in the arsenal for managing operational risk. They are invaluable for (a) supporting analysis and projections; (b) selecting individual large losses for use in stress testing models; (c) conducting loss cause analysis by reviewing loss patterns; and (d) supporting risk finance and insurance decision making.

EXHIBIT 10.2   Database Advantages and Disadvantages

perspective of analysis, situations like these point to the need to supplement databases of proprietary losses (internal databases) with information from outside the firm. Thus, practitioners have looked to databases of industry losses (external databases), and/or data from loss consortia, which have recently been formed by industry members to pool their data on a confidential basis for mutual use. Exhibit 10.2 is a matrix of advantages and disadvantages of internal and external loss databases.

CAPTURING EXTERNAL LOSS DATA

External operational risk data can come from several places. In some industries, it already exists in a raw form in the public domain—created by an industry association or another group with the self-interest in tracking and organizing industry statistics. Unfortunately, this has not generally been the case in banking, which is why vendors have developed databases and loss consortia have been formed.

The sources for finding external operational risk loss data range from newspapers to court documents, and from research reports to personal interviews. Performed diligently, hands-on research becomes a painstaking labor of love. Personal interviews can round out your information if the outside company/competitor makes that possible. Taking an even more proactive stance, sources can be created such as data sharing agreements between companies or a consortia of companies. But some remain skeptical of the prospects for these consortia given the legal implications and an extreme reluctance of firms to share their most confidential and guarded allegations and loss information. It would be ironic indeed if attempts to manage risk through loss data sharing in fact ended up creating more risk for the participants. Thus, any such consortium effort would have to be scrutinized carefully for its own control infrastructure.

Irrespective of approach, however, operational loss data are vital in the overall operational risk measurement and management process. The analysis of these losses (including causative factors), and associated risk indicators, forms the basis of the evaluation stage of a continuous cycle.[5]

External Incident and Loss Databases

The good news for practitioners today is that they have a choice when it comes to industry databases. Now there is truly a "build or buy" decision at hand. Several industry databases have come on the market in recent years.

As this book goes to print, there are only two major operational risk external databases available commercially in the industry: (1) The Zurich IC Squared First Database, which is an expansion and enhancement of the ORI CORE™ (Compilation of Operational Risk Events) Knowledgebase, and before that was the original Bankers Trust external database. (2) The second is an external database from OpVantage, a venture formed in 2001 through the combination of operational risk management consulting teams from NetRisk in Greenwich, Connecticut, and PriceWaterhouse Coopers, which also pooled their external databases.

External Databases—The Value Proposition

A well-constructed industry database can be useful through all phases of the risk management process and for a variety of users. Let's look at the applications by function, including risk identification, risk assessment and analysis, risk mitigation or control, and risk finance.[6]

Risk Identification   The risk practitioner will identify the sources of operational risk from either existing or new businesses. He may be very interested in loss descriptions, keywords, and loss causes. An example of this would be someone who wants to know which business sectors have represented the most frequent large losses for his or her peer group. Business areas could include banking, insurance, brokerage companies, energy companies, or e-commerce, for example.

Risk Assessment or Analysis   There are at least three levels of sophistication and database use in this area. At the first level, the database users will simply want to review the frequency and severity of large loss events. They want to know how many large losses have taken place, their size, and in what given business segment, region, or other criteria they occurred. A sample report would include tabular displays including totaled columns of numbers relating to the above.

At the second level, the individual wants to conduct some basic analysis such as loss class reviews, stratifications, or other similar runs. A graphical report including pie charts or bar charts would inform the user what the breakdown includes.

The third level will be to use external loss data in an exportable report format in support of loss forecasts and/or risk capital calculations. For instance, a risk manager may want to merge external database data with his or her own internal data for the purpose of creating combined loss distributions.

Critics are quick to challenge operational risk model results. So, regardless of the types of models being developed, most professionals have come to recognize the value of hard loss data in order to defend their risk and loss projections.

Risk Mitigation or Control   Auditors, control groups, operational risk committees, and hands-on risk managers are primarily interested in extracting any lessons learned from the loss record descriptions themselves. They will be interested in the various sorts from the database and in loss records relative to loss causation in order to predict, mitigate, and control events in their organizations.

Risk Finance   There are two separate and distinct user groups for this area. The first is the risk finance and insurance manager who has a responsibility to confirm that corporate programs remain highly relevant to the universe of operational risks. As in the Risk Identification section, he will want to identify risks that relate to all business lines in the firm. As in the

Risk Assessment area, the user wants to know the potential impact large event losses will have on the firm to set firmwide coverage limits at the right levels. This includes any reports generated on descriptions and loss amounts, as well as special risk finance/insurance reports. Here insurance keywords and information about how well insurance programs have responded become useful.

The second group in the risk finance and insurance area will consist of insurance brokers and underwriters who are seeking to understand operational risk better. They want broad search and sort features and are interested in descriptions, loss amounts, and insurance keywords.

THE DATA CONSORTIUM ENTITIES

Operational risk data consortia have become very visible on the operational risk management scene largely because of regulators' endorsement of the concept of data sharing. The basic idea behind loss consortia is that member participants will contribute their loss data on a confidential basis and, in exchange, receive a confidential representation of the loss data for the consortium membership overall. Tony Peccia, of CIBC (Canadian Imperial Bank of Commerce), has commented that he expects to receive "several key benefits from participating in an operational risk consortium, including (1) minimization of data handling costs for institution members; (2) creating flexibility for accessing loss information, while maintaining confidentiality; (3) building upon existing tools and best practices; (4) help in identifying predictive factors; and (5) facilitation of 'better' regulatory requirements."

As of the time of this writing in early 2001, there were three formal operational loss consortia in development and/or operation, with several other groups operating less formally on the fringes. In alphabetical order, the formal consortia are: (1) the Basel Consortium for Operational Risk, initiated by Pricewaterhouse Coopers; (2) GOLD, the Global Operational Loss Database, a data consortium promoted and managed by the British Bankers Association (BBA), and (3) the MORE Exchange (Multinational Operational Risk Exchange), which was supported by GARP at its earliest stages of development, along with NetRisk, now OpVantage, a risk management consultancy and software tools house based in Greenwich, CT.[7] There has recently been some discussion about the possible merger of the Basel Consortium and more.

Basel Consortium for Operational Risk

Pricewaterhouse Coopers (PwC) initiated this loss data consortium as an adjunct to its operational risk management consulting practice during the course of conversations with its clients beginning in about 1998. Active and highly visible in operational risk consulting, having conducted the milestone industry study for the BBA, ISDA, and RMA in 1999, PwC is counting on its size and status as an independent professional services firm to obviate any concerns about its close association, security procedures, and long-term viability. While assuming the organizing role, it has since allowed prospective members the latitude to shape development of the consortium. Members are determining the governance, data categories, and other parameters. PwC is attempting to maintain an arms-length status relative to the consortium by holding only a nonvoting seat on the steering committee, affirming that data (and their use) are owned and determined by the member institutions, and agreeing contractually that members can transfer custodian responsibilities if they choose. The consortium's objective is to promote loss data collection and the advancement of operational risk management for financial institutions. The Basel Consortium will be domiciled in Germany to gain confidentiality protections from the legal system there. PwC proposes to perform an evaluation of the quality of data provided and consequently report a quality rating to the members when they receive the information. This is intended to help members determine what degree of confidence they can put on the information received. Perhaps partly related to its choice of location, the Basel Consortium has appeared to have attracted a large following of European banks initially, but reportedly there are several United States, United Kingdom, and Australian banks that have expressed interest and attended organizing meetings, as well.

GOLD—The Global Operational Loss Database

The British Bankers' Association (BBA) has been in the forefront of operational risk discussions for a number of years, having conducted its first survey of banks in 1997 and also that year having held its first conference for members and nonmembers alike. Situated in the international banking hub of London, the BBA has always attracted numerous banks from the international banking community to its various operational risk management functions and initiatives. In addition, it has been in the business of the secure and confidential collection of sensitive bank data for over 30 years.

The BBA has taken a rather unique approach to the subject of forming a loss consortium. That is to say it is not seeking to engage in a detailed process of loss aggregation, scaling, analysis, and development of tools and models, as the other efforts have, other than to sanitize the data for confidentiality purposes and provide loss listings. Like the others, it has set out to collect data on operational loss events, but it has drawn the line there. According to John Thirlwell of the BBA, " 'Keep it simple' is a mantra which has been impressed on us by the participants who have chosen this approach because they are using the data for a variety of purposes. The members see

GOLD's simplicity as a strength rather than the weakness one might imply." Thus far, GOLD has mostly attracted banks either based in, or doing business in London, but they have not limited their loss data submissions to London-based events. Early submissions confirm that data represent activities worldwide. Reportedly, however, several bankers associations from other European nations have reached out to the BBA to explore the prospect of joint participation.

MORE Exchange

MORE was proposed and has been promoted most visibly by OpVantage, a U.S.-based (Greenwich, Connecticut) risk management software and consulting firm, in its early stages, and received promotional support from GARP in 1999. Since its introduction, OpVantage has stepped back into more of a formal advisory and Managing Agent role, and left the development of MORE in the hands of a steering committee and prospective members. Apparently based on comments from prospective participants that I have interviewed, this move was appreciated by the industry, because it has left participants free to explore a number of their own ideas and has engendered a greater sense of ownership. For instance, Tara McLenaghen of Royal Bank of Canada views MORE as "a true consortium in that the bank members are making all the decisions. This is one of the features that attracted us to join." The consortium's objective is to gather operational loss data, of course, but they are also anxious to support the advancement of industry practices in operational risk management. MORE has concluded an agreement with the Risk Management Association (RMA) to collaborate on data management. RMA is the data manager for incoming loss data with responsibilities including sanitizing of data, performing validity checks, loading data into the MORE database, serving on an advisory board, and assisting with marketing efforts.

Other Consortium Efforts

In addition to three formal consortium efforts, efforts to share data between banks regionally have actually predated the consortia themselves. For instance, British banks, Canadian banks, German banks, Scandanavian banks, and other European banks have shared data less formally for several years now. Exhibit 10.3 is an overview of the consortia and their status as of early 2001.

"Moving Mountains": The Issues and Challenges

Certainly the idea of gaining access to peer group data seems attractive enough. But there are a whole series of issues that must be sorted through

Consortium	Objective	Stated Goals	Other Advertised Benefits	Organizational Structure/Ownership
Basel Consortium for Operational Risk	To provide service to the financial service industry in operational loss data capture, information services, and the general advancement of operational risk management.	To advance operational risk management by serving the leading financial service firms in each country, in providing benchmarking services, and in operational risk quantification.	Data sanitization, rating scale of data quality, access to PwC experience with scaling and modeling; international support structure with PwC offices.	Consortium to be organized within PwC LLP entity in Germany and registered as a Foundation in Switzerland (see Confidentiality). Three parties involved: (1) Member Institutions, (2) Steering Committee, and (3) Custodian (PwC).
GOLD (Global Operational Loss Database)	To gather and provide a benchmarking of large loss events; to support risk measurement for risk capital.	To create a database of operational loss events larger than $50,000 retail; $100,000 wholesale.	Simplicity/speed of collection and response/economics of the venture.	Data owned by BBA Enterprises (the BBA's commercial arm) in trust for member banks.
MORE Exchange	To facilitate risk measurement and quantification of operational risk and to provide benchmarking data services.	To provide secure framework for data sharing, data to support operational capital-at-risk quantification, allow benchmarking, collect information on predictive factors, and influence regulatory decisions.	Data standards, data scrubbing/sanitization, web delivery, access to NetRisk models, and planned insurance developments.	MORE will be owned by the institutions that provide the data. Institutions will retain ownership of the data. NetRisk will act as a contracted Managing Agent.

Consortium	Status/Members	Governance	Technology	Data Collected/ Output Provided	Manager and Role
Basel Consortium for Operational Risk	10 letters of intent signed*; other parties have expressed interest.	Steering Committee to include one rep. from each of 1st 11 banks. PwC serves Committee in an advisory capacity, but without voting rights. Committee will determine PwC role beyond year 1.	Spreadsheets will be used in the start-up phase.	Sanitized scaled amounts will be shown as output; common currency; summary statistics by business; key indicators.	Pricewaterhouse Coopers. OpVantage being considered.**
GOLD (Global Operational Loss Database)	21 banks have signed the Participation Document and paid fee*.	Management Committee (MC) consists of 9 participant banks + BBA representative. MC also makes development and membership decisions.	Data submitted/ output received on Excel spreadsheets	Sanitized and anonymous raw data (spreadsheet of loss listings); members will sort, aggregate, analyze on their own.	BBA Enterprises, Ltd. and BBA statistical unit: data collection & scrubbing.
MORE Exchange	16 firms have signed letters of intent; 11 of them have been most active.	Current Organizing Committee will be replaced by a 7-member board.	MORE has offered two alternatives for data output: (1) via NetRisk's Web-based (Java) external database and data handling RiskOps software, or (2) via excel spreadsheets.	Sanitized scaled and unscaled data and distributions per published data standards on risk class (proximate cause), loss type (effect); business unit.	OpVantage Managing Agent (formerly NetRisk). RMA: data manager. Joint sales & marketing responsibilities.

EXHIBIT 10.3 Operational Risk Consortia: Comparative Features

* As of January 2001.
** As of June 2001.

before a firm will commit to sharing its own. Promoters of operational loss data consortia believe that they have many of the issues worked out. Others are still a bit skeptical that the entities can get past critical issues of confidentiality.

Thus, there are several levels of deliberation that an organization must traverse, however, before making a decision on participation—confidentiality being first. These levels can be characterized first as astonishment and resistance by senior managers ("You want to share WHAT?") to what I would call preliminary comfort, which might be characterized by statements like "OK, I see the benefits, but WHO are these people? Who else is in the group?" and "How will it protect and manage our data?" Last, but certainly not least, deliberations extend to impatience, characterized by "Are you getting any information yet from that operational risk consortium group we joined?" at which point you may be the one holding up the show by completing last minute due diligence and working out remaining details.

Let's look at each of the stages and the individual thresholds of comfort.[8]

"You Want to Share WHAT?"

Early on you will encounter your first major dilemma and challenge: Should you even propose to your senior management the idea of your company's participation? On one side of the argument is the hope of gaining access to benchmarking data on loss experience for peer group firms, the ability to fill out incomplete data sets for modeling purposes, and the ability to forecast areas of vulnerability that had heretofore been elusive. Weighing on the other side of this scale is the very real concern about divulging your firm's deepest, darkest loss secrets. Not so long ago the notion of releasing confidential loss data outside the walls of an institution would have been a nonstarter for many. To some it still is. Elsewhere in the industry there has been some movement on these concerns. To these firms, sharing loss data has become more acceptable, but there is certainly still an issue about what types of data might be shared. For instance, it might be acceptable for some to share data on trade fails and breaks, but there is no way that they would share litigation information.

Thus, the first threshold issue is one of simply getting comfortable with the entire notion of sharing such confidential data as information on a firm's deepest darkest secrets about mishaps, allegations, and lawsuits. There is no need to "candycoat" it. This is confidential stuff. Time will only tell how much has changed as we watch the consortia progress. Robin Phillips, VP of the Operational Risk Project at JP Morgan Chase, thinks that the industry is beyond this issue. He believes that it is "imperative that banks share these data in order to make progress on quantification. Loss data can and will be adequately sanitized by the banks at the first level, then further measures will be taken by the consortia themselves." He states that "the regulators will probably press banks even harder for data collaboration in order to move the risk capital progress along sooner rather than later."

In any event, one of the first areas for review will be the consortium's approach to confidentiality, including issues like who has access to your data, in what format will it be displayed, and, equally important, where is the consortium domiciled? What laws will apply on confidentiality and/or discovery, such as freedom of information? Mathias Naumann, of Bayersche Landesbank, believes that this is a key area of differentiation about the consortia. Being extremely sensitive to confidentiality concerns, he noted that "European banks do not want to own a consortium. They *do want to own the data,* however."

"Assuming that We Can Get Comfortable with Confidentiality, What Else Is Involved?"

At the next level, there will be a whole host of issues to deal with. They will range from getting comfortable with the ownership and management of the consortium and the data itself to definitions and data standards. They include the form, quality, and usefulness of the data output and an adequate level of participants such that the consortium is in the best position to gather sufficient data. They include administration, including technology support, legal issues, staff and management, operational risk management at the consortium itself (protection of the data, backups, uptime availability); cost of membership; and other services, unique nuances, and differentiating features. Incidentally, usefulness of the data, including a members' need for transparancy in order to assess relevance, can be in direct contradiction to other members' need for confidentiality, of course.

Rather than discussing each issue at length here, we have included an outline of some of the evaluation questions that you might want to ask with the consortium manager or member steering committee. Exhibit 10.4 outlines some of the key considerations. Many of these issues will be self-explanatory.

As one might expect, some firms feel very strongly about many of these issues. As evidence, there was a point in mid-2000 at which a number of major European banks were concerned and dissatisfied enough with the early stage efforts of one or more of the consortia that they issued a statement outlining their issues and concerns. It covered points including assurance: (1) that the consortia be balanced internationally, (2) that the members be the drivers of the process, (3) that the data be used by the members only, (4) that the contracted manager hold contractor status and be held accountable as a vendor, (5) that intellectual property rights remain with the contributors, and (6) that the database itself include precisely defined categories,

1. Objective and Membership
   a. What is (are) the stated objective(s), goal(s)?
   b. What is the target membership (industry (ies), industry sector(s), size of firm)?
   c. How many have signed up to date? What firms are willing to be identified as members?
   d. How many of these are *actually contributing* data at this point? How much data has been collected? What categories, types, etc.?
2. Ownership and Management
   a. Who owns the consortium, the data?
   b. What is the composition of management and decision making?
3. Definitions and Data Standards: Input
   a. What types of data are being collected? Loss data? Business performance, risk indicator data? Have the consortium defined risk classes? How were they developed? Who was involved?
   b. Are data standards publicized, distributed to all? In what format?
   c. Please provide key definitions, classes for comparative purposes.
   d. How does the consortium accommodate potential members who have a different view on risk classes, definitions, etc.
   e. Who assures compliance, reviews data submission, etc.
   f. How often will the consortium database be updated, new displays available?
   g. How is the consortium dealing with the usual U.S. data bias problem?
4. Data: Output
   a. In what form is the output data displayed? (what fields?)
   b. Transparency of data displays (i.e., actual loss descriptions and all info versus sanitized, etc.). If sanitized, then describe the format, or provide a sample.
5. Confidentiality and Security
   a. How has the consortium been addressed?
   b. Physical data records—Who gets (complete) (partial) access to the loss data?
   c. Manager's staff confidentiality rules.
   d. What computer security measures are taken?
6. Technology
   a. Describe process and format for gathering, storing, and analyzing the data?
   b. What application(s) is being used for data capture? For aggregation, analysis?
   c. What security access do you have in place?
   d. When and in what format can members view their data, consortium data?
   e. Print options, download options.

Continued

EXHIBIT 10.4 Key Considerations for Evaluating Consortia

7. Legal
   a. What measures have been taken to assure compliance with global anticompetitive laws and regulations?
   b. What contractual agreements govern the membership relationship? Commitments and obligations of members?
8. Staff and Administration
   a. What staff are devoted to the effort from the consortium? What assurance is there that this level will be maintained?
   b. Is there an administrative services contract? If so, what does it entail?
   c. Is the manager allowed access to and use of the data?
9. Membership Cost: What does it cost to join? Are there capital requirements, annual fees?
10. Differentiating Features
    a. What are the key differentiating features of this consortium relative to the others, in the manager's view?
    b. Exclusivity—Does the manager view the current consortia situation as a winner-take-all picture, or is there room for more than one in the industry?
11. Risk Management
    a. Redundancy and backup of the data and Web servers, if applicable.
    b. Assurance provided and liability insurance maintained by the manager.
12. Other Services: What analytics are available as part of the membership fee, if any? Are analytic services extra?
13. Member References: Interview 2 to 3 members.

EXHIBIT 10.4 Key Considerations for Evaluating Consortia

that members be given latitude on which categories to partipate in, and on the timeliness of data delivery. Hansruedi Schuetter, Group Operational Risk Manager for Credit Suisse Group, noted that it was never the banks' intent to form their own consortium, but it might have been "a last resort if none of the existing ones were to agree with our Joint Statement. . . ."

The majority of the issues relate to the acceptability of the consortium from the standpoint of its structure and operations. A threshold issue in this due diligence section, however, will be the types and status of the Consortium output itself and your own objectives for using it in the first place. For instance, Mathias Naumann of Bayersche Landesbank is primarily looking for "better information about the larger industry losses first. Smaller losses are a lesser priority for us." Others may have just the opposite view, preferring instead to gain access to large losses from a commercially available industry database, and using the consortia for more depth on smaller losses. For example, Chris Rachlin, Group Operational Risk Manager at Royal Bank of Scotland, would like to "get past the public loss events that everyone knows about, and gain access to information about losses not well covered in the large loss industry databases." He cited technology losses as one illustration.

In any event, if you are planning to use the data for risk measurement and modeling as virtually all of the consortia do, will you be able to search and sort through the data appropriately? Will you be able to map the consortium's risk or loss classes to your own and vice versa? Will you be able to review individual loss files and determine relevance to your institution? Will efforts to preserve confidentiality destroy the transparency necessary to evaluate relevance?

"Whatever Happened to that Consortium We Joined? Are We Getting Any Useful Information Yet?"

Whether you are a founding member sorting through all the due diligence issues outlined in Exhibit 10.4, or you are simply completing all the membership due diligence from the perspective of a prospective member, all this will take some time. But the reality is that this is only the beginning of your time and effort.

The real work begins when you set out to gather your own loss data. Many firms are already well into this exercise. Others have just begun. Winning the cooperation of your colleagues is the subject for an entirely different book, but suffice it to say that the challenges should not be underestimated.

Will They Fly?

Make no mistake about it, the formation of a consortium requires an enormous amount of work. The time and effort required to get a diverse (or even a roughly homogeneous) group of financial institutions together to agree on something as sensitive as sharing some of their deepest secrets, sometimes representing their darkest hours, is no insignificant task.[9]

Progress to Date

For all the reasons stated thus far, we cannot expect these ventures to come roaring out of the gate immediately with a complete array of usable industry data. In time, however, they should add significant value to the evolution of operational risk management. Having said all that, it is encouraging to note progress to date. Both the GOLD effort and the MORE Exchange had progressed to the point of having actually received data as of late 2000.

Chris Rachlin notes that Royal Bank of Scotland chose to participate in GOLD because given that the value and use of consortium data is still unproven, the BBA effort fits the bill for them because its framers have "kept the implementation simple and efficient, off to a quick start, and the independence of the BBA was key." Last but not least, given that consortia are still in the experimental state, GOLD's GBP 5000 initial participation fee is "a far more economical experiment for the bank to swallow." Charles Green of Westpac seconded this view, noting that because they are not yet decided how they will use the data, and whether they will work it into Westpac's capital allocation models, "cost was a factor" in their decision to participate in GOLD.

In contrast, the Basel Consortium and MORE have more ambitious plans for data standards, modeling, and the like; thus, it is understandable that they are lagging a bit in the progress category.

The Proof Will Be in the Data

It is quite likely that the ventures might be broad-based successes, but equally possible that they might only represent certain areas of less sensitive routine operations and settlement data. Or, they might gather up sanitized data from errors and claims accounts. However, it is difficult to believe that major corporations will be willing to share sensitive legal case information, even in a sanitized format. One of the practical problems with doing so is the fact that until a legal case is settled or finally adjudicated, any discussion of the circumstances or preliminary guesstimates as to the potential loss amount could easily prejudice the firm's defense. Even once a case is settled, the settlement is more than likely sealed in confidentiality, and if the case is adjudicated, the files might still be deemed confidential, particularly if an appeal might be planned. Thus, the likelihood of including legal cases is probably slim.

Technology

It is not at all clear than any of the consortia have dealt sufficiently with all of the issues necessary to handle vast quantities of data and potential relationships between individual data fields. Early on, one of the managers dismissed this step as an area that can be addressed easily. The intricacies and time necessary for technology data model design and technology development are often underappreciated and underestimated, however, by nontechnologist users. So, given the current indication, prospective members should probably double, triple, or perhaps even quadruple their time and expense estimates given for a robust technology. Having said that, most of the participants themselves still have much work to do in gathering their loss data internally, no less entering the data into a state-of-the-art database system. The consortia would do well, however, to focus on their technology sooner rather than later.

Making the Final Decision

It is too soon to tell which of the consortium efforts will be best, or if any such discussion will be pointless because in the end they may decide to combine or at least collaborate. In the interim, individual risk managers are beginning to cast their votes in terms of letters of intent or actual participation, but it would be unfair to judge until the consortia are fully operational.

Ultimately your own final decision may end up being based on your confidence in the group and the manager. Clearly, some are most comfortable with the BBA as an independent industry association. Others are comfortable with the MORE Exchange and OpVantage because they are current or prospective clients and are seeking expertise in various quantification or modeling methods.

A Few Words of Caution

> *Myth: Industry-wide (or external) loss databases*
> *are THE (entire) answer*

Let me be clear at the outset. I have always been an advocate of using historical external or industry loss data as a key tool in a holistic approach to operational risk management. My team began building one of the first, if not *the* first, industry-wide operational loss databases and quantitative methodologies in 1990 as an extension of our loss tracking and actuarial analysis for risk finance and insurance decision-making purposes. This early work underscored the value of historical industry loss data, but at the same time it highlighted the fallacies of relying on industry loss databases exclusively for management, or even modeling, for that matter.[10]

Industry databases are much more effective when used in combination with other advanced risk management tools. As respected risk consultant editor, and publisher of *Risk Management Reports* Felix Kloman has said, "Basing your forecasts entirely on the past is akin to riding a bobsled downhill backwards: you're inevitably going to meet a bump, bear or tree you didn't see!"[11]

The most robust, and therefore predictive, data sets will combine the causative characteristics of both industry loss data *and your firm's own internal data,* and marry the two data sets with forward-looking scenario analyses. Chapter 12 explores these methods in detail.

In addition, *industry* loss data do not provide much toward representing your firm's unique control environment characteristics. For this, the best firms:

- Use their *own* incident and loss data to represent frequency and their own control environment (e.g., What are your firm's most frequent incident and/or loss types by business and product line?).

■ Combine loss data with self-assessments and/or risk assessments by loss scenario (e.g., unauthorized activities, relationship disputes, systems fails, e-commerce hacking threats).

CONCLUSION

Without question, maintaining records of incidents and losses can be very telling when trying to understand potential loss exposure. Hypothetical scenario analyses using the methods discussed in Chapter 9 are useful enough in some occasions, but there is nothing like a real life loss case to drive the point home.

Operational losses are analogous to the use of pricing data for market risk models. They help to dimension operational risk in terms of possible outcomes just as pricing data define the range of market risk. But it is far more useful as a management tool than as an instantly supportive statistical analysis. Simply stated, management should want to know where and to what extent operational losses are impacting the bottom line.

Even so, until recently, astonishing little data have been maintained by many firms on operational risk losses, not to mention information about the factors that caused the events or about preventive measures.[12]

The British Bankers Association and OpVantage should be commended for their efforts to organize and launch industry loss databases. The question of whether these consortia will not only fly, but soar, however, will be answered by action or inaction over the coming months and years. Some are already participating and providing data. Will other firms' management teams see operational risk management as a competitive advantage or operational losses as a sign of weakness and thus back away from sharing their data? Once sanitized, will the information become so bland that it is no longer valuable to the user? Will the various consortia continue to vie for members, or will there ultimately be a single grand source for operational risk data? The answers and outcome are still unclear, but many firms seem to be warming to the idea, judging by the numbers of Letters of Intent alone. The real proof, as noted, however, will be in the actual amount and quality of data shared. Stay tuned, the picture is bound to get more interesting in the very near future.[13]

Let there be no confusion about the bigger picture. Regardless of the concerns expressed now and the degree and shape of the outcome, many participants and observers alike are cheering for these ventures not only as data services to the industry (-ies), but also in their capacity as vehicles for advancing the discipline of operational risk management on a far grander scale.

LESSONS LEARNED AND KEY RECOMMENDATIONS

■ Coordinate event and risk indicator data firmwide. Coordinate data and information collection about operational risk issues, incidents, and losses by developing a process to capture and track them, including their cost and causative factors, at both business and corporate levels firmwide. (BP Strategy #14).

- Internal loss data are far superior to external and consortia data because they have the highest relevance to the organization. Note, however:
  - Be mindful of changes in organizations and control structures over time when monitoring past losses as predictors of current and future risk environments.
  - Data standards will be essential for consistency of data capture.
  - Data should be captured and tracked by business line as an important input to risk profiling.
  - For maximum information value, losses should be tracked by business and by process, if possible. Maintain sufficient details such that the organization can learn from its past mistakes and misfortune.
  - Build or buy a data capture system that enables maintenance of a broad inventory of incidents, losses, issues, and risk indicators.
  - Set up accounting codes to track losses across businesses and risk areas, and specific codes for each type of risk that you will be tracking.
  - Use external data to supplement your internal loss data, help gauge industry losses and severity levels, and fill out the tail of a severity distribution.
  - Track as much factual information about a loss event as possible.
  - Ask yourself analytical questions about a loss incident before making the entry. (What were the causes? Could this event happen again? What were the lessons learned? What are some of the risk indicators we can use to monitor for a similar episode in the future?)
  - Formally identify and define your sets of risk indicators with management's at both the line management and corporate levels.
- When using external loss databases for benchmarking, as well as for analysis and modeling, apply these techniques:
  - Loss data should be reviewed and included or excluded depending upon their relevance to the organization.
  - External data-scaling factors should be considered in making the loss data relevant to the organization using it. Consider use of weighted or logarithmic scaling approaches.
- Scenario analysis can be used very effectively to supplement loss data in creating "synthetic data points" or simply performing stress tests on the depth and breadth of data collected.
- External loss data consortia: Give participation in industry data consortia serious consideration. Be sure that you are comfortable with privacy and confidentiality issues before joining. Review other key questions in Exhibit 10.4 including but not limited to issues of objectives, goals, definitions and data standards, output, technology and legal concerns.

CHAPTER 11

Risk Indicators and Scorecards

Cornerstones for Operational
Risk Monitoring

INTRODUCTION

"**H**ow am I doing?" Residents of New York City in the 1980s recognize this line as the familiar, often repeated question from Mayor Ed Koch. He was looking for regular feedback on his performance, like many of us in our daily business and personal lives. The line played well with citizens (at least for a time until the political climate changed and they answered with their votes), but it was noticed by students of management as a great illustration of the process of gaining regular feedback. And it is particularly relevant for students of *operational* risk management.

Indicators are everywhere. We rely on them to monitor economic and investment performance, education results, productivity gains, economic health, even the education performance of our children. Therefore, it should be no surprise that operational risk managers have begun to use risk and performance indicators as an early warning system to track their organizations' level of operational risk and create a multi-dimensioned risk profile.

Some see risk indicators as the cornerstones of both effective measurement and management of operational risk. In the measurement sense, analysts use indicators as a key variable in formula to forecast operational loss potential. In the management sense, line managers are often anxious to track multiple performance indicators as a means to confirm that their products and services are performing consistently with goals and objectives.

Where and how does an organization begin a process of operational risk tracking and measurement? What is an operational risk profile and how does an organization get a handle on it? How should a measurement methodology link to existing control functions or to line managers' own performance indicators? Which indicators are most useful? That is, which are key performance indicators (KPIs) or key risk indicators (KRIs)? All of these

---

BP STRATEGY #14, REDUX—COORDINATE EVENT AND RISK INDICATOR INFORMATION FIRMWIDE

Coordinate data and information about operational risk issues, incidents, and losses by developing a process to capture and track them, including their cost and causative factors, at both business and corporate levels firmwide. Identify and track predictive indicators and drivers of operational risks. Capture both quantitative and qualitative driver data. Provide indicator reports and scores to management levels appropriate for action.

---

questions are being discussed actively in operational risk management circles. In fact, they are indicative of the various perspectives and approaches to operational risk management. This chapter will provide some answers to those questions, along with insight on how and where indicators are being used already.

PROSPECTIVE RISK INDICATORS

Before we begin to explore risk indicators in greater detail, however, it is important that we place proper emphasis on the phrase "early warning system." The key challenges in dealing with risk indicators is in identifying or constructing metrics that serve as predictors or "drivers" of operational risk. Unfortunately, most operational indicators are trailing in nature. That is to say, they do a far better job of confirming recent history than they do in predicting the formation of operational risk storm clouds on the horizon. Beyond simply identifying indicators of risk, therefore, the risk manager must work hard to distill those that will prove to be most useful for managing the organization's future risk and potential, not simply measuring its recent loss potential.

Perhaps most important of all, risk indicators must be prospective to be useful. There is a lagged relationship between an indicator and the message it is sending. Take the example of a firm that is experiencing management change. During the course of all management changes, uncertainty abounds. Employees and managers alike are left to wonder, "How will the changes affect me?" Some hang in. Others bolt for the doors, accepting the first attractive offer that comes along. The problem with risk indicators, however, is that they may not pick up this activity quickly enough to alert others that these departures are taking place and are presenting new risk to the organization.

In fact, some firms have used the turnover indicator quite diligently, only to find that it was not flashing a warning signal at all. In fact, it was simply showing that turnover did not look too bad. The problem with this kind of usage is that in most cases there will be a lag in when the turnover actually shows up in the numbers.

This is precisely why there must be a predictive aspect to the indicators. For instance, one can assume that turnover will take place. The question is how much? The challenge, then, would be to trend forward the turnover values under optimistic, expected, and worst case scenarios, considering a range of possible scenarios and associated losses. But let's not get ahead of ourselves. Following are the basics of risk and performance indicators.

ORGANIZING THE DATA: RISK INDICATORS DEFINED

When using the term *risk indicators,* we are broadly referring to captured information that provides useful views of underlying risk profiles at various levels within an organization. These indicators seek to quantify all aspects (both tangible and intangible) that are sought by a risk manager to enable risk-based decision making. Risk indicators may be classified in a number of ways. Three classifications that my colleagues and I have found useful include indicators by type, risk class, or breadth of application to the business.[1]

- **Risk Indicator by Type:** There are at least four types of risk indicators. They include inherent risk indicators, control risk indicators, composite indicators, and model risk factors. We will illustrate these distinctive measure types using two general classes of risk: technology-related risks and people risks, such as misdeeds, mistakes, and their other actions or inactions.
- **Indicators by Risk Class:** This classification includes a mapping of the indicators to risk classes. For consistency in the book we will use people, relationships, technology/processing, physical assets, and other external risk classes. Each area implies its own set of risk indicators as drivers or predicators of risk and loss.
- **Business-Specific versus Firmwide Risk Indicators:** This classification categorizes indicators by the breadth of their application across the entire firm. Business-specific indicators are units that define an individual business type (e.g., trading businesses at a minimum would track transactions, settlements, and failed trades, whereas retail banking businesses track numbers of customer accounts, complaints, teller shortages, etc.). Conversely, there are firmwide risk indicators. Exhibit 11.1 sets the stage for our overall discussion on firmwide and business-specific risk indicators throughout this chapter.

RISK INDICATORS BY TYPE

In this first section we will illustrate and explore further the different types of indicators and their uses.[2]

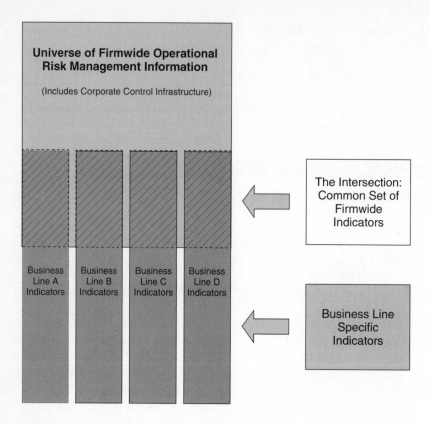

Firmwide risk indicators include training dollars spent, employee error rates, and customer complaints as illustrated in subsequent exhibits. Business line-specific measures will include unique variables by business. Also see Exhibit 11.3 for an illustration.

EXHIBIT 11.1   Risk Indicators: Firmwide versus Business-Specific

Inherent Risk or Exposure Indicators

At the most basic level, the monitoring of data that are descriptive about the business is useful to provide a context, and as a means of dimensioning exposure. Thus, these inherent risk or exposure indicators provide a dimension for inherent risk exposure. The data that support the measurement of these variables are relatively accessible across the organization, and generally inexpensive to collect. Much of these data may already be tracked by various reporting functions within the business. In addition, some operational risk managers may already maintain this information, and apply it to risk financing and/or insurance purchasing decisions, or in satisfying requests

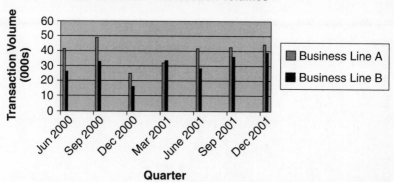

Risk variables are used to dimension risk exposure firmwide, or at the business line level. As shown here, volumes for both business lines traced a similar upward move for the majority of the period, but note the extreme values at various points in the wake of market volatility. Composite risk indicators are used to determine whether increased market volatility has a direct causal impact on operational risk levels within a business.

EXHIBIT 11.2 Transaction Volume Indicators

from insurance underwriters. Examples that have emerged in regulatory discussions include numbers of transactions, volumes of trades, value of assets in custody, and value of transactions (see Exhibit 11.2).

Individual Management Control Risk Indicators

As a second type, some organizations capture certain types of variables that are generally believed by business managers to be appropriate indicators of risk, but are not simply descriptive. Instead, they are representative of management actions or inactions. Hence we use the name management control risk indicators.

These indicators may already be tracked in some form by a given firm. Prudent managers may already monitor such indicators systematically for some classes of risks in the form of key performance indicators (KPIs). Existing processes may need to be modified, however, in order to collect data that represent the entire organization, and for all classes of risk.

Take the example of a business unit or organization that decides to embark on a mission of streamlining its operations by moving more MIS (management information system) data for key areas onto the Web for access over the Internet or its own intranet, as the case may be. Business functions affected may include purchasing, human resources, trading and settlement, and client services.

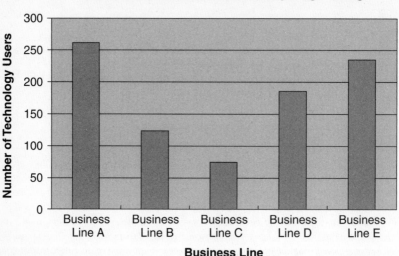

Total technology users requiring training is presented here as a firmwide risk indicator. The strength of firmwide risk indicators lies within their comparability across the organization. However, users should realize that the benefit they gain in comparability and transparency across the organization may be partially offset by the generic (nonbusiness-specific) nature of these measures.

EXHIBIT 11.3   Firmwide Indicators: Users Requiring Training

In this example, *inherent risk indicators,* such as number of servers, number of technology applications, and number of business continuity plans required, provide dimension to the technology risk profile across the organization. Similarly average transaction value, transaction volume, number of employees, and overtime serve to provide dimension to people and employee risks.

Technology management control risk indicators may specifically include the subset number of users requiring training in the new technology and will be represented as actual numbers or be weighted to reflect total employees in the department. On the other hand, employee risk indicators may include training dollars spent and employee appraisal completion rates (see Exhibit 11.3 and 11.4).

As the introduction of new technology almost always requires training to maintain productivity levels, this can be an important measure to assess risk. These indicators may be captured in terms of any meaningful unit, for example hours, dollars, or employee numbers. It is critical that the operational risk MIS is flexible and sophisticated enough to be able to accept data in any unit(s) entered.

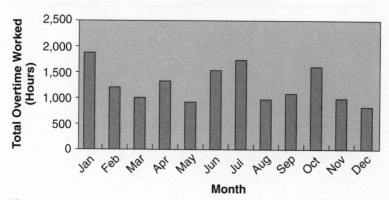

Business-Specific Indicators:
Overtime Worked

This is total overtime hours worked as a business-specific risk indicator. The analysis of business-specific indicators in isolation may prove to be only marginally beneficial. However, its intrinsic benefit may be realized when used as a variable within a group of relevant indicators (i.e., a composite).

EXHIBIT 11.4   Business-Specific Indicators

Composite Risk Indicators

A more complex use of risk indicators is the third type where, for either the inherent indicators or management control indicators, we begin to capture and monitor combinations. We call these composite risk indicators. These combinations of indicators provide an opportunity to measure multiple dimensions of risk associated with a specific class of risk, behavior, or business activity.

Tracking inherent risk variables and control-oriented risk indicators together as composites, over time, can tell some very interesting stories, as shown in Exhibit 11.5. In this case, they can show the user what his or her optimal employee/training/performance level is and whether performance is getting better or worse.[3]

Inherent and control indicators can be combined in the context of our example of a business harnessing the power of Internet-based technologies. Thus, a composite risk indicator may track the percentage of skilled technology resources required to support this transition. The percentage could be calculated as follows:

$$\frac{\text{Number of skilled technology resources, say } 14}{\text{Total number of technology resources, say } 20} = 70\%$$

It would also be invaluable if there were industry-benchmarking data on this risk indicator readily available to understand exactly where the organization

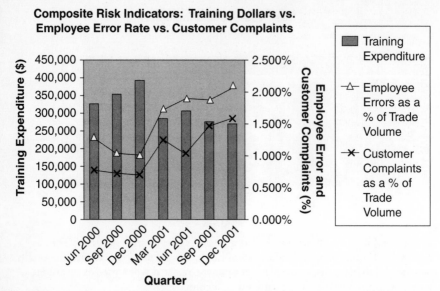

EXHIBIT 11.5   Composite Risk Indicators

As shown in this composite, there appears to be a strong correlation between declining investment in employee training, the error rates of these employees, and the rate of customer complaints. This type of indicator may be considered compelling reading by management and other interested control functions.

or business unit stands relative to other industry members (see Exhibit 11.6). In effect, a rating of seven out of ten may be more easily digested if the industry average was 7.6, for example. Such an industry benchmark may point to a shortage of skilled labor within that market and would therefore provide a perspective for any intended controls. The use of industry statistics adds perspective to the rating.

Taking the concept of composite risk indicators further, we can combine numerous inherent and/or control indicators to create operational risk indices, such as a New Application risk index or an overall technology risk index.

Operational Risk Model Factors

A fourth type entails operational risk model factors. These are essentially a subset of the previous three types of indicators. This category implies that one would not want to use all these data measures in an operational risk measurement model. For simplicity we will select certain risk drivers from those categories in order to apply the most effective ones for modeling purposes. *Factor models* will be derived from various underlying risk indi-

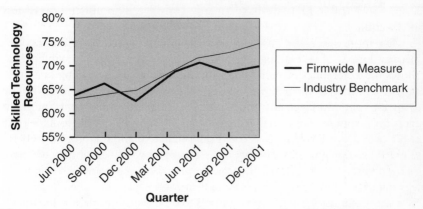

Firmwide Composite Risk Indicators: Number of Skilled Technology Resources vs. Industry Benchmark

The comparison of risk indicators to industry benchmarks adds additional perspective to the rating. This figure shows that the firmwide indicator of skilled technology resources has slipped considerably below the industry benchmark. Inferences may be drawn from this in relation to the firm's vulnerability to technical problems.

EXHIBIT 11.6 Firmwide Composite

cators that serve to characterize a risk profile. We will return to this discussion in Chapter 12.

ORGANIZATIONAL CONSIDERATIONS

Due to their inherent flexibility, risk indicators may be captured at various levels throughout the organization. For instance, at one level they may be specifically defined and captured to dimension operational risk across the entire organization. Alternatively, they may be engineered to cater specifically for risks associated with the very nature of certain business-line functions, productions, personnel, and other operational environment factors.

Thus, we often think of risk indicators as either firmwide or business specific in nature. That is to say that in order to establish a relative comparison from one business line to the next, we will identify risk indicators that can be applied to any type of business line. These are referred to as firmwide indicators, and as referenced earlier, will include generic variables such as numbers of people, systems, and customers. While these variables help to relate one business to the next, by making them comparable, they may become a bit generic for the individual line manager. By soliciting management input into the definition of indicators at various levels, however, and committing management to their systematic measurement, the risk manager increases the potential for buy in and credibility to the process. In the end, the trick is to find an intersection between firmwide and business line indicators. Returning to Exhibit 11.1, we have already considered an illustration of this intersection.

The more successful risk indicator programs benefit from the involvement and input of several management levels and consist of a flexibility that allows for different perspectives. During the course of fine-tuning one operational risk management program, and while seeking measures appropriate to Investment Management operations, we targeted some front-line managers for response. These managers focused more on risk indicators for risks at the operations level, as may have been predicted, and therefore closely resembled existing performance measures. However when senior management, and ultimately the CEO, of the organization were interviewed, their focus was found to be more on composite indicators, such as combined key people risks within the asset management team, and on drivers for relationship risks.[4]

PRACTICAL CONSIDERATIONS: DEFINITION, DATA COLLECTION, STANDARDS, AND EMPHASIS

The most effective operational risk management programs will blend business line and corporate initiatives. Clearly, working closely with management from all levels within the organization is essential for the long-term commitment and credibility of the risk measurement process.

Risk indicator definitions will consider the rationale for the risk indicator, description of rating or measurement criteria, and the sources of data. Once defined, procedures must be implemented to ensure the systematic collection of accurate and timely data and to monitor and analyze risk indicators.

Each risk indicator may also be weighted in accordance with its significance, or predictive capabilities, to ensure accuracy and relevance throughout the various levels of the organization. Once measured, this set of risk indicators in practice must be continually validated and refined together with the management responsible. Naturally, as the business environment is subjected to continual change, underlying indicators may also require enhancement, to preserve integrity and perhaps predictive capabilities.

It is natural that organizations select and define risk indicators to a large extent based on the availability of appropriate data. A word of caution is important here, however. The best firms select indicators based on their predictive value first, and data availability second, not the other way around. In any event, although data may be readily available for many variables and risk indicators, it should be noted that a full set of effective composite indicators would generally impose even more responsibilities for data collection and reporting.

The capture of operational loss data is becoming a fundamental feature within the risk management framework of many firms. Analysis of these losses (including causative factors) in combination with associated risk indicators forms the evaluation stage of the operational risk monitoring life cycle. This evaluation should consider whether the risk measures have been validated as relevant, including whether they were proven to bear some direct relationship to the propensity for losses. We will explore this concept further in Chapter 13 on Risk Profiling.[5]

SCORECARD SYSTEMS: THE NEXUS OF RISK ASSESSMENT AND RISK INDICATORS

The continual challenge in using indicators, then, remains that of identifying those that are both predictors of risk *and* for which data are readily available. Indicators that do not meet both tests are of limited value to management. Thus, capturing data remains a key focal point. But as noted already, some indicators can meet both tests and still be of limited value because of timeliness concerns.

Whether the problem lies with data or timeliness, one solution is to set up a scoring system for converting softer risk assessment information into risk indicators. An example of this would involve a typical 1–3, 1–5, or 1–10 range for scoring the answers to risk assessment or self-assessment questionnaires.

Robert Simons, Professor of Business Administration at Harvard Business School, outlined his approach to operational risk scoring in a 1999 article entitled *How Risky is Your Company?* He has applied a five point scoring system in the context of a "risk exposure calculator." His work has focused on three key indicators of risk: excessive growth (e.g., pressures for performance, expansion rates), culture (e.g., treatment of entrepreneurial risk taking, internal competition), and information management (e.g., transaction complexity, gaps in performance measures, and decentralized risk taking). The very nature of his indicators, of course, represents areas that are difficult to quantify and therefore must be represented through a scoring system. His system is simple enough. Each of nine areas is scored from 1 to 5. The areas carry equal weights. Thus, an organization's overall score is the result of simple addition, and the overall score indicates the relative vulnerability of the organization to operational risk and loss.[6]

Following is another approach written and contributed by Joseph Swipes on behalf of Dresdner Bank and its New York branch.

CASE ILLUSTRATION

Creating KRI Scores from Qualitative Reviews at Dresdner Bank

The time for quantifying qualitative operational risk data has arrived. Quantification allows for risk managers to analyze the results of operational risk exercises performed throughout an organization efficiently

Risk Subcategory—Human Capital

Question Number	Question Weight	Answer Weight	Risk Score	Scoring Legend
1	4	5	1.43	4.1–5 Excellent
2	3	3	0.64	3.1–4 Above Average
3	2	4	0.57	2.1–3.0 Adequate
4	4	1	0.29	1.1–2.0 Poor
5	1	3	0.21	0–1 Very Poor
6	0	0	0	
7	0	0	0	
	14		3.14	

Risk Subcategory—Unauthorized Activities

Question Number	Question Weight	Answer Weight	Risk Score
1	4	5	2.5
2	1	1	0.13
3	3	2	0.75
	8		3.38

EXHIBIT 11.7   Dresdner Risk/Self-Assessment Scoring

and identify areas where significant operational risk exists. In addition, quantification allows a risk manager to benchmark processes and controls against preestablished standards. Finally, quantification proceeds to a more efficient risk capital allocation.

To quantify the qualitative operational risk profile, a scoring mechanism must be applied. There are several scoring methodologies that work well. While each has its own unique features, the commonality between scoring methodologies is that they normalize the data. It is well known that different lines of business have operational risks that are unique to each business. As such, the number of operational risks associated with each line of business will vary. Whether the number of risks associated with a particular line of business are 50 or 500, in order to compare results across lines of business, one must employ a mathematical means of normalizing the data. Exhibit 11.7 illustrates an example of a scoring methodology that employs data normalization.

The operational risk profile should be dynamic. It will be updated as often as new data (risk/self-assessment, key performance indicators, etc.) are collected. Any significant deviations from the previous risk profile should be escalated for possible remedial action. Remedial action would depend primarily on management's operational risk appetite and the significance of the increase in the operational risk profile if the additional exposure were accepted.

As a risk manager, this type of consolidated risk reporting allows me to identify with ease areas where significant operational risk exists. In addition, it allows me to see how changes in processes and controls affect an area's operational risk exposure. My main concern when developing this type of analysis was that I would be unable to compare, for example, a capital markets operation with a custody operation. However, after running a few pilots, it became clear that the scoring mechanism worked effectively by giving me an accurate portrayal of an area's operational risk exposure. I also found that a user could easily retrofit the scoring mechanism with other types for consolidated risk reporting and analysis.

When applying the scoring mechanism to the results of the risk/self-assessment, key performance indicators, and unexpected operational incidents, the results provide line and senior management with a snapshot of an area's operational risk exposure in one consolidated report for easy analysis rather than producing several reports for grueling interpretation. It also provides the risk manager with an almost real-time measurement of the operational risk exposure that exists within an organization.

■ ■ ■

CASE ILLUSTRATION

Converting Risk Scores to Heat Maps at Deutsche Bank

Another step in the process is to create a reporting format from the scores. One popular graphic for this is the heat map. Robert Huebner contributed a heat map format on behalf of Deutsche Bank. As shown in Exhibit 11.8, Deutsche Bank also uses a scoring approach in comparing the results of its risk assessment process, then illustrates and ranks them in a heat map format for ease of aggregate reporting and clear communication.

A number of banks have recently come out in favor of combining both qualitative and quantified risk indicators in the form of scoring systems and scorecards. One such advocate is Mark Lawrence of ANZ Group. After a review of several assessment and quantification methods, including business measures or "scalars" such as revenues, assets, benchmarking, statistical analysis, and causal modeling, ANZ settled on an elaborate system of enterprise-wide scorecards because they "avoid many of the problems inherent in the analysis of historical data, and can be much more forward looking, by capturing the knowledge and experience of the experts who design the scorecards."[7]

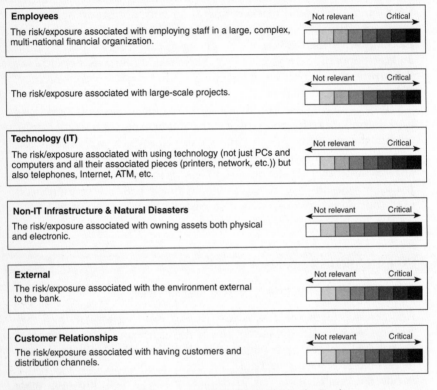

Overall Evaluation by Risk Category

Once you have read the questionaire and answered all the questions, please place a cross in the grid next to each of the categories. Your evaluation should indicate the level of importance the risks have in your whole business division. This evaluation enables you to weigh the risk categories each against the others and to sort them in order of their potential risk impact. Please use the 8 levels to make your evaluation. White means a low level of importance in the business division, black stands for a high level of importance. Any other evaluation can be expressed by using the 6 levels in between.

Employees

The risk/exposure associated with employing staff in a large, complex, multi-national financial organization.

Not relevant — Critical

The risk/exposure associated with large-scale projects.

Not relevant — Critical

Technology (IT)

The risk/exposure associated with using technology (not just PCs and computers and all their associated pieces (printers, network, etc.)) but also telephones, Internet, ATM, etc.

Not relevant — Critical

Non-IT Infrastructure & Natural Disasters

The risk/exposure associated with owning assets both physical and electronic.

Not relevant — Critical

External

The risk/exposure associated with the environment external to the bank.

Not relevant — Critical

Customer Relationships

The risk/exposure associated with having customers and distribution channels.

Not relevant — Critical

EXHIBIT 11.8   Converting Risk Scores to Heat Maps Deutsche Bank

■ ■ ■

"BACK-TESTING" RISK INDICATORS AND SCORES: SOME CASE EXAMPLES

Had risk indicators been used effectively, one could argue that the likes of Barings and Sumitomo might well have focused their resources on mitigating their operational risk exposure prior to suffering their debilitating financial losses.

Many readers will be familiar with the circumstances surrounding the collapse of Barings Bank (refer back to Chapter 8, Exhibit 8.4) and the series of control deficiencies that were exposed during investigations. Among these findings, it became clear that the blame for Barings' loss cannot be targeted solely at Nick Leeson; it must be shared throughout the management of the bank, reflective of the poor control environment, lack of supervision and accountability, and clouded communications and reporting. Could risk measures have forewarned the fall of a major international bank?

In the case of Barings, the financial world is left to ponder whether the systematic analysis of appropriate risk indicators at the business-line level, and at the firmwide level, could not only have provided warning signals of the inherent and control risks of Barings Singapore operations, but also spurned management into action.

For example, a sampling of relevant risk indicators that Barings may have captured include:

1. **Inherent Risk Indicators**
   - *Junior and Senior Staff Tenure Individual Risk Indicator:* Might have highlighted the relative inexperience of the employees managing the operations from within the Singapore Office.
   - *Product Complexity Composite Risk Indicator:* While Leeson was authorized only for intraday trading in options and futures, a significant weighting is generally attributed to derivatives trading.
2. **Management Control Risk Indicators**
   - *Internal Audit Indicators, Issues Tracking, or Operations Benchmarking:* Much has already been written about whether the collapse of Barings could have been averted if management had been forced to focus on the findings of the internal audit report on Barings Futures of August 1994. Some firms score internal audit issues based on severity. In some systems, issues outstanding and past due for a specified period would have attracted a higher risk rating.

Whether or not the systematic analysis of these specific risk indicators, in conjunction with other composite indicators, would have focused Barings' management attention, and sparked appropriate action, is open to some conjecture. Indicators are not, by themselves, a panacea for control deficiencies. However, it is logical that the systematic use of indicators may have mitigated some of the control weakness evident in a number of high-profile loss events.

The process of capturing and analyzing risk indicators can facilitate management ownership of operational risks and provide a platform for the proactive management of a control environment.

The investigation into the Barings collapse cited poor supervision and confusion over management and supervisory responsibilities with the bank's matrix structure as major contributors to the bank's demise. When used as a fundamental component of an overall risk management framework, risk indicators can convert the previously intangible to the tangible for line management. They can also create a proactive concern for the management of these proxies.

Similarly, in the case of Sumitomo's rogue trader, Hamanaka, despite reasonably sound supervision controls due to the global nature of the operations in question, there was still some uncertainty as to who had control over the activities of Hamanaka. The systematic use (analysis and discussion) of risk indicators will reinforce management ownership of the control environment, as they seek to modify behavior and strengthen controls.

The ability to report periodically on risk indicators at various levels within the organization is also important. While proactive management of operational risk is imperative at a functional management level, the enterprise-wide risk profile should be a tool used for Board Supervision. Perhaps the losses sustained by Metallgellschaft may have been mitigated if there had been greater transparency in relation to controlling weaknesses. Equally, the Barings Board may have expressed greater concern had Barings Singapore reported on risk indicators in comparison to the other operations of the bank or to industry benchmarks.

Finally, generally speaking, investment banking front office operations are dominated by fiercely competitive and performance-based cultures. The remuneration policies of many banks may reward bonuses on absolute performance, despite the business line taking excessive operational risks. The use of indicators for internal or external benchmarking, or as an allocation basis for risk capital, is an effective framework in which to achieve risk-based behavioral change and reward better quality earnings.[8]

IMPLEMENTING A SYSTEM OF RISK INDICATORS

In summarizing, the best firms are found to take action toward implementing and/or refining their efforts toward risk indicator tracking and analysis as follows:

- **Identify and Define:** They work with management at all levels within the organization to begin to identify and define variables, risk indicators, and composite indicators. These measures should contain an appropriate hybrid blend of firmwide and business-line indicators.

  This may be a significant step forward for many organizations. The cultural and behavioral implications should not be taken lightly. However, as has been mentioned previously, soliciting management input from the outset will assist in establishing the credibility and longevity of the process.

- **Data Collection, Tracking, and Analysis:** They establish enduring procedures for systematic data collection, reporting, and analysis. The reporting and analysis processes are tailored to the target audience across the various levels of the organization.

■ **Validation of Indicators:** A mechanism for the periodical evaluation and update of indicators is also crucial in maintaining longevity and management faith. These measures must be responsive to the changing business environment, and should also be evaluated in the light of actual loss data, to determine predictive capabilities.[9]

REGULATORY VIEWS ON RISK INDICATORS

In keeping with the principles of risk management, as outlined by the Basel Risk Management Committee, operational risk and exposure indicators should be transparent and reasonable, with any underlying assumptions clearly communicated to end users. Transparency in risk indicators is essential for the long-term integrity of this aspect of a risk management framework. If performance assessment, such as capital allocation, is associated with their use, management will maintain a vested interest in ensuring that the indicators are responsive to risk-based behavioral improvement.[10]

CONCLUSION

Operational risk indicators are poised to become a critical component of effective operational risk management programs. Successful business managers already use key performance indicators to gauge business efficiency and profitability upsides. Risk indicators simply serve as a gauge of potential downside outcomes. When applied and presented effectively, they should serve to identify important business vulnerabilities, or as warning lights for navigating the business clear of the dangers present in the business environment. In addition, as the debate continues over operational risk modeling and regulatory capital, risk measures are almost certain to help lay part of the data foundation on which to construct durable models.

Identifying candidates for tracking risk indicators is only half the battle. Once you have a good lead on an indicator or two, your selections must pass some additional tests. First and foremost, you must confirm that they are, in fact, a predictor of operational risk, that they can serve as part of an "operational risk early warning system" and/or be used in modeling. Second, you must come up with data and/or a quantification scheme. Third, you must test your hypothesis (candidate). One is to analyze past losses and/or areas of concern in the business in order to identify causation trends. Without a qualification or measurement, we have no way to track progress of the event.

LESSONS LEARNED AND KEY RECOMMENDATIONS

■ Identify and track predictive indicators and drivers of operational risk. Capture both quantitative and qualitative driver data. Provide indicator reports and scores to management levels appropriate for action (BP Strategy #14).

- Risk and performance indicators will be used in the best firms. Studies have shown that the most successful organizations use key performance measures. Different risk indicators will be used at different levels and in different areas. A business line manager will track indicators for his or her own business process, whereas a corporate manager will be more interested in firmwide indicators or variables that can be used consistently in all areas and in all businesses, such as error rates, turnover levels, and customer complaints.

- Composite indicators are useful management tools. Tracking a variety of issues in a survey, for instance, and scoring the results in a weighted average over time has been shown to be a useful method of tracking management and system performance. In this chapter we gave the example of tracking a variety of issues in a technology environment to illustrate this point. Many of the issues, such as degree of systems support, reliability, and criticality, for instance, are difficult issues to quantify, but can be tracked, scored, scaled, and monitored over time on a scaled basis. As an overall average, the scores, or aggregate score, can be used as a performance measure.

- The best risk indicators will be forward looking or predictive in order to be useful as either a modeling or management tool.

- The risk indicators are generally managed by a central unit, whether in the business lines themselves or at a firmwide level. Regardless of the location, the management process should include a validation where the units being tracked and measured have an opportunity to review both input and output of the tracking system and corroborate the data against their own sources.

- Don't get hung up on quantification. If any organization limits itself to tracking only those indicators that can be readily quantified neatly, it may be missing more relevant issues. Relative-ranked scoring can bridge this gap.

- Keep the indicators relevant to a business; business staff and managers should be involved in the key risk indicators that are most relevant to their risk and performance.

- Model factors are different. Indicators or factors used for modeling should be more simplified. Whereas a business or profit center might use numerous indicators to track the business at hand, it can become very confusing to use all of these indicators in modeling. Responsiveness of or to changes to all of the indicators in a model can be lost in the blur of all of these multiple indicators, all moving in different directions simultaneously.

- Scorecards are an effective way of combining both qualitative and quantitative indicators and scores for a prospective representation of risk. Some firms have become staunch advocates of scorecards as their primary basis of operational risk representation and for capital allocation purposes.

CHAPTER 12

Operational Risk Analysis and Measurement

Practical Building Blocks

INTRODUCTION

One of the more significant advancements in recent years that has served to define operational risk management is the introduction of greater sophistication in risk measurement techniques. This has included the use of quantitative techniques for measurement and modeling future loss scenarios. In and of itself, this change ranks high among Best Practice advancements. Any technique that increases the confidence of forecasting potential risk and loss outcomes must be viewed as a step forward. The bottom line objective, of course, is to get ahead of loss scenarios before they develop and take action to eliminate or minimize ultimate losses.

For some, the shift away from using *only* subjective risk assessment techniques has been a natural progression; for others, it has simply added more confusion to an already complex topic. I am certainly an advocate of using analytics to advance the state of operational risk management, including but not limited to actuarially based risk capital models. However, I would certainly not suggest that the most sophisticated of these techniques are practical for firms of all sizes, cultures, and business compositions. In addition, as we learned from cases like Long Term Capital Management, they should not be the *sole method* of operational risk assessment at any firm.

Recognizing that one size does not fit all, this chapter presents a series of building blocks—a progression of metrics and analysis topics, and lays the groundwork for economic capital models and regulatory capital discussions. At the outset, we cover our objective for analysis. Then, we cover some background and introduction to data interpretation, analytics, and metrics. Next, we look at simple calculations, such as indices, cost-of-operational-risk (COOR) calculations, trend line, and expected loss calculations. We then introduce some emerging application of more sophisticated analysis in operational risk. The latter include correlations between risk indicators, actuarial analysis, and causal analysis, all with a view toward management reporting topics such as the need for an operational risk management dashboard, and the like.

Perhaps most timely, given the industry focus on the prospect of regulatory capital and the still early stage of the operational risk management discipline, this chapter also provides an important foundation for later treatment of economic capital models (Chapter 16) and regulatory developments (Chapter 17).

It is not the intent to cover a detailed technical discussion of each modeling approach in this book. The reader who wants to take the topic further should look to several excellent texts that have recently emerged on the subject (see Additional Readings at the end of the book. In addition, the reader can find several sources of good information about quantitative analysis and economic capital modeling in the bibliography to this book.)

MANAGEMENT REPORTING AND IMPLIED ANALYTICS

Experience has taught us that one of the places to begin planning for management reporting and the need for analytics is with the audience. If our goals are to influence decision making in a productive way, and spur management to act to avoid or minimize losses, then the key is to determine what information is needed to achieve that goal. What data, information, and reporting would be most useful to answering the relevant questions at a line management level, at a senior management level, or at a Board level? Knowing this will help to identify what data and analytics would be most useful. With that in mind, one of the first aspects we look at in this chapter is the relationship of analytics and management reporting. The overall objective for ORM is to create an integrated program and arsenal of information.

A logical place to begin our discussion of analytics and metrics is by revisiting our Management Reporting and Decision Tools Matrix from Chapter 8 here. Exhibit 12.1 illustrates the component parts required to support an integrated program and the management reporting that we discussed in Chapter 8. Here we add the dimension of implied data needs and analytic implications for the management reports and decision tools needed. Later, in Chapter 13, we look at the implications of the reports and system screens needed for risk monitoring.

Exhibit 12.1 shows that much can be accomplished with the basic data and some simple mathematics alone. Many of the individual reports, data needs, and implied analytics shown should be self-explanatory from the exhibit.

Management Need and Implied Reporting	Implied Data Needs	Implied Analytics and Report Format
1. Consolidated Risk Profile Dashboard	Extensive use of: • Risk indicators • Issues • Incidents • Losses	• Range from simple math to more complex analytics including regressions and simulations • Normalize to an index, benchmark • Integrate many of the other analyses outlined below
2. Risk Assessment Tracking	Numbers of assessments completed	• Percentages of totals, or against goals, benchmarks, etc. • Produce pie charts, bar graphs
3. Individual Risk Indicator Report and Monitoring	• Risk and performance indicators by business unit or by risk class. • Data capture from internal and external systems	• Bar charts, line graphs • Dials and gauges
4. Risk Indicator Composite Reviews	Risk indicators by business unit or by risk class.	Interest in: • Testing correlations between risk indicators • Testing certain indicators as predictors of losses, thus narrowing the need to track a long list
5. Customized Risk Index (indicator index) creation	Risk indicators scoring system (e.g., min-max)	
6. "Issue Display" and Management Report	Display of issues identified	Simple math (addition, percentage completed, addressed)

Continued

EXHIBIT 12.1　Sample Management Reporting Needs: Implied Data and Analytics

Management Need and Implied Reporting	Implied Data Needs	Implied Analytics and Report Format
7. Risk Management Initiative (Project) Tracking	Listing of projects	None—data display only from issues listing
8. Causal Analysis Predictor Report	Need to populate a fault tree with assumed probabilities and tree branches with outcomes from risk indicator pick list and from firm's own incident categories	Might imply the creation of a fault tree (e.g., if x, then y), use of a Baysean Belief Network
9. Incident Displays	Listing of incidents, along with data dimensions about individual incidents (e.g., numbers of incidents by type, dates, descriptions, cause [see Chapter 10 for detailed descriptions])	Nothing unique—might imply a simple tabular display of all incident types
10. Incident Trends and Forecast Needs	• Incident capture firmwide • Key risk and performance indicators for use as exposure bases	• Might imply a graphical trendline of incident types • Might imply need for regression capabilities
11. Loss Forecasting	• Access firm's own loss data along with industry loss data for combined analysis • Need to access select risk indicators to serve as exposure bases for forecasting	Might entail: • Regression, simulation, and other capabilities • Need to produce frequency, severity, and combined loss distributions Use of Extreme Value Theory
12. Monitoring Risk During Threshold Events	Data on new and old organization scenarios Losses suffered by others in industry involved in similar situations	Manager wants to produce a **Threshold Event or Accelerator Effect Report.** There is ample evidence to show that certain threshold events can accelerate the probability of losses

EXHIBIT 12.1 Sample Management Reporting Needs: Implied Data and Analytics

Management Need and Implied Reporting	Implied Data Needs	Implied Analytics and Report Format
13. Economic Risk Capital Analyses and Reports	• Loss data • Exposure data • Risk factors • Business line financial information	Depends on the approach taken—might imply anything from simple mathematics to regression analysis and Monte Carlo simulations: • Loss data-based/ actuarial analysis • Issue-based • Causal factor-based • Economic pricing • Expense-based
14. Regulatory Risk Capital Analysis and Reports	Prescribed by regulators: • exposure bases • internal loss data • industry data	Simple math only in most scenarios. Might imply the need for Monte Carlo simulations
15. Cost of Operational Risk Reports	• Loss data by class, by business • Insurance/risk finance premiums, recoveries • Risk control/response costs	In most cases requires only simple math
16. Risk Finance/ Insurance Decision Reports	• Proprietary loss data by exposure/risk class • Industry loss data	Analysis may be too labor intensive to be automated. Artificial intelligence application needed ?
17. Risk Response Reports		Example: Business Continuity Planning Status Report

EXHIBIT 12.1 Sample Management Reporting Needs: Implied Data and Analytics

OPERATIONAL RISK ANALYSIS AND DECISION TOOLS IN PRACTICE

Marcelo Cruz, formally of UBS Warburg, and a recognized leader in operational risk measurement analytics, uses the compelling example of the models underlying sophisticated weather systems, run on supercomputers, to predict hurricane paths. He has cited the example of Hurricane Lenny in 1999 in which sophisticated measurement was used to forecast its path with 90% accuracy. By predicting the path of the hurricane with high accuracy, farmers and others in the hurricane track were provided reasonable warning of the storm. The systems saved an indeterminable number of human lives. In addition, businesses were in a better position to take reasonable precautions and property losses were mitigated. He uses this as an example of the benefits of investment to supplement judgment with sophisticated measurement techniques, rather than continue to rely solely on managers' and operational risk professionals' experience and judgment alone.[1]

Our own operational risk management team at Bankers Trust has been credited with advancing operational risk management through the use of data capture and risk measurement techniques in the modeling of operational risks. In the process our work supported operational risk-based strategic decisions (i.e., business strategy investments) and helped to target areas warranting control and risk finance investments. Retracing the evolution of our own work will be helpful and instructive to others just getting started in operational risk analytics and measurement.

Our first risk measurement effort began in 1990 with scenario and single risk class modeling, expanding to operational risk actuarial and capital allocation techniques, and then to firmwide production models beginning in 1995. In production we modeled individual operational risk classes and the firm's operational risk exposure across all business lines and on a global basis. After developing a methodology to measure operational risk, we moved on to design an allocation methodology for aligning the model results with risk profiles of the individual business lines within the bank's overall portfolio. We dubbed this overall program "Operational RAROC (Risk-Adjusted Return on Capital)" because it fit under the firm's existing risk capital architecture. Internally at Bankers Trust this development work was seen as a great leap forward in operational risk management because, among other things,

---

BP STRATEGY #15—APPLY ANALYTICS TO IMPROVE ORM DECISION MAKING

One of the most significant advancements in modern operational risk management is the introduction of quantitative techniques for risk assessment and modeling of future loss scenarios. Apply analytics to support operational risk management decision making on a day-to-day business level, as well as in strategic risk–reward decision making on a portfolio level. Apply levels of analytic sophistication appropriate for your individual firm's size, culture, and business mix.

PAST	PRESENT	FUTURE
• Incidents • Losses • Risk indicators	• Risk assessment / Self-assessment • Risk indicators • Issue tracking • Fuzzy logic	• Scenario analysis • Risk mapping • Trending risk / data set • Monte Carlo simulation

EXHIBIT 12.2 Operational Risk Measurement: Getting a Handle on the Past, Present, and Future

it introduced far greater credibility to the firm's measurement of potential losses from the scenario analyses. Many firms have since joined the effort and continue to move operational risk management Best Practices forward.

To be successful in operational risk management, one must understand the differences between leading and trailing indicators, analytic tools, and risk measurement overall. We list the different approaches in Exhibit 12.2. For instance, tracking incidents, losses, and risk indicators are all examples of getting a handle on the picture of operational risk in the past. On the other hand, risk assessment, self-assessment, current risk indicators, and issue tracking are all examples of profiling operational risk in the present. Last, scenario analyses, risk maps, trending risk and data sets, and Monte Carlo simulation are all examples of profiling future risk.

All of the tools that are presented here have their use and place, but each should be evaluated for its relative strengths and weaknesses in terms of how accurately they present the past, present, and future, and how effective they are in accomplishing our risk management goals. Exhibit 12.2 lists some of the data and tools available to us today in undertaking operational risk measurement.

MODELING: WHAT IS A MODEL?

This isn't a trick question. It is actually very useful to step back for a moment and look at a few definitions. Among the definitions of models found in Webster's dictionary is: (1) "a description or analogy used to help visualize something that can be directly observed" and (2) "a system of postulates, data, and inferences presented as a mathematical description of an entity or state of affairs."

We will apply both of these definitions in this chapter. That is, we will take a very broad, and perhaps liberal, definition of modeling. For our purposes, we will define an operational risk model as any methodology or routine that provides information and helps us to make decisions regarding the management of operational risk.

Analysts often become passionate about their models. Some observers have suggested that the word might be "obsessive." As evidence, operational risk conferences are often divided into two or more streams of sessions. At one such recent conference, there was a stream dedicated to *quantification and measurement* sessions. In the other stream were sessions on softer operational risk *management* techniques. It was interesting to observe the very distinct camps that were forming between the two, but somewhat troublesome to observe the lack of patience and, dare I say, respect that some of the "modelers" shared for the "managers," and vice versa.

I will take this opportunity to remind the reader that balance between the two camps will be key to the most effective operational risk management programs.

SOME MODELING ISSUES FOR RESOLUTION

Before we begin a discussion of alternative modeling approaches, there are some additional issues that must be considered by the modeling team. They range from definitions, to scope, credibility, balancing causes and symptoms, and balancing predictive and reactive modeling features.

- **Definitions, Again:** First and foremost, there should be a universal definition of operational risk used in all of your models. If you have not yet settled on a definition of operational risk by the time you get to modeling, you should return to square one. Definitions are generally important enough in operational risk management, of course. When it comes to the subject of models, however, it is critical that all business units and staff are speaking the same language with regard to the model application. Imagine the confusion that would arise in an organization if business "A" had not defined "people risk" to include the same subclasses as business "B."
- **Representing the Organization / Granularity:** A second challenge when it comes to modeling is how best to represent the organization. Does it make more sense to construct a model and derive numbers at a firmwide, business line, profit center, portfolio, or desk level?

Initially, much of the answer to this question lies in the risk management and modeling objectives of the firm, coupled with the availability of data at the levels desired. Is the purpose of the model to derive a representative risk number at the highest levels of the firm (i.e., for the firmwide portfolio of businesses) such that only a comparative analysis is needed on a risk–reward basis between business lines and business line managers? Or, are you seeking to create incentives for the entire employee base and staff within a unit level by function? If the motivation is more toward the former, then it will be key to apply uniform model variables across the entire firm, and a top down modeling approach may suffice.

If the objective is more toward a granular assessment and calculation, then the model may require a blend of variables that apply both firmwide on the one hand, and some that are unique to the individual business on the other. In this case, the model may require both a top-down and bottom-up orientation, or be entirely driven from the bottom of the organization to the very top. As will be evident from the following sections of this chapter, a detailed bottom-up approach will require far more time and effort than a portfolio-based top-down model.

- **Risk Assessment—Depth versus Breadth:** When designing models, we will balance what is realistic as to depth and breadth of data capture and modeling. When we began our process at Bankers Trust, we had great plans to develop detailed risk assessment questionnaires and link them to scoring at multiple levels from the bottom up. The problem was that our risk assessment rigor was vastly out of sync with our resources and timetable. This became painfully apparent after having spent nearly four months in a single business line. If we were to complete a first cut at our model and capital attribution within the initial 12–18-month timeframe that we had set for ourselves, we would have to step back and be a bit more superficial at each business (i.e., top or at least mid-tier-down). Each firm will naturally establish its own such targets and balance.
- **Credibility in Sizing Operational Risk:** Whichever technique is chosen, it goes without saying that the process must be credible to the audience. If the model uses a simplistic calculation with only two variables, such as income and error rates, the conscientious business manager knows that there are dozens, if not hundreds, of indictors that drive his business and risk profile and will undoubtedly question it.
- **Balancing Causes and Symptoms:** In looking at loss outcomes and values, one may develop an estimate of the costs of operational risk, but not understand the underlying causes. To understand the drivers and recommend appropriate loss mitigation efforts, a more detailed insight is desired, but requires more detailed data. This tradeoff must be considered early on in the data collection phase, as was noted in Chapter 10 on loss databases.
- **Balancing Predictive and Retrospective Features:** We are seeking to promote proactive, not just reactive, behavior. Be careful, when developing models, that they are not based *entirely* on historical data, as it is difficult to predict the future using only historical data. As noted, the business environment and associated operational risks are continually changing. Models that represent only a historical environment do not represent

recent developments like e-commerce, wireless trading, and others, and therefore could miss part of the operational risk picture.

■ **Data Availability/Capture:** Suffice it to say that at this stage in operational risk management, our imaginations in developing and using models probably far outstrip the availability of necessary types and amounts of data to support them. To the degree that data necessary for certain analytics are not available, adjustments in the models will need to be made until this is remedied.

Now, we are ready to begin.

DATA INTERPRETATION 101: THE RETROSPECTIVE VIEW

You can observe a lot by watching.

—Yogi Berra

Before we launch into a discussion of analytic methods, we should heed some of Yogi Berra's advice and spend a moment on the basics of simple observation and data interpretations.

Clearly there is no reason to repeat the past ourselves if we can learn from the errors and misfortunes of others. However, this is certainly easier said than done.

A simple compilation of events creates a powerful risk database of real events, situations, and outcomes that we can use for direct observation. We have already discussed the value of simple observations about loss data and many of the descriptive and interpretive questions that you should ask about losses in Chapter 10. We will not repeat that material here. Suffice it to say that there is much to be gained by making simple observations and interpretations even in the absence of quantitative analysis.

Loss data containing thorough descriptions about losses, their causes, outcomes, persons involved, and loss severity (dollar amounts) can be helpful in making business decisions and are effective in presenting and winning an argument for higher risk standards and company investments. The more detail the database contains, the better.

For instance, at one time or another most risk managers have encountered the difficulty of convincing management to set up certain precautionary risk controls. The challenge can be even greater when seeking to avoid possible losses of catastrophic events that occur only infrequently, or more difficult still, perhaps have never happened. It is always best to make an argument for risk mitigation armed with as many facts as possible both in statistically probable events and in raw data. Simple observations about the data can be helpful in this regard, but oftentimes more sophisticated analysis can be even more convincing.

COST OF OPERATIONAL RISK: SIMPLE ADDITION AND SUBTRACTION

The first measurement tool, cost of operational risk (COOR), may be both the simpliest, yet most useful measurement tool of all at the firmwide level. It is used for recording and reporting costs associated with operational risk.

Risk and Insurance Management Society and Cost of Risk Calculation

This calculation has been borrowed and adapted from the calculation developed by Douglas Barlow, then risk manager of Massey-Ferguson, Ltd., and endorsed by the Risk and Insurance Management Society's (RIMS). The RIMS version has traditionally defined COR to include the sum of four basic elements:

1. Insurance and Risk Finance Costs
2. Self-Insured Loss Costs
3. Risk Control Costs
4. Risk Administration Costs

Because of changes in insurance policy limits and risk retention, this concept is more practical than monitoring trends of insurance premium costs alone over time.

Specifically, the calculation includes the sum of (1) premiums paid to insurers and reinsurers; (2) self-insured losses including losses that fall within deductibles or retention arrangements, losses above coverage limits, changes in reserves associated with outstanding or "incurred but not reported" (IBNR) losses, and losses that were insurable events, such as settlements of legal disputes, that fall outside insurable operational categories; plus (3) expenses associated with administration of the operational risk management function; minus (4) captive subsidiary earnings (e.g., investment gains).

The New Cost of Operational Risk Calculation

For application in operational risk management, we take the emphasis off insurance and risk finance a bit. Thus, we turn the calculation around to put the primary focus on operational losses, and use them as a point of reference for stress-testing a firm's risk finance and insurance programs. We then modify this concept and calculation further to include recognition of insurance proceeds as a direct offset to operational loss costs. Our objective in doing

COOR 1997–2000 (Millions)	1997	1998	1999	2000	4-Year Total
Total Operational Losses	$135	$426	$218	$72	$851
Operational Risk Management Administrative Costs	1	2	3	3	9
Self-Insurance Reserve Contributions	5	6	10	16	37
Insurance and Risk Finance Premiums	19	20	21	22	82
Total Cost of Operational Risk Before Recoveries	**$160**	**$454**	**$252**	**$113**	**$979**
Recoveries	($49)	($20)	($46)	($88)	($203)
Total Net Cost of Operational Risk (After Recoveries)	**$111**	**$434**	**$206**	**$25**	**$776**

EXHIBIT 12.3   Cost of Operational Risk (COOR)

so is to better align the concept with financial reporting and a firm's operational loss data. Thus, the new components are as follows:

1. Operational Loss Costs
   - by business line
   - by risk class
2. Plus: Operational Risk Management Administrative Costs
   - Operational risk management department
   - Other departments and expenses (e.g., Risk-assessment group, Internal Audit)
3. Plus: Insurance and Risk Finance Costs
   - Annual self-insurance reserve contributions
   - Insurance / reinsurance premiums
4. Minus: Insurance and Risk Finance Recoveries
   - Investment income on self-insurance reserves
   - Incremental residual self-insurance reserves

Exhibit 12.3 is a sample of a firmwide cost-of-operational-risk (COOR) summary calculation.

It is particularly important to look at the cost of operational risk over a long enough period of time. This probably translates to a 5–10-year calculation. There are several reasons for this: (1) There is the reality of timing mismatches that generally take place between a loss occurrence, the settlement of legal disputes or the filing of a claim, and ultimate recovery of losses under risk finance and insurance programs. (2) Because of the very nature of large infrequent events, in order to obtain a reasonably accurate picture of cost of operational risk you must capture a long enough period of time. Longer time periods will likely capture periods of both expected and unexpected loss levels. As such, they should be compared against a commensurate period of risk finance and insurance costs.

COOR Calculation Key Advantages

Use of the COOR calculation has a number of advantages. Two key ones are:

1. Once a data capture program for operational losses is functional, and assuming that the firm already tracks its current and past insurance and risk finance costs, COOR is relatively simple to calculate, and simple enough to explain to a broad audience of management and the Board.
2. The calculation can be used to track the long-term responsiveness of risk response efforts, including controls, risk mitigation investments, and risk finance and insurance programs against the firm's loss history. Long term is emphasized here to reflect the inherent nature and objective of risk finance and insurance programs as a tool to smooth costs over time.

COOR as a Benchmarking Tool

Numerous attempts have been made over time to conduct surveys of cost of risk and compare the results between firms. The difficulty of these surveys and comparisons is to establish common ground between the firms being compared. Like many benchmarks and comparisons, it is difficult to make generalizations between different-sized firms, and firms with different risk control and risk management programs and infrastructures. In addition, you often have basic differences in data collection and decisions about the level of detail to track components like losses, loss categories, risk control, and administrative categories. For these reasons, COOR is more useful as a tool to benchmark a company's own performance over time.

At the risk of stating the obvious, losses and cost of operational risk reports are important and useful for tracking the *historic costs* of operational risk and losses. The problem is that we also want to be in a position to take the analysis one step further—to project future loss and risk costs. And for that, we must apply some assumptions about the future and, in most cases, some more advanced mathematics (and analytics).

These analytics range from simple trend lines to regressions, expected loss analysis, and actuarial analysis. Later in this chapter we also look at financial statement-based analysis; factor analyses, such as causal models; a System Dynamics model; and neural networks. But before we move into modeling, let's look at some important background issues.

ALTERNATIVE MEASUREMENT METHODS: INDUSTRY PROGRESS TO DATE

The term *measurement* in the operational risk context encompases a wide variety of concepts, tools, and information bases. For instance, we know that although two firms say they use an operational VAR or RAROC methodology, it is virtually certain that, when compared, the approaches will differ. This will be a factor in progressing industry standards and regulatory guidelines for some time yet—the interpretation and application may give rise to many variations on the same theme.

In this section we review some of the methodologies currently in use or in experimentation by operational risk teams. The broad categories include (1) Financial Statement-based models; (2) Loss Scenario Models (LSMs), including Risk Mapping methods; (3) Trend Analysis for Projecting Aggregate Losses; (4) Expected Loss Calculations; (5) Loss Distribution and Statistical/Actuarial Models; and (6) Risk Indicator and Factor-based Models, including causal analysis such as Bayseam Belief Networks System Dynamics, and behavioral analysis, such as Neural Networks.[2]

Financial Statement Models

Economic pricing models use forecasting based on financial data and application of modeling. Probably the best known in operational risk circles is the use of the Capital Asset Pricing Model (CAPM). It is based on the assumption that operational risk has an influence on an institution's stock price moves and market value overall. The pricing model suggests that operational risk is the differential between credit and market risk, and a security's market value (see Exhibit 12.4).

Some firms have applied the CAPM to their financials and have derived an economic formula for operational risk. They have used CAPM's systematic risk component as a start toward dissecting components that contribute to their risk profile. Some have found the approach useful in dimensioning a figure for the aggregate operational risk to the firm's capital. Without other information, however, the approach would only be useful in considering aggregate capital adequacy. Also, in and of itself, it would lack information about specific operational risks. For instance, what loss scenarios are producing the worst possible aggregated outcome for a one-year horizon? What scenarios would represent more moderate outcomes? For this underlying information, one must look further to other models and analyses.

Firmwide Capital for Operational Risk =
$\qquad$ **Required Earnings (operational risk) / *r* (firm)**

---

where
$$r = \text{rate of return}$$

and

Required Earnings (operational risk) = *r* (operational risk) * book value (firm)

where
$$r \text{ (operational risk)} = r \text{ (firm)} - r \text{ (investment risk)}$$

where

r (firm) using CAPM= *r* (risk free) + beta (firm) * [*r* (market) − *r* (risk free)]

and

r (investment risk) = *r* (risk free) + beta (financially leveraged) * [*r* (market) − *r* (risk free)]

where
$$\text{Beta (financially leveraged)} = \text{beta (firm)} / \text{Operating Leverage}$$

EXHIBIT 12.4 Modeling Operational Risk Using CAPM

Thus, the advantages of this approach are:

- Readily available information sources
- Relative simplicity to implement

The disadvantages are:

- Taken alone it only looks at the 'big picture' (entire firm view) in terms of a capital number.
- Inability to drill down to analyze specific type of operational risk responsible for the volatility (e.g., scenario or loss).
- For the above reason, it may be difficult to sell to business lines.
- No apparent positive motivational element.

Another example of financial statement-based models involves the use of expenses as a proxy for operational risk. The idea was that "operating risk" could be expressed as a function of operating expense. These models were abandoned by many, however, as being too random. For instance, does an expense-cutting move increase risk or reduce it? The answer depends, of course, on what the move was and the care with which it was implemented.

Loss Scenario Models (LSMs)

Loss scenario models are used to attempt to convert one or more descriptive loss possibilities into a measurement outcome. There are many types of loss scenario models. For example:

- **Issue-based models** will generally be based on some formal source of issue generation, such as Internal Audit, but could also be based on the output of a control self-assessment (CSA) process. The challenge is to derive a consistent methodology for ranking and scoring the results. These can then be used as the basis for capital allocation.
- **Risk maps** are the results of a scenario analysis and are mapped onto a grid that portrays frequency and severity loss potential. These are described in further detail below.

LSM_S have been applied for years and can be useful in many ways. Exhibits 12.5 through 12.7 illustrate a very simple loss scenario model from end to end. Exhibit 12.5 illustrates an excerpt of a risk identification and assessment matrix. Individual loss scenarios like this system disruption example are then represented by probability and severity dimensions and summarized in a single exhibit like this one or series of risk inventory exhibits. The collection of exhibits is useful in representing the qualitative or descriptive nature of operational risk. By definition they are descriptive and not quantitative, but their very nature makes them useful for representing the circumstances for which data are lacking. They can also represent operational risks that are still emerging and for which only limited data are available, such as electronic commerce-related risks or risks involving intellectual capital. Another

Risk / Scenarios	Description	Loss Potential
System Disruption: Outage	Short-term service interruptions of critical systems: 1–3 hours	US $50,000–$100,000 range
System Disruption: Total Failure	Moderate to long-term disruption; three hours to several days: risk of errors during period of manual processing, if that is even feasible.	US $5 million–$40 million range

EXHIBIT 12.5 Risk Assessment Matrix

advantage is that they can capture the precise details of loss scenarios on the minds of managers surveyed. In contrast, however, their subjectivity can be their weakness, particularly when there is a need to convince the audience of the urgency of a possible outcome.

Scenario-based Model Recap—Advantages and Disadvantages   This scenario-based model attempts to summarize possible operational risk/loss outcomes for a variety of scenarios. It is often mapped into a matrix of probabilities: frequency and severity outcomes. Scenario models are reliant on the vision and breadth of knowledge and experience of the person(s) conducting the modeling.

Advantages include:

- Involves/builds business line managers' experience into profiling—enhances buy-in.
- Intuitive and easy to understand in concept.
- Sometimes effective in accentuating weak areas in a business strategy
- Can be used to highlight the need for a robust firmwide disaster recovery plan; may lead management to a structured crisis management strategy.

Disadvantages are:

- Often subjective, based on personal experience / expertise
- Can be difficult to build an entire portfolio of scenarios that are totally representative of the institution's operational risk profile

Risk Mapping Method   The second phase of a scenario-based model sometimes involves the creation of one or more risk maps. Risk mapping is one of the oldest forms of analysis for operational risks, probably because it is also simple and straightforward. Yet it can introduce a degree of sophistication over more rudimentary data observations, such as benchmarking, use of simple indicators, and the like.

Most risk maps will analyze frequency and severity separately, as each tell a different part of the story. Let's be clear about the terms first. Frequency is a measure of the number of losses, independent of the size of loss. This measure is often indexed to an exposure base, such as revenue, income, or transaction volume to reflect correlation to the extent that it exists (i.e., the greater number of losses as activity increases). Severity is a measure of average loss size, usually in monetary terms, although it could be expressed in other terms, such as length of time, as in the case of a business disruption. For context, the following are some observations on frequency and severity:

- **Loss Frequency:** When examining high-frequency/low-severity (HF/LS) losses, the analyst will find, by definition, that data are generally plentiful, which provide a larger sample size to work with, versus the inherently smaller datasets available for low-frequency/high-severity events. Frequency is also a particularly good indicator of risk because as frequency increases, so does the expected number of random (LF/HS) large losses.

  In other words, examining high-frequency events can help managers understand risks that may seem to be relatively small (because of relatively low average severity values) but contribute to a large part of the losses and harbor the potential to produce an occasional large random event. Given this, the accumulation effect of small steps in risk mitigation may have a large impact on the firm by minimizing the chance of a snowballing effect. The probability of a firm suffering from a catastrophic loss is therefore minimized.
- **Loss Severity:** Loss severity, or the average monetary value of loss events, on the other hand, is far more random.

  Tail (low-frequency/high-severity or LF/HS) events receive worldwide attention and tend to carry huge consequences. One-off catastrophic losses (e.g., Barings) are often caused by a combination of factors (i.e., inadequate staff and resources, concentration of power, lack of dual controls, and failure to heed audit findings). When allowed to accumulate, these factors, or others, can result in a loss that may lead to severe consequences.

  These events are fascinating anecdotally, and are useful for analysis of contributing risk factors, but usually statistical analysis of such individual large losses alone does not tell us anything about patterns of those factors and behavior over time—if for no other reason than we simply do not have enough observations of them!

  LF/HS losses are highly random in nature, difficult to predict (like earthquakes), and sometimes impossible to prevent completely. In essence, this is why many firms seek out insurance or catastrophic risk financing for large loss events, and why regulators are seeking to require capital for them. On a quantitative level, however, industry tail events can help managers assess the upper range of losses when compiling risk profiles.

The risk mapping process requires a user to establish a series of categories for its two map dimensions. Exhibit 12.6 illustrates these dimensions, along with a sampling of selected categories. The first step is the creation of a relationship between frequency and probability (or likelihood) categories.

Probability (or Likelihood) Categories		
Category	Probability of Event	Chance of Occurrence
Expected—Routine	100.0%	At least annually
Unexpected	10.0%	1 in 10 years
Rare	1.0%	1 in 100 years
Extremely Rare	0.1%	1 in 1000 years
Severity Categories		
Category	Annual Monetary Loss	
Normal	Less than $1 million	
Moderate	$1–9 million	
High	$10–99 million	
Extreme	$100–999 million	
Catastrophe	$1 billion+	

EXHIBIT 12.6   Risk Map Dimensions

That is, as the upper portion shows, frequencies are expressed in categories that range from expected levels to extremely rare events. For instance, the extremely rare case will be expressed as a probability of 0.1% or that of a 1-in-1000 year event. These categories are relatively standard in many risk map exercises.

Choice of the severity categories, on the other hand, is left to the discretion of the user. The dimensions shown in this particular illustration start with a normal or expected loss level range of $1 million or less and are characteristic of a larger firm. In all probability, a smaller firm would have a lower normal or expected severity category.

The results of the scenario analysis will be mapped on a grid similar to the one shown in Exhibit 12.7. Each letter in the alphabet represents a different risk subclass or loss scenario. The scenarios can be represented on the grid as datapoints, similar to that of an expected loss calculation. Alternatively, the analyst can show a range of severity possibilities depicted vertically as a representation of variance around an expected loss amount for each one of the scenarios depicted on the grid.

The risk map process often fits well together with a qualitative risk assessment process that entails interviews, a team-based Delphi risk assessment process, or some other scenario-based approach. Conceivably, it could also be linked with a control self-assessment program.

Some of the obvious advantages of the approach are its simplicity and the speed with which the analysis can be completed. In addition, it does not require

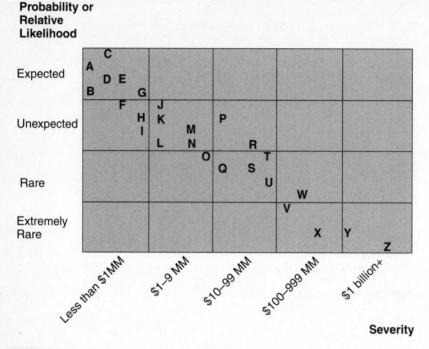

Probability or Relative Likelihood

EXHIBIT 12.7 Risk Map: Firmwide Representation

a database to complete it. Conversely, as disadvantages, it suffers from some of the same criticisms leveled against other types of scenario analysis approaches; namely, the process is subjective. However, the analyst is certainly free to supplement the subject of scenario analyses with empirical data on losses and loss experience, where available. Thus, the process presents itself nicely as a tool for hybrid qualitative–quantitative approaches.

Using Trend Analysis to Project Aggregate Losses

Aggregate loss projections attempt to calculate expected loss levels based on historical aggregate loss data by periods of time—which may be on an annual, monthly, or weekly basis. The loss data may represent the entire firm, an individual business unit, or new individual risk class. In any event, in the case of aggregate of loss analysis, there has been no attempt to separate frequency of losses from severity of those losses. For example, the analyst may have collected loss data for a business unit over the course of two years, and now wants to determine the future potential of losses for that business.

Simple forecasts of aggregate loss are developed using two variables and can be plotted on a simple x- and y-axis graphical representation. In this case, we use time as our x-axis representation and independent variable. The loss costs will be the dependent variable and plotted on the y-axis.

There are several different techniques that can be applied to project aggregate loss potential:

- **Simple Trend Line:** A line projection will generally represent a visual application of a line to historical data points available. Think of it as simply a "connecting line" spanning a few data points. This is a simple trend line. Your projection of future losses can be observed as the next point of intersection between the trend line and the future period in question. Simple trend lines can be useful where the analyst has only a few data points at his or her disposal. When more data are available, more sophisticated analysis is warranted, beginning with linear regressions.
- **Regression Analysis:** A trend line that represents the calculation of the "best fit" of a trend line to the data points available is a linear regression. Regressions are useful when we have a greater number of data points at our disposal, and where inflation has been fairly consistent over time and is expected to continue as such. In addition, the mathematical calculations involved allow us to begin to examine confidence intervals around our estimates. Exhibit 12.8 illustrates these two very simple trend analyses.

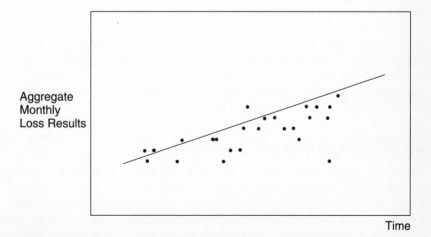

EXHIBIT 12.8 Simple Trend Line and Regression Forecasts

Insurance risk management professionals have used these techniques for as long as anyone can remember to project loss potential as a basis for making decisions about risk retentions and the need for insurance capacity (e.g., limits of coverage). In or about the 1970s, however, they recognized that these projections had limitations and that alternatives were available. So, leaning on work undertaken for a much longer time by insurance actuaries, they began to examine loss frequencies and severities in isolation. Analysts found that each of these dimensions provided useful insight into loss potential.

Expected Loss Calculations

A limitation to projecting aggregate losses is that the results provide limited insight about the causes of trends.

As the name implies, in expected loss analysis one can use the trends observed in loss frequency and severity to project future expected frequency and severity.

The concept here is straightforward enough. Simply by multiplying projected expected frequency by projected expected severity, the analyst can derive an expected loss value. For example, if it is estimated that a trading firm will suffer an average of 10 booking errors per year on a given desk, at an average value of $25,000 each, its projected average trade entry losses would be $250,000 annually for that desk.

This approach is an improvement over the others described in developing expected loss estimates. However, it doesn't provide insight into the potential for deviations from the expected values. This is why we look to more sophisticated statistical and actuarial analysis for guidance on managing expected, unexpected, and even worst case events.

We find ourselves asking for more information from the analysis. Beyond insight about the expected case results, we want to know what is the loss potential for one or more scenarios. We want to know what the worst case occurrence would be. We want to know what degree of confidence we have in the result of our analysis. All of this cries out for moving up another rung on our analytic sophistication ladder.

Loss Distribution and Statistical/Actuarial Models

Loss distributions and actuarial methods, of course, have been used by insurers and insurance risk managers for many years in projecting the potential outcomes of singular risk classes (e.g., general liability, workers' compensation, medical malpractice). Simply stated, they are derived from loss and exposure data. By capturing *representative* historical data the actuary can construct representative distributions of loss frequency and loss severity data, and has a basis for further analyses. For instance, standard statistical approaches can be used to develop a probability density function for each risk class and/or the firm as a whole.

These models are among the most commonly discussed for operational risk today, although approaches differ. At the time of this writing, however, only a handful of firms are using them for risk capital models. Commonly the source information will be operational risk event and loss data, which can in some cases be a mix of that internal and external data. Frequency and severity distributions are assembled based on the data, then simulated via a technique such as Monte Carlo to arrive at a range of possible loss outcomes; figures are produced for a stipulated time horizon and range of confidence levels.

As we continue to progress in the sophistication of our analyses, there are several other concepts and variables to consider:

- **Exposure Bases and Scaling:** Let's return to our discussion of inherent risk indicators and exposure bases in Chapter 11. The use of exposure bases implies that there is some degree of scaling that should be recognized in looking at the potential loss experience of different size organizations. Insurance actuaries examine exposure bases routinely when analyzing insurance loss experience. Traditionally, financial institution bonds have been scaled and rated on the basis of employee head count, workers compensation insurance has been scaled on the basis of payroll, and product liability insurance has been scaled on the basis of revenue. The use of exposure bases also implies that we can determine a key driver for the loss type. In the end, the use of exposure bases and scaling is a function of a correlation that exists between the relative size of the exposure base and loss potential.

- **Loss Development:** This concept represents the reality that some loss types (risk classes) take longer than others to develop to their ultimate loss costs. For instance, at one extreme, a physical damage loss, such as a fire or flood in an individual location, can be assessed and quantified within a relatively short period of time. Short in this sense is perhaps 3 to 6 months for the fire damage itself, and 6 to 18 months when considering all dimensions of the damage and indirect impact to business disruption, loss of earnings, cleanup, and reconstruction costs. In contrast, a major legal action could easily take much longer (several years) to develop to the point that the final cost of the lawsuit, its judgment, defense costs, investigation, and other associated costs are known.

- **Variance and Tail Risk:**[3] Another fundamental concept in more sophisticated risk analysis is to consider variance, or the potential variability of loss from an expected outcome. Questions regarding volatility of results, and therefore variance, require us to consider more sophisticated analysis techniques than the use of *expected* frequencies and severities alone.

The story of the line manager back in Chapter 10 who had no losses but was shocked that, despite this, he was still receiving a capital charge is a classic case of denial about variance and tail risk. This is the risk of loss involving those potential low-frequency/high-severity loss events that are so dangerous.

Operational tail risk is perhaps the dimension of operational risk most often misunderstood, and therefore also overlooked by line management. Simply stated, it is the representation of the extreme low-probability/high-severity loss events. When operational losses are plotted as a probability distribution, by definition, the vast majority of outcomes are expected to fall in the body of the distribution. Thus, people who have not ventured into statistical measures of operational risk, including variance, are by definition assessing risk at only expected levels. In other words, they are only considering losses that are known and have usually occurred. It is not until one ventures into statistical measures for extreme probabilities (i.e., 95th or 99th percentile) or at least, considers the less probable or less likely outcomes intuitively, that one is truly considering tail risk.

Let's consider the example of systems risk. In the body of the distribution, one would consider routine outages of relatively minor duration, say from ten minutes to several hours. This might be an expected and acceptable occurrence for a noncritical system. When considering a more critical system, such as money transfer, market data feed systems for trading operations, or customer service systems for funds management operations, the downtime tolerance must be lower. In the latter, more critical case, the occurrence would be unacceptable and hopefully less likely as well. For them, outages in the body of the distribution might fall in the range of seconds, if tolerated at all.

So one can identify the types of events that would naturally fall in the body of a probability distribution. We have also begun to identify those deemed less acceptable and, hopefully, less probable. Assuming then that they are either inherently less probable or have been engineered to be so, they would logically fall further out on the probability distribution—in the tail.

When combined with a risk management process, one can either map loss scenarios against probabilities and create a distribution, or actually work with empirical data. A number of firms do both. Early in our work on operational risk, we found a need to build subjective scenarios and subjective mappings against probabilities. With time, we invested in the extensive collection and collation of empirical data not only to reflect our own experience, but to track that of other firms as well. The data helped to confirm our expectations of scenarios and outcomes.

The real message here, however, is that one must consider tail risk. This can be done either by analyzing the experience of other unfortunate firms who have suffered large losses in areas that you have not, or by dreaming up some of your own worst case nightmares. The confidence of your result can be boosted, of course, by analyzing numerous events and then producing simulation results from Monte Carlo or other models. In our work at Bankers Trust, we used our database, supplemented by some hypothetical scenarios and our analytics, to produce results not only at expected levels, but also at a 99% confidence level. With the data and analytics in hand, a risk manager is then in a far better position to discuss the prospect of a tail (low-probability/high-severity) event, and perhaps more importantly, the control investment options available to reengineer its outcome. That is, through investment in control measures, a firm might reduce its probability further (although the change might be academic), or it might minimize the possible size of the outcome should the event occur.

The Data Challenge, Part II   One of the interesting problems that we did not address in Chapter 10, or have not yet addressed here, for that matter, is the practical reality of massaging loss data, working with expected losses and tail losses, and avoiding double counting for analytical purposes.

From the perspective of analytic needs, it is important to have information not only on the individual risk class, but on loss amount, current state, and a broad description of the event. Once collected, loss amounts must be adjusted for inflation to current cost levels, and to the extent possible for changes in procedures and controls. This is also the point at which you would apply scaling factors.

Because we are looking to simulate the impact of losses as they occur, the loss data used in supporting the model must be analyzed on the date the event was reported, not settled, as is normally the case with insurance actuarial models.

The next problem for many is that you still may not have enough data to be able to formulate any conclusions about the risk of loss in a given business line or attain statistical significance. Or you may not have enough to make adequate statistical calculations, or have "statistical significance." There are two component parts to this type of statistical significance. The first is one of having enough data to completely represent the body of the distribution. The other is having enough data in the tail of the distribution.

Let's start first with a key conceptual issue and look at the component data challenges and possible solutions for expected loss levels ("body-of-the-distribution" risks) and tail risk, individually:

- **Unexpected Loss and Tail Risk:** The latter can be addressed by using a large loss external database. As noted, fortunately most firms do not have many large losses of their own. If they did, chances are that they would not be around for very long to talk about them. Thus, many firms will look to central repositories of industry operational losses, whether in the form of external databases or loss consortia, in order to represent more fully the possible outcomes that might befall them, particularly when it comes to loss severities. There are several around today to choose from (see Chapter 10).

■ **Expected Losses and the Body of the Distribution:** Being confronted with insufficient data in the body of the distribution presents a slightly different problem. In attempting to represent the large loss potential, one is seeking to "borrow" the severity or size of the losses from others for analytical purposes. On the other hand, in seeking to portray the more routine or expected losses (i.e., the body of the distribution), some issues of using external data become even more pronounced. These include issues such as relevance of the loss data, like products, business lines, operations, and control environments, etc.

The emerging operational risk data consortia are, or should be, exploring either one or both of these data needs.

Internal Measurement Approach   As this book is being finalized there is much discussion about a regulatory capital proposal called the Internal Measurement Approach (IMA). The final version of this measurement option is yet undetermined, but most recently its composition consists of calculations by business type that include exposure indicators, an event probability parameter using a bank's own loss data, a parameter representing the loss given the type of event in question, and a sealing factor that regulators intend to develop in conjunction with the industry using industry data. Chapter 17 contains a more complete discussion of the IMA and other regulatory developments. Suffice to say that IMA is a developing approach that draws on both exposure bases, loss data, probabilities, and loss distributions. The intent is to reflect the value of sealed loss histories for measuring risk. It is a reasonable approach, in context. Like most methods, however, its relative success will depend on its final implementation details. At this stage, among their criticisms, opponents argue that it does not capture qualitative information about risk that is not reflected in available loss data.

CASE ILLUSTRATION

Actuarial Methods, Monte Carlo Simulation, and Loss Distributions

Bankers Trust

In the early 1990s senior management at Bankers Trust decided that the time had come to graduate from using "plug number" estimates in our economic capital models for operational risk. Following some experiments in risk assessment, we began exploring actuarial analysis and loss distribution approaches to estimate our annual exposure to operational loss. Prior to this, the plug number had come from an expense-based estimate (see "Financial Statement Models" section) relative to a select number of the firm's fee-based businesses. In essence, we knew we could do better.

In thinking about the problem, we noted some interesting parallels between insurance-related analysis and our own objective of determining exposure, or value at risk, over a one-year time horizon at a high level of confidence. It occurred to us that there is a striking similarity to the various funding studies we have done in the insurance and risk financing industries over the years. There, an organization is seeking to answer the same questions: What is my potential loss from a particular source of risk, at both an expected level and at some higher level of confidence (such as 95% or 99%)? And how do we price this on both a single-year and multiyear basis? Thus, it was an insurance-like funding study that actually formed the basis of our first actuarial risk measurement model for operational RAROC.

However, we recognized that traditional high-frequency/low-severity actuarial techniques would be only partially relevant. Because of the large loss nature of headline operational events at the time (e.g., Barings), we sensed that we would need to look at additional loss distributions more relevant to extreme events (low-frequency/high-severity).[4] This was especially true given our particular concern—protecting our capital in the face of one-in-100–year events.

The parallel was also very fresh in our minds because in 1991 we had just applied similar actuarial techniques in assessing the feasibility and forming a captive insurance company to protect the bank from large loss exposures, where conventional insurance solutions were lacking. Thus, we formed a Bermuda captive to underwrite our risk directly, and accessed the reinsurance market for risk-sharing purposes. We will reveal more on this type of undertaking in Chapter 15 on Alternative Risk Finance.

Key Considerations / Objectives for Analysis   Some of the considerations that must be addressed at the outset by a firm considering this type of approach include:

- Decide whether we are attempting to calculate an aggregate value for risk capital, or by business line.
- Confirm the time horizon (single-year or multiyear).

- Select the mathematical models.
- Select frequency/severity parameters.
- Choose a confidence level (e.g., 95%, 99%).

In terms of our own confidence levels, we recognized that in order to be consistent with our credit- and market-risk models, we needed to select a model that would help us to define the capital required to support losses incurred in a single year 99% of the time. We concluded that this capital definition required a probability distribution of aggregate losses. We also concluded that a behavioral simulation model was required, because a scenario-based model could not assign probabilities.[5]

The Monte Carlo Simulation   What is Monte Carlo Simulation? It is the process of simulating or representing an event or scenario using a series of random pairings of variables, generally referred to as iterations or trials. This situation generally involves hundreds or thousands of these iterations. We chose the latter. The samplings from Monte Carlo are such that they reproduce the aggregate distribution shape. Thus, the results of the calculation reflect the probabilities of the loss values that can occur.

Some key advantages of Monte Carlo simulations are that correlations and other interdependence can be modeled, accuracy can be improved by increasing the number of iterations, mathematical complexity can be varied (e.g., power functions, logs), and the model can be analyzed relatively easily. Much of this has been made possible, not to mention easier, in recent years with the increased availability of software for performing the calculations.[6]

In modeling event frequency and event severity separately, we chose to use the Poisson distribution for frequency and a Pareto distribution for severity because they are commonly used in analyzing insurance loss data. They also seemed appropriate based on an assessment of the key characteristics of our own operational loss data.

- **Frequency:**[7] In modeling loss frequency, we first had to determine an exposure base. As previously discussed, this is a piece of information that acts as a proxy for exposure to loss (e.g., number of transactions, square footage of office space). Recall that these would be selected from our universe of inherent risk or exposure indicators.

    We then model annual event frequency, considering changes in exposure and claims that have not yet been reported. The model considers some perspective on exposure growth. One objective might be to link operational risk estimates to economic phenomena. In that scenario we will compare the frequency trends to economic time-series data and incorporate the relationship, if any, into our model.

- **Severity:**[8] Event severity is modeled after considering how to blend supplementary data (i.e., in our case this was the external loss data in our industry loss database, or in the future this will include consortium data). The approach will differ depending on the type and quality of supplementary data.

- **"Synthetic Data Points" for New Risks:** There is a unique data problem relative to newly emerging exposures where losses are not plentiful. What about scenarios that have never been experienced or logged before, but can be imagined? Here, there is a unique concern about the lack of data to represent certain tail risk scenarios. For these, you can apply a concept that we have sometimes used in loss scenario analysis. We dubbed it the creation and use of "synthetic data points." For these cases, such as large-scale outages involving critical systems, we still want to have an option of mapping an assumed probability into our collection of empirical frequencies and severities for specified events. So, we interview experts for their insight on loss potential, then use resultant consensus estimates to represent a loss in the database. This approach is applied in only a handful of cases, but when used, we view it as important to represent the total exposure. The combination of empirical data and synthetic data provides a far more robust database than one would have in using either empirical data or hypothetical scenarios alone.

Correlation   Correlation affects the spread of results. Negatively correlated categories reduce the spread while positively correlated categories increase it.

The measurement of correlation is difficult as statistical measures of correlation are highly volatile and often need relatively large values ($> 30\%$) to be considered significant. In examining data for correlation, it is also important to adjust for the effects that you are already considering in the model, such as exposure growth and inflation. In general, results from any type of correlation study will be tempered with judgment.

The application of correlation in the simulation process depends on whether the correlation is frequency- or severity-based. Severity correlation will be implemented during the course of generating events, while frequency-based correlation will be implemented during aggregation.

As noted, because of the relative paucity of loss data available in our initial models, we were unable to conduct our analyses by business line.

Thus, our calculations were limited to simulating risk classes only. In this particular exercise, we found no strong signs of correlation between risk classes. This was confirmed during the testing process.[9]

Model Testing   We tested each of the risk classes to see how the simulations replicated the data. Ideally, the middle of the distribution should be similar to the data, but the spread of results should be wider. In addition, the joint simulation will be compared to the historical aggregate results. Satisfactory group models with inappropriate aggregate results could point to a shortcoming in the correlation process.

Based on the results of our testing, we were able to make adjustments to the model parameters, which led to improved calibration of the model.[10]

Application of Model Results   After simulating dozens of events for each of the thousands of trials (years in this case), with the appropriate considerations for correlation, exposure group, and the like, the model produced an aggregate operational loss distribution.

In addition to the aggregate results, and the ability to represent aggregate exposure for the firm, we were able to produce other useful information from our analysis. For one, we were in a position to see which risk category drove the capital constraint and drill down to see if it is frequency or severity driven. This led to better-focused risk management efforts.

The net result is that the model was useful in producing aggregate firmwide capital measures at selected confidence levels.[11]

■ ■ ■

Exhibit 12.9 is a tabular presentation of some hypothetical *business-by-business* and firmwide value-at-risk results from a loss distribution model. Exhibit 12.10 is a graphical presentation of hypothetical results *by risk class* over time. Note that diversification is assumed in both exhibits relative to the five business lines and risk classes, respectively. Thus, in both cases the diversified total is smaller than the sum of the individual parts. The time series graph is the type of trend analysis produced when an external database is combined with a firm's own internal data. The database was comprised of operational risk events that had occurred at other firms but were relevant to the user's business operations. In the time series version the analyst is in a position to analyze the reasons for the trends and pass the results over to management for appropriate action.

There has been much discussion in operational risk circles about the use of loss data in predicting future operational losses. To a large extent, past

| | (Per Confidence Interval) | | | | | | | |
	50%	75%	80%	90%	95%	99%	99.5%	99.9%
Business Line 1	#1	#5	#7	#14	#30	#182	#437	#504
Business Line 2	1	1	2	4	9	43	74	311
Business Line 3	1	3	4	9	19	75	121	258
Business Line 4	37	73	80	161	298	554	609	843
Business Line 5	2	6	6	18	39	207	370	502
TOTAL Diversified	#58	#108	#129	#243	#429	#604	#700	#1080

EXHIBIT 12.9 Operational Risk Capital Results*
*Capital reported in millions of dollars (USD).

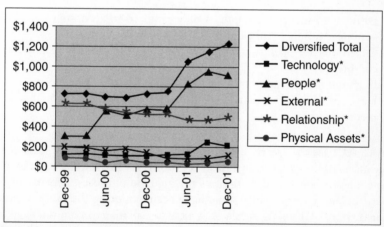

This is an hypothetical illustration of trend lines of both diversified and undiversified simulated exposure by risk class at a selected confidence level (e.g., 99%). In this scenario, the results highlight a longer term increase in the probable loss exposure, particularly in the technology and people/human capital areas. It also shows a slight upturn in external, physical asset, and relationship risk classes in the 4th quarter of 2001.

EXHIBIT 12.10 Capital by Risk Class

loss trends *have* provided a reasonably good indication of the future, but we must take into account a variety of factors in using them. As we all know, there is a fundamental shortcoming in looking solely at operational loss experience—it is a retrospective view!

Thus, for one, in using past loss data we are making a huge assumption that the future will resemble the past. All things being equal, that may not be too much of a stretch. We have already discussed supplementing past loss data with scenario analyses, "synthetic data points," and the like.

Even with all of that in our arsenal, all is not equal. We must consider the rate of change in our environment. These include the speed of change in the environment; changes in management teams, control structures, business mix, and product offerings; changes in the technological environment, in society, and so on. There is much to be said about using past loss data, but we must be comfortable with these assumptions before using them.

Advantages of the loss database and statistical/actuarial approach:

- Attempts to be predictive—ensure users are aware of its limitations.
- By definition, it is based on empirical data. It is more defensible than subjective scenarios.

Disadvantages:

- Difficult to source the depth of data required to accurately calculate a firm's operational risk capital
- Time intensive operation to gather the data; even then they may not be complete
- In its pure form, quantitative based—no qualitative assessment
- Have to ensure a risk management motivational element is built into the methodology

Extreme Value Theory As noted, most firms (thankfully) do not have many large losses of their own to include in a proprietary loss database, or, in turn, to include in their loss distributions for analytic purposes. Because of this data problem, more recently some have been exploring the use of extreme value theory (EVT). EVT is relatively new to risk managers in financial services, but has been applied to market risks in estimating value at risk for extreme positions, such as those represented by the stock market crash of 1987 or the Bond market backup of 1994.[12]

Interestingly enough, apparently it has been used even longer in operational risk situations in other industries, although perhaps its application have not been recognized as such. Dowd notes that EVT has been applied by statisticians and engineers in areas like hydroponics for estimating the height of sea walls when considering the extreme severity problem of flood risk. In many cases they have had even less data to work with than the financial services operational risk managers do![13]

EVT is focused on the extreme observations of a distribution rather than on all observations in the distribution, or in other words, the entire distribution. It applies a parametric method to compute the extreme values for the problem in question. It can be applied for a specific asset position (i.e., market risk) or risk scenario, such as flood (i.e., operational risk). The EVT explicitly takes into account the correlation between risk factors during extreme conditions.[14] It is applied when the analyst has a small number of large loss observations and is seeking to determine how the asymptotic distribution of extreme values should look.[15] Sound familiar? This is precisely why it has sparked the interest of analysts looking at extreme operational risk scenarios.

Risk Indicator and Factor-based Models

Let's return to our discussion in Chapter 11 on risk indicators and their use as factors for modeling. These methodologies originate from risk indicator information in isolation or in combination with loss information.

Risk indicator or factor models are derived from various types of data input that serve to dimension the evolution of a risk profile. There are exceptions, of course, but these often give rise to bottom-up approaches due to the granularity and nature of the information used as the source. As a simple illustration, the combination of technological operability, application viability, and technology staff competency versus system downtime suggest an interesting, albeit partial picture of the operational risk profile of a business. Exhibit 12.11 shows that when trended over time the picture can be even more informative and useful. In and of themselves, these trends only project the evolution of a risk profile. Is it evolving toward higher or lower risk? While they might be trended forward through regression analysis, they will only produce a relative future value of the individual or aggregated factors, but not necessarily a loss outcome. Thus, initially these representations are indicative of cause or causation, not *effect*, or loss outcome, as a loss scenario or actuarial model might. When these factor or causation profiles are combined with representations of outcome they begin to reach their full potential. Let's look at some examples.

One example of a model that endeavors to bridge this gap in representing firmwide risk measurement is Delta-EVT™.

The method is an interesting combination of risk factor calculations that are used to produce an operating loss distribution and extreme value theory (EVT), which is used to produce an excess loss distribution. Jack King

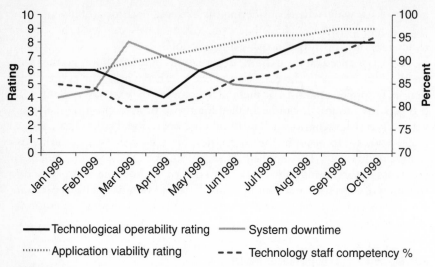

EXHIBIT 12.11   Risk Factor Trends Over Time

describes the methodology in detail in his book, *Operational Risk: Measurement and Modeling* (2001). In brief, his steps for implementation are:

1. "Establish the business model with value-adding processes and activities, and any available (historical) large losses."
2. "Determine the risk factors for the major activities in the value-adding processes and their relation to earnings (the earnings function)."
3. "Estimate operational losses using uncertainty of the risk factors propagated to the risk in earnings (Delta method)."
4. "Set the threshold of operating losses from the processes using the risk factor uncertainties and operating losses from the Delta method, and filter the large losses using the threshold."
5. "Create a set of excess losses greater than the threshold using plausible scenarios based on actual historical losses, external events, and near misses and model them using extreme value theory (EVT)."[16]

The method benefits from the qualitative use of risk factors. With careful selection, these factors can provide a more tailored and useful representation of risk than loss data alone. The method also benefits from use of loss data, to the extent available, and EVT to help develop a large loss representation, which also serve to buffet the model against criticism about subjectivity. Skeptics have expressed concern about the selection of factors, judgment applied in developing the large loss representations, and instability of the EVT tail when data are sparse. For its balance as a risk management tool, the method deserves consideration and experimentation.

Other indicator or factor-based models in development or use for operational risk management include process maps, causal analyses, such as those using Bayesian Belief Networks or System Dynamics, and behavioral models such as Neural Networks. On the following pages we will examine several illustrations of factor-based models, including a case applying Baysean Belief Networks for casual analysis in the settlement process from West LB, a discussion of the System Dynamics approach from Tillinghast/Towers Perrin, and a discussion of Neural Networks from NASA. For the most part, these methods bring value to the table as measurement and management tools for specific risks or business functions in a firm as opposed to firmwide risk measurement for VAR and risk capital applications.

CASE ILLUSTRATION

Causal Models—Bayesian Belief Networks OpVAR Project

West Landesbank

(This case was written and contributed by Karolina Kalkantara and Riaz Karim of West LB, and David Syer of Algorithmics.)

In October 2000, the London branch of WestLandesbank (WestLB) embarked upon a three-month pilot project to model the operational risk associated with the Euroclear bond settlement process. The Euroclear bond cash settlement was chosen as the initial vertical process within WestLB's Global Financial Markets division due to the transparency of determining tangible and quantifiable operational risk factors relative to other operational processes within a large investment banking environment. The working party consisted of various departments within the bank (Trade Control Market Analysis, Bond Settlement, Project Management, IT, Business Process Reengineering) as well as Algorithmics UK and Droege & Co. Management Consultancy.

The aim of the project was to provide two things: a predictive look at new transactions and a retrospective picture of the historical patterns of risk in the process. The predictive element was to rank new transactions in order of decreasing likelihood of failure, or alternatively expected cost, in a risk-adjusted sense. The retrospective element was twofold: to provide a cash-based measure of risk in the process through a daily (or monthly) operational risk VAR at various confidence levels and to report quantitatively on the historic settlement efficiency based on the data that were at hand.

The models were predictive and estimate the number and cost of failed trades (there were seven types of fails) that are likely to occur on a given day. The models constructed a predictive history of the most likely future events using Bayesian probabilities. The insight for this is derived from a model of the Bond Settlement Process. The model is said to be causal (cause versus effect); that is to say it looks for the likely cause of failure and predicts the likely effect. It achieves this by mapping out the steps in the process and says "What happens if the process fails at such and such a point (or node)?" and then "What happens if there is a system failure at the next node?" and so on, until it has "stepped through" the entire process.

Based upon historic data (we used trade files and trade fail data for a period of three months obtained from WestLB's MIS Bond system), the model attributed probabilities of failure to each trade. For the purpose of modeling, the data were split into two parts: Settled (containing 67% of the data) and Open (containing 33% of the data). The models were trained with the Settled data and their performance measured when the Open trades were entered. By supplying current market price data, related volatility, and central treasury costs of funding and inputting this information to the model, it was possible to calculate both the probability of failure and its expected monetary cost to the firm. This is the measure of operational risk inherent in the process.

The data source was obtained via the export facility of the existing MIS in the bank, which provided us with a list of all the attributes of the trades in a three-month period. Information about which of these trades had failed, and for what reason (classified into seven categories), was collected by the Settlement team itself through their internal processes and made available to us in a database. These data had been collected for some time by the Settlement team, but not analyzed in any depth, and detailed information about settlement failures was not systematically or centrally collated.

We assigned a different probability of failure to each individual transaction using the Algo WatchDog software and stored the results back into the same database that had been used to collect the transaction and fails data. The total potential cost of a failure, based on the nominal value of the transaction and the length of time that it took to resolve, were also stored in the database. In a credit risk analogy, we now had a list of all our counterparts (transactions), each with default (failure) probability and exposure (failure cost), and this enabled us to estimate a cash-based measure of risk in the Settlement process. Reports were generated showing daily VAR at 99% confidence over a period of three months (see Exhibit 12.12), to be used by operations management in their budgeting and cost setting (the firm has an internal service provider model for operations). Exhibit 12.12 illustrates a daily VAR figure for Open trades from March 1, 2000 to May 31, 2000.

The daily VAR figure was also used as a risk indicator, showing its development over time when the bank was developing new and riskier

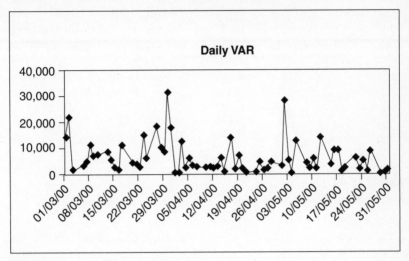

EXHIBIT 12.12 WestLB Project—Daily VAR
Source: WestLandesbank, London Branch.

Failure Code	Failure Probability	Predicted Cost (EUR)	VAR (EUR)
Code_1	20.7573%	−857.96	50.99
Code_2	0.3422%	11.32	8.40
Code_3	4.3863%	−126.80	6.60
Code_4	0.0495%	1.21	1.02
Code_5	18.4237%	−254.31	25.21
Code_6	1.8922%	104.19	2.83
Code_7	0.1906%	0.00	0.00
Total	46.0419%	−1122.35	57.96

EXHIBIT 12.13 VAR Figure for April 1, 2000
Source: WestLandesbank, London Branch.

(or less risky) practices in fixed income trading and settlement. Exhibit 12.13 illustrates the VAR figure (57.96M Euro) for a particular day (April 1, 2000), the failure probability for each fail code, and the predicted cost of failure.

In addition, we looked retrospectively at "hotspots" or "stress scenarios" by reporting on particular trade attributes, or particular historic transactions, whose attributes combined to signify a high probability of failure. These reports could be used by settlement personnel to focus their

Index	Trade Attribute	Variance Reduction	Variance Reduction Percent (%)
0	DaysLate	0.26	100.00
1	Nat_of_Cpty	0.03	11.56
2	Book_	0.03	10.31
3	Ccy_Dealt	0.02	8.90
4	Dealer	0.02	7.94
5	Industry	0.02	7.50

EXHIBIT 12.14   Trade Attributes
Source: WestLandesbank, London Branch.

Rank	Nat_of_Cpty	Number of Trades	Number of Fails	Prob (Late = True I Nationality)
1	Country_1	34	10	29.41%
2	Country_2	108	21	19.44%
3	Country_3	193	34	17.62%
4	Country_4	29	5	17.24%

EXHIBIT 12.15   Influence of Attribute Levels
Source: WestLandesbank, London Branch.

efforts on improved processes or controls and are displayed in Exhibits 12.14 and 12.15.

Exhibit 12.14 displays the trade attributes that are most important in determining trades that settled late. For example, Nationality of Counterparty is the most influential in determining failed trades (11.56%), whereas Book and Currency dealt are less influential (10.31% and 8.9%, respectively).

Exhibit 12.15 displays the influence of each attribute level of the variable Nationality of Counterparty in determining failed trades. As can be seen from the exhibit, counterparties from Country_1 were associated with 34 trades of which 29.41% (10 trades) failed.

On the predictive side, we produced the same kind of reports, focusing on a "hot list" of transactions likely to fail and an assessment of the predictive power of the model. Exhibit 12.16 shows the five most likely trades to fail on a given date (April 25, 2000) and the most likely reason for failure. Hence, the security SAFFRN05 is likely to fail be-

Book	Buy/ Sell	Amount	Sec_Code	Ccy	Fail-Code 1	Fail-Code 2	Fail-Code 3	Fail-Code 4
MBAV	B	2E + 08	ITAFRN02A	EUR		0.0000	0.0013	0.0142
TLC1	B	807654.6	SAFFRN05	USD	0.7510	0.0000	0.0000	00157
EDLQ	B	214504.8	AUS06706	AUD	0.1818	0.0000	0.5478	0.0178
EDLQ	S	214550.7	AUS06706	AUD	0.0000	0.1623	0.6410	0.0196
EDLQ	S	478795.1	SGB06005	SEK	0.0000	0.3419	0.5296	0.0352

EXHIBIT 12.16 Daily Hot List Report: Five Most Likely Trades to Fail
Source: WestLandesbank, London Branch.

	Predictivity			
	Accuracy	Success	Blind Luck	Ratio
Open	47.37%	18.00%	6.81%	2.6
Settled	65.71%	30.80%	10.41%	3.0

EXHIBIT 12.17 WestLB Project—Predictivity Results
Source: WestLandesbank, London Branch.

cause of insufficient bonds to deliver (probability = 75.1%) whereas the security SGB06005 is likely to fail because of unmatched instructions (probability = 52.96%).

The latter security (SGO009001) is expressed in Exhibit 12.17 as the Predictivity results for Open and Settled trades. *Accuracy* is defined as the quotient of the number of predicted fails and total predicted fails. *Success* is defined as the quotient of successful predictions (predicted fails that actually failed) and total predictions. *Blind luck* is the average fail rate. *Predictive power* is the ratio of success to blind luck.

From Exhibit 12.17 it follows that for the parameters chosen, the model is 2.6 times better at failure prediction than pure chance! The model's predictive power can be boosted to six times better than pure chance, by focusing on the most common kinds of transactions. A suite of associated online reports are available to support the data analyses. The firm's intention, ultimately, is to identify and calibrate all operational risk in the London Operations group through a stepwise review of each area, process by process.

■ ■ ■

CASE ILLUSTRATION

System Dynamics Approach

Another method showing promise in the developmental stage is the System Dynamics Approach. System Dynamics is a robust simulation modeling approach developed by Jay Forrester of the Massachusetts Institute of Technology. The approach involves developing a computer model that simulates the cause–effect interactions among all the key variables underlying a specific system. The following summary was written and contributed by Jerry Miccolis and Samir Shah of Towers Perrin.

There are some important distinctions between operational risks and financial risks that require a different approach to modeling operational risks than those traditionally used to quantify financial risks:

- The source of financial risks (such as volatility in interest rates, foreign exchange rates, and equity returns) are beyond a company's direct control; whereas, operational risks (such as employee fraud, technology failure, and agent misselling) are a direct consequence of a company's organization and operation. Operational risks and their magnitude vary significantly from one company to another depending on the unique combination of business processes, people, technology, organization, and culture.
- Some operational risks only impact earnings volatility, whereas other operational risks impact capital. The ones that impact capital are typically those that are characterized by low frequency and high severity. These risks have a skewed probability distribution, whereas financial risks typically have symmetric distributions. If the purpose of operational risk management is capital determination, then it will be necessary to use modeling methods suited to skewed probability distributions with fat tails.
- Whereas financial risks can be hedged, operational risks are typically managed through changes in operations such as changes in business processes, organization, technology, and training, for example.
- Finally, operational risk modeling is a relatively new endeavor for most companies. There is much less reliable historical data for risk modeling than there is for financial risk. However, in the financial services industry, initiatives to gather industry-wide data as well as efforts by individual companies to gather internal data offer promise.

For these reasons, simply applying the same methods that are now used to model financial risks is not reliable or even possible in some cases. Furthermore, it's unlikely that just one method will be appropriate for quantifying all operational risks.

In addition, representative historical operational loss data are not always available. For reasons described above, industry-wide data must be adjusted to reflect company-specific information. Even if it was possible to gather enough representative data, it's virtually impossible to determine how the operational risk will change prospectively with changes in operations. The ultimate objective, after all, is not to quantify operational risks but to reduce operational risks and its impact on capital and earnings volatility. The predominant approach to reduce these risks is through changes in how the business is managed—as opposed to hedging in the financial markets for financial risks. For these reasons, it's necessary to supplement parametric approaches based on historical data by other methods.

The System Dynamics approach offers potential to address the difficulties of modeling operational risks described above. The first step is to prepare a graphical representation (system map) of the interconnected causal relationships for the operational risk. The second step involves quantifying the cause–effect relationships between variables based on a combination of historical data and expert input. Since the data needed to model operational risks are generally sparse, this step leverages the knowledge and experience of senior managers who best understand the dynamics underlying their business. Expert input is represented as stochastic cause–effect relationships to explicitly reflect the uncertainty of the input. Finally, the results of the first two steps are combined into a computer simulation model that is used to generate scenarios for the output variables of the system being modeled. The outputs of the simulations are probability distributions for financial and operational metrics, such as profit, premium, market share, and number of policies.

An example of a system dynamics map representing the risk from a computer virus is illustrated in Exhibit 12.18. The map explicitly represents the cause–effect relationships among key variables for both the sources and consequences of a computer virus. Each relationship is quantified using a combination of industry data, internal company data, and expert input. The resulting simulation model can be used to develop a distribution of outcomes for variables such as penalties, lost business, and lost productivity.

The approach is equally applicable for modeling the risk associated with the decision to use the Internet as a distribution channel. The system dynamics simulation model will capture the interaction of variables such as brand name, marketing and advertising expenditure, complexity of product features, hit rates to website, availability of online support, and performance of competing distribution channels.

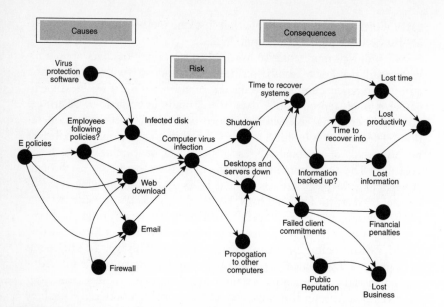

EXHIBIT 12.18   Operational Risk Modeling System Dynamics Approach
Source: Tillinghast/Towers Perrin.

In addition to addressing the unique challenges of modeling operational risks, use of system dynamics simulation models provides some additional advantages:

- It helps focus further data-gathering efforts. A simulation model can be built quickly using expert input to supplement existing data. Sensitivity analysis can identify the specific assumptions that have the greatest impact on the results. This helps an organization deploy resources to gather specific data to tighten key assumptions.
- It provides a better understanding of the dynamics of operational risks. A graphical depiction of the cause–effect relationships helps to identify interventions to manage the sources and consequences of operational risks clearly.
- It provides a means for reflecting the interactions of operational risks across the enterprise. As businesses become larger and more complex, knowledge of their underlying dynamics becomes fragmented and localized. Although many managers have a good understanding of their own functional areas, few have a solid grasp of the interactions across the enterprise. Development of a system map provides a way to combine the knowledge and experience of managers across the enterprise.

There are several disadvantages, however, in applying the system dynamics approach to model operational risks. First of all, it takes time and effort to build a simulation model. Therefore, the approach is not the ideal method for analyzing a large number of operational risks. It should be reserved for modeling the most important and complex operational risks. Also, it is not a robust method for modeling the tail of a probability distribution. For low-frequency/high-severity risks that affect capital requirements other specialized approaches are better. Thus, like Bayesian Belief Networks the System Dynamics approach is another important tool for management and monitoring of specific risks and/or parts of the enterprise.

■ ■ ■

CASE ILLUSTRATION

Applying Neural Networks to Operational Risks

NASA

Jeevan Perera of the National Aeronautic and Space Administration (NASA) in the United States has initiated experimental work on the application of neural networks to operational risk management and provided material for this section as an illustration of how a neural network model might extrapolate an operational risk conclusion from present and past data and information.

Neural networks involve modeling the brain and behavioral processes for subsequent use in computer applications. These models make use of significant amounts of complex input and data relationships, and a data mining process to arrive at a "reasoned" conclusion. They have been applied in a variety of fields including psychology, neural biology, mathematics, physics, computer science, and engineering. They represent yet another exciting opportunity for the management of operational risks.

Although it might come as a surprise, neural networks have been applied toward engineering applications at NASA. To date, they have been an effective reliability tool for concept design and planning of microelectromechanical systems (MEMS), which are small mechanical electrical devices and systems used in microspacecraft technology. He describes the data mining process for neural networks and its four steps, as follows:

1. **Identification Step:** Here we select the data and information to be used for both training and testing of the model. It is at this stage that the analyst will specify the input data and expected output. In addition, the organization will be segmented by unit (e.g., by design or fabrication teams, or by business unit).
2. **Transformation Step:** Somewhat akin to operational risk scoring, here we convert the raw input data into usable data and convert nonnumeric data into a numeric format using various techniques (e.g., mapping, sampling, feature extraction); the analyst will also compensate for outliners and sparse regions.

3. **Modeling Step:** In this step we apply one of several algorithmic schemes to learn the mathematical relationships between the inputs and outputs. These schemes might entail statistical networks, the k-nearest neighbor, logistic regression, or decision tree approaches.

4. **Analysis Step:** Last, we define performance expectations and judge the model's results against them.

As a next phase in experimentation with neural networks the challenge will be to determine whether diverse types of operational risk data will fit the mold of other uses of these models to date.

The ultimate success of using neural networks will depend on the availability of data, which of course is similar to the challenge that we have with most models, but it may, in fact, be even more important here. Because of the nature of the analytics and need to train the model, an abundance of data, along with the ability to manipulate it, is perhaps even more critical. Insufficient data or the wrong types of input will cause problems in deriving reliable correlations. Data issues probably will require application of neural networks to isolate risks or business operations for the foreseeable future.

Jeevan is optimistic that he will be able to apply neural networks to his operational risk management program at NASA. He is also confident that software is already available in the marketplace that will fit operational risk data to the various types of modeling schemes, allowing the user to select the best one. As he continues his experimentation, he cautions others to avoid work in a vacuum. As in other model development, he advises that analysts will be more successful if they include others in the process for validation of the results. He also advises practitioners to undertake a careful segmentation of the organization being modeled.

This will be an interesting space to watch (no pun intended) in the development of operational risk analysis.[17]

■ ■ ■

MODELING OPERATIONAL RISK: ADDITIONAL UNIQUE COMPLEXITIES

By definition, some of the analytical challenges of dealing with operational risk include the difficulty in modeling complexity. In addition to settling on the most appropriate means of modeling complex, multifactor risks, it is also important to recognize the need to model interdependencies. For instance, this involves the risk of loss involving transaction handoffs from one business to another (e.g., risk involving gaps in responsibility from one business to the next). Thus a model should attempt to represent these interdependencies by first identifying business lines that rely on one another (i.e., those that rely on the business in question or on which it depends), then consider the downside risk of a failed handoff.

Another area of complexity is integration risk (i.e., the risk of gaps in responsibility that result from acquisition, restructuring, or reorganization). Here too a place to start is in illustrating transaction flow.

Third, there is concentration risk. All risk maps and process models can be rendered useless if they don't consider the tail event of a single event disrupting the firm's entire operation. Thus, any firmwide representation of operational risk must look at singular concentrations such as the risk to a home office location, primary trading floor, processing center, and data centers. These variables present unique challenges for operational risk modeling.

Some tools are already available to deal more effectively with complex operational risks. For instance, stress testing (e.g., combining tail risk scenario analysis with quantification models) can and should be applied to all models as a reality check. But there is evidence that tools might already be developing to deal more effectively with complex operational risks. These might include application of fuzzy logic, as just discussed, the use of non-traditional mathematical thinking, enterprise-wide dynamic operational risk monitoring (see Chapter 13), and modeling along the line of complexity theory. W. Michael Waldrop referenced this phenomenon in his book *Complexity* in 1993,[18] and it may simply be a matter of time until the nontraditional thinking that he highlights makes its way into corporate risk management and control functions.[19]

ANALYTICS: SOME MEASURED WORDS OF CAUTION

Myth: Sophisticated analyses will save the day.

With all due respect to the editors, the February 2000 issue of *Operational Risk* might have left some readers to conclude that once they have complete risk class definitions and a good industry loss data set in hand, all they need is to acquire some actuarial models, implement a reasonable level of curve fitting, and they'll have the subject of operational risk management nailed.

Recent financial services history is replete with instances of disasters in spite of (and perhaps with contribution from) risk analysts' love for quantitative analysis. Hopefully the operational risk management discipline will not fall into the trap that some shortsighted market risk managers have. As recently as 1998, investors in Long Term Capital Management were lulled into believing that models could represent all risk. And in the wake of that debacle, and others, we were once again reminded that a mix of quantitative analysis and qualitative insight is the most effective way to understand risk.

Just as some of the more successful insurance companies benefit from applying a healthy dose of stress loss and futurist judgment to the results from their actuaries, many in operational risk management would profit from combining both quantitative and qualitative analysis. To be effective, quantitative methods must be based on a robust and relevant data set, credible methods (e.g., curves, simulations, trials, confidence levels), and tested/ used successfully in business environments. Quantitative tools can add much credibility to operational risk management by projecting a series of loss outcomes but should be kept in perspective relative to a broad-based operational risk *management* function. The best firms conduct analysis by risk class, by business activity or product line, then relate them to the strength of controls, quality of staff, management, and organization.

Balance, Revisited

From an industry perspective, much time and attention is placed today on increasingly sophisticated quantitative analysis and modeling in anticipation of regulatory operational risk capital charges. Generally speaking this has been a very positive and productive development. Although I certainly advocate further advancements in quantitative techniques, the industry and individual firms must keep these efforts in perspective. If we are not careful, these tools run a significant risk of missing the mark with respect to basic risk management needs. That is to say, the *process* of gathering the data and conducting the analysis and meeting reporting deadlines can become a self-fulfilling process in and of itself, and a distraction from behavioral modification and productive risk *management* investment, if one is not careful.

Second, although the more sophisticated modeling that we have discussed will always have a place at major financial institutions and corporations alike, use of them may not be right for every firm. In fact, for medium-sized and smaller firms, with fewer resources available for their entire risk management effort, and even for some larger organizations, sometimes simple versions of them may be more effective.

That is to say that for day-to-day management decision making, some simple analysis, reporting, and communication may in fact be more important in view of the ultimate goal of mitigating risk. And there is some truth there for larger firms as well. Too often analysts can fall in love with their models and lose focus on their interpretation, application, and practical use in day-to-day business decision making. The case of Long Term Capital Management is the poster child for this gaffe, but there are hundreds of less visible instances of this that go on in companies on a daily basis but never make it to the media.

CONCLUSION

Operational risk analysis exists to support management decision making. Generally this support comes through answering two key questions. First, how much risk is our enterprise exposed to? Second, what are the sources of these risks and how can we mitigate them? The development of more sophisticated tools has led to more insight into the answers to these questions.

The enigma about risk is that until we attempt to apply some measures to it, we have no idea where its uncertainty begins and ends. That is, what are the extremes of risk potential? It is useful to understand what expected loss potential might be, but it is probably more important to understand where the worst case loss potential lies.

The recent recognition that sophisticated analytic and risk measurement techniques can bring value to operational risk is helping to define operational risk management as a new discipline. Managers and risk practitioners are finding themselves in a position to make far better business decisions in view of better data, analytic methods, and findings. The prospect of elevating the sophistication, reliability, and confidence in loss forecasts is already contributing to the further evolution of enterprise-wide risk management. Now firms will be in a position to factor most all dimensions—credit, market, and operational risk—into their strategic and day-to-day business decisions.

LESSONS LEARNED AND KEY RECOMMENDATIONS

- Apply analytics to support operational risk management decision making on a day-to-day business level, as well as in strategic risk–reward decision making on a portfolio level. Apply levels of analytic sophistication appropriate for your individual firm's size, culture, and business mix (BP Strategy #15).
- Loss capture by business units can be combined with simple mathematics to develop loss stratifications, loss class analyses, or simple or weighted averages of past losses by business line. The results can be useful for simple observations about trends and loss causation.
- Cost of operational risk analysis, which requires extensive data input, but only simple mathematics, can be a very valuable tool for tracking the long-term cost impact of operational risk on the organization. The input components include aggregate operational losses (preferably by risk class and business unit), annual costs for risk finance and insurance, annual recoveries, risk control, and administrative costs for management of the operational risk and related control functions.
- Economic pricing models are either financial statement-based or simply expense-based. The advantage is that they involve readily available information relatively simple to implement. The disadvantages include the fact that too often they only provide a big picture results in terms of the capital number and do not provide insight as to loss types or causation.
- Examples of loss scenario models include issue-based scenarios and risk maps. These models are generally useful for providing a predictive nature, involving business managers and staff, enhancing buy-in; disadvantages include their subjectivity and ability to attain consensus in the

results overall. They also sometimes lack the credibility that comes with using hard data.

- Use of loss databases, loss distributions, and Monte Carlo simulation in actuarial analysis has become widely adopted as an industry best practice in estimating expected and extreme loss potential. Firms will have to track their own data in databases and, in many cases, supplement the data with external industry data in order to conduct the analysis. Variations on this theme have included the Internal Measurement Approach, which has been proposed among emerging measurement options for regulatory capital.

- Statistical/actuarial models use a combination of frequency and severity loss distributions and Monte Carlo simulation or extreme value theory for modeling to develop a representation of possible outcomes. They can be useful for their predictive abilities if sufficient data are available and relevant. Data remain a challenge, however. Another disadvantage is that when developed using only empirical data, the models can be retrospective in nature and must be modified to enhance predictive abilities and risk matter motivational dimensions. Hybrid models, using risk factors and in some cases, extreme value theory, along with loss data, present an interesting alternative to pure statistical/actuarial models on this theme.

- Indicator or factor-based models include process maps, causal models such as Bayesian Belief Networks and System Dynamics, and behavioral models such as neural networks. They are particularly useful when full data are available and for high-frequency/low-severity events. Analysis candidates include processing groups and typical back office operation functions. In all probability they will not be as useful for developing overall enterprise-wide risk and loss potential and aggregating results from all risk and loss classes.

CHAPTER 13

Dynamic Risk Profiling and Monitoring

INTRODUCTION

One of the hallmarks of operational risk management is the capture, analysis, aggregation, and presentation of operational risk information in more effective ways than ever before.

Chapter 8 introduced the importance of management reporting a key as focal point in risk response and mitigation efforts. It presented some of the different areas and types of risk reports. As part of that introduction, however, we also underscored the importance of distinguishing between *useful* reporting and the avalanche of information all around us on a daily basis. Thus, it is key to highlight what is meant by *quality, timely,* and *complete* information. This is where it gets challenging, of course.

When it comes to information, quality can have many connotations. First and foremost, is it quality information from the standpoint of *meeting the needs* of the audience? Is it *relevant* to the questions and risks at hand? Is it *specific* enough? Is it information that one can *act on* or is it simply interesting, but not entirely useful in a management sense?

The information and reporting must also be timely. We discussed the problem of qualitative risk assessment. Recall the challenges: By the time the detailed analyses—interviews, scenario discussions, quantitative analysis—are completed, summarized, and delivered, they are often outdated. At best, they often present the information as it stood four to six weeks ago. Even more likely, they represent the picture from two to three months ago. We have also discussed the problem of loss information is inherently retrospective in nature. The same is often true for risk indicators. Unfortunately most risk indicators are not timely. They are trailing, not leading, indicators.

With all of this in mind, our next challenge is to develop a flow of information such that management teams are kept as current as possible.

BP STRATEGY #16—IMPLEMENT DYNAMIC RISK PROFILING AND MONITORING

The most successful programs have been built around a continuum of risk tools for effective identification, assessment, mitigation, and finance. Advancements in risk monitoring include *Risk Profiling* and *Dynamic Risk Profiling*. Risk profiling recognizes the need for combining different types of assessment, measurement and control tools for a complete picture of an organization's risk. Dynamic risk profiling requires a continuous and timely process, enabled by interactive technology. Work to apply them for more effective and timely day-to-day risk management.

There are no easy answers. The good news, however, is that advances in technology are helping to speed the organization and delivery of information. In this chapter we will discuss how best to combine and present the data and information to improve quality and timeliness. Later, in Chapter 19, we will discuss the technology needed.

STAGES OF INFORMATION AND REPORTING DEVELOPMENT

Let's revisit the stages of program development to put our challenge on information and reporting into context. Many firms find themselves progressing through several key phases in evolving their operational risk management programs.

1. **Operational Risk Tracking, Aggregation, and Reporting:** At this introductory level, firms are just getting started with operational risk data and information tracking, ranging from risk and performance indicators, and qualitative operational risk issue management to incident and loss tracking. Here a reduction in the cost of operational losses is achievable based on efforts to track and report operational risk issues, incidents, and losses. It is important to realize, however, that the tracking of losses without capturing information about incidents and issues will only yield a retrospective view of the risk. Firms in this stage begin to recognize that identification of operational risk issues, before they turn into incidents, and incidents before they become losses, will bring real benefits in opportunities for risk response. The management of such issues (identified by internal audit reports, internal control reviews, and senior staff and management as well as external auditors and regulators) will inevitably lead to an improvement in the firm's control environment.

2. **Operational Risk Analysis, Risk Capital, and Risk Mitigation Pilots:** At a second level the best firms will also engage in pilot initiatives that in-

volve self-assessment and/or risk assessment. The results of these efforts are being summarized for senior management reporting. In addition, these more progressive firms are working toward a next level—continuous risk monitoring and management, a function often lost in one-time assessments and projects. The monitoring of risk indicators, from perhaps a continuous self-assessment program, is the start of a virtual information loop. Elsewhere, they are beginning to flow data to analytic assignments and risk capital efforts. Key benefits at this stage also contribute to risk cost reduction and regulatory compliance. The remediation of controls and further improvement to the risk environment will flow as well.

3. Getting Everyone Involved—Enterprise-wide Operational Risk Management: Those who have developed their programs more fully are working toward an enterprise-wide platform and toolset for involving line managers, support staff, and corporate management in the collection, aggregation, analysis, and reporting of vital operational management information. Everyone knows that risk management is most effective when practiced by those closest to the risks. In this scenario, line managers and corporate managers alike are empowered with the tools needed to monitor data and information at their respective levels throughout the firm. The key benefit at this stage is that metrics extend beyond regulatory compliance to risk- and loss-cost reduction, and cost efficiencies overall. As one example, insurance coverage terms, policy limits, retentions, and cost-effective financing can be arranged.

4. Continuous Risk Profiling—Contributing to a Competitive Edge: As operational risk management capabilities improve, it is likely that a firm's standing in the eyes of the rating agencies and the market overall will also improve; its cost structure, including, but not limited to, its cost of funding, will be reduced; and market share will increase, to name a few of the benefits. The most advanced firms are viewing a continuous profiling effort as a performance enhancement tool. They envision key risk indicators as a stepping-stone toward key performance indicators, and issue management and a platform for managing not only risk issues and control weaknesses but for prioritizing strategic risk management investments as well. The mitigation of operational risk will be more properly focused. The enhancement of performance and management achievable by the process and tools will also be evident to shareholders and customers. In addition, by benchmarking lessons learned from other firms' failings as reported in an external loss database, they can assist their own firm's earnings growth, market share, and enhanced performance and reputation. In short, when maximum benefits are reaped from a fully implemented and fine-tuned enterprise-wide program, ORM can contribute to a firm's competitive edge, advancing beyond effective risk management toward strategic advantages.

The good news is that this evolution can take place both on individual unit levels and at an enterprise-wide level. There are many types and levels of applying relevant and timely risk information.

RISK MONITORING

Risk monitoring has become a catchphrase in operational risk management of late although it is a well-established concept in risk management more generally. Recall our discussion about differentiating risk monitoring from risk management in Chapter 6. But what does risk monitoring *really* mean?

Risk monitoring only implies keeping a watch on the risks in question. The process of risk monitoring makes no representation of timeliness, the continuous nature, or the tools for surveillance of the operational risks. In market risk management, VAR analysis has become a common tool for risk monitoring. But what does risk monitoring entail in *operational* risk management? Here a firm might be using control self-assessment, actuarial analysis, or some other approach to risk monitoring. Unfortunately, some firms use only one tool, and thus practice risk monitoring from one dimension.

In evaluating the effectiveness of a monitoring effort, the first step will be to apply some perspective on its contribution. For instance, in considering the different tools and techniques that can be used in risk monitoring and reporting, a first step would be to align the tools to the various steps in the traditional risk management process. Exhibit 13.1 illustrates this alignment. This perspective forces us to think about applying multiple tools to risk monitoring, such that we gain a better perspective on the identification, assessment, control or mitigation, and financing of risks overall.

Timely and Continuous Information Management and Reporting

The second way to strengthen risk monitoring is to consider and construct it as part of a continuous flow of information. Two illustrations of risk and dynamic monitoring include monitoring internal audit issues and making efficiency improvements in operations, respectively, as follows.

Example 1: Clearing Audit Issues   The Audit Committee at Company A was concerned that issues raised in internal audit reports were not being acted upon in a timely fashion, if at all. To make matters worse, banking regulators cited the company for its lack of diligence in this area as a control weakness.

They identified many audit issues that had remained open for two years without being remedied. These included a lack of segregation of duties,

EXAMPLES:

• Accounting improprieties
• Fraud
• Improper sales practices
• Corporate sabotage
• Hurricane damage
	• Sources of losses by business unit
	  -Banking
	  -Insurance
	  -E-commerce
	• Frequency and severity analyses
	• Loss forecasts/ risk
	• Predictive analysis
	• Lessons learned
		• Quality initiatives
		• Audits
		• Control/self-assessment process
		• Remediation efforts
			• Insurance coverage and limit analyses
			• Blended financing structures
			• Risk capital

EXHIBIT 13.1 Profiling Elements of the Risk Management Process

absence of business continuity plans for certain business units, and outdated and unreliable legacy systems within critical trade settlement areas. Many of these issues had since been forgotten, for reasons that included changes in departmental management, failures in the review process, and the absence of tools enabling business units to track them on an ongoing basis.

Internal Audit recommended that they implement an action tracking system—a system for logging and tracking issues that could be seen by all of the relevant business functions, ensuring the closure of the audit points. They decided that they needed to do a better job of entering, tracking, and reporting on issues that they raised. To encourage sign-off from the Board for a new system, they used examples of events from an industry loss database to identify the risks and demonstrate the importance of managing open issues from their reports. In a short time following the implementation of a continuous tracking system, the firm experienced measurable enhancement to its control.

Example 2: Continuous Control Environment and Competitive Efficiency Improvement
Company B has just undertaken a risk review of its trade process environment. It conducted a detailed risk assessment and set up a framework for risk

mapping for its trading operation. It determined that recent budget reductions have reduced operational support staff to critically low levels and frozen headcount. Determined to maintain performance benchmarks, the manager of Operations implements a dynamic tracking and reporting system, first identifying the flow variables critical to monitoring his process and then configuring "near real time" data feeds to the Critical Risk Indicator and Critical Performance Indicator modules. With the resulting ability to pinpoint process slowdowns and recognize quickly product volume "bursts" the manager is able to institute a program of cross-training which permits him to rapidly redeploy resources to critical process nodes.

The Information Loop

As a third way of strengthening risk monitoring, Exhibit 13.2 represents the concept that operational risk information and its use should be a continuous data flow. There are many different tools available (both within a firm and available commercially) at management's disposal and various combinations of them are not necessarily right or wrong. However, it is key that they are used in conjunction with the firm's overall strategy and that they integrate with one another to provide maximum value.

The circle in Exhibit 13.2 depicts the *information loop*. The concept is that the firm will adapt the information and possibly its usage continually in each subsequent pass through the loop. For example, after analyzing the firm's loss profile in conjunction with the firm's corporate insurance policies, some of the exception clauses may be renegotiated at the next opportunity.

At a process level, we know that risk management is circular and continuous: risk assessment, risk indicator definition and tracking, issue identification and incident / loss tracking, analysis, risk mitigation / remediation, risk finance and insurance structures, reevaluation of net exposures, and the process begins all over again.

Risk identification, portfolio risk assessment, and control self-assessment are all techniques that can be applied as a first step in the process. A first objective is to identify key risk scenarios: What is the worst thing that can happen? What might keep us awake at night? This identification of key vulnerabilities to the business or control gaps can help us prioritize loss potential and apply our programs and efforts. It is straightforward enough. However, from a risk profiling standpoint the nuance is to introduce the identification of risk indicators or performance indicators that can be used to monitor the business over time.

Let's look more closely at the cycle and discuss practical tools and techniques for continuous tracking—an intuitive, but seldom practiced, management technique.

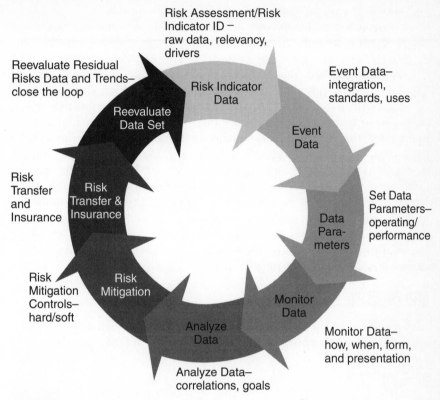

EXHIBIT 13.2 Continuous Data Flow

THE INFLUENCE OF QUALITY MANAGEMENT PROGRAMS, AGAIN

In Chapter 4 we discussed Six Sigma programs, which are related to, and have evolved from, quality management programs. These programs have not yet been as evident in financial institutions as they have been in other types of corporations. The programs themselves are very logical in flow, and relevant in the context of risk profiling. Development of operational risk management and operational risk-based performance measures bears striking similarities to the steps in a Total Quality Management (TQM) process:

1. Identification of defects, as evidenced through issue, incident, or loss
2. Categorization and ranking of the defect
3. Analysis for causal factors

4. Measurement and benchmarking of the case to others
5. Construction and implementation of a defect prevention risk control program tailored to the situation

The opportunistic risk practitioner will always look for "hooks" such as TQM programs to promote a continuous operational risk management effort.

As described in Chapter 10, operational risk events progress through an evolution of issues or circumstances that have been identified and, if left unattended, may lead to a loss sometime in the future. An example might be the presence of outdated technology. In concept, then, this issue might manifest itself as incidents. These happenings or occurrences might have resulted in an economic loss but fortunately did not. Following our example, these might take the form of system outages during off hours and no monetary loss. The third phase of progression consists of actual losses. These are incidents that have in fact resulted in monetary loss. For example, a technology failure during trading hours might result in a measurable trading loss because of the unavailability of systems.

RISK PROFILING: A STEP FORWARD

Risk profiling, as we will use the term here, can be defined as "the *combination* of two or more techniques that balance quantitative and qualitative tools and techniques in the definition and dimensioning of an organization's operational risk."

There is much that can be said in favor of risk profiling. For instance, there is great value in gathering extensive data on operational events from throughout the organization, by product, by business, or by risk class if it is organized in any of those categories. In addition, there is much value in gathering information on operational indicators, issues, initiatives, incidents, and losses. Together these can be termed a mosaic of operational risk management information. Similarly, we learned that there is extensive value in collecting data on operational events from numerous organizations globally in the form of loss databases.

For instance, Exhibit 13.3 illustrates the benefit that an individual line manager would realize in linking different areas of risk information to separate instances of unauthorized activities. In this case, a manager focuses on a recent $6.0 million loss involving an unauthorized trade. Further investigation indicates that there have been four other losses amounting to only $0.5 million but that there have been seven additional limit breaches in recent months (i.e., cases in which a trader exceeded his or her authorized limits). With access to the complete risk profile, sources indicate that there is a related audit finding on inadequate separation of duties—a situation characteristic of many other high-profile unauthorized trading losses in the in-

Risk Class or Grouping	Issue	Risk Indicator	Incidents	Losses
Technology: Unauthorized Access	Inadequate Firewall Security	Risk Assessment Rating:	# of 1999 Breaches: 0	None
People: Unauthorized Trading	Inadequate Separation of Duties	Training: Turnover: Supervisory Rating:	# of 1999 Limit Breaches: 7	1999 Freq: 5 1999 Severity: $6.5MM

EXHIBIT 13.3 Aggregated Reports: Event/Indicator Relationships

dustry. In addition, we note that risk indicators are pointing toward high recent turnover in relevant officer ranks and an inadequate supervisory rating for the area. Taken together, this profile information points to a serious risk scenario that must be addressed.

Similarly, a manager concerned about unauthorized access to certain highly sensitive systems may have been alerted to the risk from an internal audit report highlighting inadequate firewall security. Then, looking to certain risk indicators that track the relative timeliness of security software, numbers of users on the system, and values at risk, he immediately turns to incident and loss reports. He is relieved to find that there have been no reported incidents of attempted firewall breaches, and no actual losses, but can't help but wonder whether they have just been lucky. Thus the manager doubles resources devoted to upgrading security and vigilance on incidents and losses. Without question, the combination of all of these sources of information paints a much more complete picture than any one area alone.

Exhibit 13.4 indicates one version of aggregated risk profile reports by business and risk class. These reports can be very useful in citing hot spots in individual risk classes, individual business lines, or on a firmwide basis.

We have learned the value of defining ranges in volatility measures for operational loss outcomes (e.g., Value at Risk). Even if the quantification answer cannot be defined with precision, we've seen the value in sharing the range of potential outcomes with business managers such that they are in a better position to manage both the upside and downside of their operations. But for all of the positive attributes of these occasional measures, we've learned that measurement or modeling in isolation is not the same thing as management. Thus, we look to risk profiling.

In the context of a fully integrated operational risk management program, risk profiling can take on many dimensions and numerous moving

Business Line a Risk Profile				
Risk Class	Risk Index	Issue Rating	Incident Rating	Loss Rating	Aggregate Rating
People	3	4	2	4	3.3
Relationship	3	2	3	2	2.5
Technology	5	4	5	2	4.0
Physical Asset	2	2	3	2	2.3
Other / External	1	2	2	1	1.5
Combined	2.8	2.8	3	2.2	2.7

1 = Low Risk   3 = Moderate Risk   5 = High Risk

Business Line Risk Profile				
Business Line	Risk Index	Issue Rating	Incident Rating	Loss Rating	Aggregate Rating
Business Line A	2.8	2.8	3	2.2	2.7
Business Line B	3	2.5	3.5	2	2.8
Business Line C	1.8	2	2.5	3	2.3
Business Line D	4	5	4.5	3	4.1
Business Line E	3.5	3	4	4	3.6

1 = Low Risk   3 = Moderate Risk   5 = High Risk

Firmwide Risk Profile				
Risk Class	Risk Index	Issue Rating	Incident Rating	Loss Rating	Aggregate Rating
People	3	2.5	2.7	3	2.8
Relationship	4	3	5	3	3.8
Technology	2.5	3	3	2	2.6
Physical Asset	3.5	4	3	3	3.4
Other / External	3.4	2.8	3.5	3	3.2
Firmwide	3.3	3.1	3.4	2.8	3.1

1 = Low Risk   3 = Moderate Risk   5 = High Risk

EXHIBIT 13.4   Aggregated Reports: Risk Profiles

parts. Our introduction showed only a profile using indicators, issues, incidents, and losses. The objective, however, of presenting a more complete "mosaic" of information requires us to look to a number of different techniques and perspectives on risk. Therefore, taken to a higher level, some practitioners are striving toward weaving in self-assessment and risk assessment programs, scenario analysis, risk and data trends, risk capital calculations, and other dimensions for a full picture of their firm's loss potential and state of controls. Certainly, such integration is an aggressive undertaking, to say the least, but it is also representative of the ultimate enterprise-wide reporting goal. But let's not get ahead of ourselves.

Managers use profiling techniques every time they ask for a status report on their business, whether it be on market share and customer satisfaction or for operational risks, losses, and control infrastructure. All too often, however, those reports are static in nature, and just not timely enough.

> *The line manager sat in his monthly risk management committee meeting reviewing reports on system outages, settlement failures, booking errors, staff turnover and training investments, audit findings, and reams of other indicators and information activities under way to tighten controls. He glanced at his proud team of direct reports who had just spent the past five weeks compiling the data and assembling the report for this meeting. He couldn't help but find his mind wandering and realized that all of the data were anywhere from four to eight weeks out of date. Chances were high that this was not a current picture. He found himself thinking "I'll bet that the current picture is something different. There must be a better way."*

In fact, this is the problem with most risk assessment risk indicator data collection and even qualification processes. More often than not they are out of date before they are even completed and delivered. Even continuous risk monitoring and risk profiling do not make any representations about the timeliness of information.

DYNAMIC RISK PROFILING AND MONITORING: A LEAP FORWARD

In contrast, *dynamic* risk profiling goes even further. It implies the *continuous* gathering, re-calculation, and update of the component parts of the profile, linking the various tools, and reporting it all on a "real time" basis.

The concept here is to (1) differentiate between those analyses that only focus on risk at one particular point in time versus those that are continually reassessing the risk in a particular business, portfolio, or firm; (2) use a combination of tools; and (3) present a flow of information and linkage between the various tools. In fact, many traditional risk assessment approaches have fallen short of their objectives because the reports have fallen out of date within months, weeks, or even days of completion. Then, because the time

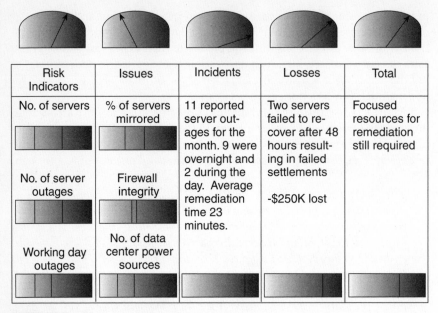

Risk Indicators	Issues	Incidents	Losses	Total
No. of servers	% of servers mirrored	11 reported server outages for the month. 9 were overnight and 2 during the day. Average remediation time 23 minutes.	Two servers failed to recover after 48 hours resulting in failed settlements -$250K lost	Focused resources for remediation still required
No. of server outages	Firewall integrity			
Working day outages	No. of data center power sources			

EXHIBIT 13.5   Designing Dials and Gauges

and effort that went into them was viewed as wasted, business managers and staff become frustrated with the process and, understandably, question the value of the assessment process.

Dynamic operational risk profiling is intended to be a highly flexible process and should be customized to the organization itself. Exhibit 13.5 illustrates one example of the combination of static and dynamic risk profiling. In this particular case, a firm has developed a technology risk index based on a combination of risk indicators, issues, incidents, and losses about its servers and outages. It adds the dimension of installing dials and gauges backed by technology such that the line manager can monitor the relative changes in each one of these variables over time. In the end, the relative success of implementing will depend as much on the design of such profiling tools as it does on the availability of data by organizational unit.

This takes us back to program objectives once again. Each firm has its own culture, style, and agenda. Any operational risk management program, including its profiling strategies, *must* be in synch at all levels.

That is, if one accepts the premise that operational risk is pervasive in an organization and an effective operational risk management program will consist of a variety of different tools and techniques, then the next hurdle is to develop a means of tracking the progress of those unique combinations of tools, programs, and systems. Ultimately, we should be striving for a continuous program of risk assessment that is effective, but not so onerous that it is never repeated, or at least not until it is too late and the loss occurs.

CASE ILLUSTRATIONS

Let's look at some Case Illustrations of the concepts of risk monitoring, risk profiling, and dynamic risk profiling. Recall that each concept can and should be applied at many levels.

The first is an illustration of the component parts of a risk profile as being used by the New York branch of Dresdner Bank. The second is a continuation of the case illustration from the Bank of Tokyo Mitsubishi and presents the concept of constructing operational risk computer screens (dashboards, if you will), for the purpose of ongoing monitoring.

The third case is Halifax Group's work in pulling together the component parts in order to provide a dynamic profile. One of the keys to their development is their work on technology in tandem with the aggregation of data and reporting tools. The technology component of the case will be covered in Chapter 19, "Operational Risk Technology and Systems."

The fourth case is from Commerzbank and presents their work combining risk profiling and fuzzy logic.

CASE ILLUSTRATION

Creating a Risk Profile

Dresdner Bank

This is a continuation of the Dresdner Bank case from Joseph Swipes in Chapter 11. The quantification of operational risk information is necessary. The question that most risk managers are faced with is how. We believe that operational risk analysis comes from three sources: risk and/or self-assessment, key performance indicator reporting, and a loss database. The data collected from these vehicles make up one's operational risk profile. Exhibit 13.6 shows how the operational risk profile is comprised.

As shown in the exhibit at Dresdner Bank we have begun to develop operational risk profiles by taking the results of the self-assessment, adding the results of the key performance indicators, and then adding any new items that arise when comparing the results of the self-assessment, incident capture application, and key performance indicators. (Incidents logged in the incident capture application should have a direct correlation to the risks being evaluated in the self-assessment and the on-going monitoring of these risks via key performance indicator reporting.) Any

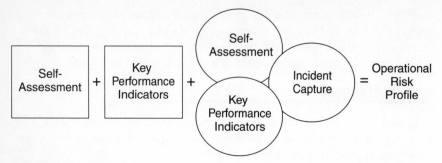

EXHIBIT 13.6   Risk Profiling–Dresdner Bank

incidents identified that are not evaluated in the self-assessment and monitored via key performance indicator reporting represent newly identified areas of risk which should be evaluated and included in the operational risk profile.

■ ■ ■

CASE ILLUSTRATION

The Operational Risk Management Dashboard

The Bank of Tokyo Mitsubishi

This case is a continuation of the contribution from Mark Balfan of The Bank of Tokyo Mitsubishi (BTM) in Chapter 9, and elaborates on their continuous profiling and reporting.

At BTM we have attempted to "modernize" the self-assessment process and use it as an Operational Risk Management tool alongside the collection of risk indicators and losses (see Exhibit 13.7). We believe that self-assessment is as valuable as the other more commonly used operational risk tools because there may not exist indicators or losses that could identify potential losses. Sometimes the self-assessment would be the only way to identify such potential risks. Since business line objectives may differ from those of Operational Risk Management, we ensure honesty through careful validation of the results.

One note of caution, however, is that self-assessment alone should not be used to quantify operational risk. It can be used as a means of allocating capital calculated through other means.

Each of the 103 questions for each business unit was assigned a value based on a simple multiplication of the frequency × severity × $(1 -$ control effectiveness). The actual value is not important, which could be debated endlessly. We use the values as a relative measure to compare across departments and across risks rather than as an absolute risk measure. From that basic building block we can do all sorts of

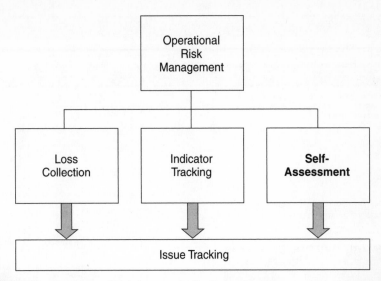

FIGURE 13.7 The Bank of Tokyo Mitsubishi Control Self-Assessment Components

analysis and aggregation. Two such analyses are presented here. They are the business unit or departmental view and the risk view. Each view is a single page and is easy for others to understand and read. A major focus of our effort was to determine how best to display information to management to ensure that they look at it. Even the best analysis in the world will fall on deaf ears if not presented in a clear and concise manner.

As shown in Exhibit 13.8, the first type of analysis, and the more traditional one, is the business unit view of risk. In this analysis we simply look at how each respondent rated itself in all of the various categories of risk. (Note: each institution must determine for itself what it considers to be high, medium, and low.) Summary information about the business is presented along the top to make the page self-contained. Such information includes head count, expenses, revenues, and a description of the business. An overall rating of the business is presented in the top right corner of the page on top of the "risk thermometer." This enables management to have a quick view of the business.

A summary of the major risks (people, process, technology, and external events) is presented at the top showing the breakout of frequency and severity, which are netted to inherent risk. Control risk is presented next, which is derived from the control effectiveness. Inherent risk and control risk are netted to come up with an overall net risk grade. We also show the number of indicators used by the business to control the risks and whether or not a loss was ever incurred.

A heat map is then displayed showing the next level of detail of our four major risk categories. Inherent risk and control risk are plotted and

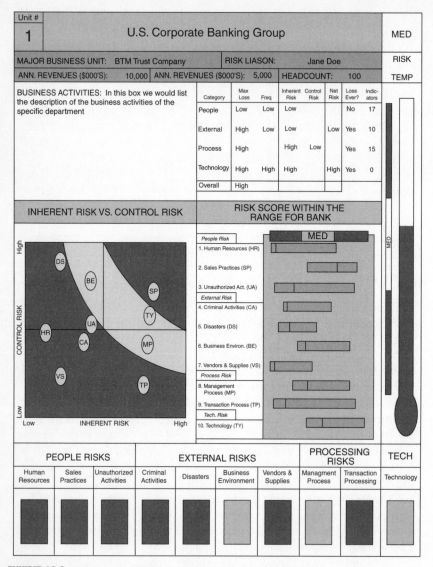

EXHIBIT 13.8 The Bank of Tokyo Mitsubishi—The Dashboard

the net result of the two can be determined based on where the circle appears on the green-yellow-red background.

In addition to showing each business's score, we also want to show management how the business scored relative to all other departments. The floating bar chart shows the total range of all scores for each of the

10 subcategories. The vertical black line in the middle of each floating bar represents where the particular business line scored within that range.

Finally, at the bottom of the page, we show a risk "dashboard" which simply summarizes information from the heat map. The value of displaying large boxes along the bottom of the page is that management can easily flip through many pages and focus their attention quickly on problem areas.

While the first analysis is more traditional, the second analysis, shown in Exhibit 13.9 is purely risk-focused. By designing the self-assessment using our risk hierarchy, all businesses were forced to respond consistently. We can now look at a cut of the data that spans all businesses while isolating just one risk. We have shown the analysis for risk #61, transaction processing (data entry), as an example. All of the other 102 risk categories are formatted exactly the same way.

Every one of our 103 risk categories has been assigned to a risk specialist whose name is shown at the top of the page along with the detailed description of the risk. Summary risk scores are shown on the top right using smiles/frowns and colors.

The next set of information displayed on the left side of the page is the three distributions of results from severity, frequency, and control effectiveness standpoints for this one risk across all businesses. This reflects how many businesses rated the risk within certain predetermined bands. These distributions are helpful to understand the range of responses as opposed to an average response. These distributions may also be used for specific quantitative analysis such as Monte Carlo simulation.

A pie chart then shows which five businesses or departments contribute the most to the particular risk. Our analysis has shown that for most risks, we usually find that the top five businesses (out of our total of 56) contribute on average about half of the total risk. Showing the top five allows management to focus their mitigation efforts on the key businesses.

A very basic risk number that we refer to as "economic risk" is then displayed below the pie chart. We are careful to call it economic risk and not capital because we don't believe that self-assessment can be used for quantifying capital. Some may use it to allocate capital that is calculated some other way such as by using historical losses. The important characteristic of the measure is not the absolute value of the number but the relative value of the number in comparing across risks.

We then present how this risk compares to all 103 risks on four different scales. In this case, we see that this risk was rated as having low severity, high frequency, good controls, and a high degree of applicability to all of our businesses. One would expect that result for a risk such as transaction processing.

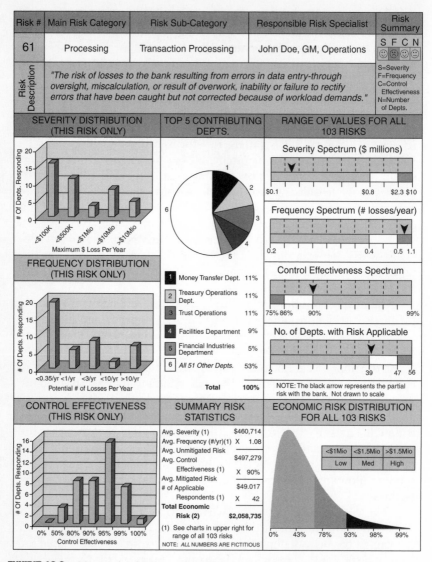

EXHIBIT 13.9   The Bank of Tokyo Mitsubishi—The Risk Level View

Finally, we show the distribution of the economic risks across all 103 risks. This particular risk, #61, is then plotted on the chart where we can see that it is more significant than 93% of all the risks. In our case the risks were fitted to a chi-squared distribution, as that was most representative of our results. Others may find a different distribution more fitting.

■ ■ ■

CASE ILLUSTRATION

Working toward Dynamic Enterprise-wide Risk Profiling

Halifax Group, Plc[1]

One of the biggest challenges to today's operational risk managers, and indeed management in general, is gaining ready access to the enterprise-wide data that drive a company's risk profile. In 1999–2000, Halifax Group Plc, a major United Kingdom retail financial services organization, working with Arthur Andersen, began analyzing its needs relative to the changing face of operational risk management and the technology required to support data capture, aggregation, and analysis.

The Halifax had gone through a considerable period of change since its conversion from a Building Society into a major United Kingdom retail financial services bank in 1997. This change, combined with aggressive expansion and development ambitions, encouraged the Halifax to address the identification and management of operational risk throughout the Group. As in the past, efforts had been concentrated around operating controls rather than risk identification.

The two main drivers for this work, one internal and one external, were:

- The need to deliver high-quality operational risk management that enables new business opportunities and increases risk-adjusted profitability through informed risk and reward decision making
- The proposed reforms to the Basel Capital Accord, introducing a new capital charge for operational risk together with stronger supervisory oversight

These and the other main drivers are illustrated in Exhibit 13.10.

Working in partnership with Arthur Andersen, Halifax developed a progressive strategy and solution appropriate for the diverse and dynamic business that the Group had become and that would meet increasing regulatory pressure.

Ammy Seth, Head of Special Risk Areas, contributed the following overview of the Group's risk management philosophy and how "The ORCA Solution" supports this.

Risk Management Philosophy

Halifax operational risk management is made up of three lines of defense: businesses; Operational Risk, including risk and group functional specialists; and internal audit.

Businesses have the primary responsibility for the management of operational risk. They have the freedom to manage operational risk as they

Significant Losses & Regulatory Pressures	Changing Business Environment

• Increase in the frequency and magnitude of losses
• Regulatory pressure
  –Increased regulatory focus and risk-based approach to supervision
  –Basel Committee operational risk capital charge
  –Financial Services and Markets Bill
• Corporate Governance initiatives such as Turnbull
	• Technology exploitation & dependency
	• E-business creating new opportunities and risks
	• Cost and expense base pressures
	• Empowerment and distribution of control responsibility
	• Outsourcing and joint ventures
	• Brand and reputation become increasingly important
	• Shareholder value, optimizing risk adjusted profits

The Need for Greater Focus on Effective Operational Risk Management

To provide protection	and	Enable business opportunities

EXHIBIT 13.10   The Operational Risk Environment—Halifax Bank, Plc

see fit but must be consistent with the groupwide standards and policies. Operational Risk's role is to provide the framework in which the businesses operate by developing and monitoring policy and identifying and reporting on groupwide risks as well as providing specialist support to the business. The risk and group functional specialists (Fraud and Investigations, Business Continuity Management, Corporate Insurance, Security and Information Risk Management) play an important role in both providing specialist risk management services to the business, such as technology risk management or fraud, as well as providing input and challenge to the policies and methodologies developed by Operational Risk. Internal audit is responsible for independently ensuring that the operational risk management process is appropriate and functioning as designed.

The model is designed in this manner so as to place accountability and ownership as close as possible to where the risks arise and to create centers of excellence that add real value across the business.

Exhibit 13.11 summarizes the relationships between the drivers, the objectives developed to respond to them, and the contributions required by the different parts of the business. Delivery of this model re-

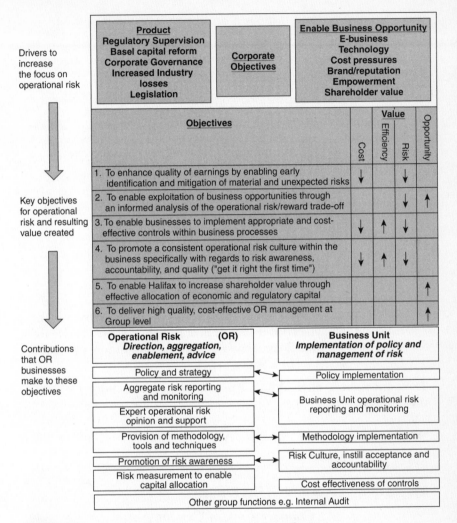

EXHIBIT 13.11 Halifax Objectives, Drivers and Contributions

quires a number of interacting approaches delivered in partnership between business areas and Operational Risk. These approaches focus on
identifying and mitigating material, unexpected risks, exploiting new
business opportunities, and enabling allocation of capital to the business. They are also an integral part of promoting a consistent risk culture by providing a structured approach to risk identification.
Operational Risk has created structured interacting methodologies for
implementation by the business areas. The methodologies will not succeed without strong support from both the businesses and Operational

Risk. Businesses retain their own process-level methodologies to address the cost-effective controls objective.

Halifax Methodologies

In brief, these interacting methodologies are:

- **Operational Risk Profiling (ORP):** Providing management self-assessment of the material risks faced by the business
- **Key Risk Indicators:** Providing early warning indications of likely hot spots enabling one piece of the causality chain for continuous improvement
- **Issues, Near Misses, and Losses:** Demonstrating how risks have crystallized through the organization
- **Capital measurement and VAOR:** Determining the amount of capital required to sustain potential exposures, resulting from operational risks by business
- **Supplemental Methodologies:** (Major Change Participation, Risk Culture surveys, Scanning and Research, Project Risk Assessments, and Strategic Planning risk assessments): Providing specific views of risks and complimenting the fundamental methodologies mentioned
- **Scorecard Methodology:** Involving the quantification of operational risks on a relative scale

These interacting methodologies are illustrated in Exhibit 13.12 on the following page.

■ ■ ■

CASE ILLUSTRATION

Applying Fuzzy Logic to Dynamic Risk Profiling

Commerzbank of Germany

(This case was contributed by Corinna Mertens of Commerzbank, Irina Sahaf of Accenture, and Hans-Peter Guellich of Risk Concepts Systems.)

Fuzzy logic is a means of adopting human decision-making processes. As such, it seeks to improve upon traditional risk evaluation approaches. The aim of this approach is to come close to the risk evaluation quality of human experts while minimizing the analysis effort by using automated decision systems.

Many operational risk assessment methods to date have some basis in historical data. For most operational risk management situations, however, historical data availability is insufficient, and even when there are sufficient data, historical losses do not represent the entire risk profile in

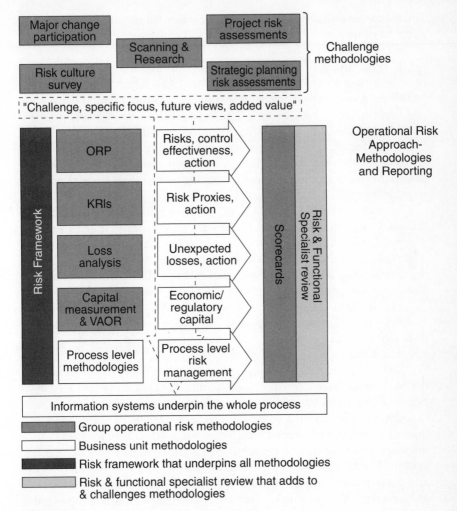

EXHIBIT 13.12 Halifax Methodologies and Reporting

isolation. Thus, purely statistical concepts and systems often lead to weak results for operational risk as management tools. In addition, important factors like management quality and other weak signals cannot be integrated readily into those risk evaluation systems.

This is where fuzzy logic comes in. It is an innovative artificial intelligence modeling technique that enables the user to apply elements of everyday language rather than mathematical formulas to describe the relation between all relevant operational risk symptoms (key performance indicators, weak control points, processes, business units, etc.). Furthermore, the theory of fuzzy logic allows the realization of a flexible and comprehensible system structure necessary for the subsequent management of uncovered operational risks. What is more, it can be applied on an enterprise-wide basis.

Commerzbank of Germany, together with Accenture and Risk Concept Systems, contributed the following case, which illustrates the bank's decision to apply fuzzy logic systems to its operational risks.

Early in their work toward defining operational risk management (ORM) and controlling, Commerzbank determined that for them the value of effective ORM was grounded in reducing the bank's exposure to operational risk and preventing potential operational risk losses from materializing. Operational Risk Controlling had to come up with a way to measure the OR status and process of risk reduction.

To realize this value proposition, Commerzbank asked Accenture to introduce their bottom-up OR identification and measurement method that would provide them with the necessary early-warning risk indicators. Their intent was that these indicators not only serve Commerzbank's business managers in analyzing and prioritizing their risks but also provide the basis for aggregated risk ratings sensitive to risk reduction measures.

The method introduced to Commerzbank's Investment Banking business covers a systematic approach to process analysis, identification of potential weak points, and definition of controls and risk indicators to assess them.

Several mathematical concepts for aggregation were explored in order to meet the requirement of aggregating the indicators into a dashboard of risk ratings for functions, processes, and organizational units.

Commerzbank chose fuzzy logic as it is suitable to adopt the human decision-making logic by using human evaluation parameters to incorporate all input criteria within the decision logic of an assessment system. In addition, fuzzy logic was chosen for its easy-to-understand and easy-to-communicate concepts, flexibility, and ability to reflect a business expert's assessment of certain critical situations. Also reflected in the fuzzy logic characteristics is the natural human reluctance to evaluate a situation solely by a single score or grade in isolation. In certain borderline cases one tends to evaluate a situation as "somewhat good, but also somewhat bad." Although fuzziness is allowed into the evaluation of a single indicator, the aggregated rating result is nonambiguous.

Thus, in an ORM context the method reflects a business manager's tendency to evaluate a situation, in which one of a set of indicators has a very negative outcome, as a situation in need of a bad rating, even if the other indicators contributing to the monitored situation are acceptable. The same indicator, if it takes on a positive value, tends to be given less weight.

The suitable properties of fuzzy logic mathematics lead to an increased effort in defining the aggregation logic, as the number of rules increase exponentially at the same time that the number of indicators or rating grades rise.

Commerzbank and its advisors solved this problem by applying the additional concept of tolerance ranges and priorities as well as a set of guidelines to the rules definition process. This defining aggregation logic hardly takes longer than defining a simplistic scoring model that consists of attributing weights and adding the weighted scores.

The resultant aggregation logic is then verified in a predefined testing process through the business expert's evaluation of certain situations. During this test phase, exceptions from the previously defined guidelines are allowed back in—experience shows that this is necessary in a minority of cases only. Hence, the risk ratings are well accepted by business managers and operational risk controllers.

To allow for corroboration of the qualitative risk ratings with actual OR losses (cause–effect relationship), internal losses are collected and allocated to the same functions, processes, and organizational units for which the risk ratings are generated.

Commerzbank reports that its early tests have shown that fuzzy logic can be seen as a helpful means of supporting its structured view of managing operational risks. Although the theory of fuzzy logic cannot replace robust statistical methods in *measuring* operational risks[2] in a capital-at-risk sense, it certainly can provide all necessary means for a more precise and accurate *assessment and management* of actual and upcoming risks related to any business activity.

Furthermore, fuzzy logic is not viewed as simply another soft computing method for modeling probabilities for random events. Rather it is complementary to those methods as it helps to build decision support systems capable of dealing with imprecise, uncertain, and incomplete information.[3]

Thus the core of the realized risk management solution for Commerzbank uses the fuzzy logic soft computing methodology as its fundament. As fuzzy logic guarantees the realistic, transparent, and comprehensible aggregation of all relevant decision parameters—which is a key success factor when realizing an integrated operational risk management system—it proved to be perfect in monitoring and managing Commerzbank's actual operational risks uncovered using Accenture's bottom-up analysis method.

Last, the fully transparent decision structure of a fuzzy logic–based risk assessment system enables the presentation of any unaddressed operational risk by easy-to-interpret graphical reports. These reports provide an innovative ability to drill down from a broad overview of Commerzbank's operational risk profile to individual issues and incidents. This case illustration is continued in Chapter 19, with insight on technology and systems support.

■ ■ ■

CONCLUSION

One-dimensional operational risk management perspectives and tactics are destined to fail in today's dynamic business environment. Complex operational risks demand a flexible series of multidimensioned solutions working in tandem. The best firms recognize this and blend a number of the tools and initiatives—from risk indicators to qualitative risk assessment, from issues tracking to quantitative analysis, and from risk systems to risk finance—into a mosaic, not exclusively as individual tiles of limited individual interest and value.[4] The speed of business today demands continuous risk monitoring for effective risk management.

Risk assessment and analysis includes, but are not limited to, dimensioning the exposures and risks identified. As operational risk management has developed in recent years, a new process has begun to emerge; a process that might be termed "risk profiling." Think of this as getting a handle on a firm's total risk being or persona. Here we attempt to form a picture of an organization's past and present, along with a view of future exposures to operational loss.

Dynamic risk profiling has taken risk monitoring one step further. It is designed and developed to empower business unit and operational risk managers to control operational risks enterprise-wide with data and tools available continuously, enabled by interactive technology. At a base level, firms will benefit from reducing risk and loss costs. When used even more strategically, these tools can serve as a competitive advantage, aiding an organization in performance, earnings, and reputation enhancement.

LESSONS LEARNED AND KEY RECOMMENDATIONS

- Too often people lose interest in elaborate risk assessment approaches after their first or second pass at it, so management must find ways to keep the process fresh and interesting to keep people's interest, enthusiasm, and involvement.
- Another problem with most risk assessment efforts is that they are outdated before they are even completed. Firms should strive for a continuous monitoring process as the best means of keeping current on business unit and overall enterprise-wide risk profiles.
- The most successful programs have been built around a continuum of risk tools for effective identification, assessment, mitigation, and finance. Advancements in risk monitoring include risk profiling and dynamic risk profiling. Work to apply them for more effective and timely day-to-day risk management (BP Strategy #16).

Insurance and Operational Risks

Aligning Conventional Programs

INTRODUCTION

How can a firm maximize the relationship between its emerging operational risk management program, its definition of risk classes, and conventional risk and insurance management programs?

One would think that conceptually, and by (risk class) definition, that
the management of operational risks should fit hand in hand with a risk and
insurance management program.

There are many good reasons to align the two functions. In fact, there
is a great deal of *potential* in offsetting operational risks with both conventional and advanced risk financing structures. In many firms, however, this
relationship has not even been explored as yet. To date the alignment has
only been evident at a few of the largest most progressive firms. The finding
of these organizations has been that insurance has not provided a complete
enough answer to the operational risk problem. In time, however, this linkage will become much more commonplace as the best firms understand their
operational risks more fully, and press insurance and risk finance providers
to develop more useful solutions.

This chapter is devoted to providing some introductory perspective on
how to approach the more conventional insurance management issues as they
relate to operational risks. In order to understand the challenges here it is necessary to examine and review some of the insurance coverages that are typically maintained at financial institutions. Then we will review the advantages
and disadvantages of them in the context of the broad universe of operational
risks (versus those referenced more conventionally as "insurance risks").
Chapter 15 is intended to provide perspective on re-engineering insurance programs, along with alternative risk financing structures in use both in banking
and finance industries, and more broadly in nonfinancial corporations. In the
limited space available, however, these two chapters cannot possibly do justice

BP STRATEGY #17—ENHANCE RISK FINANCE HEDGING OF OPERATIONAL RISKS

Align insurance and risk finance programs to operational risks. Measure program performance over time. Reengineer programs to attain an optimal coverage and cost trade-off. Since conventional insurance provides only a partial solution, enhance risk financing through the use of effective alternative risk financing structures. Use self-insurance, captive, excess-of-loss reinsurance, credit, and capital markets to construct effective protection for expected, unexpected, and catastrophic operational risks.

to all of the details and complexities of risk financing. Together they provide at best an overview of the issues and some key action steps.

OBJECTIVES FOR INSURANCE AND RISK FINANCE

In order to keep risk finance and insurance in perspective, at the outset we cannot lose sight of the key objectives. Most financial firms arrange for risk finance and insurance programs for two primary reasons. They are either seeking to (1) protect their earnings or (2) protect their balance sheet (i.e., capital structure), or perhaps both. Nonfinancial corporate firms might also arrange for risk finance and insurance to protect cash flow or liquidity, but that is not usually a prime objective for financial entities.

Ironically, these key objectives find themselves at the nexus of contention between insurers and insureds, especially when one relies on conventional insurance alone to hedge risk. That is, because very few insurance claims are settled without some degree of tension between the parties (except perhaps life insurance claims), very few of them are also actually agreed on, no less settled and paid, within the same accounting period in which the underlying loss was booked. Thus, at least from an accounting perspective, earnings for the period will not have been protected.

For the same reason of timing, the balance sheet is not protected. But here the problem is further complicated by the fact that many large financial firms cannot purchase limits of coverage large enough to protect their balance sheets.

Fortunately, the winds of change have begun to blow, however, as insurance, reinsurance, and capital market solutions have been explored to bring increased limit capacity to the traditional insurance markets, and renewed interest has been applied to other more established financing alternatives, such as captive insurance companies and creative reinsurance structures. More is presented on these alternatives in Chapter 15. But first, some background is in order.

PERSPECTIVE ON OPERATIONAL RISK HEDGING AND INSURANCE

In market risk management the prospect of hedging is often engineered directly into the trading decision, being transaction- or portfolio-based. That is to say that when considering a trade an immediate consideration is often not whether to hedge market risk, but rather how much of it can be hedged away. Because oftentimes a back-to-back hedge or portfolio hedge can be applied with minimal basis risk, the trader or risk manager understandably and naturally often talks only in terms of net exposure, unless of course the hedge fails or has some significant chance of failure.[1]

In operational risk, on the other hand, the dynamics are completely different. Operational risk is embedded in business dealings and processes and cannot be isolated and stripped out easily. In addition, its reputational consequences cannot be escaped simply because of the existence of insurance or some other hedge.[2]

We also note that in its findings relative to insurance and risk finance the Templeton Study observed that "the impact of catastrophes on shareholder value is not strongly influenced by the existence of catastrophe insurance."[3]

None of these factors are intended to imply that it doesn't matter if the firm hedges operational risk. It still has interest in offsetting the economic impact of a loss and many will strive to close the accounting gap. It is important to note that management and the board might find themselves viewed as deficient in their duties in the eyes of stakeholders if they do not explore such options.

Even though the reputation dimensions cannot be avoided, a firm certainly can hedge portions of the economic impact of operational risk either through contractual risk transfer or through risk finance and insurance techniques. The application of contractual risk transfer is often quite unique to each individual business deal, trade, or process, so we won't dwell on it here. In fact, entire books have been written on the practice. Suffice it to say that it should not be overlooked as an option.

Certainly many books have also been written on risk finance and insurance, but its relationship to definitions of operational risk is brand new. So, we *will* venture into this subject *from the perspective of operational risk management* because few if any have come at the subject from this direction to date.

DESIGNING INSURANCE PROGRAMS

Following are some of the relevant basics of insurance program design, including a discussion of coverage and limits, deductibles/retentions and risk sharing, and management responsibility.

Coverage and Limits

The term *coverage* generally refers to the insuring agreement or scope of an insurance contract. Ideally, a firm focused on operational risk would want the scope of its insurance coverage to be identical to that of its definition of operational risk.

Another key dimension of program design is that of assessing and measuring risk potential and aligning sufficient insurance coverage limits accordingly. Insurance is most useful when arranged for large loss exposures, with deductibles structured as high as reasonably practicable. Otherwise, the firm will wind up engaging in what is generally referred to as "trading premium dollars" with insurance providers (i.e., paying premiums and collecting recoveries for small losses on a regular basis.) The problem with this is that the process becomes costly from an administrative standpoint for the insured firm, not to mention the fees that the insurer will want to assess for services associated with handling these claims.

Capacity refers to the limit an insurance company can provide, or is willing to provide, whether alone or with support from reinsurers. Insurance limits, or capacity, are somewhat akin to lending limits of a bank. Thus, there is a finite amount of capacity that is available from any one insurer or from the entire market, for that matter, relative to a specific risk class or line of insurance business.

Because of limited capacity, some major insurance programs require a number of different insurers to fill a single limit. Often more than one insurer is needed to assemble the capacity of coverage that the firm needs to insure a given risk. When a buyer needs "financial capacity" that is greater than the capacity of these insurers, he must turn to multiple sources or participants. A second reason for tapping multiple insurers is to diversify the credit risk of a large insurance program between several different companies. Third, one might want to dilute the pricing leverage of one major insurer. Having several involved maintains a competitive spirit between the participants. Fourth, this diversification increases the probability that an insurance limit will be available from one year to the next. Finally, it can provide leverage in the event of disputed claims.

Risk Sharing

Despite the importance of a well-placed insurance program for large loss protection, traditional insurance no longer dominates large firms' risk fi-

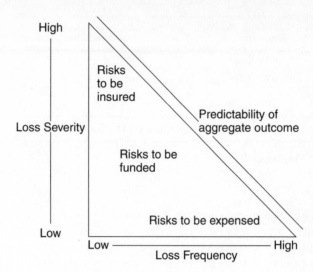

EXHIBIT 14.1 Spectrum of Risk Finance Options

nancing programs. Many firms have concluded that deductibles, retentions, and co-participations aren't necessarily bad from the perspective of an insurance buyer. In the long term companies often recognize that they will pay for their own predictable or expected losses; thus, it is generally more cost effective to retain some losses in order to avoid much of the "frictional cost" (i.e., overhead and profit margin) that one must reasonably expect insurers to charge.

For a variety of reasons, some firms actually seek out large retentions or deductibles. It can be advantageous in several ways for a firm to participate in ("self-fund") a portion of its own event risks through deductibles, self-insurance, and other risk-sharing programs. Sharing in the risk of loss with a firm's insurers through deductibles and co-participation not only results in significant savings over time, but helps to solidify a "partnership" with those insurers and illustrates to them the confidence that the policyholder corporation has in its internal controls and favorable loss history. Deductible and retention levels within these programs should be selected based on the corporation's overall financial capacity to retain risk.

Exhibit 14.1 represents the balance many firms seek between risk retention (sometimes referred to as "self-insurance") and risk transfer (in this case using conventional excess insurance). If one accepts the argument that it is more efficient to retain some level of risk, then it is simply a matter of deciding how to structure that retention level in conjunction with large loss insurance protection and management's philosophy.

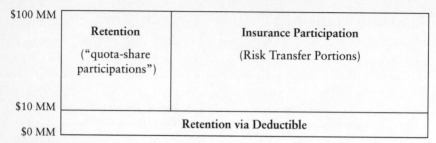

EXHIBIT 14.2   Insurance Participations

Although insurers will accept a portion of a programs' retention in the form of a deductible, they generally frown on giving up a very large portion of their primary or first layer of coverage. This layer contains expected loss levels, and thus their basis pricing and often the greatest margin for overhead and profit. It may be necessary, therefore, to split the retention between a deductible and a portion of the excess layers. The addition of a percentage participation (i.e., quota-share or "coinsurance" feature), as illustrated in Exhibit 14.2, is sometimes the best way of doing this because it illustrates to underwriters that the insured organization has confidence in its risk control measures and has incentive to manage risk at all loss levels. The partnership that it serves to forge with the underwriters is invaluable if and when it comes time to call upon them to pay for large losses. Assuming good loss experience, the application of a participation arrangement similar to the one illustrated has been shown to save large firms $1 million or more annually on their larger insurance programs such as a financial institution bond or bankers blanket bond (before losses of course).

Last, but certainly not least, risk sharing provides greater incentive internally to manage risk and avoid losses. There is ample evidence that the larger an organization's uninsured deductibles and retention, the greater its tendency toward emphasizing risk assessment and control. To the extent that we can switch the focus toward the latter, we come closer to focusing on protecting our most valued asset—public and investor confidence.

Management Responsibility

Insurance risk management practitioners in most corporations have responsibility for developing purchasing and implementing all major insurance and risk finance programs for the corporation. These programs should generally be handled centrally for the entire organization and its scope of operations (globally, if applicable) in order to reap the benefit of seamless coverage, economies of scale, and firmwide negotiating leverage.

Typical Insurance Programs

Exhibit 14.3 provides an outline of the conventional coverages typically found in one form or another at most major financial service organizations today. They range from coverage for property and liability exposures, both locally and on a global basis, that are not industry specific, to coverages that are unique to financial services, such as the blanket bond, professional liability, and in some cases, unauthorized trading coverages.

Risk Finance at Smaller Companies

Many of the same principles of risk finance in large companies hold true for smaller companies, although the premium payments are not nearly as large relative to the limits of coverage that may be required by the company. By definition, this limits a smaller company's ability to amass significant premium amounts in the self-insured vehicles we will discuss in Chapter 15.

ALIGNING COVERAGE TO OPERATIONAL RISK CLASSES

The advent of broad definitions of operational risk has served up a very effective challenge for the further evolution of risk and insurance programs in the future. Some practitioners might even argue that up to this point their insurance programs have been stunted in their evolution because of the lack of a generally accepted and aggressive enough industry target for breadth of, or simply for lack of viable competition on coverage. Firms have often found themselves caught in the trap of defining insurable risk only in the context of the coverages the insurance industry makes available to them. Perhaps even unconsciously, these organizations behaved as though they believe that if coverage cannot be readily purchased, then perhaps the risks are not insurable. This may be a bit exaggerated to make a point. But there is no question that new definitions and the broad universe of operational risks raises the bar relative to the breadth of coverage a firm should strive for.

Following are the broad coverage areas that result from an attempt at aligning conventional insurance programs to the operational risk classes outlined in Chapter 3:

- **People/Human Capital Coverage:** Relevant coverages include employee dishonesty through the Bankers Blanket Bond; Workers' Compensation and/or Employer's Liability for employee injuries that occur during the course of employment (e.g., in the United States limits are dictated by individual state statutes); and Business Travel Accident for major injuries. "Key Man Insurance" would also have conceptual relevance.
- **Relationship Risk Coverage:** Key coverages include Directors' and Officers' Liability for individual directors and officers for allegations of

Most financial service firms will have a number of individual insurance programs already in place that are relevant to operational risks. Some may have structured them to blend these coverages together. In any event, following is an outline of the major programs that will generally be structured to apply worldwide and cover all of the corporate locations. These major programs will include:

- **Local Property and Liability Insurance Programs:** All firms are confronted with traditional insurance risks that include the need for coverage for physical damage to property locations (property insurance), legal liability risks (general liability insurance), and coverage for injury to employees (referred to as "workers' compensation" or "employer's liability" insurance, depending upon the country involved). Because of individual country regulations, these programs are often arranged locally on any country-by-country basis. For instance, local regulations often dictate the types of insurance that must be purchased from insurance companies licensed (or "admitted") to provide insurance in a specific country. Again, these insurance types fall in the general categories of property (fire), general liability, and workers' compensation. Purchase of these policies from insurers not licensed or admitted in the country might result in fines, penalties, or tax assessments.
- **Blanket Crime (Financial Institution Bond or Bankers Blanket Bond):** This coverage includes employee dishonesty, on-premises theft and burglary, in-transit loss (while in possession of the company's employees or designated messengers), destruction, or forgery.
- **Securities Coverage:** Provides protection for the loss of securities being held on premises or while being transported by employees or designated messengers. Generally the limit of coverage can be structured to apply in excess of the blanket bond coverage described above.
- **Computer Crime Coverage:** Generally provides coverage for loss due to wire transfers, payment or delivery of funds as a result of fraudulent input, preparation or modification of computer instructions or data, and fraudulent electronic transmissions or communications.
- **Professional Coverage (referred to as liability or indemnity coverage for errors and omissions):** These programs are generally constructed to provide coverage relative to the performance of, or failure to perform, professional services. The details of these programs vary, but are generally structured to cover "wrongful acts," errors, omissions, or misdeeds, subject to more specific terms and conditions, of course.
- **Directors' and Officers' Liability Coverage:** As described more fully in Chapter 6, this program is generally constructed to provide coverage to directors or officers in their directorship or managerial responsibilities of governing or managing the corporation.

EXHIBIT 14.3   Typical Insurance Coverages

■ **Supplemental Global Insurance Programs:** Because local property and liability insurance programs often differ in terms and conditions from country to country, a global organization, or at least one that operates in numerous countries, will also supplement these basic programs with difference-in-conditions (DIC) insurance. This coverage is sometimes referred to as "gap" property and liability insurance coverage in that it fills gaps in other programs. It applies on a worldwide basis in excess of locally purchased insurance, where unintentional gaps in the local coverage might arise.

Typically, these supplemental global insurance programs might provide benefit in three key areas:

■ **Global Property and Business Interruption Insurance Program:** This is a global property and business interruption insurance program that can be coordinated closely (where local regulation permits) with local insurance coverages.

■ **"Earnings Protection":** The inclusion of business interruption/loss of earnings insurance on a global basis is a major benefit of DIC coverage once a loss occurs. That is, it might be constructed to provide coverage for loss resulting from a single event (e.g., physical loss of a local business and/or data processing or operations in a major city or one country, that might disrupt business operations in other cities and countries around the globe.

■ **Global Liability DIC Insurance Program:** These programs can be designed to supplement basic local liability programs, while also providing a consistent coverage, on a worldwide basis in excess of that locally, of purchased insurance or on a primary basis where unintentional gaps in local liability coverage might exist. The principle here is similar to the property DIC programs. When woven together with primary liability and excess liability coverages at the home office location, the firmwide organization can construct one comprehensive liability insurance program with hundreds of millions of dollars of coverage, as needed.

Other coverages may be present, as well, such as unauthorized trading insurance, "key man" life insurance, and employee life insurance, all of which have value as protection relative to operational risks.

EXHIBIT 14.3 Typical Insurance Coverages

"wrongful acts." Professional liability or indemnity ("malpractice") coverage for allegations of errors, omissions or wrongful acts in the performance of professional services; general liability, automobile liability, contingent liability, and non-owned aircraft liability programs all relate to specific exposures that result in bodily injury or property damage deemed to be the responsibility of the firm.

- **Technology and Processing Coverage:** Data centers, computer and telecommunications equipment, including associated loss of earnings coverage, is generally provided by a firm's property insurance program. Electronic and Computer Crime coverage is also relevant here.
- **Physical Assets Coverage:** Property and loss of earnings protection will relate here for infrastructure (buildings, contents). Also, in combination, a Bankers Blanket Bond and Excess Premises and Transit programs protect physical securities (including uncertificated securities) while on premises or in transit.
- **External/Regulatory Coverage:** While elements of protection may exist in various programs depending on the circumstances involved, the risks of external fraud and regulatory charge are difficult, at best to insure in the commercial market.

Before we get too excited about the results of our mapping, however, we must look more closely at the details. In short, we have forced an alignment. In reality, however, numerous gaps and exclusions still exist that must be addressed.

MIND THE GAPS

Those who frequent the London Underground will recognize this variation on a familiar warning. Gaps are a fact of life in insurance programs, too, but the new discipline of operational risk management will shake up the status quo on them. The process of mapping the typical financial institution insurance program against a broadly defined set of operational risks reveals both logical alignments, but some glaring gaps in coverage. (Exhibit 14.4 presents a graphic depiction of the percentage alignment and relative matches and mismatches of conventional insurance coverages to the five risk classes we have been using here.) Before we dissect the results, however, some additional conceptual observations are in order.

- **Effect (versus Cause) Orientation:** First, it is interesting to note that most insurance policies are titled and classified with the outcome of loss as their focal point. That is, in order to determine an insured loss, and the policy to which it might relate, one must focus first on the outcome. Whether it be a property loss—such as the loss of a building, computer equipment, or critical files, documents, and papers—or a liability or indemnity loss—such as a judgment, settlement, penalty, or fine—the focal point is often on the resultant loss description itself. So when aligning operational risk classes to insurance coverages, one must first focus on the loss outcome or effect, rather than the loss cause and contributing factors (e.g., employee error or misjudgment, lack of dual controls or segregation of duties), which is the more appropriate focal point for

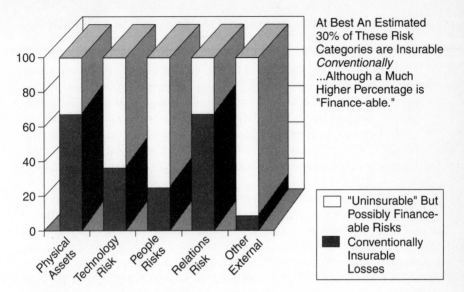

At Best An Estimated 30% of These Risk Categories are Insurable *Conventionally* ...Although a Much Higher Percentage is "Finance-able."

EXHIBIT 14.4 Aligning Operational Risks to Insurance Availability

operational risk assessment and risk mitigation. Only secondarily, when adjusting the claim, do we look at the proximate cause to confirm that policy terms, conditions, or exclusions do not exclude the loss.

■ **Limits or Capacity:** Another key issue is that of insurance capacity, or limits of coverage. As we have already discussed, firms of an appreciable size will carry significant retentions or deductibles either by choice or requirement to eliminate trading dollars over smaller loss levels. Coverage is bounded at the upper extreme by the limit of coverage. Generally speaking there is a finite capacity of coverage that can be purchased for any given risk or loss class. In some cases the capacity and/or coverage norms may seem inconsistent with more recent operational risk measurement findings. For instance, one of the most visible financial institution coverages is the Bankers Blanket (or Financial Institution) Bond, which covers employee dishonesty and crime risks. Traditionally even some of the largest financial institutions would routinely purchase only $100–200 million of coverage for these risks. This is irrespective of the fact that one could construct a loss scenario with a much larger potential, say $400–500 million or more at 95% or 99% confidence level (i.e., using a Loss Distribution Risk Measurement approach). In any event, both the retentions and limits will hinder alignment of the total loss to insurance coverage available.

■ **Terms, Conditions, and Exclusions:** Third is the issue of limitations in individual policies. Policy definitions, insuring agreements, persons or entities insured, policy territory, and exclusions are but a few of the policy features that limit the breadth of coverage for a given loss scenario. For instance, in the wake of Barings, Daiwa, and other major unauthorized trading scandals, the insurance industry responded with a new unauthorized trading insurance coverage. On the surface, once a firm purchases the coverage one might falsely assume that this risk is fully hedged and can be excluded from an analysis of exposure. It is not until the individual policy terms, conditions, and exclusions are examined, however, that it becomes clear that even within the limits of coverage there would still remain a significant amount of residual, or "basis risk."

With these and other technical observations in mind, it is instructive to continue our alignment process between the broad universe of operational risks and typical insurance coverages. This analysis involves the use of an external loss database as our point of reference for the universe of operational risks. In order to conduct the analysis, we must have access to a database with clear descriptions of the losses in question. This is particularly important because of the nuances of aligning policy terms, conditions, and exclusions to the operational loss scenarios. Even the best external databases can only provide indicative results; they generally do not contain a full enough description of the loss to make a judgment on coverage with certainty. For that matter, even with an insider's view and full information about a loss and its investigation, it is those very nuances that create claim discussions, debates, or legal actions between insurer and insured. Thus, in order to conduct an alignment analysis, we must make some broad assumptions about the circumstances of the loss cases that we are examining, and the presence of typical terms, conditions, and exclusions in policies.

Using the Bankers Trust external database (now the IC Squared First Database) and our experience in preparing, negotiating, and litigating financial institution coverage claims, on several occasions my colleagues and I examined the alignment between the database of operational losses to a hypothetical insurance program, with some broad assumptions about typical terms and conditions. We examined each loss in the database for questions about whether coverage would apply at all, whether terms and conditions might limit the amount of coverage, or whether typical policy limits might dictate only a partial recovery. Then we classified the losses either as fully covered, partially covered, unclear, or excluded with certainty. The results of our several passes on the database indicated that under a typical financial institution insurance program only 20–30% of the broad universe of operational risks would be covered.[4] Even to achieve the higher end of that range one must assume that payments would be made in cases where the claim situations contained one or more parts that might be problematic from a claim perspective (i.e., might run afoul of policy terms, conditions, or exclusions). This is probably an unlikely assumption. These are two types of gaps— "uninsurable risks" and coverage shortcomings—as follows.

- **Uninsurable Risks (Gaps between Coverages):** All industries face exposures to infrequent operational risks in key areas that are deemed uninsurable by the conventional insurance markets. Examples of these exposures for financial institutions include errors, misdeeds, and wrongful acts by employees that cause *direct loss to their firms,* fraud, regulatory change risk, certain technology risks, loss of intellectual property, certain business interruption risks, loss of key teams from other than death or injury, and an array of more specific risk scenarios. In insurance terms, these represent the gaps between policies.
- **Coverage Shortcomings of Existing Programs (Gaps within Policies):** Here the problem may be that existing insurance coverages are simply too restrictive. That is, another problem with conventional monoline insurance programs is that they present restrictions in the availability of entire classes of insurance coverage, as well as gaps in individual policies. Insurers have attempted to manage portfolio level underwriting losses on their books of business by excluding entire risk classes (e.g., certain aspects of professional liability, employment practices liability, environmental impairment liability, or contingent liability relative to real estate and other credit operations). So despite the relative completeness of a corporation's traditional monoline insurance programs in comparison to those of others in its peer group, and a firm's ability to upgrade existing coverages, problematic exclusions will exist.

Let's look at some of the problematic scenarios more closely. Exhibit 14.5 presents an illustrative list of scenarios and exclusions that present gaps in coverage within the typical insurance program.

THE NET INSURANCE COVERAGE CHALLENGE

Even the best performing insurance programs are often lacking in their charge of providing a reliable hedge from a financial management perspective (i.e., magnitude and timing of recoveries relative to losses). Perhaps more important, however, even the best insurance programs contain troublesome gaps, not necessarily relative to the norm (i.e., generally accepted insurance programs, or even a firm's peer group), but relative to its own definitions of operational risk.

Thus, recent operational risk management advances have shed light on the fact that by choice or oversight much of the insurance industry has not kept pace with operational risk trends at financial institutions. In effect, this means that despite growth in the universe of operational risk (e.g.,

In terms of broad coverage misalignments, insurance programs have not traditionally provided coverage for: (1) employee actions or inactions that cause loss to the firm itself; (2) business interruption or earnings loss other than if related to an insured *physical damage loss;* and (3) loss of revenue or earnings following loss of key people or teams through competitive recruitment, injury, or death. Needless to say, firms are also exposed for losses (4) below insurance deductibles or (5) larger than insurance policy limits, or beyond aggregate annual limit caps.

More specific coverage challenges are outlined below:

Operational Risk Class	Typical Insurance Coverage Challenges
Relationship Risks Client/counterparty-originated	■ Professional liability, if no specific coverage is in place ■ Intentional misrepresentation ■ Maintenance of customer relationship (e.g., compensation payments without legal liability) ■ Intentional breach of fiduciary duty ■ Breach of Contract ■ Fraud ■ Incorrect structuring of product (inadvertent), including modeling, pricing, etc. ■ Patent infringement ■ Money laundering ■ Failure to perform (e.g., complete a transaction, trade, etc.)
Shareholder-originated	■ Intentional misleading financial statements ■ Breach of fiduciary duty to minority shareholders
Third-party originated, being losses to a firm stemming from inter-actions with third parties.	■ Mismanagement of pension, profit sharing, welfare, or employee benefit plan ■ Breach of confidentiality ■ Unauthorized trading, unless separate coverage exists (even then, numerous exclusions may apply) ■ Anti-trust violations ■ Trade secrets infringement; liability for intellectual property

EXHIBIT 14.5 Mapping Insurance Coverages to Operational Risk Classes: Sample Coverage Challenges

<table>
<tr><td></td><td>■ Trademark & trade name infringement
■ Enforcement of environmental regulations; charges for cleanup costs</td></tr>
<tr><td>Regulator-originated</td><td>■ Suit by a regulator (e.g., improper management of pension funds)</td></tr>
<tr><td>*People Risk Class*</td><td></td></tr>
<tr><td>Employee errors</td><td>Most employee errors that cause loss to the firm itself would be excluded. Examples include:
■ Keying-in errors (e.g./errors in trade/investment instructions)
■ Losses of Intellectual Property
■ Programming errors
■ Trading losses/hedging losses due to intentional or unintentional actions/modeling or pricing errors
■ Misstatement by employee resulting in a loss of operating license</td></tr>
<tr><td>Employee misdeeds</td><td>■ Accounting manipulation/falsified records without personal gain
■ Taking or giving bribes
■ Unauthorized trading/transactions
■ Fraud (e.g., wire fraud or securities fraud)
■ Fraudulent misrepresentation
■ Losses from cross trades
■ Money laundering without personal gain
■ Liability due to market manipulation</td></tr>
<tr><td>Employee unavailability</td><td>■ Loss of intellectual capital when key employees leave the firm (including poaching)</td></tr>
<tr><td>Employment practices</td><td>■ Strikes by employees
■ Wrongful dismissal over employee's refusal to offer or cover bribes
■ Inappropriate/inconsistent application of discipline
■ Employee harassment
■ Discrimination allegations against the corporation</td></tr>
</table>

Continued

EXHIBIT 14.5 Mapping Insurance Coverages to Operational Risk Classes: Sample Coverage Challenges

Technology Risk Class

External disruption, systems failures	■ Loss of data
	■ Software bugs, errors, or other problems (e.g., programming)
	■ Systems
	■ Cost of remediations (e.g., "the Y2K-type fix")
	■ Systems integration risks (failure of systems to integrate/operate properly) following a merger, acquisition, or any other integration
	■ Systems development overruns, delays (along with associated costs) being delayed/over budget/ineffectual
	■ Hacking losses (destination of data, disruption, reputation damage, etc.)
	■ Extraordinary system maintenance costs

Physical Assets Risk Class

Criminal	■ Loss of intellectual property
	■ Negotiable/nonnegotiable securities lost/stolen on-premises in excess of blanket bond limit
	■ Lost instrument bond coverages provide "guarantees" of performance, not financial protection
	■ RICO violation/fines
	■ SEC/ERISA, etc. violations, other
Physical Disasters	■ Damage during war or war-like action/damage/subsequent business interruptions
	■ Nuclear damage and business interruption
	■ Environmental Contamination
	■ Business Interruption for other than insured property loss

External/Fraud Risk Class

Regulatory Change Risk	■ Loss of operating license as a result of employee misstatement
External Fraud	■ Loan or wire scams, with some exceptions
	■ Most forms of external fraud

EXHIBIT 14.5   Mapping Insurance Coverages to Operational Risk Classes: Sample Coverage Challenges

technological reliance risks; complexity, volume, and velocity of transactions; people/behavioral/control risks; and litigation/regulatory trend risks), most firms are forced to define and insure only the risks that underwriters have traditionally been willing to accept. Oftentimes these risk classes include only very specific and arcane classes of insurance (i.e., a "rifle shot approach" to risk finance).

Generally speaking, two primary factors have given rise to searches for risk financing alternatives. They include (1) coverage problems, uninsured losses, or the incomplete recognition of operational risk, including a determination as to whether it is reflected either in a corporation's system of distributed charges or its risk capital system and (2) cost inefficiencies caused by other program shortcomings.

In addition to analyzing uninsured risks and other coverage shortcomings, firms will assess their own needs for alternative risk finance by examining a loss ratio analysis, a cost-of-operational risk analysis, the attractiveness of self-insurance, frictional costs, and the timing of recoveries.

- **Loss Ratio Analyses:** A simple loss ratio analysis (incurred claim payments divided by insurance premiums paid) of aggregate or collective insurance programs often sheds some light on the situation. A firm's loss experience may have been excellent, resulting in only a 100% incurred loss ratio over 10 to 15 years versus the significantly higher loss ratios occurring in the property/liability insurance industry today on aggregate books of business. Obviously, no one would volunteer to incur more losses in order to "improve" their ratio because that would mean suffering the disruption and reputational damage that goes with them. In an economic sense, however these figures represent better news for insurers than they do for the corporations that hold the low loss ratios. When gauged over a sufficient period of time (not just one policy period) this measure will show how economical a company's insurance programs have been.

  In essence, the reality of coverage shortcomings can be represented through another use of historical loss ratios. Certainly not all insured companies suffer large losses. The very nature of insurance and the pooling of risk require insurers to attempt to manage their own loss ratios on their entire books of business. This causes them to tend to tweak their insurance policies over time, trimming out a bit of coverage here and there such that some of the more difficult losses slip into exclusionary provisions. In short, from an individual firm perspective, far too many operational risk losses may end up going uninsured.

- **The Cost-of-Operational Risk Analysis:** Other evidence of the depth and breadth of coverage lies in the calculation of a multi-year cost-of-operational risk (COOR) analysis as defined in Chapter 12. Even firms with one-off large loss recoveries often only find themselves able to recover 20–30% of operational losses. Note that this imbalance is partly limited by the levels of premiums and reserve contributions paid into programs, but is also partly caused by shortcomings in insurers' and reinsurers' traditional insuring agreement definitions.

- **The Attractiveness of Self-Insurance:** There is another phenomenon that might be referred to as the insured/insurer tug of war. Insurers underwrite coverage that firms prefer to self-insure. That is, both parties recognize the predictability (with high confidence) of high frequency/low severity losses. In other words, if insured, the insurance coverages offered respond to low attachment point layers of risk and risk classes that are most predictable and thus often fall into areas that are the best candidates for self-insurance.

- **Premium Dollar Trading—The Bigger Picture:** Over time, organizations of appreciable size will pay for their own event and/or operational loss costs, regardless of the risk finance technique used. In many cases it does not matter if an organization purchases insurance or if it is self-insured; over the long term, its insurance costs will adjust to pay for the actual losses incurred. Time and time again, empirical evidence and practical experience support this finding. Major corporations usually find that a fairly clear and direct relationship between insurance premiums and actual losses can be tracked over time. The period of time may be as short as 3 to 5 years, but in most cases is not more than 10 to 15 years. This fundamental insight has largely been responsible for the evolution of a broader concept of risk finance over the past 20 to 30 years.

- **Frictional Costs:** As discussed earlier, because any conventional insurance product includes certain nonloss or "frictional costs" (such as the cost of administering underwriting, claims, general overhead, profits, commissions, etc.), incentives have grown for more cost-effective financing at relatively low loss levels. In short, some insured organizations with favorable long-term loss records have a basic discomfort that their own loss costs were significantly lower than the long-term cost of their insurance coverage. The exception to this discomfort and cost imbalance, of course, is the random catastrophe insured loss occurrence, which rarely occurs at an organization, if ever. When it does occur, however, *if insured,* in a single stroke it serves to underscore the value of the insurance program.

- **Time to Recover:** It is not unusual to encounter firms whose complex losses and/or insurance claims have been mired in a court or claims system for 5 to 10 years or more.

Using the wrong benchmarks? Finally, by using traditional measures, peer group comparisons, and benchmarking information alone, some firms conclude that their risk finance programs have performed comparatively well. For instance, some firms have used loss ratio analysis in isolation to gauge the performance of their insurance programs. That is, they have looked at the percentage recovered from programs over the long term versus premium dollars expended. In essence, however, there is an inherent narrow bias to the analysis. They are only looking at the risks that they are paying to insure and by definition omitting a significant part of the landscape! Sometimes they are satisfied with the results, other times they are not. Either way, when one begins to look at the broader universe of operational risk and the other measures and issues previously outlined, they sometimes raise questions about the amount of economic benefit provided.

It is for these reasons, coupled with the coverage challenges presented by new, broad definitions of operational risk, that many are now conducting intensive studies—feasibility, then implementation, as warranted—on risk finance re-engineering.

RISK CAPITAL AND THE INFORMATION VALUE OF INSURANCE

With all of the current discussion about the development of risk capital models, some have asked whether insurance premiums might serve as an analog to capital charges, or better still, as an offset to risk capital. These are very interesting questions. In fact, there is already an analogy at most firms.

Recall our primary objectives for risk financing and insurance programs in terms of earnings and balance sheet protection. As a secondary objective, some decentralized firms already use their insurance and risk financing programs to provide information and incentives for decentralized attention to risk reduction.

There is a risk information value to insurance. Insurance premiums already serve as a proxy for the value of underlying risk. In fact, when premiums are determined by underwriters, paid by a corporate entity, and distributed throughout a firm using its internal accounting process, in essence a specific charge for risk is being levied against a business unit's earnings. The exception is that for risk classes where there is no insurance (e.g., policy exclusions, on insurable risk classes), or where a firm voluntarily takes a participation in the limit, or takes a large retention, there is often no risk charge (premium) levied. Here, a self-insured reserve may be established, and charged out.

If a firm does nothing to evolve from the traditional patchwork of monoline risk and insurance programs, and does not account for the gaps, it may simply be masking them with what might appear to be excellent loss experience on an insurable basis! In essence, if a firm buys less insurance, it takes on more risk, but under the current scenario will not recognize that

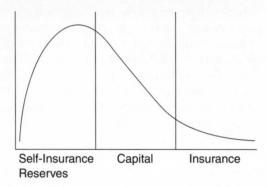

In theory, expected risks are expensed or self-funded, capital is intended for unexpected risks, and insurance should provide coverage for catastrophe risks...

Self-Insurance   Capital   Insurance
Reserves

EXHIBIT 14.6   Perception of Coverage

risk because no "premiums" will be paid. Therefore, in the context of our analogy, *when there is incomplete insurance, there is incomplete information.*

Finally, in terms of risk and coverage recognition, there is the issue of capacity of coverage (limit available to insure) operational risks, and whether the available limits are adequate to the task at hand. For one there is currently a misalignment between perception and reality of coverage availability. In short, most catastrophe insurance limits are inadequate (because of inadequate capacity in the market and unwillingness of most buyers to pay for it when it is available). This mismatch between perception and reality is illustrated in Exhibits 14.6 and 14.7.

As long as the user recognizes the potential gaps in his or her programs, there is some potential for using insurance charges as recognition of risk and applying insurance coverage as an offset to risk capital. The allocation of charges and recognition of coverage becomes even more useful, however, when insurance, its costs (premiums), and coverages are married with those of broader risk financing and serve to close many of the gaps in conventional insurance.

Thus, we find ourselves moving closer and closer to an integrated risk finance hedge for operational risks overall. Clearly, this is the objective of many who would like to see a broad hedge that not only protects a firm against the economic impact of operational losses, but also serves as a layer of protection that should be recognized in offsetting regulatory capital charges. Chapter 16 on Economic Risk Capital Modeling introduces the method we developed at Bankers Trust for offsetting risk capital with a credit for the economic benefit of risk finance programs. Chapter 17 continues this discussion vis-à-vis its regulatory implications.

In reality, insurance and capital compete for coverage of unexpected risks, because of insurance capacity shortages. Some coverage is emerging for catastrophe risks, but availability remains limited.

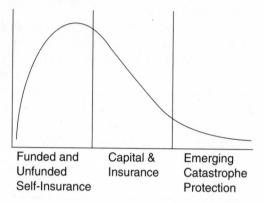

| Funded and Unfunded Self-Insurance | Capital & Insurance | Emerging Catastrophe Protection |

EXHIBIT 14.7   Reality of Coverage

MARKET TRENDS TOWARD RISK FINANCE

The growth of operational risk and its relationship to insurance often conjures up images of Nero fiddling as Rome burned. Given the financial sector's new recognition of the breadth of the operational risk universe, and relative mismatch to insurance, it seems a safe bet that there will be casualties along the way if insurers fail to keep up with the needs of their target market.

Why the predictions of gloom and doom for conventional players? Some of the evidence is borne out by the industry's own statistics. For instance, one of the industry's organizations in the United States, the Surety Association of America, has for years published the aggregated underwriting results of its member firms in the area of commercial crime insurance and financial institution bonds (Bankers Blanket Bonds). The results in the late 1980s and for much of the 1990s showed that in the areas underwritten (employee dishonesty and related coverage areas), the firms' aggregate results have paid out 20 to 40% of the premiums collected for these coverages in the form of claims. For an exception to these results one has to look back to the mid-1980s when for a few short years loss payments actually exceeded premiums.

Independent of these industry statistics, in our studies of operational risk, and analyses of the value of insurance as a hedge, we noted countless examples of crime and fraud-related losses suffered by financial firms that would not have resulted in claims covered by conventional bond coverage, or any other conventionally written coverage for that matter, because of policy term limitations. As discussed, when combined with other types of operational risks, like technology failures, disruption, data security failures, electronic commerce risks, and direct losses from employee errors, to name a few, then mapped against the entire array of conventionally available insurance coverage, the gaps are even more obvious.

What is the point of all this? There should be no confusion; it is not to attack the insurance industry, but instead to continue to prod it toward providing more effective risk financing solutions. In addition, it is intended to point out that if one thinks that operational risk can simply be insured away, they will be sadly mistaken. In statistical risk management terms, the basis risk here is enormous. Insurance has its place, but must be viewed in context of its limitation, and this is precisely why the best risk and insurance management practitioners have for years looked to supplement conventional insurance with risk financing alternatives.[5]

CONCLUSION

The intent of this chapter has been to provide the reader with some perspective on how to think about conventional insurance coverages vis a vis operational risks.

To begin with, the objectives of these programs are generally considered to be providing economic protection from operational risk, at either a balance sheet or profit-and-loss level. The problem to date, however, is that operational risks are generally defined much more broadly than insurable risks, and conventional insurance has generally been used as the primary risk financing tool available.[6]

When mapping individual insurance coverages against a broadly defined set of operational risk classes the gaps become very apparent. There are several ways to conduct this analysis. For one, an industry operational loss database can be very helpful. By reviewing the circumstances surrounding an individual loss, one can match those circumstances against the individual terms and conditions in a conventional insurance program. Because even the best of loss databases could not possibly cover all aspects of what are very complex loss scenarios, some generalizations are necessary, but generally the entries can provide useful insight into possible loss scenarios. Our analyses of actual losses indicate that perhaps only 20 to 30% of operational risks have traditionally been insurable in the conventional market.

In summary, we will evaluate and stress test existing insurance programs, and seek to improve long-term cost of operational risk results. We are raising the bar for the risk finance, insurance, and hedging markets to expand their coverage and provide much more useful product.[7]

LESSONS LEARNED AND KEY RECOMMENDATIONS

- During insurance and risk finance deliberations we must ask ourselves, are we simply looking to spread the cost of a potential loss over time, or are we looking to transfer the economic impact of it? At the end of the day, it is important to recognize that operational risk is unique because we cannot hedge it away entirely; we can hedge its economic impact but not its impact on the firm's reputation.[8]

- With sufficient data, we can stress test a firm's own insurance and risk finance programs through the calculation of the Cost-of-Operational Risk. This calculation can help us to answer some key questions. What value are the risk finance and insurance programs, given the broader scope of operational risk? How well are these programs responding? What percentage of the losses are being recovered from the risk finance and insurance programs? Are they cost effective relative to the investment required (insurance premiums or other financing costs)?

- Align insurance and risk finance programs to operational risks. Measure program performance over time.

- Challenge your insurance and risk financing programs with performance measures. Do not allow your insurance or risk financing programs to stagnate. Subject them to long-term risk measures in order to confirm their value to the organization. In addition to cost-of-operational risk calculations, such measures include loss ratio analyses, reviews of uninsured losses, analyses of the gaps between and within policies, and analyses of the attractiveness of self-insurance, to name a few options.

- In time, risk and insurance management functions will be linked to broader operational risk management programs, and they should share access to established or emerging incident and loss data capture systems. This linkage is critical in order that the firm is in the best possible position to recover from its insurance and risk finance programs.

- Concentrate your premium dollars in long-term insurance and risk finance relationships. Establish long-term relationships with a handful of insurance and risk financing providers and maintain those relationships. Quite literally, these premiums and investments in time will pay off several times over, given the scenario of a large-scale claim.

Operational Risk Finance

The Re-engineering Process

INTRODUCTION

Risk finance is a term used to describe the spectrum of prearrangements made for the payment of potential losses. Effective risk finance cannot occur in a vacuum but must follow careful risk identification, assessment, and management.

Historically, risk finance programs at large corporations have been focused primarily on the purchase of insurance. But in time it became apparent that insurance is just one form of risk finance.

Companies began the migration away from traditional insurance in the 1960s and 1970s. For many it is still the dominant risk financing vehicle, but as discussed in Chapter 14, it is no longer the most *efficient* tool for financing *all types* of risk and levels of loss. In certain aspects the conventional insurance market has become partially obsolete for large, complex corporations.

Other tools can be used to supplement or replace insurance on a more efficient and cost-effective basis. At the lower end of the loss severity axis (refer to Exhibit 14.1) is retention of risk. The vehicles include self-insurance, captive or wholly owned insurance companies, loss or experience-rated insurance plans, and risk funding (which applies concepts such as financial insurance, which is basically a banking-type plan, for funding losses). Progressive risk and insurance management groups apply some or all of these alternative risk financing tools in seeking to optimize their companies' cost of financing risk.

Because of the shortcomings in conventional insurance programs that we explored in Chapter 14, along with their problematic alignment with developing definitions and risk classes for operational risk that we also explored in Chapter 14, firms seeking to hedge these risks find themselves forced to turn to a blend of insurance and risk financing alternatives. In this chapter,

> ## BP STRATEGY #17, REDUX—ENHANCE RISK FINANCE HEDGING OF OPERATIONAL RISKS
>
> Align insurance and risk finance programs to operational risks. Measure program performance over time. Re-engineer programs to attain an optimal coverage and cost trade-off. But conventional insurance provides only a partial solution. Enhance risk financing through the use of effective alternative risk financing structures. Use self-insurance, captive, excess-of-loss reinsurance, credit, and capital markets to construct effective protection for expected, unexpected and catastrophic operational risks.

we will explore alternative risk financing possibilities. The objective here is not to provide a primer on risk financing and various alternatives. Instead, it is to illustrate how more progressive firms view and approach the re-engineering of their conventional insurance programs in order to address operational risks more effectively.

THE EVOLUTION FROM INSURANCE TO RISK FINANCING PROGRAMS

Insurance underwriters developed most individual lines of insurance over the years in response to specific market needs. For example, the Financial Institution Bond (originally the Bankers Blanket Bond) was one of the first specialty banking coverages. It was developed to respond to banks' most prominent operational risk—concerns of employee theft in banks (i.e., employee dishonesty). At the time, this was one of their first and most prominent operational risks.

As other market needs developed, insurers continued to respond accordingly, with a new insurance coverage each time (e.g., securities coverage, electronic computer crime, and more recently, unauthorized trading coverages). It all seemed responsive and logical enough on a case-by-case basis. As the market began to analyze its firmwide and enterprise-wide exposures more broadly, however, the approach has become a bit problematic. Risk and insurance practitioners were already aware of the limitations of their individual insurance contracts as outlined in their terms, conditions, and exclusions. From an enterprise-wide view of risk, however, those who were already looking to the broad universe of risk that operational definitions now represent recognized that the gaps between individual insurance policies began to appear somewhat cavernous.

Although the alternative risk financing marketplace had already been thriving in the 1970s, in the form of self-insurance, self-funded or unfunded captive insurance companies, and the like, the movement received a substantial push forward during the insurance crisis of the mid-1980s. In the early 1980s, as insurance industry losses mounted, insurance companies were faced with the prospect of either raising rates substantially in an attempt to recoup losses or exiting certain lines of unprofitable business entirely. In the United States, in particular, as insurance capacity (supply) shrank, insurance premiums skyrocketed, and insurers exited lines of business entirely, buyers were forced to consider their options. This became an important turning point for the development of the alternative risk financing marketplace. Many new captive and private insurance companies were formed during this difficult period and market tension. Bermuda confirmed its status as a global insurance center as a long list of these captive insurance companies were formed there, and a number of highly successful private insurers were developed as well. Some of the latter companies, such as ACE Insurance Company and X.L. Insurance Company of Bermuda, originally private insurers and now public companies listed on the New York Stock Exchange, have grown to become extremely successful insurers on their own.

Most important for the operational risk financing movement, risk and insurance managers discovered they could do much more with their private insurers and captives than simply play second fiddle to the established insurance and reinsurance marketplace. Although in some cases the financial benefit of these companies had already become quite impressive, for many it wasn't until the insurance crisis of the 1980s that they took on far greater prominence. Parent companies back home and industry associations alike began to commit significant amounts of capital to support these companies, and thus withheld significant market share from conventional insurers.

All the while, another interesting trend was developing. Risk and insurance managers were discovering that in addition to providing capacity for conventional lines of coverage, such as workers' compensation, casualty insurance, and product liability insurance, these companies now had the opportunity to provide entirely new lines of coverage for heretofore uninsured risks. It was based on this experience that we decided to form a captive insurance company in 1992 at Bankers Trust as a direct insurer for financial service professional liability coverage far broader than anything that the conventional marketplace was offering. Although the company was originally formed to provide this coverage entirely on its own, the reinsurance community stepped in shortly after the company was formed to provide support.

We continued to build upon the self-funding concept, to expand coverage for lines that were heretofore uninsurable. As time went on, our ultimate goal was to structure a company that could provide a broad-based operational risk insurance program.

DESIGNING ALTERNATIVE RISK FINANCE FOR OPERATIONAL RISKS

Recall from Chapter 14 that most firms' risk finance and insurance programs have been designed over the years with a view toward balancing "earnings protection" or smoothing loss accounting at relatively lower levels of risk, along with large loss coverage in striving for "balance sheet protection"; both within reasonable risk finance economics.

Two important strategies for achieving risk financing objectives include: (1) designing a broader and more holistic and aggregated coverage approach for a larger number of operational risk classes, and (2) developing better-aligned timing for accounting treatment of losses and recoveries. More specifically, then, a firm will be seeking:

- **Breadth of Coverage/Uninsured Risks:** To break away from traditional coverage definitions and expand coverages to align more directly with operational risk exposure definitions and classes. The result should be a higher percentage of operational losses "captured" in annual cost-of-operational risk (COOR) calculations. Exhibit 15.1 is an illustration of risks that are the subject of deliberations about uninsured risks and risk financing alternatives, including captives.
- **Catastrophe Protection:** To increase the limits of coverage for operational loss to a consistent catastrophe level, perhaps as high as $1 billion or more. Existing programs might range from $0 (i.e., no coverage) for some risk classes to as high as $500 million for property and related business interruption losses. A re-engineered structure might not only capture broader classes of operational risk but include some credit and market exposures as well, if appropriate and desired.
- **Timing of Recoveries:** To work toward a structure that provides improved smoothing of earnings and protection for the balance sheet during any one accounting period in the event of loss.
- **Cost:** To accomplish as much of the above as possible within reasonable levels of risk finance expenditures.

Because one of the biggest problems identified while aligning insurance to operational risks is the major gaps in coverage, we will focus primarily on addressing uninsured risk throughout the remainder of this chapter.

ALTERNATIVES FOR FINANCING UNINSURED RISK

Companies face several alternatives for financing uninsured operational risks. The following is intended to provide some perspective on re-engineering alternatives.

Traditionally captive insurance companies had been formed as a formalized means of self-insurance. They either provided coverage for their parent companies directly, or as reinsurers of an admitted commercial insurer. Their primary objective was premium cost savings.

With the advent of operational risk management, companies are equally concerned about uninsured risks as they are with constructing a more efficient balance between insurance and self-insurance. Thus, some have looked to the formation of captives, funded self insurance, and financial products to fill uninsured gaps.

For financial institutions, complex technology risks, fraud risks, unauthorized trading, and financial services' professional liability are all good examples of difficult-to-insure risks that could be addressed by risk financing alternatives. Many firms are currently uninsured in part, or completely, for these exposures. In the case of technology risks, the exposure might relate to the failure of systems for causes other than physical damage. Fraud risk has always been an area of contention between insurers and insureds. In addition, while unauthorized trading and professional liability insurance have become available, some firms may find policy terms and conditions too restrictive to provide an adequate hedge. Unauthorized trading coverages contain problematic exclusions in the areas of definitions of authorization and types of trading. Professional liability may not be broad enough, or contain problematical terms or policy exclusions. The risks consist of lawsuits for failure to exercise due care in the delivery of financial services, including financial advisory, brokerage, trust and fiduciary services, agency, evaluation, financing, mergers and acquisitions, restructuring, and risk management product structures.

Combine these examples with other operational risks that are problematic from the perspective of insurability, and an individual firm may be looking at a significant upward trend in uninsured losses. Some risk and insurance managers have often looked only at "risks that are generally insurable" when structuring their insurance coverage, eliminating from their considerations areas like external fraud, which is commonly uninsurable. With the broader focus on the entire universe of operational risks by both new operational risk teams and progressive risk and insurance managers alike, the bar has been raised in considering insurance and risk finance alternatives.

EXHIBIT 15.1 Risk Financing Alternatives and Uninsured Operational Risks

Option 1—Status Quo or Exclusive Use of Conventional Insurance

This alternative often has the illusion of being the least costly in that, all things being equal, no marginal additional premiums charges are levied on the firm and its business lines. By not being proactive, however, it allows exclusionary gaps to stagnate or widen (thereby possibly allowing loss ratios to grow less favorably, insurance programs to grow more costly, and thus less efficient over time). It also might allow risk finance costs (including but not limited to insurance market pricing, uninsured loss costs, and other financing costs) to run their course.

For all the reasons already discussed, uninsured risks also accumulate in this scenario without cost recognition to the firm (see "Insurance, Risk Capital, and Information Value of Insurance" in Chapter 14) and its business units until losses actually occur. Let's revisit the potential time lag and its related effects: losses will occur and be accounted for in one year. Their investigations and claims settlement are too often completed substantially after the fact in the event of a complex investigation and then charged to the business unit responsible.

From a management incentive standpoint, the charges wind up being applied to a business after the accounting period's results are reviewed and bonuses are paid, except in the case where accountants set a reserve for the loss during the current period. It is possible to do this when the loss is estimable, such as in the case of an unauthorized trading or unauthorized transaction event. In the case of a related legal liability, however, the outcome may not be known for years. Given the large-scale nature of some operational losses, such as fraud or legal liability cases, the firm could be facing significant "spikes" to its earnings and, dependent upon the losses, these spikes could amount to in excess of $100–200 million.

In summary, the advantages of this status quo approach are:

■ Existing programs are generally tested and reasonably well understood.
■ A firm might have been reasonably effective in capturing "insurable" losses under these programs, and with aggressive management of claims it may have kept them economical relative to premium expenditures. But studies show that only 20 to 30% of operational losses may have been insured.

There are a number of shortcomings to conventional programs when used in isolation.

■ Conventional insurance coverages are too narrow and one-dimensional in scope. They often do not align well with broad definitions of operational risk exposures; thus, firms are sometimes forced to design "in-fill" self-insurance and reinsurance structures. These are generally limited in scope and capacity because of limitations on funding. This problem will only worsen as the operational risks continue to expand.
■ The operational risk picture is outstripping these programs' track record to respond, leaving gaps between coverages.

- There is little true catastrophe protection in conventional structures, generally with the exception of very focused property and business interruption insurance coverage (e.g., $200–500 million or more) for major locations.
- Problematic terms, conditions, and exclusions make the "real time" predictability of coverage difficult, at best, within a single same accounting period. Thus, it is difficult to offset coverage against losses in any given period.
- Traditional one-dimensional or monoline pricing will probably become less cost-effective during the longer term. Monoline coverages, individually priced, do not provide a risk pricing advantage from the perspective of a portfolio or diversification effect.

Option 2—Negotiating Insurance Coverage Enhancements

Realistically, of course, no firm would simply leave its insurance program unattended, at least not intentionally. So, this second option entails a search for conventional solutions: It proposes to close gaps in existing coverages for uninsured operational risks.

Generally speaking, the first step in closing program gaps is to negotiate enhancements to existing insurance coverages. The old adage, "You won't get what you don't ask for" is particularly true when negotiating insurance coverages. It is true for all firms, but it is especially good advice for a medium-sized or larger financial institution that is negotiating firmwide coverage and wields significant clout in the marketplace. It is also true as long as competition is present in the marketplace.

Even with negotiating clout, however, there's a limit to the extent to which these gaps can be closed in the conventional insurance marketplace. None of this should come as a surprise to risk and insurance management practitioners. They have always known that gaps exist in their coverages. It had been difficult to specify the extent of the uninsured exposures, however, until recently when progress has been made toward defining the universe of operational risks, and measuring them, at least directionally, using more sophisticated analysis.

The good news is that these advancements will help both insurers and insureds move forward to negotiate for coverage enhancements and evolve programs more effectively.

Using an Operational Loss Database to Enhance Risk Finance and Insurance Programs

A company is intent on maximizing the value of its risk finance and insurance programs. It subscribes to an external loss database and sorts the industry loss records, selecting those that match its business lines, profit centers, and product offerings (e.g., investment banking, trading, *retail banking). Then, line by line it reviews loss records relative to in-surance coverage known to be responsive. Similarly, it flags all cases in which it believes that the responsiveness (i.e., breadth of terms) of cov-erage may be questionable. Addressing the latter, it negotiates the clo-sure of problematic exclusions and improves key terms and conditions (e.g., broad coverage for transaction origination and execution). Net re-sult: When losses occur, the company is better positioned to negotiate recoveries from the program. Insurance recoveries are shown to be $30 million higher in two years than they would have been without the value of the external loss database information, term changes, and skilled claims negotiation.*

Given the one-dimensional (monoline) approach to most risks by the conventional insurance industry, one should not be overly optimistic that these efforts will yield proposals to close all, or even a majority, of the major gaps relative to operational risks.

For instance, even though insurance coverages like financial services' professional liability and even newer unauthorized trading coverages have at-tempted to close key gaps in coverage, close inspection of those policies re-veals a number of problematic terms, conditions, and exclusions of coverage. Most risk and insurance management practitioners do not expect conven-tional insurance coverages to be the sole answer to the gap between tradi-tional insurance coverages and the far broader universe of operational risks in the near future.

In effect, this second option is the one that many firms have pursued. The situation is illustrated in Exhibit 15.2. It may have served them reason-ably well when benchmarked against "insurable risk" standards. Gaps in coverage can be filled with a certain amount of effort. Some are becoming increasing concerned, however, that the operational risk environment is evolving faster than conventional insurance can respond.

The advantages of this second option include:

- All of the positives from Option 1 (conventional insurance)
- Firms that can probably continue to achieve marginal advances in cov-erage with significant time and effort
- What one might expect to be a reasonable stability of programs and ex-pense, assuming a "normal" loss level

The disadvantages, on the other hand, are:

- Most of the negatives in Option 1 (conventional insurance).
- More often than not, one-off fine-tuning has been narrow, labor-intensive, and time-consuming (i.e., it can take 6–18 months to negotiate major

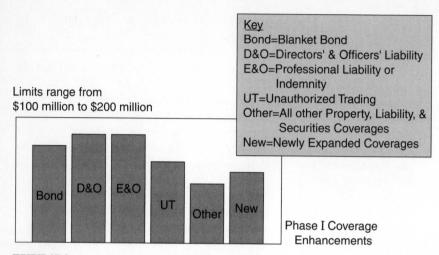

EXHIBIT 15.2   Improving Breadth of Existing Coverages

revisions to conventional coverage). There are often clear but narrow victories, considering the effort required.

- Questions of whether an operational loss hits or misses the scope of these individual policies (i.e., covered or excluded) seem to become relatively random. Because of the increasing complexity of business and losses, it is also difficult to get ahead with individual policy changes. Thus, even with fine-tuning, a firm's policies could become less economical over time when the combination of insurance premiums and uninsured losses are combined.

Option 3—Implement a Blended Aggregate or "Operational Risk Insurance Program"

In recent years, some progressive firms have been migrating toward "blended programs." One approach has been to combine and integrate major coverages such as the Bankers Blanket Bond, professional liability, and directors' and officers' liability coverages. In concept, these programs are moving in the right direction to the extent that they seek to simplify coverages and eliminate problematic terms and exclusions. It seems that the insurer has simply taken a large staple to the lines of insurance; however, with a few additional changes, these combinations can be deceiving in terms of their benefits.

Elsewhere, a variation on this theme has emerged in which the insurer actually works to re-engineer the underlying coverages, and nearly begins with a "blank sheet of paper." The concept is illustrated in Exhibit 15.3 as

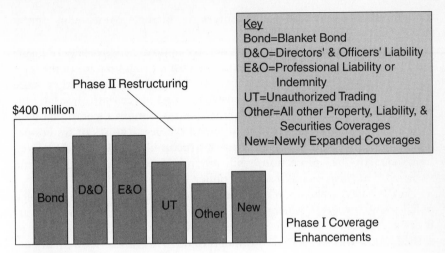

EXHIBIT 15.3 Blended Program: Restructured Operational Risk Coverage

a newly integrated program. Underwriters at Lloyds', Swiss Re, and others have underwritten some early offerings. For instance, the Organizational Liability coverage offered by certain underwriters at Lloyds' in conjunction with insurance brokers at AON, and the FIORI (Financial Institutions Operational Risk Insurance) from Swiss Re, provide aggregations of coverage. The Swiss Re program provides an aggregation of insurance, self-insurance, and capital markets coverage.

The name "operational risk insurance program" is used in quotations here because even these programs are hampered by either implied or explicit limitations in terms, conditions, and exclusions. Thus, the best firms will define their overall exposure to the entire universe of operational risks first, then confirm that these programs provide the expected coverage. One approach is to measure firmwide operational risk exposure, then carve out and price separately one's excluded risks when considering the extent of protection provided by underwriters. In any event, all costs must be considered, including both the explicit premiums and implied self-insured loss costs. If structured carefully, these aggregate programs can be very effective, but one must make sure that there is a comparison of similar terms between these programs and the other options.

Given that we had an integrated operational risk management department at Bankers Trust (risk assessment, management, risk capital, and risk financing), we were able to lever our work on the measurement of operational risks into an integration with our risk finance and insurance programs. That is to say, we sought to align our various self-insurance, captive insurance, reinsurance, and conventional insurance programs into a comprehensive net that would capture the financing of as many operational risks as possible.

During the course of these exercises, we approached a variety of insurers and reinsurers to lead this new comprehensive program. One of the reinsurers involved in these discussions was Swiss Re. Although they were unable to respond with a comprehensive solution at the time, they later introduced a program called FIORI (Financial Institutions Operational Risk Insurance). The program attempts to blend the best features of traditional insurance with that of a capital market structure, thereby providing large limit "catastrophe" protection, while attempting to eliminate many of the vagaries of a conventional insurance policy.

For instance, rather than construct a patchwork of traditional insurance policies (e.g., property, general liability, professional, and directors' and officers' liability), the program was developed and released for placement in early 2000. It was structured to respond to the five risk classes we had outlined to them in our discussions back in 1997 and 1998. They align generally to the five classes we used, but not in precise detail.[1]

Lars Schmidt-Ott of Swiss Re describes five risk classes and refers to the definition used by them as "a definition developed by Bankers Trust." He noted that the main components of this risk break down as follows:

1. **Personnel:** The risk that business performance is adversely affected by improper personnel policies, motivational issues, or internal fraud
2. **Technology:** The risk of loss resulting from systems unavailability, poor data quality, system errors, or software problems
3. **Physical Assets:** The risk of damage or loss of physical assets that negatively impact operations
4. **Relationships:** The risk of loss resulting from relationship issues such as sales practices, customer problems, and unsuitable rare relationships
5. **External:** The risk of a loss from external fraud[2]

In addition to the blended nature of risk classes shown above, other advertised benefits of the program include:

- **Catastrophe Limits of Coverage:** Capacity under the program could provide limits of over USD 1 billion.[3]
- **Multiyear program:** Program period could range upwards of three years.
- **Timely Insurance Claim Settlement:** Payments are to be made under the program within seven days, not years after the event as is so common with many complex liability and business interruption, and even some complex property, losses. Thus, they are attempting to address the timing problems already mentioned. They note, however, that the validity of a claim would be debated afterward.[4] Unfortunately, the latter stipu-

lations may well present a problem for accountants, who would need certainty of payment prior to recognizing the recovery. Thus, insureds may be no better off until the claim is ultimately settled.

Option 4—Implement a Self-Funded and/or Captive Insurance Program

A captive insurance company often represents one of several steps in what's considered a long-term departure from conventional insurance as the primary method of financing important event risks at a reasonable cost. Some firms have formed captives in order to self-fund operational risks. One such program involves a primary captive insurer formed by the corporation itself and managed by an independent firm. "Premiums" paid to the captive are determined by referencing insurance premiums the company might have paid if it chose to insure as many of its operational risks as possible with the conventional market. In addition, or alternatively, actuarial funding projections can be used to suggest an annual contribution ("premium payment") for the foreseeable future at a selected confidence level.

The way it works is that the captive issues an insurance policy to the parent organization; this contract governs the terms under which loss payments are made. If actual loss experience is better than anticipated, however, these premium amounts will be further reduced over time, thereby representing savings over what the corporation would have had to spend on conventional insurance.

Some have pursued captive insurance companies in order to reserve for their own major "incurred but not reported" (IBNR) operational risk exposures on a direct basis, and to replace relatively less economical aspects of conventional insurance programs with more efficient captive insurance. A key objective is to use these reserves to stabilize earnings in the event of significant unanticipated operational loss "spikes."

The Operational Risk Captive Mandate   In the context of operational risk, the mission of the captive will be twofold: to establish a funded reserve and to act as an "agent" of the corporation and its business lines in securing from reinsurance markets the most cost-effective external methods available for financing rare-event risk. The captive is used as a tool to formalize the firm's overall retention of both insurable and uninsurable risks and to substitute for some expensive forms of insurance gradually over time, thereby reducing the cost of operational risk for the firm. Its implementation reflects a decision by the firm to reduce its reliance on conventional insurance, while providing a new framework for the recognition, evaluation, and financing of rare-event operational risk.

When structured properly, the captive will provide earnings protection. Whether supported by statistical analysis or when reinsurance is purchased by the captive, insurance written by the captive will be structured in order to gain treatment as insurance for accounting purposes [i.e., in the United States this would reference Generally Accepted Accounting Principles (GAAP)]. In one case premiums paid for risks retained by the captive were deductible as expenses for accounting purposes assuming that they were measured and priced properly, and there was a shielding of the effective losses on the income statement. Tax issues are an entirely separate topic and will depend on a variety of issues unique to the country and situation.

In addition to earnings protection, other benefits of one such captive formed for operational risk finance include:

- Funding operational risks typically excluded from conventional programs such as direct loss from errors or omissions and fraud (see Exhibit 14.5).
- Providing accounting earnings stabilization for losses insured by the captive by substituting risk premiums annually (analogous to credit loss reserves).
- Supplementing and/or providing a surrogate for risk capital in uninsured operational risk areas. Formalizing a focal point for tracking exposures and losses, and distributing risk financing costs.
- Gaining direct access to reinsurance markets, where advantageous, to provide a greater array of alternative approaches and broad coverage by transferring part or all of certain risks when desirable and possible. This can pave the way for the purchase of large loss protection at a "wholesale level."
- The captive will provide incentives for operational risk management. Business lines will continue to retain reasonably large deductibles, reflecting those at the corporate level. While this may seem like a heavy burden, retained losses would be uninsured without the captive. Besides, leaving the deductibles with the business lines would preserve important incentives for controlling and reducing risk. At the same time, the captive insurance arrangement will provide both the business lines and corporation some protection from the effects of a very large rare-event loss.
- Reducing the parent firm's reliance on conventional insurance, as an expensive way to finance many risks, by reducing the purchase of relatively costly high frequency/low severity primary insurance coverage and offsetting it with self-insurance alternatives (in this case, captive insurance).

Other advantages can include:

- Decentralized international insurance and employee benefits—a captive can also be used as a funding vehicle for certain international property and liability insurance and/or employee benefit programs.
- Because most large companies maintain relatively high insurance deductibles, smaller subsidiaries sometimes must, for regulatory reasons,

purchase insurance to fill the gap created by the larger corporate deductibles. While the cost of this insurance to the subsidiary may seem inconsequential, it is often quite high relative to its value, and an accumulation of these purchases over all subsidiaries and over time can become a meaningful diseconomy for the firm as a whole. Captives are sometimes used to fill this gap.

The disadvantages of a captive arrangement include:

- Use as a funded vehicle for large loss uninsured risks, if losses can occur in early years when funding is insufficient to provide meaningful protection
- Favorable accounting treatment required of a credible and sophisticated risk measurement methodology (e.g., Loss Distribution Methodology)
- The cost and time to administer the company must be addressed

Option 5—Complete Self-Insurance—Cancel Most Existing Insurance Programs

British Petroleum (BP) made headlines in the early 1990s by announcing its conclusion that its balance sheet was stronger than most of its insurers and, taken in combination with their other frustrations of maintaining broad and responsive insurance, that it no longer made sense to maintain conventional insurance programs. Thus, it pursued a strategy of maintaining coverage only where absolutely necessitated by regulation or contractual agreements, and self-insuring virtually all other coverages and losses on a current expense basis.

A major firm could certainly pursue this strategy. Of the total coverage that a firm maintains annually, however, it would have to keep some programs in place. One rule-of-thumb estimate places expenditures for regulatory or contractually mandated coverages at one fourth of a company's total annual bill for conventional insurance.

The advantages of complete self-insurance are that:

- A firm could conceivably save millions of premium dollars (net) and put those savings into a self-insurance reserve, or simply return it to earnings and take any loss as a current expense.
- There would be some associated administrative savings if a firm were to cancel a significant number of its insurance coverages.

The disadvantages of complete self-insurance are that:

- Virtually all losses would be booked as current expenses. This would not be a problem in low, expected level loss cases, but given a catastrophe level loss of $1 billion or more, a firm would find itself completely un-hedged for this loss.

- An unhedged strategy will often prove inconsistent with a firm's other risk management strategies.
- A firm would find itself exposed to losses at catastrophe levels for a dis-proportionate benefit in premium savings. Of course, this assumes that the firm would have been able to arrange catastrophe coverage at the $1 billion level had it chosen to. In any event, there is a perceived benefit of having insurance coverage from the view of shareholders, regulators, and customers. This perceived value of insurance programs is difficult to measure.

Option 6—Financial Insurance Products

Attempts at addressing the problems associated with both insurance and self-insurance have resulted in exploration of a variety of financial product alternatives. Among them are:

- **Financial Insurance and/or Finite Risk Insurance:** These coverages were developed by the risk finance community for the express purpose of funding difficult-to-insure or uninsured risks, in non-financial firms, such as hazardous waste and toxic tort liabilities as well as credit risks. Given accounting pressure to recognize these risks, they were measured and products were developed to finance them over time with counter-parties. The primary objective was financial in nature, as in financing the costs over time ("timing risk") rather than transferring the underly-ing operational risks themselves. In finite risk transactions, the risk transferred typically consists of a combination of timing risk, under-writing risk (the operational risks themselves), and investment/asset risk and credit risk.[5]
- **CAT Bond Structures:** CAT Bonds, or catastrophe bonds, consist of con-tingent debt or equity issued by the firm seeking protection; the bonds' (or other financial instruments including swaps, described herein as bonds) repayment of interest and/or principal and/or maturity date is linked to a specified event or events. To date, the event(s) has (have) in-cluded hurricanes, earthquakes, or some other type of "insurable" event, but the thinking is that they might be applied more broadly to op-erational risks.

CAT Bonds are designed and issued such that their principal repayment and/or coupon payments are reduced or eliminated if certain "insurance" events occur during the bond's risk period. In this manner, catastrophe risk is transferred from the bond issuer to the bond buyer.

The advantages of financial products depend on the precise structure selected, of course. Generally speaking, however:

- They can be designed to address large limits readily.
- Uninsured risks are not a problem for financial insurance or finite risk insurance. They become a bit more challenging when seeking CAT Bond investors who may be putting some of their principal at risk. A similar challenge arises when underwriting risk is built into a finite risk transaction.

The disadvantages are that:

- Some buyers find the lack of underwriting risk transfer in financial covers to be unattractive, especially when risk charges and a profit margin is added to the principal.
- The investor market is unproven for CAT Bonds relative to a broad array of operational risks (beyond weather or earthquake-related events).

ENGINEERING A SOLUTION: BLENDING THE OPTIONS

With the advent of operational risk management as a separate discipline, along with the prospect of a generally accepted definition of risk and risk classes in the not-too-distant future, financial institutions will soon find themselves engaged in a critical reevaluation of their insurance and risk finance programs. The objective will include a fresh feasibility review of options intended to expand the programs' coverage on a cost-effective basis.

Several trends have changed the landscape of risk financing options in recent years. For one, a relatively soft insurance market in the 1990s provided an improved negotiating environment given more competitive markets. Second, the entry of capital markets into the risk financing arena provided additional opportunities to structure catastrophe protection. Third, work on operational risk analysis provides firms with additional unique leverage in negotiating risk financing coverages. Risk and loss projections, definitions, and data produced by risk analysis will serve as an important basis for evaluating alternatives and decision making relative to risk finance options.

In today's markets the most attractive option for firms aggressively pursuing risk finance reengineering will most likely involve a coordinated blend of insurance, self-insurance, and other forms of risk finance, possibly including capital markets, to be most effective and efficient overall. In essence, this approach seeks to draw from the most attractive features from the six options discussed in the previous section, and minimize as many of the disadvantages as possible. Using headline billion dollar operational losses as a reference (e.g., Barings, Daiwa) to test the design, some will structure programs that provide protection to this level or higher.

One such design offered for discussion will entail pursuing the feasibility of a recommendation that reengineers, aggregates, and expands existing coverage under risk finance programs into two "tranches" of broad "all risk" coverage for operational losses. They will provide limits up to $200–400 million, subject to exclusions, albeit minimized. A third entirely new tranche will involve a blended catastrophe facility of coverage in excess of tranches 1 and 2 and will employ a combination of insurance and either capital markets (debt) products or financial insurance. The aggregate of all three tranches will then provide coverage of approximately $1 billion or more. This structure implies the following component parts:

1. **Tranche I—Insurance and Self-Insurance Combination:** This first part will blend existing insurance, reinsurance, and self-insurance into a more cohesive whole. It entails more effective aggregation of existing coverages into one multiline and aggregated program with coverage up to $100 million. This combination is feasible; some firms have already pursued various forms of it. One interesting prospect is to leverage off of the diversification and benefits of pricing operational risks as a single broad class, rather than as individual lines of coverage. That is, rather than purchase individual monoline insurance policies, one might gain some coverage and savings by sacrificing some individuals per policy and per loss limits in exchange for an aggregate policy period limit. Some existing underwriters will respond to this request. In addition, the program will be combined with a separate self-funded, captive insurance program. The net result in this tranche or layer will be a blending of existing coverages and some simplification of contracts and terms (see Exhibit 15.2).

2. **Tranche II—New Large Loss Coverage:** A second tranche will involve construction of a new broad "All (Operational) Risk" coverage with few defined exclusions as shown in Exhibit 15.3. The limits of coverage might range between $100 million and $200–400 million. Because the attachment point (the point at which this coverage applies to a loss) of this tranche will be much higher than is the norm, a firm will be able to negotiate some significant expansions of its existing coverages here (e.g., unauthorized transactions, perhaps some language for "failure of controls"), but this remains to be seen. An alternative would be to structure part of this tranche using a spread loss coverage, which, as the name implies, simply spreads the funding of any losses in this layer over time. It might include the use of financial or finite risk insurance, for instance.

3. **Tranche III—Catastrophe Capital Markets and Insurance Blend:** This coverage will apply from the second tranche upward to $1 billion (i.e., excess of coverage provided in Phases I and II above). One possibility will be to structure a modified CAT Bond program that blends debt financing for losses with some insurance risk transfer coverage. This concept is illus-

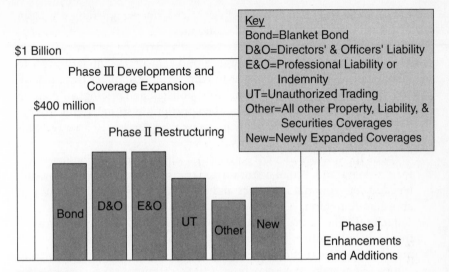

EXHIBIT 15.4 Blended Program—Insurance & Capital Markets

trated as Exhibit 15.4. Another is to apply options that are triggered by a profit downturn caused by a broadly defined class of operational losses.

The advantages to this blended program of tranches include:

- The end result will be a much broader risk transfer coverage than that provided by conventional programs (i.e., some broader coverage in the first tranche, but appreciably broader coverage in the second and third tranches given the higher coverage attachment points and receptiveness of providers to negotiate broader coverage at those levels).
- The program will provide balance sheet protection up to or in excess of $1 billion. If a CAT Bond structure is used, it might be structured to provide 20% risk transfer protection and 80% financing protection, both designed to offset drains on Tier I capital. An option structure might possibly be structured to achieve a similar result.

The disadvantages of this design are:

- The new catastrophe layer will involve significant additional cost, particularly relative to a CAT Bond or option structure.
- Aggregate limits may apply to the entire program versus current per loss or per policy limits of existing programs.
- These newer structures will require significant legal, tax, and accounting due diligence.

Action steps will include confirming the risk financing strategy and objectives, feasibility of approach, and economics:

1. **Tranche I:** Work with key insurance and reinsurance underwriters to blend existing coverages in order to reap better economics from risk diversification effects (i.e., combine risks, policies, and pricing) at levels up to $100 million or so. Determine the appropriate strategic role of captive self-funding at low levels (e.g., to expand "coverage" for technology outages, additional fraud risk).
2. **Tranche II:** New/broader coverages (e.g., supplement existing programs for external fraud, broad unauthorized transactions, rogue trades) using blended conventional insurance and reinsurance at "mid-levels" of risk above $100 million.
3. **Tranche III:** Blend capital markets with large loss insurance for catastrophe risks. Confirm the details of capital markets products. This will involve the construction of new catastrophe coverage for more truly complete coverage at levels above $200–400 million (i.e., use of CAT Bond-like structures to hedge the impact of large scale operational, market, and possibly even credit risks) (see Exhibit 15.5).

Indicative Structure: The structure will be structured as a multi-year deal, as follows:

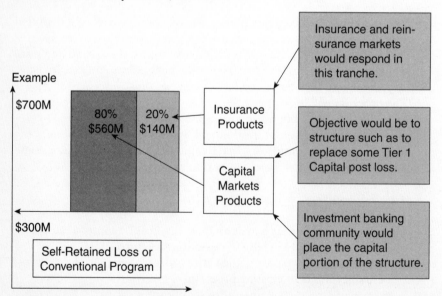

EXHIBIT 15.5 Insurance and Capital Markets Structure

A number of other considerations will come into play in order to complete the feasibility analysis and implementation of such a structure. They include:

- Consideration for protecting favored long-term insurance underwriter relationships.
- Assessing the impact of accounting/tax/legal considerations.
- Regulatory/client requirements for protection/evidence of coverage.
- Administration and service-required service elements (claims handling, inspection services) to be vended.

ANOTHER JOB FOR OPERATIONAL RISK DATA: SUPPORTING AN EVOLVING MARKETPLACE

Risk finance and insurance design and structuring are poised to become important parts of the endgame in operational risk measurement, monitoring, and management. Up until now, data and information were inadequate to support further evolution. Now, however, on the bank and corporate side, firms are developing data management systems, or at least at the outset collecting data manually for the purpose of monitoring and analyzing risk indicators, issues, incidents, and losses, and then benchmarking against losses in industry databases. The result is that these firms will be in a position to construct an operational risk profile that is essential for risk finance decision making. Armed with this information, they will be able to evaluate the strengths and weaknesses of existing and prospective financing options.

On the other side of the table, insurers and capital markets will have a need to understand the source of industry-wide and company-specific operational risks and losses before committing to funding a given client and market. Here, too, they will find the industry databases useful in understanding the dimensions of pooled industry (actuarial) risk characteristics within segments of the operational risk universe.

Thus, as data and analytics become more plentiful to both sides of the market, the market itself will be in a far better position than ever before to evolve toward new hedge and financing structures, whether in a physical or electronic marketplace.

CONCLUSION

Recently, insurers, brokers, and consultants have been promoting some new commercially available operational risk finance programs. The proof of their value will be in the policyholders' recovery rates on their operational risk losses and claims.[6]

Enhancing programs for risk finance and hedging does not simply mean expanding conventional insurance. It really means reengineering entire programs, using reserves and self-funding programs at a lower level of risk (perhaps below a $1–10 million range, depending on the size of the firm, or at an even higher level). It also entails the use of reinsurance, capital markets, and blended financial structures to provide much greater limit capacity, perhaps to as high as $1 billion or more, again depending on the size and exposures of a firm.

In combination, it means integrating these programs overall and using the new operational risk finance metrics, which will be the way to determine whether these programs are working and to what extent the old conventional programs are still relevant.[7]

LESSONS LEARNED AND KEY RECOMMENDATIONS

- Reengineer programs to optimize coverage and cost trade-off. But conventional insurance provides only a partial solution. Enhance risk financing through the use of effective alternative risk financing structures. Use self-insurance, captive, excess-of-loss reinsurance, credit, and capital markets to construct effective protection for expected, unexpected, and catastrophe operational risks (BP Strategy #17).
- Some strategic application of risk finance tools can certainly increase the odds of a more palatable hedge result for financial firms. That is, selective use of funded self-insurance, captive insurance companies, finite or funded deals intertwined as an overall risk finance program instead of, or as a supplement to, conventional insurance.
- As described in Chapter 14, there is a risk information value to insurance and risk finance. A blend of insurance, reinsurance, self-insurance, captives, and financial products may be needed; however, as described in this chapter, a firm's operational risks are fully priced and recognized in its cost structure, and ultimately included in the pricing of its own products and services. In most firms today, pricing does not yet consider operational risks, at least not explicitly.
- Finally, we must be mindful of the limitations of risk transfer. Let's say a firm has outsourced a part of its operations or even transferred the economic impact of a potential loss to an insurance company or the capital markets. If a loss occurs involving the company, its reputation will bear the brunt of the loss, even though a third party may bear the economic impact.[8]

CHAPTER 16

Economic Risk Capital Modeling

Allocation and Attribution

INTRODUCTION

We covered the various approaches to Risk Assessment (mostly qualitative) in Chapter 9, the data considerations (the operational risk data universe, databases, consortia, risk indicators) in Chapters 10 and 11, and then Risk Measurement and Analytic Building Blocks in Chapter 12. All of that background is important to factor into the development of an operational risk capital model, along with critical Risk-Adjusted Performance Measures (RAPM). For clarity, of course, each of the topics have been presented incrementally.

At this stage in the process, we are assuming that we have the results of those risk assessment and measurement exercises in hand and have been charged with seeking ways to develop operational risk capital models and performance enhancement systems from them. Thus, the endgame here is to cover a discussion of economic capital, along with attribution or allocation methodologies.

Suffice it to say that most economic capital systems are focused on answering the key question of whether the firm's capital is sufficient to support its risk profile and possible losses. Economic capital systems are most effective when used in conjunction with a performance measurement approach such as RAROC (risk-adjusted return on capital). The basic principle here is that high-risk activities will require more capital than lower risk activities in order to maintain a consistent level of balance sheet strength.

The best-managed companies already use some form of performance metrics to monitor and manage their business. Only a handful of these firms have moved on from that point, however, to weave in the allocation of the firm's capital to businesses based on their operational risk characteristics.

Thus, the first key component of the current state of best practice is to link economic capital models to performance measurement and management

> ## BP STRATEGY #18—APPLY ECONOMIC CAPITAL MODELS AND OPERATIONAL RISK-ADJUSTED PERFORMANCE MEASURES
>
> Use economic risk capital models and risk-adjusted performance measures (RAPM) to calculate, monitor, and manage the effect of operational losses on firmwide and business unit levels. Monitor capital structures on top-down and bottom-up bases. Embed the models and processes to drive strategic and tactical risk-based decisions firmwide. Work toward application of the models in product pricing.

systems such that there is a productive incentive applied for risk management. The second dimension of best practice is to integrate the analysis and calculation of capital for operational risks together with those for financial risks. So the ultimate goal here goes beyond simply the measurement of operational risk. Most risk-based capital systems are intended to position their users to make strategic and tactical business decisions based on a complete view of risk (market, credit, and now operational risk measurement as well).

The last segment of this chapter is a detailed discussion of Bankers Trust's groundbreaking operational RAROC approach, including its evolution, details of implementation, and lessons learned. It is included because of the industry's ongoing interest in our early work, and its continued relevance to recent industry developments.

ECONOMIC VERSUS REGULATORY CAPITAL MODELS

At the outset, it is important to differentiate between our discussion of economic capital and the regulatory capital discussions under way relative to the Basel Risk Management Committee. Although there is much to be said for a consistent approach to both economic and regulatory operational risk capital models, this has not always been practical with other risk classes and risk management models.

For one thing, regulators must apply consistency to their modeling components across a wide range of regions and firms, both from the perspective of size and business line composition. Unfortunately, too often the result of developing one standard is that this process forces modeling rigor to the lowest common denominator.

In contrast, the development of economic capital models is completely discretionary. These are management tools. They can be developed with as much or as little sophistication as the firm desires, depending upon its risk management needs. Thus, if the firm is seeking to drive the models from bottom up or top down, at a profit center or even a desk level, management has all of those options. One would certainly not expect this level of specificity to appear in regulatory models and regulatory capital requirements.

BENEFITS OF ECONOMIC CAPITAL MODELS AND PERFORMANCE MEASUREMENT

The most important benefit of economic capital models, when used in conjunction with performance measurement tools, is the leverage they provide in creating and supporting risk awareness and a risk aware culture over the longer term.

One of the unique aspects of operational risk is that there are literally hundreds, if not thousands, of loss scenarios that can be developed, all with different causative and contributory factors. Because of this vast spectrum, a risk practitioner is faced with the dilemma of how best to promote operational risk management throughout the firm. Do you simply choose a half dozen scenarios as your sound bites to get people's attention and hope that they catch on to all of the other scenarios that might take place? The answer is that you probably do, but the second question is how do you keep your audience's attention focused on the risk scenarios that you have chosen?

One way is by benchmarking your scenarios against other firms' losses from an external operational loss database. This approach is useful, but be forewarned that it is vulnerable to criticism. Skeptics in your audience will argue that you are describing someone else's losses, control environment, and management team, and it simply does not apply to your own. These are valid points, of course, but I would argue that the knowledge gained from that benchmarking exercise far outweighs its shortcomings, particularly if your organization does not have enough of its own large loss experiences to achieve statistical significance (thankfully).

Modeling can help us to get closer to a representative situation by focusing on a number, or series of numbers, that gets people's attention. This assumes, of course, that we are using representative data as input. For instance, these may include predictive variables from the business itself, loss experience or other observations from the firm itself, and characteristics of the management team itself. In the end, we are working our way toward a series of numbers. The fact is that it is those numbers that are what gets people's attention.

Clearly, risk-adjusted performance measures such as RAROC provide a number of strategic advantages. As noted, they help to determine whether the firm's capital is sufficient to support all of its risks. With the advent of operational risk models, firms will be in a better position than ever to answer this question when those models are used in conjunction with credit and market models. In addition, the process helps us to determine whether the firm can increase its returns without increasing its risks, or conversely reduce its risks without reducing its returns. From a performance assessment standpoint, they help to determine whether a specific activity or business is producing a reasonable return relative to its risk profile. From a risk mitigation perspective, the risks measured by the underpinnings of the RAROC approach helped to pinpoint areas requiring specific attention.

Following are the specific benefits that have come from economic capital and performance measurement models for operational risk:[1]

- They create and support a risk aware culture.
- They improve measurement of risk and risk costs (i.e., improved expense management).
- Along with enhancement of business line awareness toward operational loss potential and causative factors, they contribute observed actions toward refocusing control initiatives.
- They focus the business line's attention on open risk issues witnessed by the significant reduction in frequency and the duration over which the issues remain open (e.g., internal audit or regulatory issues).
- They position the firm to achieve enterprise-wide risk management (i.e., integration of market, credit, and operational risk management) by:
  - Expanding evaluation of new initiatives to include operational RAROC, a more wholesome analysis of the potential risk exposure representing a more efficient allocation of capital to the business lines.
  - Supporting ongoing integration of market, credit, and operational risk groups by developing a common language.
  - Supporting ongoing exploration of integrated risk finance, using insurance and capital markets tools, for integrated risks that transcend operational, market, and credit exposures.
- They improve risk recognition by business line managers and place greater focus on risk control.
- They result in risk finance cost savings (i.e., operational cost-of-risk has been reduced over time).

TOP DOWN VERSUS BOTTOM UP, AGAIN

We should pause a moment to visit the distinction between allocation and attribution in the capital sense. In order to do so, we should reference back to our discussion in Chapter 9, Risk Assessment, about top-down and bottom-up analysis. In essence, capital allocation is derived from a top-down capital calculation. In other words, under a capital allocation regime we will develop an overall estimation or calculation of capital for the entire firm on a broad level, then apply the best means for allocating that capital downward throughout the firm based on an appropriate risk profile.

In contrast, a capital attribution process is simply an extension of a bottom-up risk assessment or measurement approach. That is, we calculate risk values (i.e., the value at risk) on a product-by-product or unit-by-unit basis and aggregate risk values in a logical way to represent a firmwide view of risk. The result is that we will have completed a capital development process including capital attribution.

Undoubtedly, over the longer term, the best program will be a bottom-up, capital attribution approach. It will involve several key advantages over capital allocation. Some of those include greater accuracy at the profit center or business unit level and therefore greater relevance of the risk factors and variables to the line manager. Thus, the process will support both risk measurement and risk management.

The advantages of capital allocation, on the other hand, include the relative ease with which the program and calculation can be developed. That is, the analyst can work with aggregate values for the entire firm, whether they are aggregate representations of risk classes, loss scenarios, or simply a pooling of expected and possible losses for the entire firm. The process is simplified and streamlined. The disadvantage, however, is that its high level of simplicity keeps it somewhat removed from the line manager in terms of relevance of the individual variables and risk factors, and thus less useful to him or her on a day-to-day basis than a bottom-up line management tool.

CASE ILLUSTRATION

Operational Risk Capital Allocation—An Overview of Early Work at Bankers Trust

Bankers Trust has generally been credited with development of the first and most extensive attempt at integrating portfolio-level risk assessment, an operational loss database, use of risk factors, and statistical and actuarial modeling for operational risk. Many of the foundation concepts in Bankers Trust's Operational RAROC model have since been adopted by several other banks and promoted by consulting firms. Some have even attempted to lay claim to development of its operational value-at-risk measurement foundation (i.e., the statistical/actuarial/loss distribution risk measurement model described in Chapter 12). In addition, the Loss Distribution Approach to risk capital in discussion with the Basel Committee on Banking Supervision bears some striking similarities to its measurement foundation.

Operational RAROC Development

Development of the operational risk models at Bankers Trust (BT) was an evolutionary process. BT developed its first-generation operational risk measure as early as 1979 in the form of a percentage of expense approach. Reevaluation of that measure began in 1990. In early 1996, we introduced our first phase of a new generation of models that served to measure and allocate operational risk capital to BT business lines. They included two types of models for use in advancing operational risk management in the firm:[2]

- **Risk Measurement Model:** As described in Chapter 12, using the loss data gathered, we applied the Monte Carlo simulation to develop loss expectancies by our five risk classes and the firm as a whole.
- **Capital Allocation Model:** Using a broad array of risk factors (approximately 70), we allocated the firmwide risk capital to each of the firm's business lines and profit centers.

For our capital allocation model we engaged in additional work on new factor models using data specific to individual business lines in order to supplement our firmwide risk measurement model.[3]

The combination of these models brought to the table the value of a top-down portfolio approach toward firmwide and risk class-wide risk measurement at various levels of confidence (i.e., expected loss and outward to a 99% confidence level). In total, we had the benefit of a well-populated and information-packed loss distribution, combined with a representation of long-tail risk representation. When our allocation model was applied, we had the added benefit of a bottom-up factor-based model and representation of risk predictors that could also be quantified, traced, and trended.[4]

All of these dimensions were captured in our early stage data capture and management system for ease of data compilation, sorting, and analysis.[5]

Background Because of all of the more recent interest in approaches that bear similarities to our early work and approach, I have dusted off and elaborated on the following case overview of our early work on Operational RAROC. This section is based on an overview of our models. It was developed by Marta Johnson and me while at Bankers Trust for *Treasury and Risk Management Magazine* in 1997. It is provided courtesy of Deutsche Bank, which acquired Bankers Trust in 1999.

As an independent firm, the measurement and monitoring of risk were cornerstones of Bankers Trust's competitive strengths. With the development of a RAROC methodology for market and later credit risk during the 1970s and 1980s, Bankers Trust business lines used these risk management tools, including allocation of capital required, to make key strategic decisions about funding its businesses. For over a decade, since RAROC models were first implemented at BT, operational risk had been acknowledged as the third major component of the firm's risk portfolio. There never existed a rigorous framework with which to define, quantify, or allocate operational risk at Bankers Trust and at virtually all other financial service firms, however, until the development of our more sophisticated operational risk models.

In 1990, Bankers Trust's Chairman and CEO Charlie Sanford challenged the firm's risk specialists to answer the question, "What [was then] missing from BT's RAROC (risk-adjusted return on capital) models?" That question lead us to pioneer a series of projects that first created an inventory of long tail event risks (described briefly in Chapter 9, Risk Assessment Strategies). Then later in 1992 we initiated development of an elaborate model for analyzing operational risks under the name Operational RAROC.

As such, the impetus for investing in operational risk management systems was part evolutionary and part event-driven. It was evolutionary in response to underlying risk trends (e.g., exponential reliance on technology in the past two decades, greater product complexity, and dramatic increases in litigiousness globally) that have elevated operational risks significantly in the eyes of senior managers. On a broader level, the field of risk management has been evolving in response to the need to measure and manage operational risks more thoughtfully, thoroughly, and in a way that is consistent with other major risk classes, such as market and credit risks.

Part way into the process, development became event-driven. Early in 1994 Bankers Trust faced dissatisfaction and legal action from several customers regarding Leveraged Derivative products and services (i.e., customer disputes involving the structure and sale of derivatives by Bankers Trust and other financial services firms). All of this came to light shortly after work on the long tail event risks was expanded to include the analysis of operational risk. Clearly it raised the visibility of operational risk among all of the firm's senior managers and staff. The firm became much more intent on working to improve management information on operational risk in the wake of these high-profile events.

Elsewhere in the industry the experiences of other large, highly publicized losses elsewhere in the global financial services community (e.g., unauthorized trading, errors in hedging, pricing), as well as those of nonfinancial firms in the global market had already highlighted the potentially devastating impact of operational risk. The experiences showed that the result of an operational breakdown, at the extreme, could include the demise of a firm (e.g., Drexel Burnham Lambert and Kidder Peabody). In addition, senior management's memories of other banks' experiences with lender liability patterns in the late 1980s were still fresh and provided a viable backdrop against which to quantify, understand, and manage our own operational risks. There was concern that despite control systems and processes in place at the time, operational risk was not being recognized, measured, and managed as well as it could be due to the lack of a consistent and robust risk management framework. It was thought that as in the case of market and credit risk, such a framework could be designed to provide an incentive for managers to invest in the management of operational risk, with the objective of reducing the chance of the risk resulting in a loss, or particularly a sizable loss.

This combination of events and perspectives was powerful enough to build momentum for quantifying the firm's total global exposure to operational risk and, at the same time, develop a framework for reinforcing business line's responsibility and accounting by attributing capital based upon their operational risk profile. Thus, this elevated the requirement to quantify, allocate, and manage operational risk into one of the firm's top priorities. As with most projects, there were times when the development could have slowed or even stopped. The opposite happened: The pace of the project continued to accelerate, with its scope and depth expanding well beyond initial expectations.

Senior management was instrumental in supporting the allocation of resources required to develop Operational RAROC as an informational tool, and ultimately as a risk management tool. More importantly, they also supported the advancement of all of the RAROC capital allocations toward becoming part of the cost of capital charge for each business line, providing an expense to the profit and loss (P&L) of each based on the level of operational risk contributed to the firm.

Charlie Sanford had already requested that BT's risk management scenario analyses be expanded to the concept of "shocks" to include operational risk shock loss scenarios, thereby providing a more holistic analysis of the risks being faced. Thus, a key consideration for the project was to include operational risk in analyses used to determine the sensitivity of the firm's risk profile to an unexpected "shock" (e.g., an earthquake in Tokyo, the operational failure of a counterparty, a technology failure). Initially, the firm's operational risks were evaluated within the context of an analysis of long tail event risks (i.e., referring to the long tail of a probability distribution). We conducted interviews of senior management members and developed risk identification/mitigation techniques accordingly. This work provided the foundation for building a more robust infrastructure to perform operational risk management. A recognition along the way was that the evolution involved a nagging concern that even expected or "normal loss" risks (i.e., the body of the probability distribution) were not being measured appropriately.[6]

Operational RAROC Objectives   As with any project, the development of objectives is critical. Because there was already a risk measurement culture in place in the firm, along with existing RAROC objectives, we were able to leverage off of this foundation when developing the new operational RAROC component.

The development of our Operational RAROC models took us through the exploration and development of a variety of other program features that have become important components of an operational risk management program. We set out to develop, and place in active use, a firmwide risk management system for defining, quantifying, and attributing risk-based capital, and for providing directional underlying risk information on operational risk in its broadest possible sense, extending well beyond traditional insurable risk. So, in the end, our Operational RAROC effort became an important focal point of our operational risk management effort and supported features that served as an important foundation for our operational risk management program. It was far more than just a model.

Following is a summary of our key objectives:

- **Promote Active (Not Just Reactive) Risk Management:** Our models were to be developed with a view toward active risk management using both *directional risk predictors* (trends in underlying causative factors or indicators) and *observed risk* (loss experiences and known risk issues).
- **Enhance Risk-based Strategic Decision Making:** To develop a tool for understanding business operational risks on a business-specific basis and for making strategic risk-based decisions. To support strategic risk-based decision making by adding operational risk information to that of other (credit, market) risk classes.
- **Develop a Foundation for Better Informed Risk Finance and Insurance Decision Making:** To create linkages to risk finance that support more selective purchase of monoline insurance for cost savings (e.g., more intelligent self-funding applications) *and* the creation of blended programs that better reflect the risks being faced by the firm.

Strategies and Tactics In response, the key strategies used in developing Operational RAROC included:

- **Capital Adequacy and Allocation:** In response, we decided to model operational risk capital adequacy needs for Bankers Trust and develop an allocation system. We worked to develop a methodology for recognizing and measuring business operational loss potential and attributing risk capital, applying parameters similar to those used for market and credit risk capital (i.e., a one year time horizon; a 99% confidence level for risk analysis).
- **Support and Coverage for Control Environment:** We also decided to provide incentives for reducing operational risks and losses through

linkages with other control group issues/initiatives, including data capture from those groups and risk information reporting to business lines and control groups.

Some of the tactics applied involved the:

- **Construction of a Unique and Extensive Database of Operational Events From Numerous Organizations Globally:** Extensive global empirical loss data serves as a foundation for analytical modeling of the firm's loss potential at the 99% confidence level.
- **Directional Risk Information:** We gathered, analyzed, and disseminated consistent directional risk data for enhancement of the firm's control environment. With a focus on sources, rather than on symptoms of risk, we "mined" a vast array of operational risk data for use as factors, or risk "predictors." These included behavioral issues such as staff turnover, tenure, and training, as well as systems characteristics such as age, complexity, and support with which to allocate risk-based capital to each Bankers Trust business.
- **Risk Capital for Operational Risk Issues Outstanding:** We elected to allocate capital for outstanding risk issues, including but not limited to control and audit issues, and regulators' comments.
- **Senior Management Risk Reporting:** We introduced enhancements to existing business line performance measurement by setting the bar at different levels for businesses depending upon their allocated level of operational risk capital.

One of our key goals was to place operational risk management on a similar footing with market and credit risk management systems (in terms of risk quantification, risk profile analysis, capital allocation), and interface with all Bankers Trust business lines. We believed that it is equally important to promote proactive risk management tools for decision making at both corporate and business line levels. For instance, we believed that consistent and complete loss exposure information would add significant value when factored into priorities for investments set by line managers.

Hybrid Model Design and Implementation   As outlined in the discussion of models in Chapter 12, a truly optimal approach has not yet been identified for the industry. Each has its advantages and disadvantages. Depending on a firm's management objectives, a combination of model types may yield the best results. This was also our early conclusion at Bankers Trust given our aggressive goals. Thus in the end, we developed our operational RAROC framework and modeling process from a combination, or hybrid, of several of the approaches outlined above, attempting to represent the best features of each.

In getting started, we attempted to leverage off work that had already been completed in the market, or in the academic world. We were shocked to realize how little work was available that we could integrate into the Bankers Trust definition of operational risk. Frequently, the definitions of operational risk were viewed as too narrow, or focused on an aspect of operational risk that did not support our objectives. For example, some firms had been experimenting with valuing business operational risk using an expense-based system. But there are flaws in this approach: for example, what relation does expense have to the dimensions of risk, and does cutting costs reduce risk or increase it?

Flow charts and time studies can be developed to determine how many "hands" or systems are required to complete a transaction from start to finish. These approaches provide road maps for the controls that need to be reviewed or reconsidered. However, they do little to assist in quantifying the risks being faced by the business line.

We soon realized that we were onto something entirely new. We also realized that in order to satisfy our deliverables, we would have to start with a blank piece of paper and design the whole process, borrowing little from existing work. The advantage to this approach was that we were able to take a more strategic view of how we wanted to use the Operational RAROC components for other aspects of risk management, and we were not constrained by the assumptions of previous work.

Plan of Attack   With our key objectives in hand, along with key strategies, tactics, and the deliverables agreed upon, we put a plan in place for prioritizing resources to meet them within our set time frame. This resulted in the development of three major phases, each with major deliverables that enabled us to work concurrently on multiple objectives. These included:

1. Development of a loss database
2. Development of a risk measurement model
3. Development of an allocation model, with three subparts:
   a. Core Statistically-derived capital, and scorecard allocation model
   b. Development of risk issue tracking, and allocations
   c. Risk finance and insurance hedge allocation

Exhibit 16.1 summarizes our project worksteps. The following sections provide more detailed descriptions of our development and application of Operational RAROC.

Phase I—Development of the Loss Databases

Our internal and external databases were a key part of the foundation for risk measurement. We have already discussed database development

Our major project worksteps included actions to:
1. Define operational risks.
2. Conduct initial business line risk assessments.
3. Gather relevant internal and external operational loss data.
4. Refine the definition of operational risks.
5. Apply Monte Carlo simulation to develop loss expectancies.
6. Develop loss cause analyses/identify risk factors.
7. Gather risk assessment and risk factor or risk "predictors" data for all business lines.
8. Combine loss expectancies and risk factor or risk "predictor" analysis.
9. Complete risk-based capital allocation by business.
10. Update and repeat all data gathering and analysis on a regularly scheduled basis.

EXHIBIT 16.1   Operational RAROC Development: Primary Project Worksteps

extensively in Chapter 10, so we will not dwell on the topic any further here, with the exception of a few additional observations relative to our specific use for Operational RAROC.

Combining Proprietary (Internal) Losses and Expert Opinion   Some risks are difficult to quantify because the data are not publicly available, but to ignore them would significantly bias the overall estimate of business operational risk. One example is the cost of a technology failure. Today, a financial firm's exposure to operational risks through technology is huge, yet rarely do all the parties involved think of calculating the business impact (e.g., management and staff time spent analyzing the problem, the cost of developing "work arounds," and the cost of projects being delayed to solve the problem). For these types of risks, we chose to supplement the loss data with expert opinion on the potential exposure (i.e., the synthetic datapoints described in Chapter 12). Together, the combination was quite powerful. It enabled us to characterize the risk events with the frequency and severity distributions that both managers within the firm and industry experts had agreed upon, providing for a more wholesome array of risks being represented in the database. There may be critics who voice their objections over the use of "soft" datapoints. However, in recent years, operational risk managers have found this type of Delphi technique useful in sizing exposure to loss, particularly where datapoints are not readily available elsewhere.

External Losses and Relevance Rankings   We realized early on that not all losses would be relevant to our analysis and model and, for those that are relevant, not all would be equal in their importance to the analysis. To reflect this view, we developed a three-point scoring system in ranking the relevance of losses to be included. Those losses carrying a one ranking would be viewed as the most important or relevant to our business. We asked ourselves the questions: Did the loss occur in a financial institution? Did it occur in one of our business sectors? If the answer to these questions was yes, more than likely we included these losses in our top ranked category and included them in the analysis at full value. To the extent that the answer was no to either or both of these questions, we applied additional tests and ranked the losses in category two or category three. In any event, the losses in the second and third categories were included in our analysis database at discounted values, thereby diminishing their impact on the outcome of the analysis itself.

Phase II—Risk Measurement Model

In brief, we used severity and frequency distributions, along with sophisticated actuarial tools (including Monte Carlo simulations) to develop an aggregate distribution both on a portfolio basis and for each of the five risk categories. The resulting figures showed the amount of potential loss that could be expected for the firm overall (diversified) and in each of the five risk categories (undiversified). The distribution allowed for observation at a range of confidence levels, depending on the uses for the data. We used a 99% confidence level to be consistent with the theoretical framework used by market and credit RAROC and called the resulting number our "core" capital figure.

The total capital exposure was first derived in December 1995. In time, expansion of the database enabled us to refine the distributions for each risk class and for the total diversified capital. Trend analysis is conducted on the portfolio level representing a diversified view of the risk. Undiversified potential loss exposure was also trended and similarly used to highlight risk categories and specific types of risk whose exposure increases or decreases. For instance, the business lines required more specific trend analysis when they consider specific initiatives. (See the Actuarial and Loss Distribution method in Chapter 12 for a more detailed description of our risk measurement approach.)

In the early years of development, it became apparent that even though our loss database was growing on a weekly basis, we would not have enough data to support a bottom-up analysis and Monte Carlo simulation. It was clear that for the foreseeable period of time we would be constrained by the depth of our database. Thus, as described in Chapter 12, we were limited to producing a firmwide simulation by our five risk classes. It had been our intent from the outset to get to a point

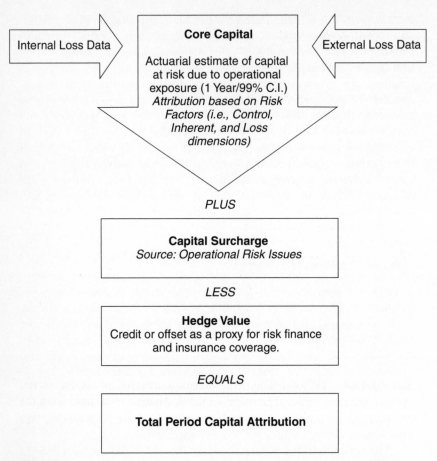

EXHIBIT 16.2 Component Parts of the Operational RAROC Attribution Model

of statistical significance in the data to be able to support a business line specific risk measurement model analysis and Monte Carlo simulation.

Our own experience certainly supports the current focus and need for the industry-wide efforts to build industry databases and loss consortia. Sufficient business-specific data will be essential to be able to support business line-by-line risk analysis.

Phase III—Scorecard Capital Allocation Model

Once again, because our limited data were unable to support bottom-up calculations by business, we were left to produce a top-down measurement model, together with a separate allocation model. In essence, this model was a scorecard system. There were three components to the allocation model: (1) statistically derived core capital, (2) risk management overlay, and (3) risk finance hedge. Following is a discussion of development and refinement of the allocation methodology. Exhibit 16.2 is a graphic depiction of the component parts.

Allocation of Statistically Derived Core Capital   How can businesses with dramatically different characteristics (e.g., check processing versus high-yield corporate finance) be compared with each other? This is a reasonable question, but one to which a reasonable answer had to be developed. Our methodology provided for relative ranking of the business lines against each other based upon the risk profiles of each. In early 1996, 20 risk factors or "predictors" were developed and applied in the model. Within two years there were nearly three times that number representing a more wholesome capture of the operational risks being faced by the business lines. Also, over time the focus of the model was refined further to be more prospective than retrospective. A richer analysis process of the internal and external loss database and a closer alignment with the project's objectives resulted in a rebalancing of the model. This shift in focus enabled us to feel more confident that the model took history into account, but also incorporated that facet of risk that is represented by the realization that "just because it hasn't happened here doesn't mean it couldn't."

Starting Point.   The loss events in the internal and external databases served as the starting point for determining the information to be used from the centralized data sources. Then two questions were asked: What types of information are predictors of control risk failures? In which risk category do the risks fall? If the centralized data sources gave us information for only one of the risk categories, say people risk, we knew this approach was not going to work. The information in the centralized data sources was analyzed against the risks that had appeared in the internal and external loss database. The risks were separated into each of the risk categories and "tested" against the loss events in the database to ensure a match between the reasons for the losses occurring and the information available from the centralized data sources.

The Components.   The methodology for developing the allocation of capital to the business lines, based on the level of operational risk they were contributing to the firm, was determined by the objectives of the project as outlined above. There are three main components of the allocation methodology, all of which stem from in-depth analysis of the events in the loss databases. To allocate the estimated capital number, a framework was developed within which we could categorize and rank the operational

Inherent Risk Factors	Control Risk Factors	Loss Experience Factors
Assess operational risks intrinsic to the business	Define operational risk dimensions over which management can exert influence	Loss frequency and severity histories by business
Inherent factors define the business; serve as exposure basis	Valuable for both active risk management MIS and for modeling	Incident tracking
Primarily used for modeling		
Examples:	*Examples:*	*Examples:*
Average transaction value	Turnover rates	Businesses' own loss experience by overall risk class
Number of employees	Training investments	
Number of system applications	Systems maintenance	Errors
	Business continuity status	Legal liabilities

EXHIBIT 16.3   Risk and Loss Indicators Application as Model Factors

risks that the business lines were taking. Our initiative resulted from a joint effort by the global risk management and internal audit teams, so that it benefited by borrowing risk analysis concepts from the audit function, such as inherent risk and control risk.

These concepts were combined with risk assessment methods and other concepts applied in risk and insurance management in the allocation of risk finance costs. The result was that the "core" capital figure was allocated using the three components—inherent risk, control risk, and loss factor—to rate the operational risks each division was taking (Exhibit 16.3 presents an illustration of the three categories). The first two categories have already been discussed in a general sense in Chapter 11, Risk Indicators.

1. **Inherent risk factors:** Those created by the nature of the business itself. They can be understood as the baseline risks associated with the choice of being in a particular industry or sector. The only way to change them is to leave the business, or change it dramatically by selling or buying a major component. Examples of inherent risks would be product complexity, product life cycle, level of automation, and the level of regulation, litigation, and compliance. The information gleaned on each division's risk factors was compared with that of each of the other business lines, and force-ranked on a relative scale.

2. **Control risk factors:** Those meant to highlight existing and potential areas of controlled weaknesses. These factors are controllable by management. Examples include staff turnover, level of product compliance training, age of technology systems, and the level of straight-through processing. Again, in our model the information gleaned on each division's risk factors was compared with that of each of the other business lines, and force-ranked on a relative scale.
3. The third component was our **loss factor.** It was a combination of the losses incurred by the business line and those losses in the external database that are relevant to the business. The internal and external losses were weighted at 80/20 providing for the bulk of the loss factor to reflect the business line's own loss experience. However, the external component provides a prospective view into the loss profile experienced by other firms in a similar business. This combination of prospective and retrospective losses enables both aspects to be taken into account in determining the allocation of capital to the business lines. Management can control the largest contributor to the factor since operational loss events can be monitored and steps implemented to minimize them.

The component scores for each division were weighted. The weighting reflects the project's objectives and was used in an attempt to achieve a balance between them. The core capital figure was allocated proportionally across the divisions, based on their total weighted score for overall operational risk.

Broader Application. Overall, this statistically-derived core capital part of the allocation methodology met our objective of risk ranking business lines against each other, even though the businesses were different. It served as a management tool to control the risk factors and internal losses: managers could reduce their overall capital charge by reducing their score on specific risk factors. We also used it to look more closely at the business lines and risk-rank them at a lower level.

In addition, the approach is representative of broader scoring methodologies that can be aligned with any top-down allocation model, whether it is quantitatively or qualitatively based.

Risk Management Overlay—Allocation of Risk Issues and Credits. A second feature of the allocation model was a ranking and scoring of outstanding risk issues and credits. Initially, we called this entire second component of the model our Operational Risk Issues Surcharge (ORIS) because it only included capital charges (i.e., disincentives). Over time, we expanded this part to include credits (i.e., incentives) and other features as well, and renamed it our Risk Management Overlay.

Operational Risk Issues Surcharge (ORIS). The surcharge issues themselves were representative of outstanding audit and regulatory issues. We developed an elaborate scheme of scoring the issues for relative severity, along with a menu of capital charges for the different characteristics of issues. We did not attempt to place a precise value on the individual risks embedded in the audit or regulatory finding, but we did attempt to track our relative scoring and capital charges to the classifications assigned by the auditors. That is, issues identified in a failed audit received a higher risk rating than those in a marginal audit, which in turn would receive a higher ranking than issues from an audit that received a "well-controlled audit" rating. In fact, we did not include any of the latter for the purposes of assigning capital charges. Other features of the issue scoring process included additional charges for issues that were past due.

It was essential to have a link between the record of the status of audit issues in the internal audit department and our operational risk group. This way, the most current status of an issue could be reflected in our operational RAROC model. Internal Audit maintained the official record on status. That is, if a business unit had questions about the status of an issue and its associated capital charge in the model, their question could only be resolved by the audit liaison responsible for their business.

Without question, this part of the model was not statistically based at all. On the other hand, it was one of the most important risk-sensitive features of the model. And it created enormous incentive for business units to clear outstanding issues. Some of our regulatory representatives noted on more than one occasion that they were particularly pleased with the incentives that this feature generated toward clearing outstanding audit concerns.

Expanding the Scope of Issues. As time went on, we worked to expand the scope of the operational risk issues surcharge. Our plan was to include other types of issues, such as technology, compliance, and legal aspects. A key determinant for inclusion was the need for a formal process and source for the information elsewhere in the firm. That is, we felt it important that operational risk be an independent unit that would track the ORIS issues identified, ranked, and scored from other sources and departments. Certainly, for instance, a firm could use issues identified and sourced in existing risk assessment programs as a feeder to this type of capital surcharge program.

Self-identified Issues. We also worked to develop incentives in this second major component of the model for issues that were identified by the business unit itself, rather than internal or external auditors. The feature involved a discount on issues that were self-identified, versus the charge that would be imposed if an auditor identified the issue. This way, a business had an incentive not only to address and clear issues than were known, but also to self-identify others at much lower capital charges that would have been ordinarily imposed if they were to later be identified by Internal Audit.

Risk Management Credits.   In time, we introduced the concept of granting capital credits for bona fide risk management investments by business units. These credits took the form of capital relief for businesses that were making measurable progress and investment. Examples of actions that qualified included upgrading their control infrastructures and their own decentralized operational risk management programs and holding productive risk management committee and team meetings that discussed, addressed, and took tangible action toward advancing the discipline of risk management in the business itself. Here too, we developed a menu of risk management hedge credits that were available to the individual business lines. The menu was made public such that the business units could work to attain these "extra credits." Introduction of this feature helped to balance the incentives and disincentives in the program overall.

As all of these features—expanded scope of types of issues, self-identified issues, and risk management credits—came together, we began to refer to this second part of the model as our Risk Management Overlay. This name reflected the fact that it was representing a broad range of risk and risk management issues, incentives, and disincentives, albeit not necessarily statistically based.

Certainly, a statistician would take issue with this second component of our model. One could argue that we were being redundant in this section relative to the statistical representation of the first model component. Certainly we saw the component as adding extra conservatism to the model. We did not see this as a problem in an economic capital model, since the entire program was designed as an internal management tool, and the feature was applied consistently to all of our business units. Certainly, this redundancy would be more of a concern if the component were to be built into a regulatory capital model, thereby placing a redundant burden of capital on industry.

Risk Finance Hedge Component   The third major component of our operational RAROC model was the inclusion of a risk finance and insurance hedge. This component was developed in recognition of the economic benefit of our risk finance and insurance programs. There should be no question these programs provide an economic benefit. Otherwise there would be little point in maintaining them, other than to meet regulatory insurance requirements.

In fact, as we discussed in Chapters 12 and 14, with some investment of time and effort on a routine basis, the firm can track the precise benefit of these programs over time using a calculation called cost of operational risk (COOR).

At Bankers Trust, we calculated our COOR over a rolling ten-year period. We then determined the percentage of recovery that our risk finance and insurance programs produced against our own universe of operational losses over ten years and applied this percentage as an offset to our quarterly capital calculations. For argument sake, let's say that, consistent with the industry analysis in the risk finance and insurance chapter, the offset amounted to 25% of historical operational losses. In this scenario, the 25% figure will be applied as an offset to operational capital as well.

In our model, we would apply a percentage to the entire firmwide calculation of capital and distribute the benefit proportionally to each business unit, consistent with its individual allocation of capital.

As one can see, this portion of the model was not particularly risk sensitive in and of itself for an individual business unit, other than the fact that it tracked proportionally to the unit's core capital allocation. We believed, however, that it was a reasonable representation of the reduction that should be shown for the value of these programs.

Interaction with Business Units and Other Corporate Groups

We tried to develop a framework to analyze operational risks within Bankers Trust and influence, in a productive risk management way through incentives, the behavior of our business line management teams.

Beginning with the early development phase in 1990–1992, there had been a considerable amount of ongoing interaction and cooperation forged with a wide variety of groups within Bankers Trust. The groups we interacted with most closely included the business lines themselves, business line controllers, business line self-assessment groups, Internal Audit, Regulatory Compliance, Legal, Credit, property management, technology risk management, risk finance, business continuity planning, human resources, and corporate controllers.

Risk measurement and modeling discussions often fall short when it comes to interaction outside of the risk management department. In our case, we worked hard to promote extensive interaction with others. In particular, all Internal Business Lines were involved with us in the gathering of uniform risk factor or "predictor" and loss data, and all corporate center internal control groups were polled to help identify risk factors and issues pertaining to all business lines or specific to a particular business.

Each group was responsible for specific aspects of risk, with some groups having a broader scope than others (Internal Audit versus business line self-assessment). There was not a significant amount of overlap (if any) among the groups, as their charters were sufficiently varied to prevent duplication. Each group approached operational risk from a slightly different standpoint resulting in a multifaceted profile for each risk being evaluated.

Numerous important behavioral lessons were learned from the interaction and are worthy of note for constructing effective operational risk modeling and capital adequacy systems. Among them, from design through implementation we found ourselves having to battle the tendency of business line representatives to reduce their capital allocations as a prime objective, in contrast to, and at the expense of, more primary risk mitigation objectives. In other words, there was a tendency to practice cost management over risk management. But through a combination of model approaches—a statistical/actuarial and scenario-based measurement approach blended with risk factor and issues-based methods—we were able to make good headway toward satisfying both objectives of risk measurement with those of providing incentive for productive risk management behavior.

Management Reporting

One of our program goals included development and implementation of operational risk management information for use by the business lines. The success of the project hinged on the use of the operational risk management information by senior management and the business lines in their measurement of performance, business decisions, and proactive risk management. From the beginning of its rollout in the first quarter of 1996, the business line allocation of Operational RAROC was reported in the management books and records of the firm. Our capital allocations were used to measure the performance of the business lines on a risk-adjusted basis and to determine where they were running compared with the hurdle rate set by the Chairman and CEO. Operational RAROC was a component in the budgeting process, and this required business lines to discuss with us their goals and strategic objective for the following year and beyond.

The process produced both business line and high-level management reporting for our management committees, the Board of Directors, and specific reports for the business lines themselves. To be proactive, management must be able to ascertain what their risk "levers" are so they can take steps to improve them. Our reports were designed accordingly.

The array of reports and graphs was too extensive to include samples of all of them here. Following is an outline of some of the reports produced:

- A risk indicator and factor scorecard by business and profit center
- Trend lines and graphs of key factors over time

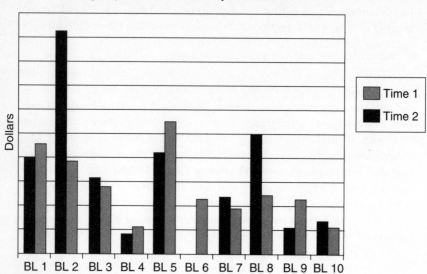

Average Operational RAROC by Business Line

EXHIBIT 16.4   Operational RAROC Capital Allocated by Business

- A summary of risk issues and investments included in the Risk Management Overlay along with surcharges and credits
- A listing of important business line losses included in the loss factor
- Loss factor graphs
- Tables and graphs of firmwide capital over time
- Business line and profit center-specific capital allocations over time
- Complete descriptions and rationale for all factors used
- A summary of the key losses, factors, or issues having a major influence in the current period
- Interpretative observations and risk management recommendations based on trends and current period results
- An outline of current period refinements to the model

For instance, Exhibit 16.4 is a high-level relative ranking of business lines provided to management with a view of how the businesses were performing on a risk-adjusted basis relative to one another over time. These types of charts would frequently prompt questions regarding the risks being run by one business relative to another.

Challenges and Solutions

As noted, our pre-rollout development phase spanned nearly five full years (1990–1995) during which time we were experimenting with internal risk assessment and risk ranking approaches, gathering loss data from internal and external sources, gathering internal exposure data for causative factor analysis and risk factors/predictors, and pilot testing various risk capital methodologies. We continued to develop and refine the project throughout the rollout phase, beginning in the first quarter of 1996.

Once the firmwide total risk capital figure was calculated using the agreed-upon methodology, rollout to the business lines began with the risk-based capital being allocated to the broadest divisional or business line level. We implemented an ongoing refinement of the allocation methodology as our rollout continued and additional data became available. In essence, then, we were in a position to provide more meaningful risk management tools to the business lines.

Some of the major challenges encountered in the initial implementation of Operational RAROC included:

- Initial project funding (always a challenge on projects, of course)
- Lack of initial focus and attention by business line managers, which is a common risk management challenge due to the inherent infrequency of large operational losses (i.e., how to gain attention to loss *potential* where *losses* have not yet occurred)
- Extremely limited number and scope of loss information impeding the ability to achieve statistical significance for analysis and forecasting
- Inconsistent risk data for relative risk ranking of business lines
- Qualified permanent staff (versus staff that was on short-term assignment) since the quantification and allocation of operational risk capital to business lines was relatively new
- Preconceived notions about definitions and data availability
- The type of statistical analysis that should be conducted (e.g., the potential for extensive correlation and regression analysis for each risk category)

Probably the most significant single hurdle for the effort was determining the most credible way to quantify the firm's global exposure to operational risk, while also supporting an active risk management agenda. Since a core competency of the Bankers Trust staff was its quantification skills, the firm's culture required a sophisticated, rigorous approach to the quantification of risk. There were multiple levels of risk that needed to be quantified in order to capture the attention of management. They included:

- Total firmwide exposure on a portfolio basis
- Total exposure for each business line

- Contribution of each risk predictor to the total and business line exposure
- Use of analytical skills consistent with those used in the existing market and credit risk models

When we began, the expectation was that the nature of operational risk did not lend itself to the type of rigorous analysis that can be performed on market, or even credit, risk data. The challenge was to find an approach that would lead to the quantification of each aspect of operational risk listed above and provide information for proactive management of the risks by business line managers.

The approach we took was to:

- Define operational risks so they encompass all phases of the business process—from origination to execution and delivery—spanning the front, back, and middle office.
- Define risk categories that correspond to responsibility for managing and mitigating risks by aligning them to resources (e.g., sales and marketing technology, human resources staff, etc.).
- Combine the risk categories and business process to create a two-dimensional system for categorizing risk with no overlap of risk categories or business processes.
- Develop a database of loss events that have been experienced by our own firm, as well as other firms.
- Develop frequency and severity distribution for the losses as a whole (diversified) and for each risk category (undiversified).

Gauging Relative Success

The benchmarks we applied to gauge our success included: (a) the construction of a credible and defensible model to calculate operational risk capital, (b) a defensible allocation process, (c) benchmarking against other financial service firms, and (d) acceptance by regulatory examiners. Following is a discussion of how we performed against these benchmarks:

- Initial capital *calculation* was completed following an intensive period of data gathering, model development, and vetting. Senior managers and management committees accepted results firmwide during the first quarter of 1996.
- Initial capital *allocations* were completed during the first and second quarters of 1996 and were under discussion with business line managers at least quarterly thereafter. Even though there had been many lively debates with individual internal business lines over relative details, there was agreement on the benefits and objectives of

the initiative, and on the framework for the allocation methodology. There was concurrence among senior business line managers that the process and methodology represented an important component in enterprise-wide risk management.

■ Operational RAROC was a tool used by senior business line management to evaluate the performance of a particular business and when considering a shift in business strategy.

Not only did Operational RAROC aid BT in quantifying its total exposure to operational risk and develop a framework within which to allocate related capital, but at the time implementation of the program brought the firm closer than any other financial service firm to practicing enterprise-wide risk management (integration of market, credit, and operational risks). It put the firm's managers in the unique and advantageous position of being able to make strategic decisions based on their "total risk" profile and risk-adjusted returns. Risk mitigation efforts became more focused and resources were redirected as needed. In addition, at a corporate level, by considering "total risk" exposure, more intelligent decisions could be made about risk finance alternatives, including, but not limited to, the purchase of insurance for operational risks.

■ ■ ■

RECONCILING TOP-DOWN MODELS

As noted at the outset of this chapter, top-down and capital allocation models harbor a number of challenges. Both types of models are complex, of course, but allocation models are easier to implement on a relative basis. In exchange for that convenience, however, a number of challenges emerge in implementation. These include the challenge of maintaining relevance to the business lines, recognizing tail risk at a line management level, and the "zero sum game".

Following are some observations about how to deal with the issues at hand.

Relevance to the Business Units

Many firms will attempt to apply one or two factors to allocate capital for a given business line. Unfortunately, all of the complexities of operational risk cannot logically be boiled down to one or two factors. As a result, models striving for this level of simplicity will suffer from a lack of relevance to line managers and their staff. An alternative is to use more factors and variables, thereby making the model more complex, or to strive for a reconciliation between the top-down calculations and bottom-up risk assessment.

Recognizing Tail Risk at a Line Management Level

One advantage of top-down models is that there is a built-in diversification effect when capital is calculated for the entire firm versus business lines individually. Simply stated, independence of events is assumed, so the calculation for the whole is less than the sum of calculations for the individual parts.

Therefore, top-down economic capital models cannot be applied in a vacuum. One way to communicate the results is to show risk-based capital calculations against a backdrop of considered business line–specific operational risk assessment.

One way to do this is to contrast MFLs (maximum foreseeable losses) to economic capital allocations as part of their broader risk management efforts, with the better line managers implementing self-assessment or independent risk assessment programs by asking themselves "What is the worst operational loss scenario for our business?" Resultant loss scenarios will be translated into both risk mitigation strategies and economic MFL estimates. Traditionally, MFLs have been used by engineers to describe the extreme loss potential for a structural failure or extreme case of fire or natural disaster.

When applied by the individual business units and for operational loss exposure classes, MFL examples might involve a large-scale failure of controls, unauthorized activities that result in a market or credit loss scenario, large-scale legal liability allegations, technology failure, large-scale external natural disasters, and related or unrelated business disruptions. Large-scale operational losses have been tracked industry-wide for all business sectors in recent years and suggest that when viewed independently any single business unit could conceivably face a loss potential well in excess of $100 million or $200 million. In some cases the number could approach $1 billion. When viewed at a 99% confidence level equivalent, these scenarios represent an *undiversified view* of operational risk by business. In contrast, when analyzed as part of a total diversified firm, the individual business will benefit in the form of a lower diversified capital allocation.

The Zero Sum Game

Related to these differences between capital attribution and capital allocation, it is important to consider the "zero sum game" problem. To recap, the distinction we make is that capital attribution is deemed to be a bottoms-up type of capital calculation. That is to say, capital is derived for each trade, transaction, or portfolio individually, and then aggregated in order to arrive at a total capital figure for the subject at hand (item or items being measured). Conversely, the capital allocation process implies that capital is derived for a portfolio, and then distributed among all the units in a portfolio or in an entire firm.

The challenges that a capital allocation process presents are many. One of the most frustrating ones for a business line manager is the notion of a zero sum game. That is, as long as we are dealing with a fixed sum of capital, we force individual business lines into a collection of capital winners and losers. For one portfolio or business to improve upon its risk profile, or "win," thereby reducing its allocation of capital, other businesses are forced to "loss," or pick up the slack for their colleagues' reduction in capital, with increases of their own. Thus, the latter groups "lose."

The system works as long as there is a clear distinction between the relative high-risk and low-risk units or businesses being measured. And even then, it works best when we are measuring relative rankings for a specific point in time. Problems begin to show up, however, as soon as we begin to look at how the units are performing on a relative basis over time.

Imagine yourself as the business manager, or member of a team, who has been working hard to hold the line on your risk profile, as described by their collection of risk indicators. You feel a justified sense of accomplishment by maintaining your aggregate risk indices at a low level, and in actuality, at levels lower than most other businesses in the firm. Now, imagine your frustration, at best, upon learning that one of the other businesses in the firm has made only marginal improvement in its already high level of risk indices, but that their improvement causes your business's capital to rise.

On the one hand an advocate of competition might argue that the situation would press both businesses to strive for better results. The reality, however, is that the zero sum turns out to be the capital allocation system's undoing. That is, the fixed sum of capital eventually causes both business managers to become critical of the system.

The zero sum game problem, therefore, presents one of the strongest arguments for bottom-up models, and capital *attribution* over top-down, capital *allocation* models.

BOTTOM-UP MODELS

Because of these challenges, the next wave of economic capital models will focus on attempting to find a solution to the bottom-up modeling challenge. For instance, the West LB case in Chapter 12 serves as an illustration of calculating the value at risk at a very detailed, individual business process level. A true bottom-up model would take values such as these and, developing respective VAR figures for all corners of the organization, ultimately drive a comprehensive value at risk for the entire firm.

In our own experience with early models we found the data problem to be one of the major challenges in using statistical and actuarial models. That is, it would have been our first choice to get one step closer to bottom-up model development than we did by developing calculations at the "middle tier." That is, to the extent that we would have had sufficient data to complete our calculations business by business, we would have been developing much more relevant figures for individual line managers. The financial services industry may well be close to realizing this development with the advent of loss data consortia. If those efforts are successful, there will be a far greater chance of having sufficient data to at least support middle tier model development.

At the time of this writing, in mid-2001, some firms, in consultation with the Basel risk management committee, seek to advance the development of "middle tier" models. We explore early model proposals in Chapter 17 on regulatory developments. Early proposals are struggling with the issue of relatively blunt calculations at the middle tier. They too will require sufficient data by the business line in order to support advancement in sophistication.

CONCLUSION

Many of the risk measurements in modeling advances discussed in Chapter 12 will have limited use unless they are integrated into a RAPM program. The combination of more sophisticated measurement, coupled with incentives and disincentives built into the performance management program, can yield very powerful results. One of the tricks, of course, is to build the RAPM measures such that they motivate individuals to manage risk, not capital.

Recent developments in operational risk management have raised the standard for all firms. Unfortunately, in today's society one cannot lose sight of the potential for criticism and liability of senior officers and directors if they do not sponsor the exploration of these more advanced techniques.

We saw our Operational RAROC methodology as representing a major breakthrough in the evolution and advancement of the risk management discipline. When coupled with our tested and proven risk measurement and monitoring methodologies for market and credit risk, we were in the best position ever to advance the measurement, management, and finance of business risks on an enterprise-wide, total, or "holistic" risk basis. Each business line's performance was measured on an adjusted integrated risk basis, supporting the firm's objective of efficiently allocating capital.

LESSONS LEARNED AND KEY RECOMMENDATIONS

Economic Capital Models:
- Use economic risk capital models and risk-adjusted performance measures (RAPM) to calculate, monitor, and manage the effect of operational losses on firmwide and business unit levels. Monitor capital structures on top-down and bottom-up bases. Embed the models and processes to drive strategic and tactical risk-based decisions firmwide. Work toward application of the models in product pricing (BP Strategy #18).
- Operational RAPM holds infinite promise. Breakthroughs in risk analytics and performance measurement are just beginning to emerge, with some anecdotal success stories and pockets of uses. Unfortunately, one cannot ignore the downside either. Keep in mind the potential for creat-

ing the wrong incentives. Also, don't lose sight of the risk of creating "analysis paralysis." Effective risk management is difficult. Creating incentives and changing behavior in a productive way is difficult. Be mindful of the tendency to take the easy path toward analysis and measurement in the absence of using those measures and results to enhance management. That last mile is often the most difficult, but the most important.

- A model (in the economic capital management sense versus regulatory capital) can be any design or construct that assists in decision making about the management of operational risk. Because operational risk is so difficult to quantify, even a very basic model can help to add value to the topic. This can be invaluable for maintaining attention to the subject firmwide and maintaining an operational risk-aware culture.

- Getting to a capital number is of considerable value for estimating and communicating the potential downside of operational risk as a whole, or by an individual risk class as a whole. Capital calculations should be developed by risk class and business type.

- Hybrid economic risk capital models can be developed using a combination of the modeling and analytic techniques. By combining the positive features of the various models, one can develop a more responsive hybrid overall that meets the needs of the firm for providing both a view of potential risk and loss, as well as the basis for risk management incentives.

- Risk-based capital allocation programs must be responsive to changes in risk profile, control structures, and risk management investment. Managers and teams want to see results from their efforts and investments. A model that is responsive will reinforce productive risk management behavior. Nothing will create nearly as much disillusionment with a risk capital program as one that is unresponsive or counter-intuitive to bona fide efforts and investment in risk reduction and mitigation.

- Beware of model behavior that creates incentives for _capital and cost_ management versus _risk_ management.

- Beware of the zero sum problem in capital allocation systems. All things being equal, improvement in the risk profile of one unit should not cause an increase in capital allocation to other units. This phenomenon can wreak havoc with your capital allocation program. Let business line numbers float independently or use a corporate "plug" number to fill the gap.

- Bottom-up capital attribution programs can be useful but require commitment and data. The amount of benefit gleaned from these programs may not always be in direct proportion to the amount of commitment, effort, and analysis committed to making them work. Beware of reaching the point of diminishing marginal returns.

- The risk measurement and economic capital model should be managed by a function independent of the business units and Internal Audit.

CHAPTER 17

Regulatory Capital and Supervision

INTRODUCTION

As this book is being finalized in late-2001, the debate seems over how best to handle the concept and details of minimum capital requirements and bank supervision of operational risk seems certain to rage on indefinitely. At this stage, any discussion between bankers and regulators about *whether* there is a significant enough impact on industry capital is misplaced. The debate has never been about *whether* there will be a capital charge, but instead, it has been about *how much* is reasonable, and whether the charge has already been captured in credit or market capital requirements.

There has been much attention, discussion, and general debate in recent years over the subject of the regulatory community's official position on operational risk. For the most part this discussion has taken a productive course and has reflected a fair amount of thoughtful reflection and interaction between the banks and regulators.

It appears clear that at the outset financial services firms will be facing a charge, albeit for most banks a relatively blunt one, with little responsiveness to underlying risk and risk control characteristics. This is despite frequent references to the three pillars of the New Basel Capital Accord from the Basel Committee on Banking Supervision: (I) minimum capital requirements, (II) the supervisory review process, and (III) market discipline. Once again, as we have seen in other areas of risk (market and credit), much of the challenge has been left with the banks to devise and propose a convincing risk-sensitive approach for regulatory consideration.

Although most of the attention has been focused on quantitative modeling techniques, more recently in 2001 the Basel Committee began to propose a qualitative balance to the regulatory discussions. The concept of Qualifying Criteria for the various measurement options has been introduced, along with a companion document that attempts to attribute definition to Sound Banking Practices. In concept this latest attempt at balance begins to track with industry best practices on operational risk.

In this chapter we explore the relative positions expressed during the course of the debate by both the industry and the regulatory community, some of the formal proposals at the time of this writing, and then provide some independent perspective. It is not productive to dwell on an up-to-the minute status of the current proposals in this forum given that they will undoubtedly continue to evolve over the coming months and years, and thus commentary here will become outdated. Thus this chapter is intended to provide a more broad and, hopefully, more lasting perspective on the subject.

Portions of this chapter are based on "Operational Risk Management and Capital Adequacy,"[1] written by myself and Matt Kimber in 2000. Many of the issues raised in that report remain relevant to the discussion today. It has been supplemented and updated, of course, to reflect more recent developments.

THE REGULATORY DEBATE

Whether a firm chooses to involve itself fully in the industry discussion on regulatory capital for operational risk, or simply monitor the discussions, it must be vigilant toward developments in order to balance the impact of any new charges on its own financial structure. No firm will want to be thrust in the position of having to maintain a level of capital over and above what it deems reasonable. Failure to monitor and manage one's regulatory position can leave a firm in a disadvantageous competitive position.

It is critically important, however, that one not lose sight of the fact that regulatory requirements and capital comprise but one facet of the management of operational risk overall. Because of the inevitable and impending inclusion of operational risk capital charges in the overall regulatory capital adequacy framework, there has been an inordinate amount of time spent on

---

BP STRATEGY #19—MONITOR THE EMERGING REGULATORY CAPITAL AND SUPERVISORY ENVIRONMENT AND POSITION ACCORDINGLY

Participate in regulatory discussions and debate. Monitor the evolution of requirements from the Basel Committee on Banking Supervision, as well as regulatory interpretations and actions on a local level. Monitor the emerging operational risk regulatory capital guidelines and options. Ensure that economic risk capital models are in sync with regulatory model developments. Position accordingly: Optimize capital models and the balance sheet.

the regulatory debate relative to other operational risk management strategies. This dedication of time is certainly understandable and warranted provided, however, that it is temporary.

ORM MYTH: AN OPERATIONAL RISK CAPITAL CHARGE IS ENTIRELY UNREASONABLE

The impact of operational risk and losses to date, industry-wide, is difficult to hide.[2] As noted in Chapter 3, based on our years of actual industry loss record-keeping ($15 billion annually), operational risk-related financial services losses have been extrapolated to have cost financial service-related entities between $45 billion and $150 billion annually over the past 20 years, depending upon how aggressive one's view may be.

With these figures in mind, any debate between bankers and regulators about whether there is a significant enough impact on industry capital must be misplaced. This is why it is no longer a question of *whether* there will be a capital charge, but rather how much is reasonable. There is also a need to confirm that the capital is not being double-counted in other calculations.

Many are becoming concerned that regulatory capital has distracted banks from the primary issues. Speaking from his personal view rather than his official capacity, one regulator expressed the view that because of the operational risk measurement challenges, much of the operational risk regulatory focus might be more appropriate under the supervisory pillar of the Basel guidelines versus the capital pillar. That is to say, for lack of a better approach, a simple charge may be appropriate so that bankers can get on with the business of *managing* risk. Thus, we may soon be focusing more on *risk management* best practices (i.e., ways of influencing productive risk mitigation behavior at the business unit level) than on the current debate over *measurement* best practices (i.e., which model to choose). Although many bankers might dispute the use of a simple charge, few would argue with the notion of getting on to the business of managing risk. That would be the best result.

There have recently been many speeches given and articles written by some of the most progressive thinkers, both in academia and the financial services industry, about operational risk management and capital adequacy, a trend that has been continuing over the past ten years. The flow has only intensified in the wake of the Basel Committee's releases (notably its paper *A New Capital Adequacy Framework,* issued in June 1999, and later its Consultative Document simply entitled *Operational Risk,* issued in January 2001).[3]

What could be added to this ongoing, and some may say contentious, debate? Before we leap to a discussion on risk capital and which methodology makes the most sense, it is essential for a firm to consider what it is trying to accomplish. For example, how important is it to derive a regulatory risk capital number if there is no process for using it to drive people toward effective risk management in their day-to-day business behavior? The obvious answer, of course, is that the capital will provide a financial cushion in the event of loss. But what about risk management value? The largest firms will, in all probability, address motivation with their economic risk capital systems, but what about smaller firms whose only involvement with risk capital will be in the regulatory context?

We certainly observed both the best and worst effects of incentives in capital systems during the course of our hands-on operational risk work during the past decade. Thus, in order to answer these questions, we must delve a little deeper into some of the objectives of a regulatory operational risk capital approach. In addition, we will discuss some of the pitfalls together with the advantages and then progress to a discussion about possible outcomes of the regulatory debate.

OPERATIONAL RISK: BACKDROP TO TODAY

The international banking community whipped itself into a frenzy over capital requirements for operational risk beginning around 1998. This has gone so far that it now seems apparent that some institutions have come full circle in their strategic thinking about operational risk, what that means to their institution, and how they could go about quantifying it in a way that suits their culture. It has been very interesting to observe the diverse approaches that have evolved over such a short period of time.

For a few the pace of this evolution has been driven by an insatiable industry desire to understand and develop risk management concepts, terminology, and tools. As of 2000, however, the emphasis had shifted almost completely from economic capital to regulatory capital. Clearly it has been regulatory pressure and the threat of regulatory capital that have caused most banks to look at risk measurement in the first place.

One result has been that some risk practitioners have been charged with the task of constructing the quantification piece, in various guises, without first locking down hands-on risk management. This has tended to result in top-down approaches and the risk of greater emphasis on *capital* management than on *risk* management. For others it has been just the reverse: they have started with a granular look at the business process and where their operational risks might lie and have subsequently moved toward a quantification process.

More recently, industry representatives became intent on ensuring that any economic capital models that they developed would first and foremost include the features and factors of regulatory proposals in order to avoid duplication of effort and leverage any existing work being developed.

In a number of regions it has been impressive to observe the openness, cooperation, and unity between industry professionals, industry bodies, and regulators. This is refreshing in today's "margin squeezing" environments, where any potential marketing angle or competitive advantage is zealously guarded. The need for information, and the problematic progress associated with setting up an operational risk framework, however, have provoked this healthy industry response. Formal and informal panels, discussion groups, and industry forums have sprung up that actively promote the dissemination of new ideas—and indeed to stress-test them intellectually.

One cannot help but observe that the hastily formed alliances appeared somewhat akin to warring tribes banding together to fight a new and common foe. Let's hope that the cooperation continues, although these groups must be careful not to promote cliques, as this endangers the creativity that is in evidence today.

THE REGULATORY PERSPECTIVE

Operational risk and regulatory capital have been around, in separate conversations, for some time, but most formal papers that have been issued by the regulatory bodies have merely committed to an *intention to implement* a structure for capital adequacy for operational risk as a separate risk class. The Basel Committee, although not a supervisory body, has been providing the industry with regulatory Best Practice guidelines and standards since 1975 and, for some time, has been paving the way for an additional risk class to be implemented into the supervisory framework. For example:

> *Banking supervisors must be satisfied that banks have in place a comprehensive risk management process (including appropriate board and senior management oversight) to identify, measure, monitor, and control all other material risks and, where appropriate, to hold capital against these risks.* (Principle no. 13 of the 1997 Basel Core Principles for Effective Banking Supervision)

New Capital Adequacy Framework

The "New Capital Adequacy Framework" issued in June 1999 by the Basel Risk Management Committee discusses a range of topics. Among them, it introduces the three pillars of its new capital framework: (I) minimum capital requirements, (II) a supervisory review process, and (III) effective use of market discipline.[4] The following quotes referenced on their website *(www.bis.org.com)* more than adequately explain the Committee's position at that time:

"However, the growing significance of these other (operational) risks has led the Committee to conclude that they are too important not to be treated separately within the capital framework."

"The Committee also proposes to develop an explicit capital charge for other risks, principally operational risk, and is exploring practical ways in which this could be done."

"Furthermore, the new framework stresses the importance of bank management, developing an internal capital assessment process, and setting targets for capital that are commensurate with the bank's specific risk profile and control environment. This internal process would then be subject to supervisory review and intervention where appropriate."

The Consultative Document

In January 2001, the Basel Committee on Banking Supervision released its Consultative Document (supporting document to the New Basel Capital Accord), simply entitled *Operational Risk*. As of mid-2001, this document was the latest official word from the regulators.

In the Consultative Document the Committee affirmed its proposal that the New Basel Capital Accord would "encompass explicitly risk other than credit and market." They noted that under the 1988 Accord, the capital buffer related to credit risk implicitly covers these risks. The document goes on to outline a series of other significant items:[5]

- The capital charge for other risks should include a range of approaches to accommodate the variations in industry risk measurement and management practices.
- The Committee is focusing the capital charge on operational risk.
- In framing its proposals, the Committee has adopted a common industry definition of operational risk, namely: "The risk of direct or indirect loss resulting from inadequate or failed internal processes, people, and systems or from external events." They note that legal risk is included, but strategic and reputation risks are excluded.
- They note that conceptually the capital charge for operational risk is intended to cover the unexpected loss portion of the loss distribution. However, the Committee proposes to calibrate the capital charge based on expected and unexpected losses but allow some recognition for provisioning and loss deduction.
- The Committee urges the industry to work on the development of codified and centralized operational risk databases using consistent definitions of loss types, risk categories, and business lines.

- Based on its survey work of a small sample of banks, the Committee has estimated that operational risk accounts for an average of 20% of economic capital.

We discuss the actual methodologies later in this chapter.

Background Perspective from Local Regulators

Regulators on a country-by-country basis will be the ones to adopt and implement the Basel Committee's outline and be responsible for the day-to-day monitoring and enforcement of any regulatory capital charge. There is no question that local supervisors have invested a tremendous amount of time toward understanding the issues and listening to their constituents. Some have and will undoubtedly continue to be more active than others.

Many of the observations that follow were contributed to the central debate. This sampling is indicative of the perspectives that have been expressed along the way.

From the United States, representatives of the Federal Reserve (the Fed) are co-chairing the Risk Management Subgroup of the Basel Committee. While the topic of operational risk management has historically been raised in virtually all U.S. bank examinations since the mid-1990s, the Federal Reserve and the Office of the Comptroller of the Currency (OCC) currently each have approached risk from the perspective of a different set of risk classes. Some reconciliation and clarity of definition would be useful as a basic starting point. From a risk measurement standpoint, we have noted interest by some U.S. regulators in operational loss data availability and risk assessment issues-based approaches.

In the United Kingdom, the Financial Supervisory Authority (FSA) was a relatively new body in the mid-to-late 1990s as the debate began and had been undergoing incremental periods of change in terms of scope and powers. Following a report commissioned by the Bank of England and completed by Arthur Andersen, the new RATE Framework "Risk Based Approach to Supervision" was released and implemented in March 1997. The FSA has been very visible throughout the process and has gone to great lengths to ensure that they capture the banking community's views and latest practices. They have been seen to immerse themselves in the undercurrent of activity with regard to operational risk evolution and have sought to ensure that they draw from all spheres of expertise on the topic.

In Germany, regulators participated, but as developments unfolded in 1998 and 1999, some representatives voiced concern over enforcement powers and about the fact that there had not been adequate time for Best Practices to have emerged.

In Japan, regulators had already been using a "box scoring approach" in the 1990s to regulatory bank risk profiling. In addition, a 25% assessment of expense had already been levied on securities firms, although at least one regulatory representative agreed that this approach is less than ideal, at least from a risk management incentive standpoint.

In Australia, the Australian Prudential Regulatory Authority (APRA) expects to follow the lead provided by overseas regulators, after careful local analysis, with discussion papers and policy statements in relation to operational risk capital. They have been seen to be active in investigating how much data is available from their major firms and which techniques now assist in the process.

Regulators in most countries have been active in evaluating firms' responses and considering their next steps. Following is a summary of some of the comments that have emerged from various regulatory discussions:

- Because of its unique characteristics, a relatively consistent view seemed to emerge that held that a separate treatment of operational risk is appropriate. In addition, clearly some believed that *additional* capital for operational risk is appropriate. In contrast, others suggested that they believed that a bank that could demonstrate sound risk controls and systems might succeed in making a case for *no additional capital.*

- On the subject of additional capital requirements (beyond 8%), apparently few if any were willing to commit to the notion that the industry is currently undercapitalized.

- Some noted that they thought it impossible to resolve "the 8% debate" until the approach to credit risk capital is settled.

- Others observed that market risk guidelines have actually freed up capital for some institutions, thus it should be possible to let overall capital percentages float—*above or below* 8%.

- One suggestion surfaced that would have applied a multiplier to aggregated regulatory capital for market and credit risk.

- Several argued that any approach should support Pillar II, Supervisory objectives (i.e., the value of risk assessments, the use of risk indicators, and control process assessments), although there was a recurring observation however, that many self-assessment efforts are probably too granular to use in modeling.

- Support waned for the use of an expense multiplier for operational risk capital after some discussion.

- Some supported the acceptance of reasonably constructed internal models but expressed concern about how to evaluate them.

- There has been a growing interest in efforts to gather industry-wide operational risk loss data.

- Last, but certainly not least, nearly all seemed to agree that any short-term approach adopted should not be contradicted later by longer term, time-tested, and more well-developed directives.

These views reflect regulators' perspectives based on their knowledge of their own corner of the industry. There are hundreds of thousands of registered banks worldwide, however, each with their own core competencies and specialties and each having been "tooled" by their environment, national culture, competition, technology, and staff. There is a plethora of influences on any particular institution, and regulators, consultants, vendors, and the banks themselves have to operate in markets around the world where there is a huge diversity of sophistication.

Indeed, there has not yet been a worldwide operational risk initiatives survey that adequately captures the full spectrum of banks, both large and small, and which reflects their relative progress in operational risk management. There are obvious reasons for this, not the least of which is who would want to bear the cost and time to sponsor this research. Nevertheless, would it not be a serious mistake for industry and the regulators to underestimate the demographics of the worldwide banking population? For example, it has been estimated that to date probably less than 10% of the worldwide banking population (in terms of pure numbers) are actively investing time and money in developing an operational risk framework. Granted, if one were to look at the aggregate asset or balance sheet size represented in these discussion groups, the percentage would be much higher. To bring this point into focus, just look to the size of the banks that have failed and/or caused the authorities and the banking community embarrassment and reputational damage.

In some cases, you need only look to your own experiences for confirmation of disparities in today's banking environments. One such view comes from observing the difficulties in managing correspondent bank relationships in Russia at a time (in the 1990s) when the emerging market businesses were growing at an astounding rate. Where there is a healthy margin to be made, there will inevitably be banking activity; however, can we, with real honesty, say that the western banks fully appreciated the differences between the institution-and-culture combination? Even though international law and standard practice should prevail, all of this is still open to interpretation. Cut off times for instructions and payments were applied on a seemingly arbitrary basis, resulting in confusion as to what was, and what was not, acceptable. Put in conjunction with high interest and compensation rates it exasperated the situation and rendered it even more fraught with risk.

Had banks factored the operational risk into the pricing of their products? For those banks that operated a capital allocation system for operational risk, had they adequately reflected the risks involved for the losses suffered?

It has been interesting to observe the regulators' proposal development in response to such factors. Clearly the proposals have had to be drafted with sufficient breadth and generalizations to be able to address and include all banks at one level or another. But there is still much work to be done in addressing a full appreciation of differences between countries and their conventions prior to finalizing the proposals, and certainly prior to implementation of them. More work will be needed to assure a level international playing field. In addition, whereas local regulators have always had the latitude to supervise as they saw fit, now supervision will likely become a key leg of the operational risk capital stool. Certainly, consistency of supervision will become more of an issue.

AN INDUSTRY PERSPECTIVE

The British Bankers Association (BBA) set up an operational risk advisory panel in 1998, with a representative sample of banks that were viewed to have an active interest in operational risk but who also embraced different approaches. One of the panel's primary objectives was to assist the BBA in lobbying the regulators on the type of frameworks that may work best for the industry as a whole. This was obviously seen as preferable to having a methodology impressed upon the industry, which may have contradicted much of the time, investment, and direction spent on the subject amongst the banks to date.

Later in 1998, the BBA panel, the International Securities Dealers Association (ISDA), and RMA, now the Risk Management Association (a U.S.-based industry body with a membership of over 3,000 financial institutions) embarked upon a survey of the financial services industry, with a view to getting a clear sense as to market consensus. The results of the survey were unveiled in early November 1999 and have since, to a certain degree, helped to crystallize the industry status in the minds of the Basel committee and regional regulators.

In the United States, the Financial Services Roundtable (formerly the Bankers Roundtable) embarked on a research project on Guiding Principles in Risk Management for U.S. Commercial Banks. The study was released in June 1999 and covered a number of risk management topics (www.bankersround.org). Specific to operational risk, it noted that meaningful measures of risk are still in the developmental stages. It went on to outline retrospective and prospective approaches such as including self-assessment or independent processes on the one hand, and the predictive use of key indicators, on the other, respectively. The study concluded that "at present, the ultimate ability of risk managers to adequately quantify operational risk is still open to debate. . . . Imposing a standard for quantification is premature. . . ." But the conclusion went on to note that ". . . the quantification of certain aspects of operational risk represents a valuable addition to the control environment and should be implemented to the extent practical."[6]

Thus *industry practice* has been developing toward the quantification of operational risk capital, but recent findings confirm that there is little or no consensus on a *standard approach* in the area.[7] A significant proportion of banks note attempts to allocate economic capital to operational risk, but reportedly nearly all are dissatisfied with both their own methodology and the behavioral incentives created. Few, if any, use measures of operational risk capital to drive business decision making or behavior. There is widespread concern that any regulatory initiative in this area may retard, or misdirect, what have been, to date, very positive initial industry developments efforts.

On balance industry response to the general proposal for regulatory risk capital has remained negative since the subject was first implied in the 1998 paper from the Basel Risk Management Subgroup. From that point forward, the industry began to articulate a series of concerns to the banking industry associations, advocacy groups, and regulatory community. In essence, industry's basic objection has been based on the following general observations:

- **Definition:** It is difficult to conceive of how you can develop a risk measure without clear consensus on a risk boundary. No positive industry standard currently exists, although the definition implied by the BBA/ISDA/RMA study, and further evolved by the IIF, helped move toward some consensus. The Committee has seized this thread for its proposals, but there is still much work needed on the specifics of risk classes and sub-classes.
- **No Additional Capital:** The industry does not believe that regulatory capital in excess of current levels is justifiable. In the context of the opening Basel proposals, it is difficult to see how a charge would not be additional for the majority of banks.
- **Duplication:** How will overlap between the various risk assessment processes (market risk, credit risk, operational risk, and supervisory review) be managed? Will the level at which current variable factors are set (market risk multiplier, target/trigger) be adjusted as a result?
- **Level Playing Field:** The level playing issue had been raised as a substantial concern for U.K. banks; more recently, Asian banks have also voiced this concern. At an international level, there is concern that any capital charge for operational risk identified through Pillar II may not be applied consistently or at all in some other jurisdictions. At a national level this is more an issue of ensuring consistency of assessment and a positive bias toward better operational risk management.
- **Behavioral Incentives:** The issue of developing positive behavioral incentives rests upon the development of a risk-sensitive assessment methodology. As outlined in the next section, all the available options have considerable flaws. There is real concern that perverse behavior will be encouraged. If the charge is blunt and at a high level, banks are much more likely to concentrate upon arbitrage/avoidance.
- **Changing Business Environment:** In parallel with the development of risk management practice, the business of banking is itself undergoing a

period of considerable change—new business, products, organizational models, competitors, e-commerce, Internet, and intranets. This rate of change augers for a flexible methodological approach.

■ **Developing Practices:** There is concern that the introduction of a prescriptive methodology will retard or misdirect industry development efforts. There is also concern that the short-term regulatory need to develop an assessment methodology might obscure the pace of development. As a consequence, any methodological solution should, from the outset, be characterized as interim and open to replacement/change as industry practice progresses. Equally there is a common opinion among many industry practitioners that a misaligned interim standard may do just as much damage even though it may be temporary.

The International Swaps and Derivatives Association (ISDA) has been very active in the regulatory debate. Most notably it began with co-sponsorship of the 1999 study entitled *Operational Risk: The Next Frontier,* along with the BBA, RMA, and Pricewaterhouse Coopers. Its active involvement continued with two key documents released in 2000. They included *A New Capital Adequacy Framework*, in February 2000, which contained its comments in the June, 1999 Basel Committee Consultative document. In its report ISDA argues that regulatory capital proposals should be brought in closer alignment with banks' own economic risk capital measures. Specifically, they argue for the reflection of four key principles in the new capital adequacy framework, three of which merit mention here:

1. "**Economic consistency:** The regulatory capital charges should be aligned more closely with banks' economic capital, and be sensitive to the same risk drivers that govern economic capital variations. The current Accord and the proposed revisions fail this test."

2. "**Simplicity:** Supervisors should seek to avoid excessive complexity in developing the new capital rules. The revised rules need to remain sufficiently simple, although robust, in order not to burden the banks with disproportionately high implementation costs."

3. "**Incentives for good risk management:** Finally, it is essential that the supervisors consider carefully whether minimum capital requirements are the appropriate tool against the forms of risk under consideration. ISDA does not believe that charging regulatory capital against operational risk is sensible, because this risk is mostly endogenous and should therefore normally be addressed by adopting proper systems and controls. Establishing minimum capital charges against operational risk would lead to arbitrage, and runs the risk of discouraging the development of adequate controls."[8]

As an extension of this position, ISDA released its *Operational Risk Regulatory Approach Discussion Paper* in September 2000. They stated that the objective in this later document was to "identify the qualitative criteria that support the appraisal of operational risk management by institutions." It goes on to state that "these qualitative criteria should be capable of being applied to the proposed quantitative regulatory approach to calculate an operational risk charge." The document then proceeds to present views on operational risk management principles, including governance and framework, qualitative assessment, and qualifying criteria for quantitative techniques. It argues for assessment by one or more approaches, including self-assessment by institutions, assessment by third parties (e.g., external auditors), and assessment by regulators. In addition, it presents a useful proposal on leading practice guidelines for ORM framework. ISDA receives kudos for its treatment of the qualitative side of the capital discussion, which has received far too little attention to date.[9]

Notwithstanding all of the above, recognizing that regulatory capital was probably inevitable, in July 2000 a group of large banks formed the Industry Technical Working Group on Operational Risk (ITWGOR), which is an independent group, but sometimes serves as a subcommittee of the Institute of International Finance (IIF). Their objective was to focus on quantitative approaches to operational risk regulatory capital. They have released a series of papers publicizing their findings. They admit that all of the members of this group are staff members of large financial institutions and that, as such, they may not represent the industry view completely, given the lack of small institution members of the group. They also note their attempt to promote simplified solutions, however, and therefore the possible application to smaller companies.

Most notably, the group's initial release formed the basis for the quantitative capital proposals included in the Basel Committee's January 2001 Consultative Document. The ITWGOR should receive ample credit for advancing the debate on quantitative approaches. Rather than dwell on the details here, we will, in essence, cover them in the regulatory section that follows. Suffice it to say that the Basel proposals bear striking similarity to portions of their work.

Before outlining the proposals, however, Exhibit 17.1 is a summary of the situation relative to both regulatory and industry objectives on risk capital.

THE REGULATORY VIEW AND ALTERNATIVE PROPOSALS

Three approaches to regulatory capital, or in essence levels of measurement sophistication, were proposed in the January 2001 Consultative Document. Generally speaking, they involve, or are intended to involve when completed, a capital incentive to move up the levels in sophistication, subject to risk measurement qualifying criteria. The proposals include the Basic Indi-

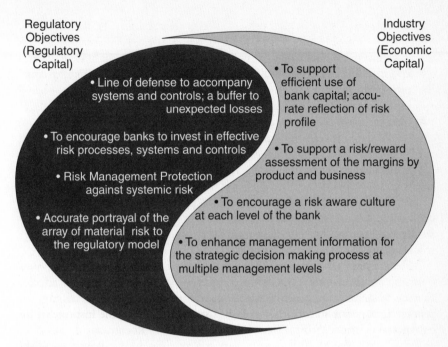

Regulatory Objectives (Regulatory Capital)

- Line of defense to accompany systems and controls; a buffer to unexpected losses
- To encourage banks to invest in effective risk processes, systems and controls
- Risk Management Protection against systemic risk
- Accurate portrayal of the array of material risk to the regulatory model

Industry Objectives (Economic Capital)

- To support efficient use of bank capital; accurate reflection of risk profile
- To support a risk/reward assessment of the margins by product and business
- To encourage a risk aware culture at each level of the bank
- To enhance management information for the strategic decision making process at multiple management levels

EXHIBIT 17.1 Seeking Common Ground

cator Approach, the Standardized Approach, and the Internal Measurement Approach, as follows.

1. **The Basic Indicator Approach** is the simplest method and links the capital charge for operational risk to a single risk indicator (really an exposure indicator) for the entire bank. Gross income is proposed as the indicator. Each bank will be required to hold capital for operational risk equal to the amount of a fixed percentage (α-alpha, which was initially proposed as 30%), multiplied by its individual amount of gross income:

$$K \text{ Firmwide} = \alpha * (\textbf{Gross Income}) \text{ Firmwide}$$

Clearly this is the simplest of the three methods, but the Committee admits that responsiveness to firm-specific needs and characteristics are sacrificed for simplicity. The pros and cons of this proposal can be summarized as follows:[10]

Pros:

- Simple to implement
- Attempts to deliver a level playing field, albeit a bit crude
- Limited scope for duplication within operational risk calculations

Cons:

- Risk insensitive/arbitrary
- Potential for confusion—different definitions of Gross Income by country/region
- Open to manipulation; potential for perverse behavior
- No risk management incentive reflected
- Could damage credibility of operational risk management as a discipline
- Does not reflect risk to new businesses or existing business where no gross income is present

2. **The Standardized Approach,** which is a more complex variant of the basic indicator approach, uses a combination of financial indicators and institutional business lines to determine the capital charge. This approach represents a further refinement along the evolutionary spectrum.

Here banks' activities are divided into a number of standardized business units and business lines. Thus, more specific indicators can be applied to each business (e.g., gross income for retail brokerage, annual average assets for retail banking). Within each business line, the capital charge will be calculated by multiplying a bank's broad financial indicator by a "beta" or risk factor. As of mid-2001 details were still sketchy on the derivation of the "beta" factor:

K Retail Brokerage = β Retail Brokerage * **(Gross Income)** Retail Brokerage

The pros and cons of this proposal are as follows:
Pros:

- More precise.
- Clear targets for firms to influence charge.
- Sets the stage for standard business unit risk weighting to be influenced by industry work.
- Internal measures can be introduced.

Cons:

- Insensitive to specific risk assessment—though less so.
- Difficulties in development and introduction consistently in the short term.
- Possible inconsistent application of qualitative assessment factors bank-by-bank and country-by-country.
- Risk of duplication. Simple sum of the results—no explicit reflection of a portfolio or diversification effect.

3. **The Internal Measurement Approach** strives to incorporate, within the supervisory-specified framework, an individual bank's own internal loss data into the calculation of its required capital. This approach provides some discretion to individual banks on the use of internal loss data to support the calculations, but the method to calculate the required capital is uniformly set by the supervisors. In this case, the supervisors will impose quantitative and qualitative standards to ensure the integrity of the measurement approach, data quality, and the adequacy of the internal control environment:

$$\text{Required Capital} = \Sigma\, i\, \Sigma\, j\, [\gamma(i, j) * \text{EI}\,(i, j) * \text{PE}(i, j) * \text{LGE}(i, j)]$$

Here, too, details are still a bit sketchy at the time of this writing, but it was suggested that the approach would be decomposed as follows:[10]

- A bank's activities would be categorized into several specified business lines and a broad set of operational loss types.
- Within each business line/loss combination, the supervisor specifies an exposure indicator (EI), which is intended as a proxy for the size or amount of operational risk for each business line.
- In addition to the exposure indicator, for each business/loss type combination banks will measure, based on the internal loss data, a parameter representing the probability of loss event (PE) as well as a parameter representing the loss given that event (PGE), and the product of EI*PE*LGE is used to calculate the expected loss (EL) for each business line/loss type combination.
- The supervisor then supplies a factor (γ the "gamma term") for each business line/loss type combination, which translates the expected loss (EL) into a capital charge.
- The overall capital charge for a particular bank is the simple sum of all the capital charges for each business line/loss type combination.

The precise details of each proposal and the mapping process for businesses, exposure indicators, and loss types have not been worked out as of mid-2001. There were also emerging discussions of 56 different cells being proposed in the resultant matrix.

Clearly, this method is the most risk responsive of the three. The pros and cons of this proposal follow:

Pros:

- More sensitive to risk profile of the bank by reflecting business lines, risk factors, and sector loss experience.
- Allows for firms to influence charge.
- Standard BU risk weighting could be influenced by industry work.

- Risk management innovation can be encouraged, somewhat.
- Quantitative method might provide a common floor, albeit loosely.

Cons:

- Difficulties in development and introduction consistently in the short term.
- Possible inconsistent application of qualitative assessment factors.
- Risk of duplication. No explicit reflection of a portfolio or diversification effect.

In summary, both the basic indicator approach and the standardized approach will be predetermined by regulators. Both the standardized and internal measurement approaches will require a decomposition of a bank's activities into specified business lines. Banks may mix application of the two approaches between individual business lines depending upon their business units' own levels of sophistication.[11]

The Committee has introduced the concept of a continuum, whereby a bank would be encouraged to evolve from the basic indicator approach to the more sophisticated standardized, rather than internal measurement, approach. Note, however, that banks are not allowed to move back to a prior approach once they have advanced.[12]

The Committee proposes a continuum of Qualifying Criteria in order for a bank to use each one of the methods. For instance, in order to qualify for the basic indicator approach, a firm would have complied with the forthcoming committee guidance on "operational risk sound practices, which will also serve as guidance to supervisors under Pillar II." For each approach there are standards for "effective risk management and control" and "measurement and validation."[13]

A potential fourth approach identified as the loss distribution approach, which would allow a bank to specify its own loss distributions, business lines, and risk types, may be available in the future.[14]

As of mid-2001, the January 2001 Consultative Document was the last detailed word in the regulatory debate on capital charges for operational risk. The document was issued for comment on May 31, 2001. In June 2001, the Bank for International Settlements reported that the Basel Committee on Banking Supervision had received more than 250 comments on its January 2001 proposals. In response, it issued an update of its position and decisions on June 25, 2001 as follows:

- "... consistent with the support that has been received on these points, the Committee remains strongly committed to the three pillars' architecture of the new Accord and to the broad objective of improving the risk sensitivity of the minimum capital requirements."

- ". . . the Committee has concluded that the target proportion of regulatory capital related to operational risk (i.e., 20%) will be reduced in line with the view that this reflects too large an allocation of regulatory capital to this risk as the Committee has defined it. The Committee is considering numerous other comments and suggestions related to operational risk."
- ". . . in light of the extremely high quality of the comments that have been received and in recognition of the Committee's desire to continue working cooperatively with the industry to achieve the best possible proposals, the Committee has determined to modify the timetable for completion and implementation of the new Accord. The Committee will release a complete and fully specified proposal for an additional round of consultation in early 2002 and will finalize the new Accord during 2002. Accordingly, the Basel Committee envisions an implementation date of 2005 for the new Accord."[15]

In addition to its formal statement, as this book goes to print, the Committee seems to be signaling some flexibility toward expanding its range of measurement approaches. As such, the resultant Advanced Measurement Approaches (AMA) may reach beyond the original Internal Measurement Approach (IMA) to include scorecard and loss distribution methods as well.

Regardless of the outcome of operational risk regulatory discussions, the regulatory community must be mindful of several key issues, as outlined in Exhibit 17.2.

CONCLUSION

The writing has been on the wall for the better part of the 1990s up through 2001. The underlying industry risks and losses incurred to date are simply too large to ignore. Regulatory capital for operational risk will be a requirement. In the words of the Basel Committee, "Such risks are too important not to be treated separately within the capital framework." One might argue that the factors that motivated their proposals include:

- A desire to recognize the impact of operational risk on capital needs, and along with it, there is a desire to capture within the capital framework businesses that are, heretofore in regulatory capital terms, almost entirely risk free (e.g., custody and fund management)
- A desire to provide incentives for sound operational risk management

The perceived need is for a balancing charge to redress an anticipated drop in regulatory capital held for credit risk. This line is also expressed in the argument that operational risk is implicit in current regulatory capital levels.

Operational risk regulation will continue to evolve, of course, as the discipline of operational risk management itself develops. In addition to assuring that adequate capital is maintained in the banking system, there are several threshold objective and success factors that ought to provide guidance for ongoing development if the regulatory community is to meet its goals of improving supervision and risk capital of the industry overall.

Objective	Success Factors and Considerations
Sound Banking Practices	The introduction of Sound Banking Practices will have a far greater impact on more effective operational risk management than an increasing sophistication of models will. Thus, regulators' primary goal should be on defining and promoting these Practices.
	Sound Practices cannot simply be a recycling of traditional controls and audit practices, however. Those practices have not been completely effective against the operational risk challenge that has emerged since the early 1990s. While they are important, the real goal must be on improving best practices and, in the process, the quality of the regulated businesses.
Useful Risk Measurement	An important success factor is to avoid conflict between regulatory models and developing economic capital models being developed for active risk management. Even better would be the considered use of internal models, where appropriate. In any event, because integrated measurement and management can yield real risk management advances and benefits for an organization, regulatory models must not be allowed to develop into a process removed from and irrelevant to the business itself.
	Both regulators and banks must remain vigilant to the trap of investing in modeling at the expense of creating risk aware cultures, quality conscious

EXHIBIT 17.2 Key Success Factors for Regulatory Risk Capital

Objective	Success Factors and Considerations
	environments, and other important risk management standards and controls. Risk measurement and modeling does not equate to risk management, nor does it guarantee *effective* risk management.
Risk Management Incentives	A key question then becomes one of asking whether the test to qualify for capital relief should be in advanced modeling or in sound banking practices, or both. Irregardless of the form that regulatory models take, the ultimate goal should be to promote operational risk management Best Practices by providing incentives to firms to link models that represent risk with performance incentives (e.g., RAPM).
Risk Finance and Insurance Advancement	The regulatory community should provide incentives for the use of risk finance and insurance programs in the form of capital relief. It is not just logical to provide some measured relief, but the move will provide incentive for the risk finance and insurance communities to improve the quality of the economic safety net that they provide. The end result will be an improvement in the economic stability of the banking industry.

EXHIBIT 17.2 Key Success Factors for Regulatory Risk Capital

The ongoing challenges will not be limited to the formulae underlying regulatory models, but will also encompass the quality and consistency of data for each firm. Another key consideration will be whether the regulatory regime will create practical and effective incentives toward risk mitigation on both institutional and industry-wide levels. In short, an unfortunate result of any capital regulation would be the creation of a process that simply creates *risk measurement and capital management* functions in institutions and misses the opportunity to promote effective *risk measurement, mitigation, and management* functions. Once again a careful balance between quantitative and qualitative methods will be key in the end.

Once the dust settles on the regulatory debate and on regulatory risk capital, one can only hope that the process involved will become only a secondary or tertiary tool amongst a handful of others of new operational risk *management* functions. Best practice risk management experience shows that it is most *effective to gather, measure, and manage based on a broad base of operational risk information and analyses*—ranging from self-assessment and scenario analysis efforts, risk drivers and indicators, to incidents and losses—from sources internal and external to the firm.

LESSONS LEARNED AND KEY RECOMMENDATIONS

- Monitor the *emerging regulatory capital and supervisory* environment and position accordingly. Participate in regulatory discussions and debate. Monitor the evolution of requirements. Financial service firms should monitor developments from the Basel Committee at the Bank for International Settlements, as well as regulatory interpretations and actions on a local level. Monitor the emerging operational risk regulatory capital guidelines and options. Ensure that economic risk capital models are in sync with regulatory model developments. Position accordingly: Optimize capital models and the balance sheet (BP Strategy #19).
- Regulatory capital is inevitable but should be evolutionary: Banks are working to advance the operational risk management discipline. It is unreasonable to think that the regulatory community can devise the perfect, comprehensive operational risk capital program at this stage. Regulatory operational risk capital guidelines should evolve in concert with advancements by best practice firms in the industry.
- Attempt to align economic capital models as closely as possible to the regulatory model evolution, without sacrificing the risk mitigation and management value of your own firm's internal modeling and management approaches. In other words, meet the requirements as efficiently as possible, while avoiding redundancy and not sacrificing internal risk management value.

CHAPTER 18

An Operational Risk Management Case Study

Managing Internet Banking Risk

INTRODUCTION

Our treatment of operational risk management would not be complete without discussing at least one individual risk scenario in some detail. After all, the portfolios of risk classes and business units that we measure and manage consist of hundreds of individual scenarios. An entire book could be dedicated to the individual risk situations that require the attention of operational risk practitioners from an enterprise-wide perspective. These situations will range from new business reviews, new technology, major acquisitions, and mergers, to a name only a few. This chapter will illustrate the value of many of the operational risk management methods discussed thus far by using a business risk case example and to illustrate the benefits these methods can bring to due diligence in a practical sense.

This case study of an Internet banking service was chosen because it is a significant and timely prospect for many banks today, and harbors numerous operational risk challenges. Internet banking is an area that most of us have experienced as customers and that most banks have undertaken. Yet it is also one that has been shown from experience to carry significant risk.

This case was contributed by David La Bouchardiere of IBM's e-Risk Management Consulting Practice in London.[1] In it he examines the main steps that one medium-sized bank (unidentified for confidentiality reasons, but herein referenced as Brick and Click Bank) took to launch its service, then describes the risks involved and what they did to reduce them. In doing so, he highlights the bank's thought process in approaching one area involving operational risks, each of the risk management methods that were used, and then explain the benefits they brought to the bank. The case study covers the full spectrum of issues from a background description and due diligence, to assessment of the risks involved, specific risk mitigation steps, and ongoing risk management measures.

LAUNCHING AND MANAGING AN INTERNET BANKING SERVICE

The Internet has changed the fundamentals of all businesses, and banking is no exception. Customers are changing: A recent study forecast over 20 million Internet investment accounts in the United States alone by 2003. Banks are changing: In fund management, credit risk and portfolio management tools are being pushed out from banks to customers because they can be automated on the Internet. Competition is changing: Even supermarkets, let alone insurance companies, are starting to become Internet banks.

What this means for banks is that they must provide a customer service that is competitive in the Internet world. Customer service is now the primary value adding function. People's involvement in service must shift from routine low-value tasks to high-value personal consultancy on issues that are important to the customer. Customer transactions must become digital and self-service. Intermediaries must evolve to add value, or perish.

Over the past two years the majority of banks have launched some form of Internet service. However, a recent survey by the British Bankers' Association showed that for many of these banks, the endeavor has carried significant risk. The following sections consider in sequence the main phases of launching the service: designing the value proposition, building the infrastructure, and operating the service.

The Launch Project

Brick and Click Bank set out on this project with a clear view that there are major rewards to be gained but also major risks to be managed. This section highlights some of these driving factors and explains the main steps the bank took as it implemented the project to launch their Internet service.

The Internet change is so fundamental that banks need to answer questions on their business vision, strategy, and implementation. To reconsider their business vision, firms are doing an analysis of their value chain. This looks at the sequence of business processes through which the firm adds value.

Common elements of the value chain are customer service improvements, productivity enhancements, and the ease of crossing national borders. But the Internet debate is still at an early stage. The Internet has the ability to gather in the same virtual place, at hardly any cost, lots of information and processing power, and a vast number of buyers and sellers. Consumers and businesses can take part in fiercely competitive auctions for literally anything that can be bought or sold. Hundreds of online exchanges and other "e-Hubs" have sprung up in business-to-business markets. These bring together firms and their suppliers to auction, negotiate, or simply compare prices.

The potential of these e-Hubs is that they can enhance economic efficiency. A recent example is the start-up of perfect.com. This website offers an automated "request-for-quote" service that allows competition on many factors besides price. It allows buyers to describe what they want: speed of delivery, supplier reputation, warranty period, and price. Suppliers then spell out their capabilities to meet those needs, and the service finds the best match between buyer and seller.

Brick and Click Bank's project to launch an Internet service involved not only considering all these revolutionary ideas, but also being realistic about what they were capable of implementing within the time and resource they had available. This came down to three main tasks: designing the value proposition, building the infrastructure, and operating the service. We consider each in turn.

Designing the Value Proposition

The Internet offers a number of specific ways for banks to increase the value of the service they offer their customers.

- **Portal:** The first is that the bank can become a portal. In other words the bank can set itself up as a good place for people to look for information—a website that offers value added services. For example, *lloydstsb.com* offers information about a range of services much wider than those the bank provides directly.
- **Aggregator:** The second way is to use the fact that the Internet makes a bank accessible by orders of more people than before. This means the bank can take the selling or the buying process and offer that service to a much larger number of people. Many Internet banks succeed because they have achieved these economies of scale as aggregators.
- **Matcher:** The third category, probably the most powerful, is referred to as being a matcher: using the Internet to match the buyers and sellers of a product or service. In this category, the Internet is assembling, in the same virtual place, a large number of buyers and sellers in a way that would be inconceivable without it. As a result, deals can be struck that are much more favorable to the buyer, to the seller, and also to the bank. This can be done at such a speed that the volume of deals can increase dramatically. Put in financial terminology, market liquidity can be substantially increased.

However, designing value propositions like these is not without risk. Banks need to pilot them in a low-risk environment, and learn from their pilots before risking their brand name in a public launch.

Building the Infrastructure

Each of the previous value propositions implied new support requirements on Brick and Click Bank's operating infrastructure. In some cases these could have been extensive. In others, these needs could have arisen urgently (e.g., to exploit a new market that has been identified only as a result of experience with the new service). The bank needed to conduct a full analysis of its proposed and potential value propositions and then assess its consequent infrastructure needs.

Technology itself is a particular challenge. In order to use the Internet, Brick and Click Bank needed to connect its web systems to its legacy operational systems. However, most banks' operational systems first need to be integrated together, and this is a complex task needing specialist skills. For example, many banks' original integrated systems design has since been overtaken by merger or acquisition. Then they need to be connected via "middleware" to the web. But choosing middleware is a long-term decision, and forecasting their future needs requires insight and experience.

Implementing the Service: Operational Risks

The operational environment for Internet services is still relatively new and different. It encompasses all the strengths and weaknesses of doing business over a network. For example, the speed and reach of the network allows communications that were previously unimaginable. Yet there are dangers, such as security breaches, vulnerability to malicious parties, and the challenge of operating a service in jurisdictions where the legal and regulatory framework may be extremely unfamiliar. It was key that Brick and Click Bank study these operational implications at the time the service was designed, and where possible, learn from the experience of those who had already explored these opportunities.

A special challenge is customer service. Banks need new business processes to exploit the Internet, but they need to be rigorously validated. For example, they might commit to an immediate email response; however, when volumes grow, this could become impossible, as during denial-of-service hacker attacks. The content of their Internet pages defines their service to customers. Yet, as their service evolves to remain competitive, the changes to these pages could become extensive and need resources they do not have. For example, some sites are merely electronic brochures, whereas others offer complex commercial transactions. Customer satisfaction is a challenging goal that requires experience, measurement, and management.

RISK IDENTIFICATION AND ASSESSMENT

The first stage of Brick and Click Bank's operational risk management due diligence was to identify risk in a way that minimized the danger that any risk might be overlooked. The bank knew from experience that once you start identifying risk, the inventory quickly becomes long and complex. They knew the best way of dealing with this was to define at the start the ownership of risk that would be accepted by the managers responsible. As risks were identified, they were grouped into categories that aligned exactly with this ownership definition.

Ownership of Risk Established

Brick and Click Bank recognized at the start that many of the risks identified would not map neatly onto the ownership responsibilities in their organization, which is often the basic reason why they are challenging risks. By focusing on ownership at the start, they organized the teamwork of taking steps to reduce the risk in a way that the responsible managers were working together, rather than against each other.

They started by talking to the sponsor of the Internet banking project to get a first cut at the risk ownership responsibilities. Next they talked with each of the responsible managers and negotiated a more detailed ownership definition with them. Then they documented these definitions and confirmed agreement with the whole management team.

Top Down versus Bottom Up

A question they faced early on was whether to identify risk top down or bottom up. Yet from experience, they knew they would in fact have to do both. They knew that the value of bottom-up identification is that it enables you to build the analysis on detailed solid facts. However, the value of top down is that it enables management to see the wood for the trees.

They began with a management brainstorm to enable them as a management team to agree on the headline risks and the actions required to mitigate them. Having done this, and having documented the outcome, they interviewed each of the risk owners to fill in the details of the risk in a bottom-up manner.

Internal Audit Consulted

As a final step in risk identification, the risk identification team enlisted the help of Internal Audit. Brick and Click Bank knew that when risks actually go wrong, it is usually because at some point, someone has missed something.

Minimizing the chance that something is missed is a special skill, usually developed in auditors.

Audit contributed the checking function, because they had the experience of looking for what might have been missed. Further, their experience was based on a detailed knowledge of the bank's organization. By this method, the bank was minimizing the danger that something might have been overlooked.

Key Risks and Steps to Mitigate Them

Banks have had significant problems launching new Internet services, and Brick and Click Bank decided to start with an exhaustive risk assessment. They used a checklist of risks that had been encountered by other banks. They held a management brainstorm meeting to identify risks in a top-down manner, and they conducted a comprehensive "walk through" of the specification of their service to also identify risks bottom up.

During the brainstorm, they discussed and agreed who in their management team would take ownership and be accountable for each of the areas of risk. In order to ensure the productivity of ongoing risk management, they structured their risk inventory into categories that aligned accurately with their agreed ownership of risk. In this way, each manager took full ownership of a well-defined category of the risks.

Having apportioned ownership in this way, Brick and Click Bank then conducted drill down interviews with each manager to define their risks in more detail. The resulting risk inventory was reviewed and checked by their audit department to minimize the possibility that any risk had been overlooked. Following is a sampling from the inventory. To put each of the risks into perspective, we show for each one its expected financial exposure, or the sum that the bank was most likely to lose, as explained in the section on risk quantification.

Value Chain Risk ($8 million)   This is the risk that the value chain might not be sufficiently exploited. Brick and Click Bank took the view that since the Internet is sufficiently new, and implementation experience is sufficiently sparse, so that there was a significant risk that they might fail to identify a value proposition opportunity. They considered that the result could be that they might fail to exploit the value chain and that this could lead to a competitor overtaking them in the future.

To mitigate this risk, they decided to compare their proposed business model with those of other banks. They also compared it with companies in other industries, such as insurance, who they thought might use the Internet to help them evolve their brand into banking. In each case, they carefully considered the differences in the business models to minimize the possibility that any opportunity was being overlooked. Admittedly, this risk is more strategic in nature than it is operational.

Supply Chain Risk ($6 million)   This is the risk that the service promised on the Internet might not be delivered. It is a type of performance risk. By its nature, the Internet leads banks into promising a level of service that might be difficult to live up to. Companies like amazon.com are successful not so much because of their website facilities, but rather because they are backed up by one of the most efficient supply chains in the world.

Brick and Click Bank took the view that because they might fail to appreciate the importance of the supply chain, this might lead them to fail to deliver the service they had promised on the Internet.

To mitigate this risk, they conducted a thorough review of their service commitments, followed by an analysis of all the requirements this placed on their service delivery facilities. The result was a thorough check on the robustness of their supply chain.

Scaling Risk ($4.8 million)   This is the risk that the business model and implementation might fail to scale. A key element of the Internet opportunity is its ability to bring economies of scale and open up the bank's business to a population of customers far greater than would otherwise be possible.

The danger, however, is that this expansion might be inhibited by some critical constraint, such as the number of people in the bank's call center, the throughput capacity of its communication network, or the ability of one of its suppliers to handle larger volumes of business. The inability to scale might result in system outages, downtime, and ultimate business interruptions.

To mitigate this risk they conducted a proof of concept study of their business model, testing its ability to handle business volumes at all the scaling points they considered necessary.

Risks to Building the Infrastructure

Following were some of the major risks identified in Brick and Click Bank's review of some of the challenges to setting up an adequate infrastructure.

Denial of Service Risk ($4.8 million)   This is the risk that there might be a serious attack on the website. Following the serious denial of service attacks on a number of prominent websites in 2000, Brick and Click Bank decided they needed to thoroughly check out their vulnerability to this risk.

Denial of service (DOS) attacks are mounted by orchestrating a large number of bogus inquiries to the website, so that it cannot handle the volume and goes down. Their main mitigation step was to significantly increase their ability to screen bogus inquiries and make it significantly more difficult to launch this type of attack. A key strategy here was that, being a bank, they could legitimately offer higher priority service to inquiries they could authenticate as being from existing customers.

Integration Risk ($3 million)   This is the risk that operational process applications might fail to integrate. Historically, most banks' operational process applications have been developed independently. When these processes are offered as part of a web service, they need to operate in a seamless, integrated manner. This needs to apply to functional screens, to the user dialogues, and to the data they use. This risk is particularly challenging when two banks have merged and need to offer a service based on inconsistent operating systems.

The main mitigation step was to conduct a review of each web-based service, check out the integration issues, and catalogue and resolve them one by one. In some areas, this involved a significant amount of redesign and redevelopment of operational applications, and it became clear this can be a major inhibitor to the launch of an Internet bank.

Pilot Risk ($2.3 million)   This entails the risk that the pilot location chosen might not be optimal. A service as complex as Internet banking is frequently piloted. Due to many factors, not least of which is customer acceptability, there is much to be gained from first learning from a well-controlled pilot. However, this leaves the bank with a critical decision: where to conduct the pilot. The risk of an ill-advised choice is that the full launch might be ill prepared, leading to potential loss of brand image.

The way the bank mitigated this risk was to conduct a comprehensive evaluation of the alternative locations for the pilot, considering all the significant factors behind the decision. This evaluation is described in detail below.

Risks to Operating the Service

Following were some of the major risks identified when Brick and Click Bank reviewed the challenges to operating the service.

"Enemy Within" Risk ($5.4 million)   Banks, regulators, and others have recently become very concerned about the "enemy within." What they mean is the scenario where a malicious party might bribe a disloyal employee to sell critical information. In this way, the intruder uses the employee's access authority to circumvent all the bank's security countermeasures.

To mitigate this risk, the bank's first step was to establish "Chinese firewalls." This means that, rather than allowing widespread access to information by all the bank's employees, a "need to know" policy was introduced, so that they could only access information judged to be needed to do their jobs.

However, this is not a straightforward matter to rule on, and the bank took some time to arrive at an appropriate set of access rules.

A second step they took was to initiate significant tracking and audit trailing of access requests to sensitive information. On a periodic basis, they now conduct reviews of these accesses. When they see trends where people seem to be accessing data without good reason, they check out the reasons.

Repudiation Risk ($0.5 million)   This is the risk that a customer might repudiate a transaction. When a transaction such as a purchase is carried out over the Internet, there is a risk that the buyer initiating the purchase might maliciously claim they never made the purchase, hoping the seller might have dispatched the goods, but then be unable to prove who purchased them. One of the weaknesses of the Internet is that impersonation is possible, and in the case of a purchase, the seller is left carrying the burden of proof.

To mitigate this risk, Brick and Click Bank used digital signatures. They insisted that each buyer authenticate their transactions with a digital signature. By using an encryption technique, these digital signatures ensure a transaction cannot be impersonated; if a purchase bears the buyer's digital signature, there can be no doubt the buyer was the person who actually placed the order.

Information Espionage Risk ($2.6 million)   This is the risk that confidential information might be stolen. There have been recent highly publicized breaches of banks' Internet security. Brick and Click Bank had no doubt that they needed to be in control of this risk and, further, to be able to reassure their clients of this.

The risk was that Internet security countermeasures might not have been comprehensively implemented. This might lead to a serious breach of confidentiality.

The mitigation action was to fully review their security exposures and ensure they implemented both the technology and security policy countermeasures required. This risk and its mitigation actions are dealt with in more detail below.

Fraud Risk ($0.5 million)   This is the risk that fraud might lead to serious financial loss. Recent surveys have suggested that Internet fraud losses are soon expected to overtake those of credit card fraud. The risk was that fraud countermeasures might not have been comprehensively implemented. A malicious party might succeed in committing fraud, leading to a serious financial and/or reputational loss.

The mitigation plan was to comprehensively assess fraud risks and fully implement the countermeasures. The countermeasures included the security of payment systems, encryption, and the use of rigorous certification and authentication procedures. A particularly effective countermeasure was the use of disk imaging and analysis. This is a method of capturing electronic evidence in a way that is forensically sound and noninvasive, in that the original media are unchanged. Yet it is rigorous enough to be accepted in evidence for litigation.

RISK ASSESSMENT AGGREGATION AND RISK MITIGATION

The second stage in Brick and Click Bank's risk management process was to assess the significance of the risks in the aggregate, particularly in view of the steps proposed to mitigate them. The bank knew from experience that to assess each risk they needed a complete analysis. This covered an objective assessment of the exposure, a clear definition of what outcome was acceptable to the business, and the plan to achieve the outcome.

The definition of the outcome was particularly important because the business needed to strike a balance between a risk reduction plan that goes far enough to make the risk acceptable, yet one that is economic and does not go past the point of diminishing returns. They knew that the ultimate test of significance and effectiveness is a quantified business case. But they also knew that before attempting to quantify the results, they first needed a complete and rigorous qualitative analysis on the nature of the risk.

In this section we also review in more detail the methods that Brick and Click Bank used to manage the risk. As discussed, their business objective was to assess all the significant risks, and to ensure the overall risk was reduced to a level acceptable to the business. We review the specific methods they used in each of the stages of risk management: identifying risk, assessing it, and reducing it. Finally we explain the approach they took in establishing a business case for managing risk, transforming this from a qualitative, intangible view into a quantified estimate of the financial sums at stake. Following are the steps taken to aggregate risk assessment.

Brick and Click Bank's Risk Inventory Compiled

As all of its risks were being identified, management was compiling a risk inventory. They also knew from experience that their managers would be far more motivated if, at the same time as identifying risks, they also identified the steps that could be taken to mitigate them. This transformed the risk identification process from solely a negative activity focused only on downside to one that was constructive. They also knew the inventory would be easier to understand if it was defined first at a headline level, and then showed the "drill down" detail under each headline. Having done all this, they arrived at a risk inventory structured as in Exhibit 18.1.

Major Internet Banking Risks	Plans to Mitigate Each Risk	Owner
Risks to designing the value proposition		
Value chain might not be exploited	Comprehensively brainstorm value proposition	Business director
Supply chain might not be robust	Destruction test design of supply chain	Logistics manager
Business model might not scale	Establish proof of concept at all scaling points	Implementation manager
Risks to building the infrastructure		
Website might suffer a denial of service attack	Stage comprehensive DOS attack testing	Website manager
Operational applications might not integrate	Test integration plans as part of proof of concept	Implementation manager
Pilot location might prove inadvisable	Comprehensively evaluate pilot alternatives	Pilot manager
Risks to operating the service		
A bribed employee might sell key information	Establish Chinese walls based on need to know	Security manager
A customer might repudiate a payment	Authenticate transactions via digital signatures	Business director
Confidential data might be stolen by a cracker	Implement technology & mgmt countermeasures	Chief information officer
Internet fraud might lead to financial loss	Take contractual & security precautions	Security manager

EXHIBIT 18.1 Risks Identified to Launch a New Internet Banking Service

Scenario Analysis The bank knew that to really understand risk, they needed to study the cause and effect scenario that leads to the loss. The value of scenario analysis is that it enables us to focus on the most likely scenarios and study them in detail. This detailed understanding of how the loss might occur maximizes our chances of taking steps to mitigate the exposure. The key to scenario analysis is to spell out the sequence of events through which the risk "goes wrong." An example of scenario analysis is given in Exhibit 18.2.

Interview Techniques Used   In building the risk assessment, the bank knew that the route to the key facts is almost always via talking to influential and, therefore, busy people. So they used formal interview techniques to capture the key facts by making the most efficient use of these peoples' time.

Before each interview, they prepared a briefing document laying out the key facts of the situation. In addition, they also prepared the structure of the interview by preparing a set of questions to be answered. They first decided the "key" question, that is, the main single question they needed to answer in the interview. An example might be "Do we need to deal with information espionage attacks?" They found this was a valuable analysis, because once they had got it right, it provided an efficient focus to make the most of the interview time.

They then searched for the subtleties that might occur in answering the key question. Examples might be "Have attacks already been attempted on us?" or "What methods might people use to launch such attacks?" From each of these subtleties, they formulated "check" questions—a group of questions designed to ensure they investigated all the subtleties raised by the key question.

Having prepared the facts, key, and check questions, they included all these in the briefing document and gave it to the manager ahead of the interview. By this means, the manager was able to prepare effectively, and the interview was carefully structured and focused on the matter to be discussed. Exhibit 18.2 is also an example of the output from such an interview, dealing with the risk of an information espionage attack.

Delphi Technique Applied   Individual opinions are rarely as valuable as those of a group, because of the wider experience base of the group. In the case of managing complex risks, this particularly applies to risks where we are dependent on in depth expertise.

To address this, the bank used a method called the *Delphi technique*. They distributed for review the risk analysis done to date to the experts in each of the specialist areas; for example, fraud, technology, or information security. They then went through an iterative process of polling these experts in order to reach a consensus of opinion on the risk analysis.

The polling was conducted in stages. In the first round, comments from the experts were included anonymously into the analysis. The result was then polled to the group as a second stage. This continued until the level of comment had reduced to an insignificant level and indicated consensus. The advantage of this technique is that it can be conducted by email and can involve experts remotely located in an efficient manner.

1. How high ** are the **exposures**?	1.1	Low: Cracker might discover **access** paths with search engines, etc.
	1.2	Med: Cracker might find network **vulnerabilities** using monitors & scanners
	1.3	High: Cracker might **attack** using spoofing, smurfing, or password crackers
2. What **evidence** leads us to believe this?	2.1	Access information has been found to be too easily **obtainable**
	2.2	Network vulnerabilities have been **identified** in trial scans
	2.3	Spoofs, smurfs, & password crackers have **succeeded** in simulated attacks
3. What **acceptable** goal do we need to aim for?	3.1	Critical access information satisfactorily **protected**
	3.2	Critical network vulnerabilities satisfactorily **screened** from scanners
	3.3	**Protection** from crackers. making risk of attack negligible
4. What is our **action plan** to achieve this?	4.1	**Monitor** databases and websites to stay informed about vulnerabilities
	4.2	**Install** firewalls, intrusion detection systems, & virtual private networking
	4.3	Implement regular audits to verify **compliance** with corporate security policy
5. Who is **accountable** for this risk?	5.1	Chief information officer
6. **Status** indicator	6.1	**Yellow:** Need database monitoring, firewalls, and security audits

The status indicator can be green, yellow, or red and are defined as follows: Green = Committed plan to close this risk in time. Yellow = Plan for such a plan. Red = No plan for a plan

**High = High probability of high financial impact. Medium = Medium prob. and/or impact. Low = Low prob. and/or impact*

EXHIBIT 18.2   Risk Assessment Example: Information Espionage Attack

Quantitative and Qualitative Assessment

The bank knew that no risk assessment can be complete without both a qualitative and a quantitative analysis. A qualitative analysis would allow them to establish a full rigorous logical analysis of the situation. They also knew it is important to delay any quantitative analysis until the qualitative one is completed. This helps to ensure that senior management must fully participate in the logic of the risk analysis and cannot "abdicate" by placing reliance on a single number. However, a quantitative analysis was then important to do two things: (1) to prioritize risks so that they spent resources on the highest priority ones and (2) to build the overall business case for risk management.

To illustrate the method they used for quantification, Exhibit 18.3 shows an example that is based on the same risk analyzed qualitatively above: an information espionage attack. The key to quantification is the scenario analysis. For example, the first scenario is that a "cracker" might discover an access path into their network. Note that "cracker" is the information espionage equivalent of a "hacker," because they crack codes, passwords, and other encrypted information.

The analysis required that they quantify two key numbers, as illustrated in Exhibit 18.3. First they needed to estimate the value of the information asset they would lose. While some people found this a new way of thinking, it was not actually that difficult. As an information asset analogy, they considered the risk of a credit card being misused during an Internet purchase. The potential loss is limited by the credit limit on the card. It is also limited by the terms of the card issuer, for example, on notification within a time limit. When they compared this scenario with what a waiter might do with a credit card when they take it out of your sight after paying for a restaurant meal, the objective value of the information asset analysis became clear.

The second number they needed to estimate was the probability that the asset might be lost. Here they used the evidence they had collected in the scenario analysis. They used the experimental data their information security people had collected when testing their own network using trial scans. The frequency with which these scans were successful was objective evidence on which they based their estimate of probability.

Loss Distribution

Having estimated the loss and the probability of loss, they were able to plot one point for their loss distribution in Exhibit 18.3. This was the point representing a 4% probability of a $20 million loss. Then they did similar estimates on the other scenarios, the finding of vulnerabilities, and the launching of an attack. These allowed them to plot two further points for a distribution. By estimating the comparative probability of zero loss, and also the maximum loss that might occur, they had plotted five points on the distribution.

Based on their experience they believed that these distributions usually have a shape called *log normal*. Thus they were able to fit the curve of the loss distribution. They used the statistical principle that the aggregated loss would, on average, be the area under the curve, to show that in this case the average loss would be $2.65 million.

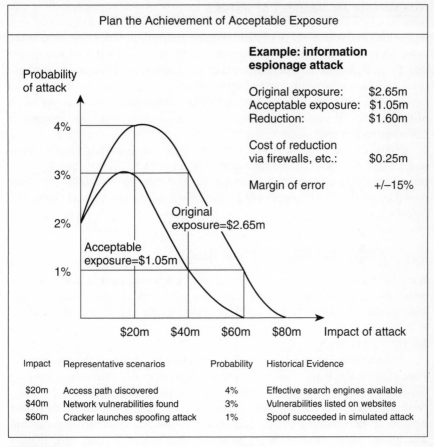

EXHIBIT 18.3 Plan the Achievement of Acceptable Exposure

Brick and Click Bank then repeated the calculation for the case where they had taken action to mitigate the risk: installing firewalls and implementing an information security policy. This resulted in the lower loss distribution curve, indicating they had reduced the average loss to $1.05 million. So the reduction they had achieved was the difference, or $1.60 million. At the same time, they knew that the mitigation actions would cost them $0.25 million, and this gave them their business case: For a cost of $0.25 million, they were estimating a return of $1.60 million.

The final step was to recognize that each of the estimates developed did contain a margin of error and to explicitly estimate what the margin was. In this case, it was estimated to be 15%, and this was considered entirely acceptable in the context of this business case.

ONGOING RISK MANAGEMENT STRATEGIES

In the risk reduction stage of risk management, the bank knew that there were several challenges to be addressed, and they used a number of methods to do this. The first was to recognize that the decision on how to reduce risk turns not only on the risk reduction achieved, but also on the reward the bank would get in return. They also concluded that the most effective way of evaluating risk controls is often an ongoing process of self-assessment.

Finally, the greatest challenge may have been to establish management governance of risk: to gain managers' commitment to the risk management process and to enable them to manage by providing them with the information they need, in terms they could understand. These methods are reviewed below.

Balance Between Risk and Reward Established

We only take risk because we want to earn a reward, so it is key to understand the balance between them, especially as they relate to operational risk. This balance enables you to analyze the significance of the reward net of the risk, to check the weakest links in the analysis, and to work on strengthening them.

In several areas, Brick and Click Bank had to establish the balance between risk and reward. For example, they had to make a decision on which country to select for their operational pilot. Here the risk–reward factors were complex, and yet they needed a precise analysis. The method they used was to do an analysis of the Strengths, Weaknesses, Opportunities, and Threats in the situation (SWOT analysis). Further, they conducted it on a quantified basis. They first established the main alternative countries for their e-banking pilot: Germany, France, and United Kingdom. In each country they identified the opportunities and threats. For example, in Germany they had the prospect of relatively wealthy customers, yet they also had the challenge of an unfamiliar regulatory regime. At the same time, they also identified the strengths and weaknesses of the e-banking service they wanted to pilot. For example, they expected it to make them more competitive through increased customer service, but the Internet undoubtedly increased the danger that they might infringe a regulatory requirement.

The SWOT analysis examined the combination of each of these strengths and weaknesses in the context of each of the opportunities and threats. It did this by considering each combination one at a time. For example, they estimated the size of the reward expected by improving customer service for wealthy customers in Germany. The method of quantification was the same as that previously described.

Decision on pilot country for e-banking start-up

E-banking factors	Germany		France		UK	
	Opportunity Wealthy customers	Threat Unfamiliar regulation	Opportunity Minitel acceptance	Threat Technology investments	Opportunity London financial centre	Threat Strong competition
Strengths						
Competitive	+$ 49m	−$ 19m	+$ 52m	−$ 6m	+$ 72m	−$ 39m
Customer service	+$ 83m	−$ 16m	+$ 110m	−$ 13m	+$ 57m	−$ 24m
Weaknesses						
Channel conflict	−$ 19m	−$ 5m	−$ 21m	−$ 7m	−$ 28m	−$ 13m
Regulatory risks	−$ 24m	−$ 43m	−$ 34m	−$ 2m	−$ 4m	−$ 3m
Average reward, net of average risk	+$ 6m		+$ 79m		+$ 18m	

EXHIBIT 18.4   Plan How to Achieve the Reward, While Taking Acceptable Risk

In this way, they completed the quantified SWOT analysis to lay out all the pros and cons of starting the pilot in each of the three alternative countries. The way they arrived at a balanced decision was to net off the quantified risks and rewards and so arrive at an estimate of reward net of risk. Exhibit 18.4 illustrates this analysis. For them, France was by far the preferred country for their pilot.

Ongoing Control Self-assessment Implemented

Usually, line managers and staff are best placed to assess their business operations and risk-reward trade-offs. If we can remove the motivation and scope for them to distort these views, self-assessments offer us the best opportunity for a complete and balanced assessment.

Brick and Click Bank started by asking the risk owners to do a self-assessment of the controls they had put in place. They eliminated the danger that some of these views might be self-serving by asking for the assessment to be corroborated by the rest of the decision-making group.

Management Governance of Risk Established

Perhaps the greatest and most important challenge to risk management is the need to gain the endorsement of the management team in the bank. Managers have a necessarily short attention span and find it hard to "see the wood for the trees." Risks are complex, and managers need a summary that highlights the important facts, without the distraction of those that are unimportant.

This is where a risk model can help. It provides managers with the information they need to manage in terms they can understand. It enables them to review an action plan and endorse it, understand a resource request and authorize it, weigh up the factors involved in an issue, and take a decision to resolve it.

The following example illustrates the risk model that was developed by the bank to enable their management team to understand what was happening. It was based on the same structure as the qualitative analysis previously described. However, rather than the typical relative ranking qualitative red / yellow / green risk indicators, the risk model used quantified assessments to indicate progress with each headline risk.

For example, the risk of an information espionage attack was shown to have an original exposure of $2.6 million, and a target acceptable exposure of $1.65 million. However, it also showed that at the time of the report, the progress to date with the implementation of risk mitigation actions had achieved a reduction to $2.0 million. The report also showed that the aggregated risk across the e-banking project started with an exposure of $37.6 million, had a plan to reduce this to $5.2 million, and to date had achieved a reduction to $31.2 million.

This progress report gave management the information first to understand in overall terms the progress that had been made towards achieving their goal. Second, it enabled them to appreciate the relative priorities of each of the risk mitigation plans. Last, and perhaps most importantly, it enabled them to drill down from the report and investigate any area that had not yet made the progress they had expected. The result was a risk model, illustrated in Exhibit 18.5.

CONCLUSION

Internet banking is here to stay, and the evidence is the volume of transactions already taking place. It has created the opportunity for new services, new businesses, and new markets. Almost every bank has implemented an Internet service. But these services differ greatly on what they offer, from simple e-mail versions of phone banking, to market moving trading sites on business-to-business e-Hubs. The question is no longer whether to invest but what is the nature of the investment.

Banks need to analyze their value chain and work out the new set of business processes that will make them most competitive. Then they need to implement those business processes and clearly focus on their risk and reward. But they need to strike a balance between offering powerful Internet services, yet remaining realistic about the implementation tasks they need to

| Top ten Internet banking risks | Plans to reduce each risk | Exposure, $m +/- 15% | | |
Ranked by exposure now		Before action	Now	Acceptable risk
Risks to designing the value proposition				
Value chain might not be exploited	Comprehensively brainstorm value proposition	8.0	8.0	0.4
Supply chain might not be robust	Destruction test design of supply chain	6.0	6.0	0.4
Business model might not scale	Establish proof of concept at all scaling points	4.8	4.8	0.8
Risks to building the infrastructure				
Website might suffer a denial of service attack	Stage comprehensive DOS testing	4.5	4.3	0.6
Operational applications might not integrate	Test integration plans within proof of concept	3.0	3.0	0.4
Pilot location might prove inadvisable	Comprehensively evaluate pilot alternatives	2.3	2.0	0.8
Risks to operating the service				
Confidential data might be stolen by a cracker	Implement technology & mgmt countermeasures	2.6	1.5	1.1
A bribed employee might sell key information	Establish Chinese walls based on need to know	5.4	0.6	0.5
A customer might repudiate a payment	Authenticate transactions via digital signatures	0.5	0.5	0.1
Internet fraud might lead to financial loss	Take contractual & security precautions	0.5	0.5	0.1
Aggregated risk exposure from Internet banking		37.6	31.2	5.2

EXHIBIT 18.5 Report Progress to Management, in Terms They Clearly Understand

undertake. The issue is managing this balance. As Bill Gates said in his book on *Business at the Speed of Thought:* "If you decline to take risks early, you'll decline in the market later."

LESSONS LEARNED AND KEY RECOMMENDATIONS

Exhibit 18.6 is an outline of the problems addressed by Brick and Click Bank. Their considered process of analysis caused them to conclude that a balance of risk management methods is key to delivering benefits and rewards from both new and existing business ventures.

Risk Management Methods	Problem Addressed	Benefit Delivered
Methods to identify risk		
Establish ownership of risk	Initially, risks do not map neatly onto existing organizational responsibilities.	Organize the teamwork between managers, so they work with, not against, each other.
Identify risk top down & bottom up	No risk assessment can be complete without both.	Bottom up ensures we are based on the facts. Top down ensures we can see the wood for the trees.
Use Internal Audit	Usually, risks go wrong because we have missed something.	Use auditors' experience of the situation to minimize the danger of missing something.
Methods to assess risk		
Compile the risk inventory	The devil in the detail quickly makes it impossible to visualize the risk.	Categorizing the inventory by ownership enables us to apportion accountability for risk.
Carry out scenario analysis	To understand risk, we need to study the cause and effect scenario that leads to the loss.	Enable us to focus on the most significant scenarios and take steps to address them.
Use interview techniques	The route to the key facts is usually via influential, and therefore busy, people.	Gather maximum information by making the most efficient use of these peoples' time.
Use the Delphi technique	The wide experience base of a group of experts is more valuable than any individual's opinion.	Consult all the experts, to ensure we benefit from their experience base.
Qualitative & quantitative basis	They are usually seen as alternatives, but are actually complementary.	Qualitative analysis establishes the logic. Quantitative analysis establishes the business case.
Methods to reduce risk		
Balance risk & reward	Taking risk is pointless unless we do it for a reward.	Select the strategy based on a conscious choice of the optimum balance between risk & reward.
Use control self-assessment	Usually, the people best placed to assess what we have done is ourselves.	Get the best assessment by removing the opportunity for us to distort our own views.
Establish management governance of risk	Risks are usually too complex for managers' necessarily short attention span.	Build a risk model, so they can focus on the key facts, and not on the distracting ones.

EXHIBIT 18.6 Summary of Risk Management Methods and Their Benefits

CHAPTER 19

Operational Risk Technology and Systems

INTRODUCTION

Technology will be a major factor for all firms as they implement enterprise-wide operational risk management. The scope of a program and its objectives will drive decisions about technology needs. Once a mandate is established, technology requirements become discernable. For instance, the firm that is focusing solely on responding to first- or second-level regulatory capital guidelines will have minimal technology and systems needs.

In contrast, one that is striving to develop an enterprise-wide monitoring and economic risk capital program will have much more extensive needs. Such a system will have to support business unit performance metrics and self-assessment on one hand, and provide a corporate repository of risk and performance data and information, along with economic and regulatory capital modeling functions and multilevel reporting, on the other. One of the biggest challenges to firms engaged in dynamic risk profiling, monitoring, and, even more broadly, enterprise-wide operational risk management will be ready access to the enterprise-wide data and information that drives a company's risk profile. For some, it may be *any* reasonable access.

The bottom line is that technology will be key in leveraging the scarce resources dedicated to operational risk management programs. This is just as true in operational risk management as it is in every other aspect of business and personal life today. Balance this, however, with one possible constraint and important reality—gaining the necessary commitment of resources.

Unfortunately, a significant commitment of resources to dedicated technology for operational risk management and enterprise risk systems may be a challenge for operational risk professionals at some firms. That may not change until the function is more fully established, and it has proven its

---

BP STRATEGY #20—LEVERAGE RISK MANAGEMENT EFFORTS THROUGH STATE-OF-THE-ART TECHNOLOGY

Assure program efficiency by leveraging technology in enterprise-wide data gathering, analysis, and information delivery. Web-enabled systems will support the flow of data and information both internally and externally. Use powerful database and data warehouse technology to prepare for the flood of data that will be required to manage operational risk effectively in the future.

---

worth to further reaches of the business community. It is incumbent upon operational risk practitioners to make that happen.

We have already addressed the data challenges in operational risk management. Now we will focus on the technology. We will also explore the concept of Operational Risk Business Intelligence in this context.

In this chapter we can only begin to scratch the surface on the many issues involved in operational risk technology, systems, and Business Intelligence. We include areas such as the evolution of operational risk management programs and systems, systems needs assessment, design issues, make-or-buy considerations, several case illustrations, and some key lessons learned, all largely from the user perspective.

EVOLUTION OF OPERATIONAL RISK MANAGEMENT TECHNOLOGY

Unlike market and credit risks, few operational risks can be readily isolated to a single trade, loan, or portfolio. Operational risks are generally far more pervasive. Thus, operational risk strategies for combating the risk must be more pervasive.

As illustrated in Exhibit 19.1, until very recently, the sum total of operational risk management analytic systems and technology consisted of spreadsheets with a few columns of data and some simplistic models. Now as the discipline is demanding much more in terms of enterprise-wide collection and access to data and information, more Web-based applications—whether over the Internet or intranets—are becoming available, supported by complex data models and warehouses. The value that these systems add consists of giving the data input, reporting, and analysis to the people who can influence risk throughout a firm on a decentralized level. Individuals are entering, analyzing, reporting, and reaping direct benefits at the local level, as well as providing data, analysis, and reports to the corporate level. There can and should be ownership at the business level and a win-win attitude

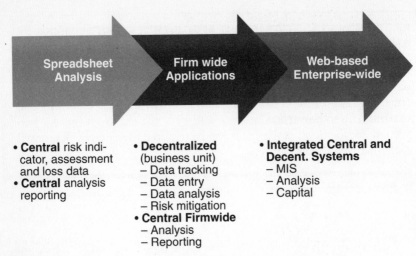

- **Central** risk indicator, assessment and loss data
- **Central** analysis reporting

- **Decentralized** (business unit)
  - Data tracking
  - Data entry
  - Data analysis
  - Risk mitigation
- **Central Firmwide**
  - Analysis
  - Reporting

- **Integrated Central and Decent. Systems**
  - MIS
  - Analysis
  - Capital

EXHIBIT 19.1 Evolution of Operational Risk Management Systems

toward the firmwide program overall between the business lines and head office.

As we move toward integrated programs and strive for a greater understanding of people risk and human behavior, operational risk MIS, analysis, and capital, it seems clear that artificial intelligence applications will also become more pervasive toward understanding behavioral and risk characteristics. As we work toward managing these complex risks, other technology-enabled tools such as the emerging use of artificial intelligence will prove valuable.

There are many aspects of broader-based operational risk management system needs that begin to resemble enterprise resource planning (ERP) systems. It is not unreasonable to believe that the best firms will demand that these systems support one another or morph together into an even more meaningful management system for the future.

In their best selling book *Unleashing the Killer App* (Harvard Business School Press), Larry Downes and Chunka Mui set the stage for developments in technology, generally. Their observations are directly relevant to operational risk management technology. One phrase, borrowed from their book, says it all: "When technologies, products, and services converge in radical, creative new ways, a 'killer app' can emerge—a new application so powerful that it transforms industries."[2]

The nexus of several key factors—the use of new tools and metrics, use of state-of-the-art web-based and database technology, and progressive managers who see the opportunity to create more effective companies—all add up to a new paradigm, and possibly the next "Killer App."[1]

CURRENT MACRO TRENDS ENABLING CHANGE

Several macro trends are important for framing a discussion about technology evolution for ORM. The first involves core information systems. The second entails third party data exchanges.

First Circle: Core Information Systems

Firms generally have developed or purchased automated applications to process and manage their critical business information. One recent trend in data processing at large organizations has been the construction of "data warehouses." In such systems, data from various applications are defined consistently so that each element can be viewed from a variety of platforms (that is, end users from different divisions, using different computer systems, will all be able to access the same database). Such systems may involve multiple tiers of systems. For example, a processing tier, a data storage tier, and presentation software may all work together to create a comprehensive system. These components may be developed, in part, with vendor software, and applications developed in-house. By enabling several applications and platforms to operate together seamlessly, such system designs provide many benefits to a business. However, this creates special management challenges in the areas of data control and data integrity, data translation, and transaction timing. Network performance and connectivity become an integral aspect of the application design and functionality.

Second Circle: Third-Party Data Exchanges

To be effective, most operational risk systems will have to link to legacy systems elsewhere in the organization and between firms over the Internet. And so the next circle involves exchanges of data with other systems and other entities. One of the ways in which automation has developed over the years is by increasing the use of systems that exchange data between organizations. An example would be electronic data interchange (EDI) systems, in which a major business and all of its suppliers exchange important data—from initiation of orders through invoicing and payment—without manual intervention. Organizations that are connected to several different EDI chains may find themselves having to comply with a number of different solutions.

As outlined in Exhibit 19.2, XML offers an unprecedented level of standardization and offers many advantages over EDI. Among them are design flexibility, faster and less complicated implementation, easy web integration, real-time or near real-time data access, and lower implementation and management costs.

- It significantly reduces the cost of data exchange with partner companies especially compared to EDI.
- It significantly lowers the cost of integrating back office legacy systems with front-office systems, including internet or Intranet sites.
- It is Worldwide Web consortium (W3C) standards-based, allowing it to integrate well with other Internet technologies and enabling it to add significant functionality and flexibility to Web interface design.
- It is language-and platform-independent in addition to open-standard based, making tools for using it generally interoperable and widely available from multiple vendors.

EXHIBIT 19.2   Key Benefits of XML

OPERATIONAL RISK BUSINESS INTELLIGENCE

In this section we look at some of the system user groups, their individual needs and priorities, and then summarize those needs into some broad Operational Risk Business Intelligence themes that will be key for the ongoing design and development of systems.

System User Groups

A needs analysis is a first important step in any discussion about technology and the development of the right operational risk system (ORS) for a given firm. The operational risk team would do well to include a discussion of technology needs when meeting with business line managers and their network of line operational risk managers.

At the outset, it is important to review the characteristics and needs of several user groups. As elsewhere in operational risk, when it comes to technology, an important distinction must be made between the technology needs relative to systems capable of supporting *operations or processing risk* and those supporting enterprise-wide *operational risk*. In the former instance, the analyst often has the luxury of extensive data since he is dealing with high-frequency low-severity events, for the most part. Thus, we discuss process risk analysis separate from other system needs such as Control Self Assessment support and enterprise-wide risk measurement.

The unique aspects of an operational risk management structure might imply one or more of the following technology needs:

Process Risk Analysis   In the operations or processing environment, the huge volumes of data will include either a separate system or specialized analytic capabilities that can be linked to existing systems for the purpose of analyzing process flows, constructing Bayesian Belief Networks, or neural networks.

An example would be as follows: Risk analyst who is seeking to assess the impact, causes, and relationships, exceptions, error counts, etc. in routine process flows of operations environments.

Risk Assessment or Control Self-Assessment (CSA) Program Administration (Enterprise-wide)   The coordination of an enterprise-wide risk assessment program is a monumental task. By definition, where a bottom-up risk assessment process is in place, a firm must put standards and formats on the desktops of individual units and participants in the process. Similarly, the results of the assessment must be transmitted to a central unit and data repository, assimilated, collated, and aggregated for reporting on both individual case and firmwide reporting purposes.

Operational Risk Data Aggregation and Monitoring (for Enterprise-wide or Business Line Application)   Leading business managers have long recognized the value of monitoring and tracking key performance and risk indicators for their business. Much of this information has been tracked "manually" by business line and corporate staff, with minimal efficiency. Here, at an enterprise-wide or business unit level, management information system (MIS) tools are needed to power efficient risk profiling: monitor and track performance relative to operational risk variables, indicators, and risk factors, as well as key issues, incidents, and loss events. All of this will be in formats that lend themselves to day-to-day hands-on management of risk. The net benefit is more effective reporting and tracking of operational risk information and progress, such that business management and risk management spends less time on data compilation and more time on the active management of risk. Examples include:

- A business line manager who needs to track the key risk indicators of his or her business
- An Internal Audit function who maintains an inventory of outstanding risk issues, their importance, priority, and status
- An operational risk manager who tracks all of the above—a variety of indicators, issues, and losses—for firmwide consolidated risk reporting

Operational Risk Measurement   As we have discussed at length in prior chapters, firms engaged in anything other than the most basic levels of operational risk measurement will require a data tracking, analysis, and reporting risk measurement framework for operational risk. Operational risks may be measured by risk class — relationship, people, technology / processing, physical asset, and other/external—by business line, or by hybrid dimensions. The analyst will require tested formats for collecting, tracking, analyzing, and reporting on risk measures (e.g., risk indicator projections) and operational risk events (e.g., issues, incidents, and losses). The focus here is on risk measurement using internal data. We address the inclusion of external data below. Examples include:

- An operational risk practitioner or committee wants to create an index of loss potential by key risk scenarios (e.g., people-related, technology-related, or relationship-related events).
- A firm wants to create risk profiles for each of its business lines and rank them one business line against another.

Economic Risk Capital Derivation (Attribution and Allocation)   Beyond the analytic building blocks and risk measurement, firms will need a foundation for the derivation of operational risk capital. Whether one subscribes to a loss distribution, factor-based modeling, or a hybrid approach, technology will be needed to provide embedded analytics and/or links to support external actuarial and statistical modeling. The risk profiling capabilities will need to support credible allocation of risk capital by business, as well as on a firmwide basis. Examples include:

- A risk analyst wants to export preformatted data by business or risk class for actuarial projections.
- A firm wants to profile its business lines and/or profit centers, using the profiles as a basis for allocation of the operational risk capital developed in the instance described above or from some other source.

Regulatory Capital Calculations   As the regulatory capital discussion stood in mid-2001, firms may have a choice of calculating regulatory risk capital based on either simple or more complex methods. In the former case, system needs will be limited, based on the fact that the analyst will only need to access basic exposure for financial data. In the more complex internal measurement or loss distribution approach being discussed, the analyst will probably require system capabilities similar to those discussed relative to risk measurement, economic capital, and external databases.

External Loss Data   Risk management practitioners have come to recognize the value of using industry data to supplement their own firms' loss histories and distributions for analysis and corporate learnings. We have discussed external loss databases and consortia at length. From a database user perspective, technology priorities all depend on their intended use of the data and databases.

Uses will range, of course, from simple database inquiries to much more complex search combinations and analytic capabilities.

The consortia and database vendors appear to be at different stages in technology development, however. Some have limited their technology investments to the use of Microsoft Excel™ or Access™, for instance, while others are using more sophisticated Microsoft, Oracle, and Sybese database programs and products to support their offerings. Be sure to explore the technology capabilities of any vendor offering closely.

CORE INFORMATION SYSTEMS: THE BROAD THEMES

We characterize our systems user group needs under a broad heading of operational risk business intelligence. We can apply either three or four general categories depending upon one's perspective and combination of the components:

1. **Data Management and Aggregation:** Access and consolidate risk data (operational or otherwise) from around the world.
2. **Risk Analysis and Measurement:** Analyze and explore your data in order to compute risk measures.
3. **Risk Reporting:** Effectively communicate risk measures.

Exhibit 19.3 from Meridien Research illustrates the model with four component parts. This illustration, developed in 1998, also appeared in a February 2000 research report by Meridien Research as a depiction of their expectation of where operational risk systems are headed. They expect that the ultimate systems will include shared resources such as "scenario generation, product and customer definitions, and reporting mechanisms [and that a] common architecture would provide for a common risk lanaguage, common risk assumptions, and the ability to better analyze the relationships between the different categories of risk."[3] Once again, we encounter common themes with credit and market risks systems. It appears that the sooner firms begin to scope and integrate operational risk needs into their enterprise-wide resource planning and/or risk systems, the better.

Data Management and Aggregation

An operational risk data warehouse is a centralized data repository. It is needed to consolidate and organize large volumes of operational data (regardless of geographic location, hardware platform, or origin) allowing decision makers to evaluate multiple dimensions of operational risk. As operational risk management matures, the need for database, data warehouse, and/or network-attached storage capabilities will gain in importance. Their presence allows application of operational risk analysis

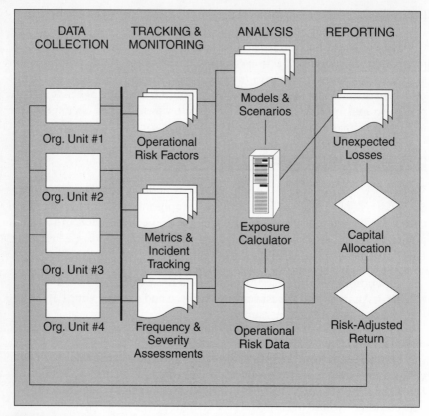

EXHIBIT 19.3   Operational Risk Solution Architecture
Excerpted from Operational Risk Management Technologies (May, 1998).
Source: Meridien Research

techniques, providing virtually unlimited perspectives on an institution's risk position, for instance, to include:

- Scenario Analysis / Current Exposure
- Projections of Potential Exposure, including Actuarial Methods / Monte Carlo VAR
- Correlation and Sensitivity Analysis
- Carsation: analysis
- Fuzzy Logic

Risk management practitioners will benefit from being able to break down or aggregate analytical results, however they are desired. Cross-classification variables allow reporting of risk measures at user-specified levels of aggregation such as firmwide, by location, by region, and by division.

■ The database architecture should support emerging open database standards. This will allow an exchange of data between common applications and other databases, ranging from word processing, spreadsheets, unrelated databases, and other applications. With XML, we are able to easily exchange data from disparate systems and databases seamlessly. While most organizations start off small and often at a department scale for collecting risk indicator and events for profiling, the need for scaling quickly arises as the scope of the ORS spreads enterprise-wide.

■ Keep in mind that the database may need to be modeled to accommodate *additional data sources* beyond the database itself, such as wire feeds, bibliographic databases, or other proprietary sources, as necessary.

Risk Analysis and Measurement

A second key theme is the need to provide more powerful risk analysis, measurement, and modeling tools. Any risk calculation is only as good as its underlying assumptions. Therefore, there has to be a modeling component that makes it possible to specify nonnormal models for incidents, losses, and risk factors and to fit these models to your data. These models can be used seamlessly in Monte Carlo-based risk measurement techniques such as Operational Value-at-Risk and Operational RAROC.

Risk Reporting Capabilities

Then comes the reporting challenge: turning the vast amounts of data generated by your organization into flexible and actionable information so that decision makers can react to quickly changing market conditions, rapidly identify new strategic directions, and uncover sources of potential problems before they materialize. Here several solutions exist—executive information systems, online analytical processing, and interactive and multidimensional data visualization—all designed to give the user the flexibility to view information at any level of aggregation or detail required. It is possible to view analysis results using Online Analytical Processing (OLAP) features interactively. Consider using Business Intelligence tools from vendors such as Business Objects or Brio or Cognos, which will enable you to "slice and dice" risk data by aggregating or drilling down on any dimension by which the results are cross-classified. In addition, the user will be able to interactively explore results using visualization tools as well, enabling you to identify outliers easily.

Use an object-oriented environment for developing the enterprise information system. Choose software that offers a wide range of business reporting objects, providing a choice of styles for dynamic display and interactive analysis. Examples of the business reporting objects include:

■ **Multidimensional Data Viewer:** Allows data to be viewed immediately in any way you choose from any possible dimension

- **Organizational Chart:** Provides graphical display of your organizational data
- **Overlapping Bar Report:** Enables different data sets to be presented together—allowing trends and comparisons to be clearly established
- **Multicolumn Report:** Summarizes data at all summary levels as tables or tables with graphics

Also look for powerful metadata. Metadata, or information about data, will help the business user understand better the meaning of specific attributes of data. For example, if we are analyzing failed trades, metadata will help define what a failed trade is, how often this data is collected, when it was last updated, what the source of data is, and all of the related information about this particular risk indicator. Use the metadata to define a complete drill-down hierarchy of your entire organization, then use this hierarchy as the framework for your data-driven Executive Information System (EIS) applications.

- **Variance Analysis and Exception Reporting:** Obtain a facility for defining and executing standard row-and-column variance reports. For instance, these reports can help pinpoint the differences between budgeted and actual values. Automatic, data-driven drill down allows business analysts to delve deeper into their data—level by level—based on the hierarchy that you have specified in the metadata. For in-depth analyses, the software should deliver capabilities for exception reporting and traffic lighting. You can specify colors to highlight exceptional data or to segment data into appropriate ranges.
- **Graphics Drill Down:** Look for graphical drill-down capabilities for use on any graphic, text, or report output. Use *hotspots* to define areas for drilling down to other reports, graphs, or data, or select keywords from the text or graph.
- **Direct Output to Business Graphics:** Provide for the ability to output to standard management reporting templates. You can create applications that actually generate new graphs whenever data values change—and modify the graphs just as easily.
- **Business Forecasting:** Allow for automated forecasting of any risk factors in your organization. Use this feature to spot trends and make informed risk/reward projections about specific aspects of your business.

SYSTEM DESIGN AND ARCHITECTURE CONSIDERATIONS

Following are five additional system design criteria that will be useful as firms consider their options relative to enterprise-wide operational risk management systems. To a lesser degree, of course, they will apply to programs requiring systems of a more narrow scope, such as those supporting a data gathering effort for economic capital systems only, or even narrower, those supporting regulatory capital calculations only.

1. **Linkage to Existing Systems:** First and foremost is the need to link to other firmwide systems, including but not limited to (ERP), Straight Through Processing (STP), credit and market risk management, and general ledger systems. The ability to access files and download data stored and information is key.

2. **Broad-based Capabilities:** In order to support ongoing enterprise-wide operational risk management or dynamic risk profiling a broad-based risk management system will be needed, not a single purpose tool (e.g., monitor and analyze indicators, issues, incidents, and losses for both management and measurement all in one system).

3. **Enterprise-wide Deployment:** If the system will be a true enterprise-wide management tool, it will be necessary to deploy to hundreds or perhaps thousands of desktops firmwide and place the tools in the hands of numerous staff members who can all influence risk, not solely in those of a single remote analysis team. For this, web-based technology will greatly ease the installation and maintenance challenge.

4. **Internal and External Data Merge Capabilities:** Cases in which a firm is seeking to combine its proprietary loss data with industry loss data for modeling or benchmarking will require unique system merge features and a platform for the user to monitor his own firm's operational risk data and profile. It also provides the ability to monitor historic industry loss data and industry-wide risk indicator benchmarking. On this front, consider working with industry data consortia like those described in Chapter 10 to standardize the attributes of loss data that is being collected. This will simplify the consolidation and reporting across the different data sets.

5. **One-time versus Continuous Processing and Reporting:** Be mindful of assessing whether a real time/continuous management tool is needed versus a periodic assessment, measurement, or analysis tool, or whether both are necessary. Following the trail of evolution in Operational Risk systems, when institutions are ready to move to more real time risk monitoring, the use of Message Oriented Middleware (MOM) with products like TIBCO and IBM's MQ Series will enable seamless linkage enterprise wide.

In addition to database and warehouse considerations, the following are a few more of the many architecture considerations that should be considered for enterprise-wide operational risk systems, depending on the functional scope and needs of the user group.

Scalability and Geographic Reach

- Database architecture must scale well *across wide geographic distribution* now and in the future without performance impact or excessive cost.
- In order to reach and enlist the participation of managers and staff firmwide, the system(s) may need to support scalability *of its user base* from initial size of a few early users to a potential user base of several thousand.
- Firms must consider whether they can leverage existing networks for global reach, or whether they can leverage the Internet. Much of this will depend, of course, on the extent of confidential information being handled. Chances are that confidential loss records may be included, and thus a secure network will probably be the default choice.

User Interface

- Don't underestimate the importance of the Graphical User Interface (GUI) and the look and feel of the system. The user screens should be relatively easy to follow, logical in their sequencing, attractive, and engaging for the user. Screens must be deliverable in *customized subsets of functionality* to users in different departments, with different levels of service and with different roles, such as administrative use screens for the central operational risk management group versus general users elsewhere in the firm.
- Ensure that a browser-based interface is used wherever possible to allow for easy rollout and maintenance.

Security and Audit Considerations

- Provide effective security against unauthorized use and intrusion, programming error, or misjudgment causing the loss of data. Establish a clear security policy within the system using a hierarchical model for establishing roles and privileges. A good security model allows for scaling over the longer term once the system grows in scope. Best Practices dictate that where possible, you should leverage an enterprise directory and Lightweight Directory Access Protocol (LDAP) to create and authenticate users and roles.
- Include automatic audit trail capabilities at design time, including information on last update and user as standard features.
- Where the Internet is used for data transmissions, current standards as of 2001 dictate that security be implemented via Secure Socket Layer (SSL) for all links through enforced 128-bit encryption. If your organization uses Public Key Infrastructure (PKI), leverage it to secure any Internet-based communication and transactions.

PUTTING TECHNOLOGY TO WORK: CASE STUDIES

Following are four Case Illustrations included to illustrate how technology systems are enabling enhanced operational risk management at individual firms. Note the objectives, challenges, benefits, and efficiency that are provided along the way. The first recounts the development of technology at J.P. Morgan (now J.P. Morgan Chase), which served to automate their Control Self-Assessment process. It was later commercialized as Horizon software. The second case from Halifax describes a data aggregation and risk-profiling system originally developed by ORI and OperationalRisk.com, then acquired and tailored by Halifax Group for its proprietary in-house use, and more recently acquired and commercialized by Algorithmics. The third is an in-house build that supports bottom-up risk assessment at Commonwealth Bank Group. The fourth describes the technology that supports data aggregation and Fuzzy logic at Commerzbank. Each of these technology cases are continuations of risk management tools and methods described in earlier chapters.

These cases are not included in any way to promote one vendor's product over another, but instead to illustrate and bring to life the process of how individual firms have chosen to apply technology to date in operational risk management. Although by association commercial products are referenced (i.e., Horizon, The ORCA Solution, which was recently re-branded as Op-Data, RCS' Time Series Aggregation product, and SOFWIN), the cases should not be interpreted as a standing endorsement of any specific product or vendor, nor are they intended to suggest the extent of systems and vendors available. These systems serve as useful illustrations of some of the leading edge developments in operational risk management and technology. Clearly there are other firms that offer CSA products, risk data aggregation and analysis technology, and systems.

CASE ILLUSTRATION

Automating the Control Self-Assessment Process

J.P. Morgan Chase

This case was contributed by Craig Spielmann of J.P. Morgan Chase and Carmine Disibio of Ernst and Young. It outlines the evolution of Control Self-Assessment (CSA) at J.P. Morgan, and, in particular, describes their technology used to support it. The resulting system became the Horizon Risk and Control Self-Assessment Tool (Horizon), which took an early lead as one of the preferred operational risk software solutions in its user sector.

Although operational risk has always been embedded in J.P. Morgan's businesses, until 1993, operational risk management was not viewed as a distinct discipline. Through much of the company's existence, operational risk at J.P. Morgan was managed implicitly through a combination of Internal Audit, Compliance, and business unit efforts. However, with the passage of the FDICIA legislation in the United States, and the increased involvement and interest in operational risk management both in the United States and the international regulatory community, the firm began to evaluate alternate methods to manage operational risk discretely.

In 1993, as a response to FDICIA, and as a first attempt at managing operational risk, J.P. Morgan embarked on a paper-based effort to document its internal control environment. These early efforts were characterized by third-party reviews and the preparation of system documentation designed to illustrate the control environment. However, these early attempts exhibited several of the shortfalls common with these paper-based, third-party control assessments. They were very time consuming to complete, they lacked the ownership and buy-in of the business line, they had a disproportionate focus on controls instead of risk, and they failed to establish and monitor the required action steps to improve the control environment.

In 1996, partly as a reaction to these shortcomings, J.P. Morgan modified its approach to operational risk management from third-party reviews and documentation of the internal control environment to that of a Control Self-Assessment (CSA). The firm's process, refreshed on a semiannual basis, consisted of evaluating risks, identifying gaps, and developing an action plan to mitigate those risks. The CSA process supported the spirit of the underlying objectives of regulatory guidelines by focusing on business and process improvement; establishing operational risk profiling and classification, standardizing risk definitions, introducing internal controls, and stimulating risk-aware management behavior.

Within J.P. Morgan, this paper-based CSA process had several distinct advantages over its predecessor's operational risk management efforts. These included the establishment of a repeatable, sustainable process that had standardized operating procedures and assessment forms. Additionally, J.P. Morgan's CSA Program transferred the responsibility for Operational Risk Management from the third-party assessor to the business unit, who completed the assessment. The shift in ownership of the process to the business unit began to improve the risk consciousness throughout J.P. Morgan, as a common risk language was established and accountability was assigned to individuals.

Despite the significant advantages of a paper-based CSA process over a third-party assessment, J.P. Morgan determined that a paper-based CSA process was plagued with practical challenges of a different kind. The paper-based nature of the tool was manually intensive and required extensive time commitments by the business unit to complete the assessment. The administrative burden imposed on the CSA sponsor and business unit resulted in great effort expended to compile and monitor completed CSAs, and left very little time to analyze the results of the CSA. As an example, under the paper-based CSA environment, J.P. Morgan conducted approximately 2,300 assessments annually, which generated 400,000 sheets of paper and 39,000 man-hours.

The manual nature of these paper-based CSAs also resulted in assessments of uneven quality among the various business units and frustration for management as firmwide aggregation, progress monitoring, and trend analysis was virtually impossible. The end result was a process that produced a deluge of paper and data, *with limited success.*

Against the backdrop of this paper-based CSA process, J.P. Morgan's Technology Risk Management Group, led by Craig Spielmann, began to develop a tool to automate it. A web-enabled architecture was selected over the less sophisticated and less scalable Lotus Notes format, reflecting J.P. Morgan's desire to make this tool available institution-wide. By 1998, this Technology team had developed a software tool to automate the CSA process, and named it Horizon Risk and Control Self-Assessment. Initially, it was only used by the Technology Group to automate their CSA process. However, by 1999 several business units and functional areas were using Horizon to automate the CSA process. During 2000, the CFO of J.P. Morgan mandated use of Horizon by all business units and functional areas preparing CSAs.

Initially Horizon was designed to automate a manually intensive process; however, other significant benefits resulted: (1) Horizon provided J.P. Morgan with the ability to score business units risk environment on a relative basis, compare business units' to each other, perform trend analysis on risk levels, and aggregate a company-wide risk profile; (2) the system provided increased accountability of the action planning process and allowed for improved monitoring of action plans; (3) it provided a central repository for best practices to be captured and shared company-wide; (4) it provided a mechanism to share risk management ideas across the company and promoted constructive competition across the company to be the best managed business unit; and (5) Horizon further "institutionalized" the CSA process within the business unit and further developed the risk culture and language within J.P. Morgan.

Horizon is a web-based, intuitively risk-focused tool. It operates on a variety of server configurations. It has a highly functional user interface, which connects to the Internet through most browsers, and uses Sybase, or other major database applications, to manage and store data. In addition, because it is scalable and flexible, Horizon can support many desktop configurations, which helps to ensure high-quality performance in remote locations.

Spielmann reports that Horizon has improved J.P. Morgan's assessment quality, productivity, management oversight, and overall operational risk management effectiveness. The increased efficiency has prompted some J.P.Morgan business units to move the CSA process to a quarterly cycle, thus getting more frequent views of their risk and decreasing the business unit's assessment completion time. The Quarterly Assessment module leads users through an intuitive risk identification, assessment, and mitigation process. The Reporting Module helps management derive maximum value from assessment data by providing a global risk profile of the business, and the Administration Module allows administrators to tailor the application to reflect the company's organizational structure.

Since its adoption, the system has provided significant benefits to various stakeholders within the organization. Senior Management now receives a consolidated view of risk across business lines and insight into how those risks are being managed. This allows them to make strategic decisions regarding the acceptance and management of risk, and to improve investment decisions on systems and business processes. Line managers get a clear understanding of the risk facing their area of responsibility and use this to drive tactical decisions and identify potential problems quickly before they become major problems or lead to losses. Risk Management and Internal Audit use the information to focus their resources on areas of higher risk and efficiently manage risk from a corporate perspective.

In 2000, J.P. Morgan rolled out Horizon company-wide with the support from Ernst & Young LLP.[4] J.P. Morgan realized other immediate benefits from its deployment of Horizon. In the short term, J.P. Morgan conducted 2,300 assessments, eliminated virtually all paperwork, and drastically reduced man hours. Today, J.P. Morgan conducts over 2,500 assessments, with each assessment taking only two to four hours, significantly down from the sixty hours per assessment with the paper-based self-assessment program.

Since its initial implementation, the system has been enhanced in several areas. In July 2000, an automated e-mail capability was added that automatically reminds action plan owners that they have an upcoming or past due date for an action they committed to complete. This has improved action plan completion performance drastically. In addition, an audit module has been added to Horizon's functionality, thus centralizing all business issues, ranging from self-assessment issues to internal and external audit, regulatory, and compliance issues in one database. Upon merging with Chase Manhattan, the combined firm has announced its decision to roll the system out enterprise-wide to support the CSA program within the combined institution. Furthermore, J.P.

Morgan Chase intends to use Horizon as an input to the capital allocation process, with the goal of allocating operational risk capital more accurately.

■ ■ ■

CASE ILLUSTRATION

Working toward Dynamic Enterprise-wide Risk Profiling

Halifax Group, Plc.

Ammy Seth, Head of Special Risk Areas at Halifax Group, contributed the following overview of the Group's operational risk management technology strategy. This case is a continuation of the Halifax case on risk profiling in Chapter 13.

Halifax appears to be on its way toward positioning itself, on the one hand, to begin gathering and aggregating all of the information needed for both economic and regulatory capital modeling. On the other hand, it is working toward levering the power of technology for continuous risk profiling—day-to-day management of operational risks groupwide.

To support our risk profiling strategy, Halifax investigated a number of technology solutions and found that software being developed by Operational Risk Inc., "The ORCA Solution," was a very good fit for its needs. Due to funding issues at Operational Risk Inc. and OperationalRisk.com in August 2000, Halifax was presented with a unique opportunity of purchasing "The ORCA Solution" software and brought it in-house as a proprietary system. As this book goes to press, it has been reported that Algorithmics has now acquired the system and commercialized it as OpData. It is working to complete the development of the software to provide a complete integrated solution for the purpose of supporting both periodic and dynamic risk profiling. This solution will deliver internal requirements for operational risk management within the Group and also functionality to support the criteria demanded by Option 3 (Internal Measurement Approach) of the New Basel Capital Accord, as well as the British Bankers' Association loss gathering initiative.

A Complete Solution Enabled by Technology (OR Suite)

The technology solution, when fully developed, will deliver part of this model and, when combined with a front-end Self-Assessment tool, existing risk assessment methodologies at the business unit level, and a flexible reporting tool, will provide the Halifax with a fully integrated solution for identifying and managing operational risk.

The Halifax intends to roll out this solution Groupwide, empowering users to gather and input a variety of operational risk management data. The system was originally built on a Unix (Sun Solaris) platform with a complex data model and database capabilities; it is now on a NT/Intel Platform to enable implementation across the Group network. It is web-based, so access is provided over the Group's own intranet.

The system is scalable and capable of growing with the organization and being brought online piece-by-piece. Following is an overview of the system's major component parts.

Self-Assessment OR Profiling (ORP) Module   This module will be based on the Halifax's existing risk-profiling framework. Business areas are required to identify and assess material risks, adequacy of controls, actions required, and confidence in their risk management performance.

It can be used as a comprehensive mechanism for identifying operational risks to each business that use other methodologies such as scanning and research and reflect varying risk cultures.

Risk Indicator Module   Halifax is gathering risk indicator data from around the Group in support of its operational risk management and measurement effort. The Risk Indicator module is intended for use in tracking, monitoring, and dimensioning a variety of risk indicators in support of an active operational risk management program. These categories include inherent risk variables, control-oriented risk indicators, composite risk indicators, and operational risk model factors.

At the most basic level, Halifax will use this module to track certain measures as a means of dimensioning exposure and active management. These include basic things like numbers of systems, workstations, process handoffs, asset size, and numbers of system users. These are their inherent risk variables. At the second level, Halifax plans to track certain variables that are generally believed by business managers to be measures of risk and therefore useful for risk management information systems' (MIS) tracking value. Examples are investment levels in system maintenance and product or service training. They refer to this second group as control-oriented risk indicators.

At a third level Halifax is able to monitor and track combinations of risk indicators as composite risk indicators. Examples of such composite indicators might be technological viability or complexity. Last, the indicators' application enables Halifax to monitor, track, and analyze model factors. These are designated variables, individual or composite risk indicators that have been selected, perhaps weighted, and/or proven to bear some direct relationship to the propensity for losses. Thus, Halifax can use them in predictive operational risk models now being explored by firms in the current dialogue about operational risk measurement and modeling for operational risk capital.

The operational risk indicators module can be used separate from, or in combination with, other parts of the product suite. It is essential that data has a common underlying framework to enable meaningful analysis (causative factors, risk categories, impacts, etc.).

Event Module   Halifax's event application module has been developed to capture, monitor, track, and analyze another important set of operational risk data that are descriptive of their own experience: Risk Issues, Near Misses, and Losses.

The first of these data sets includes descriptive information about Operational Risk Issues—various operational risk situations or circumstances. The most common example entails general or technology audit issues. Thus, situations that have been known to represent an unresolved risk situation can be tracked and rated in the system for risk severity. A "price tag," including risk pricing or risk capital, can serve to drive the point home further.

The second data set supports the tracking and analysis of Operational Risk Near Misses—events that have occurred at a bank location but have not yet resulted in a direct economic loss. The frequency of such events is a particularly good indicator of risk because frequency, whether increasing or decreasing, underscores changes in loss potential. Loss severity, or the actual cost of loss events, on the other hand, although often causing financial pain, can be far more random. Estimation of loss impact for near misses is much more defensible and transparent than pure subjective assessment.

The third and last component of the event application enables the bank to track its operational loss events that have actually resulted in economic or reputational loss. Here Halifax tracks its own experience by its business sectors, products, services, or by loss type. This database is primarily representative of larger industry events and has a variety of uses in risk management, but notably in a statistical sense can serve as a proxy for the severity loss distribution tail for analysis purposes.

External Loss Data   Halifax is participating in a British Bankers' Association scheme to share operational risk data with other members (BBA Loss Data Consortium—see Chapter 10). This is a reciprocal arrangement and in return for anonymously providing data regarding operational risk experiences, aggregate data from other participating banks is received. Halifax also received historical loss data as part of its agreement to purchase the ORCA Solution from Operational Risk Inc. (now the IC Squared First Database — see Chapter 10).

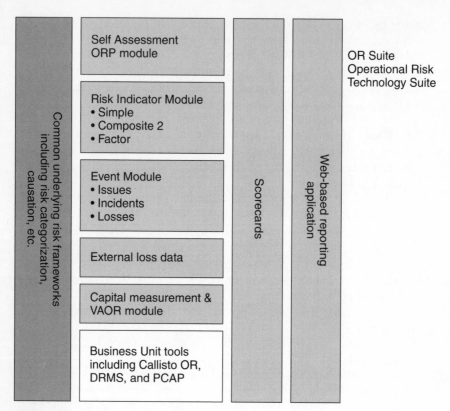

EXHIBIT 19.4   ORCA Functionality

Capital Measurement and VAOR Module   The risk profiling information and loss analysis will be used by Halifax to build the distributions required to allocate economic capital using a VAOR (Value at Operational Risk) methodology. While regulatory capital methodology is under development, the Basel Committee has indicated that Key Risk Indicators (KRIs) and objective measurement techniques will be key.

Analytics and Reporting   Halifax intends to produce reports and analyses from the application sections independently, or in combination. Options will include performing simplified "on board" analysis for simulation of future losses, or exporting data for analysis by independent actuaries or statisticians.

At its higher levels of usage, the system will be used to leverage sophisticated analytics and management techniques, enabling simultaneous evaluation and management of risk across business units and geographies, and proving the adage that a business can be stronger than the sum of the individual parts. Exhibit 19.4 illustrates the ORCA functionality.

■ ■ ■

CASE ILLUSTRATION

An In-house Build Scenario for Bottom-Up Risk Analysis

Commonwealth Bank Group

This case was contributed by Denis Taylor of the Commonwealth Bank Group. It describes their technology development in support of bottom-up risk analysis and their rationale for an in-house system build.

An integral component of our direct-assessment methodology for operational risk Economic Equity quantification is our proprietary database to facilitate the process. When implementing the Group's methodology, off-the-shelf technology solutions to operational risk were limited in their capabilities.

The Group Operational Risk Management System (GORMS) was developed in-house in conjunction with our overall operational risk management methodology. Therefore, GORMS has been developed in accordance with the precise objectives, functionality needs, and reporting requirements of the Group.

These specific needs included the following:

- Achieving consistency of implementation of our methodology across the Group.
- Providing a means for Divisional reporting and management of operational risk on an ongoing basis.
- Providing an analytical extrapolation tool to business users to convert an initial loss point estimate to a consistent standard (AA+ solvency standard).
- Facilitating the process of aggregating risks and accounting for risk correlations, through a Monte Carlo simulation. The result of this process is an Economic Equity calculation for operational risk.
- Providing a basis by which individual risks may be classified by a risk owner according to product, business process, customer segment, and delivery channel. This permits the estimation of Economic Equity on each of these bases.

While these types of information systems are not, within themselves, a panacea for implementing a consistent and coherent framework, GORMS has further contributed to a common understanding and application of our methodology throughout the Group.

The system is also used as a management decision support tool by enabling "what if" or sensitivity calculations on loss quantification, or the relative impact of changes in risk financing decisions and risk treatment initiatives.

GORMS runs on a SQL server with a Visual Basic user interface, while the Monte Carlo simulations modules were written in C++. In developing the database, independent external expert advice was sought on an ongoing basis to ensure the sound application of mathematical principles, thereby validating the approach.

Lessons learned from the exercise included:

- Proprietary systems offered the flexibility in functionality and reporting we required. However, the internal and external expert resources required to develop, support, and maintain such a proprietary system should not be underestimated.
- Independent external expert opinion on analytical modules provides a greater level of confidence in, and integrity to, the tool.
- Flexibility in technology solutions is essential if operational risk methodologies are to keep pace with business change and advances in operational risk quantification.

■ ■ ■

CASE ILLUSTRATION

Applying Fuzzy Logic Technology to Operational Risks

Commerzbank Case

This case was contributed by Corinna Mertens of Commerzbank, Irina Schaf of Accenture, and Dr. Hars-Peter Guellich of Risk Management Concepts Systems. It outlines Commerzbank's technology considerations in support of its data aggregation effort, and pilot use of Fuzzy Logic for operational risk monitoring and management. It continues their case from Chapter 13.

A market survey indicated that no software solution was available in 1998-99 that could support both a flexible risk data and rating aggregation with associated loss collection and systemization. Commerzbank and Accenture were therefore looking for a competent partner to develop an appropriate system solution that fully supports their developed method of monitoring OR.

Commerzbank was particularly interested in finding or designing a system that would meet a number of key needs in support of operational risk management firmwide. Their top priorities included:

- **Flexible Aggregation and Report Structure:** In order to develop a firmwide surveillance and monitoring system for operational risks, Commerzbank identified the need for a system logic that would support both a flexible aggregation of all identified risk indicators to a realistic risk profile and a flexible reporting structure. It was necessary to be able to drill down from a broad risk overview of Commerzbank's current risk profile to the individual risk causing indicators and symptoms.

■ **Fuzzy Logic Soft Computing Methodology:** Operational risks represent real world problems that continually confront corporations. As the available information for assessing the related risk to given operational incidents are often subjective, incomplete, imprecise, unreliable, etc., fuzzy logic was selected as the soft computing methodology best suitable to Commerzbank's requirements for dealing with such conditions.

■ **Web Accessability:** Since ORM cannot be seen at Commerzbank as a management topic purely controlled from an organization's head office, a world wide–accessible system was deemed necessary. It was decided to use a fully web-based system solution as it does not involve any PC installations and therefore immediately supports an enterprise-wide usage throughout Commerzbank's global organization. Furthermore, a web-based solution significantly reduces the later maintenance costs for system operation.

■ **Causal-based Loss Assignment:** To achieve a better insight view into the actual risks and their related losses, a causal-based loss assignment to individual risk indicators and symptoms and the collection of the according losses caused was identified as an important functionality for the later OR system.

■ **Daily Prospective Risk Rating:** In order to avoid operational losses, it was Commerzbank's goal to be capable of identifying operational problems before they were realized as losses. It was thus decided that an early warning system was needed that permanently assesses all relevant operational risks Commerzbank was confronted with.

■ **Calculation of Regulatory Capital:** It was also Commerzbank's intention to build the basis for being capable to transform all qualitatively-assessed operational risk events into their related projected regulatory capital charge for Commerzbank in total and for its individual business lines. Therefore, the intended system solution for operational risk management had to be flexible. It had to be capable of supplying all relevant information and parameters for calculating all monetary risks related to OR using any later available and accepted quantification methodology that seemed likely to develop for calculating regulatory capital.

In short, as Commerzbank saw it, losses due to operational risk are a latent threat to all banks. The value proposition of good operational risk management is to reduce the amount of losses actually incurred. Under the risk framework that the January 2001 Basel Consultative Document on Operational Risk implies, good ORM will also enable banks to reduce their capital charges. To realize this value proposition, Commerzbank's Operational Risk Management Framework had to:

- Provide a consistent approach to the identification of areas that potentially and actually create operational risk loss.
- Assess the potential threat through consistent risk measurement and thus create risk transparency for all management levels.
- Enable operational risk and loss reduction by supplying relevant cause-effect information about the loss creating areas.
- Be supported by a decentralized organization of operational risk managers and controllers to combine business and risk-controlling expertise.
- Be seen as a permanent operational risk evaluation process, thus requiring the installation of a monitoring system for the continued assessment of existing operational risks.

Commerzbank and Accenture turned to Risk Management Concepts Systems (RCS) to realize the required software, as they specialize in risk management software using Fuzzy Logic.

RCS had developed a methodology that handles time series aggregation through the use of fuzzy logic for credit risk applications.[5] This seemed an ideal foundation for handling the operational risk aggregation problem: Fuzzy logic technology offered a straightforward method for handling complicated concepts. The RCS solution, called TSA (time series aggregation), has been well received thus far in the Commerzbank's business units because it produces an intelligible rating-based approach to monitoring operational risks. The aggregation of all relevant parameters for risk assessment is handled via a transparent and comprehensible aggregation hierarchy as shown in Exhibit 19.5.

The evaluation of business risks and their aggregation into an operational risk index is performed by hierarchical aggregation of all decision parameters using intelligent decision support systems. That is, once data are scored, the fuzzy logic features of this intelligent system permit the realistic adoption of the human decision process.

The resultant TSA tool is an Internet-based standard software that can be flexibly parameterized with the needed aggregation structure of risk ratings and inverse drill down on the risk reporting. Losses are tracked and associated with the aggregation structure.

A key advantage of the Internet-based software solution is that it can be flexibly installed at the enterprise-wide or business unit level. It

Input Parameters   Parameter Aggregation   Risk Assessment Result

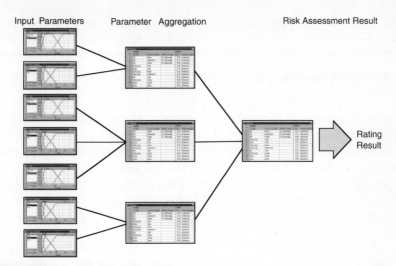

Rating
Result

EXHIBIT 19.5 Fuzzy Logic Aggregation
Source: RCS Risk Management Concept Systems (AGS).

will reach its full potential for operational risk management, however, when it is deployed across the entire corporation. The software aggregates actual losses or near losses and allows for both a bottom-up aggregation or rating that reflects the entire health of an organization, or an inverse drill-down approach that allows for rapid identification of individual "wayward" indicators at the business unit level.

The TSA system, which presently also provides access to the Zurich IC Squared First Database of external loss events, has provided a flexible and intelligible method for monitoring operational risks within Commerzbank. It is the bank's intent that, by using such a system, it will have a method for meeting both the qualitative and quantitative standards that are currently being discussed under the Basel II Accord.

At the time of this writing in early 2001, the system was still in its roll-out phase. Early indications are however, that the OR information being provided is already serving very well to manage and direct the risk analysis and reduction work.

■ ■ ■

BUILD OR BUY CONSIDERATIONS

The decision to build or buy will involve a number of important considerations, not the least of which include the availability of commercial systems in the market that will meet firms' needs and cost. Given the new market and discipline, the cases previously detailed outlined both in-house build scenarios and commercial applications developed both under contract and on commercial speculation.

Caveat Emptor: Labor and Cost Considerations

In any event, if you choose to buy a system, beware of consultants clothed as technology vendors. A technology product should not require an inordinant amount of consulting support. A client organization should have the option to use it as a stand-alone tool, if desired, and if it is capable of supporting the effort with in-house resources. Because of the complexities of operational risk and operational risk management, however, there are few, if any, off-the-shelf systems available today. For the same reasons the operational risk cannot be easily qualified, it cannot be easily generalized to all organizations.

Sometimes the result of this is what I often refer to as the consultant's "Trojan horse strategy." A consulting firm will build some screens with a glossy exterior and enough functionality to whet the prospective client's appetite, but upon further examination, it is shown that the system contains only limited functionality and requires $1 to 2 million of consulting fees to tailor the system to the client organization!

In fairness, this phenomenon is symptomatic of the unique nature of operational risk itself, but it can be a function of the consultant's strategy. Prospective clients should begin conversations with consultant-technologists with their eyes open. In some cases, million dollar studies are well worth the investment, but we all know that they are not always necessary, and are particularly unwelcome when they take a client by surprise, as in when he or she thought they were buying ready-to-use off-the-shelf technology that will require only minimal customization.

In contrast, firms such as Commonwealth Bank Group, as previously described, have gone alone (in-house). Alternatively, banks such as Standard Chartered Bank in the United Kingdom have applied products like SOFWIN, which was developed by the HSBC Operational Risk Consultancy. SOFWIN is a low-tech compact disk-based tool that enables an institution to create a "code of best practice" benchmark which is then used to analyze a consolidated database of information that has been collated across the entire organization. The goal of the software is to identify areas of weakness in the internal control structure of the organization. SOFWIN seeks to achieve this by providing a series of expert internal control type questionnaires that have essentially "done the thinking" for the organization. This type of approach is of particular value to those institutions that do not have the time, expertise, or resources available to create a best practice model for themselves. The flip side is that they may face the data and information aggregation challenge that J.P. Morgan Chase wrote about in their previously listed case.

CONCLUSION

The choice of operational risk management strategy at a given firm will drive its technology needs. Whether management is building a centralized analytic function, focused primarily on the calculation of operational risk capital, or designing a broad-based enterprise-wide effort intended to track and monitor a variety of information sources, each will require different technology resources, or at least a different level of resources.

In the end, technology will be essential to aggregate, simplify, and wire the pieces of whichever puzzle you choose, thereby connecting all of the functional areas, initiatives, and data sets, both hard and soft, firmwide. Time is money—don't waste yours with manual tracking, collection, compilations, and analytics. In addition to the scarcity of staffing resources and the need to maximize the productivity of operational risk management professionals, gather and work your numbers efficiently so you and your team can make time to get out and practice hands-on risk management.[6]

LESSONS LEARNED AND KEY RECOMMENDATIONS

- Leverage risk management efforts through state-of-the-art technology. Assure program efficiency by leveraging technology in enterprise-wide data gathering, analysis, and information delivery. Web-enabled systems will support the flow of data and information both internally and externally. Use powerful database and data warehouse technology to prepare for the flood of data that will be required to manage operational risk effectively in the future (BP Strategy #20).
- Definition of the user groups and an assessment of their needs objectives and goals are key to a successful design and implementation. Don't assume that all needs and uses are known without this step.
- Paper-based and even Spreadsheet applications will only serve to get you started. Many of us began our operational risk program by gathering risk indicators, factors, and losses and maintaining them in a spreadsheet application. This is fine for a start. However, as your mandate, program, and data universe become more complex, it becomes unworkable to manage myriad data input, organizational changes, the evolution of data standards and classification of data, and most importantly, the ability to extract different data combinations and produce management reports on demand.
- True enterprise-wide operational risk programs will require a sophisticated data collection and aggregation in a data warehouse in order to manage all the data and information needs across the firm. For instance, an array of risk measures is even more powerful when used to systematically capture, monitor, and analyze trends over time. This is best achieved as a component of an overall ORS.

- Be sure to identify all sources of data that may be available/useful in the firm, then plan to link with those systems to the extent possible.
- Leverage web-based technology wherever possible to gather risk and loss data and develop risk reporting systems firmwide.
- Aggregated operational risk reporting will become commonplace, much as portfolio market and credit risk reports have, but because of the pervasive nature of OR and ORM, they will become even broader in their reach. In addition, because of the softer issues involved, like the vagaries of human behavior (i.e., people risk), a mix of tools will be needed to fully represent operational risk. The risk complexities will also require more effective risk management programs to link initiatives and variables together not just periodically, but continuously, and with the speed of "Internet time."[7]
- Focus on technology needs sooner rather than later, inasmuch as the time required to assess needs, build, and/or acquire and customize will always take longer than anticipated. Double, or possibly triple, build-time estimates.

CHAPTER 20

The Game Plan and Action Steps

INTRODUCTION

The best risk management practitioners are continually seeking new ideas for advancing their programs and initiatives. Now that we have covered all of the essential operational risk management strategies, and associated tools, techniques and resources, the question becomes, "There is so much ground to cover, where do I begin with implementation?"

In the Introduction to this text we set out to provide a roadmap for organizations as they begin to develop enterprise-wide operational risk management programs. Throughout the book we have discussed topics ranging from corporate vision and ORM methods, to the technology needed to support them.

This final chapter will serve as a generalized game plan, albeit simplified and generalized, in the context of the Best Practice Strategies, methods, tools, and techniques presented. The plan provides some practical guidance on important areas of focus toward an otherwise far-reaching and seemingly daunting undertaking. Thus, it sums up all of these topics into an overview plan for enterprise-wide program development, first in the form of Phases of Development, then as specific action steps.

We cannot possibly cover all the issues in this short chapter, but we will strive to address some of the most important highlights.

THE VALUE PROGRESSION, AGAIN

The plan of action for an individual firm will depend on where it sits in the value pyramid we discussed in Chapter 4. Exhibit 20.1 presents a slightly different version of it. Here we have converted the pyramid to a progression, with additional detail about each stage. The idea is to present a conceptual view of development, along with associated benefits, in order to put an implementation plan into context.

The firm's starting point in the progression will depend on management perspective, and its program's current status. If it is just beginning a program,

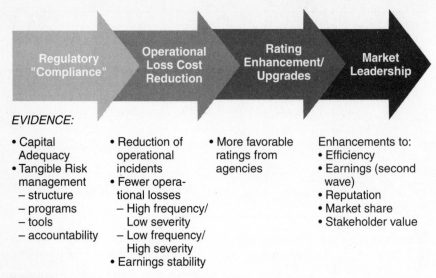

| Regulatory "Compliance" | Operational Loss Cost Reduction | Rating Enhancement/ Upgrades | Market Leadership |

EVIDENCE:

| • Capital Adequacy
• Tangible Risk management
  – structure
  – programs
  – tools
  – accountability | • Reduction of operational incidents
• Fewer opera-tional losses
  – High frequency/ Low severity
  – Low frequency/ High severity
• Earnings stability | • More favorable ratings from agencies | Enhancements to:
• Efficiency
• Earnings (second wave)
• Reputation
• Market share
• Stakeholder value |

EXHIBIT 20.1 The Operational Risk Management Value Progression

logically it will want to start at the beginning of the progression in the Operational loss cost reduction phase. Similarly, if the firm already has some risk control programs in place, but has no means of collecting incident, loss, and indicator data, it will also need to begin near the first phase. If it already has a framework in place, and data collection capabilities, then it will begin at the second Regulatory Compliance phase, and so on. The value increases demonstrably when applied across all business lines and corporate centers with full integration of management reporting and information. At the highest level, as the day-to-day business needs, the reporting, and regulatory requirements have been satisfied and the information is being applied to its fullest extent, a clear market leadership and competitive edge will begin to emerge. It is a bit ironic, of course, that recent regulatory developments have forced some firms to jump in at phase 2, before they have addressed phase 1 fully.

The design and implementation of a truly firmwide operational management program can be daunting. It is not at all uncommon to lose focus at various points along the way in implementation. Thus, it is useful to revisit our Best Practice Strategies at this point. Exhibit 20.2 is a summary outline. Let's construct action steps and projects around them. Note that our game plan may not necessarily follow the precise order that the BP Strategies were presented in the text. There the order was intended to provide a framework and conceptual flow in order to piece together the concepts in operational risk management. Here the presentation follows roughly along the business lines of generalized priorities and urgencies. That said, the order here is flexible. Naturally, the order and priorities will vary by firm, and a number of strategies

1. Define Operational Risk for the Organization
2. Demonstrate a Vision, Mandate, and Objectives
3. Foster a Culture of Integrity and Risk Management Awareness
4. Manage the Risk to the Firm's Franchise, Reputation, and Brand
5. Empower Business Units with Responsibility for Risk Management
6. Support and Leverage Corporate Units Capabilities and Contributions
7. Designate an Operational Risk Management Unit to Serve as Facilitator
8. Disseminate Useful Management Information and Reports
9. Use Incentives and Disincentives in Managing Operational Risk
10. Employ Segregation and Diversification Strategies
11. Leverage Firmwide Defenses for Business Continuity
12. Implement a Bottom-up Process to Identify, Evaluate, and Manage Operational Risks
13. Use a Portfolio-based Approach to Evaluate Firmwide Loss Potential
14. Coordinate Event and Risk Indicator Data Firmwide
15. Apply Analytics to Improve all ORM Decision Making
16. Implement Dynamic Risk Profiling and Management
17. Enhance Risk Finance Hedge Operational Risks
18. Apply Operational Risk-Adjusted Performance Measures and Economic Risk Capital Models
19. Monitor Emerging Regulatory Capital and Supervision Environment and Position Accordingly
20. Leverage Risk Management Efforts Through State-of-the-Art Technology

EXHIBIT 20.2   Operational Risk Management Best Practice Strategies

will be addressed concurrently. The point is that without some attempt at prioritization it will seem that all strategies are equal in urgency!

FRAMEWORK, MANDATE, AND ORGANIZATION

In order to cover the full spectrum of a plan and program development, we begin with framework, mandate, and organizational considerations.

Establishing the Foundation

Gauge and/or Influence Executive Management Ideology and Commitment   Review corporate statements on ideology as an important first step. The architects of the

new program will meet with appropriate senior management team members. Determine management position toward operational risk management initiatives. Read between the lines. Is management receptive to taking a fresh enterprise-wide approach to risk management, including use of many of the strategies and techniques described in the preceeding chapters, or will operational risk management only be viewed as a regulatory necessity, intended only to achieve certain baseline objectives? If the former, then work to develop context for the operational risk management within the firm's strategic vision. If the regulatory context is your reality, then deal with the current reality, but work to broaden the perspective and risk management vision.

Relevant BP Strategy: Demonstrate a Vision, Mandate, and Objectives (Strategy #2).

Develop a Mission Statement   A clear mandate is key for setting the agenda and communicating management and Board commitment outward throughout the organization. The statement will:

- Identify key program objectives, operational risk problems, issues, and opportunities
- Establish goals and timeframes
- Identify resources and communications

The mission statement will be an important backdrop for conversations with managers and staff from this point forward.

Relevant BP Strategy: Demonstrate a Vision, Mandate, and Objectives (Strategy #2)

Meet with Key Business Managers   Even if the operational risk management team is well established in the firm from other experiences and roles, time spent meeting with key line and corporate managers and staff members is an excellent investment, and will be rewarded severalfold in the future. Here, there is an opportunity to discuss all aspects of the business, identify critical processes, key vulnerabilities, and important operational risks. The key objective, however, would be to gather inside about opinions and important considerations in developing operational risk programs and models. For instance, identifying the business and performance drivers may be just the right ingredient for achieving mutual objectives—building performance measures into the program that is important to the business manager, while gaining an ally and enlisting support and enthusiasm for the operational risk program, drivers, and metrics.

Relevant BP Strategy: Empower Business Units with Responsibility for Risk Management (Strategy #5)

Gauge Corporate Culture Corporate culture will already be a clear reflection of senior management commitment. Is management focused on revenue or earnings growth only, or is there a growth-through-quality strategy? If the former is the case and risk management, risk control, and Internal Audit are viewed simply as necessary evils, then the job of formulating a firmwide strategy will be a much tougher charge. When we first began our research and analytic work at Bankers Trust, the firm already had a risk-based capital culture in place, so the idea of developing an economic capital program, Operational RAROC, was a natural progression for our team and for the firm. When we were ready to rollout our firmwide allocation scheme, the firm was in the midst of reassessing all control efforts as the firm was under seige from allegations of leveraged derivatives misdeeds, so the organization and staff were receptive, and the culture was ripe for introducing a risk-based capital allocation scheme as well.

Relevant BP Strategy: Foster a Culture of Integrity and RM Awareness (Strategy #3)

Operational Risk Management Framework Organization

Define Operational Risk for the Organization Based on initial meetings, and the firm's perspective on operational risk, craft a definition that will be useful internally. Remain mindful of developing regulatory discussions and the evolution of definitional considerations industry-wide.

Relevant BP Strategy: Define Operational Risk for the Organization (Strategy #1)

Form a Team to Coordinate ORM The structure and size of the operational risk management team will be designed commensurate with your own company, of course, being mindful of issues like the mandate for the corporate function and the level of centralization versus decentralization.

Relevant BP Strategy: Designate an ORM Unit to Serve as Facilitator (Strategy #7)

Recruit/Cultivate Top Talent The team should be comprised of a senior manager with leadership abilities. He or she must understand the vision and strategies for the business overall, have a broad working knowledge of operational risks, understand key mitigation strategies, and be capable of building and leading a diverse team of professionals. This brings us to the team membership. The team should be comprised of a diverse group commensurate with its overall mission. That is to say that if risk assessment is key at the outset, the group should include individuals with audit and self-assessment backgrounds, some product and operations backgrounds, perhaps legal and/or compliance backgrounds, perhaps strategic planning experience, and quantitative expertise. If risk finance and insurance is included, then specific expertise in these areas will be required, as well.

Relevant BP Strategy: Designate an ORM Unit to Serve as Facilitator (Strategy #7)

Establish Relationships with Key Control Groups   Concurrent with the process of meeting with key business managers, the team should forge relationships with all corporate risk and control-related groups, as well as seek to promote and leverage ORM efforts already underway for mutual benefit. This will be a key step for establishing the basis for both formal and informal operational risk task force and committee membership.

Relevant BP Strategy: Support and Leverage Corporate Units' Capabilities and Contributions (Strategy #6)

Form an Operational Risk Management Committee or Working Team   Actual formation of the committee will be the next step. It is advisable to have an executive committee member chair the committee, or at least serve as an active participant and a visible advocate for its mission and agenda.

Relevant BP Strategy: Support and Leverage Corporate Units' Capabilities and Contributions (Strategy #6)

Program Framework and Business Strategy Context   Link operational risk management to a firmwide strategy initiative for maximum impact, whether that linkage be to Six Sigma or other quality initiatives, firmwide value programs such as EVA, Enterprise-wide risk management, VAR, RAROC, or other performance initiatives. There should be a higher context and mandate than an operational risk management mission alone.

Relevant BP Strategy: Apply Economic Capital Models and Operational Risk Adjusted Performance Measures (RAPM) (Strategy #18)

Technology

Scope / Invest in Appropriate Technology Early   The mission and mandate will drive technology needs. It is never too soon to begin scoping technology needs for the program. Even if outsourced, most technology solutions will take time to develop, design, test, and implement. Begin immediately to identify primary needs and determine the appropriate course of action.

Relevant BP Strategy: Leverage Risk Management Efforts Through State-of-the-Art Technology (Strategy #20)

Risk Response Framework

The point of Chapter 8, Risk Response Framework and Strategies, was to emphasize the fact that context is needed for risk response. These strategies are key to providing the framework for enterprise-wide responsibility and accountability for operational risk management. Thus, early on in the context of the Strategies, our plan should address communications and management information, incentives and disincentives, segregation and diversification strategies, and leverage firmwide business continuity defenses, as follows:

Communications and Management Information   Identify and assess the most beneficial communications media, content, and formats early on in the process and during the course of meetings with executive management and business line management.

Relevant BP Strategy: Disseminate Useful Management Information and Reporting (Strategy # 8)

Develop Reporting Content   One of the agenda items during the course of key meetings with line managers and staff should be to discuss useful report content and format considerations. Beyond the obvious inclusion of the results of economic and regulatory capital models, determine what information would be most useful to line managers in managing the business day-to-day, such as key risk drivers, benchmarking data, industry loss information, causative factors, and studies. Include all information that a manager can interpret and use not only for operational risk management, but for business enhancement and improvement.

Determine the Forums and Media for Reporting   Determine the most effective forums for reporting on firmwide and business-specific risk assessment, mitigation, loss cost, risk capital, and other progress. Fix a frequency of reporting. Determine meetings beyond the Operational Risk Committee. Leverage senior executive committee structures for maximum visibility for issues, initiatives, and progress.

Develop Other Firmwide Programs (Orientation, NBA) Additional programs should be considered and developed, if not already in place, such as orientation programs to reinforce behavioral and conduct standards on a firmwide basis, including an awareness for risk management. Focused and periodic training with any risk awareness focus might also be advisable, or might be linked with other existing programs. As another example, a new business approval (NBA) process is an excellent way to implement a defined sign off process including legal controllers, internal audit, and operational risk unit approval before a business is initiated.

Incentives and Disincentives Identify the most effective means of providing incentives and disincentives for operational risk management. Ideally the program will involve risk adjusted performance measures, incentive compensation, and firmwide recognition activities.
Relevant BP Strategies:

- Use Incentives and Disincentives in Managing Operational Risk (Strategy # 9)
- Apply Operational Risk Adjusted Performance Measure (RAPM) (Strategy #18)

Segregation and Diversification Design the operational risk management program to extract key concentration-of-risk vulnerabilities from Internal Audit, self-assessment, and risk assessment efforts firmwide. Portfolio-level risk assessments are particularly useful for identifying physical asset risk concentrations. Internal Audits are useful for identifying the lack of dual controls or lack of segregation of duties.

Relevant BP Strategy: Employ Segregation and Diversification (Strategy #10)

Align to Business Continuity Strategies Align operational risk management iniatives to business continuity risk management programs. Avoid redunancy of effort. Create mutual leverage.
Relevant BP Strategies:

- Leverage Firmwide Defenses for Business Continuity Planning (Strategy #11)
- Manage Risk to the Firm's Franchise, Reputation, and Brand (Strategy #4)

Risk Assessment / Risk Monitoring and Profiling / Tools and Data

At this point action steps have been taken to reinforce a risk management culture as previously described, with the firm's own ORM objectives and Risk

Response Framework Strategies firmly in hand. Next, initiate risk assessment, monitoring and management programs at multiple levels firmwide. An overview of action steps follows. Exhibit 20.3 outlines some of the specific tools and techniques of this and the following sections on analytics and financial management.

Bottom-Up Risk Assessment The implementation of a bottom up risk assessment program is a major undertaking that requires support and involvement of management at all levels. Without support and commitment, the effort probably qualifies as little more than window dressing and may be something just short of futile.

Relevant BP Strategy: Implement Bottom-up Processes to Identify, Evaluate, and Manage Operational Risks (Strategy #12)

Implement Portfolio Level Risk Assessment Keep operational risks in perspective, enable firmwide risk measurement, and enterprise-wide decisions on risk-reward strategies.
Relevant BP Strategies:

- Use a Portfolio-based Approach to Evaluate Firmwide Loss Potential (Strategy #13)
- Apply Operational Risk Adjusted Performance Measures (RAPM) and Economic Capital Models (Strategy #18)

Collect Incident, Issue, and Loss Data in a Central Location It is certainly possible to collect incident, loss, and issue data manually, then enter them into spreadsheets for further analysis. In any organization of appreciable size, however, this process of collecting data manually, even with the support of e-mail, will be a considerable undertaking. Thus, once cooperation is established with units firmwide, more extensive technology will be advisable as soon as reasonably possible. One initial step would be to identify an accounting code for data entry into existing systems. Another more extensive solution would be to develop a dedicated system. Either way, process and technology will become essential to support a five enterprise-wide program.

Relevant BP Strategy: Coordinate Event and Risk Indicator Data Firmwide (Strategy #14)

Ensure Continuous Monitoring and Dynamic Profiling Do not allow risk assessment, data collection, and monitoring efforts to stagnate. Much corporate data and

Risk Management Action	The Mandate	Tools and Techniques
Risk Identification and Measurement	• Recognition and dimensioning operational risk sources and causal factors • Determining scenarios and possible loss potential	• Directional risk indicators and analysis • Inherent risk variables • Control-oriented risk indicators • Composite indicators and model factors • Operational risk MIS • Scenario Analysis • Experience-based statistical / actuarial projections • Risk capital *calculations*
Risk Response and Risk Mitigation	• Support for strategic decision-making • Understanding business operational risks • Making strategic risk-based decisions • Support for the Risk Control environment • Create appropriate incentives	• Self-assessment / Risk assessment linked to Decentralized controls • Capital *attribution or allocation* • Performance management • Goal setting • Results tracking • Risk-based incentive compensation • Operational risk-based strategic decision-making • Links to the Risk Control environment
Risk Finance and Insurance	Extend New Definition, Understanding, and Measurement Toward: • Evaluation / stress-testing of existing insurance programs • Support for ongoing risk finance decision-making • Improved cost-of-risk results • Creation of new operational risk hedges	• Re-engineering of conventional programs • Reserves and self-funding • Reinsurance • Financial structures • Integrated programs • Use of new operational risk finance metrics

EXHIBIT 20.3 Action Plan—Tools and Techniques

information can become outdated shortly after it is collected. Link data collection with real-time web-enabled technology as soon as reasonably possible to ensure accurate and timely risk information and profiles for both day-to-day and periodic strategy decisions.

Relevant BP Strategy: Implement Dynamic Risk Profiling and Management (Strategy #16)

Analytics, Model, and Management Information Systems Development

Develop Analytics and Models Appropriate for the Organization For a large, complex organization that uses sophisticated market and credit risk models, a combination of sophisticated loss distribution and causative models are probably most appropriate for operational risk management. For others, a scoring approach, (risk maps) might make more sense. Alternatively, a firm might simply consider a modified version of the regulatory proposals.

Relevant BP Strategy: Apply Analytics to Improve ORM Decision Making (Strategy #15)

Financial Management — Risk Finance, Regulatory, and Economic Capital

Risk Finance and Insurance Management A linkage should be developed early on between operational risk management and insurance and risk finance initiatives in order to align definitions, hedging objective organization information flows, and monitoring progress. This linkage will have been initiated early on during the course of business line and corporate staff meetings.

Relevant BP Strategy: Enhance Risk Finance Hedging of Operational Risks (Strategy #17)

Regulatory Analytics and Models Commensurate with the choice of sophistication analytics and models above, in the parlance of regulatory models in discussion, the firm's program sophistication will either dictate use of the Basic Indicator, Standardized, Internal Measurement approach, or possibly the Internal Measurement and Loss Distribution methods combined, depending upon the future track that regulatory developments take.

Economic Risk Capital Models More sophisticated firms will develop their own economic capital models beyond those required by regulation. If designed and developed properly, they will support both decision-making and performance management objectives. Firms that see the benefit of these tools will actually begin development of pilot versions much earlier in their program development. Ironically, however, logic would suggest for most that at this later, more developed stage we will be addressing sophisticated modeling. We know from regulatory developments, however, that action is being forced earlier on the development of many firms' programs.

Relevant BP Strategy: Monitor the Emerging Regulatory Capital and Supervisory Environment and Position Accordingly (Strategy #18)

CONCLUSION

A properly positioned operational risk management program will reflect the broad scope of the firm's associated risks. Thus, it must indeed be a far-reaching discipline. It will permeate throughout an entire organization and will require involvement of all tiers of management and employees. Its reach emphasizes the enormous challenge in managing these risks.

With this challenge in mind, this chapter, and this entire book, has been designed to help simplify the problem. By shedding some light on emerging Best Practice Strategies and case illustrations, firms will be in a position to benefit from the experience and lessons learned by others.

With these Best Practices and lessons as a foundation, risk practitioners will be poised to benefit from understanding the bigger picture on operational risk management. By addressing the key issues from definition and corporate vision, right on through to technology and regulation, firms will be in the best possible position to balance their overall operational risk profile for market leadership and maximum stakeholder value.

additional readings

INTRODUCTION

Bernstein, Peter L. *Against the Gods: The Remarkable Story of Risk.* New York: John Wiley & Sons, Inc., 1996.

Fay, Stephen. *The Collapse of Barings.* New York: W.W. Norton & Company, 1996.

Gapper, John, and Denton, Nicholas. *All That Glitters: The Fall of Barings.* London: The Penguin Group, 1996.

Jameson, Rob, Ed. *Operational Risk and Financial Institutions.* London: Risk Books and Arthur Andersen, 1998.

Pring, Martin J. *Investment Psychology Explained.* New York: John Wiley & Sons, Inc., 1993.

Root, Steven J. *Beyond COSO.* New York: John Wiley & Sons, Inc., 1998.

CHAPTER 1

Chernow, Ron. *The House of Morgan: An American Banking Dynasty and The Rise of Modern Finance.* Atlantic Monthly Press: New York, 1990.

Drucker, Peter. *Managing for Results: Economic Tasks and Risk-taking Decisions.* New York: Harper & Row, 1964.

Various Authors. *Operational Risk and Financial Institutions.* Rob Jameson (Ed.). London: Risk Books and Arthur Andersen, 1998.

CHAPTER 2

International Swaps and Derivatives Association, Inc. *Operational Risk Regulatory Approach: Discussion Paper,* September 2000 (Particular focus on the Appendix entitled Operational Risk Management Framework Leading Practice Guidelines).

Lowenstein, Roger. *When Genius Failed.* New York: Random House, 2000.

Miccolis, Jerry, Muelley, Hubert, and Gruhl, Robert, "Enterprise Risk Management in the Insurance Industry: 2000 Benchmarking Survey Report," Tillinghast-Towers Perrin, 2000.

Operational Risk: The Next Frontier. Philadelphia: RMA (and) British Bankers' Association (and) ISDA (and) Pricewaterhouse Coopers, [1999].

CHAPTER 3

Blunden, A. C., and Hill, V. J. H. "People Risk: The Human Factor — Definition and Measurement." *Operational Risk,* February 2000, pp. 13–14.

Downes, Larry, and Mui, Chunka. *Unleashing the Killer App.* Boston: Harvard Business School Press, 1998.

Gates, Bill. *Business @ The Speed of Thought: Using a Digital Nervous System.* New York: Warner Books, 1999.

Operational Risk: The Next Frontier. Philadelphia: RMA (and) British Bankers' Association (and) ISDA (and) Pricewaterhouse Coopers, [1999].

CHAPTER 4

Brocka, Bruce, and Brocka, M. Suzanne. *Quality Management: Implementing the Best Ideas from the Masters.* Homewood, Illinois: Business One Irwin, 1992.

Campbell, Andrew, and Nash, Laura L. *A Sense of Mission: Defining Direction for the Large Corporation.* Reading, MA: Addison-Wesley Publishing Company, 1992.

Collins, James C., and Porras, Jerry I. *Built To Last: Successful Habits Visionary Companies.* New York: HarperCollins Publishers, Inc., 1994.

Deal, Terrence E., and Kennedy, Allan A. *Corporate Cultures: The Rites and Rituals of Corporate Life.* Reading, MA: Addison-Wesley Publishing Company, 1982.

Eccles, Robert G., Herz, Robert H., Keegan, E. Mary, and Phillips, David M.H. *The ValueReporting Revolution: Moving Beyond the Earnings Game.* New York: John Wiley & Sons, 2001, pp. 146–147.

Heller, Robert. *The Leadership Imperative: What Innovative Business Leaders are Doing Today to Create the Successful Companies of Tomorrow.* New York: Truman Talley Books / Dutton, 1995.

Horton, Thomas R. *The CEO Paradox: The Privilege and Accountability of Leadership.* AMACOM, a division of the American Management Association, New York, 1992. (Particularly Chapter 13 - Corporate Culture: Ignore it at Your Peril.)

Pande, Peter S., Neuman, Robert P., and Cavanagh, Roland R. *The Six Sigma Way.* New York: McGraw-Hill, 2000.

Slater, Robert. *The GE Way Fieldbook: Jack Welch's Battle Plan for Corporate Revolution.* New York: McGraw-Hill, 1999.

Various Authors. *Operational Risk and Financial Institutions.* London: Risk Books and Arthur Andersen, 1998.

CHAPTER 5

Copeland, Tom, Koller, Tim, and Murrin, Jack. *Valuation: Measuring and Managing the Value of Companies.* New York: McKinsey & Company, Inc. and John Wiley & Sons, 1995.

Gottschalk, Jack A., Ed. *Crisis Response.* Washington D.C.: Visible Ink, 1993.

Knight, Rory F., and Pretty, Deborah J. *The Impact of Catastrophes on Shareholder Value.* Oxford: Templeton College, 1997.

Lynch, Peter, and Rothchild, John. *One Up on Wall Street.* New York: Penguin Books, 1989.

Lynch, Peter, and Rothchild, John. *Beating the Street.* New York: Simon & Schuster, 1993.

Mackiewicz, Andrea. *The Economist Intelligence Unit Guide to Building a Global Image.* New York: McGraw-Hill, Inc., 1993.

O'Neil, William J. *How to Make Money in Stocks.* New York: McGraw-Hill Book Company, 1988.

Schuetter, Hansruedi. "Analysis of Impact—Brand and Reputation," *E-Risk: Business as Usual?* London: British Bankers Association, 2001.

CHAPTER 6

Annon. *Focus on the Bank Director.* Washington D.C.: American Bankers Association [1984].

Blanchard, Ken, Carlos, John P., and Randolph, Alan. *The 3 Keys to Empowerment.* San Francisco: Berrett-Koehler Publishers, Inc., 1999.

Larsen, Mark W., and Maze, Mary R. *1999 Directors and Officers Liability Survey: U.S. and Canadian Results.* Chicago: Towers Perrin, 2000.

CHAPTER 8

Belcher, John G., Jr. *How to Design & Implement a Results-Oriented Variable Pay System.* New York: AMACOM, a division of American Management Association, 1996.

Drucker, Peter F. *Management Challenges for the 21st Century.* New York: HarperCollins Publishers, Inc., 1999.

Gottschalk, Jack A. *Crisis Response: Inside Stories on Managing Image Under Siege.* Detroit, MI: Visible Ink Press, 1993.

Nudell, Mayer, and Antokol, Norman. *The Handbook for Effective Emergency and Crisis Management.* Lexington, MA: Lexington Books, 1988.

Smith, Roy C., and Walter, Ingo. *Street Smarts.* Boston: Harvard Business School Press, 1994.

CHAPTER 9

Kloman, H. Felix, and Hoffman, Douglas G. "Risk Assessments: The Risk Management Process (A Bankwide Assessment of Risks Associated with Traditional and Non-Traditional Services and New Business Opportunities)." *Risk Assessments.* Washington, D.C.: American Bankers Association, 1984.

Levine, Margaret, and Hoffman, Douglas G. "Enriching the universe of operational risk data: Getting started on risk profiling." *Operational Risk* (March 2000), pp. 25–39.

CHAPTER 10

Cagan, Penny, and Manser, Rene. "Operational Risk Loss Databases." *Operational Risk* (April 2001).

Hoffman, Douglas G. "Into the valley." *Risk Professional 2* (December 2000), pp. 12–18.

CHAPTER 11

Hoffman, Douglas, and Taylor, Denis. "Risk Indicators: How to Avoid Signal Failure," *Operational Risk Special Report, Risk,* November, 1999, pp. 13–15.

Simons, Robert. "How Risky Is Your Company?" *Harvard Business Review,* May-June 1999, pp. 85–94.

CHAPTER 12

King, Jack L. *Operational Risk: Measurement and Modelling.* West Sussex: John Wiley & Sons, Ltd., 2001.

Marshall, Dr. Christopher Lee. *Measuring and Managing Operational Risks in Financial Institutions: Tools, Techniques and Other Resources.* Singapore: John Wiley & Sons (Asia) Lte Ltd 2001.

Various Authors. *VAR: Understanding and Applying Value-at-Risk.* London: Risk Publications, 1997.

Vose, David. *Quantitative Risk Analysis: A Guide to Monte Carlo Simulation Modelling.* New York: John Wiley & Sons, 1996.

Wheeler, Donald J., and Chambers, David S. *Understanding Statistical Process Control.* Knoxville, Tennessee: SPC Press, 1992.

CHAPTER 13

Gates, Bill. *Business @ The Speed of Thought: Using a Digital Nervous System.* New York: Warner Books, 1999.

Miccolis, Jerry and Shah, Samir. *Enterprise Risk Management: An Analytic Approach*. Tillinghast-Towers Perrin, 2000.

CHAPTER 14

Elliot, Curtis M., and Vaughnan, Emmett J. *Fundamentals of Risk and Insurance*. New York: John Wiley & Sons, Inc., 1972.

Kulp, C. A., and Hall, John W. *Casualty Insurance*. New York: The Ronald Press Company, 1968.

Mehr, Robert I., and Hedges, Bob A. *Risk Management: Concepts and Applications*. Homewood, Illinois: Richard D. Irwin, Inc., 1976.

Wielinski, Patrick, Woodward, Jeffrey, and Gibson, Jack. *Contractual Risk Transfer*. Dallas, TX: International Risk Management Institute, Inc. (IRMI), 1995–2001.

Williams, C. Arthur, Jr., and Heins, Richard M. *Risk Management and Insurance*. New York: McGraw-Hill Book Company, 1976.

CHAPTER 15

Head, Dr. George, ed. *Course Guide - RM 56: Risk Financing*. Insurance Institute of America.

Monti, R. George Monti, and Barile, Andrew. *A Practical Guide to Finite Risk Insurance and Reinsurance*. New York: John Wiley & Sons, Inc., 1995.

CHAPTER 16

Hoffman, Douglas, and Johnson, Marta. "Operational Procedures," *Risk 9*, no. 9 (October 1996), pp. 60–63.

Matten, Chris. *Managing Bank Capital: Capital Allocation and Performance Measurement*. New York: John Wiley & Sons, Inc., 1996.

"Next Frontier of Risk Management," *Corporate Finance Risk Management & Derivatives Yearbook 1996*, pp. 12–14.

Parsley, Mark. "Risk Management's Final Frontier," *Euromoney* (September 1996), pp. 74–78.

CHAPTER 17

Basel Committee on Banking Supervision. *Consultative Document: Operational Risk*. Bank for International Settlements, January 2001.

International Swaps and Derivatives Association, Inc. *A New Capital Adequacy Framework: Comments on a Consultative Paper Issued by the Basel Committee on Banking Supervision in June 1999*, February 2000.

International Swaps and Derivatives Association, Inc. *Operational Risk Regulatory Approach: Discussion Paper,* September 2000.

Kimber, Matt, and Hoffman, Douglas G. "Operational risk management and capital adequacy: A frontal assault on capital?" *Operational Risk* (March 2000), pp. 71–83.

Working Group on Operational Risk and Institute of International Finance. *Response to the Basel Committee on Banking Supervision Regulatory Capital Reform Proposals,* May 2001.

CHAPTER 19

Downes, Larry, and Mui, Chunka. *Unleashing the Killer App.* Boston: Harvard Business School Press, 1998.

Paggett, T., Wilson, D., and Pinkstone, I. "Technology to Tackle Operational Risk," *Operational Risk, Risk Professional,* March 2000.

Williams, Deborah. *Time for a New Look at Operational Risk.* Newton: Meridien Research, Inc., February 2000.

Operational Risk Management: Bibliography of Sources

BACKGROUND INFORMATION ON RISK

1. "Mastering Risk." *Financial Times. www.ftmastering.com.* Ten Tuesday installments, starting on April 25, 2000, and ending on June 27, 2000. This is one of the most extensive discussions of risk management ever published in the general business press. Topics included a history of risk management, decision tree analysis, value-at-risk, product liability, bribery, systemic risk, e-commerce risk, and an introduction to crisis management.

2. *Operational Risk and Financial Institutions.* Risk Publications. 1998. Brings together essays by a number of risk professionals. Includes both introductory and more in-depth discussions of operational risk. Topics include trends, measurement and management, retail banking applications, processing errors, securities fraud, and model risk. The charts— covering a variety of topics including descriptions of the large loss events—are especially worth investigating.

3. "Operational Risk: A Special Report." *Risk Magazine* insert. November 2000. Includes state-of-the-art discussions by most of the prominent thinkers in the industry on operational risk methodology, systems, programs, and solutions.

4. *Operational Risk.* March 2000. A special issue published by Risk Professional magazine. Includes several key operational risk articles, including "Enriching the Universe of Operational Risk Data: Getting Started on Risk Profiling" by Douglas Hoffman and Margaret Levine, and "Operational Risk Management and Capital Adequacy: A Frontal Assault on Capital?" by Douglas Hoffman and Matt Kimber. Additional articles include "Towards a Grand Unified Theory of Risk" by Roland Kennett, and "Technology to Tackle Operational Risk" by Tim Pagett.

5. *Managing Operational Risk in Financial Markets.* Amanat Hussain. Butterworth-Heinemann, 2000.

This bibliography was prepared by Penny Cagan of Zurich IC Squared.

6. *Operational Risk: Measurement and Modeling.* Jack Leon King. John Wiley & Sons, 2001.

7. *Managing Operational Risk: 20 Firmwide Best Practice Strategies.* Douglas G. Hoffman. John Wiley & Sons, 2002.

8. *Journal of Portfolio Management.* May 1999. This 25th anniversary issue is devoted to the history of risk management, and includes articles by a group of risk pioneers, including Merton Miller, Frank J. Fabozzi, and Tanya Styblo Beder.

9. *Dictionary of Financial Risk Management.* 1999. Frank J. Fabozzi Partners. By Gary L. Gastineau and Mark P. Kritzman. This basic reference source contains robust definitions of key terms.

10. *Operational Risk: The Next Frontier.* December 1999. Information about the study is available at the following site: *www.isda.org/a5200_2.html.* This study is based on a series of interviews with 55 global financial institutions located in North America, Europe, and Asia. It includes a discussion of operational risk, management structures, senior management reporting, operational risk capital, insurance strategies, and tools. An executive summary and table of contents is available at the British Bankers Association site: *www.bba.org.uk.* The report concludes with an observation of seven major trends, including an industry-wide acceptance of operational risk management as a core competency.

11. *Time for a New Look at Operational Risk.* February 2000. Meridien Research. Includes an overview of operational risk, an appraisal of available vendor solutions, and case studies. *www.meridien-research.com.*

12. *Risk Budgeting: A New Approach to Investing.* Edited by Leslie Rahl. Risk Books. 2000. Chapters are dedicated to a variety of topics, including crisis and risk management, and the dangers of historical hedge fund data.

13. "A Walk on the Wild Side: Financial Risk Sources on the Web." Penny Cagan. *Econtent.* 12/01/1999.

14. "Are You the Risk Manager of Tomorrow?" Charles Fishkin. *The RMA Journal.* February 2001.

15. "The Knowledge Factory." Charles Fishkin. *MiddleOffice.* Autumn 2000.

16. "The Silent Risk." Charles Fishkin. *FOW.* December 2000.

17. "Arming the Corporate Everyman." Charles Fishkin and Penny Cagan. *FOW.* July 2001.

18. "Seizing the Tail of the Dragon." Penny Cagan. *FOW.* July 2001.

19. "Capital Market Solutions for Op Risks: Does a Credit Derivative Model Make Sense?" Penny Cagan. *Operational Risk.* June 2001.

20. *Value at Risk: The New Benchmark for Managing Financial Risk.* Phillippe Jorion. McGraw Hill, 2000. The new version of Jorion's ear-

lier groundbreaking book on VAR includes chapters on operational risk and integrated risk management.

21. *Famous First Bubbles: The Fundamentals of Early Manias.* Peter M. Garber. The MIT Press, 2000. Includes in-depth discussions of "Tulipmania" in the 1770s in Holland and the "South Sea Bubble." Provides interesting analogies to modern day "bubbles."

22. "Planting Seeds for a New Competitive Edge." Banking 2000, Summer 2000. *www.bankingmm.com/sumed/p66.html.* A timely discussion of operational risk, and where the industry currently stands in terms of regulations and current thought.

23. *Enterprise Risk Management in the Insurance Industry: 2000 Benchmarking Survey Report.* Tillinghast-Towers Perrin. *www.tillinghast.com.* This survey of insurance executives finds that although many are aware of the extreme importance of having an operational risk program, they are dissatisfied with their own progress with addressing operational issues on an enterprise-wide basis. The insurance executives cited technology, interest rates, distribution channels, reputation/rating, and expenses as the most important types of risk faced by their companies. In addition, the chief barriers to integrating operational risk into a firm's risk management program include having the right tools (50% of those surveyed).

INDUSTRY PERIODICALS

1. *Risk. www.riskpublications.com. Risk* magazine is a monthly devoted to all aspects of risk management. This is the premier source for risk information, and always a good place to start your research.

2. *Operational Risk. www.watersinfo.com. Operational Risk* is a monthly newsletter with more of a micro focus on operational industry personnel and issues than *Risk* magazine.

3. *Wall Street and Technology. www.wstonline.com. Wall Street Technology* is one of the best sources for information on technology, software, and vendor trends in the financial services industry.

4. *Treasury and Risk Management. www.treasuryandrisk.com.* Almost every issue includes a major discussion of an operational risk.

5. *Middle Office. www.fow.com/magazine/magazine.htm.* A journal of firmwide risk management.

6. *Risk Professional. www.llplimited.com/cat98/rm3.htm.* The official publication of the Global Association of Risk Professionals (GARP).

7. *Derivatives Strategy. www.derivativesstrategy.com.*

8. *Institutional Investor. www.iimagazine.com.* A good basic business journal with occasional discussions of risk related topics.

9. *US Banker. www.usbanker.faulknergray.com/.*

10. *The Industry Standard. www.thestandard.com.* Full-text print and online journal with essential coverage of e-commerce, the Internet, and the new "net economy."
11. *Risk Management Reports. www.riskreports.com. Risk Management Reports* were started in 1974 by Felix Kloman as an "irreverent, opinionated, and iconoclastic monthly commentary on strategic risk management."
12. *Business Insurance. www.businessinsurance.com.*
13. *International Risk Management. www.grmn.com.*
14. *Risk Management. www.rims.org.* From the Risk and Insurance Management Society.
15. *Banking 2000. www.bankingmm.com.* A quarterly online publication from Silverline Publishing. Almost every issue includes several major articles devoted to risk management topics. Recent issues have included articles on operational risk, data management, e-commerce, and Internet banking.

KEY WEBSITES

1. Institute of International Finance (IIF). *www.iif.org.* The IIF has recently initiated a discussion on operational risk, and associated news releases and discussions are expected to appear on its website.
2. International Association of Financial Engineers. *www.iafe.org.* The IAFE has established an operational risk committee.
3. The International Swaps and Derivatives Association. *www.isda.org.* ISDA's site provides access to Market Surveys, a list of publications, notices of conferences, recommended readings, and useful links.
4. The Group of Thirty. *www.group30.org.* The Group of Thirty's site includes a catalog of the organization's primary publications and documents.
5. Risk News. *www.risknews.net.* This is a new offering from *Risk* magazine and includes real-time risk related headlines and events. A good source for daily monitoring of the risk industry.
6. Financial Technology Network. *www.financetech.com.* Includes links to Wall Street & Technology, Insurance & Technology, Bank Systems & Technology, and Trade Shows and Conferences.
7. CIBC Financial Products. *www.schooolfp.cibc.com.* CIBC Financial Products has constructed an in-depth educational website devoted to all aspects of risk. This is one of the richest content sites on the web in terms of content.
8. FinanceWise. *www.financewise.com.* Financewise is a search engine owned by Risk publications that focuses exclusively on financial content and risk management providers. This is one method of streamlining an Internet search and retrieving more focused results.

9. Bank for International Settlement (BIS). *www.bis.org*. This site provides access to most BIS studies, documents, news releases, initiatives, documentation, and Best Practices guidelines.

10. Meridien Research. *www.meridien-research.com*. Meridien is a premier market research firm that specializes in the financial services industry and is one of the first such organizations to evaluate operational risk applications.

11. Algorithmics. *www.algorithmics.com*. Algorithmics is a vendor of risk management software, and its well-designed site includes case studies and recently published market overviews, including a discussion of its mark-to-future methodology.

12. Philippe Jorion's webpage. *www.gsm.uci.edu/~jorion*. This site includes the selected full text of Professor Jorion's case studies, including a discussion of Orange County.

13. IFCI Risk Watch. *http://ifci.ch*. IFCI's site includes text in a nicely formatted grid of selected regulatory documents from BIS, IOSCP, and G-30, among others.

14. Robert Tomski Associates' Operational Risk site. *www.oprisk.freeserve. co.uk*. In-depth background information of operational risk, with links to key regulatory documents. Includes a detailed historical outline of operational risk events.

15. RiskWorld. *www.riskworld.com*. This is an interesting website that focuses on risk issues in the corporate community. Recent headlines cover soft drink contamination and the rate of injury among flight attendants.

16. Erisks.com. *www.erisks.com*. Erisks.com is a portal offering from Oliver Wyman. Daily news stories, cases studies, and stress scenarios are included.

17. Barra. *www.barra.com*. Barra specializes in analytic models, software, consulting, and money management services. This site provides in-depth discussions of Barra's predicted betas and information relating to Barra models and indices.

18. Risk metrics. *www.riskmetrics.com*. Former J.P. Morgan-affiliated group devoted to providing risk management research, data, software, and consultation services, and benchmark risk management products.

19. Value at Risk Resources. *www.gloriamundi.org*. A metasite for information on VAR. This site provides an excellent bibliography of VAR books, articles, and research, and includes links to VAR software vendors, risk-related regulations, conferences, and courses.

20. Global Association of Risk Professionals. (GARP) *www.garp.com*. Includes access to GARP documents and discussions.

21. Contingency Analysis. *www.contingencyanalysis.com*. This site provides over 1,000 pages of information on financial risk management topics.
22. Institute of Internal Auditors. *www.theiia.org*.
23. Risk and Insurance Society. *www.rims.org*.
24. RiskCare. *www.riskcare.com*. This site includes daily risk management news, and short movies on a variety of topics, including footage of Nick Leeson being led away to prison.
25. The Board of Governors of the Federal Reserve System. *www.bog.frb. fed.us*. The fed site includes a complete text of many of its reports and working papers, recent studies, statistics, and links to the regional member banks.
26. The Bank of England. *www.bankofengland.co.uk*. This site includes full-text documents, recent speeches, minutes from Monetary Policy Committee Meetings, results of the Treasury Bill auctions, inflation reports, press releases, monetary and banking statistics, working papers, and regulatory documents.
27. The Financial Services Authority. *www.fsa.gov.uk*. The UK's FSA provides the full-text of reports, and press releases covering a variety of topics.
28. The Bundesbank. *www.bundesbank.de/index_e.html*. Includes monthly economic reports, statistics, special topics, and regulatory-position statements.
29. Zurich IC Squared. *www.ic2.zurich.com*. The IC Squared group has purchased the old CORE database from Operationalrisk.com and has renamed its offering FIRST (Financial Institution Risk Scenario Trends.) The group's website provides an introduction to its unusual and innovative approach to managing risk.
30. RiskNews. *www.risknews.net*. This daily risk related news offering from *Risk* magazine provides a convenient source for tracking daily news stories and key events.
31. Complinet. *www.complinet.com*. A compliance related news story based in the United Kingdom that provides excellent summaries of key securities, operations, human resources, and technology issues and incidents.

ARTICLES: FINANCIAL APPLICATIONS OF OPERATIONAL RISK

1. "Case Study—Weighing the Dragon: Operational Risk Measurement at ANZ (Parts I and II)." *Operational Risk*. October 2000 and November 2000. Mark Lawrence of ANZ Bank takes the reader through a step-by-step process of designing and implementing an operational risk program. This series of articles does a wonderful job pulling together all the key issues and strategies that are involved in such an enterprise-wide endeavor.
2. "Banking Services: Risk Enters the Real Works—As the Bank for International Settlements Revises its Capital Adequacy Framework, Bert

Bruggink and Alice Van Den Tillaart Offer an Alternative Way of Calculating Operational Risk." *The Banker.* September 2000.

3. "Operational Risk Reduction: William Higgins Argues That it Is Vital That Banks Put an Operational Risk Reduction Model in Place Now." *The Banker.* July 2000.

4. "Managing Operating Risks: a Control Issue." Rodd Zolkos. *Business Insurance.* February 28, 2000. Operational risk panel discussion at the American Bankers Association's annual insurance risk management conference.

5. "Lesson from a Swiss Bank." Ramon Dzinkowski. *Strategic Finance.* January 2000. Felix Fischer, the head of the risk management program at UBS, discusses the challenges and pitfalls of defining, measuring, and managing operational risk, with an emphasis on strategy. He estimates that UBS's data collection efforts (encompassing funding/liquidity risk, operations risk, clerical risk, IT or systems risk, legal risk, liability risk, compliance risk, physical risk, crime risk, reputation risk, and personnel risk) represents 25% of the total risk for the bank.

6. "Knowledge Is Power—Sort of." *USBanker.* January 2000. Discussion of study released on operational risk by British Bankers Association, International Swaps and Derivatives Association, Robert Morris and PriceWaterhouseCoopers. The survey found that banks have a long way to go in the process of identifying and quantifying operational risk.

7. "Firms Grope for Definition." David Sherreff. *Euromoney.* December 1999. Examination of the banking industry's reaction to the Basel Committee's recently released definition of operational risk: "Operational risk is the risk of direct or indirect loss resulting from inadequate or failed internal processes, people and systems, or from external events."

8. "Market Volatility Drives Escalating Operational Risk." *Global Investor.* December 1999/January 2000. A rare but very important discussion on how volatility in the financial markets increases operational risk—particularly in back office operations.

9. "Operational Lapses Cost the Industry $7 Billion." Rob Garver. *American Banker.* November 18, 1999. Discussion of a PriceWaterhouseCoopers report on operational risk. According to the survey, financial institutions lost $7 billion in 1998 due to failed internal controls and other operational risks.

10. "Comment: Risk Strategy Should Involve Entire Company." William M. Saubert. *American Banker.* November 3, 1999. Discussion of A.T. Kearney survey on risk spending.

11. "Countering the Domino Effect." Orla O'Sullivan. *US Banker.* August 1999. Deborah Williams, a Meridien Research director referred to by some as a "guru" in the risk management industry, discusses with the author enterprise-wise software packages, and the limitations of currently

available tools. According to Williams, all the spectacular incidents in recent years—including Barings, Kidder Peabody, Sumitomo, and Daiwa—have been operational risk failures.

12. "Fund Managers Fail Operational Risk and Efficiency Audit." Sudip Roy. *Global Investor.* February 1999. Addresses the importance of adopting straight-through processing as a tool for mitigating risk.

13. "Finding Value in a Collection of Losses." Matt Kimber. *Operational Risk Manager* (LLP Publishing). June 2000. An easy-to-read and fun approach to designing and using a loss database.

14. "Debunking Op Risk Myths." *Operational Risk.* March 2000. Newsletter from Risk Publications, Douglas Hoffman.

15. "How to Avoid Signal Failure." Doug Hoffman & Denis Taylor. *Risk.* November 1999.

16. "Getting the Measure of Operational Risk." Rob Jameson. *Risk.* November 1998.

17. "The Benefits of Sharing." Dan Mudge. *Risk.* January 2000.

18. "Made-to-Measure: Operational Risk Capital." Robert Ceske, Angelina Colombo, Lara Swann. *Operational Risk Management.* Autumn 2000.

19. "Share and Share Alike." Robert Ceske, Lara Swan. *Risk Professional.* November 1999.

20. "Quantifying Event Risk: The Next Convergence." Robert Ceske, Jose Hernandez. *Journal of Risk Finance.* Spring 2000.

21. "Controlling the Documentation Vortex." Charles Fishkin. *MiddleOffice.* Spring 2000.

22. "Electronic Derivatives Markets and Operational Risk Analysis." *Operational Risk.* May 2000.

23. "Hidden Dangers: Identifying Operational Risk in Collateral Management." Charles Fishkin. *MiddleOffice.* Summer 2000.

24. "Indicators of Operational Risk." Charles Fishkin. *Derivatives Week.* September 18, 2000.

25. "Software Roundup: Op Risk Software—The Leading Contenders." Rob Jameson and John Walsh. *Operational Risk.* June 2000. Includes operational risk managers' software wishlist and overview of available vendors. Comments on ORI: "ORI's offerings build a flexible platform for the management and analysis of a wide range of op risk information."

ARTICLES: CORPORATE AND OTHER APPLICATIONS OF OPERATIONAL RISK

1. "E-merging Risks." Emily Q. Freeman. *Risk Management.* July 2000. A discussion of operational issues and solutions in cyberspace.

2. "Top Priority on Bottom Line." Sally Roberts. *Business Insurance.* March 20, 2000. Discusses the transfer of business risk from the balance

sheet of corporations to the insurance market. Includes discussion of how United Grain Growers identified and transferred exposure to a series of identified risks.

3. "Risk Management." Mark Hall. *Computerworld*. January 17, 2000. Overview of operational risk management issues in the technology sector, with specific emphasis on e-commerce.

4. "The Final Frontier of Risk." Russ Banham. *Reactions*. May 1999. Discussion of new operational risk policies being written for nonfinancial corporations, including Mead Corp, and United Grain Growers.

5. "Operational Risks, Bidding Strategies, and Information Policies in Restructured Power Markets." Ray Dennis. *Decision Support Systems*. January 1999. Overview of the development of advanced analytical tools for the measurement of operational risk in power systems.

6. "Avoiding the Pitfalls of Risk." Ed Blount, *Infoworld*. April 1999.

KEY OPERATIONAL RISK REGULATORY DOCUMENTS

From the Bank for International Settlements, Basel Committee on Banking Supervision

1. *The New Basel Capital Accord*. January 2001. Includes additional supplements on Credit Risk, Internal Ratings-Based Approach, Asset Securitization, Interest Rate Risk, and Operational Risk. The general tenor of the document involves a shift from crude measures instituted under the 1988 Accord to more finely tuned ones that do a better job capturing the risk sensitivity of an individual institution. This involves a shift away from the one size fits all, single risk measure, broad-brush approach to one that emphasizes banks' own internal methodologies, supervisory review processes, and discipline. The scope of the document is broad and aims to cover a variety of solutions for banks that fall at various points on the risk management spectrum. The overall goal of the Basel Committee is to provide banks with incentives (in the form of capital discounts) for instituting proper risk management controls. The Committee's recommendations remain essentially unchanged for market risk measures, but offer revolutionary changes for credit risk, and propose an operational risk capital charge (20% of the total capital charge) for the first time.

2. *The New Basel Accord. Operational Risk Supplement*. January 2001. What is most notable about the supporting document on Operational Risk is the Basel Committee's request for industry commentary on a number of topics, including data collection, risk indicators, indirect losses, and insurance solutions. The Committee's primary goal is to "enhance operational risk assessment efforts by encouraging the industry to develop methodologies and collect data related to managing operational risk." Previously, the Basel Committee referred to operational risk as

simply "all other risks." The 2001 recommendations represent the first time the regulatory body has addressed operational risk directly. This is near monumental in the development of the discipline. Under the old 1988 Accord, the Basel Committee made an implicit assumption that "all other risks" were included under the capital buffer that was related to Credit Risk. In the new recommendations, the Committee acknowledges that the 1988 Accord made rather crude calculations covering market and credit risks, and that the newer Accord recommends capital calculations based on more accurate assumptions. The new more finely tuned recommendations reduce the amount of capital that is put aside for "other risks" under the more broad-brushed approach. Hence, the Basel Committee is recommending capital requirements that cover operational risk directly, based on a three-pronged "evolutionary approach" based on the readiness and sophistication of member banks. Banks are essentially provided with capital discounts under this approach if they can demonstrate a well-managed and properly controlled operating environment. The essence of the Basel Committee's approach is based on a supposition that the capital charge for a typical bank will be less at each progressive step on the evolutionary spectrum.

3. *The Relationship Between Banking Supervisors and Banks' External Auditors.* February 2001. *www.bis.org/publ/bcbs78.htm.* Recommends increased communication between bank supervisors and external auditors, and provides guidance on the relationship between the two parties.

4. *Other Risks (OR) Discussion Paper.* Revised April 2000. Available online at the following site: *www.sib.co.uk/basel/publications/bis_other_risks042000.pdf.* This consultative document from the Basel Committee provides a revision of the regulatory committee's 1998 capital adequacy guidelines. The focus of the document is to propose a capital adequacy framework for *other risks*. The Basel Committee's Risk Management Group targets identified risks other than market and credit risk as the focus of this discussion paper, including client relationship exposure, valuation risk, legal and documentation risk, technology and processing risk, transactional exposure, safe custody risk, in-house fraud, external fraud, liquidity, business, reputational, and strategic risks. The committee stresses the importance for establishing proper capital adequacy guidelines in light of two developments: (1) Newly developed and finely tuned credit calculations mean that the previous assumption that the capital buffer for credit risk implicitly covered operational risk is no longer true, and (2) developing banking practices such as securitization, outsourcing, specialized processing operations, and developing technologies will contribute to an environment of increased operational risk. The committee also recommends an internal capital assessment approach that decomposes activities into business lines and risk categories, and aggregates the total into an overall capital charge.

5. *Operational Risk Management.* September 1998. Available online at the following site: *www.bis.org/publ/index.htm.* This document is the committee's first attempt to address operational risk directly and systematically. The document isolates internal controls and corporate governance as the "most important types of operational risk" and concludes that such breakdowns can lead to financial losses through human error, fraud, or unsupervised and uncontrolled business practices. Other risks identified by the committee include technology failures and major disasters. The document is based on interviews with 30 major banks, and highlights the following concerns: (1) Incentives for business line managers to adhere to operational risk Best Practices are needed. The identified incentives include capital allocation for operational risk activities, performance based on operational risk measures, and the requirement that all business lines present operational risk data to top levels of management. (2) Banks need to develop frameworks for managing operational risk—at best, most are only in the early stage of doing so. (3) Banks have immediate data collection needs. This data is needed in order to create operational risk models of the order that already exist for model and credit risk projections. There is currently very little historical and time-series data available for such projections. The required data includes internal audit ratings or internal self-assessments, operational indicators such as volume, turnover or rate of errors, losses, and income volatility.

6. *Framework for Internal Control Systems in Banking Organizations.* September 1998. Available online at the following site: *www.bis.org/publ/index.htm.* This document provides a discussion of the Basel Committee's 13 principles for establishing internal controls. The report attempts to identify the types of control breakdowns that can occur. Control failures that are discussed include the following: (1) Lack of adequate management oversight and accountability and failure to develop a strong control culture. (2) Inadequate recognition and assessment of the risk of certain banking activities. (3) The absence or failure of key control structures and activities, such as segregation of duties, approvals, verifications, and account reconciliation. (4) Inadequate communication of information between different levels of management. (5) Inadequate or ineffective audit programs and monitoring activities. The document also stresses the role of internal auditors within a banking organization.

7. *Core Principles For Effective Banking Supervision.* September 1997. Available online at the following site: *www.bis.org/publ/index.htm.* This document includes a discussion of the Basel Committee's 25 core principles. The discussions attached to principles 14 (internal controls) and 15 ("know-your-customer" and due diligence rules) directly deal with operational issues, although other sections of the document are of additional interest.

8. *New Capital Adequacy Framework.* June 1999. Available online at the following site: *www.bis.org/publ/index.htm.* This robust document includes an introduction to the Basel Committee's new capital adequacy framework that replaces the 1988 Accord, and proposed approaches to establishing such guidelines. The committee acknowledges that most banks use modified versions of the 1988 Accord, but it also recognizes the validity of newer methods, including internal credit ratings and portfolio models. It extends the pool of risks that the earlier Accord identified to include operational and "other" risks categories. The committee states in the document that hard-to-quantify risks, such as reputational and legal risks, are important to understand and measure, and recommends a capital charge for this category of risks. It suggests that a "simple benchmark" can be established from a category of indicators, including off-balance-sheet exposures and operating costs.

9. *Consultative Paper on Customer Due Diligence.* January 2001. *www.bis.org/publ/bcbs77.htm.* This paper presents a "qualitative top-down" approach to operational risk and the establishment of Best Practices within a banking environment. Key discussions include know-your-client (KYC) initiatives and the establishment of anti-money laundering programs. The paper states that without proper due diligence procedures in place, a bank becomes vulnerable to reputational, operational, legal, and concentration risks.

From ISDA

10. *Operational Risk Regulatory Approach. Discussion Paper.* October 2000. This paper's primary objective is to "identify qualitative criteria that support the appraisal of operational risk management by institutions." The paper makes a case for establishing good operational risk principles and a management framework. It also discusses the challenges for regulators in their efforts to implement a qualitative approach.

From the Federal Reserve Bank of New York

11. *Building a Coherent Risk Measurement and Capital Optimization Model for Financial Firms.* Tim Shepheard-Walwyn and Robert Litterman. February 1998. Available online at the following site: *www.ny.frb.org.* Includes a discussion of how financial firms are using internal models to measure and allocate capital against credit, market, and enterprise-wide risks. The document provides an interesting definition of operational risk: "Operational risk can be seen as a general term which applies to all risk factors which influence the volatility of the firm's cost structure as opposed to its revenue structure."

12. *Regulatory Capital and the Supervision of Financial Institutions: Some Basic Distinctions and Policy Choices.* Arturo Estrella. January 2000. A discussion of regulatory capital for banks, with substantial but not absolute overlap with the BIS's 1999 recommendations.

From the Office of the Superintendent of Financial Institutions (OSFI)

13. *Supervisory Framework: 1999 and beyond.* August 1999. Available online at the following site: *http://www.osfi-bsif.gc.ca/AndreE/supervis.htm*. Canada's Office of the Superintendent of Financial Institutions (OFSI) has drafted a framework for a series of basic risk principles including: (1) Better evaluation of risks through separate assessment of inherent risks and risk management processes. (2) Greater emphasis on early identification of emerging risks and system-wide risks. (3) Cost effective use of resources through a sharper focus on risk. (4) Reporting of risk-focused assessments. OSFI recommends a six-step risk management process that includes analysis, planning, action, documentation, reporting, and follow-up.

From the Financial Services Authority (FSA)

14. *Risk-Based Approach to Supervision of Banks.* June 1998. Available online at the following site: *http://finaserv02.uuhost.uk.uu.net/pubs/policy/p10.pdf*. This paper discusses the Financial Services Authority's risk-based approach to the supervision of banks, and its framework for merging the RATE (Risk Assessment, Tools of Supervision, Evaluation) and SCALE (Schedule 3 Compliance Assessment, Liaison, Evaluation) methodologies. A step-by-step description of both RATE and SCALE and the FSA's regulatory responsibilities are included. In addition, the FSA states that it is "committed to adopting a flexible and differentiated risk-based approach to setting standards and to supervision, reflecting the nature of the business activities concerned, the extent of risk within particular firms and markets, and the quality of firms' management controls and the relative sophistication of the consumers involved."

From the Bank of England

15. Handbook in Central Banking. No. 7. *Basic Principles of Banking Supervision.* Derrick Ware. May 1996. Available online at the following site: *www.bankofengland.co.uk/cgi-bin/empower.exe*. Includes a discussion of "systemic problems" that failures within any one bank can contribute to

the banking system, operational risks, and ownership/management risks. The document recommends against the excessive concentration of risk in any one sector and stresses the importance of segregation of duties. It also targets the role of the internal auditor as one of great importance in relation to systems and controls.

From the European Commission

16. *A Review of Capital Requirements for EU Credit Institutions and Investment Firms.* November 1999. Available online at the following site: *http://www.ecb.int.* A consultative document that complements the Basel Committee review on the capital adequacy of banks with emphasis on credit risk. The document, however, does devote significant space to "other risks" and recommends a specific capital charge aimed to cover operational, legal, and reputational risk.
17. *Commission Services' Second Consultative Document on Review of Regulatory Capital for Credit Institutions and Investment Firms.* February 2001. This document updates the previously issued one above, and contends on specific European Union concerns. It also offers capital adequacy suggestions for credit and investment companies, and solicits comments before May 31, 2001. It provides an European context to the recent consultative paper on capital requirements released by the Bank for International Settlements.

From Global Association of Risk Professionals

18. *An Approach to Modelling Operational Risk in Banks.* October 1999. *www.garp.com.* Discussion of the Reliability Theory in predicting operational risk events.
19. *Operational Risk: Current Issues and Best Practices.* July 1999. A slide show of GARP's approach to operational risk.

From the British Bankers Association

20. *Operational Risk Data Pooling.* February 2000. *www.bba.org.uk.* An overview of the conclusions from meetings of the BBA Operational Risk Advisory Panel members on an effort to share operational risk data.
21. *The New Capital Adequacy Framework.* 1999. The BBA recommends requiring a benchmark operational risk capital charge based upon high level business activity indicators.
22. *Operational Risk Management Survey.* The first three chapters of the joint study with ISDA and RMA titled: *Operational Risk: The Next Frontier* is available online at the BBA's site.

From the Industry Technical Working Group

23. *The Internal Measurement Approach to Operational Risk Regulatory Capital.* (Option 3). October 13, 2000. The Industry Technical Working Group on Operational Risk responds to the Basel request for response to the internal measurement approach (option 3) to its recommendations for calculating operational risk. This is a technical paper, which befits a rather complicated capital approach.
24. *Working Paper on Operational Risk Regulatory Capital.* July 2000. The Industry Technical Working Group on Operational Risk. Provides a brief discussion of the three methods for establishing capital charges (single indicator, standardized lines of business, internal risk-based approach).
25. *The Evolutionary Framework: Qualifying Criteria for Each Stage and Other Qualitative Factors.* Industry Technical Working Group. October 2000. Describes a recommended framework for advancing along the evolutionary framework of capital charges (from option one—basic indicator approach—through option three—the internal measurement approach.) The methodology here is based on an earlier paper published by the Bank of Japan titled "Internal Risk-Based Approach."
26. *Response to RMG Request of 1 Nov 2000. Data & Definitions.* Industry Technical Working Group. November 2000. Data Standards based on a consensus reached among a small group of representatives from primarily U.S. and Canadian-based mid-sized banks during a two-day conference.

From the Institute of International Finance, Inc.

27. *Report of the Steering Committee on Regulatory Capital: Response to the Basel Committee on Banking Supervision, Regulatory Capital Reform Proposals.* May 2001. *www.iif.com.* The IIF steering committee on regulatory reform has recommended that banks be allowed to use their own internal rating systems. The organization also held a series of private meetings with a group of industry representatives, and has been critical of the BIS' "business line approach" as a valid method for operational risk assessment.
28. *Report of the Steering Committee on Regulatory Capital: Response to the Basel Committee on Banking Supervision, Regulatory Capital Reform Proposals.* May 2001. *www.iif.com.*

From the Bank of Japan

29. *Measuring Operational Risk in Japanese Major Banks.* June 2000. Discussion of the new focus among Japanese banks on operational risk and their mostly "bottom-up" approach. The document includes discussions of scenario analysis, methods for allocating capital, and the importance of internal data and external data.

30. *Internal Risk-Based Approach: Evolutionary Approaches to Regulatory Capital Charge for Operational Risk.* 1999. This paper discusses the Bank of Japan's Internal Risk Approach which is viewed as a bridge between the basic approach and the more complicated "full model" one. The paper presents recommendations for the "evolutionary" journal through the various levels of complexity.
31. *Challenges and Possible Solutions in Enhancing Operational Risk Measurement.* 2000. A summary of responses to its earlier "Measuring Operational Risk" paper.

INTRODUCTION

1. The Basel Committee on Banking Supervision (The Basel Committee) was established at the end of 1974 by the central bank governors of the Group of Ten countries. It meets regularly four times a year and has about thirty technical working groups and task forces which also meet regularly. One of these groups is the Risk Management Group (RMG), formerly the Risk Management Subgroup.

   The Committee's members come from Belgium, Canada, France, Germany, Italy, Japan, Luxembourg, the Netherlands, Spain, Sweden, Switzerland, the United Kingdom, and the United States. Countries are represented by their central bank and also by the authority with formal responsibility for the prudential supervision of banking business. The present chairman of the Committee is Mr. William J. McDonough, President and CEO of the Federal Reserve Bank of New York.

   The Committee does not possess any formal supranational supervisory authority, and its conclusions do not, and were never intended to, have legal force. Rather, it formulates broad supervisory standards and guidelines and recommends statements of Best Practice in the expectation that individual authorities will take steps to implement them through detailed arrangements—statutory or otherwise—which are best suited to their own national systems. In this way, the Committee encourages convergence towards common approaches and common standards without attempting detailed harmonisation of member countries' supervisory techniques.

   In 1988, the Committee decided to introduce a capital measurement system commonly referred to as the Basel Capital Accord. This system provided for the implementation of a credit risk measurement framework with a minimum capital standard of 8% by the end of 1992. Since 1988, this framework has been progressively introduced not only in member countries but also in virtually all other countries with active international banks. In June 1999, the Committee issued a proposal for a New Capital Adequacy Framework to replace the 1988 Accord. The proposed capital framework consists of three pillars: minimum capital requirements, which seek to refine the standardised rules set forth in the

1988 Accord; supervisory review of an institution's internal assessment process and capital adequacy; and effective use of disclosure to strengthen market discipline as a complement to supervisory efforts (*source*: www.bis.org).
2. Peter L. Bernstein, *Against the Gods: The Remarkable Story of Risk,* New York: John Wiley & Sons, Inc., 1996, pp. 18–21.
3. Press release announcing the CORE Loss Database (Operational Risk, Inc.), January, 2000.
4. *Source*: IC Squared First Database of operational loss events, which has evolved from Operational Risk, Inc.'s CORE (Compilation of Operational Risk Events) Loss Knowledgebase™, and before that it was the external database at Bankers Trust.
5. Margaret Levine and Douglas G. Hoffman, "Enriching the universe of operational risk data: Getting started on risk profiling," *Operational Risk*. London: Informa Business Publishing, March 2000; p. 25.
6. Doug Hoffman, "Debunking Op Risk Myths," *Operational Risk,* March 2000.
7. Ibid.

CHAPTER 1. OPERATIONAL RISK 101: AN EXECUTIVE SUMMARY

1. Except where noted otherwise, this chapter is based on and/or reprinted from Chapter 2 of *Operational Risk and Financial Institutions,* London: 1998, entitled "New Trends in Operational Risk Measurement and Management," pp. 29–42, by Douglas G. Hoffman. Reprinted with permission from Risk Books and Financial Engineering, Ltd.
2. Doug Hoffman, "Commentary: Debunking Op Risk Myths," *Operational Risk,* March 2000.
3. Douglas Hoffman, "Operational Risk Management: A Board-Level Issue," *Bank Accounting & Finance,* Winter 2000–2001, p. 27.
4. Ibid.
5. Peter Drucker, *Managing for Results: Economic Tasks and Risk-taking Decisions.* Harper & Row, New York, 1964.
6. Douglas Hoffman, "Operational Risk Management: A Board-Level Issue," *Bank Accounting & Finance,* Winter 2000–2001, p. 26.
7. Ibid., pp. 26–27.
8. Ibid., p. 26.
9. Douglas Hoffman, "Operational Risk Management: A Board-Level Issue," *Bank Accounting & Finance,* Winter 2000–2001, pp. 28–29.
10. This section is excerpted from Doug Hoffman, "Debunking Op Risk Myths," *Operational Risk,* March 2000. Reprinted with permission of Risk-Waters.

11. Douglas Hoffman, "Operational Risk Management: A Board-Level Issue," *Bank Accounting & Finance*, Winter 2000–2001, p. 29.
12. Ibid.
13. Ibid.

CHAPTER 2. THE BEST PRACTICE STRATEGIES

1. Douglas G. Hoffman, "New Trends in Operational Risk Measurement and Management," *Operational Risk and Financial Institutions*, London: Risk Books and Arthur Andersen, 1998.
2. Note that even though there is a separate section entitled Risk Mitigation Strategies, one might argue that many of the other strategies, such as Business Line Responsibility, have a risk mitigation orientation as well. But to drive home the importance of establishing an organizational framework, logic and convenience causes us to classify them under the heading "Framework."
3. Douglas Hoffman, "Operational Risk Management: A Board-Level Issue," *Bank Accounting & Finance*, Winter 2000–2001, p. 22.

CHAPTER 3. WHAT IS OPERATIONAL RISK?

1. The Basel Committee on Banking Supervison, *Consultative Document: Operational Risk* (Basel: Bank for International Settlements, 2001), p. 2. The Committee had adopted this "common industry definition" of operational risk for the purpose of framing its proposals as of January 2001. We might like to imply by this quote from an influential and standard-setting global regulatory body that there is full consensus on the definition of operational risk. But in reality, there is not, at least not *full* consensus just yet as evident by the references to definitions and risk classes throughout this book.
2. Reprinted with permission from Douglas G. Hoffman, "New Trends in Operational Risk Measurement and Management," *Operational Risk and Financial Institutions*, London: Risk Books and Arthur Andersen, 1998, p. 29.
3. The Zurich IC Squared First Database is an expanded and enhanced version of the ORI CORE™ (Compilation of Operational Risk Events) Knowledge-base, and prior to that was the Bankers Trust external database.
4. Ibid., p. 30.
5. Ibid.
6. Ibid.
7. Bruce Jurin, "Operational Risk Analysis: A Shareholder Value Perspective," OpRisk 98, Risk-Waters Conferences, New York, November 1998.

8. Larry Downes and Chunka Mui, *Unleashing the Killer App,* Boston: Harvard Business School Press, 1998, p. 21.
9. Timothy Boyle and Douglas Hoffman, "The Relevance of Insurance to Operational Risks," *Review of the Bankers Trust External Database,* 1997.
10. Reprinted with permission from Douglas G. Hoffman, "New Trends in Operational Risk Measurement and Management," *Operational Risk and Financial Institutions,* London: Risk Books and Arthur Andersen, 1998, pp. 29–30.
11. Reprinted with permission from Douglas Hoffman, "Operational Risk Management: A Board-Level Issue," *Bank Accounting & Finance,* Winter 2000–2001, p. 24.
12. Reprinted with permission from Douglas G. Hoffman, "New Trends in Operational Risk Measurement and Management," *Operational Risk and Financial Institutions,* London: Risk Books and Arthur Andersen, 1998, p. 38.
13. Ibid.
14. Douglas G. Hoffman and Marta Johnson, "The Development of Operational RAROC (Risk-Adjusted Return on Capital) at Bankers Trust," Submission for *Treasury and Risk Management's* Alexander Hamilton Award, September 1997.
15. Reprinted with permission from Douglas G. Hoffman, "New Trends in Operational Risk Measurement and Management," *Operational Risk and Financial Institutions,* London: Risk Books and Arthur Andersen, 1998, p. 38.
16. Ibid.
17. Hoffman and Johnson, Ibid., pp. 11–12.
18. Ibid.
19. Douglas G. Hoffman, "New Trends in Operational Risk Measurement and Management," *Operational Risk and Financial Institutions,* London: Risk Books and Arthur Andersen, 1998, p. 30.
20. Hoffman and Johnson, Ibid., p. 11.
21. Ibid., p. 12.
22. Reprinted with permission from Douglas G. Hoffman, "New Trends in Operational Risk Measurement and Management," *Operational Risk and Financial Institutions,* London: Risk Books and Arthur Andersen, 1998, p. 30.
23. Hoffman and Johnson, Ibid., p. 10.
24. RMA (and) British Bankers' Association (and) ISDA (and) Pricewaterhouse Coopers, *Operational Risk, The Next Frontier,* p. 29.
25. Rob Jameson, ed., "NetRisk Makes Public Loss Data Methodology—Exclusive," *Operational Risk,* February 2000, pp. 1–3.

26. The Working Group on Operational Risk (WGOR), "The Internal Measurement Approach to Operational Risk Regulatory Capital (Option 3)," October 13, 2000.

27. Ibid., p. 4.

28. The WGOR notes that "near misses are not loss events, and therefore, by definition, do not attract capital. However, financial institutions may choose to track these events for operational risk management purposes."

29. The Working Group on Operational Risk (WGOR), Ibid., p. 8.

30. The WGOR offers the clarification that "although we recommend that these loss types be used as standards for regulatory purposes each firm may wish to have different grouping, with the requirement that the internal grouping be complete and mappable into the regulatory standard loss categories."

31. The Basel Committee on Banking Supervision, *Consultative Document: Operational Risk,* Basel: Bank for International Settlements, 2001, p. 2.

32. Institute of International Finance, *Report of the Working Group on Operational Risk: Response to the Basel Committee on Banking Supervision Regulatory Capital Reform Proposals,* May 2001.

CHAPTER 4. THE REAL OPPORTUNITY: CREATING MORE EFFECTIVE COMPANIES

1. H. Felix Kloman, "A Fairly Poisonous Cocktail," *Risk Management Reports,* April 2000.

2. Robert G. Eccles, Robert H. Herz, E. Mary Keegan, and David M. H. Phillips, *The Value Reporting Revolution: Moving Beyond the Earnings Game,* New York: John Wiley & Sons, 2001, pp. 146–147.

3. Ibid.

4. Douglas Hoffman, "Operational Risk Management: A Board-Level Issue," *Bank Accounting & Finance,* Winter 2000–2001, p. 27.

5. Ibid.

6. James C. Collins and Jerry I. Porras, *Built To Last: Successful Habits Visionary Companies,* New York: HarperCollins Publishers, Inc., 1994, pp. 68–71.

7. Geoffrey Colvin, "America's Most Admired Companies," *Fortune,* February 21, 2000, pp. 110–111.

8. Technically, the term Six Sigma is a statistical reference: 6 standard deviations, or in terms of the Six Sigma discipline, 3.4 errors, defects, complaints, etc., and of a sample of 1,000,000.

9. Peter S. Pande, Robert P. Newman, and Roland R. Cavanagh, *The Six Sigma Way,* New York: McGraw-Hill, 2000, p. xi.

10. Ibid. p. 15.

11. Ibid. p. 14.
12. James C. Collins and Jerry I. Porras, *Built To Last: Successful Habits Visionary Companies,* New York: HarperCollins Publishers, Inc., 1994, pp. 138–139.
13. This section reprinted from Chris Rachlin, "Operational Risk In Retail Banking," *Operational Risk and Financial Institutions,* London: Risk Books and Arthur Andersen, 1998, p. 125, with permission from Chris Rachlin and Financial Engineering, Ltd.

CHAPTER 5. OPERATIONAL RISK AND MARKET PERCEPTION: FRANCHISE, REPUTATION, AND BRAND RISK

1. Jim Kartalia, "Reputation at Risk?" *Risk Management,* New York: Risk Management Society Publishing, Inc., July 2000.
2. "Bloomberg on the Weekend," Bloomberg Business News Radio, WBBR, New York, January 6, 2001.
3. Rory F. Knight and Deborah J. Pretty, *The Impact of Catastrophes on Shareholder Value,* Oxford: Templeton College, 1997, p. 4.
4. Robert Slater, *The GE Way Fieldbook: Jack Welch's Battle Plan for Corporate Revolution,* New York: McGraw Hill, 2000, p. 233.
5. Admittedly, American Airlines may have a different policy today, but the story underscores how negative customer experiences can have far-reaching and long-lasting effects on market perceptions.
6. Joanne Muller, "Ford: It's Worse Than You Think," *Business Week,* June 25, 2001, pp. 80–89.
7. Peter Lynch with John Rothchild, *One up on Wall Street,* New York: Simon and Schuster, 1989, Penguin Books, 1990, pp. 155–156.
8. William J. O'Neill, *How to Make Money in Stocks,* New York: McGraw-Hill, Inc., 1995, p. 4.
9. Roy C. Smith and Ingo Walter, *Street Smarts,* Boston: Harvard Business School Press, 1997, p. 285.
10. Douglas G. Hoffman, "New Trends in Operational Risk Measurement and Management," *Operational Risk and Financial Institutions,* London: Risk Books and Arthur Andersen, 1998, p. 39.
11. Douglas Hoffman, Marta Johnson, and Pat Medapa, "Reputation Risk Management," an Analysis using the Bankers Trust External Database, 1997.
12. Rory F. Knight and Deborah J. Pretty, *The Impact of Catastrophes on Shareholder Value,* Oxford: Templeton College, 1997.
13. Ibid., p. 1.
14. Ibid., p. 4.
15. Ibid.

16. This section is based on "Reputation Risk Management," an Analysis using the Bankers Trust External Database, 1997, by Douglas Hoffman, Marta Johnson, and Pat Medapa.
17. Jack A. Gottschalk, *Crisis Response: Inside Stories on Managing Image under Siege,* Detroit: Visible Ink Press, 1993, p. 138.
18. Beth Snyder Bulik, "The Brand Police," *Business 2.0,* Brisbane, CA: Imagine Publishing, Inc., p. 146.
19. Ibid., p. 150.

CHAPTER 6. THE ENTERPRISE-WIDE FRAMEWORK: CORPORATE GOVERNANCE, MANDATE, AND ROLES

1. Andrew J. Berry, "Risk Assessment: Bankers Trust's Approach," *BankRisk: Practical Approaches to Business Risk Management,* Stamford, CT: Towers Perrin, September, October 1994, p. 5.
2. Douglas Hoffman, "Operational Risk Management: A Board-Level Issue," *Bank Accounting & Finance,* Winter 2000–2001, p. 21.
3. Ibid.
4. Ibid.
5. Steven J. Root, *Beyond COSO: Internal Control to Enhance Corporate Governance,* John Wiley & Sons, Inc., New York, 1998, pp. 77–80.
6. James W. Bean, "The Audit Committee's Roadmap," *Corporate Governance,* AICPA, 1999.
7. Steven J. Root, *Beyond COSO: Internal Control to Enhance Corporate Governance,* John Wiley & Sons, Inc., New York, 1998, pp. 80–82.
8. Anthony Carey and Nigel Turnbull, "The Boardroom Imperative on Internal Control," *Financial Times,* April 25, 2000, Mastering Risk—Part 1, pp. 6–7.
9. Jack L. King, *Operational Risk: Measurement and Modelling,* John Wiley & Sons, Inc., Chichester, 2001, pp. 41–42.
10. Group of Thirty, *Derivatives: Practices and Principles,* New York: Group of Thirty, 1993.
11. Bank of England, *Report of the Board of Banking Supervions Inquiry into the Circumstances of the Collapse of Barings,* London: HMSO Publications, 1995, and Phillipe Jorion, *Financial Risk Manager Instruction Manual,* (New York: Carli Management Corporation, 2000).
12. Counterparty Risk Management Policy Group, *Improving Counterparty Risk Management Practices,* New York: Counterparty Risk Management Policy Group, 1999, and Phillipe Jorion, *Financial Risk Manager Instruction Manual,* (New York: Carli Management Corporation, 2000).
13. Douglas Hoffman, "Operational Risk Management: A Board-Level Issue," *Bank Accounting & Finance,* Winter 2000–2001, p. 23.

14. Douglas G. Hoffman, "Risk and Insurance Management: Perspective and Positioning," *BankRisk: The Bank Risk Management Quarterly,* Third Quarter, 1989, p. 3.
15. Douglas G. Hoffman, "Risk and Insurance Management: Perspective and Positioning," *BankRisk: The Bank Risk Management Quarterly,* Third Quarter, 1989, p. 2.
16. Douglas Hoffman, "Operational Risk Management: A Board-Level Issue," *Bank Accounting & Finance,* Winter 2000–2001, p. 23.
17. Ibid., p. 29.
18. Douglas G. Hoffman and Marta Johnson, "The Development of Operational RAROC (Risk-Adjusted Return on Capital) at Bankers Trust," Submission for *Treasury and Risk Management's* Alexander Hamilton Award, September, 1997.
19. HSBC Presentation on Risk Assessment and Control, Risk-Waters Conferences, New York, January 1997.
20. Tillinghast—Towers Perrin, *1999 Directors and Officers Liability Survey: U.S. and Canadian Results,* Chicago, Illinois, 2000, pp. 71–72.
21. Douglas Hoffman, "Operational Risk Management: A Board-Level Issue," *Bank Accounting & Finance,* Winter 2000–2001, pp. 21–22.

CHAPTER 7. THE OPERATIONAL RISK MANAGEMENT GROUP

1. Matt Kimber and Douglas G. Hoffman, "Operational Risk Management and Capital Adequacy: A Frontal Assault on Capital?" *Operational Risk,* Anindya Bhattacharyya, ed., London: Informa Business Publishing, 2000, pp. 76–77.
2. This section based on Douglas G. Hoffman, "Risk Management: Perspective and Positioning," *BankRisk: The Bank Risk Management Quarterly,* Third Quarter, 1989, pp. 6–9.
3. Douglas G. Hoffman, "Bank Shorts: Running Lean" *BankRisk: The Bank Risk Management Quarterly,* Fourth Quarter, 1989, p. 16.
4. Doug Hoffman, "Commentary: Debunking Op Risk Myths," *Operational Risk,* March 2000.
5. Ibid.

CHAPTER 8. RISK RESPONSE FRAMEWORK AND STRATEGIES

1. Douglas Hoffman, "Operational Risk Management: A Board-Level Issue," *Bank Accounting & Finance,* Winter 2000–2001, p. 27.
2. Ibid.
3. Heny K.S. Daryanto and Arief Daryanto, "Theoretical Perspectives: Motivational Theories and Organisation Design," and William P. Flinn,

"The X, Y and Z of Management Theory," Chapman University (http://members.home.net/wflinn/xyz.htm).

4. Ibid.
5. *The Wall Street Journal,* June 2000.
6. "Managers Are Starting to Gain More Clout over Their Employees," *The Wall Street Journal,* 30 January 2001, p. B1.
7. Joe Kolman, Interview with James Lam, *Derivatives Strategy,* October 1987, p. 42.
8. Roy C. Smith and Ingo Walter, *Street Smarts: Linking Professional Conduct with Shareholder Value in the Securities Industry,* Boston: Harvard Business School Press, 1997, pp. 25–28.
9. Douglas Hoffman, "Operational Risk Management: A Board-Level Issue," *Bank Accounting & Finance,* Winter 2000–2001, p. 27.
10. Ibid.
11. Douglas G. Hoffman and Marta Johnson, "The Development of Operational RAROC (Risk-Adjusted Return on Capital) at Bankers Trust," Submission for *Treasury and Risk Management's* Alexander Hamilton Award, September, 1997.
12. Tom Copeland, Tim Koller, and Jack Murrin, *Valuation: Measuring and Managing the Value of Companies,* New York: McKinsey & Company, Inc. and John Wiley & Sons, 1995, p. 118.
13. Douglas Hoffman, "Operational Risk Management: A Board-Level Issue," *Bank Accounting & Finance,* Winter 2000–2001, p. 27.

CHAPTER 9. RISK ASSESSMENT STRATEGIES

1. Douglas Hoffman, "Operational Risk Management: A Board-Level Issue," *Bank Accounting & Finance,* Winter 2000–2001, p. 25.
2. Doug Hoffman, "Commentary: Debunking Op Risk Myths," *Operational Risk,* March 2000.
3. Ibid.
4. This section is largely reprinted with permission from Douglas G. Hoffman, "New Trends in Operational Risk Measurement and Management," *Operational Risk and Financial Institutions,* London: Risk Books and Arthur Andersen, 1998, p. 32.
5. This section is largely based on an article by Margaret Levine and Douglas G. Hoffman, "Enriching the Universe of Operational Risk Data: Getting Started on Risk Profiling," *Operational Risk,* London: Informa Business Publishing, March 2000, pp. 25–39.
6. Douglas Hoffman, "Operational Risk Management: A Board-Level Issue," *Bank Accounting & Finance,* Winter 2000–2001, p. 25.

CHAPTER 10. DATABASES AND CONSORTIA: WORKING THROUGH THE DETAILS

1. Margaret Levine and Douglas G. Hoffman, "Enriching the universe of operational risk data: Getting started on risk profiling," *Operational Risk,* London: Informa Business Publishing, March 2000, pp. 25.
2. Douglas G. Hoffman, "New Trends in Operational Risk Measurement and Management," *Operational Risk and Financial Institutions,* London: Risk Books and Arthur Andersen, 1998, pp. 37–38.
3. This section is largely reprinted from Margaret Levine and Douglas G. Hoffman, "Enriching the Universe of Operational Risk Data: Getting Started on Risk Profiling," *Operational Risk,* London: Informa Business Publishing, March 2000, pp. 27–28, with permission.
4. Ibid., pp. 28–29.
5. Ibid., p. 30.
6. Ibid., p. 29.
7. This section is reprinted from an article written by Doug Hoffman for *Risk Professional* magazine, entitled "Into the Valley," and published in the December 2000/January 2001 issue with permission.
8. Ibid.
9. Ibid.
10. Doug Hoffman, "Commentary: Debunking Op Risk Myths," *Operational Risk,* March 2000.
11. Ibid.
12. Margaret Levine and Douglas G. Hoffman, "Enriching the Universe of Operational Risk Data: Getting Started on Risk Profiling," *Operational Risk,* London: Informa Business Publishing, March 2000, p. 25.
13. Doug Hoffman, "Into the Valley," *Risk Professional,* December 2000/January 2001, p. 12.

CHAPTER 11. RISK INDICATORS AND SCORE CARDS: CORNERSTONES FOR OPERATIONAL RISK MONITORING

1. This section reprinted with permission from Denis Taylor and Douglas G. Hoffman, "Avoiding Signal Failure," *Operational Risk Special Report, Risk,* November 1999, p. 13.
2. Ibid.
3. Douglas Hoffman, "Operational Risk Management: A Board-Level Issue," *Bank Accounting & Finance,* Winter 2000–2001, pp. 25–26.
4. This section reprinted with permission from Denis Taylor and Douglas G. Hoffman, "Avoiding Signal Failure," *Operational Risk Special Report, Risk,* November 1999, p. 15.
5. Ibid.

6. Robert Simons, "How Risky Is Your Company?" *Harvard Business Review,* May/June 1999, p. 87.
7. Mark Lawrence, "Marking the Cards at ANZ," *Operational Risk: A Risk Special Report,* November 2000, pp. S9–S10.
8. Taylor and Hoffman, Ibid., p. 14.
9. This section reprinted with permission from Denis Taylor and Douglas G. Hoffman, "Avoiding Signal Failure," *Operational Risk Special Report, Risk,* November 1999, p. 15.
10. Ibid.

CHAPTER 12. OPERATIONAL RISK ANALYSIS AND MEASUREMENT: PRACTICAL BUILDING BLOCKS

1. Marcelo Cruz, "Latest Techniques for Measuring and Pricing Operational Risk," *Op Risk 2000, Risk-Waters Conferences*, New York, February 10–11, 2000.
2. This section is partially based and reprinted with permission from Chapter 2 of *Operational Risk and Financial Institutions,* London, 1998, entitled "New Trends in Operational Risk Measurement and Management," pp. 29–42, by Douglas G. Hoffman. Reprinted with permission from Risk Books and Financial Engineering, Ltd. Portions also reproduced with permission from Matt Kimber and Douglas G. Hoffman, "Operational Risk Management and Capital Adequacy: A Frontal Assault on Capital?" *Operational Risk,* London: Informa Business Publishing, March 2000, pp. 71–83.
3. This section is partially reprinted with permission from Douglas G. Hoffman, "New Trends in Operational Risk Measurement and Management," *Operational Risk and Financial Institutions,* London, 1998, p. 33.
4. The prior experience of private catastrophe insurers born in the 1980s out of the insurance crisis of that era was also particularly relevant. At that time, new insurers were stepping in to provide large loss coverage in sectors where conventional insurance had disappeared due to difficult financial market conditions, poor underwriting results and constricted supply, or insurance "capacity." These coverages included large loss liability coverages being provided by the new Bermuda insurers. It was striking that we both had the same concerns.
5. Dave Sommer, FCAS, MAAA, "Quantifying Operational Risk," *Risk-Waters Conferences,* London, May 10, 1999.
6. David Vose, *Quantitative Risk Analysis: A Guide To Monte Carlo Simulation Modelling,* West Sussex: John Wiley & Sons Ltd., 1996, p. 11.
7. Dave Sommer, FCAS, MAAA, "Quantifying Operational Risk," *Risk-Waters Conferences,* London, May 10, 1999.
8. Ibid.
9. Ibid.

10. Ibid.
11. Ibid.
12. Francois Longin, "From Value at Risk to Stress Testing: The Extreme Value Approach," *Journal of Banking and Finance* 24, 2000, p. 1098.
13. Kevin Dowd, Ph.D., "The Extreme Value Approach to VaR—An Introduction," *Financial Engineering News,* Issue 11, August 1999, p. 1.
14. Francois Longin, "From Value at Risk to Stress Testing: The Extreme Value Approach," *Journal of Banking and Finance* 24, 2000, p. 1110.
15. Kevin Dowd, Ph.D., "The Extreme Value Approach to VaR—An Introduction," *Financial Engineering News,* Issue 11, August 1999, p. 1.
16. Jack L. King, *Operational Risk: Measurement and Modelling,* John Wiley & Sons, Ltd., Chichester, 2001, p. 66.
17. Based on presentation by Jeevan Perera with permission, "Industry Case Study: Utilising Neural Networks to Quantify Operational Risk, "RiskWaters Conference," February 11, 2000.
18. W. Michael Waldrop, *Complexity: The Emerging Science at the Edge of Order and Chaos,* 1992.
19. Reprinted with permission from Douglas G. Hoffman, "New Trends in Operational Risk Measurement and Management," *Operational Risk and Financial Institutions,* London: Risk Books and Arthur Andersen, 1998, pp. 36–37.
20. Douglas G. Hoffman, "New Trends in Operational Risk Measurement and Management," *Operational Risk and Financial Institutions,* London: Risk Books and Arthur Andersen, 1998, p. 37.

CHAPTER 13. DYNAMIC RISK PROFILING AND MONITORING

1. Company Information: Halifax Group, Plc had total assets of £183bn in 2000. The company earned pre-tax profits of £1.9bn for the year. It has 20 million customers, 3.4 million shareholders, and 37,000 staff members.
2. Doug Hoffman, "Debunking Op Risk Myths," *Operational Risk,* March 2000.
3. Marcelo Cruz, "Modelling and Measuring Operational Risk," *Journal of Risk,* 1(1), 1998, pp. 63–72
4. C. V. Altrock, *Fuzzy Logic & Neuro Fuzzy Applications in Business and Finance,* 1997, p. 277.

CHAPTER 14. INSURANCE AND OPERATIONAL RISKS: ALIGNING CONVENTIONAL PROGRAMS

1. Douglas G. Hoffman, "New Trends in Operational Risk Measurement and Management," *Operational Risk and Financial Institutions,* London: Risk Books and Arthur Andersen, 1998, p. 39.

2. Ibid.
3. Rory F. Knight and Deborah J. Pretty, *The Impact of Catastrophes on Shareholder Value,* Oxford: Templeton College, 1997, p. 5.
4. Timothy Boyle and Douglas Hoffman, "The Relevance of Insurance to Operational Risks," Review of the Bankers Trust External Database, 1997.
5. This section reprinted with permission from Douglas G. Hoffman, "New Trends in Operational Risk Measurement and Management," *Operational Risk and Financial Institutions,* London: Risk Books and Arthur Andersen, 1998, pp. 40–41.
6. Douglas Hoffman, "Operational Risk Management: A Board-Level Issue," *Bank Accounting & Finance,* Winter 2000–2001, p. 28.
7. Ibid.
8. Ibid.

CHAPTER 15. OPERATIONAL RISK FINANCE: THE RE-ENGINEERING PROCESS

1. Roland Avery and Paul Milton, "Insurers to the Rescue?" *Operational Risk,* London: Informa Business Publishing, March 2000, p. 66.
2. Lars Schmidt-Ott, "An Appeal for an Operational Risk Derivatives Market," *Operational Risk,* London: Informa Business Publishing, March 2000, pp. 55–56.
3. Roland Avery and Paul Milton, "Insurers to the Rescue?" *Operational Risk,* London: Informa Business Publishing, March 2000, p. 64.
4. Ibid., p. 65.
5. Douglas Hoffman, "Operational Risk Management: A Board-Level Issue," *Bank Accounting & Finance,* Winter 2000–2001, p. 28.
6. R. George Monti and Andrew Barile, *A Practical Guide to Finite Risk Insurance and Reinsurance,* John Wiley & Sons, Inc., New York, 1995.
7. Ibid.
8. Ibid.

CHAPTER 16. ECONOMIC RISK CAPITAL MODELING: ALLOCATION AND ATTRIBUTION

1. Douglas G. Hoffman and Marta Johnson, "The Development of Operational RAROC (Risk-Adjusted Return on Capital) at Bankers Trust" (Submission for *Treasury and Risk Management's* Alexander Hamilton Award), September 1997.
2. Douglas G. Hoffman, "New Trends in Operational Risk Measurement and Management," *Operational Risk and Financial Institutions,* London: Risk Books and Arthur Andersen, 1998.
3. Ibid.

4. Ibid.
5. Ibid.
6. This section adapted from Douglas G. Hoffman and Marta Johnson, "The Development of Operational RAROC (Risk-Adjusted Return on Capital) at Bankers Trust," (Submission for *Treasury and Risk Management's* Alexander Hamilton Award), September 1997.

CHAPTER 17. REGULATORY CAPITAL AND SUPERVISION

1. Matt Kimber and Douglas G. Hoffman, "Operational Risk Management and Capital Adequacy: A Frontal Assault on Capital?" *Operational Risk,* London: Informa Business Publishing, March 2000, pp. 71–83.
2. This section based on an article by Doug Hoffman, "Commentary: Debunking Op Risk Myths," *Operational Risk,* March 2000.
3. Basel Committee on Banking "A New Capital Adequacy Framework: Consultative Paper," Basel: Bank for International Settlements, June 1999, and "Consultative Document: Operational Risk," *Basel Committee on Banking Supervision, Supporting Document to the New Basel Capital Accord,* January 2001.
4. Basel Committee on Banking Supervison, "A New Capital Adequacy Framework: Consultative Paper," *Basel: Bank for International Settlements,* June 1999, p. 5.
5. "Consultative Document: Operational Risk," *Basel Committee on Banking Supervision, Supporting Document to the New Basel Capital Accord,* January 2001.
6. The Financial Services Roundtable, "Guiding Principals (sic) in Risk Management for U.S. Commercial Banks: A Report of the Subcommittee and Working Group on Risk Management Principles," June 1999, pp. 37–39.
7. RMA (and) British Bankers' Association (and) ISDA (and) Pricewaterhouse Coopers, *Operational Risk—The Next Frontier,* p. 7.
8. International Swaps and Derivatives Association (ISDA), "A New Capital Adequacy Framework: Comments on a Consultative Paper Issued by the Basel Committee on Banking Supervision in June 1999," pp. 6–7.
9. International Swaps and Derivatives Association, Inc., "Operational Risk Regulatory Approach Discussion Paper," September 2000, pp. 1–23.
10. "Consultative Document: Operational Risk," *Basel Committee on Banking, Supervision, Supporting Document to the New Basel Capital Accord,* January 2001, pp. 6–9.
11. Ibid., p. 4.
12. Ibid.
13. Ibid., pp. 11–14.

14. Ibid., p. 11.
15. Basel Committee on Banking Supervision, "Update on the New Basel Capital Accord," June 25, 2001 (www.bis.org).

CHAPTER 18. AN OPERATIONAL RISK MANAGEMENT CASE STUDY: MANAGING INTERNET BANKING RISK

1. David La Bouchardiere is with IBM's Global Services e-Risk Management Consulting Practice, London +44 (0)207 202 3517.

CHAPTER 19. OPERATIONAL RISK TECHNOLOGY AND SYSTEMS

1. Section reprinted with permission from Douglas Hoffman, "Operational Risk Management: A Board-Level Issue," *Bank Accounting & Finance*, Winter 2000–2001, p. 29.
2. Larry Downes and Chunka Mui, *Unleashing the Killer App: Digital Strategies for Market Dominance*, Harvard Business School Press, Boston, 1998.
3. Deborah Williams (Research Director), "Time for a New Look at Operational Risk," Meridien Research, Inc., February 2000, p. 7.
4. In 1999, J.P. Morgan entered into an arrangement with Ernst & Young LLP to incorporate Horizon into Ernst & Young's operational risk service offerings. Capitalizing on the lessons learned during the J.P. Morgan Horizon deployment, Ernst & Young has developed a comprehensive operational risk management framework and implementation approach, which incorporates Horizon's process-driven approach with Ernst & Young's other operational risk management tools. With Ernst & Young's assistance, five global institutions ranging from major financial institutions, insurers, and energy companies have adopted Horizon as a key component of their operational risk management framework, utilizing the Horizon tool as the qualitative foundation of their operational risk management programs.

   Since the initial Horizon deployment, Ernst & Young has continued to provide assistance to J.P. Morgan. "Working with other organizations in developing their operational risk management solutions, we found that the integration of the self-assessment process with other operational risk components is critical to the acceptance and long term success of an operational risk management program," states Carmine DiSibio, partner with Ernst & Young. Carmine continues, "The trap most organizations fall into is not fully developing their operational risk management methodology and framework before embarking on an operational risk management pilot project. This causes them to not consider the interactions of piloted tool and methodology with other business processes and other initiatives throughout the organization."

5. Guellich, H-P., "Experience with New Soft Computing Concepts for Rating Systems," *Rating Community*, 2000, pp. 45–50.

6. Margaret Levine and Douglas G. Hoffman, "Enriching the universe of operational risk data: getting started on risk profiling," *Operational Risk,* London: Informa Business Publishing, March 2000, pp. 33.

7. Doug Hoffman, "Commentary: Debunking Op Risk Myths," *Operational Risk,* March 2000.